lonely planet

Andalucía

John Noble
Susan Forsyth
Des Hannigan

LONELY PLANET PUBLICATIONS
Melbourne • Oakland • London • Par

ANDALUCÍA

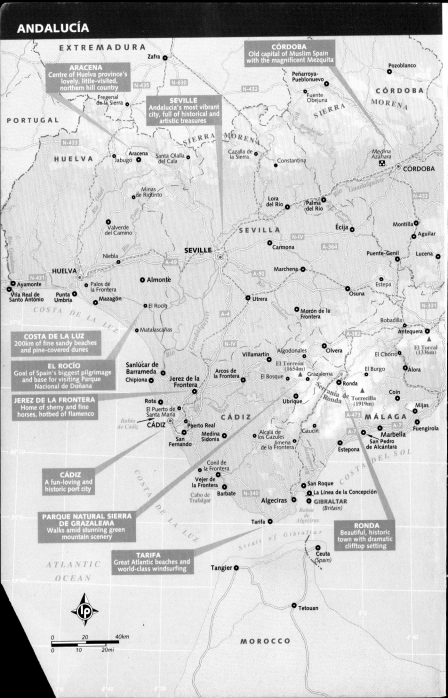

EXTREMADURA

Zafra

ARACENA
Centre of Huelva province's lovely, little-visited, northern hill country

Fregenal
de la Sierra

PORTUGAL

N-433

HUELVA

Aracena
Jabugo
Santa Olalla
del Cala

Minas
de Riotinto

Valverde
del Camino

Niebla

HUELVA

Ayamonte
Vila Real de
Santo António
Punta
Umbría
Palos de
la Frontera
Mazagón

Almonte

El Rocío

COSTA DE LA LUZ
200km of fine sandy beaches
and pine-covered dunes

Matalascañas

EL ROCÍO
Goal of Spain's biggest pilgrimage
and base for visiting Parque
Nacional de Doñana

JEREZ DE LA FRONTERA
Home of sherry and fine
horses, hotbed of flamenco

CÓRDOBA
Old capital of Muslim Spain
with the magnificent Mezquita

Pozoblanco

Peñarroya-
Pueblonuevo

CÓRDOBA

Fuente
Obejuna

SIERRA MORENA

SEVILLE
Andalucía's most vibrant
city, full of historical and
artistic treasures

Cazalla de
la Sierra

Medina
Azahara

CÓRDOBA

Constantina

Lora
del Río
Palma
del Río

Río Guadalquivir

Montilla

SEVILLA
Écija
Aguilar

Carmona
Puente-Genil
Lucena

SEVILLE

Marchena

Estepa

Almonte
Utrera
Osuna

Morón de la
Frontera

Bobadilla

Antequera

Algodonales
Olvera
El Torcal
(1336m)

El Chorro

**Sanlúcar de
Barrameda**
Villamartín
El Torreón
(1654m)
Grazalema
El Burgo
Álora

Chipiona
Arcos de
la Frontera
El Bosque
Ronda
Coín

**Jerez de la
Frontera**
Serranía de
Ronda
Torrecilla
(1919m)
Mijas

Rota
Ubrique
MÁLAGA

El Puerto de
Santa María
CÁDIZ
A-473

CÁDIZ
Puerto Real
Gaucín
Marbella

Bahía
de Cádiz
Medina
Sidonia
Alcalá de
los Gazules
San Pedro
de Alcántara

San
Fernando
Jimena
de la Frontera
Estepona

CÁDIZ
A fun-loving and
historic port city

Conil de
la Frontera

COSTA DEL SOL

Vejer de
la Frontera

**PARQUE NATURAL SIERRA
DE GRAZALEMA**
Walks amid stunning green
mountain scenery

Cabo de
Trafalgar
Barbate
Algeciras
GIBRALTAR
(Britain)

Tarifa
Bahía
de
Algeciras

RONDA
Beautiful, historic
town with dramatic
clifftop setting

TARIFA
Great Atlantic beaches and
world-class windsurfing

Ceuta
(Spain)

Tangier

**ATLANTIC
OCEAN**

COSTA DE LA LUZ

Strait of Gibraltar

Tetouan

0   20   40km
0   10   20mi

MOROCCO

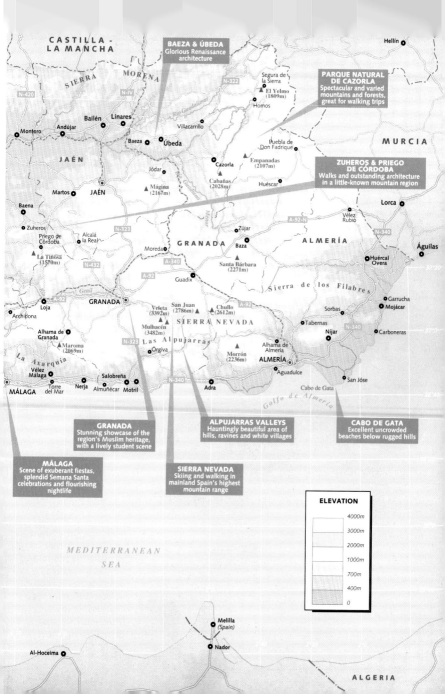

Andalucía
3rd edition – January 2003
First published – January 1999

Published by
Lonely Planet Publications Pty Ltd ABN 36 005 607 983
90 Maribyrnong St, Footscray, Victoria 3011, Australia

Lonely Planet offices
Australia Locked Bag 1, Footscray, Victoria 3011
USA 150 Linden St, Oakland, CA 94607
UK 10a Spring Place, London NW5 3BH
France 1 rue du Dahomey, 75011 Paris

Photographs
Many of the images in this guide are available for licensing from
Lonely Planet Images.
w www.lonelyplanetimages.com

Front cover photograph
Architectural features of the Mezquita of Córdoba (Bill Wassman)

ISBN 1 74059 279 4

Printed by SNP SPrint (M) Sdn Bhd
Printed in Malaysia

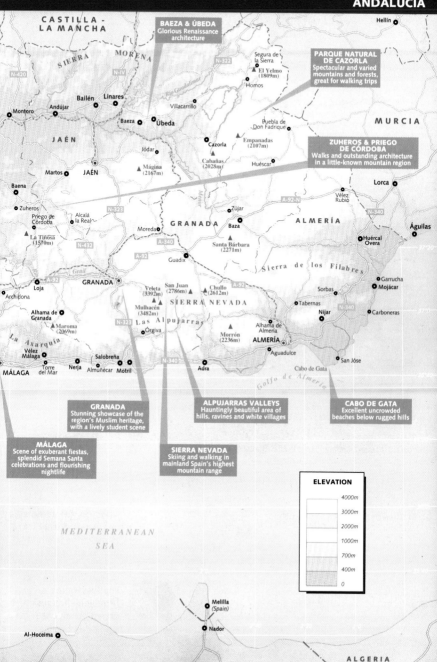

ANDALUCÍA

CASTILLA-LA MANCHA

Hellín

SIERRA MORENA

BAEZA & ÚBEDA
Glorious Renaissance architecture

N-420

N-IV

N-322

Segura de la Sierra

PARQUE NATURAL DE CAZORLA
Spectacular and varied mountains and forests, great for walking trips

Montoro

Andújar

Bailén

Linares

Río Guadalimar

El Yelmo (1809m)

Homos

MURCIA

Baeza

Úbeda

Villacarrillo

JAÉN

Jódar

Cazorla

Empanadas (2107m)

Puebla de Don Fadrique

Lorca

Baena

Martos

JAÉN

Mágina (2167m)

Cabañas (2028m)

Huéscar

ZUHEROS & PRIEGO DE CÓRDOBA
Walks and outstanding architecture in a little-known mountain region

Zuheros

Priego de Córdoba

Alcalá la Real

N-323

GRANADA

Zújar

Vélez Rubio

A-92-N

ALMERÍA

Águilas

N-340

La Tiñosa (1570m)

N-432

Moreda

Baza

Santa Bárbara (2271m)

Huércal Overa

Sierra de los Filabres

Garrucha

Archidona

Genil

A-92

LOJA

GRANADA

Guadix

A-340

Veleta (3392m)

San Juan (2786m)

Chullo (2612m)

A-92

SIERRA NEVADA

Sorbas

Tabernas

Mojácar

Alhama de Granada

Maroma (2069m)

Mulhacén (3482m)

Las Alpujarras

N-323

Orgiva

Morrón (2236m)

Alhama de Almería

Níjar

Carboneras

ALMERÍA

La Axarquía

Vélez Málaga

Salobreña

Aguadulce

VÉLEZ MÁLAGA

Torre del Mar

Nerja

Almuñécar

Motril

N-340

Adra

Cabo de Gata

San Jóse

MÁLAGA

Golfo de Almería

GRANADA
Stunning showcase of the region's Muslim heritage, with a lively student scene

ALPUJARRAS VALLEYS
Hauntingly beautiful area of hills, ravines and white villages

CABO DE GATA
Excellent uncrowded beaches below rugged hills

MÁLAGA
Scene of exuberant fiestas, splendid Semana Santa celebrations and flourishing nightlife

SIERRA NEVADA
Skiing and walking in mainland Spain's highest mountain range

ELEVATION

4000m
3000m
2000m
1000m
700m
400m
0

MEDITERRANEAN

SEA

Melilla (Spain)

Al-Hoceima

Nador

ALGERIA

Andalucía
3rd edition – January 2003
First published – January 1999

Published by
Lonely Planet Publications Pty Ltd ABN 36 005 607 983
90 Maribyrnong St, Footscray, Victoria 3011, Australia

Lonely Planet offices
Australia Locked Bag 1, Footscray, Victoria 3011
USA 150 Linden St, Oakland, CA 94607
UK 10a Spring Place, London NW5 3BH
France 1 rue du Dahomey, 75011 Paris

Photographs
Many of the images in this guide are available for licensing from
Lonely Planet Images.
w www.lonelyplanetimages.com

Front cover photograph
Architectural features of the Mezquita of Córdoba (Bill Wassman)

ISBN 1 74059 279 4

text & maps © Lonely Planet Publications Pty Ltd 2003
photos © photographers as indicated 2003

GR and PR are trade marks of the FFRP (Fédération Française de la
Randonnée)

Printed by SNP SPrint (M) Sdn Bhd
Printed in Malaysia

HUELVA PROVINCE   184

CÁDIZ PROVINCE   211

GIBRALTAR   259

MÁLAGA PROVINCE   269

CÓRDOBA PROVINCE   314

GRANADA PROVINCE   334

Contents – Text

Contents – Maps

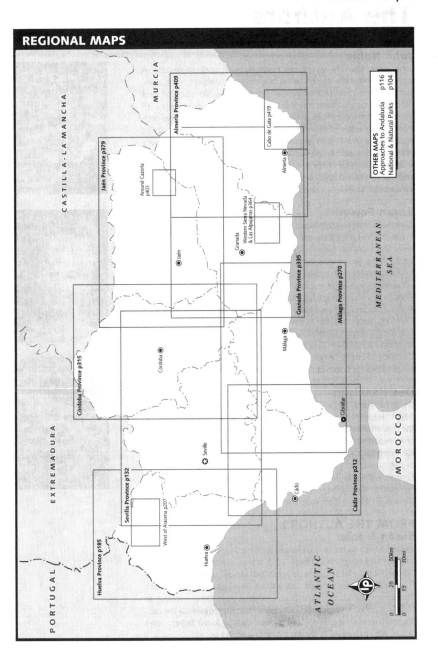

REGIONAL MAPS

PORTUGAL

EXTREMADURA

CASTILLA-LA MANCHA

MURCIA

Huelva Province p185

Sevilla Province p132

West of Aracena p207

Córdoba Province p315

Jaén Province p379

Around Cazorla p403

Almería Province p409

Cabo de Gata p419

Huelva

Seville

Córdoba

Jaén

Granada

Western Sierra Nevada & Las Alpujarras p364

Almería

Granada Province p335

Málaga Province p270

Cádiz Province p212

Cádiz

Málaga

Gibraltar

ATLANTIC OCEAN

MEDITERRANEAN SEA

MOROCCO

0   25   50km
0   15   30mi

The Authors

John Noble

John comes from the cool, green Ribble Valley in northern England. A degree in philosophy somehow led to a career in newspaper journalism, but increasing interruptions for travel eventually saw him abandon Fleet Street for a Lonely Planet trail that has seen him cover, at last count, 19 countries from Indonesia to Mexico and Brazil to Uzbekistan. He has been coordinating author of many multiauthor LP titles, including *Brazil*, *Spain*, *Russia, Ukraine & Belarus* and four editions of *Mexico*. John and his wife and coauthor Susan Forsyth, and their children Isabella and Jack, have lived in an Andalucian hill village since the mid-1990s. Investigating Andalucía's untrammelled hill country and remote, ancient villages is still among his favourite pastimes – as is discovering delectable new tapas bars!

Susan Forsyth

Born and raised in Melbourne, Australia, Susan spent a decade teaching in the Victorian state education system. Distracted by her regular visits to Indonesia, Susan sought work in Asia and headed off to Sri Lanka for a year's stint as a volunteer lecturer. There she met her husband, writer John Noble, and before long she began writing for LP, set up home in Europe and had two children. An original author of LP's *Andalucía* and *Spain* guides, Susan has worked on several editions of *Mexico*, as well as *Australia*, *Indonesia*, *Sri Lanka* and *Travel with Children*. Susan and family live in Andalucía, where her children are acquiring a distinct *andaluz* demeanour and super-fluency in the local version of *castellano*. Susan likes to get away from her desk to the Costa de la Luz, to enjoy the squeaky white sand, good waves and what passes for beach culture in this part of the world.

Des Hannigan

Try as he might, Des could not find the start of the Hippie Trail in the 1970s. He went to sea instead and spent 15 years as a fisherman on the unkind waters of Britain's Atlantic approaches. Then he took up news reporting in the mistaken hope that it might make for an easier life. From hack work he moved into guidebook work and has written, or contributed to, guides to Rhodes, Corfu, Southern Spain, Northern Europe, and North Pakistan, as well as several walking and rock climbing guides. Des updated the Denmark section of LP's *Scandinavian Europe*. He lives in Cornwall, England.

FROM THE AUTHORS
Susan & John

We would like to thank Isabella and Jack for their patience during our long working hours on this book. Also, thanks to Karen Abrahams and Simone Kempf of Los Caños de Meca and James Stuart of Vejer de la Frontera for their local insight on the Costa de la Luz. Tourist-office staff throughout the region have been enthusiastic in their response to endless questions. We would like to record our appreciation of the continual interest in our journeys and books shown by John's father, Derek Noble, who passed away during the writing of this book.

Des Hannigan

A big thank you to the very helpful staff in tourist offices throughout Andalucía and in Gibraltar. Special thanks for their insight and good company, to: Nando Viedma and Beatriz Martinez in Cazorla; Clive Jarman and Tom Jones in Zuheros; Donny Mackinnon in Mojácar; Bautista Martinez Ceprian in Santa Elena; Christine Hofer in El Chorro; Anna Moore in Comares; Rebecca Sutton and Damaris Bowker in Ronda; Antonio Cuaresma Sancha in Aroche; and to the many patient, good-humoured Andalucians who furnished me with information, explanation and hospitality along the way. Thanks, above all, to John Noble and Susan Forsyth for writing the original guide and the second edition, which was such a pleasure to work from.

This Book

John Noble and Susan Forsyth researched and wrote the first two editions of Andalucía, and were joined by Des Hannigan and Heather Dickson for this third edition. John and Susan updated the introductory chapters, Sevilla Province, Cádiz Province and Granada Province; Des Hannigan updated Huelva Province, Gibraltar, Málaga Province, Córdoba Province, Jaén Province and Almería Province; and Heather Dickson wrote the Places to Eat, Entertainment and Shopping sections of Seville, Granada, Córdoba, Málaga and the Costa del Sol.

FROM THE PUBLISHER

This edition of Andalucía was produced in Lonely Planet's Melbourne office. Editing was coordinated by Kim Hutchins, with invaluable assistance from Simone Egger, Tegan Murray, Tony Davidson, Evan Jones, Sally O'Brien, Pete Cruttenden, Darren O'Connell and Anastasia Safioleas. Helen Rowley and Kusnandar drew the maps, with help from Cris Tsismetzis, Karen Fry, Csanad Csutoros, Jimi Ellis, Chris Thomas and Sarah Sloane. Quentin Frayne compiled the Language chapter, and Anastasia Safioleas, Bridget Blair and Isabelle Young compiled the index. David Burnett sorted out production glitches along the way.

The book was designed and laid out by Cris Gibcus, who also selected the images. Thanks to Pepi Bluck for assistance with illustrations, and to Lonely Planet Images for the photographs. Annika Roojun designed the cover.

Senior production staff Bridget Blair, Meredith Mail, Isabelle Young, Mark Griffiths and Adriana Mammarella steered the project from start to finish. Thanks also to Tim Ryder and Heather Dickson in the London office.

Foreword

ABOUT LONELY PLANET GUIDEBOOKS

The story begins with a classic travel adventure: Tony and Maureen Wheeler's 1972 journey across Europe and Asia to Australia. There was no useful information about the overland trail then, so Tony and Maureen published the first Lonely Planet guidebook to meet a growing need.

From a kitchen table, Lonely Planet has grown to become the largest independent travel publisher in the world, with offices in Melbourne (Australia), Oakland (USA), London (UK) and Paris (France).

Today Lonely Planet guidebooks cover the globe. There is an ever-growing list of books and information in a variety of media. Some things haven't changed. The main aim is still to make it possible for adventurous travellers to get out there – to explore and better understand the world.

At Lonely Planet we believe travellers can make a positive contribution to the countries they visit – if they respect their host communities and spend their money wisely. Since 1986 a percentage of the income from each book has been donated to aid projects and human rights campaigns, and, more recently, to wildlife conservation.

> Although inclusion in a guidebook usually implies a recommendation we cannot list every good place. Exclusion does not necessarily imply criticism. In fact there are a number of reasons why we might exclude a place – sometimes it is simply inappropriate to encourage an influx of travellers.

UPDATES & READER FEEDBACK

Things change – prices go up, schedules change, good places go bad and bad places go bankrupt. Nothing stays the same. So, if you find things better or worse, recently opened or long-since closed, please tell us and help make the next edition even more accurate and useful.

Lonely Planet thoroughly updates each guidebook as often as possible – usually every two years, although for some destinations the gap can be longer. Between editions, up-to-date information is available in our free, quarterly *Planet Talk* newsletter and monthly email bulletin *Comet*. The *Scoop* section of our website covers news and current affairs relevant to travellers. Lastly, the *Thorn Tree* bulletin board and *Postcards* section carry unverified, but fascinating, reports from travellers.

Tell us about it! We genuinely value your feedback. A well-travelled team at Lonely Planet reads and acknowledges every email and letter we receive and ensures that every morsel of information finds its way to the relevant authors, editors and cartographers.

Everyone who writes to us will find their name listed in the next edition of the appropriate guidebook, and will receive the latest issue of *Comet* or *Planet Talk*. The very best contributions will be rewarded with a free guidebook.

We may edit, reproduce and incorporate your comments in Lonely Planet products such as guidebooks, websites and digital products, so let us know if you don't want your comments reproduced or your name acknowledged.

How to contact Lonely Planet:
Online: ⒺⒺ talk2us@lonelyplanet.com.au, Ⓦ www.lonelyplanet.com
Australia: Locked Bag 1, Footscray, Victoria 3011
UK: 10a Spring Place, London NW5 3BH
USA: 150 Linden St, Oakland, CA 94607

Introduction

Andalucía – the south of Spain, a stone's throw from Africa – has fascinated foreign travellers since the early 19th century when Romantic voyagers and writers were captivated by its fiestas, its music, its exotic, semi-oriental past, its southern heat, its dramatic mountains and sparkling seas, and its unique flamenco music and dance.

Though modernity has hit Andalucía with a jolt in recent decades, and to some people it conjures up images of concrete, package-holiday resorts, much of what gripped those early travellers lives on. Andalucians remain gregarious, relaxed and in love with life, still with a quaintly flexible notion of time. Their fiestas are always full-blooded affairs, full of colour, noise and spectacle – from the relatively solemn processions of Semana Santa (Holy Week) to the unadulterated hedonism of night-long music, dancing and drinking at summer *ferias* (fairs).

The Islamic civilisation that swept the Iberian Peninsula in the 8th century flourished longest (until 1492) in Andalucía. It not only left behind magnificent buildings such as the Alhambra in Granada and the Mezquita in Córdoba, but also made a deep imprint on the landscape, townscapes, people and even the food of modern Andalucía. Flamenco, the music that says 'Spain' to the outside world but which is Andalucía's own, has Islamic roots, as does the guitar, another felicitous Andalucian invention.

The more recent Christian centuries have given Andalucía a great deal of its fascinating folklore and a superb legacy of Gothic, Renaissance and baroque architecture. The great artists Velázquez, Murillo and Picasso all hailed from Andalucía, as did the great writer Federico García Lorca. In the 18th century Andalucía was one of the birthplaces of that quintessential Spanish activity, bullfighting, which continues to thrive there today.

Seville, Grànada, Málaga, Córdoba and Cádiz are cities with a fascinating heritage of history, art and architecture. They also provide a vibrant nightlife which often kicks on until dawn. A great start to a night out is to

tour a few bars to sample the delicious snacks known as tapas. An excellent accompaniment to many tapas is sherry, Andalucía's very own variety of wine.

The region's climate – sizzling in July and August, temperate in winter – is part of its appeal. The potent combination of sun, sea and sand has turned the Costa del Sol, west of Málaga, into one of the world's most densely packed tourist zones. You'll be delighted to discover that other stretches of the Andalucian coast, such as Cabo de Gata in the east and the Atlantic Costa de la Luz in the west, have far better beaches and far fewer people.

Away from the cities and beaches, much of Andalucía is rugged mountain chains and picturesque white villages where for centuries time has at best ambled along. From the mysterious Las Alpujarras valleys and the green and damp Sierra de Grazalema to the rocky crags of beautiful Parque Natural de Cazorla, you'll find a wealth of excellent walking and a profusion of beautiful flora and unusual fauna.

The coasts and countryside offer endless scope for the growing bands of active travellers who are heading for Andalucía: from world-class windsurfing and kitesurfing at Tarifa to championship skiing and snowboarding in the Sierra Nevada, and horse riding or mountain biking all over the place, you need never sit still for a moment.

Still deeply traditional, yet changing fast with the times, Andalucía yields fascinating surprises wherever you go. And the more you explore it, the deeper its fascination grows.

Facts about Andalucía

HISTORY

Andalucía stands where the Mediterranean Sea meets the Atlantic Ocean and Europe gives way to Africa. From prehistoric times to the 17th century, this critical location put Andalucía at the forefront of Spanish history and at times made it a mover of European and even world history. Then several centuries of economic mismanagement turned Andalucía into a backwater, a condition from which it has only emerged since the 1960s, helped by its leading place in Spain's tourism industry.

In the Beginning

A bone fragment found in 1976 near Orce, in Granada province, could be the oldest known human remains in Europe. It is probably one to two million years old and is believed to be from the skull of an infant *Homo erectus* – an ancestor of modern *Homo sapiens*. From the much later Neanderthal era comes 'Gibraltar Woman', a skull dating from about 30,000 BC, found in 1848.

The Palaeolithic or Old Stone Age, which lasted beyond the end of the last Ice Age to about 8000 BC, was somewhat less cold in Andalucía than in more northerly regions. Thick forests and varied fauna developed, permitting hunter-gatherer humans to live here in reasonable numbers. Many traces of their presence remain, notably some impressive rock art (see Painting, Sculpture & Metalwork under Arts later in this chapter).

The Neolithic or New Stone Age reached eastern Spain from Egypt and Mesopotamia in around 6000 BC, bringing a host of innovations such as the plough, crops, livestock raising, pottery, textiles and villages. Between 3000 and 2000 BC, what was probably Spain's first metalworking culture arose at Los Millares, near Almería. This Chalcolithic or Copper Age saw the emergence in Andalucía of megalithic culture, during which tombs known as dolmens were built of large rocks. Spain's best dolmens are near Antequera.

The next big technological advance was bronze, an alloy of copper and tin, stronger than copper. In about 1900 BC, El Argar, near Antas in Almería province, became probably the first Bronze-Age settlement on the Iberian Peninsula (occupied by Spain and Portugal).

Tartessos

By about 1000 BC, a flourishing culture rich in agriculture, animals and metals had arisen in western Andalucía. Phoenician traders, largely from Tyre and Sidon in present-day Lebanon, arrived to exchange perfumes, ivory, jewellery, oil, wine and textiles for Andalucian silver and bronze. The Phoenicians set up trading settlements on the coast at Adra (west of Almería), Almuñécar (which they called Sex), Málaga (Malaca), Cádiz (Gadir) and Huelva (Onuba). Cádiz, possibly founded as early as 1100 BC, may be the oldest city in Europe. In the 7th century BC the Greeks came too, trading much the same goods. The Phoenicians and Greeks brought Andalucía the potter's wheel, writing, the olive tree, the vine, and animals such as the donkey and hen.

The culture of western Andalucía in the 8th and 7th centuries BC, influenced by the Phoenicians and Greeks, is known as the Tartessic culture. The Tartessians worshipped Phoenician-type gods and possessed advanced methods of working gold. Iron, however, was the most important metal. The name comes from Tartessos, a place somewhere in this area which was described centuries later by Greek, Roman and biblical writers as the source of fabulous riches. Whether Tartessos was a city, a state or just a region no-one knows. Some argue that it was a trading settlement on the site of modern Huelva, others believe it may lie beneath the marshes near the mouth of the Río Guadalquivir, and yet others equate it with the lost continent of Atlantis.

Iberians

From the 6th century BC the Phoenicians and Greeks were pushed out of the western Mediterranean by Carthage, a former Phoenician colony in modern Tunisia which came to dominate regional trade. Tartessic culture weakened and the people known as Iberians, from farther north in Spain, set up a number of small, often one-village statelets in Andalucía.

Romans

The Carthaginians inevitably came into conflict with a new Mediterranean power, Rome. After losing out to Rome in the First Punic War (264–241 BC), which was fought for control of Sicily, Carthage conquered southern Spain. The Second Punic War (218–201 BC), in which Carthaginian general Hannibal marched his elephants over the Alps towards Rome, brought Roman legions to Spain. Rome ended Carthaginian ambitions on the Iberian Peninsula with a victory at Ilipa in 206 BC. The first Roman town in Spain, Itálica (Santiponce, near Seville), was founded near the battle site soon afterwards.

Although it took Rome 200 years to subdue the rest of the Iberian Peninsula, Andalucía settled quickly into Roman ways and became one of the most civilised and wealthiest areas of the empire outside Italy. Rome imported Andalucian products such as wheat, vegetables, grapes, olives, copper, silver, lead, fish and *garum* (a spicy seasoning derived from fish). Andalucía also gave Rome two emperors, Trajan and Hadrian, both from Itálica.

In the 1st century BC Rome divided the Iberian Peninsula into three provinces: Baetica, covering most of Andalucía, southern Extremadura and southwestern Castilla-La Mancha, with its capital at Corduba (Córdoba); Lusitania (Portugal and northern Extremadura); and Tarraconensis (the rest, including far-eastern Andalucía). The Via Augusta road ran from Rome to Gades (Cádiz), passing through Tarraco (Tarragona in Catalunya), Corduba, Astigi (Écija), Carmo (Carmona) and Hispalis (Seville; Sevilla in Spanish).

Rome gave Andalucía aqueducts, temples, theatres, amphitheatres, circuses and baths. It also bequeathed Spain its language (Spanish is basically colloquial Latin 2000 years on), the basis of its legal system, a sizable Jewish population (Jews spread throughout the Mediterranean part of the Roman Empire), and Christianity, which probably arrived in the 3rd century AD with soldiers from North Africa and with merchants. The new religion took root among the wealthier urban classes in Andalucía even before Emperor Constantine made it the empire's official religion in AD 313.

Visigoths

By the late 3rd century, the Roman Empire was weakening and under attack from the north and east. When the Huns arrived from Asia in the late 4th century, displaced Germanic peoples moved westwards, some overrunning the Iberian Peninsula. One Germanic group, the Visigoths, took Rome in 410. Having spared the emperor, they made a pact with him to rid the Iberian Peninsula of other invaders in return for lands in southern Gaul (France). But early in the 6th century, the Visigoths were pushed out of Gaul by yet another Germanic people, the Franks. The Visigoths then settled in the Iberian Peninsula, and Toledo, in central Spain, became their capital.

The long-haired Visigoths, numbering about 200,000, had little culture of their own and tended to ape Roman ways. Their rule over the relatively sophisticated Hispano-Romans was precarious, and undermined by strife among their own nobility. Ties between the Visigoth monarchy and the Hispano-Romans were strengthened in 587 when King Reccared converted to Catholicism from the Visigoths' Aryan version of Christianity (which denied that Christ was God).

The Muslim Conquest

By 700, with famine in Toledo, strife among the aristocracy and chaos throughout the peninsula, the Visigothic kingdom was falling apart. This paved the way for the Muslim invasion of 711, which set Spain's destiny apart from the rest of Europe.

Following the death of the prophet Mohammed in 632, Arabs had spread through the Middle East and North Africa, bringing Islam with them. If you believe the myth, they were ushered onto the Iberian Peninsula by the sexual exploits of the last Visigoth king, Roderic (Rodrigo). Ballads and chronicles relate how Roderic seduced young Florinda, the daughter of Julian, the Visigothic governor of Ceuta in North Africa; and how Julian sought revenge by approaching the Muslims with a plan to invade Spain. In dull fact, Roderic's rivals probably just appealed for outside help in the struggle for the Visigothic throne.

In 711 Tariq ibn Ziyad, the Muslim governor of Tangier, landed at Gibraltar with around 10,000 men, mostly Berbers (indigenous North Africans). He had some of Roderic's Visigoth rivals as allies. Roderic's army was decimated, probably near the Río Guadalete or Río Barbate in Cádiz province, and he is thought to have drowned as he fled. Visigothic survivors fled north.

Within a few years, the Muslims had taken over all of the Iberian Peninsula except for small areas in the Asturian mountains in the far north.

Al-Andalus

The Muslims (often referred to as Moors) were to be the dominant force on the Iberian Peninsula for nearly four centuries, a potent force for 170 years after that and a lesser one for a further 250 years. Between wars and rebellions, the Muslim areas of the peninsula developed the most cultured society of medieval Europe. The name given to the Muslim territories, Al-Andalus, was probably an Arabisation of the Visigothic name for the Roman province of Baetica, *landa-hlauts*, and lives on in the modern name of what was always the Muslim heartland – Andalucía.

Al-Andalus' frontiers were constantly shifting as the Christians strove to regain territory in the stuttering 800-year Reconquista (Reconquest). Up to the mid-11th century, the frontier stretched across the Iberian Peninsula from just south of Barcelona to what's now northern Portugal. The small Christian states that developed north of this frontier were too weak and quarrelsome to pose much of a threat for 350 years. Al-Andalus itself also suffered internal conflicts, and Muslims and Christians even struck up alliances against their own kind.

Muslim political power and culture centred first on Córdoba (756–1031), then Seville (c. 1040–1248) and lastly Granada (1248–1492). In the main cities, the Muslims built beautiful palaces, mosques and gardens, established large, bustling *zocos* (markets) and public bathhouses (which most people attended about once a week), and opened universities. In the countryside, they built on the Hispano-Roman agricultural base by improving irrigation and introducing new fruits and crops, such as oranges, lemons, peaches, sugar cane and rice.

Although military campaigns against the northern Christians could be bloodthirsty affairs, the rulers of Al-Andalus allowed freedom of worship to Jews and Christians under their rule. Jews, on the whole, flourished, but Christians in Muslim territory (Mozarabs; Spanish *mozárabes*) had to pay a special tax, so most either converted to Islam (to become known as *muladíes*, or Muwallads) or left for the Christian north.

The Muslim ruling class was composed of various Arab groups prone to factional friction. Below them was a larger group of Berbers, holding mainly second-rank positions and living on second-grade land. Berbers rebelled on numerous occasions.

The Arabs and Berbers didn't bring many women with them and, before long, Muslim and local blood merged. There was even frequent aristocratic intermarriage with the northern Christians, for tribute, appeasement or alliance. The famous 10th-century Córdoba caliph Abd ar-Rahman III, whose grandmother was a Basque princess, had fair hair and blue eyes.

Cordoban Emirate (756–929) Initially, Muslim Spain was a province of the Emirate of Ifriqiya (North Africa), part of the Caliphate of Damascus, which ruled the Muslim world. In 750 the Omayyad caliphal dynasty was overthrown by a revolutionary group called the Abbasids, who

soon shifted the caliphate to Baghdad. One Omayyad escaped the slaughter and somehow made his way to Córdoba, where in 756 he managed to set himself up as an independent emir, Abd ar-Rahman I. It was he who began the construction of Córdoba's great Mezquita (mosque).

Abd ar-Rahman I's Omayyad dynasty more or less unified Al-Andalus for long periods, although Muslim leaders near Christian frontiers often resisted central Cordoban authority, and prolonged resistance was waged in Andalucía itself by Omar ibn Hafsun, a Muwallad rebel based at the hilltop hideout of Bobastro (Málaga province). Ibn Hafsun gained a large following and at one stage controlled territory from Cartagena to the Strait of Gibraltar. His 40-year rebellion was carried on for a further 10 years by his sons after his death in 917.

Cordoban Caliphate (929–1031) In 929 Abd ar-Rahman III (912–61) decided that he would bestow upon himself the title of caliph (meaning deputy to Mohammed and therefore supreme religious, political and military leader of the Muslim world) to assert his authority in the face of the Fatimids, who were becoming a growing Muslim power in North Africa. Thus Abd ar-Rahman III launched the caliphate of Córdoba, during which Al-Andalus reached its greatest power and lustre.

At its peak, the caliphate encompassed most of the Iberian Peninsula south of the Río Duero, plus the Balearic Islands and some of North Africa. Córdoba became the biggest, most dazzling and most cultured city in Western Europe, thriving on agriculture and the work of its skilled artisans. Astronomy, medicine, mathematics, philosophy, history and botany flourished. Abd ar-Rahman III's court was frequented by Jewish, Arabian and Christian scholars. Even Christians from northern Spain came to be treated by its renowned doctors.

Later in the 10th century, the fearsome Cordoban general Al-Mansur (or Almanzor) terrorised the Christian north with 50-odd *razzias* (forays) in 20 years. In 997 he destroyed the cathedral at Santiago de Compostela in northwestern Spain – home of the cult of Santiago Matamoros (St James the Moor-Slayer), which was a crucial inspiration to Christian warriors. Al-Mansur also conquered Morocco and, though not caliph, effectively ruled Al-Andalus. But after the death of Al-Mansur's son in 1008, the caliphate imploded in a devastating civil war. In 1031 it disintegrated into dozens of *taifas* (small kingdoms), ruled by local potentates, often Berber generals.

Rise of Sevilla In Andalucía, Granada and Sevilla were the strongest *taifas*. Sevilla's Abbasid dynasty, controlling the trading and agricultural wealth of the lower Guadalquivir valley, was soon able to start absorbing other *taifas*; it did this by various means, including suffocating the rulers of Morón, Arcos and Ronda in the bathhouse of Seville city's Alcázar palace. By 1078, Sevilla's writ ran all the way from southern Portugal to Murcia, restoring a measure of peace and prosperity to Andalucía.

Almoravids Meanwhile, the small northern Christian states were getting themselves into more threatening shape. Castile (Castilla in Spanish), which was originally a small principality within the kingdom of León, emerged as the dominant force in the 11th century.

When Alfonso VI of Castile took Toledo in central Spain in 1085, Seville begged for help from the Almoravids, a strict Muslim sect of Saharan Berbers who had conquered Morocco. The Almoravids came, defeated Alfonso, and went back to Morocco. They then returned in 1091 to help themselves to Al-Andalus too.

Aghast at what they saw as the decadence of Al-Andalus, the Almoravids ruled it from Marrakech as a colony, and persecuted Jews and Christians (many of whom fled north into Christian territory). But the charms of Al-Andalus seemed to relax the austere grip of the Almoravids. Revolts spread across Al-Andalus from 1143 and within a few years it had again split into *taifas*.

Almohads A new, strict Muslim Berber sect, the Almohads from the Atlas Mountains, displaced the Almoravids in Morocco and then started nibbling at Al-Andalus. So too did the Christians: Portugal, an emerging Christian kingdom in the west of the Iberian Peninsula, took Lisbon from the Muslims in 1147. The Almohads invaded Al-Andalus in earnest in 1160, bringing it under full control by 1173. But what they ruled was considerably less than the Al-Andalus of its 10th-century heyday: the frontier now ran from south of Lisbon to north of Valencia.

The Almohads made Sevilla capital of their whole realm (which included Algeria, Tunisia and Morocco) and revived arts and learning, building a big new mosque in Seville city.

In 1195, King Yusuf Yacub al-Mansur thrashed Castile's army at Alarcos, south of Toledo, but this only had the effect of temporarily uniting most of the Iberian Peninsula's Christian states against him. In 1212 the combined armies of Castile, Aragón and Navarra routed a large Almohad force at Las Navas de Tolosa in northeastern Andalucía (Jaén province); this was the beginning of the end for Al-Andalus.

The Almohad state cracked in a succession dispute after 1224, and the Christians took full advantage. Castile's Fernando III (El Santo, the Saint) took the strategic town of Baeza, in northeastern Andalucía, in 1227. León took the key towns of Extremadura in 1229 and 1230, while Aragón took the Valencia region in the 1230s. Fernando III took Córdoba easily in 1236, and won Jaén in 1246 by agreeing to respect the frontiers of the Emirate of Granada, a wedge of territory carved out of the disintegrating Almohad realm by one Mohammed ibn Yusuf ibn Nasr. Ibn Nasr agreed to pay half his income in tribute to Castile and sent a troop of cavalry to join Fernando's attack on Almohad Sevilla, which fell, after a two-year siege, in 1248.

Nasrid Emirate of Granada Portugal's defeat of the Muslims in 1249 left the Granada emirate, known as the Nasrid emirate after ibn Nasr, as the only Muslim state on the Iberian Peninsula. It comprised roughly the modern provinces of Granada, Málaga and Almería, plus bordering bits of Cádiz, Sevilla, Córdoba and Jaén, and had a population of about 300,000, of whom some 50,000 were in Granada itself.

The Nasrids ruled from Granada's lavish Alhambra palace. The city saw the final flowering in Spain of Muslim culture and the state prospered as a result of an influx of Muslim refugees from conquered lands. In between bouts of fighting, Granada continued trading with Christian Spain, selling silk, dried fruits, sugar and spices, and buying salt, oil and other staples. The emirate reached its greatest glory in the 14th century under Yusuf I and Mohammed V, who were the creators of the chief splendours of the Alhambra.

Castilian armies eventually began nibbling at the emirate in the 15th century. Granada's final downfall was precipitated by two things. One was Emir Abu al-Hasan's refusal in 1476 to pay any more tribute to Castile. The other was the unification in 1479 of Castile and Aragón, the peninsula's biggest and most powerful Christian states, through the marriage of their monarchs Isabel and Fernando (Isabella and Ferdinand). The Reyes Católicos (Catholic Monarchs), as the pair are known, launched the final crusade of the Reconquista – against Granada – in 1482.

By now, Granada's rulers were riven by harem jealousies and other feuds. Matters degenerated into a civil war which allowed the Christians to push across the emirate, besieging towns and devastating the countryside. They captured Málaga (whose people were mostly sold off as slaves) in 1487, and Granada itself, after an eight-month siege, on 2 January 1492.

The surrender terms were fairly generous to the last emir, Boabdil, who got the Alpujarras valleys south of Granada as a personal fiefdom. He stayed there only a year, however, before leaving for Africa. The Muslims were promised respect for their religion, culture and property, but this didn't last long.

The Muslim Legacy

The medieval Muslims left a deep imprint on Andalucía – and not just because of the palaces, castles and mosques that rank among its greatest monuments today. For a start, many, if not most, Spaniards are, through medieval interbreeding, partly descended from the Muslims.

The typically narrow, labyrinthine street plan of Andalucian villages and towns is of Muslim origin, as are the predilection for fountains and running water and the use of plants as decoration. Muslim architectural tastes and crafts were adopted by Christians in and outside Al-Andalus (the Muslim territories), and many of them remain in use in Spain today. Flamenco song, though brought to its modern form by *gitanos* (Roma people) in post-Muslim times, has clear Islamic roots. The Spanish language contains numerous words of Arabic origin, including *arroz* (rice), *alcalde* (mayor), *naranja* (orange) and *azúcar* (sugar). Many of the foods eaten in Andalucía today were introduced by the Muslims, and in many places the irrigation and terracing systems on which foods are grown date back to Muslim times. Lots of today's Andalucian churches were originally built many centuries ago as mosques.

It was through Al-Andalus that much of the learning of ancient Greece was transmitted to Christian Europe. The Arabs, during the course of their conquests in the eastern Mediterranean, had absorbed Greek science and philosophy, translating classical works into Arabic and developing such sciences as astronomy and medicine. There were two places in southern Europe in the Middle Ages where the Islamic and Christian worlds met and through which this knowledge could find its way north – one was southern Italy, the other was Al-Andalus.

13th- & 14th-Century Christian Andalucía

Much of the Muslim population who fled from areas that fell to the Christians in the 13th century went to Granada or North Africa. The new Christian rulers gave smallholdings to Christian settlers in an attempt to repopulate the countryside. They also handed out large tracts of land to the nobility as well as to the knightly crusading orders – such as the Orden de Santiago (Order of Santiago) and the Orden de Calatrava – who had played a vital part in the Reconquista.

Muslim raids from Granada often caused the lesser settlers to flee or sell their lands to the nobility and orders, whose holdings thereby increased. Thus originated the *latifundia* (huge estates) that have been a problematic feature of rural Andalucía ever since.

By 1300, rural Christian Andalucía was almost empty. The landowners turned much of it over to sheep, ruining former food-growing land.

Fernando III's son Alfonso X (El Sabio, The Learned; 1252–84) made Seville one of his capitals and launched something of a cultural revival, gathering scholars around him, particularly Jews, who knew Arabic and Latin and could translate ancient texts into Castilian Spanish.

Initially, Mudejars (Muslims who remained in Christian territory) faced no reprisals. But in 1264 the Mudejars of Jerez rose up against new taxes and rules that required them to celebrate Christian feasts and live in ghettos. After a five-month siege they were expelled to Granada or North Africa, along with the Mudejars of Seville, Córdoba and Arcos.

Meanwhile the Castilian nobility, contentedly rich from wool production on their huge estates, permitted Jews and foreigners, especially Genoese, to dominate Castilian commerce and finance.

The Black Death and a series of bad harvests ravaged Christian Andalucía in the 14th century. Discontent eventually found its scapegoat in the Jews, resented for their involvement in tax collecting and money-lending, who were subjected to pogroms around the peninsula in the 1390s. As a result, some Jews converted to Christianity (they became known as *conversos*); others moved to Granada.

The Catholic Monarchs

The pious Isabel and Machiavellian Fernando were an unbeatable team. They checked the power of the Castilian nobility, excluding them from the royal administration, and granted Andalucian land to their own supporters. They also reformed a corrupt clergy. By the time Fernando died in 1516 (12 years after Isabel – both are buried in Granada), Spain was united under one rule for the first time since Visigothic days.

Persecution of the Jews The urge for unity was not just territorial. The Catholic Monarchs revived the Inquisition – originally founded in the 13th century to deal with heretics in France – to root out those who didn't practise Christianity as the Catholic Church wished them to. The Spanish Inquisition focused most of all on *conversos*, accusing many of these converted Jews of continuing to practise Judaism in secret. Jews were considered Muslim allies. The Inquisition's first tribunal was held in Seville in 1481. In its three centuries of existence, the Inquisition was responsible for perhaps 12,000 deaths, 2000 of them in the 1480s.

Under the influence of Grand Inquisitor Tomás de Torquemada, in 1492 Isabel and Fernando ordered the expulsion from their territories of every Jew who refused Christian baptism. Around 50,000 to 100,000 Jews converted, but some 200,000, the first Sephardic Jews (Jews of Spanish origin), left for other Mediterranean destinations. The bankrupt monarchy seized all unsold Jewish property. A talented urban middle class was decimated.

Persecution of the Muslims Cardinal Cisneros, Isabel's confessor and overseer of the Inquisition, was given the task of converting the Muslims of the former Granada emirate. He carried out forced mass baptisms, had Islamic books burnt and banned the Arabic language. This, combined with expropriations of Muslim land, sparked a revolt in 1500 that, beginning in the Alpujarras valleys, spread right across the former emirate, from Ronda to Almería. Afterwards, Muslims were ordered to convert to

Through marriage and belief, Isabel, Catholic crusader, united Spain under a single rule

Christianity or leave. Most, an estimated 300,000, underwent baptism and stayed, becoming known as Moriscos (converted Muslims). But their conversion was barely skin-deep and they never assimilated to Christian culture.

Seville & the Americas

In April 1492 the Catholic Monarchs granted the Genoese sailor Christopher Columbus (Cristóbal Colón to Spaniards) funds for a voyage across the Atlantic in search of a new trade route to the Orient. Columbus' finding of the Americas (for his story, see the boxed text 'The Four Voyages of Christopher Columbus' in the Huelva Province chapter) opened up a whole new hemisphere of opportunity for Spain, and especially for the river port of Seville.

During the reign of Carlos I (Charles I; 1516–56), the first of the new Habsburg dynasty, Spain occupied vast tracts of the American mainland. Ruthless but brilliant conquerors such as Hernán Cortés and Francisco Pizarro, who subdued the Aztec and Inca empires respectively with small bands of adventurers, were, with their mix of brutality and bravery, gold lust and piety, the natural successors to the crusaders of the Reconquista.

The new colonies sent huge quantities of silver, gold and other treasure back to Spain, where the crown was entitled to one-fifth of the bullion (the *quinto real*, or royal fifth). Seville became the hub of world trade, a cosmopolitan melting pot of money seekers, and remained Spain's major city until late in the 17th century, even though little Madrid was made the national capital in 1561.

The prosperity was shared to some extent by Cádiz and the lower Guadalquivir area, and less so by cities such as Jaén, Córdoba and Granada. But eastern Andalucía still depended on technologically backward agriculture and artisanry. A small number of big landowners did little with large tracts of territory except raise sheep on them, while those peasants who still lived off the land lacked any way of improving their lot.

Seville's cosmopolitan status opened up urban Andalucía to new European ideas and artistic movements. Lavish Renaissance and, later, baroque buildings sprouted and Seville became a focus of Spain's artistic golden age. New universities in Seville (1505), Granada (1531) and Baeza (1542) spread the humanist ideas of the Renaissance, which led to a questioning of Roman Catholic dogma by so-called *protestantes* or *alumbrados* (enlightened ones) in a few centres. These nascent flickers of Protestantism were soon snuffed out by the Inquisition.

Morisco Revolt & Expulsion

Felipe II (Philip II; 1556–98) was a fanatical Catholic who, as well as spurring the Inquisition to renewed persecutions, in 1567 forbade Moriscos to use the Arabic language, Arabic names, Morisco dress or practise certain Morisco customs. The Moriscos were blamed (with reason) for some of the frequent raids on Spanish coasts from North Africa. A Morisco revolt in the Alpujarras spread across southern Andalucía and took two years to put down, resulting in the deportation of the Moriscos from eastern to western Andalucía and more northerly parts of Spain. Among other things, this ruined the Granada silk industry. The Moriscos were finally expelled altogether from Spain by Felipe III between 1609 and 1614.

Decline

Even under Carlos I, Spain had been spending much of its new wealth on European wars, wasting any chance of the country becoming an early industrial power. There was no plan to absorb the American wealth, or to cope with the inflation it caused. The gentry's disdain for commerce and industry allowed Genoese and German merchants to dominate trade, and left the countryside full of sheep and cattle ranches, with Spain running a trade deficit because grain had to be imported. Most Andalucians had no land or property.

In the 17th century, under the last three ineffectual Habsburg kings, Spain's European wars continued while silver shipments from the Americas shrank disastrously. In Andalucía, epidemics and bad harvests killed some 300,000 people – including half of Seville in 1649. Coming after the expulsions of the Jews and Moriscos, this left Andalucía distinctly underpopulated. The lower Guadalquivir, Seville's lifeline to the Atlantic, became increasingly silted-up and in 1717 the Casa de la Contratación, the government office controlling commerce with the Americas, was transferred to Cádiz.

The 18th Century

Under the Bourbon dynasty (still in place today) Spain made a limited recovery in the 18th century. This was the age of the Enlightenment, with its faith in reason, science and social planning. The monarchy financed incipient industries, such as Seville's tobacco factory. A new road, the Carretera General de Andalucía, was built from Madrid to Seville and Cádiz. Along the Andalucian section, Carlos III's reforming minister Pablo de Olavide founded a couple of dozen new towns, with straight streets, broad squares and German and Flemish settlers. The idea was both to repopulate empty, lawless areas and to modernise Andalucía's agriculture. But the project was opposed by the big landowners (who didn't like releasing land) and the church (because many of the settlers were Protestants), and had little success.

New land was opened up for wheat and barley, however, and trade through Cádiz (which was in its heyday) grew. Free-trade decrees in 1765 and 1778 made it legal for additional Spanish ports to conduct commerce with the Americas, which stimulated the growth of Málaga. New settlers from other parts of Spain boosted Andalucía's population to about 1.8 million by 1787.

Napoleonic Invasion & the Cádiz Cortes

When Louis XVI of France (a cousin of Spain's Carlos IV) was guillotined in 1793, Spain declared war on France. Two years later, with French forces occupying northern Spain, Spain switched sides, pledging military support for France against Britain in return for French withdrawal from Spain. In 1805 a combined Spanish-French navy was beaten by a British fleet under Admiral Nelson off Cape Trafalgar (which lies between Cádiz and Gibraltar). This terminated Spanish sea power.

Two years later, Napoleon Bonaparte and Spain agreed to divide Portugal, Britain's ally, between the two of them. French forces poured into Spain, supposedly on the way to Portugal, but by 1808 this had become a French occupation of Spain, with Napoleon forcing Carlos IV to abdicate to his brother, Joseph Bonaparte (José I). In the ensuing Spanish War of Independence, or Peninsular War, the Spanish populace took up arms in guerrilla fashion and, with help from British and Portuguese forces led by the Duke of Wellington, drove the French out by 1813.

During the war, few Spanish cities kept the French at bay, but Cádiz withstood a two-year siege from 1810 to 1812. A national parliament which convened in Cádiz during the siege adopted a new constitution for Spain which proclaimed sovereignty of the people and reduced the rights of the monarchy, nobility and church.

Liberals vs Conservatives

The Cádiz constitution set the scene for a century of struggle between Spanish liberals, who wanted vaguely democratic reforms, and conservatives who wanted to maintain the status quo. Fernando VII,

son of Carlos IV, revoked the new constitution, persecuted opponents and even reestablished the Inquisition. In 1820 in Las Cabezas de San Juan, in Sevilla province, Colonel Rafael de Riego made the first of 19th-century Spain's many *pronunciamientos* (pronouncements of rebellion) in the name of liberalism. But French troops put Fernando back on the throne in 1823 (Riego was captured in Jaén and hung, drawn and quartered in Madrid).

Between 1813 and 1825, Mexico and most of Spain's South and Central American colonies took advantage of Spain's problems to win their independence – desperate news for Cádiz, which had been totally reliant on trade with the colonies.

The Disamortisations of 1836 and 1855, when liberal governments ordered church and municipal lands to be auctioned off to reduce the national debt, pleased the bourgeoisie, who could build up new estates. But they were a disaster for the peasants who lost municipal grazing lands.

Despite being home to one-quarter of Spain's population of 12 million in 1877, Andalucía declined into one of Europe's most backward, socially polarised areas. At one social extreme were the bourgeoisie and the very rich aristocratic landowners. At the other were a small number of poor people with regular jobs and a large number of even poorer *jornaleros* – landless agricultural day labourers who were without work for a good half of the year and who, with their families, probably comprised three-quarters of the population. Illiteracy, disease and hunger were rife. The Industrial Revolution had reached northern Spain in the late 18th century, but it had barely touched the south.

In 1873 a liberal government proclaimed Spain a republic – a federal grouping of 17 states. The republic was totally unable to control its provinces, where numerous cities and towns declared themselves to be independent. Some even declared war on each other, as happened between Sevilla and nearby Utrera. This 'First Republic' lasted only 11 months, with the army ultimately restoring the monarchy.

Anarchism & Socialism

In the face of lost grazing lands, erratic, miserably paid work and hunger, some Andalucian peasants emigrated to Latin America. Others staged uprisings, always savagely put down. The anarchist ideas of the Russian Mikhail Bakunin gained a big following in Andalucía, especially in the lower Guadalquivir area, where the estate owners' monopoly on cultivable land was most complete. Bakunin advocated strikes, sabotage and revolts as the path to a spontaneous revolution of the oppressed that would usher in a free society of voluntary cooperation between autonomous groups of people.

The powerful anarchist union, the Confederación Nacional del Trabajo (CNT; National Labour Confederation), was founded in Seville in 1910. Anarchist trade unionists, known as syndicalists, saw the general strike as the main weapon to achieve an anarchist society. But major anarchist actions in Andalucía, such as the occupation of Jerez de la Frontera by 4000 labourers armed with sticks one day in 1891, brought violent repression. Waves of anarchist strikes occurred between 1902 and 1905, and 1917 and 1918.

Socialism, with its aim of steady change through parliamentary processes, won less support in Andalucía. By 1919, the CNT had 93,000 members in Andalucía, compared with the 12,000 of the socialist Unión General de Trabajadores (UGT; General Union of Workers), and 7000 in Catholic unions.

In 1923 an eccentric general from Jerez, Miguel Primo de Rivera, launched a mild military dictatorship, which won the cooperation of the UGT, while anarchists went underground. Primo achieved more industrialisation, better roads, punctual trains, new dams and power plants. But he was unseated in 1930 as a result of an economic downturn and discontent in the army.

The Second Republic

When a new republican movement scored sweeping victories in Spain's municipal elections in April 1931, King Alfonso XIII departed in exile to Italy. The Second Republic that ensued (1931–36) was an idealistic, tumultuous period that ended in civil war.

The Left in Charge (1931–33) La Niña

Bonita (the Pretty Child), as the Second Republic was called by its supporters, was welcomed by leftists and the poor, but conservatives were alarmed. Elections in 1931 brought in a mixed government including socialists, centrists and Republicans, but the anarchist CNT preferred strikes and violence to bring on the revolution.

A new constitution in December 1931 outraged Catholics by stopping government payment of priests' salaries, legalising divorce and banning clerical orders from teaching. The constitution promised land redistribution, which pleased the Andalucian landless, but failed to deliver much.

The Right in Charge (1933–36) Anarch-

ist disruption, an economic slump, the alienation of big business and disunity on the left all helped the right win the 1933 election. A Catholic party, Confederación Española de Derechas Autónomas (CEDA; Spanish Confederation of Autonomous Rights) won the most seats. Another new force on the right was the fascist Falange, led by José Antonio Primo de Rivera, son of the 1920s dictator. The Falange practised blatant street violence. The left, including the emerging Communists, called increasingly for revolution.

By 1934 violence was spiralling out of control. When workers committees that had taken over the northern mining region of Asturias were viciously quashed by generals Millán Astray and Francisco Franco and the Spanish Foreign Legion (set up to fight Moroccan tribes in the 1920s), all Spain was polarised into left and right.

Popular Front & Army Uprising In the

February 1936 elections the Popular Front left-wing coalition narrowly defeated the right-wing National Front. Violence continued on both sides of the political divide. The CNT now had over one million members and peasants were on the verge of revolution.

On 17 July 1936 the Spanish garrison in Melilla in North Africa revolted against the leftist government, followed the next day by some garrisons on the mainland. The leaders of the plot were five generals. On

19 July one of them, Francisco Franco, flew from the Canary Islands to Morocco to take command of his legionnaires. The civil war had begun.

The Civil War

The Spanish Civil War split communities, families and friends. Both sides committed atrocious massacres and reprisals, in the early weeks especially. The rebels, who called themselves Nationalists, shot or hanged tens of thousands of supporters of the Republic. Republicans did likewise to those they considered Franco sympathisers, including some 7000 priests, monks and nuns. Political affiliation often provided a convenient cover for settling old scores. Altogether, around 350,000 Spaniards died in the war.

In Republican-controlled areas, anarchists, Communists or socialists ended up running many towns and cities. Social revolution followed. In Andalucía this tended to be anarchist, with private property abolished and churches and convents often burned and wrecked. Large estates were occupied by the peasants and around 100 agrarian communes were established. The Nationalist campaign, meanwhile, quickly took on overtones of a holy crusade against the enemies of God.

Nationalist Advance The basic battle lines were drawn within a week of the rebellion in Morocco. Cities whose garrisons backed the rebels (most did) and were strong enough to overcome any resistance fell immediately into Nationalist hands – as happened at Cádiz, Córdoba, Algeciras and Jerez. Seville was in Nationalist hands within three days and Granada within a few more. Author Hugh Thomas, in his authoritative work *The Spanish Civil War* (first published in 1961), estimates that 4000 people were executed by the Nationalists in and around Granada after they had taken the city. There was slaughter in Republican areas too. An estimated 2500 people were murdered in a few months in anarchist Málaga. A gang from Málaga killed over 500 people in Ronda in the first month of the war.

From Seville, Nationalist troops mopped up most of western Andalucía by the end of July. Málaga fell, with little resistance, to Nationalist and Italian troops in February 1937. When the Nationalists captured Republican towns they took bloody revenge for any supposed atrocities carried out there: thousands were executed after they took Málaga.

After the fall of Málaga there was little shift in the military position in Andalucía for the rest of the war. Almería and Jaén provinces, the eastern half of Granada province and the north of Córdoba province all remained Republican until the end of the war in 1939.

General Franco emerged as the undisputed Nationalist leader in late 1936, styling himself Generalísimo (Supreme General). Before long, he also adopted the title Caudillo, roughly equivalent to the German Führer.

Foreign Intervention The scales of the war were tipped in favour of the Nationalists by support from Nazi Germany and Fascist Italy in the form of weapons, planes and 92,000 men (the majority of them from Italy). The Republicans had some Soviet planes, tanks, artillery and advisers, and 25,000 or so French soldiers fought on their side, along with as many other foreigners in the International Brigades.

Nationalist Victory The Republican government moved from the besieged city of Madrid to Valencia in late 1936. The diversity of political persuasions on the Republican side erupted into fierce street fighting in Barcelona in May 1937, with the Soviet-backed Communists crushing the anarchists and Trotskyites. The Republican government moved to Barcelona in the autumn of 1937.

In 1938 Franco swept eastwards, isolating Barcelona from Valencia, and the USSR withdrew from the war. The Nationalists took Barcelona unopposed in January 1939 and Madrid in March. Franco declared the war won on 1 April 1939.

Franco's Spain (1939–75)

After the civil war, instead of reconciliation, more blood-letting ensued. An estimated 100,000 Spaniards were killed, or died in prison, after the war. A few Communists and Republicans continued their hopeless struggle in small guerrilla units in the Andalucian mountains and elsewhere until the 1950s.

Franco kept Spain out of WWII, but afterwards Spain was excluded from the United Nations (UN) until 1955 and suffered a UN-sponsored trade boycott which helped turn the late 1940s into the *años de hambre* (years of hunger) – which were particularly hungry in poor areas such as Andalucía where, at times, peasants subsisted on soup made from grass and wild herbs.

Franco ruled absolutely. He was commander of the army and leader of the sole political party, the Movimiento Nacional (National Movement). Army garrisons were maintained outside every large city and the jails were full of political prisoners. Catholic orthodoxy was fully restored: most secondary schools were entrusted to the Jesuits, divorce was made illegal and church weddings compulsory. Crime rates were low and strikes were illegal.

From 1939 to 1975 General Francisco Franco ruled over every aspect of Spanish life

In the late 1950s a new breed of technocrats in government engineered an economic boom. In Andalucía, despite some new industries and the launch of mass foreign tourism on the Costa del Sol, many villages still lacked electricity, reliable water supplies and paved roads to the outside world. Between 1950 and 1970, 1.5 million Andalucians left to find work elsewhere. Some went to other European countries, but more to Barcelona, Madrid and other Spanish cities. Although tourism created jobs for Andalucians, it also brought culture shock to what was still an old-fashioned, traditional society.

New Democracy

Franco chose Alfonso XIII's grandson, Prince Juan Carlos, as his successor; Juan Carlos took the throne, aged 37, two days after Franco's death in 1975. Much of the credit for the ensuing transition to democracy goes to the king. The man he appointed prime minister, Adolfo Suárez, pushed through the Francoist-filled Cortes (Parliament) a proposal for a new, two-chamber parliamentary system. In 1977 political parties, trade unions and strikes were all legalised, the Movimiento Nacional was abolished and Suárez's centrist party won nearly half the seats in elections to the new Cortes. The left-of-centre Partido Socialista Obrero Español (PSOE; Spanish Socialist Workers' Party), led by a young lawyer from Seville, Felipe González, came in second.

Spanish society enjoyed a sudden liberation after Franco. Contraceptives, homosexuality, adultery and divorce were legalised, and it was during this era that the *movida* – the late bar and club scene that enables people almost anywhere in Spain to party all night – emerged.

Government by the PSOE & PP

In 1982 Spain made a final break with the past by voting the PSOE into power with a big majority. Felipe González was to be prime minister for 14 years, taking several other Andalucians into high office with him. The party's young, educated leadership came from the generation that had opened the cracks in the Franco regime in the late 1960s and early 1970s. It made big improvements in education, launched a national health system, and legalised narcotics and abortion (in the face of drug and alcoholism problems, public use of narcotics was banned in 1992).

In 1986 Spain joined the European Community (EC), now the European Union (EU), which brought on its second post–civil war economic boom, lasting until 1991, and cut unemployment to 16%. The PSOE, however, began to figure in a series of scandals. Most damaging was the GAL affair, named after the Grupos Antiterroristas de Liberación, death squads that had murdered 28 suspected Basque terrorists in the mid-1980s. Eventually a dozen senior police and PSOE men were jailed in connection with GAL.

In the face of all this and a post-1991 economic slump, the PSOE lost the 1996 general election to the Partido Popular (PP; People's Party), a centre-right party under the leadership of a former tax inspector, José María Aznar. After four years of steady economic progress and no scandals, Aznar and the PP won again in 2000.

Andalucía since Franco PSOE government at national and regional level eradicated the worst of Andalucian poverty with grants, community works schemes and a generous dole system. The left-of-centre party has dominated Andalucía's regional government in Seville since 1982. Expo '92, the world fair held in Seville in 1992 – the same year as the Barcelona Olympic Games, and exactly five centuries on from the pivotal year of Spanish history, 1492 – brought hundreds of thousands of visitors and boosted the international image of Seville and Andalucía, plus the new high-speed Alta Velocidad Española (AVE) railway from Madrid to Seville.

Since the economic slump of the early to mid-1990s, Andalucía, like Spain as a whole, has become steadily more prosperous. The unemployment rate has almost halved, even though it remains above the national average, and wages in Andalucía are now only a little below the national average. Steady growth in tourism and industry, a construction boom and massive EU subsidies for Andalucian agriculture have all helped.

The widespread air of prosperity and confidence would certainly surprise any Andalucian returning home today after 50 years on Mars. So too would the bright lights and high-rise public housing blocks in the cities; the glitzy shopping centres; the transformation of long stretches of useless, barren coast into tightly packed concrete international holiday resorts; the motorcycles in place of donkeys; the rarity of hunger; universal schooling, the high level of youth literacy and the large numbers of university students; the relaxation of old codes of dress and morality; the loud new music; and the prevalence of drugs and drink among the young. Yet not everything would be unfamiliar. Andalucians still remain a close-knit bunch, oriented first to their family, second to their village or town, third to their district, fourth to their province, and finally, about equally to Andalucía and Spain. They know they must still stick together because the good times have not yet lasted quite long enough to obliterate the memory of the bad ones.

GEOGRAPHY

Andalucía stretches 550km from east to west and between 90km and 250km from north to south. Its 87,000-sq-km area – about the same size as Portugal – comprises 17% of Spain. It has 460km of coastline along the Mediterranean Sea, and a 240km seaboard on the Atlantic Ocean. The two coasts meet at the Strait of Gibraltar, where the town of Tarifa, just 15km from Africa, is continental Europe's most southerly point.

Andalucía has four main geographic regions, all running roughly east–west across it: the Sierra Morena, the Guadalquivir valley, the mountains and the coastal plain.

Sierra Morena

The Sierra Morena, a range of hills that rarely tops 1000m, rolls across the north of Andalucía, straddling the borders with the neighbouring regions, Extremadura and Castilla-La Mancha. The area has a few mining towns, but most of it is very sparsely populated and divided between evergreen oak woodlands and scrub and rough pasture used for grazing. Different bits of the Sierra Morena have their own names, such as the Sierra del Viento in Sevilla province and the Sierra de Aracena in Huelva province.

Guadalquivir Valley

The fertile valley of the 660km Río Guadalquivir, Andalucía's longest river, stretches across Andalucía south of the Sierra Morena. The Guadalquivir flows approximately westwards from Jaén province through Córdoba, then bends south through Seville to enter the Atlantic at Sanlúcar de Barrameda. From the lower Guadalquivir, a broad plain stretches west across Huelva province and southeast into Cádiz province. Before entering the ocean, the Guadalquivir splits into a marshy delta known as Las Marismas del Guadalquivir, which includes the Parque Nacional de Doñana.

The Guadalquivir is navigable as far upstream as Seville, and used to be navigable up to Córdoba. The river and the surrounding rich agricultural country have made these two cities the main seats of political power in Andalucía since Roman times. The plains rolling north and south from the river as far downstream as Seville are known as *la campiña*.

The name Guadalquivir derives from the Arabic Wadi al-Kabir (Great River): the Romans called it the Betis and the ancient Greeks the Tartessos.

The Mountains

Between the Guadalquivir valley and the Mediterranean coast rises the Cordillera Bética, a band of rugged mountain ranges which widens out from its beginnings in southwest Andalucía to a breadth of 125km or so in the east. Beyond Andalucía, the mountain chain continues east across the Murcia and Valencia regions, then re-emerges from the Mediterranean as the Balearic islands of Ibiza and Mallorca.

In Andalucía, the *cordillera* divides into two main chains: the more northerly Sistema Subbético and the southerly Sistema Penibético. Both begin in the green, rainy hills southwest of Ronda. The two chains are separated by a series of valleys, plains and basins, such as the Llanos de Antequera, the Vega de Granada, the Hoya de Guadix and the Hoya de Baza.

In northeast Andalucía, the Sistema Subbético turns into the picturesque and complicated collection of 2000m-plus ranges – now running almost north–south – of the Parque Natural de Cazorla in Jaén province, source of the Río Guadalquivir.

The Sistema Penibético includes the 75km-long Sierra Nevada, southeast of Granada, with a series of 3000m-plus peaks, including Mulhacén (3482m), the highest mountain on mainland Spain.

The Coastal Plain

Andalucía's coastal plain varies in width from 50km in the far west to virtually nothing in parts of Granada and Almería provinces, where the Sierra de la Contraviesa and Sierra de Cabo de Gata drop away in sheer cliffs to the Mediterranean. Where the plain is wide enough, it supports much vegetable and fruit growing.

Andalucía's most important ports are Almería, Málaga, Algeciras, Cádiz and Huelva. Tourist development has turned the 75km-long Costa del Sol from Málaga to Estepona into one almost continuous built-up strip. Elsewhere, the coast runs between smaller fishing, farming and resort towns, with – especially around the Cabo de Gata promontory east of Almería and along the Atlantic coast (called the Costa de la Luz) – plenty of fine, long, sandy beaches, which for much of the year are distinctly underpopulated. As well as the Marismas del Guadalquivir, further wetlands mark the mouths of several rivers along the Atlantic coast.

Dams & Desert

Nearly all Andalucía's rivers are dammed at least once in their course to supply water and hydroelectricity. You'll come across large reservoirs throughout the region. The exception is the very dry Almería province, which contains extensive semi-desert areas of bare, eroded terrain with enough resemblance to the Arizona badlands to have been used as the location of many Western movies!

CLIMATE

There's a marked difference between the coastal and interior climates. Inland, the weather can be pretty inclement from November to February and frying hot in July and August. On the coasts, temperatures are temperate in winter and not quite so hot in summer.

In July and August, daytime temperatures will typically reach 36°C in Seville and Córdoba and climb to only a little less in Granada and Jaén. Along the coasts, expect temperatures of about 30°C. Winter weather (November to February) is unpredictable: winters can be predominantly dry and warm (raising the danger of drought) or there can be many weeks of rain, with the possibility of flooding.

From December to February, average daytime highs hover around 16°C on the coasts and in Seville, and reach around 13°C in Granada and Jaén; Granada gets close to freezing at night.

From October to March Andalucía receives, on average, a similar amount of rain to London. But there's little rain between June and September. With the prevailing winds coming from the Atlantic Ocean, western Andalucía is damper than the east. In fact, the Sierra de Grazalema, west of Ronda, is the wettest part of Spain and the town of Grazalema receives over 2200mm of rain per year. Meanwhile, the Cabo de Gata promontory in Almería province is the driest place in Europe, with just 100mm of rainfall a year.

Tarifa, at Andalucía's southernmost point, where the Atlantic Ocean meets the Mediterranean Sea, experiences strong winds most of the time – wonderful for windsurfers.

In the mountains, temperatures are always several degrees cooler than down on the plains and you can expect more rain and, in winter, some snow. The Sierra Nevada is snow-covered above about 3000m most of the year.

Sea temperatures hover around 20°C along most of the coast from July to October, and around 15°C from December to April.

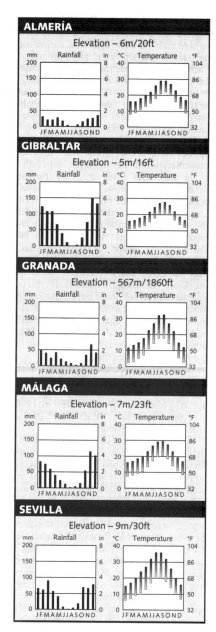

ECOLOGY & ENVIRONMENT

Andalucía's relative lack of industry and, until recently, its fairly traditional agriculture have left it with a pretty clean environment. Each year, the **Foundation for Environmental Education** (**w** *www.fee-international.org*) awards blue flags to 60 or 70 Andalucian beaches, indicating that they meet certain international standards of hygiene, facilities and environmental management.

There are, however, a number of black spots. Slackly controlled tourism-based construction and development, especially along the coasts, leads to the destruction of coastal woodlands, threats to coastal ecosytems and some pollution of the seas. Large amounts of untreated sewage enter the sea along the coast of the Axarquía region east of Málaga. Air pollution by industry is a concern in the Huelva area and there have been scares over fertilisers that may have polluted the drinking water of the lower Guadalquivir basin. Intensive vegetable growing under ugly expanses of plastic greenhouse in the arid Almería region raises fears that the underground aquifers on which it depends will be bled dry (see the boxed text 'The Plastic Sea' in the Almería Province chapter).

There are also occasional disasters, such as the damage to areas around the Parque Nacional de Doñana caused by a big leakage of poisonous mining wastes in 1998 (see the boxed text 'Black Tide' in the Huelva Province chapter).

It was the Romans who began to cut Andalucía's extensive woodlands and forests for timber, fuel, weapons and space for agriculture. They and the Muslims opened up large areas to agriculture through irrigation and terracing of the hillsides. Later, overgrazing by huge sheep flocks eroded much topsoil – most of the Guadalquivir wetlands have been formed by deposited sediment in the past 3000 years – and imperial Spain's demand for shipbuilding timber decimated many native forests. Many animal species have been drastically depleted by hunting. Protection given to many animal and bird species has helped some, but it's probably too late for others.

Conservation

Environmental awareness in Spain took a leap forward in the 1980s under the PSOE national government, which gave regional administrations responsibility for most environmental matters. In 1981 Spain had 35 environmentally protected areas, covering 2200 sq km. Today there are over 400, covering more than 25,000 sq km, and Andalucía is the leader in this field (see the special section 'Andalucía's National & Natural Parks'). Not that protected areas are always perfectly protected: environmentalists have to stay alert against corrupt officials turning a blind eye to illicit building, quarrying, hunting and so on in protected areas. Ever since the Parque Nacional de Doñana, whose wetlands are a bird habitat of huge international importance, was declared in 1969, battles have had to be fought against agricultural and tourism schemes around its fringes which threaten to reduce or pollute the park's water supplies.

Water

Potentially, Andalucía's worst environmental problem is drought, which struck in the 1950s and '60s and the early 1990s. This is despite huge investment in reservoirs (which cover a higher proportion of the land in Spain than in any other country in the world).

The national government wants to spend billions of euros on diverting water from the Río Ebro, which flows across northern Spain, southwards to help agriculture in the arid Valencia and Murcia regions and Almería in eastern Andalucía. But the Plan Hidrológico Nacional (National Water Plan), proposing this, faces intense opposition from farmers and others along the Ebro and from ecologists concerned about the effects on the delicate balance of the large Ebro delta in Catalunya.

GOVERNMENT & POLITICS

Since 1978 Spain has been a constitutional monarchy. The national parliament, the Cortes Generales, comprises the Congreso de los Diputados (lower house) and Senado (upper house). Both houses are elected by free universal suffrage. Spain is divided into

17 autonomous communities, each with its own regional parliament, government and supreme court. Andalucía is one of the autonomous communities, and its parliament sits in Seville, with 109 members who are chosen by universal suffrage every four years. The executive government, called the Junta de Andalucía, is headed by a president. The parliament and executive have been controlled by the left-of-centre PSOE party ever since autonomy began in 1982 – although in recent years the PSOE has governed without an absolute parliamentary majority after the break-up of a coalition with the communist Izquierda Unida (IU; United Left), which usually gets 15% to 20% of the vote. Manuel Chaves has been the junta's president since 1990.

The policy areas that are controlled at autonomous-community level vary from one community to another. Andalucía, the most populous autonomous community, has more powers than most, including over industry, agriculture, tourism, education, health, social security, environmental conservation and non-national roads and railways. But, since the national government has a far larger budget than that of the autonomous community, many of the important decisions are still made in Madrid.

Each autonomous community consists of one or more provinces. Andalucía has eight, all named after their capital cities: Almería, Cádiz, Córdoba, Granada, Huelva, Jaén, Málaga and Sevilla. The provinces are further subdivided into city, town and village administrative units called *municipios* (municipalities), each with an elected council headed by a mayor.

ECONOMY

Andalucía will probably always lag behind more industrialised parts of Spain in economic terms, but it hasn't done at all badly in recent years. In 2002 unemployment in Andalucía was running at 19%, the lowest rate since the 1970s and down from 35% in 1994. Average monthly wages in Andalucía were around €1800, only a little below the national average. Andalucian unemployment was still well above the Spanish national rate

of 11.5%, but many people undoubtedly get away with registering as unemployed (to qualify for dole) while working at the same time! The 'submerged' economy is estimated to account for at least a quarter of Andalucian income.

A major factor in economic growth has been a big increase in agricultural production. The year-round growing of vegetables under hideous seas of plastic, using water pumped up from deep underground, has transformed the parched province of Almería, which now employs some 30,000 mainly North African immigrants. Huge EU subsidies for olive oil and sunflower oil have helped to modernise and improve efficiency in these crops, centred chiefly in the provinces of Jaén, Córdoba and Sevilla. (Jaén alone produces about 10% of the world's olive oil; see the boxed text 'Essential Oil' in the Jaén Province chapter).

Tourism continues to do well, accounting for over 10% of the Andalucian economy. Costa del Sol hotels recorded 1.95 million overnight stays in August 2001, up from 1.64 million in August 1997, with about two-thirds of the guests being foreigners. A boom in 'residential tourism' – holiday homes and expatriate immigration – helped to fuel an amazing construction boom all along the holiday *costas* (coasts) in the late 1990s and early 2000s. The introduction of the euro in 2002 undoubtedly contributed to the boom, as Spaniards, Germans and others sought to invest 'black' cash in property so that they would not have to declare it for exchange into euros. The construction boom was particularly intense in Málaga province, where unemployment halved between 1994 and 2002.

Poverty has not been eradicated, although benefits for the unemployed have softened its effects since the 1980s. According to regional government figures, 26% of Andalucians in 2002 remained 'poor'. Poverty has tended to migrate from the countryside to the cities, where young people, immigrants and single women with children are among the worst off. Cádiz province has the highest unemployment rate in Andalucía, 28% in 2002, and Almería province the lowest, 11%.

Just 2% of Andalucian landowners still own about half of Andalucía's land, and the 'big five' – the Duques de Arcos, Infantado, Medinaceli, Medina Sidonia and Osuna – retain vast estates. The estates now tend to be efficiently farmed, but mechanisation has not provided many new jobs. There are still tens of thousands of *jornaleros* – landless, seasonally employed agricultural day-labourers.

The Expo '92 world fair in Seville failed to spark a takeoff of hi-tech industries in Andalucía, and the region remains underindustrialised. Such industry as exists is concentrated mainly in the western Seville-Huelva-Cádiz triangle, with some in Málaga, Córdoba and Granada.

Agriculture still provides one job in eight (one in six in some provinces). In addition to olives and sunflower oil, traditional agricultural products include pork, wool, beef, wine, grains and cork. Fishing is still important – Andalucía has one of the biggest fishing fleets in Spain.

POPULATION & PEOPLE
Population
Andalucía has a population of 7.4 million – almost exactly one person for every foreign tourist per year. The population comprises 18% of the Spanish total and Andalucía is the most populous of Spain's 17 regions. Of Andalucía's eight provinces, Sevilla has the most people (1.75 million), followed by Málaga (1.3 million), Cádiz (1.13 million), Granada (813,000), Córdoba (770,000), Jaén (646,000), Almería (533,000) and Huelva (462,000).

The population is very much weighted to the provincial capitals. The cities of Seville (population 703,000), Málaga (534,000), Córdoba (314,000), Granada (243,000) and Huelva (141,000) are all five times as big as any other town in their provinces. Only a handful of non-capital cities – Jerez de la Frontera (185,000), Marbella (111,000), Algeciras (105,000) and Dos Hermanas (101,000) – top the 100,000 mark.

Andalucians like to live together, in cities, towns or villages. Country farmsteads and cottages are rarely actually lived in these days – their owners will travel out to them daily from their villages by car, motorcycle or mule or donkey, or just use them at weekends.

Spain has one of the lowest birth rates in the world (about 1.2 children per woman; Andalucía is slightly above the national average) and in 2001 the UN predicted that Spain's population would fall from 40 million to 31 million by 2050. Many pundits argue that it must encourage immigration in order to maintain its workforce, its production and its tax and welfare systems.

People
The ancestors of today's Andalucians include prehistoric hunters from Africa; Phoenicians, Jews and Arabs from the Middle East; Carthaginians and Berbers from North Africa; Visigoths from the Balkans; Celts from central Europe; Romans; and northern Spaniards, who were themselves descended from a similar mix of ancient peoples. By the time the remaining identifiable Jews and Muslims were expelled in the 15th to 17th centuries, all these influences were intermingled. In the past 1000 years there have been three major influxes to the Andalucian ethnic soup: the *gitanos*, who arrived in the 15th century, the sun-seeking northern European expatriates, whose 19th-century trickle became more of a tide in the late 20th century, and the work-seeking migrants from the Third World (chiefly Morocco but also from other African and Latin American countries).

Gitanos Spain has around 600,000 *gitanos* (Roma people, formerly called Gypsies) – more than any other country in Western Europe – and about half of them live in Andalucía. The *gitanos'* origins are uncertain, but they are thought to have come from India, from where they headed west in about the 9th century AD. One migration route led to Istanbul and then into Europe, where some *gitanos* eventually reached Spain in the 15th century, most heading to the south. Another route from India, it's thought, led to Egypt (hence, some reckon, the word Gypsy) and then across North Africa to Andalucía.

Promised Land?

Every year dozens, some years hundreds, of people from Morocco and other African countries drown attempting to cross the Strait of Gibraltar to gain clandestine entry into Andalucía. They die when their overloaded small boats capsize in the treacherous waters of the strait, or when they can't manage to swim the last few hundred metres to the shore after their boats dump them. Thousands more each year (over 20,000 in 2001) are intercepted by coastguards or police and sent back. No-one knows how many escape capture: in 1999 the Spanish police estimated that they caught only 15% of illegal immigrants from Morocco. For the risky strait crossing and the hope of work in Europe the migrants may pay anything up to the equivalent of €1200. The beaches of Cádiz province, near southern towns such as Tarifa and Algeciras, are the favoured drop-off points, but the Canary Islands – a much longer journey of 15–20 hours west from Morocco – and Almería province are also the destinations of many boats.

In the past, the lucky ones who avoided the coastguards and police tended to move on through Spain into other EU countries. Today, as the Spanish economy improves and Spaniards themselves become less and less ready to do dirty or menial jobs, increasing numbers of immigrants are staying in Spain. In 2001, 214,000 of the 943,000 foreigners legally resident in Spain were Moroccans. A further 64,000 were from other African countries. Of the 164,000 legal foreigners in Andalucía, 100,000 were from non-EU countries, principally Morocco but also sub-Saharan Africa and Latin America. An estimated 30,000 legal and illegal migrants, mainly illiterate North African males in their 20s, work on intensive vegetable cultivation in plastic-sheeting greenhouses in Andalucía's Almería province, often in extremely poor conditions and for much lower wages than Spaniards would receive for the same work. The illegals are vulnerable to all manner of exploitation, even including kidnap and ransom demands by Moroccan gangs operating in Spain.

In 2000, some 200,000 illegal foreigners in Spain (mainly in the provinces of Madrid, Barcelona, Murcia and Almería) made use of a new Ley de Extranjería (Aliens Law) to legalise their position, but a revised law in 2001 made things more difficult for anyone hoping to follow in their footsteps. It is now easier for Spain to expel illegal immigrants, and Spanish bosses hiring illegal labour now face heavy fines.

Spain criticises Morocco for not doing enough to stem the tide of migrants. But migration to Spain, France and other European countries is a safety valve for a country that has 20% unemployment and no social welfare. Moroccans working overseas send the equivalent of over €2 billion back to Morocco.

Spain's reputation for racial tolerance is being put to the test by the surge in immigration. Tensions in Almería's El Ejido area boiled over in 2000 in a wave of violent attacks on Moroccans after three Spaniards were murdered by Moroccans. A government survey that year found that half of Spaniards consider their own society to be 'quite or very racist'.

Spain began enacting laws against the *gitanos* in 1499 and continued doing so for a long time. Early laws were chiefly intended to stop them wandering. Others tried to extinguish the *gitano* identity by forbidding them to own horses, work as blacksmiths or use *gitano* names, language or dress. King Carlos III in 1783 permitted *gitanos* to do whatever work they could on the impossible condition that they abandon their customs. They remained on the fringes of society. Along the way they created flamenco music and dance (see Arts later in this chapter).

Today, most Andalucian *gitanos* lead a settled life in cities, towns and villages, but *gitano* quarters are often the poorest parts of town. *Gitanos* rub along all right with other Spaniards, but still tend to keep – and be kept – to themselves. Marriages between *gitanos* and non-*gitanos* are still unusual even now.

For more information on Spanish *gitanos*, a good place to start is the trilingual (English, Spanish and Romani) website of the *gitano* organisation **Unión Romaní** (**W** *www.unionromani.org*).

Foreigners In 2002 Andalucía had 164,000 legal foreign residents, of whom 64,000 were from EU countries (principally Britain, Germany, Scandinavia and France) and the rest chiefly from Morocco and Latin America. The number constitutes 13% of the legal foreign population in Spain. The legal foreign residents are probably at least equalled by others from both the EU and the Third World who live full time in Andalucía without legal documentation. In addition, an estimated 400,000 northern Europeans own properties in Andalucía (chiefly in coastal areas of Málaga province) and live there part time.

EDUCATION

Seven of Spain's 17 regions have taken charge of their own education systems, and Andalucía is one of them. Schooling is compulsory throughout Spain until the age of 16. Children move from primary to secondary school at the age of 12. Two-thirds of children attend free state schools; most of the rest go to state-subsidised Catholic coeducational schools. In very general terms, Spanish education can be characterised as well-organised but not particularly imaginative. Extracurricular activities in state schools are few.

Around 55% of school leavers go on to vocational training or to the *bachillerato*, a two-year academic course leading to higher education or higher-grade vocational studies. Around 40% of Spaniards now attend university, which is where professions such as teaching and nursing as well as more academic disciplines are taught. Dropout rates, however, are high: only 10% to 12% of students complete their courses successfully.

Each of Andalucía's eight provincial capitals has a publicly run university. To enter university, students must obtain their *bachillerato* and pass an entrance exam. They can then do either a three-year course leading to the degree of *licenciado* or *diplomado* (roughly equivalent to bachelor's degrees), or a five- or six-year course leading to a *licenciatura*, *arquitecto* or *ingeniero superior* degree (roughly equivalent to a master's degree). University fees vary between about €300

and €500 a year; around one-seventh of students get grants. Higher education is also available in institutes devoted to physical education, tourism and the performing arts.

Illiteracy is far less widespread than it was 30, or even 15, years ago, thanks to universal schooling, adult education and job-training schemes. Adult illiteracy is now under 10%. Around 60% of illiterates are women and nearly all illiterates were born before 1960. Their school years passed in an age when even the level of primary school attendance was patchy.

ARTS
Flamenco

The passionate combination of song, music and dance known as flamenco is Andalucía's most characteristic art. Flamenco emerged among *gitanos* in the lower Guadalquivir valley in the late 18th and early 19th centuries: its origins may have included music and verses of medieval Muslim Andalucía, songs brought to Andalucía by the *gitanos* themselves and even Byzantine chant used in Visigothic churches.

The earliest flamenco was *cante jondo* (deep song), a tortured lament that grew from the experience of the marginalised *gitano*. *Jondura* (depth) is still the essence of flamenco, and some of the early *jondo* forms are still sung – notably the *martinete*, whose only accompaniment is the sound of a hammer striking an anvil, an echo of the smithies where many *gitanos* worked.

A flamenco singer is known as a *cantaor* (male) or *cantaora* (female); a dancer is a *bailaor/a*. Most of the songs and dances are performed to a blood-rush of guitar from the *tocaor/a*. Flamenco's scales and rhythms can certainly be difficult for the average beginner to tune in to, but it's hard to remain unmoved by its emotional intensity, whether expressing inconsolable desolation over death or up-tempo excitement about love.

Technically speaking, flamenco is in the Phrygian mode, in which the interval between the first and second notes of an eight-note scale is a semitone. In conventional Western music the interval is a whole tone.

Andalucians have always loved dancing, and it was only natural that dance (*baile* in flamenco contexts) should soon accompany song. *Toque* (guitar-playing) for a long time functioned solely as accompaniment to singing and dance. Percussion is provided by tapping feet, clapping hands and sometimes castanets. The traditional flamenco costume – for women, the shawl, fan and long, frilly *bata de cola* dress; for men, flat Cordoban hats and tight black trousers – dates from Andalucian fashions in the late 19th century, when flamenco first took to the public stage.

Flamenco Legends The first person to make a living from flamenco was El Fillo, from the Cádiz area, born about 1820. His name lives on in the term *voz afillá*, which refers to the classic raw, powerful, booze-and-baccy-soaked *jondo* voice.

The great singers of the late 19th century were Silverio Franconetti, from Seville, and Antonio Chacón, from Jerez. The early 20th century threw up Seville's La Niña de los Peines, the first great *cantaora*, and Manuel Torre, from Jerez, whose singing, legend has it, could drive people to rip their shirts open and upturn tables.

La Macarrona, from Jerez, and Pastora Imperio, from Seville, the first great *bailaoras*, took flamenco to Paris and South America. Their successors La Argentina and La Argentinita turned flamenco dance into a theatrical show, forming dance troupes and triumphing in Paris and America in the 1920s and '30s. The fast, dynamic, unfeminine dancing and wild lifestyle of Carmen Amaya (1913–63), from Barcelona, made her the *gitano* dance legend of all time. Her longtime partner Sabicas was the father of the modern solo flamenco guitar, inventing a host of techniques now considered indispensable.

The leading *jondo* singers of the mid-20th century were Antonio Mairena and Manolo Caracol. Mairena kept the flame of pure flamenco alive at a time when it seemed that the lightweight, debased flamenco of the *tablaos* – 'clubs' with second-rate, touristic shows emphasising the sexy and the jolly – was in danger of taking over.

The Guitar is Born

Clapton, Cooder and King owe everything to Andalucía. It was the Arabs who developed an ancient Middle Eastern stringed instrument, the cithara, into a four-string lute. The 9th-century Córdoba court musician Ziryab added a fifth string and this instrument was widespread in Spain for centuries. Around the 1790s a sixth string was added, probably by a Cádiz guitar maker called Pagés. In the 1870s Antonio de Torres of Almería brought the guitar to its modern shape by enlarging its two bulges and placing the bridge centrally over the lower one to give the instrument its carrying power.

Flamenco puro got a new lease of life in the late 1960s and '70s through singers such as Terremoto from Jerez; Enrique Morente from Granada, with his clear, tenorish voice; La Paquera from Jerez, a stormingly powerful *bulería* singer; and above all, El Camarón de la Isla from San Fernando near Cádiz. Camarón's screaming, raucous voice, his great range and his wayward lifestyle made him a legend well before his early death in 1992 after years of an uncontrollable drug problem. Camarón was said to be one possessed of *duende* (spirit), an undefinable transforming magic possessed by the very greatest flamenco performers – the kind of thing that made Manuel Torre's listeners tear open their shirts.

The one flamenco name likely to be known to the uninitiated is Paco de Lucía (born 1947), from Algeciras. De Lucía absorbed forms and techniques so fast that by the time he was 14 his teachers had nothing left to teach him. He then proceeded to transform the guitar, formerly the junior partner of the flamenco trinity, into an instrument of solo expression with new techniques, scales, melodies and harmonies that took him far beyond traditional limits. De Lucía can sound like two or three people playing together. The double album *Paco de Lucía Antología* is an excellent introduction to his music.

Flamenco Today Flamenco may be going through its true golden age right now. Never has it been so popular or so innovative. Several stars mentioned earlier are still going very strong. Enrique Morente is the leading figure of contemporary male *cante*. And new generations continue to broaden flamenco's audience.

Big-name singers today include José Mercé, from Jerez, whose *Del Amanecer* (Of the Dawn; 1999) is one of the most exciting flamenco albums of recent years; José Menese from Seville; rising young stars Estrella Morente (Enrique's daughter) and Arcángel; and versatile Carmen Linares, whose 1996 double album *Carmen Linares en Antología* is a journey through 150 years of female *cante*. Other first-rate singers include Remedios Amaya and Aurora Vargas among women, and El Cabrero, Juan Peña 'El Lebrijano', Calixto Sánchez and Vicente Soto 'Sordera' among men.

Dance, always the readiest of flamenco arts to cross boundaries, has reached its most adventurous horizons in the person of Joaquín Cortés, born in Córdoba in 1969. Cortés' hugely popular touring ensemble fuses flamenco with contemporary dance, ballet and jazz, to music at rock-concert amplification; Cortés himself may dance half-naked, or in women's clothes.

Antonio Canales, born in Seville in 1962, is more of a purist. His dance company has done successful shows on bullfight and *gitano* themes. Further classy flamenco dance companies are led by Sara Baras, born in Cádiz in 1971 (who had a big success with her 2001 show *Juana La Loca*), Seville's Cristina Hoyos, and Eva La Yerbabuena. Top individual *bailaoras* include Manuela Carrasco and Concha Vargas (both from Lebrija), Juana Amaya and the innovative Belén Maya.

Guitarists to keep an eye out for include Cádiz's Manolo Sanlúcar, Vicente Amigo, Juan and Pepe Habichuela from Granada's voluminous Montoya family of flamenco performers, and Tomatito, from Almería, who used to accompany El Camarón de la Isla.

Flamenco Fusion Given a cue, perhaps, by Paco de Lucía, 1970s musicians began mixing flamenco with jazz, rock, blues, rap and other musical genres. This *nuevo* (new) flamenco greatly broadened flamenco's appeal. The seminal recording was a 1977 flamenco/folk/rock album, *Veneno*, by the group of the same name centred on Kiko Veneno (see Pop & Rock under Other Music later in this chapter) and Raimundo Amador, both from Seville. Amador and his brother Rafael formed Pata Negra, which produced four fine flamenco/jazz/blues albums culminating in *Blues de la Frontera* (1986). Raimundo now performs solo, staging some memorable blues and flamenco concerts with the likes of BB King – the album *Noche de Flamenco y Blues* (1998) preserves one such event for posterity.

The group Ketama, whose key members are all from the Montoya flamenco family of Granada, are named after a Moroccan hashish town and mix flamenco with African, Cuban, Brazilian and other rhythms. Two of their best albums are *Songhai* (1987) and *Songhai 2* (1995). Radio Tarifa emerged in 1993 with *Rumba Argelina* (Algerian Rumba), a mesmerising mix of flamenco, North African and medieval sounds, which has been followed by a new album every four years: first *Temporal* (Storm), then *Cruzando el Río* (Crossing the River).

The latest generation is led by artists such as Cádiz's Niña Pastori, who arrived in the late 1990s singing jazz- and Latin-influenced flamenco. Her albums *Entre dos Puertos* (Between Two Ports; 1997), *Eres Luz* (You are Light; 1999), *Cañailla* (2000) and *María* (2002) are all great listening. Navajita Plateá, two brothers from Jerez, are somewhere between flamenco and pop: their *Desde Mi Azotea* (From My Terrace; 1999) was one of the biggest-selling flamenco albums of recent years.

Seeing Flamenco See under Entertainment in this book's city and town sections, and also Entertainment and Public Holidays & Special Events in the Facts for the Visitor chapter, for tips on where and when to catch live genuine flamenco in Andalucía.

The swirling dress of a flamenco dancer, exotically patterned tilework, and the striped interior of the Mezquita in Córdoba all reflect the mosaic of colours and shapes that is Andalucía

The birthplace of the guitar, Andalucía marries a fascinating heritage of history, art and architecture with a thoroughly modern lifestyle

Flamenco Forms

There are several song types *(palos)*. The *siguiriya*, an expression of intense despair about loss or death, is the biggest test of a singer's ability. It's thought to have originated in Jerez de la Frontera, one of the three key cities of flamenco's lower Guadalquivir heartland. The *soleá*, marginally less anguished, probably came from the Triana district of Seville, for centuries a *gitano* quarter. The livelier *alegría* is a contribution from the third city, Cádiz. Jerez is also the home of the *bulería*, the fastest, most upbeat *palo*.

Non-*jondo*, relatively light forms include the *tango*, originally from Cádiz, and its derivatives the *guajira*, *rumba* and *colombiana*, all with influence from Latin America. The home of the *fandango* is Huelva, but other areas also have varieties of *fandango* – such as Málaga's *malagueña* and Granada's *granaína*. Almería's *taranta* is not dissimilar.

Coplas (flamenco songs) are made up of short, rhyming bursts called *tercios*; the underlying rhythm is called the *compás*.

The *saeta*, an outburst of religious adoration by an onlooker at a Semana Santa (Holy Week) procession, was flamenco-ised around the start of the 20th century. These days *saetas* are usually stage-managed.

The very popular *sevillana* is not flamenco at all. This dance with high, twirling arm movements, consisting of four parts each coming to an abrupt halt, is probably an Andalucian version of a Castilian dance, the *seguidilla*.

Carlos Saura's film *Flamenco* (1995) is as good an introduction to the subject as you could have, featuring many of the best artists, including Paco de Lucía, Manolo Sanlúcar and Joaquín Cortés.

Other Music

See Public Holidays & Special Events in the Facts for the Visitor chapter for information on music festivals.

Pop & Rock The Spanish music scene is busy and vibrant. Andalucian summers are filled with happy, danceable pop but the region has its share of more progressive outfits. Very few performers are untouched by the flamenco tradition: little flamenco guitar runs or that distinctive wail in the voice can creep into the hardest of rock and even into Andalucian rap.

One of the most interesting characters is the singer-songwriter Kiko Veneno, who has spent most of his life around Seville and Cádiz. Though also a practitioner of flamenco fusion (see Flamenco earlier in this chapter), he's more in a rock/R&B camp now. After his 1970s collaboration with Raimundo Amador, Kiko accompanied

El Camarón de la Isla for a while (writing Camarón's big hit 'Volando Voy'; 'I Go Flying'), then disappeared from the music scene for a while. He eventually found his way back with three 1990s albums – *Échate un Cantecito* (Sing Yourself a Little Song), *Está muy bien eso del Cariño* (The Love Thing's Going Fine) and *Punta Paloma* – then *La Familia Pollo* (The Chicken Family; 2000). Kiko mixes rock, blues, African and flamenco rhythms with lyrics that range from humorous, *simpático* snatches of everyday life to Lorca poems. His retrospective albums *Puro Veneno* (Pure Poison; 1997) and *Un Ratito de Gloria* (A Moment of Glory; 2001) are excellent introductions to his music.

Another evergreen is Joaquín Sabina from Úbeda (Jaén province), a prolific producer of lyrical rock-folk with a protest theme for more than two decades. Sabina is one who, thankfully, has not let his anger die: 'I'll always be against those in power' and 'I feel like vomiting every time I sit in front of a telly', he has proclaimed in recent interviews. His live appearances get fewer and ever more popular. The 2000 double album *Nos Sobran Los Motivos* (More Reasons

Than We Need) is a good one to start with; of the earlier albums, *Pongamos Que Hablo de Madrid* (Let's Suppose I'm Talking About Madrid; 1987) includes several classic songs.

Granada band Lagartija Nick, whose music has been described as 'technopunk', 'psychedelic metal' and a 'tyrannical storm of sound', made waves through a partnership with flamenco doyen Enrique Morente that included the 1996 album *Omega*, an interpretation of Federico García Lorca's poetry collection *Poeta en Nueva York* (Poet in New York) as well as songs by the Lorca-influenced Leonard Cohen. Their most recent productions are *Lagartija Nick* (2000) and *Ulterior* (2001). Of *Lagartija Nick*, one reviewer commented that the band deprived pop of such basics as melody or refrain.

Other performers well worth watching out for include Hermanas Sister, a Málaga-based *madrileño*-and-Englishwoman duo whose repertoire includes Janis Joplin and Red Hot Chili Peppers numbers; Seville's female hip-hop revelation, Mala Rodríguez; Los Perdidos from Fuengirola, with a powerful mix of rock, Latin, reggae, rap, flamenco and anger; blues-rockers The Blackberry Clouds and mainstream band Danza Invisible, both from Málaga; Granada indie band Los Planetas; and Tabletom, an avowedly hippy band that has been mixing blues, jazz, Frank Zappa and Málaga hedonism since the 1970s and which has accumulated several generations of admirers.

Andalucian performers apart, there's often a chance to see other top Spanish bands at the many concerts and festivals staged in summer. Keep an eye out for the likes of Madrid indie quartet Dover; Barcelona R&B outfit Jarabe de Palo; balladeer Alejandro Sanz; Catalan rumba band Estopa; Asturian bagpipe rockers Hevia; heavy rockers Extremoduro from Extremadura; Celtas Cortos from Valladolid, reminiscent of the Pogues; and guitarist Javier Vargas (who comes with a Carlos Santana recommendation).

One musical area that *is* untouched by flamenco, born outside Spain but tailor-made for the Spanish propensity to dance all night, is techno, house and electronic dance music in general. Andalucía has its share of late-night clubs with DJs. Perfomers to watch out for include Javy Unión from Seville (hard-techno, techno-house, house) and Jordi Slate (electro-break beat), Miguel Picasso (house, funky and deep house, tribal) and Felipe Volumen (techno-house), all of whom hail from the Málaga area.

Classical Arguably the finest Spanish classical composer of all, Manuel de Falla, was born in Cádiz in 1876. He grew up in Andalucía before heading off to Madrid and Paris, then returned in about 1919 to live in Granada until the end of the civil war, when he left for Argentina.

De Falla's three major works, all intended as ballet scores, have deep Andalucian roots: *Noches en los Jardines de España* (Nights in the Gardens of Spain) evokes the Muslim past and the sounds and sensations of a hot Andalucian night, while *El Amor Brujo* (Love, the Magician) and *El Sombrero de Tres Picos* (The Three-Cornered Hat) are rooted in flamenco. *El Amor Brujo*, a *gitano* love story with a supernatural touch, was the mainstay of Spanish dancers for decades.

Andrés Segovia from Jaén province was one of the major classical guitarists of the 20th century, and Málaga's Carlos Álvarez ranks among the top baritones of the opera world today.

That, however, exhausts the list of important Andalucian contributions to classical music. The region is more notable for the music it has inspired from others – such as Rossini's opera *Il Barbiere di Siviglia* (The Barber of Seville) and Mozart's *Don Giovanni*, which drew on a 17th-century Spanish play by Tirso de Molina that presented the immortal character of Don Juan (see the boxed text 'Andalucía Through Romance-Tinted Spectacles' later in this chapter). Falla's friendship in Paris with the French composers Ravel (of *Bolero* fame) and Debussy *(Ibéria)* no doubt encouraged their Hispanic leanings.

Literature

Muslim Period The 11th century saw a flowering of both Arabic and Hebrew poetry. The Arabic was chiefly love poetry, by the likes of Ibn Hazm and Ibn Zaydun from Córdoba, and Ibn Ammar and Al-Mutamid, a king, from Seville. The latter pair, initially friends, fell out, and Al-Mutamid hacked Ibn Ammar to death with an axe. Of the Jewish poets, Judah Ha-Levi, considered one of the greatest of all post-biblical Hebrew writers, divided his life between Granada, Seville, Toledo and Córdoba, before deciding that a return to Palestine was the only solution for Spanish Jews. Samuel Ha-Nagid's work dealt a lot with war because he was also Granada's top general.

The philosopher Averroës, or Ibn Rushd (1126–98), from Córdoba, wrote commentaries on Aristotle that tried to reconcile science with religious faith, and had great influence on Christian thought in the 13th and 14th centuries. Averroës expressed the inward, spiritual approach to Islam of Al-Andalus' rulers at the time, the Almohads. This remarkable polymath was also a judge, astronomer, mathematician and personal physician and adviser to two Almohad rulers.

Siglo de Oro In Andalucía Spain's literary *Siglo de Oro* (Golden Century), roughly the mid-16th to the mid-17th centuries, began with the circle that gathered in Seville around Christopher Columbus' great-grandson Álvaro Colón. The group included the playwrights Juan de la Cueva and Lope de Rueda, as well as Fernando de Herrera, who addressed his love poetry to Colón's wife.

Córdoba's Luis de Góngora (1561–1627) is considered the greatest Spanish sonneteer and, by many, the greatest Spanish poet. Góngora manipulated words with a majesty that has defied attempts at critical explanation; his metaphorical, descriptive verses are above all intended as a source of sensuous pleasure. Some of them celebrate the more idyllic aspects of the Guadalquivir valley.

Góngora's contemporary Miguel de Cervantes (1547–1616) was no Andalucian but he did spend 10 troubled years here procuring oil and wheat for the Spanish navy and as a collector of unpaid taxes. In his Andalucian years Cervantes also procured for himself an indecent number of lawsuits, spells in jail and even excommunications – no doubt grist to the mill for the inventor of the novel. *El Ingenioso Hidalgo Don Quijote de La Mancha* (The Inventive Hidalgo Don Quijote of La Mancha) started life as a short story designed to make a quick peseta, but Cervantes had turned it into an epic tale by the time it appeared in 1605. Quijote and his companion, Sancho Panza, conducted most of their deranged ramblings on the plains of La Mancha, but did stray into the Sierra Morena for a few crazed episodes. Some of Cervantes' short *Novelas Ejemplares* (Exemplary Novels) chronicle turbulent 16th-century Seville.

19th Century Andalucian literary creativity didn't flower again until the time of José María Blanco White (1771–1841), who was born into an Irish Catholic merchant family in Seville but fled from the Napoleonic invasion to England. His *Letters from Spain* (1822), widely read in England, chronicled Andalucian life and customs in a detail that didn't disguise his contempt for its 'superstition' and 'fanaticism'.

Serafín Estébanez Calderón, with *Escenas Andaluzas* (Andalucian Scenes; 1846), and Fernán Caballero, with *La Gaviota* (The Seagull; 1849), portrayed Andalucian customs in a manner influenced by the foreign Romantics' interest in 'exotic' Andalucía (see the boxed text 'Andalucía Through Romance-Tinted Spectacles' later in this chapter).

The Generations of '98 & '27 The Generation of '98 was a loose collective of intellectuals who shared a deep disturbance about Spain's national decline symbolised by the loss of its last overseas colonies in 1898. Antonio Machado (1875–1939), the leading poet of the group, was born in Seville but spent most of his adult life outside Andalucía, except for a few years as a teacher in Baeza, where he completed *Campos de Castilla* (Fields of Castile), a set of melancholy poems evoking the landscape of Castile. Machado's friend Juan Ramón Jiménez (1881–1958), from Moguer near Huelva, touchingly and amusingly brought to life his home town in *Platero y Yo* (Platero and I), a prose poem that tells of his childhood wanderings around Moguer with his donkey and confidant, Platero. Jiménez, the 1956 Nobel literature laureate, stands as a kind of bridge between the Generation of '98 and the later Generation of '27, who took their name from the readings and talks they organised in Seville in 1927 for the tercentenary of the death of their hero, Luis de Góngora.

The loose-knit Generation of '27 included the poets Rafael Alberti, from El Puerto de Santa María, and Vicente Aleixandre (the 1977 Nobel laureate) and Luis Cernuda, both from Seville. Artist Salvador Dalí, film maker Luis Buñuel and composer Manuel de Falla were also associated with them, but the outstanding figure – and for many, the

major Spanish writer since Cervantes – was Federico García Lorca, from Granada.

Federico García Lorca Federico Lorca (1898–1936) was a musician, artist, theatre director, poet, playwright and much more. Though charming and popular, he felt alienated – by his homosexuality, his leftish outlook and, probably, his talent itself – from his stuffy home town Granada ('a wasteland populated by the worst bourgeoisie in Spain') and from Spanish society at large. Lorca identified with Andalucía's marginalised *gitanos* and longed for spontaneity and vivacity. He eulogised both Granada's Islamic past and what he considered the 'authentic' Andalucía (to be found in Málaga, Córdoba, Cádiz – anywhere except Granada).

As a student in Madrid in the early 1920s Lorca met many of those who would go on to become the Generation of '27. Lorca

Andalucía Through Romance-Tinted Spectacles

The very backwardness and poverty of 19th-century Andalucía spurred travellers from northern Europe to develop the Romantic image of Andalucía – a mysterious, sensuous, materially poor but spiritually rich land of almost oriental adventure. The picturesque decay of Andalucía's cities; its *gitano* flamenco music and dance; its legend-filled past; its people's love of fiesta, fun and bullfighting; its rugged, brigand-haunted mountains; its heat; its dark-haired, dark-eyed people – all these contributed to an exotic image that's hard to shake off even today.

One of the first Romantic writings to be set in Andalucía (Seville, in this case) was *Don Juan*, the masterpiece of Britain's Lord Byron, who came to Andalucía in 1809 and wrote the mock-epic poem near the end of his life in the early 1820s. In 1826 France's Viscount Chateaubriand published a melancholic novella, *Les Aventures du Dernier Abencerage* (The Adventures of the Last Abencerraj), in which a Muslim prince of Granada returns to his city after the Christian conquest. The Alhambra was established as the quintessential symbol of exotic Andalucía in *Les Orientales* (1829) by French writer Victor Hugo (who didn't visit Granada), and *Tales of the Alhambra* (1832) by the American Washington Irving (who lived in the palace for a few months). *Carmen*, a violent novella of *gitano* love and revenge in Seville, written in the 1840s by another Frenchman, Prosper Mérimée, added subtropical sensuality to the Andalucian mystique. Georges Bizet's 1875 opera, based on Mérimée's work, fixed the stereotype of Andalucian women as full of fire, guile and flashing beauty.

Russian composer Mikhail Glinka went to Granada in 1845 and, fascinated by *gitano* song and guitar, returned home to write Spanish-flavoured music that influenced many of his successors. Among them was Rimsky-Korsakov, who popped into Cádiz for three days' shore leave from the Russian navy – resulting in his delightful *Capriccio Espagnol* (Spanish Caprice; 1887).

Alexandre Dumas came close to summing it all up when he characterised Andalucía as a 'gay, lovely land with castanets in her hand and a garland on her brow'.

won major popularity with *El Romancero Gitano* (Gypsy Ballads), a colourful 1928 collection of verses on Andalucian *gitano* themes, full of startling metaphors and with the simplicity of flamenco song. This was followed between 1933 and 1936 by the three tragedies for which he is best known: *Bodas de Sangre* (Blood Wedding), *Yerma* (Barren) and *La Casa de Bernardo Alba* (The House of Bernardo Alba) – brooding, dark but dramatic works dealing with themes of entrapment and liberation, passion and repression. Lorca was executed by the Nationalists in the early stages of the civil war.

Recent Writing Most of Spain's post–civil war literary lights have hailed from farther north, but Antonio Muñoz Molina, who was born in Úbeda, in Jaén province, in 1956, is one of the country's leading contemporary novelists, possessed of depth, imagination and great storytelling ability. Probably his best novel to date is *El Jinete Polaco* (The Polish Jockey; 1991), set in 'Mágina', a fictionalised Úbeda, in the mid-20th century. Also acclaimed is Molina's 1995 memoir of nightmare military service, *Ardor Guerrero* (Warrior Ardour).

Poet, novelist and essayist José Manuel Caballero Bonald was born in Jerez de la Frontera in 1926. His 1962 novel *Dos Días de Septiembre* (Two Days in September) treats the social inequalities of rural Andalucía using experimental narrative techniques such as stream of consciousness. *Ágata Ojo de Gato* (Agate, Cat's Eye; 1974) comes close to magical realism; it's an allegorical work that is set in Andalucía although not in any recognisable time or place. In *Campo de Agramante* (Field of Agramante; 1992) Bonald continues to experiment with language and evokes the Andalucian atmosphere.

Antonio Gala (born 1930), from Córdoba, has succeeded as a playwright, poet and novelist. Gala sets much of his work in the past, which he uses to illuminate the present. *La Pasión Turca* (Turkish Passion; 1993) is his best-known novel.

Architecture

Andalucía's most famous buildings – the Alhambra in Granada and the Mezquita in Córdoba – represent the supreme lasting achievements of the Islamic period (AD 711–1492). For a detailed look at Muslim architecture in Andalucía, see the special section 'Muslim Architecture in Andalucía'.

Apart from a few Phoenician tombs (as at Almuñécar) and megalithic dolmens (as at Antequera), Andalucía's most significant pre-Muslim structures are Roman – notably, at Itálica, near Seville, which possesses the biggest of all Roman amphitheatres, a bathhouse and a theatre. The Roman town sites of Baelo Claudia and Ronda la Vieja are also well worth a visit, as is the necropolis at Carmona. The Romans bequeathed Andalucía the happy invention of the interior patio, an idea later taken up by the Muslims.

Gothic Christian architecture reached northern and western Andalucía with the Reconquista in the 13th century. The prevailing style at the time was Gothic, which had started to infiltrate Spain from France in the 12th century, with its pointed arches, ribbed ceilings, flying buttresses and fancy window tracery. Gothic's technical innovations enabled the building of much bigger structures than previously – notably big cathedrals. Seville's cathedral, the biggest in Spain, is almost entirely Gothic.

Spanish Gothic cathedrals have a number of differences from French and English ones. They tend to be wider (sometimes because they were built on the sites of square mosques), to have the choir *(coro)* and a chapel containing the high altar *(capilla mayor)* in the middle of the building, to have many side chapels, and to feature retables *(retablos)*. The retable is a large, often three-part, sculptural altarpiece, designed to illustrate Christian stories and teachings and elaborately carved with apostles, saints, angels and so on. A retable can fill the whole width of the nave behind the altar, and there are often smaller ones for side altars too.

There are dozens of Gothic or part-Gothic churches, castles and mansions in Andalucía. Many buildings that began life in Gothic times were finished or added to later, so they ended up as stylistic hotch-potches. Such are the cathedrals at Jerez de la Frontera (Gothic, Mudejar, baroque and neoclassical) and Málaga (Gothic, Renaissance and baroque).

The final flourish of Spanish Gothic was Isabelline Gothic, from the time of the Catholic Monarchs, whose own burial chapel – the Capilla Real in Granada – is the supreme work in this style. Isabelline Gothic features sinuously curved arches and tracery, and facades with lace-like ornament and low relief sculptures (including lots of heraldic shields). Another fine example is the facade of the Palacio de Jabalquinto in Baeza.

Renaissance The Renaissance in architecture was an Italian-originated return to disciplined ancient Roman and Greek ideals of harmony and proportion, with columns and classical shapes such as the square, circle and triangle predominating. Many Andalucian Renaissance buildings feature elegant interior courtyards lined by two tiers of wide, rounded arcades.

In Spanish architecture, the Renaissance had three phases. First came plateresque, taking its name from the Spanish for silversmith, *platero*, because it was primarily a decorative genre, with effects resembling those of silverware. Round-arched portals were framed by classical columns and stone sculpture (often including heraldry, in a carryover from Isabelline Gothic).

Next came the more purist Renaissance style, whose ultimate expression is the Palacio de Carlos V in Granada's Alhambra, designed by the Rome-trained Pedro Machuca.

The last and plainest phase was Herreresque, after Juan de Herrera (1530–97), creator of the grand and austere palace-monastery complex of El Escorial, near Madrid, and Seville's Archivo de Indias.

All three phases were spanned in Jaén province by Andrés de Vandelvira (1509–75), who gave the town of Úbeda one of the finest ensembles of Renaissance buildings in the country (see the boxed text 'Andrés de Vandelvira' in the Jaén Province chapter). Vandelvira was much

influenced by Burgos-born Diego de Siloé (1495–1563), who had studied in Italy and was chiefly responsible for the cathedrals of Granada, Málaga and Guadix.

This was an era in which the nobility could build gorgeous urban mansions with delightful central patios surrounded by harmonious arched galleries – piles like the Palacio de Lebrija and Casa de Pilatos in Seville or the Palacio de Vázquez de Molina in Úbeda. Today, some Renaissance mansions have been converted into some of Andalucía's most beautiful and atmospheric hotels.

Hernán Ruiz, who specialised in 'improving' on surviving Islamic buildings, stuck a Renaissance bell tower atop Seville's Giralda minaret, and plonked an entire cathedral *inside* the Mezquita at Córdoba.

Baroque The reaction to Renaissance sobriety came in the colours, sense of motion and dramatic, top-heavy effect of baroque, which reached its peak of elaboration (some say over-elaboration) in the 18th century. Andalucía was one of the places where baroque blossomed most brilliantly.

Baroque was at root classical, but crammed a great deal of ornament onto facades and stuffed interiors full of ornate stucco sculpture and gilt paint. Retables reached extremes of gilded extravagance.

Before full-blown baroque there was a kind of transitional stage, exemplified by more sober works such as Alonso Cano's 17th-century facade for the Granada cathedral. Then came a burst of greater exuberance. The most extravagant work is termed Churrigueresque after a Barcelona family of sculptors and architects named Churriguera.

Seville has probably as many baroque churches per square kilometre as any city in the world. However, the church at La Cartuja monastery in Granada, by Francisco Hurtado Izquierdo (1669–1728), is one of the most lavish baroque creations in all of Spain. Hurtado's followers adorned the small town of Priego de Córdoba with seven or eight baroque churches. Écija is another small place that received a disproportionate share of baroque attention because of its prosperity at the time.

Neoclassicism Throughout Europe in the mid-18th century, the cleaner, restrained lines of neoclassicism came into fashion – another return to Greek and Roman ideals, in keeping with the Enlightenment philosophy prevailing in learned circles. Cádiz, which was in its heyday, has the biggest neoclassical heritage in Andalucía. But the single most notable neoclassical building is Seville's very large, almost monastic Antigua Fábrica de Tabacos (Old Tobacco Factory), built to house an early state-supported industry.

19th & 20th Centuries The 19th century brought revivals of all sorts of earlier architectural styles, in a sort of yearning for past glories at a time of decline. Andalucía experienced some neo-Gothic, and even a bit of neobaroque, but most prevalent were neo-Mudejar and neo-Islamic.

Mansions such as the Palacio de Orleans y Borbón, in Sanlúcar de Barrameda, and public buildings ranging from train stations in Seville and Almería to markets in Málaga and Tarifa were constructed in imitation (often pleasing) of past Muslim architectural styles. For the 1920s Exposición Iberoamericana, fancy buildings in almost every past Andalucian style were concocted in Seville.

During the Franco period, historic buildings in Seville were demolished to make way for new roads and developments. Drab, Soviet-style blocks of workers housing sprang up in many cities. New public buildings such as Huelva's city hall exhibited a bland classicism similar to that favoured by Stalin and Mussolini.

It was also during this era that long stretches of Andalucía's coasts began to be lined with scrappy concrete seaside hotels and resorts – a breed of development that is today still characterised by piecemeal, hotchpotch planning.

Since Franco, the major positive impetus has been Expo '92 in Seville, which brought the city several spectacular new bridges over the Guadalquivir and a sea of avant-garde exhibition pavilions on the Isla de la Cartuja.

Painting, Sculpture & Metalwork

Andalucian art goes back to the Stone Age and reached its creative peak during the 17th century.

Pre-Christian Art Stone Age hunter-gatherers left impressive rock paintings of animals, people and mythical figures in caves such as the Cueva de la Pileta near Ronda, the Cueva de los Letreros near Vélez Blanco and the Cueva de los Murciélagos near Zuheros. The later Iberians left fine stone sculptures of animals, deities and other figures, often with Carthaginian or Greek influence. The archaeological museums in Seville and Córdoba and Jaén's Museo Provincial have good Iberian collections.

The Roman artistic legacy is at its best in mosaics, with some wonderful examples at Itálica, Carmona and Écija (all in Sevilla province), and in Córdoba's Alcázar de los Reyes Cristianos and the Córdoba and Seville archaeological museums.

See the special section 'Muslim Architecture in Andalucía' for information on the decorative arts of the Muslim period in Andalucía.

Gothic & Renaissance Art Seville, the most powerful and richest city of post-Reconquista Andalucía, was long the region's artistic epicentre. One of the earliest masterpieces of Andalucian Christian art is Seville cathedral's huge Gothic main retable (1482), designed by a Flemish sculptor, Pieter Dancart, and carved with more than 1000 gilded and painted biblical figures. Around this time, Frenchman Lorenzo Mercadante de Bretaña and his local disciple, Pedro Millán, brought a new naturalism and detail into Sevillan sculpture. Then Seville's 16th-century boom threw it open to the humanist and classical trends of the Renaissance. Alejo Fernández (1470–1545), an artist of probable German origin who moved to Seville in 1508, ushered in the Renaissance in painting; the Italian Pedro Torrigiano (1472–1528) did the same for sculpture. Southern Spain in the 16th century, however, produced no-one of the stature of the great Greek-born El Greco, who spent his career in Toledo.

A 16th-century master artisan known as Maestro Bartolomé created some of Spain's loveliest *rejas* (wrought-iron grilles) in churches in Granada and Jaén province.

Siglo de Oro The stiff, idealised schemes of Mannerism, the transition from Renaissance to baroque art, presided over the late 16th century. But early in the 17th century a more naturalistic approach, heralding baroque, was taken by Seville artists such as Francisco Pacheco and Juan de Roelas. With its large, colourful, accessible images, the baroque movement took deep root in Andalucía. Great Seville artists of this, Spain's artistic Golden Century, included the mystical Francisco de Zurbarán; Diego Velázquez, who left Seville in his 20s to become an official court painter in Madrid and ultimately the major artist of Spain's cultural golden age; and the masters of full-blown baroque Bartolomé Esteban Murillo, Juan de Valdés Leal and sculptors Juan Martínez Montañés and Pedro Roldán. See the boxed text 'The Golden Century in Seville' in the Sevilla Province chapter for more on all these major figures.

Velázquez's friend Alonso Cano (1601–77) studied under the influential Pacheco in Seville, but did some of his best work in Granada and Málaga cathedrals. A gifted architect as well as painter and sculptor, Cano led a turbulent life in which he moved to Madrid, only to end up being tortured there for the murder of his wife (which he didn't commit), and later moving to Granada. Málaga-based Pedro de Mena (1628–88), the most sought-after Andalucian sculptor of his age, produced a welter of saints, child Christs and other religious work. The last major Andalucian baroque sculptor was Granada's José de Mora (1642–1724), who seems to have had only one model for his numerous Virgin sculptures – his wife, Luisa de Mena.

18th & 19th Centuries An impoverished Spain in this period produced just one outstanding artist – the great Francisco Goya (1746–1828), from Aragón in northern Spain. Goya recorded Andalucian bullfights at Ronda, and tradition has it that he painted his famous *La Maja Vestida* and *La Maja Desnuda* – identical portraits of one woman, clothed and unclothed – at a royal hunting lodge in what is now the Parque Nacional de Doñana. A few Goya works are on view in Andalucía in places such as Seville cathedral and the Oratorio de la Santa Cueva in Cádiz.

The 19th-century *'costumbrista'* painters (artists depicting the 'typical' characters, types and costumes of the region) of Seville – chief among them José Domínguez Bécquer – turned out sentimental pictures of *gitanos*, dancers and so on for tourists.

Andalucian art museums have rooms full of late-19th- and early-20th-century historical art and paintings influenced by non-Spanish movements such as Impressionism. Many are pleasing landscapes infused with the region's radiant light, but Andalucía produced no outstanding practitioners in this period.

20th Century Pablo Picasso (1881–1973) was born in Málaga, but moved to Galicia (northwest Spain) when he was nine and to Barcelona a few years later. He revisited Málaga for annual holidays from 1891 to 1900, painting landscapes and fishing scenes, but never returned thereafter, settling in France for good in 1904. Picasso's career involved many abrupt changes. His sombre Blue Period (1901–04) was followed by the merrier Pink Period; later, with Georges Braque, Picasso pioneered cubism. A much-postponed new Picasso museum may finally open in Málaga in 2003, with a large collection of his works donated by his daughter-in-law, Christine Ruiz-Picasso, finally giving his native city a slice of the Picasso pie.

Other talented 20th-century artists followed Picasso's footsteps out of Andalucía, among them the Granada-born abstract expressionist José Guerrero (1914–91). He moved to Paris in the 1940s and then to New York, where he found fame in the 1950s. A museum dedicated to him opened in Granada in 2000. Among the more notable artists who actually worked in Andalucía have been Córdoba's Julio Romero de Torres (1880–1930), a painter of dark, sensual female nudes; Huelva's Daniel Vázquez Díaz (1882–1969), a portraitist who also did a set of murals on the Columbus story in the Monasterio de La Rábida; and Carmen Laffón, a realistic, intimate painter of everyday things, born in Seville in 1934. Leading contemporary artists working in Andalucía include Chema Cobo, born in Tarifa in 1952, and Pedro García Romero, born in Aracena in 1964.

SOCIETY & CONDUCT

Andalucians have a great capacity for enjoying themselves, but their reputation for being lazy seems entirely unjustified. As someone put it, they work, but they don't have a work ethic.

They're economical with saying *'Gracias'* ('Thank you'), but this does not signify unfriendliness. One small way in which people express their fellow-feeling is a general *'Buenos días'* ('Good morning') to all present when they enter a shop or bar, or an *'Adiós'* ('Goodbye') when they leave. Andalucians are generally tolerant, often welcoming towards the millions of foreigners who come to spend money in Andalucía each year, but they don't usually attempt serious communication with foreigners, especially non–Spanish speakers. A strong 'us-and-them' mentality remains; invitations to Andalucian homes are something special.

Andalucians are gregarious and the family is of paramount importance, with children always a good talking point. At the same time, they're an individualistic, proud people. But short of blatantly insulting someone, it's not easy to give offence.

Gender roles are more defined in Spain than in northern Europe and north America, and perhaps particularly so in Andalucía. While many women have jobs outside the home, they tend to do most of the domestic work too. Things are a little less extreme in the bigger cities and among the young, but in the villages you'll notice that nearly all pushchair (stroller) pushers are women and you won't see many men shopping for food or women standing at bars.

Most people like to look their best and take every opportunity to dress up – though not often to the extent of a formal suit and tie. They know that foreigners don't go to

Latin Lovers

According to a survey by a condom company in 2001, Andalucians are the least sexually faithful of all Spaniards, 45% of them claiming that at some time during their lives they had had more than one lover. They also ranked as the most promiscuous, with an average of 10.9 sexual partners per lifetime (against a national average of 5.5). Andalucians lose their virginity at an average age of 17.1 years, against the national average of 18 (the ages are lower for men than for women and lower for the under-30s than for the over-30s). According to another survey by the same company a few years earlier, Spaniards in general did not conform to the stereotypical image of Latin lovers, having sex an average of 71 times a year, against a world average of 109.

quite the same lengths, but you may feel uncomfortable in an un-fresh T-shirt, jeans and trainers in some restaurants or discos – some places wouldn't let you in, in any case.

Time

The Spanish, and perhaps especially the Andalucian, attitude to time is more relaxed than in most other Western cultures. But things that need a fixed time – trains, buses, cinemas, bullfights – get one, and it's generally stuck to.

What is different is the daily timetable. The Spanish *tarde* (afternoon) doesn't really start until about 4pm and goes on to 9pm or so. In the hot summer months, people stay outside till very late at night, enjoying the coolness. At fiestas, don't be surprised to see a merry-go-round packed with tiny children at 3am. And Friday and Saturday nights, year-round, barely begin until midnight for those heading out to bars and clubs.

Siesta

Contrary to popular belief, most Andalucians do not sleep in the afternoon. The siesta, if taken, is generally devoted to a long lunch and lingering conversation. Then again, if you've stayed out until 6am...

Treatment of Animals

Dangerous though it is to generalise, and leaving aside the issue of bullfighting for a moment, Andalucians appear to respect animals about as much as most other Western Europeans – but they don't mollycoddle them. They value them above all for their usefulness – as beasts of burden or farming help (horses, mules, donkeys), as guardians (dogs) or ratcatchers (cats), and above all, of course, as food – and will treat them well as long as they remain useful.

Hunting wild animals and birds (with a gun, for food) is a popular country pursuit, but is controlled fairly closely so that populations are not depleted. Spaniards eat more meat than any other people in the EU, over half of it pig meat. But vegetarianism is increasing among the young.

As for bullfighting, it's so ingrained in the culture as a sport-cum-art-cum-fiesta that the question of whether it's cruel or not just doesn't frame itself to many Andalucians (except perhaps in terms of the very real danger to the bullfighters). Plenty of people are uninterested in the activity, but few actively oppose it. If pressed, they might comment that the bulls live a particu-larly good life before they die in a fight, and that they wouldn't have been bred at all if there was no bullfighting. Spanish animal-rights and anti-bullfighting organisations include the **Asociación para la Defensa de los Derechos del Animal** (ADDA, Association for the Defence of Animal Rights; ☎ 934 59 16 01; W www.addaong.org; Calle Bailén 164, Local 2 interior, 08037 Barcelona). Another antibullfighting organisation is the **World Society for the Protection of Animals** (headquarters ☎ 020-7587 5000; W www.wspa .org.uk; 89 Albert Embankment, London SE1 7TP, UK).

RELIGION
Roman Catholicism

It's impossible not to notice the importance of the Roman Catholic church in Andalucía, as throughout Spain. So many of the big occasions are religious fiestas; so many of the finest buildings are cathedrals or churches. The great majority of Spaniards have church baptisms, weddings and funerals. According to surveys, 90% of Andalucians say they are Catholics. This is hardly surprising in a country whose very existence is the result of a series of medieval anti-Muslim crusades.

Since 1978 Spain has had no official religion, but the government still finances the church with enormous subsidies, and many schools are still run by religious orders and groups.

The country also has a deep-rooted anti-clerical tradition, going back to the days when the church and nobility were very rich and most other people very poor. The church was considered one of the main enemies by the Andalucian anarchists and other 19th-century Spanish revolutionaries. This hostility reached a bloody crescendo in the civil war, when some 7000 priests, nuns and monks were killed in Spain. The revolutionary spirit lives on in Andalucía (where 15% to 20% of people vote communist) and so does the anti-church tradition.

Despite avowing Catholicism, only 20% of Andalucians call themselves churchgoers. Those who do go to church are often old, poor, female and live in rural areas. But Catholicism is so ingrained that men who hardly ever go to church vie for membership of the brotherhoods that carry holy images in Easter processions, and families spend an average of €2000 on special clothes and festivities for a child's first communion. There's still plenty of truth in the 20th-century philosopher Miguel Unamuno's quip: 'Here in Spain we are all Catholics, even the atheists'.

Other Faiths

Protestantism was eradicated by the Inquisition in the 16th century. Today, the few Protestants in Andalucía are nearly all northern European expatriates. The Jehovah's Witnesses also have a sizable presence.

Muslims and Jews played an enormous role in medieval Spain, but were firmly stamped on at the end of that period (see History earlier in this chapter). In recent years, however, the number of Muslims in Spain has grown fast. By 2002 there were an estimated 500,000, of which 80,000 were in Spain's North African enclaves, Ceuta and Melilla. Some 20,000 to 25,000 were former Catholics, converted to Islam in the previous 20 years, and about 10,000 were students.

The rest of them were legal and illegal immigrants. Most Muslims in Spain come from North Africa, especially Morocco. Perhaps 60,000 to 70,000 Muslims are in Andalucía. Many labour in the greenhouses of Almería province, but most tourists are more likely to meet those who live or work in Granada's old Muslim quarter, the Albayzín.

The Jewish community numbers a few thousand people, many of them from Morocco. In 1982 Sephardic Jews (Jews of Spanish origin) were officially invited to return to Spain, 490 years after expulsion by the Catholic Monarchs.

LANGUAGE

Spanish is spoken throughout Andalucía. Most Spaniards who encounter foreign tourists on a regular basis speak at least a little English and/or German, and often prefer to use them rather than put up with a foreigner stumbling along in pidgin Spanish. Away from the main tourist routes, however, the more Spanish you speak, the better: just being able to understand some of the signs around you and some words on the menu, or having a few words of Spanish to say to an elderly, monolingual *pensión* proprietor, can make a big difference. See the Language chapter at the back of this book for details and local pronunciation.

MUSLIM ARCHITECTURE IN ANDALUCÍA

The most spectacular legacy of Andalucía's Islamic centuries (from AD 711 to 1492) is a collection of exotic buildings – palaces, mosques, minarets, fortresses – that makes this region visually unique in Europe and also sets it apart from the rest of the Muslim world. Andalucía was always the heartland of Al-Andalus (as the Muslim-ruled areas of the Iberian Peninsula were known), and its Islamic architectural heritage is by far the richest in Spain, with an influence that is still deeply felt at home and in the Maghreb (North-West Africa) today.

After the Christian Reconquista (Reconquest), many Spanish Muslim buildings were converted to Christian use. Many Andalucian churches today either stand on the site of mosques or are simply converted mosques (as most famously at Córdoba), many church towers were originally built as minarets, and the tangled streets of many a Spanish town centre have their origins in labyrinthine Muslim-era street plans. Granada's Albayzín district is just one famous case in point.

The Omayyads

Islam – the word means 'Surrender' (to the will of Allah, God) – was founded by the prophet Mohammed in the Arabian city of Mecca in the 7th century AD. With its teaching that those who fell in the holy war against the infidel would go directly to paradise, Islam spread rapidly to the north, east and west (first reaching Spain in 710). After Mohammed died in 632, the leader of Islam was known as the caliph (deputy). The first caliphs were chosen from among Mohammed's companions, but in about 660 Muawiya, a late convert to Islam from among Mecca's richest families, seized power and instituted a hereditary caliphate. This was the Omayyad dynasty, which governed from Damascus, Syria, from 661. In 750 the Omayyads were deposed and massacred by a group of non-Arab Muslim revolutionaries known as the Abbasids. Just one of the Omayyad family, Abu'l-Mutarrif Abd ar-Rahman bin Muawiya, escaped. Aged only 20, he headed for Morocco, his mother's native land, and thence to Spain. Winning the support of many Muslims, in 756 he set himself up as an independent emir, Abd ar-Rahman I, in Córdoba. This was the beginning of the Omayyad dynasty of Al-Andalus, which lasted till 1009.

The Abbasids meanwhile set up their caliphal capital far to the east, at Baghdad. Al-Andalus, at the western extremity of the Islamic world, became the last outpost of Omayyad culture, rejecting – consciously or unconsciously – the arts of the Abbasid-ruled Middle East. Some building types common in the medieval Middle East, such as mausoleums and khans (lodging places for merchants and travellers), are rare in the Maghreb and the Iberian Peninsula – which explains why more energy went into religious architecture in the Muslim west than in the Muslim east.

Inset: Geometrically patterned tilework, the Alhambra, Granada (Photograph by Sara-Jane Cleland)

The Horseshoe Arch Omayyad architecture in Spain was enriched by styles and techniques taken up from the Christian Visigoths, whom the Omayyads had replaced as rulers of the Iberian Peninsula. Chief among these was what became almost the hallmark of Spanish Islamic architecture, the horseshoe arch – so called because it narrows at the bottom like a horseshoe, rather than being a simple semicircle. It was probably the Visigoths who had first used the horseshoe arch in architecture (as in the church of Santa Comba de Bande in Galicia, northwest Spain, built around 670).

The Mezquita of Córdoba

The oldest significant surviving Spanish Muslim building is also arguably the most magnificent and the most influential. The Mezquita (Mosque) of Córdoba was founded by emir Abd ar-Rahman I in AD 785 and underwent major extensions under his successors Abd ar-Rahman II in the first half of the 9th century, Al-Hakim II in the 960s and Al-Mansur in the 970s. Córdoba was these rulers' capital, and the Mezquita was Córdoba's Friday Mosque, always the most prestigious and important building in an Islamic city, where adult males must go for prayers every Friday at noon.

The 8th-Century Mosque

Abd ar-Rahman I's initial mosque, built by both local and Syrian artisans, was square, divided into two rectangular halves: a covered prayer hall and an open ablutions courtyard where the faithful would wash before entering the prayer hall. The prayer hall was divided into 11 'naves' by lines of two-tier arches in stripes of red brick and white stone. Both two-tier arches and similar striped effects had been used in Omayyad Syria and perhaps also in pre-Muslim Spain, but their use in the Córdoba Mezquita was truly innovative. The columns available for building the Mezquita were relatively short ones, from the church that had previously occupied the site and from other buildings in Córdoba and elsewhere. The two tiers enabled the builders to gain enough height for a roof to cover a large area: the mosque would otherwise have been uncomfortably low-ceilinged. The

DAMIEN SIMONIS

Right: Intricately carved stonework, the Mezquita, Córdoba

arches of the lower tier are horseshoe-shaped, while the upper arches, supporting the roof, are semicircular and thicker.

The later enlargements of the mosque extended these lines of arches to cover a total area nearly 120 metres square, one of the biggest of all mosques. These arcades afford ever-changing perspectives, vistas disappearing into infinity and plays of light and rhythm that rank among the Mezquita's most mesmerising and unique features.

One element of the Mezquita that definitely came from the Middle East was its 'basilical' plan, similar to many early Christian churches, with the central nave broader than the others and leading to the mihrab, the niche indicating the direction of Mecca (and thus of prayer) that is crucial to the layout of any mosque. A basilical plan had been used at one of the most important Muslim shrines, the Al-Aqsa mosque in Jerusalem.

The 10th-Century Mosque The most important of the later extensions to the Córdoba mosque was that of Al-Hakim II. Al-Hakim's father Abd ar-Rahman III had taken the title of caliph for himself and his successors, in rivalry to the Abbasids and other would-be caliphs, and as a result the architecture of 10th-century Córdoba is sometimes called 'caliphal'. Al-Hakim's basic alteration, like that of Abd ar-Rahman II a century earlier, was to lengthen the naves of the prayer hall, creating a new mihrab at the south end of the central nave. What was special this time was the splendour of the new mihrab and its flanking portals, and the treatment given to the royal enclosure in front of them, the *maksura*, where the caliphs and their retinues would have prayed. The arches within and around the *maksura* are an almost forest-like combination of interwoven horseshoe and multilobed arches, much more intricate and sophisticated than any others in the Mezquita. Equally special are the ribbed domes over the *maksura*, lavishly decorated with

OLIVER STREWE

Left: Lavishly decorated walls, the Mezquita, Córdoba

heavenly motifs and each held up by four interlocking pairs of parallel ribs, a highly advanced technique by the standards of 10th-century Europe.

The *maksura* helped to form a kind of transverse axis to the building, an aisle running along in front of the wall containing the mihrab – known as the qibla wall because, like the mihrab, it indicates the qibla or direction of Mecca, to which the faithful turn when praying. This transverse axis, in conjunction with the central nave, creates the T-plan that features strongly in many mosques, having first appeared in clear form in the 9th-century Sidi Ogba Mosque at Kairuan, Tunisia.

The greatest glory of Al-Hakim II's extension was the portal of the mihrab itself – a horseshoe arch with a rectangular surround known as an *alfiz*, surmounted by a blind arcade (a row of arch shapes in relief on the surface of the wall). For the decoration of the portal, Al-Hakim sent to the Christian emperor of Byzantium (modern Istanbul), Nicephoras II Phocas, for a mosaicist capable of imitating the superb mosaics of the Great Mosque of Damascus – one of the great 8th-century Syrian Omayyad buildings, whose mosaics were probably also crafted by Byzantine artisans. The Christian emperor sent the Muslim caliph not only a mosaicist but also a gift of 1600kg of gold mosaic cubes, and the shimmering golden mosaics that resulted give the Córdoba mihrab area something of the mysterious character of a Byzantine church. Its splendour served not only to suggest the Islamic paradise but also to glorify the caliph.

The later broadening of the Mezquita by Al-Mansur meant that the mihrab no longer stood in the centre of the south wall. The plan of Al-Hakim II's building is further obscured by the Christian cathedral that was subsequently plonked right in the middle of the mosque. But it is still quite possible to work out, when you are in the Mezquita, the dimensions of each phase of its construction.

Decorative Motifs

The mosaic decoration around Al-Hakim II's 10th-century mihrab portal exhibits all three of the decorative types allowable in Islamic holy places: stylised inscriptions in classical Arabic; geometric patterns; and stylised plant and floral patterns.

At this early stage of Hispano-Islamic art, the plant and floral decorations were still relatively naturalistic: later they become more stylised, more determined by geometry and more repetitive. In the 11th century, vegetal decoration started to leave behind the naturalistic forms inherited from classical antiquity and to adopt the more mathematically conceived patterns known as arabesques or *atauriques*. By the time Granada's Alhambra was built, in the 14th century, vegetal and geometric decorative forms had become almost indistinguishable.

Medina Azahara

In 936 Caliph Abd ar-Rahman III built himself a new capital just west of Córdoba. Medina Azahara, named after the caliph's favourite wife, Azahara, was planned as a royal residence, palace and seat of government, set away from the hubbub of the city in the same manner as the Abbasid royal city of Samarra, north of Baghdad – to which it may have been conceived as a rival. Medina Azahara's chief architect was Abd ar-Rahman III's son, Al-Hakim, who later embellished the Córdoba Mezquita so successfully. In contrast to Middle Eastern palaces, whose typical reception hall was a domed *iwan* (hall or room opening to a forecourt on one side), Medina Azahara's reception halls had a 'basilical' plan, each with three or more parallel naves – similar to mosque architecture.

Though Medina Azahara was wrecked during the collapse of the Córdoba caliphate, less than a century after it was built, it has now been partly reconstructed. It's easy to see that it was a large, splendid place, even if it didn't quite match the fabled grandeur and luxury of Samarra.

Other Omayyad Mosques

Relatively few other buildings survive from the Omayyad era in Spain. The ablutions courtyard of the 9th-century **Friday Mosque** in **Seville** remains, beside the Parroquia del Salvador church. One of the most charming of all Muslim buildings in Spain is the little 10th-century **Mezquita** (Mosque) at remote **Almonaster la Real** in Huelva province. Though later converted into a church, the original mosque remains more or less intact. It's like a miniature version of the Córdoba Mezquita, with rows of arches forming five naves, the central one being the widest and leading to a semicircular mihrab in the east wall. The mosque's three-storey minaret (the tower from which the Muslim faithful are called to prayer), square like all Andalucian minarets, now functions as the church's bell tower.

11th-Century Palaces

Most of the 'petty kings' of the turbulent *taifa* (small kingdoms) period would have lived in palaces of some kind, but few of these remain. Some horseshoe arches in the Salón de Embajadores of the **Alcázar** in **Seville** may have survived from an 11th-century palace constructed here by the *taifa* ruler Al-Mutamid. The **Alcazaba** at **Málaga**, though rebuilt later, still has a group of 11th-century rooms with a caliphate-style row of horseshoe arches. Within the **Alcazaba** at **Almería** is the Palacio de Almotacín, constructed by the city's strongest *taifa* ruler.

The most important *taifa* palace in Spain, and the most impressive Spanish Islamic building outside Andalucía, is the **Aljafería** in the northern city of **Zaragoza**. Its almost square plan harks back to the 8th-century desert palaces of Syria but also clear, in the design of its mihrab and its complex patterns of the interlocking arches, is the influence of the 10th-century Córdoba Mezquita. Pointed horseshoe arches and mixtilinear arches (with part-curved, part-straight lines) are here added to the existing cocktail of multilobed arches and round horseshoe arches, providing an inspiration for increasingly elaborate arches in later centuries.

CHRISTOPHER GROENHOUT

DONALD C & PRISCILLA ALEXANDER EASTMAN

CHRISTOPHER GROENHOUT

Top left: Exterior of the Mezquita at night, with its stone walls punctuated by ornate gates

Top right: The 16th- and 17th-century tower of Córdoba's Mezquita was built on the remains of the original Arab minaret

Middle: Founded by Abd ar-Rahman I in 785, the Mezquita in Córdoba is the oldest significant surviving Muslim building in Spain

Bottom left: Mesmerising geometric mosaic, the Alhambra

Bottom right: Intricately patterned stonework, the Alhambra

BETHUNE CARMICHAEL

CHRISTOPHER WOOD

CHRISTOPHER WOOD

NEIL SETCHFIELD

DAN HERRICK

JESSE MECHLING

SARA-JANE CLELAND

DAN HERRICK

Top left: Carved detail of the Patio de las Doncellas in the Alcázar, Seville

Top right: Seville's Alcázar is more palace than castle

Middle top: The Alcázar's Baños de Doña Maria de Padilla, a grotto which replaced the patio's original pool in which, it's imagined, Maria de Padilla liked to bathe

Middle bottom left: The Jardines del Partal in the gardens of the Alhambra

Middle bottom right: Decorative stone pattern, the Alhambra

Bottom: Arches in the Alhambra

MUSLIM ARCHITECTURE IN ANDALUCÍA

Fortifications

With its borders constantly under threat and its subjects often rebellious, it's hardly surprising that Al-Andalus boasts more Muslim-era castles and forts than any comparably sized territory in the Islamic world.

CHRISTOPHER WOOD

Caliphate Era The 10th century saw many forts built in Al-Andalus' border regions, and numerous fortified garrisons constructed in the interior. Designs were fairly simple, with no outer walls, and rectangular towers that were rarely higher than the walls. Entrances were usually simple gates, with no outer defences. Two of the finest forts from this period are the oval-shaped one at **Baños de la Encina** in Jaén province and the hilltop **Alcazaba** dominating the city of **Almería**.

Taifa Period In this 11th-century era of internal strife and power struggles, many towns bolstered their defences. A fine example is **Niebla** in Huelva province, which was strengthened by walls with massive round and rectangular towers. So was the **Albayzín** area of Granada. Niebla's gates show a new sophistication, with barbicans (double towers defending the gates) and bends in their passageways.

Almohad Fortifications The Almohads, in the 12th and early 13th centuries, rebuilt many city defences, as at Seville, Córdoba and Jerez de la Frontera. Córdoba's **Torre de la Calahorra** and Seville's **Torre del Oro** are well constructed bridgehead towers. The Torre del Oro, at a corner of the city wall, did not actually guard a bridge but probably had a sister tower on the far bank of the Río Guadalquivir, enabling a chain to be stretched between the two for defensive purposes.

Nasrid Fortifications Many forts and town defences in Andalucía were restored as the Nasrid emirate of Granada strove to survive in the 13th, 14th and 15th centuries. Fortifications at **Antequera**, **Ronda** and **Archidona**, and **Málaga's Castillo de Gibralfaro**, were among those strengthened. Big rectangular corner towers as at Málaga and Antequera suggest the influence of the Christian enemy. The most spectacular fort of the era – though better known as a palace – is Granada's **Alhambra**.

Right: Stone battlements of the 10th-century Muslim castle, Baños de la Encina, Jaén province

The Almoravids

The rule of the Berber Almoravids from Morocco from the late 11th to mid-12th centuries yielded few notable new buildings in Spain, but did result in ideas from the Córdoba Mezquita and other Andalucian buildings being carried to Morocco. It was also in Almoravid Morocco, at the great mosque at Tlemcen, that one of the most eye-catching features of Hispano-Islamic design makes its first appearance in the Muslim west, introduced from Iran or Syria: this was the *muqarnas* vault – 'stalactite' or 'honeycomb' vaulting, composed of hundreds or thousands of tiny cells or niches, used chiefly as cladding in the transitional zones between domes and their supports.

The Almohads

The second wave of Moroccan Berbers to conquer Al-Andalus, the Almohads constructed huge Friday mosques for large populations in the main cities of their empire, among them Seville. The design was simple and purist, with large prayer halls conforming to the T-plan of Al-Hakim II's extension to the Córdoba Mezquita. Cupolas or stucco *muqarnas* vaults surmounted the bays where the naves meet the qibla transept. On walls, large panels with designs of interwoven lozenges were created with specially fired bricks. From the late 12th century, tall, square, richly decorated minarets appear. The minaret of the Seville mosque, now known as **La Giralda**, is the masterpiece of surviving Almohad building in Spain, with its beautiful brick panels. The prayer hall of the **Seville mosque** was demolished in the 15th century to make way for the city's cathedral, but the mosque's courtyard (now called the **Patio de los Naranjos**) and its northern gate, the **Puerta del Perdón**, survive.

Another Almohad mosque, which is more of a palace chapel than a large congregational affair, stands inside the Alcázar of **Jerez de la Frontera**. This tall and austere brick building is based on an unusual octagonal plan inscribed within a square.

CHRISTOPHER WOOD

Many rooms and patios in the **Alcázar**, the palace-fortress across the street from the cathedral in **Seville**, date from Almohad times, but only the Patio del Yeso has substantial surviving Almohad remains. One side of this courtyard, with its flower beds and a water channel, is adorned with a superbly delicate trelliswork of multiple interlocking arches. The Almohad capital, Marrakech, was famous for its parks with lakes and ponds, and the Alcázar's lovely gardens are probably also of Almohad origin.

Left: Door detail inside the Alcázar of Seville

The Alhambra

Granada's magnificent palace-fortress is the only surviving large medieval palace anywhere in the Muslim world. The Alhambra was the redoubt of the Nasrid emirs of Granada, whose state – the last Muslim state on the Iberian Peninsula – endured from 1249 to 1492. It's a palace-city in the tradition of Medina Azahara but also, because of the time and place in which it was built, a fortress, with 2km of walls, 23 towers, four gates and a fortress-within-a-fortress, the Alcazaba. Also within its walls were seven separate palaces, mosques, garrisons, houses, offices, baths, a royal cemetery, a summer residence (the Generalife) and exquisite gardens.

The Alhambra's designers were supremely talented landscape architects, combining nature and architecture in uniquely successful ways by the use of pools, running water, meticulously clipped trees and bushes, flower beds, windows framing vistas, carefully placed lookout points, and contrasts of heat and cool and light and dark. The conjunction of fountains, pools and gardens with royal reception halls was developed to a degree of perfection suggestive of the paradise described in the Quran. The pools are usually rectangular, with water flowing over shallow dishes into the pool below. The reception rooms are domed, with vaults of stucco *muqarnas* or wood. In keeping with the Alhambra's partial role as a pleasure palace, many of its defensive towers also functioned as miniature summer palaces.

A great variety of densely ornamented arches adorns the Alhambra. The achievement of the Nasrid architects lay less in innovative ground plans than in the refinement of existing decorative techniques to new peaks of delicacy, elegance and harmony. Their media included sculptured stucco, marble panels, carved and inlaid wood, epigraphy (with endlessly repeated inscriptions of 'There is no conqueror but Allah'), and colourful tiles. Plaited star patterns in tile mosaic have since covered walls the length and breadth of the Muslim world, and Nasrid Granada is the dominant artistic influence in the Maghreb even today.

STEVE DAVEY

The peak of Granada's splendour, and the building of the finest parts of the Alhambra, came under the emirs Yusuf I (1333–54) and Mohammed V (1354–59 and 1362–91). Yusuf I was responsible for the Alhambra's **Palacio de**

Right: Ornate Arabic window dressing, the Alhambra, Granada

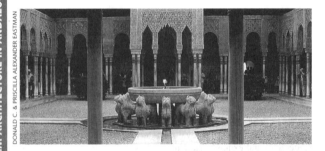

DONALD C. & PRISCILLA ALEXANDER EASTMAN

Comares (Comares Palace) and Mohammed V for its **Palacio de los Leones** (Palace of the Lions). The Palacio de Comares' stucco-and-wood facade resembles a harmonious, subtly patterned wall hanging. Within the Palacio de Comares, the marquetry ceiling of the Salón de Comares (Comares Hall) stands out for its brilliance, with more than 8000 small wooden panels representing the seven levels of the Islamic heavens, capped by a cupola representing the throne of Allah. This ceiling served as the model for Muslim-style ceilings in state rooms for centuries afterwards.

The Palacio de los Leones focuses on the celebrated Patio de los Leones (Patio of the Lions), with its central fountain channelling water through the mouths of 12 stone lions. The colonnaded gallery surrounding the entire patio was an innovation, as are the projecting colonnaded pavilions at the ends. Of its reception rooms, the Sala de Dos Hermanas (Hall of Two Sisters) features a fantastic *muqarnas* dome of 5000 tiny cells, recalling the constellations.

Bathhouses

Cleanliness and the public bathhouse *(hammam)* were such features of life in Al-Andalus that the Muslims' Christian enemies came to view washing with huge suspicion and believed bathhouses to be dens of wild orgies. To make their point, some Spanish monks took pride in wearing the same woollen habit uninterrupted for a whole year, and the phrase *'Olor de Santidad'* (Odour of Sanctity) became a euphemism for particularly offensive BO. After the Christian conquest of Andalucía, the Moriscos (Muslims who converted to Christianity) were expressly forbidden from taking baths.

Be that as it may, Muslim bathhouses survive in some Andalucian towns today. They generally contained a changing room, cold room, temperate room and hot room, in succession, with the heat in the hot rooms being provided by underfloor systems called hypocausts. Good examples of bathhouses, with their rooms lined by arched galleries and lit by star-shaped skylights, are at **Granada** (the **Baño de Comares** in the Alhambra and **El Bañuelo** in the Albayzín), **Jerez de la Frontera** (in the Alcázar), **Jaén**, **Ronda** and **Segura de la Sierra**.

Left: Patio de los Leones within the Alhambra; the fountain consists of 12 water-spouting lions

Mudejar & Mozarabic Architecture

The label Mudejar – from Arabic *mudayan*, 'domesticated' – was given to Muslims who stayed on in areas reconquered by the Christians. It was hardly surprising that the conquering Christians should employ the talents of gifted Muslim artisans, and as a result, a number of Mudejar buildings, though not built for Muslim use, are effectively part of Spain's Muslim heritage. The classic example is the exotic **Palacio de Don Pedro**, built in the 14th century for a Christian king of Castile, inside the Alcázar of **Seville**. The king for whom it was built, Pedro I, maintained friendly relations with Mohammed V of Granada, who sent many of his best artisans to Seville to work on Pedro's palace. As a result the Palacio de Don Pedro is effectively a Nasrid building, and is one of the best of its kind.

One hallmark of Mudejar style is brick and/or stucco-based geometrical decorative designs, often further embellished with tiles. Elaborately carved timber ceilings are also a mark of the Mudejar hand. *Artesonado* is the word used to describe ceilings with interlaced beams leaving regular spaces for decorative insertions. True Mudejar ones generally bear floral or simple geometric patterns. Mudejar and Christian Gothic styles are often found side by side in the same building.

You'll find Mudejar or part-Mudejar churches and monasteries all over Andalucía – in Seville, Carmona, La Rábida, Moguer, Aracena, Aroche, Jerez de la Frontera, Arcos de la Frontera, Vejer de la Frontera, Antequera, Baeza and Salobreña and in the villages of Las Alpujarras, among other places. Mansions such as the **Casa de Pilatos** in Seville and the Parador hotel in **Carmona** also boast Mudejar sections.

The term Mozarabic, from *musta 'rib* (Arabised), refers to Christians who lived or had lived in Muslim-controlled territories in the Iberian Peninsula. Though Christians and Jews were by and large permitted to practice their religions in Muslim territory, many Christians still fled north to Christian-controlled areas, and it was in reconquered territories such as León that most Mozarabic architecture was constructed. Mozarabic architecture was, unsurprisingly, much influenced by Muslim styles. It includes, for instance, the horseshoe arch. The only significant remaining Mozarabic structure in Andalucía – but well worth seeking out for its picturesque setting and poignant history – is the rock-cut church at **Bobastro**.

Facts for the Visitor

HIGHLIGHTS

Travel highlights are such personal things, and most parts of Andalucía have their own unique attractions. But here are a few relatively indisputable highlight destinations to help plan your explorations.

Cities & Towns

Seville (Sevilla in Spanish) is Andalucía's most vibrant city. Málaga is not far behind in terms of its people's capacity for fun, though it lacks Seville's range of great historical and artistic treasures. Granada is an absolute must because of its peerless Muslim heritage, and it has the most international atmosphere of Andalucía's cities thanks to its many foreign students and travellers. Córdoba, too, possesses an unmistakable Muslim heritage.

Among smaller cities and towns, our favourites include down-to-earth, fun-loving Cádiz; Jerez de la Frontera, the sherry capital also famed for its horses and flamenco; Ronda, astride a dramatic gorge with beautiful hill country close by; Arcos de la Frontera, a white town spilling over a rocky ridge; and Cazorla, an old-fashioned place that's also the gateway to the beautiful Parque Natural de Cazorla. All these places, except Cádiz, have a clear imprint from the Islamic past. Baeza and Úbeda, near Cazorla, are full of lovely architecture from the early post-Reconquista (Reconquest) centuries.

Coasts

Andalucía's best coasts are near its extremities. East of Almería, the arid Cabo de Gata peninsula is strung with excellent and, by Spanish standards, underpopulated beaches, backed by stark, rugged coastal hills.

In western Andalucía, the 'Costa de la Luz' (Coast of Light) stretches almost 200km from Tarifa to the Portuguese border. The slightly cooler Atlantic waters and breezes are a small price to pay for many fine, long, sandy beaches, backed by pine-covered dunes. Small places like Tarifa (with its international windsurfing and kitesurfing

scene), Bolonia, Zahara de los Atunes, Los Caños de Meca, Sanlúcar de Barrameda and La Antilla are among the most enjoyable of all Andalucía's resorts – most of them little known to the outside world, though popular enough with Andalucians. They're interspersed with cities and ports such as Cádiz, Huelva and Isla Cristina and with extensive wetlands vital to wildlife – most famously the Parque Nacional de Doñana.

Hill Country

Andalucía has some beautiful mountain and hill areas, great for walking, mountain biking, climbing or just cruising around. The thickly forested Parque Natural de Cazorla in Jaén province is perhaps the most stunning – its mountains are among the most rugged and spectacular, and in Segura de la Sierra you'll find one of the most dramatically located villages in Spain.

The Alpujarras valleys on the southern flank of the Sierra Nevada, southeast of Granada, form an otherworldly, hauntingly beautiful zone of arid hillsides and ravines, dotted with oasis-like white villages. The Sierra Nevada itself contains mainland Spain's highest peak, Mulhacén (3482m), and is a major goal for energetic walkers.

The Sierra Morena, rolling along Andalucía's northern rim, rarely more than 1000m high, attains great verdure and beauty in areas like the Parque Natural Sierra Norte and Parque Natural Sierra de Aracena y Picos de Aroche. These areas are far off the regular foreign tourist's trail.

Further lovely, green mountainous areas lie around the town of Ronda, mostly in the Parque Natural Sierra de Grazalema and the Serranía de Ronda. A little farther east, Andalucía's most awesome gorge, El Chorro, has been carved out by the Río Guadalhorce.

SUGGESTED ITINERARIES

Where to go depends on what you're interested in: exploring the marvellous monuments from Andalucía's fascinating past;

enjoying its beaches and seas; roaming its spectacular mountain and country areas; or partying in its up-all-night cities. Here are a few ideas to help you get as broad a taste of Andalucía as possible in a limited time.

One Week
You have to travel fairly hard to experience much in one week. For the major monuments and three contrasting and fascinating cities, make a beeline for Seville, Córdoba and Granada. Alternatively, do an eastern or western circuit. An eastern circuit could combine Granada with Las Alpujarras – a beautiful slice of mountainous, rural Andalucía – and finish in Córdoba (or Málaga – another rewarding city). In the west, Seville can be combined with the historic port of Cádiz, or the sherry capital Jerez de la Frontera, or a couple of days on Cádiz province's Costa de la Luz (Coast of Light); complete the week with Córdoba or Málaga.

Two Weeks
The Seville–Córdoba–Granada axis should be the hub of your trip. You could easily devote two weeks to these three cities alone, maybe with a few trips out to places such as Carmona, Sanlúcar de Barrameda or Jerez de la Frontera from Seville; Zuheros from Córdoba; or Las Alpujarras from Granada. For a wider-ranging trip, in the west consider Ronda, Tarifa, the Costa de la Luz, Cádiz, the Sierra de Grazalema, the Parque Nacional de Doñana and the Sierra de Aracena. In the east, consider the architectural splendours of Jaén, Úbeda and Baeza and the beautiful, mountainous Parque Natural de Cazorla; or go for a laid-back beach stint at spectacular Cabo de Gata. The city of Málaga makes a lively start or end to any trip.

One Month
Travelling consistently, you could cover most of the 'Two Weeks' options in one trip; or select a limited number of destinations and take time to savour them.

Two Months
With this amount of time you can cover everywhere we've mentioned previously,

select some off-the-beaten track destinations of your own, and throw in some genuine relaxation time too.

PLANNING
When to Go
Andalucía can be enjoyable any time of year, though the weather between November and February is hit-or-miss. Climatically, the ideal months to visit are April, May, June, September and October. At these times the countryside is at its most colourful and you can rely on good to excellent weather. July and August temperatures can be extreme, reaching up to 45°C inland. July and August are also the high-season months, with a crush of tourists pushing room prices up in most places. On the positive side, they're also the peak months for colourful fiestas.

If you plan to pursue some specific activity such as walking or skiing, choose your season carefully – see Activities later in this chapter, and regional chapters, for more information.

Maps
Michelin's 1:400,000 *Andalucía – Costa del Sol* is excellent for overall planning and touring, with an edition published each year. It's widely available in and outside Andalucía – look at petrol stations and bookshops.

Maps provided by tourist offices are often adequate for finding your way around cities and towns. So are those in phone directories, which come with indexes of major streets. For something more comprehensive, most cities are covered by one of the Spanish series such as Telstar, Escudo de Oro, Alpina or Everest, all with street indexes – available in bookshops. Check their publication dates, though.

On the Internet, **w** www.multimap.com has street maps of the main Andalucian cities, with a street-name search facility.

The Centro Nacional de Información Geográfica (CNIG), the publishing arm of the Instituto Geográfica Nacional (IGN), covers about three-quarters of Andalucía in its 1:25,000 (1cm to 250m) *Mapa Topográfico Nacional* sheets, most of which are up to date. The CNIG also publishes a 1:50,000 series, as does the Servicio Geográfico del Ejército (SGE, Army Geographic Service); the SGE's, called *Serie L*, tends to be more up-to-date (most of its Andalucía sheets have been revised since the mid-1990s). Other CNIG maps include a *Mapa Guía* series of national and natural parks, mostly at 1:50,000 or 1:100,000 and published in the 1990s. CNIG maps may be labelled CNIG, IGN or both.

The Junta de Andalucía, Andalucía's regional government, also publishes a range of Andalucía maps, including a *Mapa Guía* series of natural and national parks. These have been published recently and are widely available, although are perhaps better for vehicle touring, with a scale of 1:75,000. Other Junta maps include 1:10,000 and 1:20,000 sheets covering the whole of Andalucía – good maps but sales outlets for them are few.

The best maps for walkers in the Sierra Nevada, Las Alpujarras, Parque Natural de Cazorla and the Cabo de Gata area are the 1:40,000 and 1:50,000 maps published by Editorial Alpina.

You're only likely to find a limited range of maps in or near the areas they cover, so it's a good idea to try to obtain them in advance. **Editorial Alpina** maps can be ordered online at w www.editorialalpina.com and sent to any country in the world. **Stanfords** (☎ 020-7836 1321; w www.stanfords.co.uk; 12-14 Long Acre, London WC2E 9LP, UK) has a good range of Spain maps and you can order them online.

In Spain, seek out any specialist map or travel bookshops: there's a list of them on the Internet at w www.copt.junta-andalucia.es/jsp/bienve.jsp. **LTC** (☎ 954 42 59 64; e ltc-mapas@sp-editores.es; Avenida Menéndez Pelayo 42-44, 41004 Seville) is the best map shop in Andalucía, selling most Junta maps as well as SGE and CNIG maps. Another good map shop is **Luque Libros** in Córdoba (see Orientation under Córdoba in the Córdoba Province chapter).

The **CNIG** (☎ 915 97 95 14, fax 915 35 29 13; w www.cnig.es; Calle General Ibáñez de Íbero 3, 28003 Madrid) sells its own and

other maps (including the SGE's *Serie L* 1:50,000 maps) through its website. The CNIG also has sales offices in Andalucía's eight provincial capitals, including:

Granada (☎ 958 29 04 11) Avenida Divina Pastora 7 & 9
Málaga (☎ 952 21 20 18) Calle Ramos Carrión 48
Seville (☎ 954 64 42 56) Avenida San Francisco Javier 9, Edificio Sevilla 2-8° (módulo 7)

The **SGE** has a map shop (☎ 917 11 50 43, fax 917 11 14 00) at Calle de Darío Gazapo 8 (Cuartel Alfonso X), 28024 Madrid, open 9am to 1.30pm Monday to Friday. You can also order maps from here by fax or mail, though the procedure is complicated.

See Car & Motorcycle in the Getting Around chapter for recommendations for road atlases.

What to Bring

It's worth keeping in mind that everything you bring, you have to carry, and that you can buy most things you may need once there.

If you'll be doing any walking at all with your luggage, a backpack is the obvious answer. One whose straps and openings can be zipped inside a flap is preferable. A small daypack and a padlock or two are useful additions.

TOURIST OFFICES
Local Tourist Offices

All cities and many smaller towns and even villages in Andalucía have at least one tourist office (*oficina de turismo*). Staff are knowledgeable and increasingly versed in foreign languages. Offices are usually well stocked with printed material. Opening hours vary widely.

Tourist offices in Andalucía may be run by the local town hall, by local district organisations, by the government of whichever province you're in, or by the regional government, the Junta de Andalucía. There may be more than one of these in larger cities, each offering information on the territory it represents. The Junta's environmental department, the Consejería de Medio Ambiente, has visitor centres in many environmentally protected areas – *parques naturales* and so on. If a place has no tourist office, the town hall can often help with information.

You'll find details of useful tourist offices in destination sections throughout this book.

Tourist Offices Abroad

You can get information on Andalucía from Spanish national tourist offices in 22 countries, including:

Canada (☎ 416-961 3131, ⓔ toronto@tour spain.es) 2 Bloor St W, 34th floor, Toronto M4W 3E2

France (☎ 01 45 03 82 57, ⓔ paris@tourspain .es) 43, rue Decamps, 75784 Paris, Cedex 16

Germany (☎ 030-882 6543, ⓔ berlin@tour spain.es) Kurfürstendamm 63, 10707 Berlin Branches in Düsseldorf, Frankfurt am Main & Munich

Italy (☎ 06-6920 0453, ⓔ roma@tourspain.es) Piazza di Spagna 55, 00187 Rome

Netherlands (☎ 070-346 59 00, ⓔ lahaya@tour spain.es) Laan Van Meerdervoor 8A, 2517 AJ The Hague

Portugal (☎ 21-354 1992, ⓔ lisboa@tourspain.es) Avenida Sidónio Pais 28-3° Dto, 1050-215 Lisbon

UK (☎ 020-7486 8077, ⓔ londres@tourspain.es) 22-23 Manchester Square, London W1U 3PX

USA (☎ 212-265-8822, ⓔ oetny@tourspain.es) 666 Fifth Ave, 35th floor, New York, NY 10103 Branches in Chicago, Los Angeles & Miami

You'll find details of the other offices, and links to several offices' own websites, on the **Turespaña** website (ⓦ *www.tourspain.es*).

VISAS & DOCUMENTS
Passport

Citizens of the 15 EU member states and Switzerland must carry their national identity card or a full valid passport (UK Visitor passports are not acceptable) when travelling to Spain. All other nationalities must have a full valid passport.

If your passport's expiry date is only a few months away, you may not be granted a visa should you need one.

By law, you are supposed to have your ID card or passport with you at all times in Spain. You will usually need one of them for registration when you take a hotel room.

Visas

Spain is one of 15 countries that have signed the Schengen Convention, an agreement whereby all EU member countries (except the UK and Ireland), plus Iceland and Norway, abolished checks at internal borders by the end of 2000. The other EU countries are Austria, Belgium, Denmark, Finland, France, Germany, Greece, Italy, Luxembourg, the Netherlands, Portugal and Sweden. Legal residents of the Schengen countries (regardless of their nationality) and citizens of the UK and Ireland need no visa to visit a Schengen country. Nationals of many other countries, including Australia, Canada, Israel, Japan, New Zealand, Switzerland and the USA, do not need a visa for tourist visits of up to 90 days in Spain, although some of these nationalities may be subject to restrictions in other Schengen countries.

Citizens of other countries should check with a Spanish consulate, and consulates of any other country they will be visiting, about visa requirements for any visit.

The standard tourist visa issued when necessary by Spanish consulates is the Schengen visa, valid for up to 90 days. You must apply for the visa in person at a consulate in your country of residence. Schengen visas cannot be extended and you can apply for no more than two of them in any 12-month period. It's worth applying early for your visa, especially in the busy summer months. In the UK, single-entry visas for a 30-day stay cost UK£15.50. Multiple entry visas valid for 90 days cost UK£21.70. A multiple-entry visa will save you time if you plan to leave Spain – say for Gibraltar or Morocco – and then re-enter. Visas are free for spouses and children of EU nationals. Various transit visas also exist – people who need a visa for Spain may do so even if just changing planes at a Spanish airport.

A Schengen visa issued by one Schengen country is generally valid for travel in all other Schengen countries. Since passports are often not stamped on entry (unless you arrive by air from outside the Schengen area), the 90-day validity can sometimes be interpreted flexibly, since no-one can prove how long you have been in the country.

Residence Nationals of EU countries, Norway and Iceland wanting to stay in Spain longer than 90 days are supposed to apply during their first month for a resident's card. This is a lengthy bureaucratic procedure: consult a Spanish consulate before you go.

Other nationalities who want to stay in Spain longer than 90 days are also supposed to get a resident's card – start the process aeons in advance.

Travel Insurance

A travel-insurance policy to cover theft, loss and medical problems is a good idea (see Health later in this chapter for further information on medical insurance). Travel agents will be able to make recommendations. Check the small print: some policies specifically exclude 'dangerous activities', which can include scuba diving, motorcycling, even trekking. You may prefer a policy that pays doctors or hospitals directly, rather than you having to pay on the spot and claim later. If you have to claim later, make sure you keep all documentation. Check whether the policy covers ambulances or an emergency flight home.

Buy travel insurance as early as possible. If you buy it in the week before you leave home, you may find, for example, that you are not covered for delays to your trip caused by strikes.

Paying for your airline ticket with a credit card often provides limited travel accident insurance, and you may be able to reclaim payment if the operator doesn't deliver.

Driving Licence & Permits

All EU countries' licences (pink or pink-and-green) are accepted in Spain. (But note that the old-style UK green licence is not accepted.) Licences from other countries are supposed to be accompanied by an International Driving Permit, although in practice, for renting cars or dealing with traffic police, your national licence will suffice. The International Driving Permit, valid for 12 months, is available from automobile clubs in your country. For other documents needed to drive to or in Spain, see The UK under Land in the Getting There & Away chapter.

Hostel Cards

A valid hostel card is needed at all 19 youth hostels of Inturjoven, the official Andalucía hostel organisation – see Accommodation later in this chapter.

Student, Teacher & Youth Cards

These cards can get you worthwhile discounts on travel, and reduced prices at some museums, sights and entertainment venues.

The International Student Identity Card (ISIC), for full-time students, and the International Teacher Identity Card (ITIC), for full-time teachers and academics, are issued by student travel organisations such as STA Travel (see Air in the Getting There & Away chapter for more information).

Anyone under 26 can get a Euro<26 card (Carnet Joven in Spain), which is available in Europe to people of any nationality, or an International Youth Travel Card (IYTC; or the GO25 card), available worldwide. These give similar discounts to the ISIC and are issued by many of the same organisations. The more useful discounts on offer for Euro<26 card holders include 20% or more off many train fares, 20% off some ferry fares, 10% off some bus journeys with the Alsa, Socibus and Secorbus companies, 10% off lodging in Andalucía's Inturjoven hostels, 30% off Avis car rentals, and discounts at some museums.

Asatej in Seville and Usit Unlimited in Seville and Granada (see city sections for details) sell the ISIC, Euro<26 and IYTC cards for around €5 per card. For information, see W www.istc.org and W www.euro26.org.

Copies

It is a wise precaution to photocopy all important documents (passport data and visa pages, credit cards, travel insurance policy, air/bus/train tickets, driving licence etc) before you leave home. Leave one set of copies with someone at home and keep another with you, separate from the originals.

Another option for storing details of your vital travel documents is Lonely Planet's online Travel Vault. You can create a personal Travel Vault free at W www.ekno.lonely planet.com. It will be password-protected and accessible by Internet at any time.

EMBASSIES & CONSULATES
Spanish Embassies & Consulates

Here is a list of Spanish embassies and consulates in selected countries:

Australia (☎ 02-6273 3555, W www.embaspain
.com) 15 Arkana St, Yarralumla, Canberra, ACT
2600
Consulates: In Melbourne (☎ 03-9347 1966) &
Sydney (☎ 02-9261 2433)

Canada (☎ 613-747-2252, e spain@docuweb.ca)
74 Stanley Ave, Ottawa, Ontario K1M 1P4
Consulates: In Toronto (☎ 416-977-1661) &
Montreal (☎ 514-935-5235)

France (☎ 01 44 43 18 00, W amb-espagne.fr)
22, Ave Marceau, 75381 Paris, Cedex 08
Consulates: In Paris (☎ 01 44 29 40 00) 165
Blvd Malesherbes, 75840; Lyon (☎ 04 78 89
64 15); Marseille (☎ 04 91 00 32 70); &
Toulouse (☎ 05 61 52 05 50)

Germany (☎ 030-254 00 70, W www.spanische
botschaft.de) Lichtensteinallee 1, 10787 Berlin
Consulates: In Düsseldorf (☎ 0211-43 90 80);
Frankfurt am Main (☎ 069-959 16 60); &
Munich (☎ 089-98 47 90)

Ireland (☎ 01-269 1640) 17A Merlyn Park, Balls
Bridge, Dublin 4

Italy (☎ 06-684 04 01, e ambespit@correo
.mae.es) Palacio Borghese, Lardo Fontanella di
Borghese, 19, 00186 Rome
Consulates: In Rome (☎ 06-687 14 01) Via
Campo Marzio 34, 00186; Genoa (☎ 010-56
26 69); Milan (☎ 02-632 88 31); & Naples
(☎ 081-41 11 57)

Netherlands (☎ 070-302 49 99, e ambespnl@
mail.mae.es) Lange Voorhout 50, 2514 EG The
Hague
Consulate: Amsterdam (☎ 020-620 38 11)

New Zealand See Australia

Portugal (☎ 213 472 381, e embesppt@correo
.mae.es) Rua do Salitre 1, 1250 Lisbon
Consulates: In Lisbon (☎ 213 472 792) Rua do
Salitre 3, 1299; Elvas (☎ 268 622 419); & Porto
(☎ 222 563 915)

UK (☎ 020-7235 5555, e embespuk@mail.mae
.es) 39 Chesham Place, London SW1X 8SB
Consulates: In London (☎ 020-7589 8989) 20
Draycott Place, SW3 2RZ; Manchester (☎ 0161-
236 1262); & Edinburgh (☎ 0131-220 18 43)

USA (☎ 202-452-0100, W www.spainemb.org)
2375 Pennsylvania Ave NW, Washington, DC
20037
Consulates: In Washington (☎ 202-728-2330)
2375 Pennsylvania Ave NW, DC 20037; Boston
(☎ 617-536-2506); Chicago (☎ 312-782-
4588); Houston (☎ 713-783-6200); Los
Angeles (☎ 213-938-0158); Miami (☎ 305-
446-5511); New Orleans (☎ 504-525-4951);
New York (☎ 212-355-4080); & San Francisco
(☎ 415-922-2995)

Embassies & Consulates in Spain

All foreign embassies are in Madrid, but
many countries also have consulates in
Andalucian cities – there are nearly 40 in
Seville. Málaga, Almería and Cádiz are
among other cities with some foreign consulates. Embassies and consulates include:

Australia (☎ 91 441 60 25, W www.spain.em
bassy.gov.au) Plaza del Descubridor Diego de
Ordás 3, Madrid
Consulate: (☎ 95 422 09 71) Calle Federico
Rubio 14, Seville

Your Own Embassy

It's important to realise what your own embassy – the embassy of the country of which you are a
citizen – can and can't do to help you if you get into trouble. Generally speaking, it won't be much
help in emergencies if the trouble you're in is remotely your own fault. Remember that you are
bound by the laws of the country you are in. Your embassy will not be sympathetic if you end up
in jail after committing a crime locally, even if such actions are legal in your own country.

In genuine emergencies you might get some assistance, but only if other channels have been exhausted. For example, if you need to get home urgently, a free ticket home is exceedingly unlikely –
the embassy would expect you to have insurance. If you have all your money and documents stolen,
it might assist with getting a new passport, but a loan for onward travel is out of the question.

Some embassies used to keep letters for travellers or have a small reading room with home newspapers, but these days the mail-holding service has usually been stopped and even newspapers tend
to be out of date.

Canada (☎ 91 432 32 50, W www.canada-es.org)
Calle de Núñez de Balboa 35, Madrid
Consulate: (☎ 95 222 33 46) Edificio Horizonte,
Calle Cervantes, Málaga
France (☎ 91 423 89 00, W www.ambafrance.es)
Calle Salustiano Olózaga 9, Madrid
Consulates: In Seville (☎ 95 422 28 96) Plaza
de Santa Cruz 1; & Málaga (☎ 95 222 65 90)
Calle Duquesa de Parcent 8
Germany (☎ 91 557 90 00, W www.embajada-
alemania.es) Calle de Fortuny 8, Madrid
Consulate: (☎ 95 423 02 04) Edificio Winterthur,
Avenida de la Palmera 19, Seville
Ireland (☎ 91 436 40 93) Paseo de la Castellana
46, Madrid
Consulates: In Seville (☎ 95 421 63 61) Plaza de
Santa Cruz 6; & Fuengirola (☎ 95 247 51 08)
Galerías Santa Mónica, Avenida de los Boliches
Italy (☎ 91 423 33 00) Calle Lagasca 98, Madrid
Consulate: (☎ 95 422 85 76) Calle Fabiola 10,
Seville
Morocco (☎ 91 563 10 90) Calle de Serrano 179,
Madrid
Netherlands (☎ 91 353 75 00) Avenida del
Comandante Franco 32, Madrid
Consulate: (☎ 95 422 87 50) Calle Placentines 1,
Seville
New Zealand (☎ 91 523 02 26) Plaza de la
Lealtad 2, Madrid
Portugal (☎ 91 782 49 60) Calle Pinar 1, Madrid
Consulate: In Madrid (☎ 91 577 35 85) Calle
Lagasca 88; & Seville (☎ 95 423 11 50)
Avenida del Cid 1
UK (☎ 91 700 82 00, W www.ukinspain.com)
Calle de Fernando el Santo 16, Madrid
Consulates: In Málaga (☎ 95 235 23 00) Edificio
Eurocom, Calle de Mauricio Moro Pareto 2; &
Granada (☎ 958 27 47 24), Carmen de San
Cristóbal, Carretera de Murcia s/n
USA (☎ 91 587 22 00, W www.embusa.es)
Calle de Serrano 75, Madrid
Consular agency: In Seville (☎ 95 423 18 85)
Paseo de las Delicias 7; & Fuengirola (☎ 95
247 48 91) Apartment 1C, Avenida Juan
Gómez 8, (mailing address: Apartado de
Correos 236, 29640 Fuengirola)

CUSTOMS

Duty-free allowances for entering Spain from outside the EU include 2L of wine (or 1L of wine and 1L of spirits), and 200 cigarettes or 50 cigars. Duty-free allowances for travel between EU countries were abolished in 1999. There are no restrictions on the import of *duty-paid* items into Spain from other EU countries for personal use.

MONEY

You can get by easily enough with a credit or debit card enabling you to withdraw cash from Automatic Teller Machines (ATMs), but it's sound thinking to take two cards (if you have them) and a few travellers cheques too. The combination gives you a fallback if you lose a card or for some reason can't use it.

Overall, when you take into consideration commissions, handling fees, exchange rate differentials and other factors, visitors from outside the euro zone will get most value for their money by making purchases by credit or debit card, with ATM withdrawals not far behind as second-best value. Obtaining euros by exchanging travellers cheques or non-euro cash gives less value for your money.

Currency

Spain's currency is the euro (€), made up of 100 céntimos. The currency comes in coins of 1, 2, 5, 10, 20 and 50 céntimos and 1 and 2 euros, and notes of 5, 10, 20, 50, 100, 200 and 500 euros.

All euro notes and coins, whichever country mints them, are legal tender in all euro-zone countries. Coins of each denomination are all identical on the side showing the value. The design of the obverse varies according to the country minting the coin: Spain's show the cathedral of Santiago de Compostela (€0.01, €0.02 and €0.05), writer Miguel de Cervantes (€0.10, €0.20 and €0.50) and King Juan Carlos I (€1 and €2). The €500 note – one of the world's most valuable banknotes – shows two of the bridges over the Río Guadalquivir at Seville.

Exchange Rates

Exchange rates as this book went to print were:

currency	unit		euros
Australia	A$1	=	€0.57
Canada	C$1	=	€0.65
Japan	¥100	=	€0.83
Morocco	Dr10	=	€0.96
New Zealand	NZ$1	=	€0.49
UK	UK£1	=	€1.60
USA	US$1	=	€1.02

Adiós, Peseta

Thanks to a long programme of preparatory publicity about the euro, most Spaniards adopted it *sin problemas* when the changeover from Spain's previous currency, the peseta, happened in early 2002. The euro's value had been fixed at 166.386 pesetas back in 1999, giving the relatively straightforward approximate conversion rate of 1000ptas = €6. Many prices had been quoted in both currencies for some time before the changeover, to get people used to the idea, and this continued afterwards.

The introduction of the euro undoubtedly pushed up the cost of living, with many retailers and service providers seizing the chance to tack a few per cent on to prices, confident in the knowledge that few customers would be carrying pocket calculators checking peseta–euro conversion rates. Although official statistics tried to play this down, some economists claimed that prices of everyday goods went up by 15% to 20%. Tourists were hit too: Andalucian room prices in 2002 averaged about 20% higher than two years previously, an increase far above the rate of inflation.

Exchanging Money

Spain's international airports have bank branches, ATMs and exchange offices, and seaports and road crossings into Spain will have at least one or the other close by. If coming from Morocco, be sure to get rid of any dirham before you leave.

For those with money in the form of plastic cards, most banks have ATMs. Cash or travellers cheques can be exchanged at virtually any bank or exchange office. Banks are plentiful and tend to offer the best exchange rates. They mostly open from about 8.30am to 2pm Monday to Friday, and 9am to 1pm Saturday.

Exchange offices – usually indicated by the word *cambio* (exchange) – exist mainly in tourist resorts. Generally they offer longer opening hours and quicker service than banks, but worse exchange rates.

Travellers cheques usually bring a slightly better exchange rate than cash, though that's offset by the charges for buying them in the first place.

In many places, the more money you change, the better the exchange rate you'll get. Wherever you change, it's worth asking about commissions first, and confirming that exchange rates are as posted (posted rates may not have been recently updated). Commissions may be different for travellers cheques and cash, and may depend on how many cheques, or how much in total, you're cashing. A typical commission is 2.5% to 3%, with a minimum of €2 to €4, but there are places that have a minimum of €6 or

even €12. Places that advertise 'no commission' usually offer poor exchange rates.

Travellers Cheques These can be replaced if they are lost or stolen. In Spain you usually can't use them like money to actually make purchases. Thomas Cook, Visa and American Express (AmEx) are widely accepted brands with efficient replacement policies. AmEx offices cash their own travellers cheques commission-free – but you might still gain by going to a bank or exchange office because their exchange rates may be more favourable.

Get most of your cheques in fairly large denominations (the equivalent of €100 or more) to save on any per-cheque commission charges.

It's vital to keep your initial receipt, plus a record of your cheque numbers and the ones you have used, separate from the cheques themselves. For AmEx travellers cheque refunds you can call ☎ 900 99 44 26 from anywhere in Spain.

ATMs & Plastic Money The exchange rate used for credit- and debit-card transactions is usually more in your favour than for cash exchanges.

You can use plastic to pay for many purchases and to withdraw cash from banks and ATMs. Always report a lost card straight away: in Spain you can call ☎ 902 37 56 37 for AmEx cards, ☎ 900 97 44 45 for Visa, ☎ 900 97 12 31 for MasterCard or

EuroCard, and ☎ 91 547 74 00 for Diners Club.

International Transfers To have money transferred from another country, you need to organise someone to send it, through a bank or a rapid international money-transfer service such as **Western Union** *(Spain ☎ 900 63 36 33;* ⓦ *www.westernunion.com)* or **MoneyGram** *(Spain ☎ 900 20 10 10;* ⓦ *www.moneygram.com)*, and a bank (or transferservice agent) in Spain to collect it from. If there are funds in your home bank account, you may be able to instruct the bank yourself.

To set up a transfer through a bank, the sender will need exact details of the Spanish bank branch where you want to collect the money – its name, address, city and any contact or code numbers required. Fees for this service depend on the banks concerned – Spanish banks may charge around €20 for their part in it.

Security

Keep only a limited amount of money as cash, and the bulk in more easily replaceable forms such as plastic cards or travellers cheques. If your accommodation has a safe, use it. If you have to leave money in your room, divide it into several stashes and hide them in different places.

For carrying money on the street, the safest thing is an unobtrusive moneybelt or wallet that you can keep under your clothes. Watch out for people who touch you or seem to be getting unwarrantedly close, in any situation. When using ATMs, be wary of anyone who offers to help you, even if your card is stuck in the machine.

Costs

If you are extremely frugal, it's just about possible to scrape by on €25 to €30 a day by staying in the cheapest possible accommodation, avoiding restaurants except for an inexpensive set lunch, minimising visits to museums and bars, staying away from the more expensive cities such as Seville, and generally not moving around too much. A more comfortable economy budget would be €50 to €60 a day. This could allow you

€15 to €20 for accommodation; €2 for breakfast (coffee and a pastry); €6 to €10 for lunch or dinner; €5 for another, lighter meal; €6 to €12 for public transport and admission fees to museums, sights or entertainment venues; and a bit over for a drink or two, intercity travel and a little shopping.

If you've got €125 to €150 a day you can stay in excellent accommodation, rent a car and eat some of the best food Andalucía has to offer.

Ways to Save Two people can travel more cheaply (per person) than one by sharing rooms. Rooms for three or four people are available in many places and work out even cheaper per person. You'll also save by avoiding the peak tourist seasons, when most room prices go up: these vary from region to region, but generally run from about July to mid-September. A student or youth card (see Visas & Documents, earlier), or a document such as a passport proving you're over 60, brings worthwhile savings. A few museums and sights are cheaper for EU passport holders.

Tipping & Bargaining

The law requires menu prices to include service charge, and tipping is a matter of personal choice – most people leave some small change if they're satisfied, and 5% is usually plenty. Porters will generally be happy with €1.50.

The only places in Spain where you are likely to bargain are markets – though even there most things have fixed prices – and, occasionally, cheap hotels, particularly if you're staying for a few days.

Taxes & Refunds

In Spain, value-added tax (VAT) is known as IVA (**ee**-ba, *impuesto sobre el valor añadido*). On accommodation and restaurant prices, it's 7% and is usually (but not always) included in the prices you'll be quoted. On retail goods and car hire, IVA is 16%. To ask 'is IVA included?', say *'¿está incluido el IVA?'*.

Visitors are entitled to a refund of the 16% IVA on purchases costing more than €90.15 from any shop if they are taking them out of the EU within three months. Ask the shop for a Cashback refund form showing the price and IVA paid for each item and identifying the vendor and purchaser. Then present the refund form to the customs booth for IVA refunds at the airport or port from which you leave the EU. You will need your passport and a boarding card that shows you are leaving the EU. The officer will stamp the invoice and you hand it in at a bank in the airport or port for the reimbursement.

POST & COMMUNICATIONS
Postal Rates
At 2002 rates, a postcard or letter weighing up to 20g costs €0.50 from Spain to other European countries, and €0.75 to the rest of the world. An aerogram costs €0.50 to anywhere in the world.

Registered *(certificado)* mail costs an extra €2.10. *Urgente* service, which means your mail may arrive two or three days quicker than normal, costs an extra €1.75 for international mail.

Sending Mail
Stamps are sold at most *estancos* (tobacconist shops with 'Tabacos' in yellow letters on a maroon background), as well as at post offices *(oficinas de correos)*. Main post offices in cities and towns are usually open from about 8.30am to 8.30pm Monday to Friday and 9am to 1.30pm on Saturday. Village offices may be open shorter hours. *Estancos* usually open for normal shop hours.

It's quite safe to post mail in the yellow street postboxes *(buzones)* as well as at post offices. Mail to other Western European countries normally arrives within a week; to North America within 10 days; to Australia and New Zealand within two weeks.

Receiving Mail
Delivery times are similar to those for outbound mail. Poste-restante mail can be addressed to you at poste restante (or better, *lista de correos*, the Spanish name for it), anywhere in Spain that has a post office, with the name of the province following that of the town. Mail will be delivered to the place's main post office unless another

one is specified in the address. Take your passport when you go to pick up mail.

AmEx card or travellers cheque holders can use the free client mail-holding service at AmEx offices in Spain (Seville, Granada, Marbella, Madrid and Barcelona).

Spanish addresses have a five-digit postcode, use of which may help your mail arrive a bit quicker. Villages, towns and small cities have one postcode for the whole place (for example, 29400 for Ronda). But the biggest cities each encompass several different postcodes. The postcodes given in this book for these larger places (Andalucía's eight provincial capitals, plus Algeciras and Jerez de la Frontera) are those for mail addressed to the *lista de correos* at main post offices.

Telephone
Andalucía is well provided with street pay phones, which are easy to use for both international and domestic calls. These blue phones accept coins and/or phonecards *(tarjetas telefónicas)* issued by the national phone company Telefónica. Phonecards come in €6 and €12 denominations and are sold at post offices and *estancos*.

Coin pay phones inside bars and cafés – usually green – are normally a little more expensive than street pay phones. Phones in hotel rooms can be a good deal more expensive: managements set their own rates, so ask about costs before using one.

Costs A three-minute pay-phone call costs around €0.15 within your local area, €0.35 to other places within the same province, €0.45 to other Spanish provinces and €1.15 to €1.35 to Spanish mobile phones (numbers starting with 6). All these calls are 10% to 20% cheaper (about 50% cheaper to mobile numbers) from 8pm to 8am Monday to Friday, and all day Saturday and Sunday. A three-minute pay-phone call to other EU countries or the USA costs about €1, and to Australia €4.50. There's no cheap period for international calls.

Calls to Spanish numbers starting with ☎ 900 are free. Calls to other numbers starting with ☎ 901 to ☎ 906 vary. A common one is ☎ 902, for which you pay about €0.35 for three minutes from a pay phone.

Calls from private lines cost about 25% less than calls from pay phones.

A variety of discount cards are available which can significantly cut call costs, especially for international calls. Most of these are not slot-in cards but work through special access numbers. If you're thinking of buying one, look closely into call costs (including any taxes payable, such as IVA) and find out exactly from where you can use the card.

Domestic Dialling Spain has no telephone area codes. All numbers have nine digits and you just dial that nine-digit number, wherever in the country you are calling from.

Dial ☎ 1009 to speak to a domestic operator, including for a domestic reverse-charge (collect) call *(una llamada por cobro revertido)*. For directory inquiries dial ☎ 1003; calls cost approximately €0.30.

International Dialling To make an international call from Andalucía, dial the international access code (☎ 00), then the country code, area code and number you want. For international reverse-charge calls, dial ☎ 900 followed by the code for the country you're calling:

Australia	☎ 99 00 61
Canada	☎ 99 00 15
France	☎ 99 00 33
New Zealand	☎ 99 00 64
UK	☎ 99 00 44
USA	☎ 99 00 11 (AT&T), ☎ 99 00 13 (Sprint), ☎ 99 00 14 (MCI) or ☎ 99 00 17 (Worldcom)

Codes for other countries are often posted up at pay phones. You'll get straight through to an operator in the country you're calling.

Alternatively, in most places you can get an English-speaking international operator on ☎ 1008.

Mobile Phones Spaniards adore mobile phones *(teléfonos móviles)*. By 2002 there were about 26 million mobiles in the country. Shops on the high street of every Andalucian town sell phones with prepaid cards from around €70.

Spain uses GSM 900/1800, compatible with the rest of Europe and Australia but not with the North American GSM 1900 or the totally different system used in Japan (though some North Americans have GSM 1900/900 phones that do work here). If you plan to take your own mobile to Spain, it's sensible to:

• Check with your mobile network provider that your phone is enabled for international roaming.
• Check with your provider the current costs of international roaming services. You will probably also pay to receive calls or listen to voicemail abroad. Sending text messages might be cheaper, but you might be charged twice per message (once by your own operator and once by the overseas operator) for messages to or from home. It's worth asking about special international traveller services which offer cheaper calls abroad in return for a monthly fee.
• Consider buying an alternative SIM card for use on a local network in Spain. These are sold at some Spanish international airports and holiday destinations and even by some specialist retailers in other countries.
• Take a continental adaptor for the charger plug.
• Note your phone's number, serial number (IMEI number) and your operator's customer services number. This will help if your phone is stolen.

Calling Andalucía from Abroad Spain's country code is ☎ 34. Follow this with the nine-digit number you are calling.

ekno Communication Service

Lonely Planet's ekno global communication service provides low-cost international calls. It also offers free messaging services, email, travel information and an online travel vault, where you can securely store all your important documents. You can join online at ⓦ www.ekno.lonelyplanet.com, where you will find the local-access numbers for the 24-hour customer-service centre.

Fax

Most main post offices have fax service: sending one page costs about €2.25 within Spain, €7 to elsewhere in Europe and €13.30 to North America or Australasia. However, you'll often find cheaper rates at shops or offices with 'Fax Público' signs.

Email & Internet Access

You'll find cybercafés and other public Internet points in most Andalucian cities and towns where you can access the Web for typically €1 to €2 per hour. If you have a Web-based email account, you can access it anywhere in the world from any Internet-connected computer. Several email accounts are available free, such as **ekno** (W *www.ekno.lonelyplanet.com*) (see ekno Communication Service, earlier), **Yahoo!** (W *www.yahoo.com*) and **Hotmail** (W *www .hotmail.com*).

If you intend to travel with a portable computer, remember that the power supply voltage in Spain may vary from that at home, so take a universal AC adaptor for your appliance. You'll also need a plug adaptor for Spain – often it's easiest to buy these before you leave home. To cope with telephone sockets that may be different from those at home, take a US RJ-11 telephone adaptor that works with your modem. You can almost always find an adaptor that will convert from RJ-11 to the local variety. For more information on travelling with a portable computer, check out W www.teleadapt.com or W www.warrior.com.

Major Internet service providers such as **AOL** (W *www.aol.com*) and **CompuServe** (W *www.compuserve.com*) have dial-in nodes throughout Europe including Seville, Málaga and other Spanish cities. It's best to download a list of the dial-in numbers before you leave home.

DIGITAL RESOURCES

The Web is a rich resource for travellers. You can research your trip, hunt down bargain air fares, book hotels, check on weather conditions or chat with locals and other travellers about the best places to visit (or avoid).

A good place to start your Web explorations is the **Lonely Planet** website (W *www.lonelyplanet.com*). You'll find succinct summaries on travelling to most places on earth, postcards from other travellers, and the Thorn Tree bulletin board where you can ask questions before you go or dispense advice when you get back. You can also find travel news and the subWWWay section links you to the most useful travel resources elsewhere on the Web.

The following are among the best wide-ranging English-language websites on Andalucía. You'll find more specialised sites recommended in specific sections of this book.

All About Spain (W www.red2000.com/spain) This site contains sections on cities, bullfighting, flamenco, food, nightlife and more.

Andalucia.com (W www.andalucia.com) A broad compendium of practical and background information resides here, from country hotels to bus timetables, flamenco to natural parks.

Andalucía There's Only One (W www.anda lucia.org) The official tourism site of the Junta de Andalucía; includes a tourist atlas with photos, locator maps and detailed information on every city, town and village; detailed information on golf courses, marinas and language schools; descriptions of 200 walks and 150 mountain-bike rides; information on flamenco and the Muslim heritage; and an online booking facility for accommodation, activities and hire cars.

OKSpain (W www.okspain.org) The site of the Spanish tourist offices in the USA, this has lots of good links.

Spanish Tourist Office in London (W www.tour spain.co.uk) You'll find good practical stuff here.

Turespaña (W www.tourspain.es) The site of the Spanish overseas tourism promotion body, with hotel prices, links to Spanish tourist offices worldwide, language schools and lots of other useful practical stuff.

BOOKS

Andalucía has fascinated foreign writers for two centuries, inspiring a wealth of literature in English and other languages. For any reading material you particularly want, stock up before you go: local availability of foreign-language books is patchy.

Most books are published in different editions by different publishers in different countries. As a result, a book might be a hard-cover rarity in one country while it's readily available in paperback in another. Fortunately, bookshops and libraries search by title or author, so your local bookshop or library is best placed to advise you on the availability of the following recommendations.

Lonely Planet

You'll find detailed route descriptions for many of Andalucía's best walks in *Walking in Spain*. If you're travelling in Spain beyond Andalucía, the guides on *Spain*, *Madrid*, *Valencia & the Costa Blanca*, *Barcelona, Catalunya & the Costa Brava*, and the *Canary Islands* will point you in the right directions. *World Food Spain* by Richard Sterling is a trip into Spain's culinary soul, from tapas to *postres* and the *menú del día* to the *carta de vinos*, with a comprehensive culinary dictionary. The *Spanish phrasebook* will give you something to say in between ¡hola! and ¡adiós!

Travel

Washington Irving was an American who took up residence in Granada's Alhambra palace when it was in an abandoned state in the 1820s. His *Tales of the Alhambra* (1832), easy to find in Granada, weaves a series of enchanting stories around the folk with whom he shared his life there.

A Handbook for Travellers in Spain by Richard Ford (1845) remains a classic not only for telling how things were then in places we see now, but also for its irascible, witty English author. Unfortunately, the most easily available edition costs around UK£75.

The Bible in Spain by George Borrow (1842) is an English clergyman's view of 19th-century Spain in which he tried to spread the Protestant word. You might be able to track this down relatively cheaply.

Laurie Lee set off from his Gloucestershire home on foot, aged 19, in 1934. He walked from northern Spain to Andalucía, playing his violin for a living. *As I Walked Out One Midsummer Morning* (1969) delightfully evokes the sights, smells and contrasting moods of turbulent pre–civil war Spain. He was rescued by the Royal Navy

when the civil war broke out while he was living in a village he calls Castillo (probably Almuñécar). Lee returned to his old haunts in Andalucía in the 1950s, a trip recorded in *A Rose for Winter* (1955).

History & Society

Michael Jacobs' *Andalucía* (1998) admirably elucidates Andalucía's history in a book of broader compass (see Culture & Arts later in this section).

Most histories of Spain pay major attention to pre-1700 Andalucía, since it was the hub of Islamic Spain and then of early imperial Spain. A colourful and not over-long survey of the whole saga is *The Story of Spain* (1990) by Mark Williams. *Moorish Spain* by Richard Fletcher (1992) is a fascinating short history of Al-Andalus, concentrating to a large extent on Andalucía. Michael Jacobs' *In the Glow of the Phantom Palace* (1999) investigates the cultural and monumental legacy of Al-Andalus in both Spain and North Africa, tackling the legends and the reality on a journey from Granada to the Sahara desert.

Andalucía since 1700 is less written about, but Gerald Brenan worked much about the region's problems and politics into The Spanish Labyrinth (first published 1943), a fascinating unravelling of the political and social movements of pre–civil war Spain. See under Living in Andalucía, following, for more on Brenan.

The murky story of one of the civil war's most infamous atrocities, the killing near Granada of writer Federico García Lorca, is chillingly pieced together in *The Assassination of Federico García Lorca* (1979) by Ian Gibson.

On the civil war as a whole, Hugh Thomas' *The Spanish Civil War* (first published 1961) is *the* classic account; it's long and dense, yet readable and humane.

Two excellent, wide-ranging introductions to modern Spain are *Fire in the Blood* (1992) by Ian Gibson and *The New Spaniards* (1995) by John Hooper, a former Madrid correspondent for the *Guardian*. *Death in the Afternoon* (1932) is Ernest Hemingway's book about bullfighting.

Living in Andalucía

In the 1920s Englishman Gerald Brenan settled in Yegen, a remote village in Las Alpujarras south of Granada, aiming to educate himself unimpeded by British mores and traditions. *South from Granada* (1957) is his classic, perspicacious and humorous account of local life punctuated by visits from members of the Bloomsbury set. In 1949 Brenan returned to Andalucía to explore Franco's Spain, an experience recounted in *The Face of Spain* (1950).

Alastair Boyd's *The Sierras of the South* (1992) evokes life in the hills around Ronda in the 1950s and '60s, when foreigners were a rarity. Naturalist Nicholas Luard does a similar job for the hinterland behind the coastal towns of Tarifa and Algeciras in the 1960s and '70s in *Andalucia: A Portrait of Southern Spain* (1984). His wife Elisabeth Luard tells of life with their four children in *Family Life* (1996), a book sprinkled with Andalucian recipes but which ends like a sledgehammer with a terrible family tragedy.

Driving Over Lemons (1999), the big hit of recent English-language writing about Spain, is the entertaining tale of amiable writer-cum-sheep-shearer-cum-drummer Chris Stewart's small farm in Las Alpujarras, south of Granada. Stewart published a sequel-cum-prequel, *A Parrot in the Pepper Tree*, in 2002.

If it's *you* that's contemplating 'Living in Andalucía', have a look first at *Living and Working in Spain* by David Hampshire (2000) or *You and the Law in Spain* by David Searl. If the nightmarish bureaucratic tangle these books reveal doesn't put you off, continue pursuing your dream.

Culture & Arts

It's hard to better James Woodall's *In Search of the Firedance* (1992) as an introduction to flamenco. In this unfortunately now hard-to-get book, Woodall explains the different forms of flamenco, tells us about the great artists, visits all the main flamenco hubs and explores its *gitano* (Roma people) and Islamic roots. *¡Flamenco!* by Gwynne Edward (2000) also traces the flamenco story, with the aid of wonderful photos by Ken Haas. Ian Gibson's *Federico García Lorca* (1990) is an excellent biography of Andalucía's most celebrated writer.

Andalucía by Michael Jacobs (1998) runs comprehensively, eruditely and irreverently through the region's culture and history, from Muslim architecture to Lorca and the Sevillan golden age to flamenco, adding informed comment on today's Andalucía, plus a 140-page gazetteer of places and sights. It's great for those of us who wonder whether the street we're staying on is named after a 16th-century playwright or a 19th-century general.

Fiction

Ernest Hemingway's gripping civil war novel *For Whom the Bell Tolls* (1941) – probably the most read of all English-language books set in Spain – only touches on Andalucía but it warrants reading in any Spanish context. Hemingway experienced the war as a journalist, as did Arthur Koestler, who was imprisoned by the Nationalists when they took Málaga, and almost executed – an experience on which his fine novel *Darkness at Noon* (1940) is based.

See Literature under Arts in the Facts about Andalucía chapter for information on works by Andalucian writers.

Flora & Fauna

Wildlife Travelling Companion Spain by John Measures (1992) covers 150 of Spain's best sites for viewing flora and fauna – many of them in Andalucía – with details of how to reach them. It also contains a basic field guide to some common animals and plants. Bird-watchers will find *Where to Watch Birds in Southern Spain* (second edition, 2001) by Ernest Garcia & Andrew Paterson invaluable, but will also want a field guide such as *Collins Field Guide: Birds of Britain and Europe* by Roger Tory Peterson, Guy Mountfort & PAD Hollom.

For botanists, there's the classic *Flowers of South-West Europe, A Field Guide* by Oleg Polunin & B E Smythies (1973), and *A Selection of Wildflowers of Southern Spain* by Betty Molesworth Allen (1993).

Food

The Flavor of Andalusia by Pepita Aris (1996) gives recipes for some 50 typical Andalucian dishes, plus interesting background on the region's food, but is hard to find. Numerous books on the diverse field of Spanish cookery include plenty of Andalucian material: among the best are *Spanish Cooking* by Pepita Aris (2000) and Lonely Planet's *World Food Spain* by Richard Sterling (2000).

NEWSPAPERS & MAGAZINES
Spanish Press

Spain has a thriving and free press. Spaniards have never taken to the idea of 'popular' newspapers. Among the major daily national newspapers, the liberal *El País* is hard to beat for solid reporting. *Marca*, devoted entirely to sport (mostly football), is the bestselling national daily paper. Every sizable city in Andalucía has at least one daily paper of its own and these are often useful for what's-on and transport information. Among the best are Seville's *El Correo*, Granada's *Ideal* and Málaga's *Sur*.

Foreign-Language Press

At least a dozen local English-, German- and Scandinavian-language newspapers and magazines are published along the holiday coasts of Málaga, Granada and Almería provinces. Most are simply vehicles for estate agents' ads, occasionally useful for the town maps they contain. An exception is the Málaga-published weekly free newspaper *Sur in English*, which reviews local news, with translations of some articles from the Spanish *Sur*. You can often pick it up at tourist offices and hotels and in some shops, especially in Málaga province: it comes out on Friday. The *Costa del Sol News* (Thursday) is a weekly newspaper (€0.75) geared mainly to resident expats. The *Reporter*, a free monthly magazine found on the Costa del Sol, usually has a few interesting features. La Herradura's *Coastal Gazette* is 'dedicated to the restoration of beer-drinking as a true art form'.

Newspapers from Western European countries and international press such as the *International Herald Tribune*, *Time* and *Newsweek* reach major cities and tourist areas on the day of publication. Monday to Saturday, the *International Herald Tribune* comes with an eight-page English-language version of the same day's *El País*.

RADIO & TV

The coastal areas have at least six English-language radio stations. Most carry BBC or British independent radio news on the hour several times a day. You'll get a lot of music and some talk on Spectrum (105.5MHz FM), Central (98.6MHz and 103.8MHz), Global Radio (96.5MHz), Sunshine Radio (99.4MHz), Onda Cero International (OCI; 101.6MHz) and Coastline (97.7MHz) – we've listed them in approximate ascending order of audience age. OCI provides Spanish news in English from 9.30am to 10am, Monday to Friday. Radio Gibraltar is on 91.3MHz FM.

El País publishes province-by-province wavelength guides in its *Cartelera* (What's-on) section.

The standard Spanish broadcast channels include: state-run TVE1 and TVE2 (La 2); national independent channels Antena 3, Tele 5 and Canal Plus (this last is a pay channel, giving non-subscribers impossibly fuzzy pictures on most programmes); and a few regional or local channels.

PHOTOGRAPHY

Most main brands of film are widely available, and processing is generally efficient. A roll of print film (36 exposures, ISO 100) costs around €4 to €5 and can be processed for around €10 – there are often better deals if you have two or three rolls developed together. The equivalent in slide *(diapositiva)* film is around €5 plus €5 for processing.

Your camera and film will be routinely passed through airport x-ray machines. These shouldn't damage film but you can ask for hand inspection if you're worried. Lead pouches for film are another solution.

Some museums and galleries ban photography, or at least flash, and soldiers can be touchy about it. It's common courtesy to ask – at least by gesture – when you want to photograph people.

Bright midday sun tends to bleach out your shots. You get more colour and contrast earlier and later in the day.

Lonely Planet's *Travel Photography* offers expert advice and is designed to take on the road.

TIME

All mainland Spain is on GMT/UTC plus one hour during winter, and GMT/UTC plus two hours during the daylight-saving period, which runs from the last Sunday in March to the last Sunday in October. Most other Western European countries have the same time as Spain year-round, the major exceptions being Britain, Ireland and Portugal. Add one hour to these three countries' times to get Spanish time.

Spanish time is normally USA Eastern Time plus six hours, and USA Pacific Time plus nine hours. But the USA tends to start daylight saving a week or two later than Spain, so you must add one hour to the time differences in the intervening period.

In the Australian winter subtract eight hours from Sydney time to get Spanish time; in the Australian summer subtract 10 hours. The difference is nine hours for a few weeks in March.

Morocco is on GMT/UTC year-round, so is two hours behind Spain during Spanish daylight saving, and one hour behind at other times of year.

ELECTRICITY

Electric current in Spain is 220V, 50 Hz, as in the rest of continental Europe, but just a few places are still on 125V or 110V (sockets are often labelled where this is the case). Voltage may even vary in the same building. Don't plug 220V (or British 240V) appliances into 125V or 110V sockets unless they have a transformer. North American 60 Hz appliances with electric motors (such as some CD and tape players) may perform poorly.

Plugs have two round pins, again like the rest of continental Europe.

WEIGHTS & MEASURES

The metric system is used. Like other continental Europeans, the Spanish indicate decimals with commas and thousands with points.

LAUNDRY

Self-service laundrettes are becoming slightly more common in big cities (they charge around €5 to wash and dry a load), but small laundries are much more usual: they normally wash, dry and fold a load for about €9. The Spanish word for both types of place is *lavandería*. Some youth hostels and camping grounds and a few budget *hostales* (guesthouses) have washing machines for guests' use.

TOILETS

Public toilets are not common, but it's OK to wander into many bars and cafés to use their toilet even if you're not a customer. It's worth carrying some toilet paper with you as many toilets lack it.

HEALTH

Most travellers experience no health problems. Your main potential risks are likely to be sunburn, dehydration, foot blisters and insect bites, or mild gut problems at first if you're not used to olive oil. Generally the health precautions you should take in Andalucía are the same as anywhere else in the developed world.

Predeparture Planning

Immunisations It is recommended you seek medical advice at least six weeks before travel. You should have a tetanus-diphtheria booster if necessary, you might consider immunisation against hepatitis A (though this disease is of low prevalence throughout Western Europe), and you could think about hepatitis B vaccination if you might have sexual contact with the local population, stay longer than six months in southern Europe, or be exposed through medical treatment. Hepatitis B vaccine is now widely recommended for infants and for children aged 11 or 12 who did not complete the series as infants.

Health Insurance Visitors from other EU countries, as well as Norway, Iceland and

Liechtenstein are entitled to free Spanish national health emergency medical care if they have an E111 form, which you must get in your home country before you come. You will probably still have to pay at least some of the cost of medicines bought from pharmacies, even if a doctor has prescribed them (unless you are a pensioner), and perhaps for a few tests and procedures.

An E111 is no good for private consultations or treatment, which includes all dentists and some of the better clinics and surgeries, or for emergency flights home. If you want to avoid paying for these, you'll need to take out medical travel insurance. See Travel Insurance under Visas & Documents earlier in this chapter for more information. In Britain and Ireland, E111s are issued free by post offices. Just supply name, address, date of birth and National Insurance number. You are required to provide a photocopy of the E111 when you see a doctor in Spain, so it makes sense to get a couple of copies when you get the form.

Many US health insurance policies stay in effect, at least for a limited period, if you are travelling abroad. Most non-European national health plans (including Australia's Medicare) don't, so you must take out special medical insurance.

Other Preparations If you wear glasses, consider taking a spare pair and your prescription. If you need a particular medication carry an adequate supply, as it may not be available locally. Take part of the packaging showing the generic name, rather than the brand, to make getting replacements easier.

Water

Domestic, hotel and restaurant tap water is safe to drink in most of Spain. The city of Málaga, however, is one place where many people prefer to play it safe by drinking bottled water. Safe bottled water is available everywhere, for €0.40 to €0.80 for a 1.5L bottle in shops and supermarkets.

Ask *'¿es potable el agua?'* if you're in any doubt about water quality. Water from public spouts and fountains is not reliable unless it has a sign saying 'Agua Potable'.

Natural water, unless it's straight from a definitely unpolluted spring, or running off snow or ice with no interference from people or animals, is not safe to drink unpurified.

Medical Services

For serious medical problems and emergencies, the Spanish public health service rivals any in the world. Seeing a doctor about something more mundane can be less enchanting, because of queues and obscure appointment systems, though you should still get decent attention in the end. The expense of going to a private clinic or surgery often saves time and frustration: you'll typically pay €15 to €30 for a consultation (not counting medicines). All dental practices are private.

If you need to see a doctor quickly, or need emergency dental treatment, one way is to go along to the emergency *(urgencias)* section of the nearest hospital. Many towns also have a Centro de Salud (Health Centre) with an emergency section. Take as much documentation as you can when you deal with medical services – passport, insurance papers, E111 with photocopies. Tourist offices, the police and your accommodation can all tell you where to find medical help. You could also contact your country's consulate for advice. For an ambulance call ☎ 061. Many major hospitals and other emergency medical services are listed in this book's city sections.

Pharmacies *(farmacias)* can help with many ailments. A system of duty pharmacies *(farmacias de guardia)* operates so that each district has one open all the time. When a pharmacy is closed, it posts the name of the nearest open one on the door. Lists of duty pharmacies are often given in local papers.

Environmental Hazards

Altitude Sickness Lack of oxygen at altitudes over 2500m affects most people to some extent. Less oxygen reaches the muscles and the brain, requiring the heart and lungs to work harder. Mild symptoms include headache, lethargy, dizziness, difficulty sleeping and loss of appetite. Acute Mountain Sickness (AMS) has been fatal at 3000m, although 3500 to 4500m is the usual range.

Paracetamol or aspirin can be taken for headaches, but if symptoms persist or become worse, *immediate descent is necessary*; even 500m can help.

Heat Exhaustion Dehydration and salt deficiency can cause heat exhaustion. Take time to acclimatise to high temperatures, drink sufficient liquids and don't do anything too physically demanding.

Salt deficiency is characterised by fatigue, lethargy, headaches, giddiness and muscle cramps; adding extra salt to your food is the remedy.

Heatstroke This serious, occasionally fatal, condition can occur if the body's heat-regulating mechanism breaks down. Long, continuous periods of exposure to high temperatures and insufficient fluids can leave you vulnerable. The symptoms are: feeling unwell, not sweating very much (or at all) and a high body temperature (39°C to 41°C, 102°F to 106°F). Where sweating has ceased, the skin becomes flushed and red. Severe, throbbing headaches and lack of co-ordination will occur. The sufferer may be confused or aggressive, and eventually will become delirious or convulse. Hospitalisation is essential, but in the interim get victims out of the sun, remove their clothing, cover them with a wet sheet or towel and then fan continually. Give fluids if they are conscious.

Prickly Heat This itchy rash, caused by excessive perspiration trapped under the skin, usually strikes people who have just arrived in a hot climate. Keeping cool, bathing often, drying the skin and using a mild talcum or prickly heat powder, or resorting to air-conditioning, may help.

Sunburn You can get sunburnt surprisingly quickly, even through cloud. Use a sunscreen, a hat, and barrier cream for your nose and lips. Calamine lotion or a commercial after-sun preparation is good for mild sunburn. Protect your eyes with good quality sunglasses, particularly if you will be near water, sand or snow.

Infectious Diseases

Diarrhoea A change of water, food or climate can cause a mild bout of diarrhoea, but a few rushed toilet trips with no other symptoms are not indicative of a major problem.

Dehydration is the main danger with any diarrhoea, particularly in children or the elderly. Under all circumstances *fluid replacement* is the most important thing to remember. Weak black tea with a little sugar, soda water, or soft drinks allowed to go flat and diluted 50% with clean water are all good. With severe diarrhoea a rehydrating solution is preferable to replace minerals and salts lost. Commercially available oral rehydration salts (ORS) are very useful; add them to boiled or bottled water.

In an emergency you can make up a solution of six teaspoons of sugar and a half teaspoon of salt to a litre of boiled or bottled water. You need to drink at least the same volume of fluid that you are losing in bowel movements and vomiting. Urine is the best guide – if you have small amounts of dark urine, you need to drink more. Keep drinking small amounts often. Stick to a bland diet as you recover.

Gut-paralysing drugs such as loperamide or diphenoxylate can be used to bring relief from the symptoms, but they do not cure the problem. Only use these drugs if you do not have access to toilets – for example, if you *must* travel. They are not recommended for children under 12 years. Do not use these drugs in more serious cases such as diarrhoea with fever, profuse watery diarrhoea, persistent diarrhoea not improving after 48 hours, or severe diarrhoea. In these situations you should seek medical help urgently.

Fungal Infections Fungal infections most commonly occur in hot weather and are usually found on the scalp, between the toes (athlete's foot) or fingers, in the groin and on the body (ringworm). You get ringworm (which is not a worm) from infected animals or other people.

To prevent fungal infections wear loose, comfortable clothes, avoid artificial fibres, wash frequently and dry carefully. If you get an infection, wash the area at least daily with a disinfectant or medicated soap and water. Apply an antifungal cream or powder like tolnaftate. Try to expose the area to air or sunlight as much as possible, and wash all towels and underwear in hot water, change them often and let them dry in the sun.

Hepatitis A general term for inflammation of the liver, hepatitis is common world-wide. The symptoms include fever, chills, headache, fatigue, feelings of weakness and aches and pains, followed by loss of appetite, nausea, vomiting, abdominal pain, dark urine, light-coloured faeces, jaundiced (yellow) skin and yellowing of the whites of the eyes. Hepatitis A, transmitted by contaminated food and drinking water, is not common in Spain. There are almost 300 million chronic carriers of Hepatitis B in the world and it's more prevalent in Spain than in northern Europe, the US or Australia. It is spread through contact with infected blood, blood products or body fluids. The symptoms of type B may be more severe than type A and may lead to long-term problems.

HIV & AIDS Infection with the human immunodeficiency virus (HIV; in Spanish, VIH) may lead to acquired immune deficiency syndrome (AIDS; in Spanish, *sida*), a fatal disease. Any exposure to blood, blood products or body fluids may put the individual at risk. The disease is often transmitted through sexual contact or dirty needles. Sharing needles has always been the most common cause of AIDS in Spain. By 2001 the annual number of new cases of AIDS in Spain (around 2300) was one-third of what it was in the mid-1990s. Andalucía accounts for about 14% of Spanish cases.

Sexually Transmitted Diseases (STDs) Hepatitis B and HIV/AIDS (see the relevant sections earlier for more details) can be transmitted through sexual contact. Other STDs include gonorrhoea, herpes and syphilis; common symptoms are sores, blisters or rashes around the genitals, and discharges or pain when urinating. In some STDs, such as wart virus or chlamydia, symptoms may be less marked or not observed at all, especially

in women. Syphilis symptoms eventually disappear but the disease continues and can cause severe problems in later years. While abstinence from sexual contact is the only 100% effective prevention, using condoms (*condones* or *preservativos*) is also effective. The different STDs each require specific antibiotics.

Cuts, Bites & Stings
Wash cuts and scratches well and treat any cut with an antiseptic such as povidone-iodine. Where possible, avoid bandages and Band-Aids, which can keep wounds wet.

Insects, Scorpions & Centipedes Bee and wasp stings are usually painful rather than dangerous. However, in people who are allergic to them severe breathing difficulties may occur and require urgent medical care. Calamine lotion or a sting relief spray will give relief; ice packs will reduce pain and swelling.

Scorpion stings are notoriously painful but Spanish scorpions are not considered fatal. They often shelter in shoes or clothing, so shake these out before you put them on when camping. Some Andalucian centipedes (*escolopendras* or *ciempiés*) have a very nasty, but not fatal, sting. The ones to steer clear of are those composed of clearly defined segments, which may be patterned with, for instance, black and yellow stripes.

Also beware of the hairy, reddish-brown caterpillars of the pine processionary moth (*procesionarias*), which live in easily discernible silvery nests in pine trees in many parts of Andalucía and have a habit of walking around in long lines. Touching the caterpillars' hairs can set off a severely irritating allergic skin reaction.

Mosquito and other insect bites can be a nuisance but Spanish mosquitoes don't carry malaria. You can avoid bites by covering your skin and using an insect repellent.

Jellyfish With their stinging tentacles, jellyfish (*medusas*) generally occur in large numbers or hardly at all, so it's fairly easy to know when not to go into the sea. Dousing in vinegar will deactivate any jellyfish stingers which have not 'fired'. Calamine lotion, antihistamines and analgesics may reduce the reaction and relieve the pain.

Ticks Check all over your body if you have been walking through a potentially tick-infested area (such as woodlands or fields in spring or summer), as ticks can cause skin infections and other more serious diseases. If a tick is found attached, press down around its head with tweezers, grab the head and gently pull upwards. Avoid pulling the rear of the body.

Snakes The only venomous snake that is even relatively common in Spain is Lataste's viper (*víbora hocicuda* or *víbora de Lataste* in Spanish). It's a triangular-headed creature, up to 75cm long, and grey with a zigzag pattern. It lives in dry, rocky areas, away from humans. Its bite can be fatal and needs to be treated quickly with a serum which state clinics in major towns keep in stock.

Women's Health
Antibiotic use, synthetic underwear, sweating and contraceptive pills can lead to fungal vaginal infections in hot climates. Good personal hygiene, loose-fitting clothes and cotton underwear may help prevent them. Fungal infections, characterised by a rash, itch and discharge, can be treated with a vinegar or lemon-juice douche, or with yogurt. Nystatin, miconazole or clotrimazole pessaries, or vaginal cream, are the usual treatments.

Sexually transmitted diseases are a major cause of vaginal problems. Symptoms include a smelly discharge, painful intercourse and sometimes a burning sensation when urinating. Medical attention should be sought, and male sexual partners must also be treated. For more details see the earlier section on Sexually Transmitted Diseases.

Less Common Diseases
Leishmaniasis This is a group of parasitic diseases found in many parts of the Mediterranean. *Leishmania infantum*, the strain found in Spain, is characterised by irregular bouts of fever, substantial weight loss, swelling of the spleen and liver, and anaemia. It can be fatal for children under five and people with deficiencies of the immune system, such as AIDS sufferers. It is transmitted when sandflies (which are more akin to mosquitoes than flies and may be found anywhere in country areas near the Mediterranean coasts) bite dogs carrying leishmaniasis, then bite humans. Avoiding sandfly bites is the best precaution: cover up and apply repellent. Sandflies are most active at dawn and dusk. The bites are usually painless but itchy. If you suspect leishmaniasis, seek medical advice as laboratory testing is required for diagnosis and treatment.

WOMEN TRAVELLERS
Women travellers should be ready to ignore any stares, catcalls and unnecessary comments, though in fact harassment is not frequent. Learn the word for help *(socorro)* in case you need to draw other people's attention. Men under about 35, who have grown up in the post-Franco era, are less sexually stereotyped than their older counterparts. But you still need to exercise common sense about where you go solo. Think twice about going alone to isolated stretches of beach or country paths, or down empty city streets at night. It's highly inadvisable for a woman to hitchhike alone – and not a great idea even for two women together.

Topless bathing and skimpy clothes are acceptable in many coastal resorts, but people tend to dress more modestly elsewhere.

Each province's national police headquarters has a special **Servicio de Atención a la Mujer** *(SAM)*, literally Service of Attention to Women. The national **Comisión de Investigación de Malos Tratos a Mujeres** *(Commission of Investigation into Abuse of Women; emergency ☎ 900 10 00 09)* maintains a 24-hour free emergency line for victims of physical abuse anywhere in Spain.

GAY & LESBIAN TRAVELLERS
Gay and lesbian sex are both legal in Spain; 16 is the age of consent.

Andalucía has lively gay scenes in Seville, Granada, Málaga and Torremolinos, but there are gay-and-lesbian-friendly bars or clubs in all major cities. Most Spanish receptionists have difficulty understanding that two people of the same sex might want to share a double bed. One lesbian traveller suggested that to avoid confusion and wasted time, it can be a good idea for one of the pair to do the checking in before the other appears.

Websites such as W www.gayinspain.com, W www.guiagay.com and W www.cogailes.org have long listings of bars, clubs, discos, saunas, beaches, bookstores, associations and cruising spots. Gayinspain and Cogailes have message boards too. Cogailes is the site of the **Coordinadora Gai-Lesbiana**, a Barcelona-based gay and lesbian organisation that operates a free national information telephone line in English, Spanish and Catalan on ☎ 900 60 16 01, from 6pm to 10pm daily.

The **Asociación Andaluza de Lesbianas y Gais** (NOS; Calle Lavadero de las Tablas 15, Granada) runs the **Teléfono Andaluz de Información Homosexual** (☎ 958 20 06 02). The **Federación Colega** (W www.colega web.net) works for Andalucian gay and lesbian solidarity, rights and acceptance, and has branches in all eight provincial capitals.

DISABLED TRAVELLERS

Some Spanish tourist offices in other countries provide a basic information sheet with useful addresses for disabled travellers, and can give details of accessible accommodation in specific places.

Wheelchair accessibility in Andalucía is improving. Fuengirola, for instance, has equipped two beaches for the disabled, with specially adapted showers and sunbed areas, reserved toilets and parking, and aluminium wheelchairs that can be taken into the sea without going rusty. Nearly all Andalucian youth hostels have rooms adapted for the disabled, but poor accessibility is still the norm in other budget accommodation. All new public buildings are now required to have wheelchair access, but most public buildings predate the law. Unfortunately, many hotels that claim to be accessible actually retain problem features.

Holiday Care (☎ 01293-774535; W www .holidaycare.org.uk; 2nd floor, Imperial Buildings, Victoria Rd, Horley, Surrey RH6 7PZ, UK) produces an information pack on Spain for people with special needs. Tips range from accommodation with disabled access to equipment-hire services and advice on tour operators and getting to your destination in Spain. The **Cruz Roja Española** (Spanish Red Cross; ☎ 915 33 45 31; W www.cruzroja.es; Calle Doctor Federico Rubio y Galí 3, 28003 Madrid) can provide some help with travel arrangements.

SENIOR TRAVELLERS

There are reduced prices for people aged over 60, 63 or 65 at some museums and sights, and occasionally on transport. Many of the luxurious paradors (see the boxed text 'Old-Fashioned Luxury' later in this chapter) offer discounts for people over 60.

TRAVEL WITH CHILDREN

Andalucians as a rule are very friendly to children. Any child whose hair is less than jet black will get called *rubia* (blonde) if she's a girl, *rubio* if he's a boy. Accompanied children are welcome at all kinds of accommodation, and in virtually every café, bar and restaurant. Andalucian children stay up late and at fiestas it's commonplace to see even tiny ones toddling the streets at 2am or 3am. Visiting kids like this idea too, but can't cope with it quite so readily.

As well as the obvious attraction of beaches, playgrounds are fairly plentiful in Andalucía, and many places have excellent special attractions such as amusement parks (for example Seville's Isla Mágica, and Tivoli World on the Costa del Sol), aquaparks, aquariums – and let's not forget Mini Hollywood and other Western movie sets in the Almería desert (see destination chapters for details).

Most children are irresistibly drawn to the ubiquitous street-corner *kioscos* selling sweets or packets of *gusanitos* (corn puffs) for a few céntimos. The magnetism of these places often overcomes children's inhibitions enough for them to carry out their own first Spanish transactions.

Children benefit from cut-price or free entry at many sights and museums. Those under four years of age travel free on Spanish trains and those aged four to 11 normally pay 60% of the adult fare.

Lonely Planet's *Travel with Children* has lots of practical advice, and first-hand stories from many Lonely Planet authors and others.

USEFUL ORGANISATIONS

The **Instituto Cervantes** (W *www.cervantes.es*) exists to promote the Spanish language and the cultures of Spanish-speaking countries. It has branches in over 30 cities around the world. It's mainly involved in Spanish teaching and in library and information services.

DANGERS & ANNOYANCES

Andalucía is generally a pretty safe place. The main thing you have to be wary of is petty theft (which of course may not seem so petty to you if your passport, money and camera go missing).

Theft & Loss

Most risk of theft occurs in tourist resorts, big cities, and when you first arrive in a city and may be unaware of danger signs. The main things to guard against are pickpockets, bag snatchers and theft from cars. See Security under Money earlier in this chapter for hints on safeguarding your money.

If anything valuable does get stolen or lost and you want to make an insurance claim, you'll need to report it to the police and get a copy of the report. For help replacing your passport, contact your embassy or consulate.

Terrorism

The Basque terrorist organisation ETA occasionally explodes bombs or commits murders in Andalucía, as in other parts of Spain. Before travelling to Spain, you can consult your country's foreign affairs department for any current warnings.

EMERGENCIES

Spain is introducing a single free number, ☎ 112, for all emergency services – police, ambulance, fire and rescue. Operators who speak English, French and German are available. This number is supposed to be operative throughout Andalucía by 2003. If you have no luck with it, the following emergency numbers may be useful.

Medical

Throughout Andalucía, you can call ☎ 061 or ☎ 902 50 50 61 for an ambulance or emergency medical help. See under Health earlier in this chapter for more on Spanish medical facilities and health problems. If you're seriously ill or injured, someone should tell your embassy or consulate.

Police

Spain has three main types of police. The **Policía Nacional** *(National Police; ☎ 091)* cover cities and bigger towns. The uniformed contingent wears blue; many are in plain clothes, some of them forming special squads dealing with drugs, terrorism and the like. A further contingent is to be found shuffling paper in bunker-like police stations called *comisarías*. The **Policía Local** *(Policía Municipal – Local or Municipal Police; ☎ 092)* are controlled by city and town councils and deal mainly with minor matters such as parking, traffic and bylaws. They wear blue-and-white uniforms. The responsibilities of the green-uniformed **Guardia Civil** *(Civil Guard; often but not always ☎ 062)* include roads, the countryside, villages and international borders.

If you need to go to the police, any of them will do, but you may find the Policía Local are the most approachable. Further police numbers, and locations of main stations, are given in city and town sections of this book.

Fire

The fire brigade *(bomberos)* is on ☎ 080 in most cities, but ☎ 085 in Cádiz, Jerez de la Frontera and Algeciras, ☎ 953 25 15 95 in Jaén and ☎ 952 77 43 49 in Marbella.

LEGAL MATTERS

If arrested you will be allotted the free services of a duty solicitor *(abogado de oficio)*, who may speak only Spanish. You're also entitled to make a phone call. If you use this to contact your embassy or consulate, it will probably be able to do no more than refer you to a lawyer who speaks your language. If you end up in court, the authorities are obliged to provide you with a translator.

Drugs

Spain's liberal drug laws were severely tightened in 1992. The only legal drug is cannabis, and then only for personal use – which means very small amounts. There are some bars where people smoke joints openly, although public consumption of any drug is supposedly illegal. The only sure guideline is to be very discreet if you do use cannabis. It would be very unwise in hotel rooms or guesthouses.

Travellers entering Spain from Morocco, especially with a vehicle, should be prepared for intensive drug searches.

BUSINESS HOURS

In Andalucía, people generally work from about 9am to 2pm from Monday to Friday and then again from 5pm to 8pm. Most shops are usually open these hours on Saturday too (although sometimes without the evening session). Big supermarkets and department stores generally stay open all day Monday to Saturday, from about 9am to 9pm. Many government offices don't bother opening afternoons any day of the week.

PUBLIC HOLIDAYS & SPECIAL EVENTS

Spain has 14 official holidays a year – some are holidays nationwide, some only in one village. The list of holidays often changes a bit from year to year. If a holiday date falls on a weekend, sometimes the holiday is moved to the Monday. If a holiday falls two days away from a weekend, many Spaniards take the intervening day off too – a practice known as making a *puente* (bridge).

The two main periods when Spaniards go on holiday are Semana Santa (Holy Week, leading up to Easter Sunday) and the six weeks from mid-July to the end of August. At these times accommodation in resorts can be scarce and transport heavily booked.

There are usually nine official national holidays:

Año Nuevo (New Year's Day) 1 January
Viernes Santo (Good Friday) 18 April 2003,
  9 April 2004
Fiesta del Trabajo (Labour Day) 1 May
La Asunción (Feast of the Assumption) 15 August
Fiesta Nacional de España (National Day)
  12 October
Todos los Santos (All Saints' Day, the traditional
  day for paying respect to the dead) 1 November
Día de la Constitución (Constitution Day)
  6 December
La Inmaculada Concepción (Feast of the
  Immaculate Conception) 8 December
Navidad (Christmas) 25 December

In addition, the Andalucía regional government normally sets three holidays and local

---

The Times They Are Always A-Changing

Opening hours of museums, monuments and other sights in Andalucía change frighteningly often. Apart from opening different hours for different days of the week (which often include shorter hours on Sunday and not at all on Monday), many places change their hours with the seasons. But don't expect much pattern to the changes: summer hours might be longer than winter hours because there's more daylight, or shorter because it's too hot in the afternoon, or nonexistent because the staff have all gone on holiday. And everything can be thrown into complete confusion around public holidays.

Many tourist offices provide a list of opening hours of local sights *(horario de monumentos)*, but this won't always be up to date. The only sure way to check a place's opening hours is to phone ahead, or get a tourist office to phone for you. Unfortunately, the places whose hours change more often than any others are tourist offices themselves. Well, this is Andalucía – go and have a drink and tapas while you wait for it to reopen.

councils a further two. The three regional holidays are usually:

Epifanía (Epiphany) or **Día de los Reyes Magos** (Three Kings' Day) 6 January – children receive presents and, in many towns, Reyes Magos cavalcades *(cabalgatas)* tour the streets the evening before, tossing sweets to the crowds.
Día de Andalucía (Andalucía Day) 28 February
Jueves Santo (Holy Thursday, the day before Good Friday) 17 April 2003, 8 April 2004

Local holidays in some places include:

Corpus Christi late May or June (19 June 2003, 10 June 2004)
Día de San Juan Bautista (Feast of St John the Baptist, King Juan Carlos I's saint's day) 24 June
Día de Santiago Apóstol (Feast of St James the Apostle, feast day of Spain's patron saint) 25 July

Festivals

Andalucians indulge their love of colour, noise, crowds, pageant, dressing up and partying at innumerable exuberant local fiestas. Every little village and every city *barrio* (district or quarter) holds several festivals every year, each with its own unique twist. Many fiestas are religion-based but still highly festive.

Most places hold their *feria* (main annual fair) in summer, with concerts, parades, fireworks, bullfights, fairgrounds, dancing and an all-night party atmosphere.

There's always a festival happening somewhere in Andalucía. Main local festivals are noted in city and town sections of this book, and tourist offices can supply detailed information.

The monthly what's-on magazine *El Giraldillo* also has a section devoted to upcoming fiestas. Dates of many are given on the **Andalucía There's Only One** *(W www .andalucia.org)* website, and you'll find information on the most important events in city and town sections throughout this book. The most outstanding events include:

February/March
Carnaval (Carnival) Fancy-dress parades and general merrymaking happen in many places (the wildest in Cádiz) in February and/or March, usually ending on the Tuesday 47 days before Easter Sunday.

March/April
Semana Santa (Holy Week) The week leading up to Easter Sunday sees parades of lavishly bedecked holy images, long lines of *nazarenos* (penitents, sometimes hooded), and big crowds, in almost every city, town and village. In major cities there are daily processions from Palm Sunday to Easter Sunday; smaller places may omit Monday and Tuesday. Seville has the most famous celebrations; Málaga, Granada, Córdoba, Arcos de la Frontera, Jaén, Baeza, Úbeda and Huércal-Overa also stage spectacular processions. Village events can be just as unique and touching. The website Guía de la Semana Santa (W guia.semanasanta.andal.es) provides links to hundreds of related sites.

April
Feria de Abril (April Fair) Seville stages this week-long party in late April.
Romería de la Virgen de la Cabeza Hundreds of thousands of pilgrims mass at the Santuario de la Virgen de la Cabeza near Andújar, Jaén province, on the last Sunday in April.

May
Feria del Caballo (Horse Fair) Held at Jerez de la Frontera in early May, this features music, dance and other events as well as lots of colourful equestrian activities.
Cruces de Mayo (May Crosses) Crosses are placed in squares and patios in many towns, notably in and around Granada, on about 3 May. They are decorated with flowers and become the focus for temporary bars, food stalls, music and dancing.
Concurso de Patios Cordobeses (Courtyard Competition) Scores of beautiful private courtyards open to the public for two weeks in early May in Córdoba.

May/June
Romería del Rocío (Pilgrimage to El Rocío) This festive pilgrimage of up to one million people to El Rocío in Huelva province is held on Pentecost weekend, the seventh day after Easter (7–9 June 2003; 29–31 May 2004).

June
Hogueras de San Juan (Bonfires of San Juan) Bonfires and fireworks, especially on beaches, are the heart of this midsummer celebration on 23 June. Many thousands of people camp overnight along Andalucía's beaches.

July
Día de la Virgen del Carmen (the feast day of the patron of fisherfolk) On 16 July, the Virgin's image is carried into the sea, or paraded upon it amid a flotilla of small boats, at many coastal towns.

August
Feria de Málaga (Málaga Fair) This most animated of all the summer *ferias* runs for nine days from one weekend to the next in mid-August.

September

Moros y Cristianos (Moors and Christians) This re-enactment on 14 and 15 September of the 1568 Muslim rebellion in Válor, Granada province, is the most colourful of several Andalucian events commemorating Muslim/Christian conflicts.

September/October

Fiestas de Otoño (Autumn Festival) Jerez de la Frontera's three-week grape harvest celebrations in September/October, with horse races and parades, flamenco dancing and an air show.

Music & Dance Festivals Given Andalucians' love of music and partying, it comes as no surprise that the calendar is peppered with music and dance festivals. Every town's and village's summer fair features plenty of live performances, and in the bigger towns and cities these often include the top names of the Spanish music and dance world. Many towns stage one- or two-night *fiestas de flamenco* in June, July or August, getting going around midnight: the three big ones for aficionados are the Potaje Gitano, Caracolá Lebrijana and Gazpacho Andaluz (see following). Ask tourist offices for exact dates, or check the music section of *El Giraldillo*. Here's a selection of Andalucía's major music and dance festivals (you'll find more on many of them in the destination sections):

May

Costa Pop The port of Málaga hosts a massive all-night concert by top Spanish and Latin pop performers, attended by 100,000 or more fans, one night in late May.

June/July

Potaje Gitano The 'Gitano Stew' is a top flamenco festival, held in Utrera, Sevilla province, on a Saturday in June.

Festival Torre del Cante Another June flamenco event, this is held in Alhaurín de la Torre near the Costa del Sol.

June/July

Caracolá Lebrijana This Saturday night flamenco festival in Lebrija, Sevilla province, is staged in June or July (*caracol* means snail).

Festival Internacional de la Guitarra Córdoba stages the International Guitar Festival over two weeks in late June or the first half of July.

Festival Internacional de Música y Danza This is a 2½-week international festival of mainly classical music and dance in Granada, in late June and

early July. Some events are staged in beautiful historic sites.

Festival Internacional de Itálica This series of dance events includes everything from classical ballet to contemporary. It happens in Seville in late June and July.

July

Espárrago Rock (Asparagus Rock) This three-day festival at Jerez de la Frontera features indie and alternative rock – the line-up in 2002, for example, included Iggy Pop, Garbage and Bunbury. In recent years Espárrago Rock has been held over a weekend in mid-July.

Cubano y Flamenco Top Cuban bands (playing traditional Cuban sounds) and Andalucian flamenco stars tour Sevilla province together for two weeks in July.

July/August

Gazpacho Andaluz This flamenco festival takes place in Morón de la Frontera in July or August.

Castillo de Cante The 'Castle of Cante' is a one-night flamenco song festival in Ojén, near Marbella, on the first or second Saturday of August.

September

Bienal de Flamenco Staged in Seville in September of even-numbered years, the Bienal attracts the largest assembly of big flamenco names.

November

Festival Internacional de Jazz This jazz festival is held in several Andalucian cities during November.

December

Fiesta Mayor de Verdiales Verdiales are an exhilarating brand of folk music unique to the Málaga area: the biggest celebration of the genre happens at Puerto de la Torre, Málaga, on 28 December.

ACTIVITIES

There's so much to do in Andalucía apart from seeing sights and sitting on beaches. Spanish tourist offices – locally and in other countries – have information or contact details for organisers of many activities, and the Junta de Andalucía publishes useful guides to activities such as hiking, horse riding, diving, mountain biking, sailing, fishing and golf, sold in several languages at its tourist offices for a few euros. The Junta's official tourism website, ⓦ www.andalucia.org, also has some useful background and contact details. For information on entire holidays focused on particular activities, see Organised Tours in the Getting There & Away chapter.

Walking

Andalucía's rugged landscape provides some beautiful walking areas, mostly in mountainous regions such as the Parque Natural de Cazorla (Jaén province); the Sierra Nevada and Las Alpujarras (Granada province); the Sierra de Grazalema and other hill areas near Ronda (Cádiz and Málaga provinces); the Parque Natural Sierra de Aracena y Picos de Aroche (Huelva province); the Cabo de Gata peninsula (Almería province); and the Parque Natural Sierras de Tejeda, Almijara y Alhama (Málaga and Granada provinces).

In some of these areas you can string together day walks into a trek over several days, sleeping in a variety of *hostales*, camp sites or occasionally mountain refuges or wild camping. Further information on walking is given in this book's regional chapters, and over two weeks' worth of Andalucía's best walking is detailed in Lonely Planet's *Walking in Spain*. Tourist offices – especially visitor centres in natural parks and other protected areas – can help with walking information. For information on maps, see Planning at the beginning of this chapter.

Paths Some of Andalucía's many walkable trails are well signed with route numbers. On others just the odd spot of paint on a stone might tell you you're heading in the right direction. Elsewhere, you're left entirely to your own devices.

The two main categories of walking routes in Spain are *senderos de Gran Recorrido* (GRs, long-distance footpaths, some of them several hundred kilometres long) and *senderos de Pequeño Recorrido* (PRs, shorter routes suitable for day or weekend hikes). Not all, however, are fully marked or maintained. There are also plenty of paths which are neither GRs nor PRs.

The GR-7, a long-distance path being created across Europe from Greece to Tarifa (Cádiz province), enters Andalucía near Almaciles in northeast Granada province, then divides at Puebla de Don Fadrique, with one branch heading through Jaén province and the other through Las Alpujarras southeast of Granada. Signposting of this path throughout Andalucía is in progress.

Natural and national parks and other protected areas may restrict visitors to limited zones and routes – and ban wild camping – but usually have marked walks through some of their most interesting areas.

Seasons April to mid-June and September through to mid-October are generally the most pleasant times for walking, but conditions in the high Sierra Nevada are relatively easy only from July to early September. The weather in high mountains is unpredictable.

Climbing

Mountainous Andalucía is full of rocky crags that invite climbing *(escalada)*. More than 3000 climbs – over half of them in Málaga province – are equipped with bolts. The sheer walls of El Chorro gorge in northwest Málaga province are the main magnet, with over 400 charted climbs of every degree of difficulty. Other climbing areas and centres include the Sierra Nevada, El Torcal near Antequera, the Sierra de las Nieves near Ronda, Casares near Estepona, the Sierra de Grazalema and the Parque Natural de Cazorla. *Andalusian Rock Climbs* by Chris Craggs is a good guide.

Mountain Biking

Mountain bikers can test their muscles on hundreds of kilometres of good and bad tracks in Andalucía. Tourist offices often have information on routes. The Spanish for mountain bike is *bici todo terreno* (BTT) or *bici de montaña*.

A growing number of places rent out mountain bikes in Andalucía, usually for around €10 a day.

Skiing & Snowboarding

The popular Sierra Nevada ski resort southeast of Granada is Europe's most southerly, and its runs and facilities are good enough to have staged the world alpine skiing championships in 1996. The season normally runs from December to April.

Windsurfing

Tarifa (Cádiz province), west of Gibraltar, is one of Europe's top windsurfing spots, with strong breezes year-round and long, sandy beaches. The winds can also be good at nearby Barbate and Los Caños de Meca and you can rent or buy equipment and have tuition in all three places. Conditions are less suitable along the Mediterranean coasts but some Costa del Sol beaches and La Herradura (Granada province) can be OK.

Kitesurfing

Kitesurfers use boards like windsurfers but the 'sail' is high in the air and they're attached to it by a body harness and long strings. This sport has gained popularity fast because the equipment is cheaper than for windsurfing, and you can practise it in lighter winds. Tarifa is the hub, with equipment rental and sales, and classes available, but if you have the gear you can kitesurf on the Mediterranean coast too.

Surfing

The most ridable waves are in winter on the Atlantic coast, at places like El Palmar and Los Caños de Meca, both in Cádiz province. You can rent boards in Vejer de la Frontera.

Diving & Snorkelling

The rockier parts of the Mediterranean coast – between Nerja and Adra, and from Cabo de Gata to Mojácar – offer some interesting snorkelling. The best diving spots include La Herradura and Castell de Ferro, both near Almuñécar, and El Pozo del Esparto on the Almería coast. You'll find diving trips, and gear rental, available in these places.

Sailing

Sailing is naturally a popular activity along Andalucía's coasts and over 40 marinas and mooring places are strung between Ayamonte on the Portuguese border and Garrucha in Almería province. The biggest are the flashy Puerto Banús and Benalmádena on the Costa del Sol, and Almerimar near Almería, each with over 900 moorings.

Paragliding

Paragliding (*parapente* in Spanish) involves taking a running jump off a hill top with a rectangular parachute behind you, then staying aloft with the aid of thermal winds. Andalucía's paragliding capital is Valle de Abdalajís, east of El Chorro (Málaga province). The air currents are also good around La Herradura, on the Granada coast.

Golf

Around 700,000 tourists a year come to Andalucía primarily to play golf. Andalucía has 58 golf courses, two-thirds of them dotted along or near the Costa del Sol between Gibraltar and Málaga. Green fees at most clubs cost between €40 and €65. Top courses, such as Valderrama, Sotogrande, and Las Brisas and Aloha at Marbella, are more costly (over €200 at Valderrama, which is the most expensive). Useful information sources include W www.andalucia.org and the free paper *Andalucía Costa del Golf*, available from some tourist offices.

Golf Service (W *www.golf-service.com*) offers discounted green fees and tee-off time reservations.

Horse Riding

Chief breeding ground of the Spanish thoroughbred horse (also known as the Andalusian), Andalucía is steeped in equestrian tradition. There are plenty of fine trails to ride, and a growing number of stables to take you on a guided ride or even a long-distance trek. Check this book's sections on El Rocío, Tarifa, Las Alpujarras, Los Caños de Meca, Parque Natural de Cazorla, Parque Natural de Hornachuelos, Alájar and Sierra de las Nieves. The cost can range from €7 to €25 for an hour or about €40 to €70 for a ride of five hours or so.

Anyone with an interest in horses should put Jerez de la Frontera on their itinerary. The town holds a number of exciting annual equine events and its Royal Andalucian School of Equestrian Art and the nearby Yeguada del Hierro breeding centre are fascinating to visit at any time.

Wildlife-Watching

See the special section 'Andalucía's National & Natural Parks' for more on the species to be found in Andalucía.

Birds Andalucía is a magnet for bird-watchers year-round. March and April, when you can see many wintering species and some arriving summer visitors, are good months. The Strait of Gibraltar is a particularly exciting viewing site (see the boxed text 'High-Fliers over the Strait of Gibraltar' in the Cádiz Province chapter). You'll find information on other bird-watching spots – including details on the greater flamingo, perhaps Andalucía's most spectacular bird – in several other sections of this book, including Isla Cristina, Laguna de Fuente de Piedra, Paraje Natural Marismas del Odiel, Parque Nacional de Doñana, Parque Natural Sierra de Grazalema and El Cabo de Gata. See also Books earlier in this chapter for useful publications. A favourite gathering ground for bird enthusiasts is the observatory of the **Sociedad Española de Ornitología** *(Spanish Ornithological Society, SEO/Birdlife;* ⓦ *www.seo.org)* on the fringe of the Parque Nacional de Doñana.

Other Wildlife The Bahía de Algeciras and Strait of Gibraltar harbour plenty of dolphins and some whales. Boat trips to see them are a popular attraction from Tarifa (Cádiz) and Gibraltar.

The Parque Natural de Cazorla is good for spotting Andalucía's larger mammals. You stand a good chance of seeing ibex in the upper altitudes of the Sierra Nevada, Sierra de las Nieves and Sierra Almijara. Easier to see than any of these are Gibraltar's colony of 'apes' (actually Barbary macaques).

COURSES

A spot of study is a great way not only to learn something but also to meet people and get an inside angle on local life.

Language

The **Instituto Cervantes** (see Useful Organisations earlier in this chapter) offers a great deal of information on Spanish-language courses in Andalucía, through the website ⓦ www.cervantes.es and through its branches worldwide. Another Internet source is the **Spanish Directory** (ⓦ *www .europa-pages.com/spain)*.

Seville, Granada and Málaga are the most popular places in Andalucía to study Spanish, but there are also schools in most other main cities and in coastal towns such as Tarifa, El Puerto de Santa María, Nerja, Marbella and Almuñécar. Check the Web or at tourist offices for details.

University courses often last a term, though they range from two weeks to a year. Private language schools are generally more flexible about when you can start and how long you study. Most places cater for a wide range of levels, from beginners up. Many courses have a cultural component as well.

Costs vary widely. University courses offer some of the best value, with a typical four-week course of 20 one-hour classes a week for around €400 to €500. Many places offer accommodation with families, in student lodgings or in flats – generally from around €200 to €300 a month with no meals to €500 to €700 for full board.

Most schools can furnish detailed information on what they offer. Things to think about when choosing one include how intensive the course is (this varies at different schools), class sizes, who the other students are likely to be and whether you want organised extracurricular activities. Personal recommendations from previous students count for a lot in selecting your school. It's also worth asking whether a course will lead to any formal certificate. The Diplomas Oficiales de Español como Lengua Extranjera (DELEs) are qualifications awarded by Spain's Ministry of Education and Science (for a complete beginner, approximately 40 hours of classes are required to achieve the most basic DELE qualification).

It's easy to arrange private classes in many places: check notice boards in universities and language schools, or small ads in the local press. Expect to pay around €15 per hour for individual private lessons.

Arts & Culture

Many of the universities and schools offering language courses also offer other courses in Spanish history, literature and culture. The Instituto Cervantes is, again, a good source of information. See the Seville and Granada sections for information on some courses in Spanish dance and/or guitar. The magazine *El Giraldillo* (available from tourist offices) carries ads for flamenco classes and courses. See also Dance Tours in the Getting There & Away chapter.

WORK

Andalucía has high official unemployment figures, but the recent economic boom has provided more and more ways of turning a penny during a temporary stay. If you have any contacts follow them up – word of mouth counts for a lot.

Regulations

Nationals of EU countries, Norway and Iceland are allowed to work in Spain for up to 90 days without a visa. Virtually everyone else is supposed to obtain a work permit from a Spanish consulate in their country of residence and, if planning to stay more than 90 days, a residence visa (see Visas & Documents). These procedures are well-nigh impossible unless you already have a job contract, and you should set things rolling long before you go to Spain. That said, plenty of people do work, discreetly, without bothering to tangle with the bureaucracy.

Opportunities

Tourist Resorts Work in the areas with high expatriate populations, especially on the Costa del Sol in summer, is a distinct possibility, particularly if you get there early in the season and are prepared to stay a while. The huge expat and foreign tourist scene provides plenty of openings for temporary, part-time work. Look at notice boards, and check the local press, including *Sur in English*, which carries ads for secretaries, receptionists, salespeople, waiters, bar staff, nannies, chefs, baby-sitters and cleaners as well as 'liners', 'closers' and other types required to sell timeshare properties to foreign holidaymakers. The more Spanish you can speak, the better your chances, of course.

Language Teaching Having some relevant qualifications and a knowledge of Spanish obviously help for this option. There are

several language schools in most cities and often one or two in smaller towns. Getting a job is harder if you're not an EU citizen. Giving private lessons is an option, though you're unlikely to earn a living wage from it.

Sources of information on possible teaching work – school or private – include universities, language schools and foreign-language bookshops. Some of these have notice boards where you may find work opportunities, or where you can advertise your own services. The local press is also worth scanning or placing an advertisement. Language schools are listed under 'Academias de Idiomas' in the Yellow Pages.

Boat Crew Gibraltar is the best place to look for work as a crew member on a yacht or cruiser. In high summer, a few places a week come up there on craft sailing the Mediterranean, and from November to January there's the possibility of working your passage to the Caribbean. Puerto Banús is the next best place to try. You're unlikely to be paid for this work.

ACCOMMODATION

The annual *Guía de Hoteles, Pensiones, Apartamentos, Campings y Casas Rurales*, published by the Junta de Andalucía and available from some tourist offices and bookshops in Andalucía for about €5, lists most of the region's places to stay, including camp sites, facilities and approximate prices. Two useful accommodation websites, with online booking service, are **InterHotel** (**w** *interhotel.com/spain/en*) and **Andalucía There's Only One** (**w** *www.andalucia.org*).

Camping

Andalucía has over 130 officially graded camp sites *(campings)*. Some are well located in woodland or near beaches or rivers, others are stuck away near main roads on the edges of towns and cities. Very few are near city centres.

Sites are officially rated 1st class (1^aC), 2nd class (2^aC) or 3rd class (3^ac). There are also a few not officially graded, usually equivalent to 3rd class. Facilities range from reasonable to very good, though any site can be crowded and noisy at busy times. Even a 3rd-class site is likely to have hot showers, electrical hook-ups and a cafeteria. The best sites have heated pools, supermarkets, restaurants, laundry service and children's playgrounds. Sizes vary, some cater for under 100 people, others can take over 5000 people.

Camp sites usually charge per person, per tent and per vehicle – typically €3 to €4 for each. Children usually pay a bit less. Many sites are open year-round, but some close from around October to Easter. Occasionally you come across a *zona de acampada* or *área de acampada*, a country site with minimal or no facilities, little or no supervision and probably no charge. Tourist offices can always direct you to the nearest camp site.

With certain exceptions – such as many beaches and environmentally protected areas – it is permissible to camp outside camp sites (though not within 1km of official ones). Signs may indicate where wild camping is not allowed. You'll need permission to camp on private land.

Youth Hostels

Most of Andalucía's 20-odd youth hostels (*albergues juveniles*, not to be confused with *hostales* – see the next section) are affiliated to **Inturjoven** (W *www.inturjoven.com*), the official Andalucía youth hostel organisation. Inturjoven hostels are mostly good, modern places with a good number of twin rooms as well as small dormitories with bunks. Sheets are provided and most rooms have private bathrooms. Hostels don't have cooking facilities but they do have dining rooms (*comedores*), usually serving meals at good prices. You can book places in any Inturjoven hostel through the Inturjoven website, or on Inturjoven's reservations line (☎ 902 51 00 00, 9.30am-7.30pm Mon-Fri), or through the hostel itself.

Prices for a bed in any Inturjoven hostel, including breakfast, are €8.50/10.90/12.90 in the low/mid-/high season for under-26s, and €11.50/15.20/17.25 for people aged 26 or over. At many hostels it's mid- or high season from June to September and for certain short peak periods at other times of year, and low season the rest of the time. Hostels in Almería, Córdoba, Granada, Huelva, Málaga and Seville are mid- or high season all year. Any Inturjoven hostel can supply full price information and details for all the others – as can the Inturjoven website.

To stay in an Inturjoven hostel you need a youth hostel card. If you don't already have

When the Price is Right

Accommodation prices given in this book are high-season prices unless stated otherwise – so you can expect some pleasant surprises during the low season. Many places to stay have separate price structures for high season (*temporada alta*), shoulder season (*temporada media*) and low season (*temporada baja*), all of which are usually displayed on a notice in reception. Hoteliers are free to charge less than the posted prices, which they quite often do, or more, which happens less often.

High season depends on where you are, but in most places it's summer – which can mean a period as short as mid-July to the end of August or as long as Easter to October. The Christmas–New Year period, Semana Santa (the week leading up to Easter Sunday) and local festivals that attract lots of visitors are also high season in many places. We note major seasonal pricing trends in Places to Stay sections, and as a rule the prices we give include the 7% value-added tax (IVA).

Differences between low- and high-season prices tend to be biggest in coastal resorts, where you'll typically pay 25% less in February than in August, but it can be 50% less. Some places to stay in Seville charge three times as much during Semana Santa and the Feria de Abril as they do in winter.

Many establishments, especially the cheaper ones, vary their prices according to demand. Some will forget about IVA if you don't require a receipt, and even in high season some will charge less than we quote if business is slow. At any time you may be able to obtain a discount if you stay for more than a couple of nights.

one from a youth hostel or hostel organisation in your own country, you can get a Hostelling International (HI) Card, valid till 31 December of the year you buy it, at any Inturjoven hostel or any of the 140 or so other hostels in the Red Española de Albergues Juveniles (REAJ), the Spanish affiliate of HI. For the HI card, you pay in instalments of €3 for each of the first six nights you spend in a hostel, up to €18.

Some hostels are often heavily booked by school or youth groups, but inconvenient night-time curfews or daytime closing hours are rare.

The annual HI Europe hostels directory lists all Inturjoven and other REAJ hostels. It's available at hostels and hostel offices.

Just a few Andalucian hostels are run by organisations other than Inturjoven. Some of these do not require hostel cards.

Hostales, Hospedajes, Pensiones & Hotels

Officially all these establishments are classified as either *hoteles* (from one to five stars) or *pensiones* (one or two stars). In practice, places to stay use all sorts of titles, especially at the budget end of the market.

In broad terms, the cheapest places are those that just advertise beds *(camas)*, *fondas* (traditionally a basic eatery and inn combined, though one or other function is now often missing) and *casas de huéspedes* or *hospedajes* (guesthouses). All such places will be bare and basic, with shared bathrooms. In winter don't hesitate to ask for extra blankets. Singles/doubles in these

types of place cost around €9/15 to €12/20. A *pensión* (basically a small private hotel) is usually a small step up from the above categories, in standards and price. Some cheap establishments forget to provide soap, toilet paper or towels; don't hesitate to ask for these necessities.

Next up the scale are *hostales*, little different from *pensiones* except that some are considerably more comfortable, and most rooms tend to have private bathrooms. Some *hostales* are bright, modern and pleasant; others are less so. Prices for singles/doubles range from around €12/18 for the cheapest, with shared bathroom, to as much as €40/50 at the best *hostales*.

Establishments calling themselves *hotel* range from simple places where a double room could cost €25 up to super-luxury, five-star places where you would pay €300. Even in the cheapest hotels, rooms are likely to have an attached bathroom and there'll probably be a restaurant.

Some of Andalucía's most charming places to stay are small- or medium-sized hotels with economical or mid-range prices from around €40 to €70 a double. Many such establishments occupy old town houses or rambling country properties with pleasant gardens and pools. They tend to be atmospheric places, and their manageable scale encourages personal attention.

Most places to stay have a range of rooms at different prices. At the bottom end, prices vary according to whether the room has a washbasin *(lavabo)*, shower *(ducha)* or full bathroom *(baño completo)*. At the

---

Old-Fashioned Luxury

Spain's paradors, officially *paradores de turismo*, are a chain of 86 high-class hotels dotted around the country (16 of them in Andalucía). Many – such as those at Carmona, Jaén, Úbeda and Granada – are in converted castles, mansions or monasteries, and are highly atmospheric places to stay. Singles/doubles in the low season start at €60.45/75.55 and you're looking at about €90/115 in the high season – even more at Granada, which is the most expensive parador in Spain. Special offers can make paradors more affordable and there are often deals for the over-60s and 20- to 30-year-olds. You can check out the current offers at W www.parador.es, or by contacting the paradors' central reservation service, the Central de Reservas (☎ 915 16 66 66, fax 915 16 66 57; e info@parador.es; Calle Requena 3, 28013 Madrid) or one of their 20 overseas booking offices (listed on the website).

top end you may pay more for a room on the outside of the building or with a balcony, and will often have the option of a suite. Many places have rooms for three, four or more people where the per-person cost is much lower than in a single or double – good news for families. Checkout time is nearly always noon.

Note that *una habitación doble* (a double room) might have one double bed *(cama matrimonial)* or two single beds *(dos camas individuales)*. If one or other option is important to you, specify it.

Reservations In the low season there's generally no need to book ahead, but when things get busier it's advisable to do so, and at peak periods it can be essential if you want to avoid a wearisome search for a room. At many places, a phone call is all that's needed.

Casas Rurales

The booming interest in Andalucía's countryside has led to many new places to stay opening in rural areas, in Andalucía as elsewhere. These *casas rurales* are usually comfortably renovated village houses or farmhouses, with just a handful of rooms. Some have meals available; some just provide rooms; some offer self-catering accommodation. Prices typically range between €12 and €20 per person per night.

Tourist offices can usually provide leaflets on local country accommodation and direct you to any local agencies where you can book. **Rural Andalus** *(☎ 952 27 62 29;* W *www.ruralandalus.es; Calle Montes de Oca 18, 29007 Málaga)* represents nearly 500 rural properties including some hotels. It's particularly strong on rural areas of Málaga province, but houses are offered in most parts of Andalucía. **Red Andaluza de Alojamientos Rurales** *(Andalucian Country Lodgings Network; ☎ 902 44 22 33;* W *www .raar.es)* offers around 400 rural accommodation possibilities.

Apartments, Houses & Villas

In many places in Andalucía there are well-equipped, self-catering apartments, houses and villas to rent. A simple one-bedroom apartment for two or three people might cost as little as €18 a night, though more often you're looking at twice that, and prices can jump further in high seasons. These options are worth considering if you plan to stay several days or more, in which case there will usually be discounts from the daily rate.

Tourist offices can supply lists of places for rent, and in Britain the travel sections of the broadsheet press carry private ads for such places. British-based house and villa agencies (don't expect low prices) include **Magic of Spain** *(☎ 08700-270400;* W *www.magictravel group.co.uk)*, **Individual Travellers Spain** *(☎ 08700-773773;* W *www.indiv-travellers .com)*, **Spain at Heart** *(☎ 01373-814222;* W *www.spainatheart.co.uk)*, **Simply Spain** *(☎ 020-8541 2222;* W *www.simply-travel .com)*, and **Travellers' Way** *(☎ 01527-573724;* W *www.travellersway.co.uk)*.

Also see under Casas Rurales earlier.

FOOD

Andalucian cooking is typically Mediterranean in its liberal use of olive oil, garlic, onions, tomatoes and peppers. Traditionally, it's simple peasant fare based on fresh ingredients and with a hint of herbs and spices reflecting Roman, Jewish, Arabic, *gitano* and New World influences. The Arabic is the most distinctive: among other things the Muslims introduced oranges, lemons, apricots, aubergines, mint, spinach, *escabeche* (a marinade used for pickling), the *churrasco* (barbecued meat) and spices such as cinnamon and cumin. They are also credited with the now almost-worldwide order of serving courses: soup followed by hors d'oeuvres, then meat, then sweet dishes.

Stews based on various types of soaked, dried bean are a traditional staple of home cooking. Fish *(pescado)* is eaten almost everywhere, and there's a great variety of excellent seafood *(mariscos)*, especially from the Atlantic coast. A quick deep-fry in very hot olive oil is the most common method of cooking fish and seafood in Andalucía. A fine way to sample the Andalucian style, especially if there are a couple of you to share it, is to order a *fritura* or *frito variado*, which is deep-fried seafood's equivalent of a mixed grill. A good *sopa de mariscos* (seafood soup) can almost be a meal in itself.

Throughout Andalucía, the fruit and vegetables are delicious and fresh, for the growing season is almost year-round.

Andalucian food remains pretty traditional and conservative, experimentation with adventurous combinations is rare except in some of the more ingenious tapas bars of Seville.

For a culinary glossary, see Food in the Language chapter.

Provincial Specialities

Most restaurants provide quite a range of fare, but you'll notice changes of emphasis from one area to another. In the hill country, hams are cured and game dishes abound. On the coasts, seafood predominates and seafood soups, fried fish and sardines grilled on spits *(espetos)* over driftwood fires are all common. Here are some of the gastronomic traditions of Andalucía's eight provinces:

Almería The basic cuisine of arid Almería is a simple affair focused on chickpeas, grains, seafood and plenty of fresh irrigation-grown vegetables.

Cádiz The Cádiz coastline has fantastic seafood, used in a multitude of mouthwatering tapas and main dishes. Cádiz city is the home of *pescaíto frito* (deep-fried fish). Sherry is added to meat dishes in Jerez de la Frontera. The French and English, who played a big role in the sherry industry in Jerez, have also influenced the cuisine.

Córdoba At the heart of the culinary changes introduced by the Muslims was Córdoba. Today, some of Córdoba city's classy restaurants prepare food in medieval styles – concoctions such as garlic soup with raisins, or meats stuffed with dates and pine nuts. Few authentic recipes survive from the Muslim era, but there is enough information to approximate, especially on *cocina Mozárabe* – the food of Christians who lived under Muslim rule. At grassroots level, Córdoba is strong on vegetable dishes and has good cured meats.

Granada The province of Granada includes Spain's highest peaks and a semi-tropical coastline. It is known for its mountain-cured hams and warming meat dishes, but seafood and tropical fruits feature too.

Huelva There's excellent seafood here at the western end of Andalucía – *chocos* (small cuttlefish) are a local passion. But

---

From Little Acorns, Great Hams Grow

'Appetising' may not be the word that leaps to mind when you first set eyes on a dozen pigs' back legs dangling from the ceiling of a bar. But to most Spaniards there's no more mouthwatering prospect than a few thin, succulent slices of this cured *jamón* (ham). Try two or three slices as a *tapa*, or have it in a *bocadillo* (sandwich), or get a *ración* (meal-sized serving of a *tapa*).

Most of these hams are *jamón serrano* (mountain-cured ham, although nowadays the climatic conditions of the mountains can be reproduced in sheds and cellars at any altitude). The best *serrano* is *jamón ibérico*, also called *pata negra* (black leg), from the black (or dark brown) Iberian breed of pig, and the best *jamón ibérico* is *jamón ibérico de bellota*, from swine fed on *bellotas* (acorns).

Considered to be the best *jamón* of all is the *jamón ibérico* of Jabugo, in Andalucía's Huelva province, which comes from pigs free-ranging in the Sierra Morena oak forests. The best Jabugo hams are graded from one to five *jotas* (Js), and JJJJJ *(cinco jotas)* hams are said to come from pigs that have never eaten anything but acorns.

Ordinary, uncured cold ham, by the way, is called *jamón York*. It's dull as ditchwater after you've tasted *serrano* or *ibérico*.

Huelva is best known for its cured meats, especially hams from Jabugo.

Jaén The province of Jaén is the home of olive oil, which is added liberally to many dishes. It's also known for its game dishes, such as venison, wild boar and partridge, and *rin-rán* – a salad of potato, olives, red peppers and *bacalao* (salted cod).

Málaga This province is famed for its fried fish and seafood. Another favourite is *boquerones* (anchovies), often eaten raw after being marinated in vinegar, oil and garlic. Seafood soups are common. Ronda, in Málaga's mountains, has tasty game and stews. *Ajo blanco* (cold garlic and almond soup) and *migas* are further Málaga specialities: at their most basic, *migas* consist simply of crumbly fried flour and water, but they can be enlivened with fish, garlic, peppers or dried tomato.

Sevilla Cuisine here is a touch more sophisticated than elsewhere in Andalucía. Seville city was the first port of arrival for the new foodstuffs from the Americas that radically changed European cookery – potatoes, avocados, turkey, tomatoes, peppers, dried beans and chocolate. Today, it's the tapas capital of Andalucía.

Meals

The Spanish eating timetable is at its most extreme in Andalucía, so it's a good idea to reset your stomach clock unless you want to eat only with other tourists.

Breakfast Andalucians, like most Spaniards, usually start the day's eating with a light *desayuno* (breakfast), usually consisting of coffee with a *tostada* (toasted roll or slice of bread available with an infinite variety of toppings). This often happens around 10am, when many take a break from work. You may get the chance to specify what type of bread you want for your *tostada* – we thoroughly recommend *molletes*, tasty soft rolls.

Churros con chocolate – long, deep-fried doughnuts to dip in thick hot chocolate – make a rich, calorie-laden breakfast.

If you're hungry, a *tortilla* is a good option. Eggs *(huevos)* also come *fritos* (fried), *revueltos* (scrambled) or *cocidos* (boiled).

Lunch This is usually the main meal of the day, eaten between 2pm and 4pm, and known as *la comida* or *el almuerzo*. It can consist of several courses, starting with a soup and/or salad, continuing with a main course of meat or fish with vegetables, or a rice dish or bean stew, and ending with dessert.

In addition to the possibility of ordering from *la carta* (the main menu), you nearly always have the option of the budget traveller's best friend, the *menú del día* (daily set meal). This usually gives you a starter, a main course, a *postre* (dessert), bread and wine, with a choice of two or three dishes for each course. The *menú* is usually posted up outside and typically costs €6 to €10.

Some restaurants also offer *platos combinados*, a kind of halfway house between the *carta* and the *menú*, combining several items on one plate.

Ordering à la carte (*la carta* – not *el menú*, which means the *menú del día*) is more expensive, but the food will be better. Note that prices for fish and seafood are sometimes given by weight, which is potentially misleading. Vegetarians beware: 'vegetable' dishes may contain more than just vegetables – for example, beans with bits of ham.

Desserts have a low profile – *helado* (ice cream), fruit and *flan* (caramel custard) are often the only choices.

Dinner The evening meal, *la cena*, tends to be lighter than lunch and may be eaten as late as 10pm or 11pm. Andalucians sometimes go out for a bigger dinner in a restaurant, but before about 9pm you're unlikely to see anyone but foreigners doing this. Only a few restaurants offer their *menú del día* in the evening.

In-Between Times It's not a bad idea to go to a bar or café for a *merienda* (snack) around 11am or noon and again around 6pm or 7pm. Tapas apart, one great Spanish snack is the *bocadillo*, a long white-bread roll filled with cheese or ham or salad or *tortilla* or whatever else you fancy.

Put a Lid on it – Tapas & Raciones

The saucer-sized snacks known as tapas are part of the Spanish way of life and come in infinite variety. The word *tapa* means 'lid'. Today's snacks supposedly originated in the sherry area of Andalucía in the 19th century, when bar owners placed a piece of bread on top of a drink to deter flies; this developed into the custom of putting a salty titbit such as olives or a piece of sausage, on the bread to encourage drinking.

Today, tapas have become a cuisine in their own right and each Spanish region and city has its specialities. Sometimes they're free, though this custom has all but disappeared in many areas. The majority of tapas cost between €0.60 and €1.20 (it's worth checking before you order as some are a lot more expensive). Tapas are not a cheap way of eating if you're very hungry, as you'd need half a dozen to approximate the quantity of a decent-sized dinner.

Simple tapas include olives, cheese, omelette and *charcutería/chacinas* (pork products). Other varieties include chickpeas with spinach *(garbanzos con espinacas)*, a small serving of pork *solomillo* (sirloin) or *lomo* (loin) with garnish, *brochetas* or *pinchos* (mini-kebabs on sticks), *flamenquines* (deep-fried, breaded veal or ham) or *boquerones* (anchovies), which might be marinated in vinegar or fried in batter.

There's infinite scope for adventurous chefs to combine flavours and textures. Seville is out in front, where you can sample courgettes with Roquefort cheese or mushroom-filled artichoke hearts.

Seafood tapas are a highlight. Sample the best shellfish in the sherry triangle of Cádiz province – from Atlantic *conchas finas* (Venus shell, the biggest of the clams) to *cangrejos* (tiny crabs, cooked whole) or *búsanos* (sea snails or whelks). *Langostinos a la plancha*, jumbo prawns grilled with coarse-grained salt, are a taste sensation.

Offal such as *sesos* (brains), *callos* (tripe), *criadillas* (bull or sheep testicles), *riñones* (kidneys) and *hígado* (liver) may appear in a small earthenware dish, simmering in a tomato sauce or gravy. More to some people's taste are salad tapas such as *pipirrana* (based on diced tomatoes and red peppers), *salpicón* (the same with bits of seafood), *ensaladilla* (Russian salad) and *aliño* (any salad in a vinegar-and-oil dressing).

Bars usually display a range of tapas on the counter. They may also have a tapas menu or a blackboard listing what's available. Otherwise, things can be a mite confusing. A place that appears not to have tapas may actually specialise in them! You just have to ask what tapas are available.

A *ración* is a meal-sized serving of these snacks. A *media-ración* is half a *ración*. Two different *media-raciones* amount to something like a full meal. A *tabla* is a selection of tapas – typically some combination of hams, sausages, cheeses and *ahumados* (smoked fish); like a *ración*, it's good for a group of people to share.

Types of Eatery

Cafés & Bars If you want to live like locals, you'll spend plenty of time in bars and cafés. Bars come in many guises, such as *bodegas* (old-fashioned wine bars), *cervecerías* (beer bars), *tascas* (bars specialising in tapas), *tabernas* (taverns) and even *pubs*. In many of them you'll find tapas to eat; others may serve more substantial fare too. You'll often save 10% to 20% by eating at the bar rather than at a table. (The outside table area of a café, bar or restaurant, known as a *terraza*, is usually even more expensive.)

Restaurants Throughout Andalucía, plenty of *restaurantes* serve good, straightforward food at affordable prices, often featuring local specialities. There are also some classy, high-quality *restaurantes*, and some woeful places – particularly in tourist haunts.

A *mesón* is a simple restaurant attached to a bar with home-style cooking, and a *comedor* is usually the dining room of a bar or *hostal* – the food is likely to be functional and cheap. A *venta* is (or once was) a roadside inn, often off the beaten track – the food can be delectable and inexpensive. A *marisquería* is a seafood restaurant, while a *chiringuito* is a small open-air bar or kiosk, or sometimes a more substantial beachside restaurant.

Italian restaurants are common in Andalucía and there are some good Arabic restaurants in Granada and Málaga. Andalucía boasts only a few avowedly vegetarian restaurants. Vegetarians will find that salads in most restaurants are a good bet. A reliable vegetarian dish is *pisto*, a fry-up of courgettes, green peppers, onions and potatoes.

Markets Andalucía's *mercados* (markets) are fun places to visit. Buy a selection of fruits, vegetables, cold meat, sausage, olives, nuts and cheese, pick up some bread from a bakery, stop in at a supermarket for a bottle of wine and head for the nearest picturesque picnic spot. If you shop carefully, you could put together a filling meal for as little as €3 per person.

Traditional Andalucian Dishes

Stews In the past the *cocido*, a one-pot feast of meat, sausage, beans and vegetables, was a mainstay of the Andalucian diet. It's time-consuming to prepare, but in Andalucian villages the smell of chickpeas cooking still wafts through the streets around lunch time. A *cocido* can actually provide a three-course meal, with the broth eaten first followed by the vegetables and then the meat.

More usual nowadays is a simpler kind of stew, the *guiso,* which comes in three traditional types – *las berzas*, with cabbage and either beef or pork; *el puchero*, chicken and bacon broth with turnips and mint; and *los potajes*, with dried beans and *chorizo* sausage.

Gazpacho True *gazpacho*, a very typical Andalucian dish, is a cold soup of blended tomatoes, peppers, onion, garlic, breadcrumbs, lemon and oil. It's sometimes served in a jug with ice cubes, with side dishes of chopped raw vegetables such as cucumber and onion. Its close relatives – all cold soups containing oil, garlic and breadcrumbs – include *salmorejo cordobés*, Cordoban *gazpacho* cream with hard-boiled eggs as a garnish, and *ajo blanco*, pounded almond and garlic soup from Málaga province, often garnished with grapes.

Gazpacho developed in Andalucía among *jornaleros*, agricultural day labourers, who were given rations of bread and oil. They soaked the bread in water to form the basis of a soup then added oil and garlic and whatever fresh vegetables were at hand. All the ingredients were pounded using a mortar and pestle resulting in a relatively refreshing and nourishing dish.

Paella Andalucian versions of Spain's most famous dish often include seafood and/or chicken. On the Costa del Sol, peas, clams, mussels and prawns, and a garnish of red peppers and lemon slices is a popular combination. In Seville and Cádiz, big prawns and sometimes lobster are added. Paella is cooked in a wide, two-handled metal pan – best on a wood fire outdoors. Its flavour comes from the simmering rice absorbing the juices of the other ingredients, and the yellow colour traditionally comes from saffron, but since saffron is expensive today, food colouring or paprika *(pimentón)* are more commonly used. A lot of restaurants will only serve paella to a minimum of two people as it's not worth the effort of preparing a single portion.

DRINKS
Nonalcoholic Drinks

Coffee In Andalucía the coffee is good, and strong unless you specify otherwise. A *café con leche* is about 50% coffee, 50% hot milk; ask for *grande* or *doble* if you want a large cup, *en vaso* if you want it in a glass and *sombra* if you want lots of milk. A *café solo* is a short black; *café cortado* is a short black with a little milk.

Tea In cafés and bars, *té* is invariably weak. Ask for milk to be separate *(leche aparte)*, otherwise you'll end up with a cup of lukewarm milky water with a tea bag thrown in. Many places also have *té de manzanilla* (camomile tea). *Teterías* (Islamic-style tea-rooms) are fashionable in some cities, serving all manner of teas and herbal *infusiones*.

Chocolate Spaniards brought chocolate back from Mexico and adopted it enthusiastically. As a drink, it's served thick; sometimes it even appears among *postres* (desserts) on menus. Generally, it's a breakfast drink consumed with *churros*.

Soft Drinks Orange juice *(zumo de naranja)* is the main freshly squeezed juice available, but it's not cheap at around €1.50 a glass. Boxed juices come in all varieties in shops, and are good and cheap.

Refrescos (cool drinks) include the usual international brands of soft drinks, local brands such as Kas and expensive *granizado* (iced fruit crush).

Clear, cold water from a public fountain or tap is an Andalucian favourite – but check that it's potable. For tap water in restaurants, ask for *agua de grifo*. Bottled water *(agua mineral)* comes in innumerable brands, either *con gas* (fizzy) or *sin gas* (still). A 1.5L bottle of still water can cost anywhere between €0.40 and €0.80 in a supermarket.

A *batido* is a flavoured milk drink or milk shake. *Horchata* is made from the juice of tiger nuts, sugar and water: it tastes like soya milk with a hint of cinnamon. You'll come across it both fresh and bottled.

Wine

Wine production in Spain began in Andalucía when the Phoenicians, who founded Cádiz possibly as early as 1100 BC, introduced vines. Spanish wine *(vino)* is strong due to the sunny climate. It not only accompanies meals but is also a popular bar drink – and it's cheap: a bottle costing €5 from a supermarket or €12 in a restaurant will be decent wine. Cheap *vino de mesa* (table wine) may sell for less than €1.50 a litre in shops.

You can order wine by the glass *(copa)* in bars and restaurants: the *vino de la casa* (house wine) may come from a barrel or jug at €1 or less per glass.

Wine Terminology You can judge the quality of Spanish wine to a certain extent from the label. Apart from sherry, most of Spain's best wines come from the north of

the country. DOC stands for Denominación de Origen Calificada and refers to wine from areas that have maintained high quality over a very long period. Rioja, in northern Spain, is the only DOC so far. DO, Denominación de Origen, is one step down from DOC. There are 50-odd DO areas around Spain. A DOC or DO label tells you that the wine has been produced to certain supervised standards by serious wine growers, although each DOC and DO covers a wide range of wines of varying quality (usually indicated by the price).

Wine made for immediate drinking is called *vino joven*, while *vino de crianza* is wine that has been stored for certain minimum periods: if red, two full calendar years with a minimum of six months in oak; if white or rosé, one calendar year. The title Reserva requires three years' storage for reds and two for whites and rosés. Gran Reserva wines are particularly good vintages, which must have spent at least two calendar years in storage and three in the bottle; they're mostly reds.

Sherry *Jerez* (sherry), Andalucía's most celebrated wine, is produced in the towns of Jerez de la Frontera, El Puerto de Santa María and Sanlúcar de Barrameda.

A combination of climate, chalky soils that soak up the sun but retain moisture, and a special maturing process called the *solera* system (see the boxed text 'The Solera Process' in the Cádiz Province chapter) produces these unique wines.

The main distinction in sherry is between *fino* (dry and straw-coloured) and *oloroso* (sweet and dark, with a strong bouquet). An *amontillado* is an amber, moderately dry *fino* with a nutty flavour and a higher alcohol content. An *oloroso* combined with a sweet wine results in a 'cream sherry'. A *manzanilla* – officially not sherry – is a camomile-coloured, unfortified *fino* produced in Sanlúcar de Barrameda: its delicate flavour is reckoned to come from sea breezes wafting into the *bodegas* (wineries).

The website Ⓦ www.sherry.org provides a good introduction on the subject of sherry and the firms that make it.

Other Andalucian Wines In southern Córdoba province the Montilla-Moriles DO produces a wine that is very similar to sherry but, unlike sherry, is not fortified by the addition of brandy – the *fino* variety is the most acclaimed. Andalucía's other DO is Málaga: sweet, velvety 'Málaga Dulce' has pleased palates from Virgil to Shakespeare and the ladies of Victorian England, until the vines were blighted around the beginning of the 20th century. Today the Málaga DO area is Andalucía's smallest. You can sample Málaga wine straight from the barrel in some of the city's numerous bars.

Almost every village throughout Andalucía has its own simple wine – cheap country wine is simply known as *mosto*. Eight areas in the region produce distinctive, good, non-DO wines that can be sampled locally: Aljarafe and Los Palacios (Sevilla province), Bailén, Lopera and Torreperogil (Jaén province), Costa Albondón (Granada province), Laújar de Andarax (Almería province) and Villaviciosa (Córdoba province).

The Big Bottle

Spaniards have always liked a party, especially one in the open air. But when teenagers started taking to the streets in their hundreds of thousands to carouse through Friday and Saturday nights, it became a social crisis.

Young people joined in these huge open-air parties because it's much cheaper than drinking in bars and they're far from parental observation. For €10 or less a group of friends can buy a litre bottle of spirits, 2L of soft drink, a bag of ice and some big plastic mugs to mix it all up in. Fruit liqueurs and cask wines are even cheaper. The huge gatherings resulted in residents being unable to sleep, rubbish strewn about the streets and plazas, bar owners losing a lot of business, and parents being anxious about their kids.

The Botellón (Big Bottle) phenomenon began in the mid-90s. By 2002, well over half a million young Spaniards were reckoned to be indulging each weekend. Some towns and cities dreamt up imaginative schemes to keep their adolescents off the streets: in Málaga, free classes in creative hairdressing, self-defence, henna tattoos, dance, swimming, basketball and much more were offered from 11pm to 2am on Friday and Saturday nights. In Benalmádena teenagers could take tuition in seduction techniques. In Dos Hermanas, near Seville, free sandwiches, coffee, hot chocolate and alcohol-free cocktails were given out. Jerez de la Frontera staged all-night movie marathons and late-night concerts, and let young people convert an old winery into a youth community centre.

These efforts had some success but the Botellón crowds didn't diminish. In Madrid the mayor sent police to keep people carrying alcohol out of the most popular Botellón plazas on weekend nights. Citizens' groups all over Andalucía grew ever angrier with their city halls for doing nothing to control the Botellón. A neighbourhood group from Seville's El Arenal district won a court order obliging their city hall to take steps against the Botellón.

Finally in May 2002 the national government proposed a new law which would ban drinking in public places when it affected 'public tranquillity and free movement', except where authorised by local administrations. The law also fixed the minimum age for purchasing alcohol to 18 (previously 16 in most of the country), and enabled local administrations to limit the hours alcohol could be sold from petrol stations and shops without special licences (it was from small grocery and food shops that the Botellón folk were buying much of their booze). City halls were thus handed the hot potato of keeping their grown-ups happy without alienating their youth. Málaga immediately announced that the Botellón would be banned from one of its most popular sites in the city, Plaza de la Merced, when the law took effect. But whatever ideas the legislators and politicians thought up, it seems clear that nothing easily deters Spain's teenagers from getting together to have a good time.

Other Alcoholic Drinks

Beer The most common ways to order a *cerveza* (beer) is to ask for a *caña*, which is a small draught beer, or a *tubo*, a larger draught beer (about 300mL) in a straight glass. If you just ask for a *cerveza* you may get bottled beer, which tends to be a bit more expensive. A small bottle (250mL) is called a *botellín* or a *quinto*; a bigger one (330mL) is a *tercio* or a *media*. San Miguel, Cruzcampo and Victoria are all decent Andalucian beers.

Mixed Drinks, Spirits & Liqueurs *Sangría* is a wine and fruit punch, sometimes laced with brandy. It's refreshing going down, but can leave you with a sore head! You'll see jugs of it on tables in restaurants, but it also comes ready-mixed in bottles at around €2 for 1.5L. *Tinto de verano* is a mix of wine and sweet carbonated water.

Chupitos, particularly popular with the younger pub-crawling crowd, are highly potent little cocktails intended to be knocked back.

Coñac (Spanish brandy) is popular and cheap. Most of it is made in Andalucía – mainly in the sherry towns, but also in Málaga and in Córdoba province. In bars, you'll notice locals starting the day with a coffee and a *coñac*, or a glass of *anís* (aniseed liqueur).

Spirits produced in Spain are generally much cheaper than imports. Málaga's Larios gin is an example. *Ron* (rum) is produced in Málaga and Motril (Granada province), the only areas in Europe that grow sugar cane.

Andalucía also produces a wide range of *licores* (liqueurs). *Aguardiente* is a colourless, grape-based liqueur. When spiked with aniseed, it becomes an *anís* or *anisado* (anisette). *Pacharán*, a red liqueur made with aniseed and sloes (the fruit of the blackthorn) is very popular in Andalucía.

ENTERTAINMENT

You need never go short of entertainment in Andalucía. The nightlife is wild and just sitting in a café and watching the animated street life is never dull.

Listings

Local papers often carry fairly thorough entertainment listings. Try to pick up *El Giraldillo*, a good Spanish-language monthly what's-on listing for all Andalucía, from tourist offices. Tourist offices can help with specific inquiries and may have further what's-on publications.

On the Internet, W spain.viapolis.com provides city-by-city what's-on listings; W www.clubbingspain.com and W espaciodj.com point you to the best clubs and tell you who's on at them; and W www.ideal.es/indyrock keeps you in touch with upcoming indie festivals and concerts.

Bars & Clubs

Wild and very late nights, especially on Friday and Saturday, are an integral part of the Andalucian scene, even in small towns. Many young Andalucians don't think about going out till midnight or so. Bars, in all shapes, sizes and themes, are the main attractions until at least midnight. Some play great music, which will get you vibrating before moving on to a club till dawn. Andalucía provides the gamut of dance music if you know where to look (check this book's individual city Entertainment sections). Some clubs won't let you in wearing jeans or trainers. It's worth being aware, by the way, that the word *'club'* in nightlife contexts in Spain can refer not only to dance clubs but also to sleazy pick-up joints.

Live Pop, Rock & Jazz

Most towns have at least one bar or café with live music at the weekend. In the major cities there's something happening every night and a big choice at weekends.

The Spanish rock and pop scene is large and lively, and foreign touring bands put in fairly frequent appearances in Andalucía, especially in summer. Live music of many types is an essential ingredient of many fiestas. Jazz and blues have good followings, with venues in most big cities.

Flamenco

Flamenco is easiest to catch in the summer, when a number of towns stage flamenco festivals and others include flamenco events in a wider-ranging *feria* or fiesta. Such flamenco nights are typically long-drawn-out open-air affairs, rarely getting going till after midnight and sometimes lasting till dawn, aided by copious quantities of alcohol.

The rest of the year you'll find there are intermittent big-name performances in theatres, but also regular flamenco nights at bars and clubs in some cities – often just for the price of your drinks. Flamenco fans also band together in clubs called *peñas*, which stage live performance nights – most will admit genuinely interested visitors and the atmosphere here can be very intimate.

Unless asked otherwise, tourist offices may steer you towards *tablaos*, regular shows for largely undiscriminating tourist audiences, usually with high prices.

The website of the **Centro Andaluz de Flamenco in Jerez** (**w** *caf.cica.es*) includes a detailed calendar of flamenco festivals and lists of *peñas flamencas* (flamenco clubs, many of which will admit interested outsiders).

See Public Holidays & Special Events in this chapter for major flamenco festivals. There's further information in the Flamenco section in Facts about Andalucía. Seville, Jerez de la Frontera and Granada are flamenco hotbeds, but you'll often be able to find something in Málaga, Cádiz or Córdoba – and, erratically, in many other places too.

Cinemas

Cinemas abound and are inexpensive, though foreign films are almost always dubbed into Spanish. In the major cities a few cinemas show foreign films with Spanish subtitles – look for the letters v.o.s. *(versión original subtitulada)* in listings.

SPECTATOR SPORTS
Football

Soccer *(fútbol)* rivals bullfighting as Spain's national sport. Every weekend from September to May, millions follow the national Primera División (First Division) on TV. Spaniards take their teams' fortunes very seriously!

Andalucía's three best teams are Sevilla, Málaga and Real Betis (of Seville), all usu-ally to be found around the middle of the Primera División table. In 2002 Recreativo de Huelva won promotion from the Segunda División to make it four Andalucian teams in Spain's top flight for season 2002–03. Huelva has a place in every Spanish football lover's heart for it was there that football was introduced to Spain in the 1870s by British sailors, and Recreativo was the first football club in Spain when founded in 1889. Season 2002–03 was only 'Recre's' second ever in the top division.

League games are mostly played on Sunday, with a few on Saturday. Games in the Copa del Rey (Spain's FA Cup equivalent) are held midweek at night. For upcoming fixtures see the local press or the sports paper *Marca*, or visit **Planet Fútbol** (**w** *www.diariosur.es/planetfutbol*).

Bullfighting

The bullfight *(corrida)* is a pageant with a long history and many rules, not simply a ghoulish alternative to the slaughterhouse. Many people feel ill at the sight of the kill, and the preceding few minutes' torture is undoubtedly cruel, but aficionados will say that fighting bulls have been bred for conflict and that before the fateful day they are treated like kings. The bull is better off, it is said, dying at the hands of a matador (killer) than in the abattoir *(matadero)*. The *corrida* is also about many other things – a direct confrontation with death, bravery, skill and performance. Although many Spaniards themselves consider it a cruel activity, many others view it as an art and there is no doubting its popularity.

Contests of strength, skill and bravery between man and beast are no recent phenomenon. The Romans probably staged Spain's first bullfights. *La lidia*, as the modern art of bullfighting on foot is known, took off in an organised fashion in Spain in the mid-18th century. Andalucía was one of its birthplaces and has been one of its hotbeds ever since. Before then, bullfighting on horseback was a kind of cavalry-training-cum-sport for the gentry. (Horseback bullfights, known as *corridas de rejones*, still take place – and the equestrian skills displayed can be enthralling.)

Three generations of the Romero family from Ronda in Andalucía's Málaga province established most of the basics of bullfighting on foot.

For information on antibullfighting organisations see Treatment of Animals under Society & Conduct in the Facts about Andalucía chapter.

El Matador & La Cuadrilla Only champion matadors make good money, and some actually make a loss. The matador must pay a supporting team *(cuadrilla)*, pay for the right to fight a bull, and rent or buy an outfit and equipment.

The *cuadrilla* has quite a few members. Firstly, there are several *peones*, junior *toreros* (bullfighters) who come out to distract the bull with great capes, manoeuvre him into the desired position, and so on. Then come the *banderilleros*, who race towards the bull and attempt to plunge a pair of colourfully decorated *banderillas* (short prods with harpoon-style ends) into his withers. This is intended to goad the animal into action. In the next stage of the fight, the horseback *picadores* shove a lance into the withers, greatly weakening the bull.

Then there is the matador. The matador's dress could be that of a flamenco dancer. At its most extravagant, the *traje de luces* (suit of lights) is an extraordinary display of bright, spangly colour. All the *toreros* (matadors, *banderilleros* and so on) wear the black *montera*, the hat that looks a little like a set of Mickey Mouse ears. The *torero's* standard weapons are the *estoque* or *espada* (sword) and the heavy silk and percale *capa* (cape). The matador alone also employs a different cape – the *muleta*, a smaller piece of cloth held with a bar of wood used for a number of different passes.

La Corrida Bullfights usually begin about 6pm and, as a rule, six bulls are on the day's card, with three different matadors fighting two bulls each. Each fight takes about 15 minutes.

The spectacle begins with the bull entering the arena, then being moved about by the junior bullfighters. The matador then appears and displays moves *(faenas)* with the bull, such as pivoting before its horns. The more closely and calmly the matador works with the bull, the greater the crowd's approbation. After a little of this, the matador strides off and leaves the stage first to the *banderilleros*, then to the *picadores*, before returning for the final session. When the bull seems tired out and unlikely to give a lot more, the matador chooses the moment for the kill. Facing the animal head-on, the matador aims to sink the sword cleanly into its neck for an instant kill – the *estocada*. It's an awful lot easier said than done.

A good performance followed by a clean kill will have the crowd on its feet waving handkerchiefs in appeal to the president of the fight to award the matador an ear of the animal. The president usually waits to gauge the crowd's enthusiasm before finally flopping a white handkerchief onto his balcony. If the fight has been exceptional, the matador might *cortar dos orejas* – cut two ears off. And a matador who does really, really well may be awarded the tail too *(dos orejas y rabo)*.

Matadors If you're spoiling for a fight, it's worth looking out for the big names among the matadors. They are no guarantee you'll see a high-quality *corrida*, as that also depends on the animals themselves. Names to look for include: Enrique Ponce, a serious class act from Jaén province; Julián 'El Juli' López, born in Madrid in 1982 (he graduated to senior matador status at the extraordinarily early age of 15); José Tomás, another young superstar; Morante de la Puebla, highly popular in Seville, his home town; and Finito de Córdoba, the great hope of *his* city.

Ethics of the Fight Anyone in doubt about the danger to the human participants in this contest of bravery should remember that people *do* die in the ring. Today, however, the risk is reduced by the fraudulent practice known as the *afeitado* – filing down the bull's horns. Filing not only makes the bull slightly less anxious to attack its tormentors but also impairs its judgment of distance and angle. When moves were made to stop this practice in 1997, the matadors went on strike.

When & Where The official bullfighting year in Andalucía runs from Easter Sunday to October, though it's possible to see a *corrida* at other times of the year on the Costa del Sol. Most *corridas* are held as part of a city or town fiesta. Few rings have regular fights right through the season, Seville being an exception.

The big bang that launches Andalucía's bullfighting year is Seville's Feria de Abril (April Fair), with fights almost daily during the week of the fair and the week before it. It's Seville, too, where the year ends with a *corrida* on 12 October, Spain's National Day. Here are some of the other major fight seasons on the Andalucian bullfight calendar:

Late April or early May
  Fiesta de Jerez de la Frontera
Late May or early June
  Feria de Nuestra Señora de la Salud Held in Córdoba, a big bullfighting stronghold
  Feria de la Manzanilla Held in Sanlúcar de Barrameda
  Corpus Christi Held in Granada
June to August
  El Puerto de Santa María & the Costa del Sol Fights happen most Sundays: those on the Costa del Sol tend to be frequented by tourists but most Sundays there's a respectable fight in one of the rings (such as Fuengirola, Marbella, Torremolinos and Mijas)
August
  Fiestas Colombinas Held in Huelva from approximately 3 to 9 August
  Feria de Málaga Held in mid-August
  Feria de la Virgen del Mar Held in Almería in the last week of August
September
  Corrida Goyesca Held in Ronda from around 6 to 8 September, with select, stylish matadors fighting in costumes of the type shown in Goya's bullfight engravings
  Corridas in Jaén province Held mostly in mid- or late September, including at Úbeda, Cazorla and Linares, site of the 1947 death of the legendary matador Manolete

Bullfighting magazines such as the weekly *6 Toros 6* carry full details of who's fighting where and when, and posters advertise up-

coming fights locally and give ticket information. In addition to the top *corridas*, which attract the big-name matadors and big crowds, there are plenty of lesser ones in cities, towns and villages. These are often *novilleras*, in which immature bulls *(novillos)* are fought by junior matadors *(novilleros)*.

If you're interested in knowing more about bullfighting, ⓦ www.red2000.com/spain/toros is a good place to start.

Other Sports

The Jerez de la Frontera Grand Prix in the World Motorcycle Championship, held in May, is one of Spain's biggest sporting events, attracting around 150,000 spectators.

Basketball *(baloncesto)* is also popular. Andalucía's most successful teams in the Liga ACB national professional league are Unicaja of Málaga and Caja San Fernando of Seville.

Andalucía stages several major professional golf tournaments each year. Events, venues and dates change: the Volvo Masters, played in recent Novembers at Montecastillo, Jerez de la Frontera, is traditionally the final tournament of the season on the European Circuit. In 1999, Andalucian Ryder Cup star Miguel Ángel Jiménez, from Churriana near Málaga, became the first Spaniard to win the Volvo.

SHOPPING

You can find some very attractive and reasonably priced handicrafts in Andalucía. There's surprising variation in what you find from one area to another, with many products being sold only close to where they are made. Apart from craft shops – abundant in tourist areas – you may pick up crafts at markets in villages or towns, and even in department stores such as the nationwide El Corte Inglés chain. There are also flea markets *(mercadillos)* and car boot sales *(rastros)* around the region where you can at times find incredible bargains.

For general shopping, most towns have a shopping zone where you can buy just about anything. Large, glossy, air-conditioned, purpose-built *centros comerciales* (shopping centres) are also springing up on the fringes of towns and cities over Andalucía. If you have a car, these offer the convenience of a lot of different shops in one place, but they're not high on local atmosphere.

Pottery

Pottery comes in many attractive regional varieties – crockery, tiles, plant pots and more – and is cheap. Islamic influence on design and colour is strong. In Granada, the dominant colours are white splashed with green and blue, often with a pomegranate as the centrepiece of the pattern. In Córdoba the product is finer, with black, green and blue borders on white. Úbeda, another noted pottery centre, typically employs a green glaze.

Leather & Horse-Riding Equipment

Andalucian leather goods can be a bargain. You can still get good prices on jackets, bags, belts, shoes and boots in many places. Exquisite riding boots can be purchased in 'horsey' places like Jerez de la Frontera and El Rocío. Most sizable towns have at least one shop devoted to riding gear: not only boots, hats, saddles etc, but also the embroidered blankets, pom-poms and tassles with which Andalucians deck their mounts at festival times.

Embossed, polychrome leather products such as poufs make a good, not-too-bulky present: you simply roll up the leather and insert the filling back at home. Córdoba produces some of the finest embossed leather.

Other Crafts

Gold and silver jewellery abounds – some of the best is the filigree made in Córdoba. There's some pleasing woodwork available, such as Granada's marquetry boxes, chess sets and more. Basketwork is most evident on the coasts.

Clothes & Shoes

City centre shopping zones and *centros comerciales* are full of stylish clothes and footwear at good prices. Every major city centre has a small cluster of flamenco shops, selling embroidered shawls, hand-painted fans, flat-top Cordoban hats and of course lots of highly colourful flouncy dresses – these days not just in Polkadots but also in some gorgeous floral and wilder prints.

ANDALUCÍA'S NATIONAL & NATURAL PARKS

Flamingos wheeling over the Doñana marshes... ibex clinging to the crags of Mulhacén...dolphins leaping in the Bahía de Algeciras...stags trotting through the Cazorla forests... Just a few of the wildlife wonders waiting to be seen by anyone with a little determination while travelling in Andalucía. The region is a nature lover's delight; from the prehistoric fir forests of the rainy Sierra de Grazalema to the dwarf palms of the semidesert Cabo de Gata; from the Sierra Nevada's unique high-altitude gentians to the evergreen oak forests of the Sierra Morena, rolling along Andalucía's northern borders. Much of Andalucía remains wilderness barely touched by human hand, or countryside managed in traditional, sustainable ways. Its landscapes never cease to surprise with their unexpected beauty.

Most of the most spectacular and ecologically important country is under official protection: Andalucía has the biggest environmental protection programme in Spain, possessing more than 90 protected areas covering some 17,000 sq km. This amounts to 20% of Andalucian territory, and more than 60% of the total protected area in the whole country.

Along with official protection – largely an achievement of the regional government, the Junta de Andalucía, since the 1980s – have come infinitely improved levels of public information and access to these often remote, challenging areas. Visitor centres and information points; maps, leaflets and guidebooks; marked footpaths; more and better rural accommodation; active-tourism firms that will take you walking, riding, wildlife-watching, paragliding, climbing, caving, canyoning, canoeing – all of these now enable almost anyone to venture forth and explore the untamed side of this exciting region.

In this special section we introduce the animal and plant life of Andalucía and the two national and 23 natural parks *(parques nacionales* and *parques naturales)* where, by and large, the best and closest encounters with Andalucian nature are to be had.

Inset: The griffon vulture is found in Andalucía's mountain regions (Photograph by David Tipling)

Right: Striking rock formations, Torcal de Antequera

ANDERS BLOMQVIST

Flora

The variety of Andalucian flora is astonishing, as anyone who witnesses the spectacular wildflower displays in spring and early summer will testify. Andalucía has around 5000 different plant species, of which some 150 are unique to the region. This abundance is largely due to the fact that, during the last ice age, many plants that were killed off further north were able to survive at this southerly latitude.

High-Altitude Plants The mountain areas are responsible for a lot of Andalucía's botanical variety. The Sierra Nevada, southeast of Granada, with mainland Spain's highest mountain, Mulhacén (3482m), is home to some 2100 of Spain's 7000 plant species. About 60 of these are unique to the Sierra Nevada. The Cazorla natural park in northeast Andalucía, another mountainous region, has 2300 plant species, 24 of them found nowhere else. When the snows melt, the alpine and subalpine zones above the tree line bloom with small, rock-clinging plants and high pastures full of **gentians, orchids, crocuses** and **narcissi**.

Forest & Woodlands Many mountain slopes are clothed in **pine** *(pino)* forests, often commercial. The tall **black pine** *(pino larico* in Spanish), with horizontally spreading branches clustering near the top, likes terrain above about 1300m. The **maritime pine** *(pino resinero* or *pino marítimo)*, with its rounded top, can grow all the way up to elevations of 1500m. The **Aleppo pine** *(pino carrasco)*, with a bushy top and separated, often bare branches, flourishes below 1000m. The lovely **umbrella pine** *(pino piñonero)*, with its broad, umbrella-like top and edible kernels, prefers low-lying and coastal areas – it's highly characteristic of the Doñana area around the mouth of the Río Guadalquivir.

The natural vegetation of many lower slopes and gentler hill country is **Mediterranean woodland**, with trees adapted to a warm, fairly dry climate, such as the **wild olive** *(acebuche)*, **carob** *(algarrobo)*, and three types of oak: the evergreen **holm** or **ilex oak** *(encina)* and **cork oak** *(alcornoque)*, and the **gall oak** *(quejigo)*, whose leaves fall in spring. These types of oaks are generally shorter, more gnarled and smaller and pricklier in the leaf than the tall deciduous oaks of more temperate regions, which are generally known as *robles* in Spanish. Human intervention has left sadly little Mediterranean woodland intact. The best stands are in the Sierra de Grazalema and Los Alcornocales natural parks in Cádiz province.

The rare **Spanish fir** *(pinsapo)*, a handsome, dark-green relic of the extensive fir forests around the Mediterranean in the Tertiary period (which ended approximately 2.5 million years ago), survives in significant numbers only in the Sierra de Grazalema, Sierra de las Nieves and Sierra Bermeja, all in southwest Andalucía, and in northern Morocco. The Spanish fir likes north-facing slopes up to 1800m. It can grow up to 30m high and lives for up to 500 years.

Along river valleys you will often find a rich variety of deciduous trees including the **poplar** *(álamo)*, **ash** *(fresno)*, **willow** *(sauce)*, **maple** *(arce)*,

Dehesas

In some areas, such as the Sierra Morena, the Parque Natural Los Alcornocales and lower parts of the Sierra de Grazalema, evergreen oaks form a vital component of extensive woodlands-cum-pastures known as *dehesas*, which provide a delightful example of sustainable symbiosis between humans, plants and animals.

The cork oak's thick outer bark is stripped every ninth summer for cork; you'll see the visible scars – a bright terracotta colour if they're new – on some trees. The holm oak can be pruned about every four years and the offcuts used for charcoal. Meanwhile, livestock can graze the pastures, and in autumn pigs are turned out to hungrily gobble up the fallen acorns, a diet considered to produce the tastiest ham of all. *Dehesas* were mostly created long ago by the felling or burning-off of the original Mediterranean forest for pasture which was replanted with these useful trees.

elm *(olmo)* and **alder** *(aliso)*. In summer many watercourses are lined with the unmistakable bright pink flowers of **oleander** *(adelfa)* bushes.

At ground level Andalucía's forests sprout some 2000 species of **fungi** *(setas)* in autumn. Many of these are edible and appear in markets and country restaurants. Some others are poisonous – and the decisions on which are which are best left to the local experts!

Definitely not natural but in some areas the dominant feature of the landscape – especially in Jaén and Córdoba provinces – are lines upon lines upon lines of **olive** *(olivo)* trees, stretching over the rolling horizon and far beyond. Andalucía produces about 20% of the world's olive oil (see the boxed text 'Essential Oil' in the Jaén Province chapter). Other food-bearing trees grown in many parts of Andalucía are the **almond** *(almendro)*, with its beautiful pink winter blossom, and the **chestnut** *(castaño)*, with incredible star-bursts of catkins in mid-summer. Widely cultivated for timber, though now unfashionable because of its insatiable thirst, is the **eucalyptus** *(eucalipto)*.

Scrub & Steppe Where there are no trees and no agriculture, the land is likely to be either scrub *(matorral)* or steppe *(estepa)*. Scrub occurs where forests were felled and the land was later abandoned (though some of its plants can also occur in the understorey of Mediterranean woodland). Herbs like **lavender** *(lavanda)*, **rosemary** *(romero)*, **fennel** *(hinojo)* and **thyme** *(tomillo)* are typical, as are **gorse** *(tojo)*, **juniper** *(enebro)*, **heather** *(brezo)* and shrubs of the **cistus** *(jara)* family. Orchids, gladioli and irises may flower beneath these shrubs, some of which are themselves colourful in spring.

Steppe is produced by constant overgrazing or occurs naturally in hot, very dry areas such as the southeast of Almería province. Here, plant life is generally sparse, often with cacti, but some areas can bloom with colour after rain.

Fauna

The region's wildlife is among the most diverse in Europe, thanks to Andalucía's varied and often untamed terrain, which has allowed the survival of several species that have died out in other countries – though some are now in perilously small numbers. Many animals are nocturnal but if you want to see wildlife, and know where to look, you're unlikely to go home disappointed.

Mammals A small number of **wolves** *(lobos)* survive in the Sierra Morena along Andalucía's northern border (Jaén and Córdoba provinces). In 1986 the wolf was declared in danger of extinction in Andalucía and, in an effort to protect it from hunters, farmers are now awarded compensation if their animals are attacked by wolves. But the wolf population – probably not more than 100 – remains dangerously low. Around 2000 wolves survive in other parts of Spain.

Things are better for the **ibex** *(cabra montés)*, a stocky mountain goat whose males have distinctive long horns. Andalucía has an ibex population of perhaps 12,000. The ibex spends summer hopping agilely around high-altitude precipices and descends lower in winter. Around 5000 ibex live in the Sierra Nevada, 2000 or more in the Cazorla natural park, 1500 in the Sierras de Tejeda y Almijara, 1000 in the Sierra de las Nieves and a few hundred each in the Sierra de Grazalema and Sierra Mágina.

The **Pardel** or **Iberian lynx** *(lince ibérico)*, a beautiful feline unique to the Iberian Peninsula and smaller than the lynx of northern Europe, is the world's most endangered cat. Its numbers have been reduced, to probably about 400 in Spain and fewer than 50 in Portugal, by hunting and by a decline in the number of rabbits, its staple diet. Now stringently protected, it lives in wild southern and western woodlands, including Andalucía's Doñana national and natural parks (where a total of perhaps 50 remain) and Parque Natural Sierras de Andújar. The zoo at Jerez de la Frontera has launched an in-captivity breeding programme to try to save the lynx from extinction.

Less uncommon beasts include the mainly nocturnal **wild boar** *(jabalí)*, which likes thick woods, marshes and farmers' root crops; the **red deer** *(ciervo)*, **roe deer** *(corzo)* and **fallow deer** *(gamo)*, in forests and woodlands of all types; the nocturnal **genet** *(gineta)*, rather like a short-legged cat with a black-spotted white coat and a long, striped tail, in woodland and scrub; the mainly nocturnal **Egyptian mongoose** *(meloncillo)*, in woods, scrub and marshes, especially in southwestern Andalucía; the **red squirrel** *(ardilla)*, in mountain forests; the nocturnal **badger** *(tejón)*, in woods with thick undergrowth; the **fox** *(zorro)*, common in scattered areas; the **otter** *(nutria)*; and the **beech marten** *(garduña)*, in deciduous forests and on rocky outcrops and cliffs. The **mouflon** *(muflón)*, a wild sheep, has been introduced to the Cazorla natural park and a couple of other areas for hunting.

Gibraltar is famous for its colony of **Barbary macaques**, the only wild monkeys in Europe. The Bahía de Algeciras and Strait of Gibraltar harbour plenty of **dolphins** *(delfines;* common, striped and bottle-nosed) and some **whales** *(ballenas;* pilot, killer and even sperm), and boat trips to see them are an increasingly popular attraction from Gibraltar and Tarifa.

Birds Andalucía is a magnet for bird-watchers (see Activities in the Facts for the Visitor chapter for more information).

Raptors Andalucía has 13 resident raptor (bird-of-prey) species and several other summer visitors from Africa. You'll see some of them circling or hovering over the hills in many parts of Andalucía.

The Sierra Morena is a stronghold of Europe's biggest bird, the rare **black vulture** *(buitre negro)*. The few hundred pairs in Spain are probably the world's biggest population.

Another emblematic and extremely rare bird is the **Spanish imperial eagle** *(águila imperial)*, found in no other country. Its white shoulders distinguish it from other imperial eagles. Of the 130 pairs remaining, about 30 are in Andalucía, of which seven (at the last count) are in the Parque Nacional de Doñana. Poisoned bait put out by farmers or hunters is the imperial's greatest enemy.

Other large birds of prey in Andalucía include the **golden eagle** *(águila real)* and several other eagles, and the **griffon vulture** *(buitre leonado)* and **Egyptian vulture** *(alimoche)*, all found in mountain regions. Among smaller birds of prey, many of them found around deciduous or lowland woods and forests, are the common **kestrel** *(cernícalo)* and **buzzard** *(ratonero)*, the **sparrowhawk** *(gavilán)*, various **harriers** *(aguiluchos)*, and the acrobatic **red kite** *(milano real)* and **black kite** *(milano negro)*. You may see black kites over open ground near marshes, rivers and rubbish dumps.

Storks The large, ungainly **white stork** *(cigüeña blanca)*, actually black-and-white, nests from spring to summer on electricity pylons, trees and towers – sometimes right in the middle of towns – in western Andalucía. Your attention will be drawn to it by the loud clacking of beaks from these lofty perches. A few pairs of the much rarer **black stork** *(cigüeña negra)*, all black, also nest in western Andalucía, typically on cliff ledges. In spring both types migrate from Africa across the Strait of Gibraltar, relying heavily on thermals and updraughts to soar along their way. There are just two places where the seas are narrow enough for the stork to get into Europe by this method. One is the Bosphorus, the other is the Strait of Gibraltar, where flocks of as many as 3000 white storks gather to sweep northward in January or February.

RAY TIPPER

Right: White stork

RAY TIPPER

Water Birds Andalucía is a haven for water birds, mainly thanks to large wetlands along the Atlantic coast, such as at the mouths of the Guadalquivir and Odiel rivers. Hundreds of thousands of migratory birds, including an estimated 80% of Western Europe's wild ducks *(patos)*, winter in the Doñana wetlands at the mouth of the Guadalquivir, and many more call in during spring and autumn migrations.

Laguna de Fuente de Piedra, near Antequera, is Europe's main breeding site for the **greater flamingo** *(flamenco)*, with as many as 16,000 pairs rearing chicks in spring and summer. This beautiful pink bird can also be seen in several other places, including Cabo de Gata, Doñana, the Bahía de Cádiz and the Marismas del Odiel.

Other Birds Among the most colourful of Andalucía's many other birds are the **golden oriole** *(oropéndola)*, seen in orchards and deciduous woodlands in summer (the male has an unmistakable bright yellow body); the orange-and-black **hoopoe** *(abubilla)*, with its distinctive crest, common in open woodlands, on farmland and golf courses; and the gold, brown and turquoise **bee-eater** *(abejaruco)*, which nests in sandy banks in summer. Various **woodpeckers** *(pitos* or *picos)* and **owls** *(búhos)* inhabit hill-country woodlands.

Other Fauna From spring to autumn, Andalucía is a paradise for butterfly and moth enthusiasts. Most of Europe's **butterflies** *(mariposas)* are found in Spain. There are several **bat** *(murciélago)* species, **salamanders** *(salamandras)*, **chameleons** *(camaleones;* most numerous in the Axarquía region), numerous **lizards** *(lagartos)*, and **snakes** *(serpientes)*. See Cuts, Bites & Stings under Health in the Facts for the Visitor chapter for more information on dangerous beasts.

Left: Greater flamingos

Protected Areas

Responsibility for nature conservation in Spain is divided between the national government in Madrid and regional governments such as the Junta de Andalucía. There are at least 17 different categories of protected area, some used countrywide, others only cropping up in one or two regions as local policies dictate. All protected areas can be visited, but degrees of access vary. So do degrees of actual protection: environmentalists and dedicated environmental officials wage an endless struggle against the efforts of developers, industrialists and the more pliable officials to nibble away at legally established conservation guidelines.

In the following brief summaries, CMA stands for Consejería de Medio Ambiente, CV for Centro de Visitantes (Visitor Centre), PI for Punto de Información (Information Point) and TO for Tourist Office. 'Towns' and 'Villages' refer to good launching points for visits, in or just outside the parks.

You'll find detailed information on many of the parks in this book's provincial chapters. For official information, try W www.mma.es, the website of the national environment ministry, or W ww.cma.junta-andalucia.es, the site of the Junta de Andalucía's environmental department. These sites are in Spanish but the diagrams, maps, lists and pictures are informative even if the text means nothing to you.

Parques Nacionales National parks are declared by the national parliament and administered jointly by the national and regional governments. National parks are areas of exceptional importance for their fauna, flora, geomorphology or landscape and are the most strictly controlled protected areas. They tend to have sparse human population and may include reserve areas closed to the public, or restricted areas that can only be visited with permission. Some unscrupulous or (to give them the benefit of the doubt) ignorant tourism operators will make out that every little nature reserve, hunting reserve or periurban park on their doorstep is a 'national park'. Take no notice of them: Spain has just 13 *parques nacionales*, two of which are in Andalucía.

Doñana

Provinces: Huelva, Sevilla
Area: 507 sq km
Towns/Villages: El Rocío, Matalascañas, Sanlúcar de Barrameda
Information: CV El Acebuche (☎ 959 44 87 39); CV Fábrica de Hielo (☎ 956 38 16 35), Sanlúcar de Barrameda

Extensive wetlands near the mouth of the Río Guadalquivir, vital to Europe's water birds; 250 bird species are found here. Also dune and woodland habitats, home to several large mammal species. Visits by 4WD tour only.

Sierra Nevada

Provinces: Granada, Almería
Area: 862 sq km
Towns/Villages: Pradollano (ski station), Pampaneira, Capileira, Trevélez, Laujar de Andarax
Information: CV El Dornajo (☎ 958 34 06 25); PI Pampaneira (☎ 958 76 31 27); CV Laujar de Andarax (☎ 950 51 35 48)

Spain's biggest national park. Covers the upper reaches of the Sierra Nevada, a spectacular wilderness with 15 3000m-plus peaks, a large ibex population and many endemic plants and insects. In summer (the walking season) bus services provide access into the park.

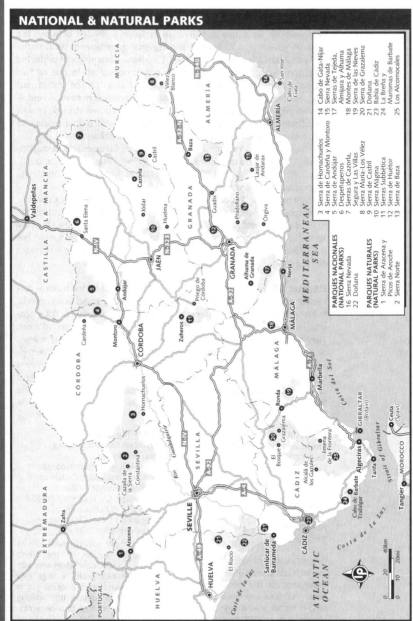

NATIONAL & NATURAL PARKS

PARQUES NACIONALES (NATIONAL PARKS)
16 Sierra Nevada
22 Doñana

PARQUES NATURALES (NATURAL PARKS)
1 Sierra de Aracena y Picos de Aroche
2 Sierra Norte
3 Sierra de Hornachuelos
4 Sierra de Cardeña y Montoro
5 Sierra de Andújar
6 Despeñaperros
7 Sierras de Cazorla, Segura y Las Villas
8 Sierra María-Los Vélez
9 Sierra de Castril
10 Sierra Mágina
11 Sierras Subbética
12 Sierra de Huétor
13 Sierra de Baza
14 Cabo de Gata-Níjar
15 Sierra Nevada
17 Sierras de Tejeda, Almijara y Alhama
18 Montes de Málaga
19 Sierra de las Nieves
20 Sierra de Grazalema
21 Doñana
23 Bahía de Cádiz
24 La Breña y Marismas de Barbate
25 Los Alcornocales

Parques Naturales Natural parks are declared and administered by regional governments; in Andalucía's case this means they're administered by the Junta de Andalucía's Consejería de Medio Ambiente (Environment Department). Andalucía's 23 natural parks account for most of its protected territory and include most of its most spectacular country.

Natural parks are intended to protect not only nature but also human cultural heritage, and to promote economic development that's compatible with conservation. Many of them include roads, villages or even small towns, with accommodation often available within the park. Camping is often restricted to organised sites. In some parks there are networks of marked walking trails. Like national parks, they may include areas which can only be visited with permission.

Bahía de Cádiz
Province: Cádiz
Area: 105 sq km
Towns: San Fernando, Cádiz, El Puerto de Santa María
Information: CMA (☎ 956 27 48 42) & TOs, Cádiz

Wetland/estuary/beach/dune habitat for birds, fish, shellfish

Cabo de Gata-Níjar
Province: Almería
Area: 497 m
Villages: El Cabo de Gata, San José, Las Negras, Agua Amarga
Information: CV Las Amoladeras (☎ 950 16 04 35)

Spectacular coastal park with nice sandy beaches, volcanic hills and cliffs, a flamingo colony and semidesert vegetation

Despeñaperros
Province: Jaén
Area: 75 sq km
Village: Santa Elena
Information: CV Puerta de Andalucía (☎ 953 66 43 07), Santa Elena

Area of forest and rocky pinnacles, traversed by the major pass into Andalucía from north; habitat of boar, deer, occasional wolves

Doñana
Provinces: Huelva, Sevilla, Cádiz
Area: 553 sq km
Towns/Villages: El Rocío, Matalascañas, Sanlúcar de Barrameda
Information: Pl Cuesta de Maneli (☎ 95 504 49 21); CV Bajo de Guía (☎ 956 36 07 15), Sanlúcar de Barrameda

Four separate areas providing a buffer for Doñana national park: wetlands, dunes, beaches, woodlands and similar fauna

La Breña y Marismas de Barbate
Province: Cádiz
Area: 48 sq km
Towns/Villages: Barbate, Los Caños de Meca
Information: CMA (☎ 956 27 48 42), Cádiz; Barbate TO (☎ 956 43 39 62)

Umbrella pine forest, beaches, 100m cliffs, wetlands

Los Alcornocales
Provinces: Cádiz, Málaga
Area: 1686 sq km
Towns/Villages: Ubrique, Alcalá de los Gazules, Tarifa, Jimena de la Frontera, Cortes de la Frontera
Information: Park office (☎ 956 41 33 07), Alcalá de los Gazules; CV Huerta Grande (☎ 956 67 91 61), Pelayo; CV Cortes de la Frontera (☎ 95 215 45 99)

Magnificent large park, with great cork oak forests rolling over the southwestern end of the Cordillera Bética, Andalucía's main mountain chain

Montes de Málaga
Province: Málaga
Area: 50 sq km
Towns/Villages: Málaga, Colmenar
Information: Ecomuseo Lagar de Torrijos (☎ 95 104 21 00)

Hilly, forested area near Málaga city

Sierra de Aracena y Picos de Aroche

Province: Huelva
Area: 1869 sq km
Towns/Villages: Aracena, Jabugo, Cortegana, Aroche, Santa Olalla del Cala
Information: CV Cabildo Viejo (☎ 959 12 88 25), Aracena

Verdant, rolling Sierra Morena country with old stone villages and good walking routes. Source of Spain's best *jamón serrano* (cured ham).

Sierra de Baza

Province: Granada
Area: 538 sq km
Towns/Villages: Baza, Charches
Information: CV Narváez (☎ 958 00 20 00)

Mountainous island of botanical variety rising from the plains of northeast Granada province

Sierra de Cardeña y Montoro

Province: Córdoba
Area: 385 sq km
Towns/Villages: Cardeña, Montoro
Information: CMA (☎ 957 23 25 04) & TOs, Córdoba

Wooded, hilly Sierra Morena park, with walking routes

Sierra de Castril

Province: Granada
Area: 127 sq km
Town: Castril
Information: CV Castril (☎ 958 72 00 59)

Transition zone between Granada's northeastern *altiplano* (high plain) and the high Cazorla mountains

Sierra de Grazalema

Provinces: Cádiz, Málaga
Area: 535 sq km
Towns/Villages: El Bosque, Ubrique, Cortes de la Frontera, Ronda, Grazalema, Zahara de la Sierra
Information: PI El Bosque (☎ 956 72 70 29); Grazalema TO (☎ 956 13 22 25); CV Zahara de la Sierra (☎ 956 12 30 14); CV Cortes de la Frontera (☎ 95 215 45 99)

Beautiful, damp, hilly region with Mediterranean woodlands, big Spanish fir grove and large griffon vulture colony – good walking country

Sierra de Hornachuelos

Province: Córdoba
Area: 672 sq km
Village: Hornachuelos
Information: CV Huerta del Rey (☎ 957 64 11 40)

Transition zone between the cultivated Guadalquivir valley and the rolling *dehesas* of the Sierra Morena, with high populations of wild boar and red deer and Andalucía's second-biggest black vulture colony. Has walking trails; also popular with hunters.

Sierra de Huétor

Province: Granada
Area: 122 sq km
Towns/Villages: Granada, Viznar
Information: CV Puerto Lobo (☎ 958 54 04 26)

Pine-forested mountains with rocky outcrops and deep gulleys, northeast of Granada city

Sierra de las Nieves

Province: Málaga
Area: 186 sq km
Towns/Villages: Ronda, El Burgo, Yunquera, Tolox
Information: PI Palacio de Mondragón (☎ 95 287 84 50), Ronda; Yunquera TO (☎ 95 248 25 01)

Dramatic, empty mountain region southeast of Ronda, with good walks, deeply eroded valleys, ibex, Spanish firs and spectacular vistas

Sierra Mágina

Province: Jaén
Area: 200 sq km
Towns/Villages: Jódar, Huelma
Information: CV Castillo de Jódar (☎ 953 78 76 56)

Isolated massif of 2000m-plus limestone mountains, with Mediterranean woodlands, unique plants, walking trails; famous for wild mushrooms

Sierra María-Los Vélez

Province: Almería
Area: 226 sq km
Towns/Villages: Vélez Blanco, Vélez Rubio, María

Information: CV Almacén del Trigo (☎ 950 41 53 54), Vélez Blanco

Beautiful mountain region, often snowy in winter, with ancient rock paintings, walking trails and a spectacular castle

Sierra Nevada
Provinces: Granada, Almería
Area: 858 sq km
Towns/Villages: Pradollano (ski station), Capileira, Trevélez, Laujar de Andarax, etc
Information: CV El Dornajo (☎ 958 34 06 25); Pl Pampaneira (☎ 958 76 31 27); CV Laujar de Andarax (☎ 950 51 35 48)

Covers the lower slopes of the Sierra Nevada, surrounding the Parque Nacional Sierra Nevada. Includes much of the lovely Las Alpujarras region on the south side of the range, with timeless villages of Muslim origin set amid orchards, woodlands and tumbling streams. Wonderful walking territory.

Sierra Norte
Province: Sevilla
Area: 1648 sq km
Towns/Villages: Constantina, Cazalla de la Sierra
Information: CV El Robledo (☎ 95 588 15 97), Constantina

Rolling Sierra Morena country; good walks, long panoramas, gorgeous spring wildflowers; Muslim-origin villages with castles and impressive churches.

Sierra de Andújar
Province: Jaén
Area: 740 sq km
Town: Andújar
Information: CV Las Viñas de Peñallana (☎ 953 54 90 30)

Large area of Sierra Morena with very sparse human population, a few wolves, lynx and Spanish imperial eagles, and lots of red deer. The Santuario de la Virgen de la Cabeza is the scene of a huge mass pilgrimage every April.

Sierras de Cazorla, Segura y Las Villas
Province: Jaén
Area: 2143 sq km
Towns/Villages: Cazorla, Hornos, Segura de la Sierra, Santiago de la Espada
Information: CV Torre del Vinagre (☎ 953 71 30 40)

Spain's largest protected area, a spectacular region of craggy mountains and deep river valleys, thickly forested and with abundant, relatively easy-to-see wildlife: red and fallow deer, wild boar, mouflon, ibex, 140 nesting bird species. Great walks, picturesque, historic villages.

Sierras de Tejeda, Almijara y Alhama
Provinces: Málaga, Granada
Area: 407 sq km
Towns/Villages: Nerja, Cómpeta, Alcaucín, Alhama de Granada
Information: CMA (Málaga ☎ 95 204 11 48 • Granada ☎ 958 24 83 02)

Covers the mountains straddling the Málaga/Granada provincial border. Has a sizable ibex population and is one of the last Andalucian redoubts of the yew (*tejo*). Good walks to the summits.

Sierras Subbéticas
Province: Córdoba
Area: 316 sq km
Towns/Villages: Zuheros, Priego de Córdoba
Information: CV Santa Rita (☎ 957 33 40 34)

Mountains, canyons, wooded valleys, castles, cave paintings, enjoyable walks

Right: Entering one of the tunnels on the Río Borosa walk, Parque Natural de Cazorla

JOHN NOBLE

Other Protected Areas Other categories of protected areas in Andalucía include *paraje natural* (natural area; there are 31 of these) and *reserva natural* (nature reserve; numbering 28). These are generally smaller, little-inhabited areas, with much the same goals as natural parks. *Parajes naturales* include Atlantic-coast wetlands such as the **Marismas del Odiel** near Huelva; some dramatic geological features in Málaga province such as the **Desfiladero de los Gaitanes** (El Chorro Gorge), the **Torcal de Antequera** and the **Sierra Crestellina** near Casares; and the **Sierra Pelada y Rivera del Aserrador**, south of Aroche in Huelva province, home to one of the world's biggest colonies of the rare black vulture. *Reservas naturales* are mostly under 10 sq km in area and include inland lakes such as **Laguna de Fuente de Piedra** in Málaga province, Spain's major flamingo habitat.

Some Spanish wilderness areas – about 900 sq km in Andalucía – are *reservas nacionales de caza* (national hunting reserves). These are often located inside protected areas such as *parques naturales*. They're usually well conserved for the sake of the wildlife that is to be hunted – which has to be exploited in a 'rational' manner. Hunting, though subject to restrictions, is a deeply ingrained aspect of Spanish life. Public access to hunting reserves is usually pretty open and you might walk or drive across one without even knowing it. If you hear gunshots, though, caution is advisable!

Getting There & Away

AIR

Andalucía has excellent air connections with other European countries. From Britain, it's usually cheaper to fly than to go overland or by sea.

The peak season for flights to Andalucía is mid-June to mid-September, although Easter is also busy.

Airports & Airlines

Málaga is Andalucía's main international airport and the cheapest flights available usually go there. Almería, Seville, Jerez de la Frontera and Gibraltar also receive some international flights. Granada airport receives internal Spanish flights only (you can get there with a transfer at Madrid or Barcelona).

Major airlines such as Spain's Iberia, British Airways (BA), Air France, Alitalia, Lufthansa Airlines and Scandinavian Airlines fly into Málaga and, in some cases, other Andalucian airports. They're generally an expensive way to fly, though advance-purchase tickets may be competitively priced and they're worth checking for special offers.

Other scheduled airlines include Monarch Airlines (from England to Málaga and Gibraltar); LTU International Airways, Air Berlin and Hapag-Lloyd from Germany to several Andalucian airports; Transavia from the Netherlands; Swiss from Switzerland; Sterling from Scandinavia; and two Spanish airlines, Air Europa and Spanair, both flying from several European countries and, in Air Europa's case, the USA.

The cheapest fares are often found on 'no-frills' airlines such as easyJet and Go (each from several UK airports to Málaga), Buzz (London to Jerez), bmibaby (East Midlands Airport, England, to Málaga), Virgin Express (to Málaga from Brussels; to Málaga from London, Copenhagen and Gothenburg, with connections at Brussels) and Basiq Air (Netherlands to Málaga).

Charter flights provide further inexpensive options from many European countries.

See the individual destination sections in this chapter for more details. Most charters go to Málaga, though Almería, Jerez de la Frontera and Seville also receive some. Non–EU passport holders are not allowed on some charter flights.

Iberia and/or its franchised carrier Air Nostrum fly domestic routes to/from all five of Andalucía's airports (not including Gibraltar). Other Spanish airlines such as Air Europa and Spanair provide further domestic flights.

Buying Tickets

With a bit of research – ringing around travel agents, checking Internet sites, perusing ads in the press – you can often get yourself a good deal. Start as early as you can: the cheapest tickets generally need to be bought well in advance, and at peak holiday periods it can be difficult to get a flight at short notice. It's usually cheaper to travel midweek and outside the main holiday periods.

Full-time students and those under 26 years (under 30 in some countries) are eligible for some special deals. Children under two years generally travel for 10% of the adult fare (or free, on some airlines) if they don't occupy a seat; they don't get a baggage allowance. Children aged between two and 12 years can usually occupy a seat for 50% of the regular fare or 67% of a discounted fare (but usually pay full fare on charter flights and no-frills airlines); they do get a baggage allowance.

Often there is nothing to be gained by buying a ticket direct from an airline. The cheapest deals are released to selected travel agents. But one important exception to this rule is the no-frills airlines who sell direct to travellers. Unlike the 'full-service' airlines, these carriers often make one-way tickets available at around half the return fare, making it easy and inexpensive to put together a ticket that allows you to fly into one place and out of another.

The other exception is booking on the Internet. Many airlines, full-service and no-frills, offer some excellent fares to Web surfers. They may sell seats by auction or simply cut prices to reflect the reduced cost of electronic selling.

Many travel agencies around the world have websites, which can make the Internet a quick and easy way to compare prices. There are also an increasing number of online agents, such as ⓦ www.travelocity.co.uk and ⓦ www.deckchair.com, who operate only on the Internet.

The cheapest flights may be advertised by obscure agencies. Most such firms are honest and solvent, but there are some rogue outfits. Paying by credit card generally offers protection, as most card issuers provide refunds if you can prove you didn't get what you paid for. Similar protection can be obtained by buying a ticket from a bonded agent, such as one covered by the Air Travel Organiser's Licence (ATOL) scheme in the UK (ⓦ www.atol.org.uk).

After you've made a booking or paid your deposit, call the airline and confirm that the booking has been made.

Travellers with Special Needs

If warned early enough, airlines can often make special arrangements for travellers, such as wheelchair assistance at airports or vegetarian meals on board. For babies, 'skycots', baby food and nappies should be provided by the airline if requested in advance. The disability-friendly website ⓦ www.allgohere.com has an airline directory providing information on the facilities offered by various airlines.

Departure Tax

Air fares are usually quoted with taxes included, but sometimes you have to add them to the ticket price. Taxes depend where you are flying to and from but generally range between about €8 and €20 per flight.

The Rest of Spain

Flying within Spain is most worth considering if you're in a hurry and you're making a longish one-way or a return trip.

Spain's biggest airline, Iberia, and its franchised carrier Air Nostrum fly daily (in some cases several times a day) nonstop from Madrid and Barcelona to all of Andalucía's airports, and from Bilbao and Valencia to Seville and Málaga. Iberia one-way/return fares from Madrid to Seville, for instance, are around €120/200. Cheaper return tickets (around €110) are available if you return within two weeks but stay at least one Saturday night. The equivalent Barcelona–Málaga fares are around €190/250 and €180.

Air Europa's nonstop routes include Madrid–Málaga, Barcelona–Seville, Palma de Mallorca–Granada, Palma de Mallorca–Seville and Bilbao–Málaga. Spanair flies Barcelona–Málaga, Madrid–Jerez, Madrid–Málaga, Madrid–Seville and Palma de Mallorca–Málaga. Both these airlines offer connections at Madrid to/from many other Spanish cities. Their standard fares are similar to Iberia's, but they're well worth checking for special deals: at the time of writing, Air Europa offers included Barcelona–Seville or Madrid–Málaga for €48/73 one way/return.

The UK & Ireland

The weekend national newspapers have ads and information on cheap fares. In London also try the *Evening Standard*, *Time Out* and the free magazine *TNT*.

No-Frills Airlines You buy flights direct from these budget airlines, not through travel agents, and can usually obtain a small discount by buying on the airlines' websites. You often don't get a ticket, just a confirmation number to quote at check-in. On board, you pay extra for all food and drink. Fares on a flight increase as tickets sell, so if you book well in advance you can find some real bargains. The no-frills market is highly competitive, with new routes emerging all the time and super-bargain deals being widely advertised when business is slow. Once one-way UK–Spain fares top about UK£70 it's time to start thinking about alternatives.

Easyjet flies from London Gatwick, Luton and Liverpool to Málaga and other Spanish airports, with one-way fares starting at around UK£35. At Luton you can connect with easyJet flights to/from Belfast and several Scottish airports.

Go flies to Málaga and other Spanish cities from London Stansted, Bristol and East Midlands airports. The cheapest fares are around UK£40 each way, but to be eligible you need to fly both ways with Go. Like easyJet, Go has connections to other British airports.

Buzz flies from London Stansted to Jerez and also to Murcia, which is outside Andalucía but worth considering as it's only about 200km from Almería. One-way fares start at around UK£70 to Jerez and UK£50 to Murcia.

Bmibaby flies daily from East Midlands to Málaga (starting at around UK£45 one way) and a few times weekly to Murcia.

Virgin Express offers London–Málaga flights starting at around UK£80 one way, with a connection in Brussels.

CityJet flies Dublin–Málaga with fares starting at around €300 return.

Discount & Charter Flights Discounted tickets for scheduled flights and tickets for charter flights are sold by travel agencies, which advertise in the press and on the Internet. Most British travel agents are registered with ABTA (Association of British

Travel Agents). If you have bought a flight ticket from an ABTA-registered agent that goes out of business, ABTA will guarantee a refund or an alternative. Unregistered agencies are riskier but sometimes cheaper.

Charter flights can be among the cheapest of all flights, though you must often fly back within a fairly short period (one or two weeks is typical). Arrival and departure times can be inconvenient – even more so if they are delayed – and remember that if you miss your charter flight, you have lost your money. Try these agencies for good deals from anywhere in the UK:

Avro (☎ 0870 036 0111, W www.avro.com)
JMC (☎ 0870 010 0434, W www.jmc.com)
Lunn Poly (☎ 0870 165 5000, W www.lunnpoly.com)

Some discount agencies are better established than others and have a long track record of reliability; they may also sell non-discounted fares. **STA Travel** (☎ 0870 160 0599; W www.statravel.co.uk; 86 Old Brompton Rd, London SW7), with 44 other branches around the UK, caters especially to students and travellers under 26, but sells tickets to all travellers. Other recommended agencies include:

Flightbookers (☎ 020-7757 2000, W www.ebookers.com) 177–178 Tottenham Court Rd, London W1
Trailfinders (☎ 020-7937 1234, W www.trail finders.co.uk) 215 Kensington High St, London W8, with branches in Glasgow, Dublin, Belfast, Bristol, Birmingham, Cambridge, Manchester and Newcastle-upon-Tyne

Also worth looking into for cheap flights are:

Spanish Travel Services (☎ 020-7387 5337, W www.apatraveluk.com) 138 Eversholt St, London NW1 1BL – this firm also organises city breaks, accommodation on the Costa de la Luz and in rural areas, and a range of other services in Spain
Tarleton Direct (☎ 01604-633633, W www.tarle tondirect.co.uk) 353 Wellingborough Rd, Northampton NN1 4ER – Tarleton sells charter flights to Almería from London Gatwick, Manchester, Birmingham and Glasgow for about UK£140 to UK£200 return

Some ticket agencies work largely, or only, via the Internet. You can get quotes, book and pay (by credit card) online. Many of those already mentioned offer online booking. Also worth checking are:

- ⓦ www.lastminute.com
- ⓦ www.dialaflight.com
- ⓦ www.airnet.co.uk
- ⓦ www.opodo.co.uk and
- ⓦ www.expedia.co.uk

The range of discount and charter fares is broad. Advertised UK£69 London–Málaga return fares are often unavailable if you try to buy them, or turn out to be nearer UK£100 when you add taxes, late-booking surcharges etc. But with luck you can get a return charter flight for under UK£100 at most times of year except in the summer high season. Discounted tickets with scheduled airlines are likely to be between UK£100 and UK£150. From other British airports, return fares average UK£20 to UK£50 more than from London. From Ireland, getting to London first may save you money. Fares to Seville and charter flights to Almería are similar to Málaga fares. Otherwise, flying into any Andalucian airport other than Málaga will generally cost a bit more.

Scheduled Airlines On BA and Iberia, economy return fares between London and Málaga or Seville generally range from UK£150 to UK£250. BA flies from London to Gibraltar for similar fares. All these BA flights are operated by a franchise carrier, GB Airways.

Monarch Airlines flies from Luton to Málaga and Gibraltar and from Manchester to Málaga. The cheapest available one-way/return fares range from about UK£50/90 to UK£145/250 depending when you travel and when you book.

Air Europa flies daily from London Gatwick to Málaga, with a transfer at Madrid, with regular return fares starting at around UK£240, but special offers can cut that to about UK£140.

Aer Lingus flies Dublin–Málaga direct; fares start at around €150 each way.

Continental Europe

Except for very short hops, air fares often beat overland alternatives on cost. For information and bookings Europewide, try ⓦ www.opodo.com.

France Charter or discounted return flights from Paris to Málaga or Seville start at around €250. Airlines flying direct include Corsair, Air France and Iberia. Air Europa and Spanair offer competitive fares, with a connection at Madrid.

France's student travel agencies can usually supply discount tickets to travellers of all ages. **OTU Voyages** (☎ 01 44 41 38 50; ⓦ www.otu.fr; 39 av Georges Bernanos, 75005 Paris) has a central Paris office and many other branches around the country.

Another place to look for good fares is **Nouvelles Frontières** (☎ 08 25 00 08 25; ⓦ www.nouvelles-frontieres.fr; 87 blvd de Grenelle, 75015 Paris), with other branches around the country.

A useful website is ⓦ www.anyway.fr.

Germany Return flights to Málaga from most German airports can usually be found for €200 to €250. There are some deals under €200 on airlines such as Hapag-Lloyd, Air Berlin and LTU International Airlines if you can meet the conditions. However, you may need to pay €300 or more in high summer or for late bookings, or for another Andalucian airport besides Málaga.

A recommended agency is **STA Travel** (☎ 030 311 0950; ⓦ www.statravel.de; Goethesttrasse 73, 10625 Berlin), with other branches in major cities around the country. Online agencies worth consulting include: ⓦ www.justtravel.de, ⓦ www.lastminute.de and ⓦ www.expedia.de.

Netherlands & Belgium The no-frills airline Basiq Air, owned by Transavia, flies daily from Amsterdam and Rotterdam to Málaga, with one-way fares starting around €80. For other fares from the Netherlands, try **Holland International** (☎ 070 307 6307), with offices in most Dutch cities, or ⓦ www.airfair.nl.

Liberal quantities of olive oil, fresh ingredients, succulent cured hams and fine wines are all staples of traditional Andalucian cuisine

From religious celebrations to fighting bulls, Andalucians indulge their love of colour, noise, crowds, pageant and partying at innumerable festivals and events throughout the year

Contacting Airlines

Here are some selected airline contact details:

Aer Lingus
W www.aerlingus.com
Spain: ☎ 91 541 42 16
UK: ☎ 0845 973 7747
US: ☎ 800-IRISH AIR
Ireland: ☎ 0818 365000

Air Berlin
W www.airberlin.com
Spain: ☎ 901 11 64 02
Germany: ☎ 01801-737 800

Air Europa
W www.air-europa.com
Spain: ☎ 902 40 15 01
UK: ☎ 0870 240 1501
US: ☎ 212-921 2381
France: ☎ 01 42 97 40 00

Air Nostrum
W www.iberia.com
Spain: ☎ 902 40 05 00
UK: ☎ 0845 601 2854
US: ☎ 800-772 4642

Air Plus Comet
W www.aircomet.com
Spain: ☎ 91 203 63 00
US: ☎ 212-983 1277,
877-999 7587

Basiq Air
W www.basiqair.com
Spain: ☎ 902 11 44 78
Netherlands: ☎ 0900 227
4724

bmibaby
W www.bmibaby.com
Spain: ☎ 902 10 07 37
UK: ☎ 0870 264 2229

British Airways
W www.britishairways.com
Spain: ☎ 902 11 13 33
UK: ☎ 0845 773 3377
US: ☎ 800-AIRWAYS
Gibraltar: ☎ 79300

Buzz
W www.buzzaway.com
Spain: ☎ 91 749 66 33
UK: ☎ 0870 240 7070

CityJet
W www.cityjet.com
Ireland: ☎ 01-844 5566

easyJet
W www.easyjet.com
Spain: ☎ 902 29 99 92
UK: ☎ 0870 600 0000

GB Airways
W www.britishairways.com
Spain: ☎ 902 11 13 33
UK: ☎ 0845 773 3377
US: ☎ 800-AIRWAYS
Gibraltar: ☎ 79300

Go
W www.go-fly.com
Spain: ☎ 901 33 35 00
UK: ☎ 0870 607 6543

Iberia
W www.iberia.com
France: W www.iberia.fr
Spain: ☎ 902 40 05 00
UK: ☎ 0845 601 2854
US: ☎ 800 772 4642
France: ☎ 08 20 07 50 75
Ireland: ☎ 01-407 3017
Morocco: ☎ 022-279600
Portugal: ☎ 21-355 81 51

LTU International Airways
W www.ltu.de
Spain: ☎ 95 204 86 96
US: ☎ 866-266 5588
Germany: ☎ 0211-94 18 888

Monarch Airlines
W www.fly-crown.com
Spain: ☎ 95 204 83 47
UK: ☎ 0870 040 5040
Gibraltar: ☎ 47477

Portugália Airlines
W www.pga.pt
Spain: ☎ 902 100 145
UK: ☎ 0870 755 0025
Portugal: ☎ 21-842 55 59

Royal Air Maroc
W www.royalairmaroc.com
UK: W www.royalairmaroc.co.uk
Spain: W www.royalairmaroc-es
.com
France: W www.royalairmaroc.fr
Spain: ☎ 902 21 00 10
UK: ☎ 020-7439 4361
US: ☎ 800-344 6726
Morocco: ☎ 0900 00 800
France: ☎ 08 20 82 18 21

Spanair
W www.spanair.com
Spain: ☎ 902 13 14 15
France: ☎ 01 53 43 26 35
Germany: ☎ 01805-680 681

Virgin Express
W www.virgin-express.com
Spain: ☎ 91 662 52 61
UK: ☎ 020-7744 0004
Belgium: ☎ 070 35 36 37
Denmark: ☎ 35 25 68 00
Sweden: ☎ 020 84 74 46

Virgin Express flies Brussels–Málaga with one-way fares from €100. Recommended Belgian agencies include **Connections** (☎ 02550 01 00; W www.connections.be; 19-21 rue du Midi, 1000 Brussels), a student- and youth-travel specialist, and **Nouvelles**

Frontières (☎ 02 547 44 44; W www.nou velles-frontieres.be; 2 blvd Maurice Lemmonier, 1000 Brussels). Both have branches in other Belgian cities.

Portugal Portugália Airlines flies daily nonstop between Lisbon and Málaga. One-way/return tickets are available for around €245/265 on websites such as W www .opodo.com – poor value one way, but the return fare is only marginally more than for routings via Madrid with airlines such as Iberia or Spanair.

The USA

The only direct flights between the USA and Andalucía at the time of writing are the twice-weekly (Wednesday and Thursday) flights between New York and Málaga by the Spanish airline Air Plus Comet. Plenty of flights with transfers in Madrid or another European city are available using airlines such as Delta, Continental, American Airlines, Iberia, British Airways, Air France, Lufthansa and Air Europa. Fares via Barcelona, London, Paris or Frankfurt are not necessarily more expensive than via Madrid.

Discount travel agents can be found through the *Yellow Pages* or the major daily newspapers. The *New York Times, Los Angeles Times, Chicago Tribune* and *San Francisco Chronicle* all produce weekly travel sections in which you'll find a number of travel agency ads. The Internet is another useful source of fare information and bookings; try W www.travelocity.com, W www .or bitz.com, W www.expedia.com, W www .lowestfare.com, W www.smarterliving .com, W air.onetravel.com, or W www .discount-airfare.com.

America's largest student travel organisation, **STA Travel** (☎ 800-777 0112; W www .statravel.com), has offices in several major cities. It sells youth, adult, teacher and student air fares.

Booking well ahead, you should be able to get a New York–Málaga return ticket for around US$650 to US$750 in low season or US$1000 to US$1150 in high season. Booking just a week or two before travel can add hundreds of dollars to those prices.

Price differences between the east and west coasts are generally between US$100 and US$300.

Standby & Courier Flights Standby one-way fares are often sold at 60% of the full price. **Airhitch** (☎ 800 326 2009; W www .airhitch.org) is a specialist: one-way fares from the USA to Western Europe can cost under US$200.

Courier flights are occasionally advertised in the newspapers, or you could contact air-freight companies listed in the phone book. You may even have to visit the company – they aren't always keen to give information over the phone. Most flights depart from New York. A New York–Madrid low-season return fare can cost less than US$300. Arrangements often have to be made a month or more in advance. For more information, contact the **International Association of Air Travel Couriers** (IAATC; ☎ 561-582 8320; W www.courier.org).

Canada

Canada's main student-travel organisation, **Travel CUTS** (☎ 800 667 2887; W www.travel cuts.com), known as Voyages Campus in Quebec, has offices in all major cities. Otherwise, scan the ads for fares in the *Globe & Mail, Toronto Star, Montreal Gazette* and *Vancouver Sun*, or check some of the websites mentioned under The USA earlier. Round trips from Montreal or Toronto to Málaga cost between about C$1000 and C$1800 depending on when you fly and when you book. The best fares are usually with some combination of Air Canada, British Airways, Iberia and Spanair, with a transfer in Madrid or London. Flights from Vancouver cost anything from C$200 more.

Morocco

Iberia and Royal Air Maroc fly from Málaga to Casablanca daily with a code-sharing arrangement. Return fares are around €240 to €300. Morocco's Regional Air Lines flies direct from Málaga to Casablanca (around €260/300 one way/ return) and Tangier (€165/285) daily. You can book through Spanair.

Iberia's franchised carrier Air Nostrum flies daily nonstop to Melilla, the Spanish enclave on the Moroccan coast, from Málaga, Almería and Granada, with return fares starting at around €125 (€145 from Granada).

Australia

As there are no direct connections from Australia to Spain, you will have to fly to Europe via Asia, the Middle East or (less often) America, and change flights, if not airlines, at least once.

Sydney–Málaga return tickets on mainstream airlines through reputable agents start at around A$2000 for February departures, and A$2500 for August.

The Saturday editions of the *Age* in Melbourne and the *Sydney Morning Herald* advertise cheap fares. **STA Travel** (☎ 13 17 76; W *www.statravel.com.au*) and **Flight Centre** (☎ 13 16 00; W *www.flightcentre.com.au*) are well-known dealers in cheap air fares. The website W www.travel.com.au is worth consulting too. Remember that heavily discounted fares can often be found at your local travel agent.

New Zealand

Fares are advertised in the *New Zealand Herald* travel section. **STA Travel** (☎ 0508 782872; W *www.statravel.co.nz*) and **Flight Centre** (Auckland ☎ 0800 243544; W *www .flightcentre.co.nz*) are popular travel agencies with offices around the country. The cheapest Auckland–Madrid fares are generally via Asia or the USA. Expect to pay around NZ$2400 for a return flight during the low season. Round-the-world tickets can sometimes be cheaper.

Flights from Andalucía

For flights out of Andalucía, look into the no-frills carriers and local agencies such as **Flightline International** (☎ 902 20 22 40; W *www.flightline.es*), **Servitour** (☎ 902 40 00 69; W *www.servitour.es*) and **Travelshop** (☎ 95 246 42 27; W *www.thetravelshop .com*). Advertisements in local foreign-language papers such as *Sur in English* are worth a look too. Bargain one-way fares from Gibraltar to London are sometimes available from British Airways (operated by GB Airways) or Monarch Airlines.

Outside peak seasons you might find one-way Málaga–London tickets for under €100; in August they may be €200. You can always go to Málaga airport early in the morning and ask around for standby tickets. You might not get a flight that day – but if you do it will be cheap. For agencies selling flights out of Almería, see the Almería section in the Almería Province chapter.

The Granada and Seville city sections in the Granada Province and Sevilla Province chapters in this book have details of student-travel agencies in those cities.

LAND

If you're travelling overland to Spain, check whether you require visas for the countries you pass through. An excellent website providing European train timetable information in English and German is operated by **Die Bahn** (W *www.bahn.de*).

The Rest of Spain

You could reach Andalucía in a day from almost any corner of Spain by bus, train or your own vehicle. On some long-haul runs buses are cheaper and/or quicker than trains; on others it's the opposite.

Bus Daily buses to all main and many smaller Andalucian cities leave from Madrid's **Estación Sur de Autobuses** (☎ 91 468 42 00; Calle Méndez Álvaro; metro Méndez Álvaro). In Barcelona, buses to Andalucía go from the **Estació del Nord** (☎ 93 265 65 08; Carrer d'Alí Bei 80; metro Arc de Triomf). Buses from Barcelona stop at the main cities and towns along Spain's Mediterranean coast. Other buses to Andalucía include services to Seville from Extremadura, Castilla y León and Galicia.

Here are examples of journey times and one-way fares for bus travel within Spain:

from	to	fare (€)	duration (hrs)
Barcelona	Granada	50	12–14
Cáceres	Seville	14	4
Madrid	Córdoba	10.25	4½
Madrid	Málaga	17	6

Train Most main-line trains of **Renfe** *(Red Nacional de Ferrocarriles Españoles, Spanish National Railways; countrywide information & reservations ☎ 902 24 02 02; **W** www.renfe .es)* are reliable and quick. The quickest are the AVE (Alta Velocidad Española) trains, which cover the 471km from Madrid to Seville, via Córdoba, in around 2½ hours, reaching speeds of 280km/h. (If an AVE arrives more than five minutes late due to a delay attributable to Renfe, you get a refund; but don't get excited, as this happens extremely rarely.)

For train information you can go to a station or Renfe's city centre ticket offices, call Renfe's national information and reservations number, or visit Renfe's helpful website, which provides all schedules and fares, offers online booking and gives locations of other ticket sales points (in English and Spanish).

The map 'Approaches to Andalucía' shows the rail routes into Andalucía from other parts of Spain.

Daytime Trains The terms *grandes líneas* and *largo recorrido* refer to trains travelling 400km or more. Most have 1st- and 2nd-class carriages (usually called *preferente* and *turista*, respectively), and all except some night trains have catering. Basic long-distance daytime trains are *diurnos*. More comfortable, marginally more expensive daytime trains with fewer stops are called InterCity. Even more comfortable and expensive trains are called Talgo. A Talgo 200 is a Talgo that uses the high-speed AVE line between Madrid and destinations such as Málaga, Cádiz, Huelva and Algeciras.

The most expensive way to go is to take the AVE on the Madrid–Córdoba–Seville line. Even in *turista* class, passengers have access to everything from videos and telephones to children's games and facilities for the disabled.

Regionales and *cercanías* are local, shorter-distance trains – see the Getting Around chapter.

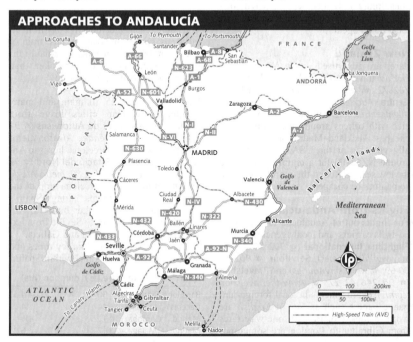

APPROACHES TO ANDALUCÍA

Road Distances (km)

	Almería	Barcelona	Bilbao	Cádiz	Córdoba	Gibraltar	Granada	Huelva	Jaén	Madrid	Málaga	Seville
Almería	---											
Barcelona	809	---										
Bilbao	958	620	---									
Cádiz	484	1284	1058	---								
Córdoba	332	908	796	263	---							
Gibraltar	346	1124	1110	127	314	---						
Granada	166	868	829	355	166	256	---					
Huelva	516	1140	939	219	232	291	350	---				
Jaén	228	804	730	367	104	336	99	336	---			
Madrid	563	621	395	663	400	714	434	632	335	---		
Málaga	219	997	939	265	187	127	129	313	209	544	---	
Seville	422	1046	933	125	138	197	256	94	242	538	219	---

Night Trains The most basic type of overnight train, the *estrella*, usually has seats, couchettes and sleeping compartments. The more common *trenhotel* is a sleek, comfortable, expensive sleeping-car-only train. First class on these tends to be called *gran clase*, and 2nd class *turista*.

Couchettes, called *literas*, are fold-out bunk beds (generally six to a compartment). A couchette ticket costs about €9 more than a seat. More comfortable sleeping accommodation ranges from shared cabins to luxury singles. Prices depend on the distance you travel.

Reservations On most trains you don't need to book in advance, but for busy services it's advisable to do so. Bookings can be made at stations, Renfe offices, many travel agents, by telephone to the national reservations number ☎ 902 24 02 02, and online at W www.renfe.es (except for overnight and international trains and some short-distance local services). Whichever way you book, there's usually no booking fee.

Costs A time saving of a couple of hours on a faster train can mean a big hike in the fare.

Fares quoted elsewhere in this guide are basic 2nd-class seat fares.

Your fare depends first on the type of train. Then it's a question of class. On daytime trains you generally have the easy choice of *turista* (2nd class) or *preferente* (1st class). AVEs also have a super-1st class called *club*. Night trains offer varied combinations of *turista* or *preferente* seats, couchettes and *camas* (sleeping compartments).

In some cases, especially AVE and Talgo 200 trains, the fare also depends on the time you travel. The cheaper times are called *valle* and the more expensive *llano*.

The following fares available from Madrid to Seville illustrate the range of possibilities:

train	class	
	one-way fare (€)	duration (hrs)
Talgo	*turista/preferente*	
	45.50/66	3½
Talgo 200	*turista/preferente*	
	51.50/76.50	3¼
AVE (*valle*)	*turista/preferente/club*	
	52.50/78.50/94	2½
AVE (*llano*)	*turista/preferente/club*	
	62/92/110.50	2¼–2½

Examples of other one-way 2nd- or *turista*-class seat fares include:

from	to	fare (€)	duration (hrs)
Barcelona	Granada	46–47	11¼–12¼
Cáceres	Seville	14.05	5¾
Marid	Córdoba	24–45.50	1¾–5½
Madrid	Málaga	29.50–52	4¼–7¾

Return fares in Spain are generally 20% less than two one-way fares. Children aged under four years travel free; those from four to 11 (to 12 on some trains) get 40% off the cost of seats and couchettes. The Euro<26 card (see Visas & Documents in the Facts for the Visitor chapter for details) gives 20% off Spanish long-distance and regional train fares, and 25% to 40% off the fast AVE and Talgo 200 services.

Car & Motorcycle Spain's main roads are good. You can drive from Barcelona to Málaga in eight hours (though at a sane pace it's closer to 11).

The main highway from Madrid to Andalucía is the N-IV to Córdoba, Seville and Cádiz. For Jaén, Granada, Almería or Málaga, get off at Bailén. The N-401 becoming the N-420, heads from Madrid to Córdoba via Toledo and Ciudad Real.

From the ferry ports at Santander or Bilbao or the French border at Irún, the most direct route is to head for Burgos, from which it's a pretty straight 240km to Madrid. The main Irún–Bilbao and Bilbao–Burgos highways are each subject to tolls of about €12.

The A-7 leads down the Mediterranean side of Spain from La Jonquera on the French border as far as Murcia. Tolls between La Jonquera and Alicante total €43.90, and toll-free alternative roads tend to be busy and slow. At Murcia the toll-free N-340 takes over as the main road and continues to Almería: branch off it along the A-92-N for Granada and Málaga.

The N-630 heads all the way down to Seville from Gijón on Spain's north coast, through Castilla y León and Extremadura.

See the Getting Around chapter for some general information on driving in Spain.

Bicycle If you get tired of pedalling, it's often possible to take your bike on a bus (usually you'll just be asked to remove the front wheel). To take a bike on a train, you must comply with numerous conditions. On long-distance trains you have to be travelling overnight in a sleeper or couchette, and you have to remove the pedals and pack the bike in a specially designed container.

The UK

Bus Buses from Britain to Andalucía cost more than the cheapest flights. **Eurolines** *(UK* ☎ *0870 514 3219 • Málaga* ☎ *95 236 33 45;* **w** *www.eurolines.com)*, a confederation of European coach companies, runs two or three times weekly from London's Victoria coach station to Córdoba, Seville (34½ hours) and, with a change of buses in Madrid, to Jaén, Granada (33 hours), Málaga (35 hours), Torremolinos, Fuengirola, Marbella (37 hours), Estepona and Algeciras (38 hours). One-way/return fares to all stops in Andalucía are UK£91/139 (a little less for 13- to 25-year-olds and 60-or-overs, a little more during July and August). Euro-apex return fares, on which you must book a week ahead and return within a month of going, are UK£84.

Train The simplest and quickest route from London involves the Eurostar Channel Tunnel service from Waterloo to Paris, changing from Gare du Nord to Gare d'Austerlitz in Paris, taking an overnight sleeper-only train to Madrid's Chamartin station, and then taking an AVE or Talgo 200 to Andalucía. You will probably also have to change stations in Madrid. The best services to central and western Andalucía use the expensive AVE line from Madrid's Atocha station for part of their route.

Leaving Waterloo at about 2pm, you can reach Seville by 12.30pm the next day, or Málaga at 4.30pm. Fares vary according to the time of year and day of the week you travel, how far ahead you book, your age and in all likelihood the train driver's daughter's birthday, but you're looking at around UK£235 return to Seville if you book 30 days ahead (a little less to Málaga or Granada, or if you're under 26).

To cut costs – and add time – you can take a more economical Paris–Madrid service such as the 11.55pm (departing from Paris Montparnasse station and changing trains at Irún on the France–Spain border), and catch a cheaper train from Madrid to Andalucía.

For information on rail travel from Britain, contact **Rail Europe** (☎ *0870 584 8848;* ⓦ *www.raileurope.co.uk; 179 Piccadilly, London W1)* or **Eurostar** *(UK ☎ 0870 518 6186, France ☎ 08 36 35 35 39;* ⓦ *www .eurostar.com).* For information and bookings on Spanish railways in the UK, contact **Prestige International UK** (☎ *020 7499 9100;* ⓦ *www.spanishrail.co.uk; Berkeley Square House, Berkeley Square, London W1).* For more on trains within Spain, see under The Rest of Spain earlier.

Car & Motorcycle If you just want to drive *in* Andalucía, it's not usually worth taking your own vehicle. Two people should be able to get return flights from London to Málaga and two weeks' car hire for a total of UK£350 to UK£500, depending on the time of year. But if you plan to stay in Andalucía several weeks and want a car most of the time, driving from home can work out cheaper.

The options for getting your vehicle from Britain to continental Europe are threefold: you can use Eurotunnel – the Channel Tunnel car train from Folkestone to Calais; or put your vehicle on a cross-channel ferry to France; or use the direct vehicle ferries from England to Bilbao or Santander in northern Spain (from which it's possible to reach Andalucía in one long day).

Using Eurotunnel or a ferry to France, then driving pretty hard to Andalucía, should cost between UK£600 and UK£800 for a return trip for two people, including petrol, food and one night's accommodation each way en route. To this, add about UK£70 each way for road tolls if you use the quickest routes.

Eurotunnel *(UK ☎ 0870 535 3535 , France ☎ 03 21 00 61 00;* ⓦ *www.eurotunnel.com)* runs around the clock, with up to four crossings (35 minutes) an hour. You pay for the vehicle only. Economy return fares, booked a minimum 14 days ahead, range from about UK£280 to UK£380 for a car and UK£150 to UK£210 for a motorcycle, depending on the season, day of week and time of day.

See under The Rest of Spain earlier in this chapter for a summary of routes through Spain, and under Sea later for more details of the ferry options.

Paperwork & Preparations Proof of ownership of a private vehicle (Vehicle Registration Document for UK-registered cars), driving licence, roadworthiness certificate (MOT), and either an insurance certificate or a 'Green Card' should always be carried when driving in Europe. See Visas & Documents in the Facts for the Visitor chapter for further information on driving licences.

Third-party motor insurance is a minimum requirement throughout Europe. If you live in the EU, your existing motor insurance will probably provide automatic third-party cover throughout the EU: this is certainly the case with all UK car insurance policies. But check with your insurer about whether you will also be covered for medical or hospital expenses or accidental damage to your vehicle. You might have to pay an extra premium if you want the same protection abroad as you have at home. A European breakdown assistance policy such as the AA Five Star Service or the RAC Eurocover Motoring Assistance is also a good investment.

The Green Card is an internationally recognised document showing that you have the minimum insurance cover required by law in the country visited. It is provided free by insurers. If you're carrying an insurance certificate that gives the minimum legal cover, a Green Card is not essential, but it has the advantage of being easily recognised by foreign police and authorities.

Also ask your insurer for a European Accident Statement form, which can simplify matters in the event of an accident.

In Spain it's compulsory to carry two warning triangles (to be used in the event of a breakdown). If the car is from the UK or Ireland, remember to adjust the headlights for driving in mainland Europe (motor accessory shops sell stick-on strips which deflect the beams in the required direction).

In the UK, further information is available from the **RAC** (☎ *0870 572 2722;* ⓦ *www .rac.co.uk*) or the **AA** (☎ *0870 550 0600;* ⓦ *www.theaa.co.uk*).

Rental If you plan to rent a car in Andalucía, it's a good idea to organise it before you leave. So many car-hire firms now offer booking by Internet that this is easily accomplished, either with a local agency in Spain (usually the cheapest option), a major international car-hire company such as Avis, Hertz etc (the most expensive option), or a British firm such as Holiday Autos and Transhire, which act as an intermediary between you and local renters in other countries (the intermediate option in price). As a general rule, it's considerably cheaper to pick up your car at a major tourist point such as Málaga or Almería airport, or resorts on the holiday coasts, than at places such as Seville or Granada in inland Andalucía.

If you're thinking of using one of the big international companies, you can save a lot of money by booking through their British branches (even by phone or Internet from Spain) than through their Spanish offices: a sample comparison of the Avis' UK and Spain websites as we researched this edition gave us prices of UK£131 and €387 (about UK£244), respectively, for the same small car to be rented for the same August week from Málaga airport.

Holiday Autos (☎ *0870 400 0099;* ⓦ *www .holidayautos.co.uk*) offers cars for pickup at any airport and a variety of other locations in Andalucía, with prices for four-seat cars starting at around UK£80 a week in winter and UK£110 a week in August. **Transhire** (☎ *0870 789 8000;* ⓦ *www.transhire.com*) also has good rates and numerous Andalucian pickup locations. Both firms offer on-line booking. Many Internet air-ticket sites also offer car hire.

Booking direct with local Spanish agencies can cost even less and in many cases can also be done by Internet: see Car & Motorcycle in the Getting Around chapter for further details, and for general information on driving in Spain.

Bicycle People do make their way to Andalucía by bike – best in spring, early summer or autumn. Bicycles can also travel by air: usually you can check them in as a piece of baggage, but confirm this with the airline in advance, preferably before you pay for your ticket.

France

Bus Eurolines (*Paris* ☎ *08 36 69 52 52;* ⓦ *www.eurolines.com.fr*) runs to several Andalucian cities from numerous points around France. For example, Paris–Granada (24 hours) costs €125/210 one way/return (€113/189 if you're under 26 or over 60).

Train Most routes enter Spain at Irún, on the Bay of Biscay, or Portbou on the Mediterranean, and all involve at least one change of train (usually in Madrid). The only direct train between France and Madrid is the overnight, sleeper-only *trenhotel* (No 409) leaving Paris Austerlitz about 7.45pm and arriving at Madrid Chamartin at about 9am. Couchette tickets purchased at least seven days in advance for travel between mid-September and mid-June cost €55 one way. Standard one-way/return couchette fares are €111/189 (€122/208 from mid-June to mid-September), but it's a bit less for those under 26 and over 60.

Trains from Madrid (usually Atocha station) get you to the main Andalucian cities in a few hours for between €26 and €62.

Car & Motorcycle See the UK section earlier for general information on taking a vehicle across Europe. The main highways from France into Spain run to Barcelona and San Sebastián at either end of the Pyrénées. There are good routes from both borders (see under The Rest of Spain earlier for a note on tolls).

Portugal

Bus Portugal's **EVA Transportes** (*Lisbon* ☎ *213 147 710; Terminal Rodoviário Arco do Cego • Albufeira* ☎ *289 587 526; Ribeira Parque • Beja* ☎ *284 313 620; Rodoviária do Alentejo • Faro* ☎ *289 899 760; Avenida da República 5 • Lagos* ☎ *282 762 944; Rossio de*

São João) and Spain's **Damas** *(Seville ☎ 95 490 80 40; Estación de Autobuses Plaza de Armas • Huelva ☎ 959 25 69 00; Estación de Autobuses)* run joint services between Portugal and Andalucía. Buses from Lisbon to Seville (€28.25, 4½ hours) go via Beja, Serpa, Rosal de la Frontera and Aracena, leaving Lisbon at 8.30am Tuesday, Thursday and Saturday, and starting back from Seville (Plaza de Armas bus station) at 9.30am Monday, Wednesday and Friday. (It's also possible to cover the same route any day by changing from a Portuguese to a Spanish Casal bus at the frontier – Vila Verde de Ficalho on the Portuguese side, Rosal de la Frontera on the Spanish – but this takes about 10 hours, costing about €23 in all. Two services go daily in each direction.) EVA and Damas also run twice each way daily between Lagos and Seville (€14.80, 4½ hours) via Albufeira and Huelva, and (except Sundays from October to March) between Faro and Huelva (2¼ hours) via Tavira, Vila Real de Santo António and Ayamonte. The latter service has connections to/from Albufeira at Faro, and to/from Seville at Huelva: a Faro–Seville trip (four hours) costs €10.45.

The Spanish company **Alsa** *(☎ 902 42 22 42; W www.alsa.es)*, part of the Eurolines confederation, travels three or four times a week from Lisbon's Terminal Rodoviário Arco do Cego to Málaga bus station (€49 one way, 14½ hours), via Setubal, Évora, Elvas, Badajoz, Seville (Plaza de Armas bus station; €32, eight hours), Cádiz (Viajes Rico, Glorieta Ingeniero La Cierva; €41, 9½ hours), Algeciras and the Costa del Sol. Under-26s and over-60s pay 10% less.

Transportes Agobe *(☎ 902 15 45 68; W www.agobe.es)*, based at Almuñécar, Granada province, runs three buses a week from Lisbon to Granada (13 hours) via Albufeira, Huelva, Seville, Málaga and Almuñécar, with one in each direction continuing to/from Porto. One-way fares from Lisbon to Seville/Granada are €30.05/ 51.10. Departure and ticket points in Portugal include:

Porto *(☎ 225 898 130)* Eurotour Viagens, Campo 24 de Agosto

Lisbon *(☎ 217 966 148)* Viagens Samar, Avenida do Roma 114B; also stops at the Care do Oriente
Albufeira *(☎ 289 514 053)* Rua 5 de Octubro 33

In Spain, Agobe's departures are from main city bus stations.

Train No railway crosses from Portugal into Andalucía, but trains run along the Algarve to Vila Real de Santo António, where there's a ferry across the Río Guadiana to Ayamonte in Andalucía (€3.50 for a car and driver, €1.80 for a motorcycle and rider, €1 for other adult passengers and foot passengers). You can get between Lagos and Vila Real by changing trains at Faro and in some cases Tunes too (five decent connections daily). Ayamonte is linked by bus to the nearest Spanish train station, at Huelva, 50km east.

You can travel from Lisbon to Seville, or vice versa, in about 16 hours by changing trains (and waiting four or five hours at night) at Cáceres in Spain's Extremadura. Departure from Lisbon's Santa Apolónia station is around 10pm daily. The *turista* seat fare from Lisbon to Seville is €43.10 one way.

Car & Motorcycle From Lisbon, head for Beja and Serpa and cross into Spain at Rosal de la Frontera, where the N-433 runs 160km to Seville via Aracena. From the Algarve a modern road bridge crosses the Río Guadiana just north of Vila Real de Santo António. See the UK section earlier in this chapter for general information about taking your own vehicle across Europe.

Elsewhere in Europe

Buses of **Eurolines** *(W www.eurolines.com)* run to Andalucía from Germany *(☎ 069-79 03 50)* and Switzerland. Direct trains run at least three times a week from Geneva, Berne, Zürich, Turin and Milan to Barcelona, where you can transfer to an Andalucía-bound train.

Morocco

Eurolines *(Málaga ☎ 95 236 33 45, Casablanca ☎ 022 44 81 08, Tangier ☎ 039 93 11 72)* runs several weekly buses from Jaén, Granada, Málaga and the Costa del Sol to

Casablanca, Marrakesh, Fès and other places in Morocco, via Algeciras–Tangier ferries. Granada to Casablanca (23 hours) costs €70/115 one way/return.

You can transport vehicles by ferry from several Andalucian ports (see under Sea, following, for details).

SEA
Portsmouth–Bilbao

P&O Portsmouth (UK ☎ 0870 242 4999, Spain ☎ 94 423 44 77; W www.poportsmouth .com) operates a ferry from Portsmouth to Bilbao. As a rule, there are two sailings a week except for a few weeks in January, when there's no service, and the month of February (once weekly). Voyage time varies between 29 and 35 hours.

Standard one-way/return fares for two people with a car range from around UK£275/525 in winter to UK£535/970 in August. This includes the cheapest cabin accommodation. Cabins are compulsory – all have a shower and toilet.

The ferries dock at Santurtzi, about 14km northwest of central Bilbao.

Plymouth–Santander

Brittany Ferries (UK ☎ 0870 556 1600, Spain ☎ 942 36 06 11; W www.brittanyferries.com) operates a twice-weekly car ferry from Plymouth to Santander (23 hours sailing time), between mid-March and mid-November. For two people with a car, return fares with seats/cabin range from about UK£435/540 to UK£725/880 depending on the season.

To/From Britain via France

For the Eurotunnel car train service through the Channel Tunnel, see The UK under Land earlier in this chapter.

The quickest and busiest ferry route, with around 60 crossings daily at peak times, is Dover–Calais, operated by **P&O Stena Line** (☎ 0870 600 0600; W www.posl.com), **SeaFrance** (☎ 0870 571 1711; W www.sea france.com) and **Hoverspeed** (☎ 0870 240 8070; W www.hoverspeed.co.uk).

Fares are volatile and you should research the latest options and offers. In August a Dover–Calais return ticket for a car and two people can cost UK£375. But if you travel at off-peak times (early morning, late at night, midweek, winter) you could pay only UK£220. Booking in advance helps too: tickets bought early in the year (by about early April) can cost well under UK£200.

Other routes include Newhaven–Dieppe (Hoverspeed), Portsmouth–Caen (Brittany Ferries) and Portsmouth–Cherbourg (P&O Portsmouth).

Ferrysavers (☎ 0870 442 4223; W www .ferrysavers.com) offers an online booking service and comparisons of cross-Channel sailing options.

Morocco

You can sail to the Moroccan ports of Tangier and Nador and to Ceuta or Melilla (Spanish enclaves on the Moroccan coast) from Almería, Málaga, Algeciras, Gibraltar or Tarifa. The routes are: Almería–Melilla, Almería–Nador, Málaga–Melilla, Málaga–Ceuta, Gibraltar–Tangier, Algeciras–Tangier, Algeciras–Ceuta and Tarifa–Tangier (note that only people with a passport or residence document from an EU country are allowed on this last route). A Cádiz–Tangier service has operated in the past but was not running at the time of writing. All routes usually take vehicles as well as passengers.

The quickest and cheapest sailings are from Algeciras and Tarifa, with those from Algeciras being much more frequent. Usually at least 25–30 sailings a day go from Algeciras to Tangier (taking 1 to 2½ hours) and 15–20 to Ceuta (30 minutes to 1½ hours), with many more between mid-June and mid-September when hundreds of thousands of ex-pat Moroccans return home from Europe for holidays. However, arriving at Tangier can be a big hassle because of the hustlers around the port and it's a good idea not to take this route on your first trip to Morocco. It's much more painless to sail to Ceuta or Melilla. The border crossing into Morocco itself is more straightforward from Melilla than from Ceuta, but sailings to Melilla can take eight hours and are much less frequent (just one a day from Almería and one a day from Málaga for most of the year). Passenger seat fares to

Melilla are little more than to Algeciras or Ceuta, but if you want a cabin or are taking a car, it gets more costly.

The most prominent ferry company, with sailings from Algeciras, Málaga and Almería, is the Spanish government–run **Trasmediterránea** (*Spain ☎ 902 45 46 45, Tangier ☎ 039 935076, UK ☎ 020-7491 4968;* Ⓦ *www.trasmediterranea.es*). The other main operators from Algeciras are **EuroFerrys** (*☎ 956 65 11 78;* Ⓦ *www.euro ferrys.com*) and, to Ceuta only, **Buquebus** (*☎ 902 41 42 42*). There's little price difference between the rival lines. One-way passenger fares from Algeciras are about €23 to Tangier and €21 to Ceuta. Two people with a small car pay around €120 to Tangier and €100 to Ceuta. On the Melilla and Ceuta routes there's a 10% discount for return tickets, and Euro<26 cardholders and EU citizens aged 60 or more get a 20% discount on passenger fares.

If you're taking a car, book well ahead for August or Easter travel. Anyone crossing from Morocco to Spain with a vehicle should be prepared for rigorous searches on disembarking at Ceuta and Melilla and on the mainland.

For more details see the Getting There & Away entries for Algeciras, Almería, Gibraltar, Málaga and Tarifa.

Canary Islands
A weekly car ferry sails from Cádiz – see the Cádiz section of the Cádiz Province chapter for details.

ORGANISED TOURS
Many companies offer tours to Andalucía, sometimes combining it with other parts of Spain. Special-interest tours include horse riding, walking, bird-watching, cycling and wine trips. Spanish tourist offices can often provide long lists of tour firms. The following is just a tiny sample of tours available.

Short Breaks
Kirker Holidays (*☎ 020 7231 3333;* Ⓦ *www .kirkerholidays.com; 3 New Concordia Wharf, Mill St, London SE1 2BB, UK*) offers short breaks from London, staying in good

hotels in Seville, Granada, Córdoba and Carmona. As a rule, they will set you back around UK£400 per person for three nights, breakfast included.

Walking Holidays
Andalucía has become a highly popular walking holiday destination, and the number of options for guided trips is growing all the time.

Headwater Holidays (*☎ 01606-72 00 33;* Ⓦ *www.headwater-holidays.co.uk; The Old School House, Chester Rd, Castle, Northwich, Cheshire CW8 1LE, UK*) offers one-week walking holidays in Las Alpujarras, the Sierra de Aracena, the Sierra Norte of Sevilla province and the Ronda-Grazalema area for between UK£657 and UK£997 including flights from London. **Exodus** (*☎ 020-8675 5550;* Ⓦ *www.exodus.co.uk; 9 Weir Rd, London SW12 0LT, UK*), with agents worldwide, does one-week walking trips in similar areas a little cheaper, and also a two-week Alpujarras walking holiday for UK£889 to UK£975 – all including flights from London. The **Walking Safari Company** (*☎ 01572-82 13 30;* Ⓦ *www .walkeurope.com; 29A Main St, Lyddington, Oakham, Rutland LE15 9LR, UK*) does walking holidays in the Ronda and Arcos de la Frontera areas for around UK£1370 including flights. **Rustic Blue** (*☎ 958 76 33 81;* Ⓦ *www.rusticblue.com; Barrio de la Ermita, 18412 Bubión, Granada*) offers one-week walking holidays in Las Alpujarras and the Sierra Nevada for UK£480 plus flights.

Other British providers of Andalucía walking holidays include **Inntravel** (*☎ 01653-62 90 00;* Ⓦ *www.inntravel.co.uk; Hovingham, York YO62 4JZ*) and the **Walking Safari Company** (*☎ 01572-82 13 30;* Ⓦ *www.walk europe.com; 29A Main St, Lyddington, Oakham, Rutland LE15 9LR*).

A leading Dutch operator is **Sindbad Reizen** (*☎ 020-521 8484;* Ⓦ *www.sindbad.nl; Buiksloterweg 7A – 1031 CC Amsterdam*).

Country Walkers (*☎ 800 464 9255;* Ⓦ *www.countrywalkers.com; PO Box 180, Waterbury, VT 05676, USA*) offers a week of Alpujarras walking and Granada in the region of US$2300 plus flights.

Golf Holidays

Longshot Golf Holidays (UK ☎ 01730-26 86 21; w www.longshotgolf.co.uk) includes some of Andalucía's best courses in its holidays. A one-week trip in May can cost UK£450, including flights, car hire and B&B accommodation. The website w www.ifyougolf.com offers hundreds of holidays in Spain, with a week's accommodation plus flights from Britain and car hire (but not the golf itself) starting around UK£350.

Wine Tours

Winetrails (UK ☎ 01306-71 21 11; w www.winetrails.co.uk) runs one-week Andalucía walking and wine tours for around UK£750 plus flights.

Horse-Riding Tours

With Andalucía's great equestrian tradition and so much spectacular country to cross, horseback holidays are booming in popularity. **In The Saddle** (UK ☎ 01256-85 16 65; w www.inthesaddle.com) organises trail-riding in the Alpujarras and Sierra Nevada costing UK£1075 to UK£1135 for a week with full board, and riding holidays based at the Hotel Dos Mares near Tarifa for UK£730 to UK£1040 with half board, all including flights from London. **Ride World Wide** (UK ☎ 01837-825 44; w www.rideworldwide.com) provides trail-riding holidays in the Doñana national park area and Las Alpujarras, at UK£800 to UK£1195 plus flights, medical insurance and drinks. Rustic Blue (see Walking Holidays) offers one-week riding holidays in Las Alpujarras and the Sierra de la Contraviesa for UK£790 plus flights. **Equitor** (UK ☎ 01865-51 16 42) and Inntravel (see Walking Holidays) are other operators. Further options are available from **The Compleat Traveller** (w www.ridingholidays.com).

Cycling Tours

This is another field that's growing in popularity and possibilities. **Discover Adventure** (☎ 01722-74 11 23; w www.discoveradventure.com; 4 Netherhampton Cottage, Netherhampton Rd, Netherhampton, Salisbury SP2 8PX, UK) offers one-week

mountain-bike tours in the Sierra Nevada, Alpujarras and Sierra de Cazorla for UK£695 to UK£755, including flights but not bike hire (UK£95), insurance (UK£32) or evening meals (about UK£50). **Rough Tracks** (☎ 07000 560 749; w www.roughtracks.com; Alexandra Rd, Frome, Somerset BA11 1LX, UK) does a similar trip with comparable prices.

The British-run **Ciclo Montaña España** (☎ 958 76 52 00; w www.tuspain.com/ciclo; Calle Cortijo 2, Mecina Fondales, La Taha, 18414 Granada) offers one-week mountain-bike holidays in the Alpujarras–Sierra Nevada area for around UK£240 plus flights.

Language Tours

Caledonia Languages Abroad (☎ 0131-621 77 21; w www.caledonialanguages.co.uk; The Clockhouse, Bonnington Mill, 72 Newhaven Rd, Edinburgh EH6 5QG, UK) organises trips with language study and activities components in several Andalucian cities. **AmeriSpan** (☎ 215-751 1100; w www.amerispan.com; PO Box 40007, Philadelphia, PA 19106-0007, USA) can set you up with language courses in Seville, Granada or Marbella.

Nature & Bird-Watching Tours

Country Connoisseurs (☎/fax 01428-72 79 29; w www.odspain.com; 2 Wey Lodge Close, Liphook, Hants GU30 7DE, UK) offers 10-day spring migration bird-watching trips combining Morocco, the Strait of Gibraltar and Doñana national park for UK£1500 including flights. **Naturetrek** (☎ 01962-73 30 51; w www.naturetrek.co.uk) does one-week Flowers of Western Andalucía and Doñana & Extremadura (bird-watching) trips for around UK£900 to UK£1000 from Britain. Another company to check out is **Cox & Kings** (☎ 020-7873 5010; w www.coxandkings.com).

Cultural Tours

Martin Randall Travel (UK ☎ 020-8742 3355; w www.martinrandall.com), **The British Museum Traveller** (☎ 020-7436 7575; w britishmuseumtraveller.co.uk) and

ACE Study Tours *(UK ☎ 01223-83 50 55, US ☎ 877-465 9050; W www.study-tours.org)* all offer tours with expert guides, delving into Andalucía's fascinating architecture, art, archaeology and history. Some typical prices are UK£1000/1700 for seven/11 days.

Dance Tours

You can learn tango in Granada, salsa in Seville or flamenco in Jerez with **Dance Holidays** *(UK ☎ 01293-527722; W www.danceholidays.com)*. One-week trips cost between UK£379 and UK£489 including flights from the UK and accommodation.

Getting Around

You will probably find that a combination of trains and buses best suits your needs if you're using public transport. Train services are good between some cities, nonexistent between others. Buses get to just about every town and village, but their frequency and convenience varies enormously.

Touring Andalucía on your own wheels has many advantages – roads are generally good (though country roads can be badly surfaced), you can get well off the beaten track and you have much more flexibility about where you go and when.

AIR

There are no direct flights between cities within Andalucía.

BUS

Most larger towns and cities have one main *estación de autobuses* (bus station) where all out-of-town buses stop. In smaller places, buses tend to operate from a particular street or square, which may be unmarked. Ask around; locals generally know where to go and there's usually a specific bar that has schedule information and may sell tickets. Services to small villages may run just once a day – or not at all on Saturday or Sunday.

During Semana Santa (Holy Week), July and August it's advisable to buy long-distance bus tickets a day in advance. Occasionally, a return ticket is cheaper than two singles. Travellers aged under 26 should inquire about discounts on intercity routes.

TRAIN

Good or reasonable train services, with at least three direct trains each way daily (often more), run on the following routes:

Algeciras–Ronda–Bobadilla–Antequera–Granada
Córdoba–Málaga
Málaga–Torremolinos–Fuengirola
Seville–Jerez de la Frontera–El Puerto de Santa María–Cádiz
Seville–Córdoba
Seville–Huelva
Seville–Bobadilla–Málaga
Seville–Antequera–Granada–Guadix–Almería

Apart from these routes, trains between Andalucía's main cities and towns tend to be infrequent and journeys often involve changing trains at the small junction station of Bobadilla, where lines from Seville, Córdoba, Granada, Málaga and Algeciras all meet. Except for the Málaga–Torremolinos–Fuengirola line, no trains run along any of Andalucía's coasts. But with a little perseverance you *can* reach a surprising number of places by train, including Jaén, the Sierra Norte of Sevilla province and the Sierra de Aracena.

On some routes such as Córdoba–Málaga, Córdoba–Seville–Cádiz and Córdoba–Ronda–Algeciras you can use long-distance trains heading into or out of Andalucía (for information on long-distance trains, see The Rest of Spain under Land in the Getting There & Away chapter). But more often you'll use the cheaper *regional* or *cercanía* trains. *Regionales* run between Andalucian cities, stopping at towns en route. Most are classed as Tren Regional Diésel (TRD) or, slower and a bit cheaper, Andalucía Exprés (AE). AEs are in turn a bit quicker and more expensive than the most basic Regional (R) trains. *Cercanías* are commuter trains that link Seville, Málaga and Cádiz with their suburbs and nearby towns.

You can consult the schedule and fares of every train in Spain on the website of the national rail authority, **Renfe** *(Red Nacional de Ferrocarriles Españoles; Spanish National Railways; countrywide information ☎ 902 24 02 02; ⓦ www.renfe.es)*. On Renfe's website and its national information and reservations line you can reserve tickets for TRDs and daytime long-distance trains.

CAR & MOTORCYCLE

The Land section in the Getting There & Away chapter covers ways of getting a vehicle to Andalucía from other countries and from other parts of Spain, and the paperwork needed to drive in Spain. It also contains a chart of road distances between cities in Andalucía and elsewhere in Spain. For information about hitching see later in this chapter.

There are only two toll roads in Andalucía: the Autopista del Sol between Fuengirola and Guadiaro, west of Málaga (€10.55 June to September and Semana Santa, €6.50 otherwise), and the A-4 from Seville to Cádiz (€5.65).

Road Rules

As elsewhere in continental Europe, drive on the right and overtake on the left. The minimum driving age is 18 years. Rear seat belts, if fitted, must be worn. The blood-alcohol limit is 0.05% (0.03% for drivers with a licence less than two years old) and breath-testing is carried out on occasion. Nonresident foreigners may be fined on the spot for traffic offences. You can appeal in writing (in any language) to the **Jefatura Provincial de Tráfico** (*Provincial Traffic Headquarters*) and if your appeal is upheld, you'll get your money back – but don't hold your breath for a favourable result.

Motorcyclists are supposed to have their headlights on at all times, and crash helmets are obligatory on bikes of 125cc or more. A licence is required to ride any bike or scooter. The minimum age for a machine of more than 125cc is 18; for bikes of 50cc to 125cc the minimum age is 16; and for bikes under 50cc the minimum age is 14.

The speed limit is 50km/h in built-up areas, 90km/h or 100km/h outside built-up areas, and 120km/h on *autopistas* (toll highways) and *autovías* (toll-free dual carriageways).

Selected One-Way Bus & Train Fares

from	to	bus fare (€)	duration (hrs)	type of train	train fare (€)	duration (hrs)
Granada	Almería	10	2¼	AE	10.10	2¾
				TRD	11.10	2¼
Granada	Seville	14.90	3	AE	15.10	3¼
				TRD	16.65	3
Granada	Trevélez	5.25	3¼			
Jaén	Cazorla	6.10	2			
Málaga	Córdoba	9.50	2½	Estrella	*turista* 14.50	2½
					preferente 19	
				InterCity	*turista* 15	2¼
					preferente 20	
				Talgo 200	*turista* 12–13.50	2–2¼
					preferente 17–20	
				Talgo	18.50	2¼
Málaga	Seville	12	2½	TRD	13.35	2½
				AE	12.10	3
Seville	Cádiz	8.70	1¾	R	7.05	1¾
				AE	8.05	1¾
				Talgo 200	*turista* 11	1½
					preferente 16.50	
				Talgo	*turista* 14	1½
					preferente €18.50	

(Note: Trains listed are *turista* (2nd) class only unless stated otherwise; *preferente* = 1st class)

Road Maps & Atlases

Michelin's *Andalucía – Costa del Sol* map (see Planning in the Facts for the Visitor chapter) is pretty good for finding your way round. Michelin also publishes the good *Michelin Spain & Portugal* road atlas (called *Michelin España & Portugal Atlas de Carreteras* in Spain). Both of these are widely available in and outside Spain. In Spain, the atlas costs about €16 and the map about €5.50. Several other good road atlases are available, including the government-published *Mapa Oficial de Carreteras* (€16) and one produced by the Campsa petrol company. Petrol stations and bookshops are the places to look for all these publications.

Road Assistance

The **Real Automóvil Club de España** *(RACE; ☎ 91 594 74 00;* **w** *www.race.net)* operates a 24-hour, countrywide emergency breakdown assistance service. This is available to members of some foreign motoring organisations, such as Britain's RAC and AA – ask your national association for its special contact numbers.

Petrol

Gasolina prices vary slightly between service stations and fluctuate with oil prices and tax policy. Lead-free *(sin plomo)* petrol usually comes in two versions: 95 octane, often called Eurosúper, at around €0.85/L, and 98 octane, with names like Súper Plus, at about €0.90/L. Lead replacement petrol (Eco Super 97), which replaced the now banned leaded Súper, costs €0.89, and diesel (or *gasóleo*) about €0.70/L.

Rental

See the Car & Motorcycle section under The UK in the Getting There & Away chapter for information and advice on booking hire cars before you come to Andalucía, which is worth considering. The cheapest deals available locally are usually from local firms: at Málaga airport, in Nerja, along the Costa del Sol and in the Almería resorts there are heaps of agencies and you can hire a small four-seat car for around €140 a week (as little

as €110 in winter), including unlimited mileage, collision damage waiver, insurance and 16% IVA (value-added tax). Many firms offer online booking. Away from the holiday coasts, rates may be double that.

One established local firm with good prices is **Helle Hollis** *(☎ 95 224 55 44;* **w** *www.hellehollis.com),* with offices at Málaga airport, Fuengirola, Marbella and Nerja. Helle Hollis charges €132 to €142 a week in summer for small four-seat cars such as an Opel Corsa or Seat Ibiza, and €167 or more for family cars. Winter prices can be 25% lower. **Crown Car** *(☎ 95 217 64 86;* **w** *www.costanet.es/crown),* at Málaga airport, Marbella, Sotogrande, Torre del Mar, Nerja and Almuñécar, offers competitive rates. Wherever you hire from, make sure you understand what is included in the price.

You need to be aged at least 21 (23 with some companies) and to have held a driving licence for a minimum of one year (sometimes two years). It's much easier, and often obligatory, to pay with a credit card. See Visas & Documents in the Facts for the Visitor chapter for information on driving licences.

Rental outlets catering for motorcycles and mopeds are rare and usually expensive. **Moto Mercado** *(☎ 95 247 25 51;* **w** *www .rentabike.org; Avenida Jesús Santos Rein s/n, Los Boliches, Fuengirola)* has 50/125/250/600/750cc bikes for €24/30/42/69/90 a day (less if you rent for three days or more). It also has branches in Torremolinos and Marbella.

City Driving & Parking

Driving in the bigger cities can be a little nerve-racking at the start. Road rules and traffic lights are generally respected, but the pace, jostling and one-way systems take a little getting used to.

Parking in cities can be a headache. Underground or multistorey car parks are common enough in the bigger cities, and well enough signposted, but they're not cheap (typically around €1 per hour or €10 to €15 for 24 hours). Street parking space can be hard to find during working hours (about 9am to 2pm Monday to Saturday and 5pm to 8pm

Monday to Friday). You just have to be patient until you find a place. Blue lines on the street usually mean you must pay at a nearby meter to park during working hours (usually around €0.50 an hour). Yellow lines mean no parking. Take care not to park in prohibited zones, even if other drivers have (you risk being towed, which will cost around €60).

In certain areas of cities where street parking space is particularly prized, you may see self-appointed attendants trying to wave you into available spaces, 'supervising' parking on waste ground, and so on. It's standard practice to give them €0.50 or €1; they may keep some kind of an eye on your vehicle and they are usually in fairly obvious need of cash. Sometimes they'll even give you a receipt showing that you've just made a donation to some charity or cooperative.

Safer at Last?

Every year 5000 to 6000 people die on Spain's roads. The average of around one death per 7000 people each year makes Spain's roads nearly three times as dangerous as Sweden's or Britain's, and 50% riskier than Italy's, but safer than those of Portugal (one death per 4500). Half of those who die on Spain's roads are aged between 15 and 35. In 2002 Spain finally introduced punishments in line with many other EU countries in an effort to improve its miserable road-safety record. Spaniards can now lose their licences for three months and be fined up to €600 if they exceed speed limits by more than 50% or drive under the influence of drugs or alcohol. Three such offences within two years can bring a ban for life. Talking on a mobile phone while driving is also now illegal.

Increased use of motorcycle crash helmets – until recently unfashionable – provides further hope for saving lives. In Málaga province, for example, one-third of accidents in 2000 involved motorbikes, with 73% of the riders involved not wearing helmets. Two years later, after a police clampdown, some 80% of riders in Málaga city were habitually wearing helmets.

BICYCLE

Bicycles are increasingly available for hire in main cities, coastal resorts and inland towns and villages which attract tourism. They're often mountain bikes *(bicis todo terreno)*. Prices range from €10 to €20 a day. Day rides and touring by bike are particularly enjoyable in spring and autumn and there are plenty of tracks. Ask at the local tourist office for track routes.

Some regional trains have space for bicycles, others don't. Ask before buying tickets. Bikes are generally permitted on *cercanía* trains. Bikes can also be carried on most intercity buses if the front wheel is removed.

HITCHING

Hitchhiking is never entirely safe and we don't recommend it. Travellers who decide to hitch should understand that they are taking a small but potentially serious risk. People who do choose to hitch will be safer if they travel in pairs and let someone know where they are planning to go.

Hitching is illegal on *autopistas* and *autovía*, and difficult on other major highways. You can try to pick up lifts before the toll-booths on tollways. Otherwise, you need to choose a spot where cars can safely stop prior to highway slipways, or use minor roads.

LOCAL TRANSPORT

Cities and larger towns have efficient bus systems, but in most places accommodation, attractions and main-line bus and train stations are usually within fairly comfortable walking distance of each other. All Andalucía's airports except Jerez de la Frontera are linked to city centres by bus – in Málaga's case also by train. Gibraltar airport is within walking distance of downtown Gibraltar and of the bus station in La Línea de la Concepción, Spain.

Taxis are plentiful in larger places and even many villages have a taxi or two. Fares are reasonable – a typical 3km trip should cost about €3 (airport runs cost a bit extra). Intercity runs cost around €0.60/km. You don't have to tip taxi drivers but a little rounding up doesn't go amiss.

ORGANISED TOURS

Guided tours of the major cities are an option, but as a rule it's cheaper and not a great deal more trouble to do it under your own steam. Of more potential use are trips in national and natural parks (see individual destination sections for details), some of which are hard to penetrate if you don't have your own vehicle. Guides' local knowledge can be illuminating. The only way the general public is permitted to enter the Parque Nacional de Doñana is by guided tour.

Sevilla Province

The wonderful city of Seville (Sevilla in Spanish) is the highlight of the province, but countryside lovers will enjoy heading north to the Parque Natural Sierra Norte. In the east, you can visit fascinating old towns such as Carmona, Écija, Osuna and Estepa.

Seville

postcode 41080 • pop 702,520

Seville is Andalucía's biggest and most exciting city. It takes a stony heart not to be captivated by its unique atmosphere – stylish, ancient, proud, yet also fun-loving and intimate. One of the first people recorded as falling in love with Seville was the 11th-century Muslim poet-king Al-Mutamid. The place is working its enchantment every bit as well today.

Except along the Río Guadalquivir – navigable to the Atlantic Ocean 100km away, and the source of Seville's greatness in times past – this is not a city of great long vistas. Its crowded centre unfolds more subtly as you wend your way through narrow streets and small squares, stopping for a drink or a bite in some of the wonderful bars and cafés. Similarly, the city's two great monuments – the Muslim Alcázar and the Christian cathedral – reveal most of their glories only once you're inside them.

A great city in Muslim times and again in the 16th and 17th centuries, Seville has seen bad times too, so it knows how to enjoy the good ones when they come. Every April for more than a century, Seville has thrown one of Spain's biggest parties, the Feria de Abril (April Fair: see Special Events later in this section for details). A couple of weeks before the *feria*, the city's Semana Santa (Holy Week) processions are among the most magnificent in Spain.

Outside its fascinating inner city, Seville enjoys some good green parks on the fringes of the centre. It's also one of the homes of flamenco and bullfighting, and has great

Highlights

- Marvel at the cathedral and Alcázar, Seville city's great monuments
- Visit the Museo de Bellas Artes, full of fantastic paintings from the golden age of Spanish art
- *¡Tapea!* Join with the locals and sample the tapas bars of Seville, Andalucía's tapas capital
- Experience Seville's jumping nightlife
- Witness Seville's Semana Santa processions, probably the most emotive and spectacular in Spain
- Enjoy the rolling hills of the Sierra Morena and the spring wildflowers in the Parque Natural Sierra Norte

nightlife. But above all, Seville is an atmosphere. Being out among its celebratory, happy crowds on a warm night is an unforgettable experience. To put it in one Spanish word, the city has *alegría*; Sevillans most certainly know how to enjoy life!

There are a couple of catches. Seville is expensive. You might pay €60 here for a room that would cost €30 elsewhere in Andalucía. And prices go even higher during the two big festivals. Another thing to bear in mind is that Seville gets *very* hot in July and August: locals, sensibly, leave the city then.

SEVILLA PROVINCE

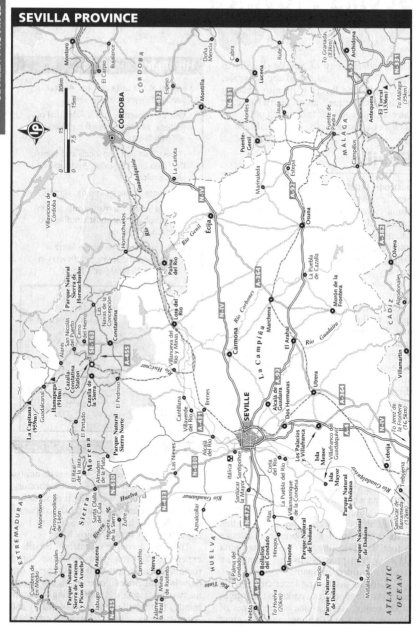

HISTORY
Beginnings

It was Phoenician influence in the Seville area that gave rise to the ancient Tartessos culture in the 8th and 7th centuries BC, when iron replaced bronze for the first time in Andalucía, and a new method of working gold was developed.

The Roman town of Hispalis, probably founded in the mid-2nd century BC, was a significant river port, but was overshadowed by Córdoba. Later, Hispalis became a Visigothic cultural centre, especially in the time of St Isidoro (AD565–636), Spain's leading scholar of the Visigothic period.

The Taifa Kings

Under the Muslims, who called it Ishbiliya, Seville initially played second fiddle to Córdoba. After the collapse of the Córdoba caliphate in 1031, Seville became the most powerful of the *taifa* (small kingdom) states into which Muslim Spain broke up. Its Abbadid dynasty rulers Al-Mutadid (1042–69) and Al-Mutamid (1069–91) were both poets too. Al-Mutamid presided over a languid, hedonistic court in the Alcázar.

Almoravids & Almohads

When Toledo in central Spain fell to the Christians in 1085, Al-Mutamid asked the Muslim fundamentalist rulers of Morocco, the Almoravids, for help against the growing Christian threat. The Almoravids took control of all of Muslim Spain before being replaced by another strict Muslim Berber sect from North Africa, the Almohads, in the mid-12th century. Arts and learning revived under the Almohads: Caliph Yacub Yusuf made Sevilla province capital of the whole Almohad realm, building a great mosque where the city's cathedral now stands. His successor, Yusuf Yacub al-Mansur, added the Giralda tower.

Reconquista

Almohad power dwindled after a disastrous defeat by the Christians at Las Navas de Tolosa, in Jaén province (1212). The Castilian King Fernando III (El Santo, the Saint) went on to capture several major Andalucian cities – including Seville in 1248.

Fernando brought 24,000 Castilian settlers to Seville. His intellectual son Alfonso X made it one of his capitals and by the 14th century it was the most important Castilian city. But the monarch who perhaps loved Seville more than any other was Pedro I (1350–69) – see Alcázar later in this section for more on this infamous king. Pedro's court included many Jewish financiers and tax collectors, which provoked racial jealousies. A pogrom which emptied the Jewish quarter in 1391 signalled the end of 'three cultures' tolerance.

The Catholic Monarchs, Fernando and Isabel, set up court in the Alcázar for several years as they prepared for the conquest of the Emirate of Granada, the last Muslim stronghold on the peninsula, which fell in 1492.

Seville's Golden Age

Seville's biggest break was Columbus' discovery of the Americas in 1492 (see the boxed text 'The Four Voyages of Christopher Columbus' in the Huelva Province chapter). In 1503 the city was given an official monopoly on Spanish trade with the newly found continent. Galleons disgorged cargos of gold and silver at El Arenal, a sandy riverbank area where the Plaza de Toros de la Real Maestranza now stands, and Seville rapidly became one of the biggest, richest and most cosmopolitan cities on earth, a magnet for everyone from beggars and *pícaros* (card and dice tricksters) to Dutch bankers, Italian merchants and the clergy of its more than 100 religious institutions. Seville was labelled the *puerto y puerta de Indias* (port and gateway of the Indies), the Babylon of Spain and even the New Rome. Its population jumped from about 40,000 in 1500 to 150,000 in 1600, lavish Renaissance and baroque buildings sprouted, and many figures of Spain's artistic *Siglo de Oro* (Golden Century) did the bulk of their work here (see Arts in the Facts about Andalucía chapter).

The Not-So-Golden Age

A plague in 1649 killed half the city and, as the 17th century wore on, the Río Guadalquivir became more and more silted-up and difficult for the increasingly big ships of the day to navigate; many ships foundered on a sandbar at the mouth of the river near Sanlúcar de Barrameda. Cádiz began to take much of the American trade. By 1700 Seville's population was down to 60,000 and in 1717 the Casa de la Contratación, the government office controlling commerce with the Americas, was transferred to Cádiz. Another Seville plague in 1800 killed 13,000 people. It's said that the Napoleonic troops occupying the city from 1810 to 1812 stole 999 works of art when they left.

A certain prosperity returned in the mid-19th century with the beginnings of industry. The first bridge across the Guadalquivir, the Puente de Triana (or Puente de Isabel II), was built in 1845, and the old Almohad walls were knocked down in 1869 to let the city expand. Romantic travellers were attracted by Seville's faded grandeur, but the majority in the city and in the countryside remained very poor.

The 20th Century

Middle-class optimism was expressed by Seville's first international fair, the Exposición Iberoamericana of 1929. The fair's architects tried to inspire a new future with buildings that looked back to the city's glorious past.

Seville fell very quickly to the Nationalists at the start of the Spanish Civil War despite resistance in working-class areas (which brought savage reprisals). Urban development in Franco's time did little for the look of the city, with numerous historic buildings being demolished. Things looked up in the early 1980s when Seville was named capital of the new autonomous Andalucía and the left-of-centre Partido Socialista Obero Español (PSOE) party, led by Sevillan Felipe González, came to power in Madrid (see History in the Facts about Andalucía chapter for details). The city received another big thrust forward from the Expo '92 international exhibition, held to mark the 500th anniversary of the discovery of America. As well as millions of extra visitors and a boost to its international image, Expo brought Seville eight new bridges across the Guadalquivir, the super-fast AVE

(Alta Velocidad Española) rail link to Madrid, and thousands of new hotel rooms.

Almost inevitably, Expo was a source of controversy too. Costs escalated in the run-up to 1992, and no-one seemed to know what to do with the site afterwards. In 1997, amid allegations that large sums had disappeared into private pockets and PSOE coffers, the national Accounts Tribunal reported that Expo had lost around 35 billion pesetas (about €210 million).

The historic heart of the city retains the picturesque decay that attracted the 19th-century Romantics. Bureaucratic delay, political squabbling and lack of funds for renovation remain as characteristic of Seville as grand projects such as the Olympic stadium built for the 1999 World Athletic Championships. Seville made unsuccessful bids to host the 2004 and 2008 Olympics. Madrid may take over from Seville when Spain tries again for 2012.

ORIENTATION

Seville straddles the Río Guadalquivir, with most places of interest on the east bank. The central area is mostly a tangle of narrow, twisting old streets and small squares, with the exceptions of Plaza Nueva and Avenida de la Constitución. The latter runs south from Plaza Nueva to the Puerta de Jerez, a busy intersection marking the southern edge of the central area. The area between Avenida de la Constitución and the river is called El Arenal. Just east of Avenida de la Constitución are the city's major monuments: the cathedral, with its tower (La Giralda), and the fortress-palace, the Alcázar. The quaint Barrio de Santa Cruz, east of the cathedral and Alcázar, offers some budget accommodation. The true centre of Seville, El Centro, is a little farther north, around Plaza de San Francisco and Plaza Salvador.

Transport terminals are on the periphery of the central area: Santa Justa train station is 1.5km northeast of the cathedral, on Avenida Kansas City; Plaza de Armas bus station is 900m northwest of the cathedral near Puente del Cachorro; and Prado de San Sebastián bus station is 650m southeast of the cathedral on Plaza San Sebastián.

Maps

The main tourist office hands out a reasonable city map but you can buy better ones, with street indexes, in bookshops. Compare their publication dates before parting with your money (around €4.50).

INFORMATION
Tourist Offices

The **main tourist office** (☎ *95 422 14 04; Avenida de la Constitución 21; open 9am-7pm Mon-Fri, 10am-2pm & 3pm-7pm Sat, 10am-2pm Sun, closed holidays*) is often very busy. There are also two very helpful **municipal tourist offices**: one south of the centre (☎ *95 423 44 65; Paseo de las Delicias 9; open 8.30am-2.45pm Mon-Fri*); the other by the Puente de Triana (☎ *95 422 17 14; Calle de Arjona 28; open 8am-8.45pm Mon-Fri, 8.30am-2.30pm Sat & Sun, 9am-7pm daily during Semana Santa & Feria de Abril*). Staff at the Calle de Arjona office are very switched on and can answer anything you toss at them. They have lots of printed material to give away. There are also **tourist offices** at the airport (☎ *95 444 91 28*) and Santa Justa train station (☎ *95 453 76 26*).

Money

There's no shortage of banks and ATMs in the central area. Santa Justa train station has ATMs and an exchange office. The ATM in the post office (see Post & Communications, following) offers more security than those on the street. The **American Express (AmEx) office** (*Plaza Nueva 8*) is open from 9am to 8pm Monday to Friday, 10am to 1.30pm Saturday.

Post & Communications

The **main post office** (*Avenida de la Constitución 32; open 8.30am-8.30pm Mon-Fri, 9.30am-2pm Sat*) is conveniently located near the cathedral. There are plenty of pay phones around the centre, and call centres (*locutorios*) offering cheap international calls have started to appear. One such is **Ciber Alcázar** (*Calle San Fernando 35; open 10am-11pm Mon-Fri, noon-11pm Sat & Sun*), where calls to Australia and the USA cost €0.21 per minute.

Seville has heaps of cybercafés and other public Internet/email services, including:

Ciber Alcázar Calle San Fernando 35; 5/60 minutes €0.15/2; this is also a cheap international call centre (see Post & Communications, earlier)

Ciber easytech@ Avenida Menéndez Pelayo 16, in same building as Viajes Asatej (see Travel Agencies, later); €1.50 for 54 minutes

Cibercenter Calle Julio Cesar 8, near Plaza de Armas bus station; open 9am to 9pm Monday to Friday, 10am-2pm Saturday; 10/30/60 minutes €0.75/1.50/2.50

CiberSevill@ Calle Pérez Galdós, €0.03/1.80 per minute/hour, minimum €0.70.

The E-m@il Place Calle Sierpes 54, El Centro; open 8am to 11pm Monday to Friday, noon to 9pm Saturday and Sunday; 10/30/60 minutes €0.70/1.50/2.20

Sevilla Internet Center Calle Almirantazgo 2, just off Avenida de la Constitución, in spacious premises with other office services too; open 9am to 10pm Monday to Friday, noon to 10pm Saturday and Sunday; €0.05 per minute, two-hour package €3.60

Digital Resources

The following websites are useful:

About Sevilla Provides comprehensive coverage of what the city has to offer, in English.
  W www.aboutsevilla.com

Sevilla5 Gives useful tourist information, in Spanish, English and German.
  W www.sevilla5.com

Sevilla Cultural Tells you what's on and gives arts and music background plus some tourist information, in Spanish, English and French.
  W www.sevillacultural.com

Sevilla Online Provides information on sights, language schools, tours, entertainment, bars and nightlife, festivals, transport and so on, in English and Spanish.
  W www.sol.com

Travel Agencies

Viajes Asatej (☎ *95 441 25 56, 902 44 44 88;* W *www.asatej.com; Avenida Menéndez Pelayo 16*) is completely geared to providing student and youth travel services, including cheap flights. **Usit Unlimited** (☎ *902 25 25 75; Avenida de la Constitución • Calle Mateos Gago 2, Barrio de Santa Cruz*) is another student/youth travel agency represented in Seville.

SEVILLE

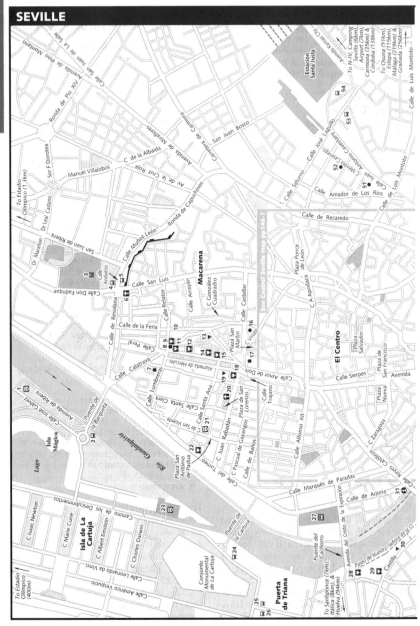

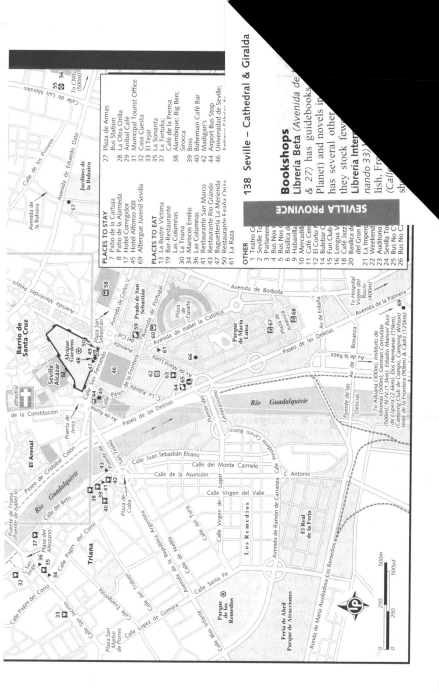

SEVILLA PROVINCE

Bookshops
Librería Beta (Avenida de ___
& 27) has guidebooks ___
Planet) and novels in ___
has several other ___
they stock fewer ___
Librería Inter ___
nando 33) ___
lish, Fre ___
(Calle ___
sh ___

PLACES TO STAY
7   Patio de la Cartuja
8   Patio de la Alameda
17 Hotel Corregidor
45 Hotel Alfonso XIII
69 Albergue Juvenil Sevilla

PLACES TO EAT
13 La Ilustre Victima
19 Bar-Restaurante
30 La Triana
34 Las Columnas
36 Mariscos Emilio
41 Restaurante San Marco
43 Restaurante Río Grande
47 Restaurante La Merienda
50 Baguettería Espña Orza
61 La Raza

27 Plaza de Armas Bus Station
28 La Otra Orilla
29 Anibal Café
31 Municipal Tourist Office
32 Casa Cuesta
33 El Tejar
35 La Sonanta
37 La Tertulia;
    Café de la Prensa
38 Alambique; Big Ben;
    Sirocca
39 Boss
40 Bohemian Café Bar
42 Madigan's
44 Airport Bus Stop
46 Universidad de Sevilla;
    Antigua Fábrica de

OTHER
1   Teatro C
2   Seville To
3   Parlamen
4   Bus Nos C
5   Bus Nos C
6   Basílica d
9   Habanilla
10 Mercadill
11 Café Cem
14 El Corto
15 Bulebar C
16 Fun Club
18 Lengua V
20 Café Jazz
    Basílica d
    del Gran
21 La Imperd
22 Weekend
23 Auditorio
24 Sevilla To
25 Bus No C
26 Bus No C

a Constitución 9 (including Lonely English, and maps. It shops around town but r English-language books. *lacional* **Vértice** *(Calle San Fer-* las a large range of books in Eng- nch and German. **La Casa del Libro** *Velázquez 8)* is a big, central book- op with guidebooks and novels in English.

LTC *(☎ 95 442 59 64; Avenida Menéndez Pelayo 42-44)*, near the Barrio de Santa Cruz, is with little doubt the best map shop in Andalucía (see Maps in the Facts for the Visitor chapter). LTC also sells Spanish-language guidebooks.

Laundry

Tintorería Roma *(☎ 95 421 05 35; Calle Castelar 2C; open 9.30am-1.30pm & 5pm-8.30pm Mon-Fri, 9am-2pm Sat)* will wash, dry and fold a load of washing for €6. Though it advertises a one-hour service, allow half a day. **Vera Tintorería** *(☎ 95 454 11 48; Avenida Menéndez Pelayo 11)* will wash and dry 4kg for €7.20. It's located in a little passageway almost next to the LTC map shop.

Medical Services & Emergency

There's a **Centro de Urgencias** *(Emergency Medical Post; ☎ 95 441 17 12; cnr Avenida Menéndez Pelayo & Avenida Málaga)* near Prado de San Sebastián bus station. The main general hospital is the **Hospital Virgen del Rocío** *(☎ 95 501 20 00; Avenida de Manuel Siurot s/n)*, 1km south of the Parque de María Luisa.

The **Policía Nacional office** *(☎ 95 422 88 40; Plaza Concordia)* is 900m north of the cathedral.

Dangers & Annoyances

Seville has a reputation for petty crime against tourists – pickpockets, bag snatchers and the like. Until recently, we didn't think the reputation was justified. However, there is no doubt that the Casco Antiguo (Old City Centre) has a security problem. Robberies with violence are on the increase and local residents have asked for increased police presence in the Casco Antiguo. Locals are as much at risk as tourists, with thieves interested in mobile phones and fashionable clothes, shoes and accessories.

CATHEDRAL & GIRALDA

Seville's immense cathedral *(☎ 95 421 49 71; cathedral & Giralda adult/student or child under 12/senior €6/1.50/1.30, admission free Sun; open 11am-6pm Mon-Sat, 2pm-7pm Sun; ticket office closes one hour before scheduled closing time)* stands on the site of the main Almohad mosque, with the mosque's minaret, La Giralda, still towering beside it. After Seville fell to the Christians in 1248 the mosque was used as a church until 1401. Then, in light of the building's decaying state, the church authorities decided to knock it down and start again. Legend has it that they agreed: 'Let us create such a building that future generations will take us for lunatics'. They certainly got themselves a big church. The main building (excluding the Patio de los Naranjos), one of the largest cathedrals in the world, is 126m long and 83m wide. It was completed by 1507 – all in Gothic style, though work done after its central dome collapsed in 1511 was mostly in Renaissance style.

The sheer size of the broad, five-naved cathedral is obscured by a welter of interior structures and decoration typical of Spanish cathedrals – which adds up to a storehouse of art and artisanry as rich as in any church in Spain. Don't forget to look up from time to time to admire the marvellous Gothic vaulting. At least one strategically placed mirror enables you to do this with ease.

The entry system and timetable for visiting the cathedral and Giralda change frequently. Current regulations are usually posted up fairly clearly. At our last check the main entrance was next to the Puerta de los Príncipes on the southern side of the cathedral; the entrance on Plaza Virgen de los Reyes, beside the Giralda, was for guided groups only. From about 8.30am to 2pm on Sunday a series of masses is held in the cathedral: with discretion, visitors can also look around at this time.

SEVILLE CATHEDRAL

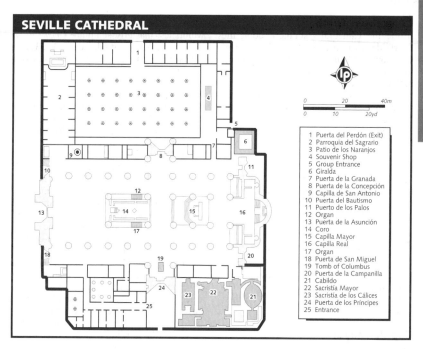

1 Puerta del Perdón (Exit)
2 Parroquia del Sagrario
3 Patio de los Naranjos
4 Souvenir Shop
5 Group Entrance
6 Giralda
7 Puerta de la Granada
8 Puerta de la Concepción
9 Capilla de San Antonio
10 Puerta del Bautismo
11 Puerto de los Palos
12 Organ
13 Puerta de la Asunción
14 Coro
15 Capilla Mayor
16 Capilla Real
17 Organ
18 Puerta de San Miguel
19 Tomb of Columbus
20 Puerta de la Campanilla
21 Cabildo
22 Sacristía Mayor
23 Sacristía de los Cálices
24 Puerta de los Príncipes
25 Entrance

Exterior

The bulky exterior of the cathedral gives few hints of the treasures within, apart from the **Puerta del Perdón** on Calle Alemanes (a legacy of the Islamic building) and the one neo-Gothic and two Gothic **doorways** on Avenida de la Constitución. These last are sculpted with 15th-century terracotta reliefs and statues by Lorenzo Mercadante de Bretaña and Pedro Millán.

More impressive from outside is **La Giralda**, the 90m-high brick tower on the northeastern side of the cathedral (but entered from inside the cathedral). The Giralda was the minaret of the mosque, constructed between 1184 and 1198 at the height of Almohad power. Its proportions and decoration, and its colour, which changes with the light, make it perhaps Spain's most perfect Islamic building. Its four sides are each divided into three vertical sections, the outer ones with delicate brick patterns and the central ones with windows. The topmost parts of the Giralda – from the bell level up – were added in the 16th century, when Spanish Christians were busy 'improving on' surviving Islamic buildings.

The bronze weathervane representing Faith, a symbol of Seville known as **El Giraldillo**, which tops the Giralda, is a copy. The 16th-century original was removed in 1997 to prevent further damage by the elements. It may eventually reappear in one of the city's museums.

Southern & Northern Chapels

The chapels along the southern and northern sides of the cathedral hold riches of sculpture, stained glass and painting. Most of the stained glass dates back to the 16th century. Near the western end of the northern side is the **Capilla de San Antonio** housing Murillo's large 1666 canvas depicting the vision of St Anthony of Padua; thieves cut out the kneeling saint in 1874 but he was later found in New York and put back.

Columbus' Tomb

Inside the cathedral's southern door, the Puerta de los Príncipes, stands the tomb of Christopher Columbus (Cristóbal Colón). The great sailor's remains – or rather, his probable remains, for no-one's 100% sure that the real ones didn't get mislaid somewhere in the Caribbean – were brought here from Cuba in 1899. The monument shows four sepulchre-bearers representing the four kingdoms of Spain at the time of Columbus' voyage: Castile (carrying Granada on the point of its spear), León, Aragón and Navarra. In 2002, investigators began a series of DNA tests on various known and claimed Columbus family corpses in order to establish finally where the famous navigator lies.

Coro

In the middle of the cathedral you will see the large choir *(coro)* with 117 carved Gothic–Mudejar stalls. The lower ones have marquetry representations of the Giralda. Vices and sins are depicted on their misericords.

Capilla Mayor

East of the choir is the Capilla Mayor (Main Chapel). Its Gothic retable is the jewel of the cathedral and reckoned to be the biggest altarpiece in the world. Begun by Flemish sculptor Pieter Dancart in 1482 and finished by others in 1564, the sea of gilded and polychromed wood holds over 1000 carved biblical figures. At the centre of the lowest level is the 13th-century silver-plated cedar image of the Virgen de la Sede, patroness of the cathedral.

Sacristía de los Cálices

South of the Capilla Mayor is the entrance to rooms containing some of the cathedral's main art treasures. The westernmost room is the Sacristía de los Cálices (Sacristy of the Chalices), built between 1509 and 1537. Goya's painting of the Seville martyrs, *Santas Justa y Rufina* (1817), hangs above the altar. These two potters died at the hands of the Romans in AD 287: the Giralda and cathedral in the background are anachronistic. The other art dates from the 16th and

17th centuries, including Juan Martínez Montañés' masterly sculpture *Cristo de la Clemencia* (Christ of Clemency; 1603) and Zurbarán's painting *San Juan Bautista* (1640).

Sacristía Mayor

This large domed room east of the Sacristía de los Cálices is a plateresque creation of 1528–47: the arch over its portal has carvings of 16th-century foods. Pedro de Campaña's 1547 *Descendimiento* (Descent from the Cross), above the central altar at the southern end, and Zurbarán's *Santa Teresa*, to its right, are two of the cathedral's most masterly paintings. Murillo's *San Isidoro* (reading) and *San Leandro* face each other across the room: the pair were leaders of the Visigothic church in Seville. This room also holds 17th-century images of San Fernando (Fernando III) and La Inmaculada (Mary, the Immaculate), and the Custodia de Juan de Arfe, a huge 475kg silver monstrance made in the 1580s by the celebrated Renaissance metalsmith Juan de Arfe, all of which are carried in Seville's Corpus Christi processions. In one of the glass cases are the city keys handed over to the conquering Fernando III in 1248.

Cabildo

The beautifully domed *cabildo* (chapter house), in the southeastern corner of the cathedral, was built between 1558 and 1592 for meetings of the cathedral hierarchy. It was designed by Hernán Ruiz, architect of the belfry atop the Giralda. At the base of the dome, above the archbishop's throne at the southern end, is a Murillo masterpiece, *La Inmaculada*. Eight Murillo saints adorn the dome at the same level.

Eastern Chapels

East of the Capilla Mayor, against the eastern wall of the cathedral, are more chapels. They're usually roped off, which prevents you getting a close view. This is a pity, because the central chapel is the **Capilla Real** (Royal Chapel), containing the tombs of two great Castilian kings. The silver-and-bronze tomb of Fernando III stands in front of the altar (he's mummified inside); the tombs of his son, Alfonso X, and wife, Beatrice of Swabia, are at the sides. The Capilla Real has a separate entrance from Plaza del Triunfo. It is not supposed to be open for tourist visits, though masses are held in the Capilla Real and you may find you can take a look.

La Giralda

In the northeast corner of the cathedral you'll find the passage for the climb up to the belfry of the Giralda. The ascent is quite easy, as a series of ramps – built so that guards could ride up on horseback – goes all the way up. The climb affords great views of the forest of buttresses and pinnacles that surround the cathedral, as well as of the city beyond.

Patio de los Naranjos

Immediately beyond the Giralda access, and planted with more than 60 orange trees, this was originally the courtyard of the mosque. The font where Muslims performed ablutions before entering the mosque remains in the centre of the patio. Hanging from the ceiling in the patio's southeastern corner are a stuffed crocodile – a gift to Alfonso X from the Sultan of Egypt – and an elephant's tusk, said to have been found in the Roman amphitheatre at nearby Itálica. The impressive Puerta de la Concepción, a 20th-century addition to the cathedral's structure, is on the patio's southern side. Immediately opposite is the beautiful Islamic Puerta del Perdón, through which you leave the cathedral precinct.

ALCÁZAR

South of the cathedral across Plaza del Triunfo, the Alcázar *(Fortress; ☎ 95 450 23 23; admission €5; open 9.30am-7pm Tues-Sat, 9.30am-5pm Sun & holidays Mar-Oct; 9.30am-5pm Tues-Sun & holidays Nov-Feb)* is more palace than castle. It's a beautiful place that shouldn't be missed, not least for its associations with the lives and loves of several rulers, above all the extraordinary Pedro I, who was known either as El Cruel or as El Justiciero (the Justice-Dispenser), depending which side you were on.

Audio guides (€3) are available in English, Spanish, French, German and Italian.

History

The Alcázar was founded as a fort for the Cordoban governors of Seville in 913. It has undergone many expansions and reconstructions in the 11 centuries since then, making it a complicated building to understand, but in the end only adding to its fascination.

Seville's prosperous 11th-century rulers built a palace called Al-Muwarak (The Blessed) in what's now the western part of the Alcázar. East of this, the 12th-century Almohad rulers added another palace around what's now the Patio del Crucero. Christian Fernando III moved into the Alcázar when he captured Seville in 1248, dying here four years later. Several later Christian monarchs used the Alcázar as their main residence. Fernando's son Alfonso X replaced much of the Almohad palace with a Gothic one (which has now become the Salones de Carlos V). Between 1364 and 1366 Pedro I created the Alcázar's crown jewel, the sumptuous Mudejar Palacio de Don Pedro, partly on the site of the old Al-Muwarak palace.

The whole complex was further adapted and expanded by later rulers, who also created the Alcázar's beautiful gardens.

Patio del León

From the ticket office just inside the **Puerta del León** (Lion Gate) you emerge into the Patio del León (Patio of the Lion), which was the garrison yard of the original Al-Muwarak palace. Off its southeastern corner is the **Sala de la Justicia** (Hall of Justice), with beautiful Mudejar plasterwork and an *artesonado* ceiling (wooden ceiling with interlaced beams); this room was built in the 1340s by the Christian king Alfonso XI, who disported here with his mistress Leonor de Guzmán, reputedly the most beautiful woman in Spain. Alfonso's sexual exploits left his heir Pedro I with five illegitimate half-brothers and a severe case of sibling rivalry. Pedro is said to have ordered a dozen relatives and friends murdered in his efforts to stay on the throne. Don Fadrique, one of the half-brothers, met his maker right here in the Sala de la Justicia.

The room gives on to the pretty **Patio del Yeso**, part of the 12th-century Almohad palace reconstructed in the 19th century.

Patio de la Montería

The rooms on the western side of this patio, the Hunting Patio, were part of the Casa de la Contratación founded by the Catholic Monarchs in 1503 to control the American trade. The **Salón del Almirante** (Admiral's Hall) houses 19th- and 20th-century paintings showing historical events associated with Seville. The **Sala de Audiencias** (Hall of Audiences) is hung with the shields of admirals of the Spanish fleet and the *Virgen de los Mareantes* (Virgin of Sailors) by Alejo Fernández, painted in the 1530s and the earliest known painting on the subject of the discovery of the Americas. Columbus, Fernando El Católico, Carlos I, Amerigo Vespucci and native Americans can all be seen sheltered beneath the cloak of the Virgin in her role as protector of sailors. This room also contains a model of Columbus' ship, the *Santa María*. An adjacent room houses an international collection of strikingly pretty fans.

Palacio de Don Pedro

Whatever else Pedro I may have done, posterity owes him a big thank you for creating this palace, which rivals Granada's Alhambra in its splendid design and decoration. The entrance is on the southern side of the Patio de la Montería. The palace is also called Palacio de Mudejar.

Though unable to trust many of his fellow 'Christians' from closer to home, Pedro had a long-standing alliance with the Muslim emir of Granada, Mohammed V, the man responsible for much of the decoration of the Alhambra's magnificent Palacio Nazaríes. So in 1364, when Pedro decided to build a new palace within the Alcázar,

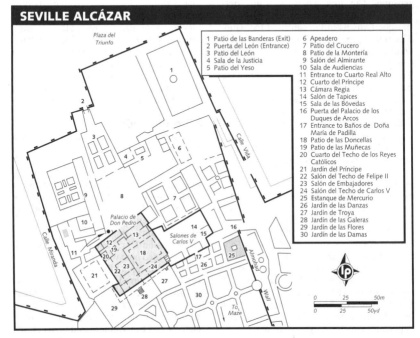

SEVILLE ALCÁZAR

Plaza del Triunfo

1 Patio de las Banderas (Exit)
2 Puerta del León (Entrance)
3 Patio del León
4 Sala de la Justicia
5 Patio del Yeso
6 Apeadero
7 Patio del Crucero
8 Patio de la Montería
9 Salón del Almirante
10 Sala de Audiencias
11 Entrance to Cuarto Real Alto
12 Cuarto del Príncipe
13 Cámara Regia
14 Salón de Tapices
15 Sala de las Bóvedas
16 Puerta del Palacio de los Duques de Arcos
17 Entrance to Baños de Doña María de Padilla
18 Patio de las Doncellas
19 Patio de las Muñecas
20 Cuarto del Techo de los Reyes Católicos
21 Jardín del Príncipe
22 Salón del Techo de Felipe II
23 Salón de Embajadores
24 Salón del Techo de Carlos V
25 Estanque de Mercurio
26 Jardín de las Danzas
27 Jardín de Troya
28 Jardín de las Galeras
29 Jardín de las Flores
30 Jardín de las Damas

Palacio de Don Pedro

Salones de Carlos V

Calle Vida

Calle Miranda

Almohad Wall

To Maze

0   25   50m
0   25   50yd

Cuarto Real Alto

The Alcázar is still a royal palace. As recently as 1995 it staged the wedding feast of the Infanta Elena, daughter of King Juan Carlos I, after her marriage in Seville's cathedral. The Cuarto Real Alto (Upper Royal Quarters), the rooms reserved for the Spanish royal family in and around the Palacio de Don Pedro, can now be visited on a guided tour. Tickets (€3) are sold in the southwestern corner of the Patio de la Montería, from where the tours start. Around 12 half-hour tours, for a maximum of 15 people, are given daily, alternately in Spanish and English. You can book in advance on ☎ 95 456 00 40. Highlights of the visit include a beautiful 1504 Italian Renaissance tile retable in the chapel, Pedro the Cruel's bedroom, with marvellous Mudejar tiles and plasterwork, and the 14th-century Salón de Audiencias, still the monarch's reception room.

Mohammed sent along many of his best artisans. These were joined by Jews and Muslims from Toledo, and others, mainly Muslim, from Seville. Their work, drawing on the traditions of the Almohads and caliphal Córdoba, represented the best of contemporary architecture and design. It's a unique synthesis of Iberian Muslim art.

Inscriptions on the Palacio de Don Pedro's relatively austere **facade**, facing the Patio de la Montería, encapsulate the unusual nature of the enterprise. While one records that the building's creator was 'the very high, noble and conquering Don Pedro, by the grace of God king of Castile and León', another intones repeatedly that 'There is no conqueror but Allah'.

Inside the entrance, the left-hand passage leads to the wonderful **Patio de las Doncellas** (Patio of the Maidens), which is surrounded by beautiful arches and with some exquisite plasterwork and tiling. The doors at the two ends are among the finest ever made by Toledo's carpenters. The upper galleries were added in 1540.

The **Cámara Regia** (King's Quarters), on the northern side of the Patio de las Don-

cellas, has two rooms with stunningly beautiful ceilings and more wonderful plasterand tilework. The rear room was probably the monarch's summer bedroom.

From here you can move west into the small **Patio de las Muñecas** (Patio of the Dolls), the heart of the palace's private quarters, with delicate Granada-style decoration on its lowest level. The mezzanine and top gallery were added in the 19th century for Queen Isabel II, using plasterwork brought from the Alhambra. The **Cuarto del Príncipe** (Prince's Room), to the north, has superb ceilings and was probably the queen's bedroom.

The spectacular **Salón de Embajadores** (Hall of Ambassadors), at the western end of the Patio de las Doncellas, was the throne room of Pedro I's palace – as it had been, in earlier form, of the Al-Muwarak palace (Al-Mutamid held literary soirees here). Pedro retained the door arches, heavily reminiscent of the Medina Azahara palace near Córdoba, from the Al-Muwarak palace. The room's fabulous wooden dome of multiple star patterns, symbolising the universe, was added in 1427. The dome's shape gives the room its alternative name, *Sala de la Media Naranja* (Hall of the Half Orange). The coloured plasterwork is equally magnificent. It was in this room that Pedro laid a trap for the so-called Red King, who had temporarily deposed Pedro's buddy Mohammed V in Granada. During a banquet, armed men suddenly leapt from hiding and seized the Red King and his retinue of 37, all of whom were executed outside Seville a few days later.

On the western side of the Salón de Embajadores the beautiful **Arco de Pavones** – named after its peacock motifs – leads into the **Salón del Techo de Felipe II**, with a Renaissance ceiling (1589–91). The **Salón del Techo de Carlos V**, along the southern side of the Patio de las Doncellas, has another fine ceiling (1540s) and used to be the palace chapel.

Salones de Carlos V

Reached by a staircase from the southeastern corner of the Patio de las Doncellas, these rooms named for Carlos V are the much-remodelled rooms of the 13th-century Gothic palace built by Alfonso X. It was here that Alfonso's intellectual court gathered and, a century later, Pedro I installed the mistress he loved, María de Padilla (notwithstanding the fact that he was already married to a French princess). The **Sala de las Bóvedas** (Hall of the Vault) is now adorned with beautiful tiles made for Felipe II in the 1570s by Cristóbal de Augusta. The **Salón de Tapices** (Tapestry Room) has a collection of huge 18th-century tapestries showing Carlos I's 1535 conquest of Tunis from the Turkish-backed pirate Barbarossa.

Patio del Crucero

This patio outside the northern side of the Salones de Carlos V was originally the upper level of the central patio of the 12th-century Almohad palace. At first it consisted only of walkways along the four sides and two cross-walkways which met in the middle (thus its name, Patio of the Crosses). Below grew orange trees, whose fruit could be plucked at hand height by the privileged folk strolling along the upper walkways. María de Padilla must have liked strolling around picking oranges, because the patio is also known as the Patio de María de Padilla.

The patio's whole lower level had to be built over in the 18th century after earthquake damage.

Gardens & Exit

From the Salones de Carlos V you can go out into the Alcázar's large gardens, the perfect place to wind down a little after some intensive sightseeing. The gardens in front of the Salones de Carlos V and Palacio de Don Pedro date back to Muslim times, but were mostly brought to their present form in the 16th and 17th centuries. Immediately in front of the buildings is a series of small linked gardens, some with pools and fountains. From one, the **Jardín de las Danzas** (Garden of the Dances), a passage runs beneath the Salones de Carlos V to the so-called **Baños de Doña María de Padilla** (María Padilla Baths). Here you can see the vaults beneath the Patio del Crucero – originally that patio's lower level – and a

grotto which replaced the patio's pool, in which, judging by the place's name, María de Padilla must have liked to bathe.

Farther out in the gardens is a **maze**. The gardens to the east, the other side of a long Almohad wall, are 20th-century creations. There's quite a good café near the wall. From the gardens you can return to the corner of the Salones de Carlos V, where a passage leads north to the **Apeadero**, a 17th-century entrance hall now housing a collection of carriages. From here you leave the Alcázar via the **Patio de las Banderas** (Patio of the Banners).

ARCHIVO DE INDIAS

The Archive of the Indies (☎ 95 421 12 34), on the western side of Plaza del Triunfo, has since 1785 been the main archive on Spain's American empire. Unfortunately it was closed for supposedly two years of restoration work in 2001. Its 8km of shelves hold 80 million pages of documents dating from 1492 through to the end of the empire in the 19th century. Researchers can still consult much of the archive with special permission. Before the current closure to the general public, there were rotating displays of fascinating maps and documents, often including manuscripts written by Columbus or Cervantes or conquistadors such as Cortés or Pizarro. The 16th-century building, designed by Juan de Herrera, was originally Seville's Lonja (Exchange) for commerce with the Americas. For an update on opening hours, check at the tourist office.

BARRIO DE SANTA CRUZ

This area east of the cathedral and Alcázar was Seville's medieval Jewish quarter (judería). Today it's a tangle of quaint, winding streets and lovely squares with flowers and orange trees. If you're not staying in the area, wander through it anyway: there are some good places to stop off for food or drink as you go.

The judería, which extended to just east of Calle Santa María La Blanca, came into existence after the Christian Reconquista (Reconquest) of Seville in 1248 and was emptied by a pogrom in 1391. **Plaza Doña Elvira** is a

Completed in 1507, Seville's cathedral is one of the largest in the world

Vaulted ceiling inside Seville's cathedral

Seville cathedral's blue-striped dome

The 13th-century Torre del Oro, Seville

Interior, Barrio de Santa Cruz, Seville

Plaza de España, Seville

Seville's horse-drawn carriages make a pleasant way to see the city sights

very pretty spot, with tiled benches beneath the orange trees.

On Plaza de los Venerables is the **Hospital de los Venerables Sacerdotes** (☎ 95 456 26 96; admission €3.60; open 10am-2pm & 4pm-8pm daily). Used from its inception in the 17th century until the 1960s as a residence for aged priests, it is now open for guided visits, but you may find it closed in August. You can visit the lovely central courtyard, the old living quarters, several art exhibition rooms (one with an interesting collection of prints of Seville), and the church with murals by Juan de Valdés Leal and fine sculptures by Pedro Roldán. The district's most characteristic square is **Plaza de Santa Cruz**, whose central cross, made in 1692, is one of the finest examples of Seville wrought-iron work.

A few steps away is the **Casa de Murillo** (Calle Santa Teresa 8; admission free; open 10.30am-1.30pm & 4pm-6.30pm Mon-Fri), where the famous painter lived. The permanent exhibits are minimal, but you might find an interesting temporary show. You may also find a good exhibition at the **Casa de la Memoria de Al-Andalus** (☎ 95 456 06 70; Calle Ximénez de Enciso 28; admission €1; open 9am-2pm & 6pm-8pm daily), which is dedicated to Andalucía's Muslim era. One interesting room is dedicated to influential women of the time – poets, teachers and even a judge.

EL CENTRO

The real centre of Seville is the densely packed zone of narrow, crooked streets north of the cathedral, broken up here and there by squares around which the city's life has revolved for aeons.

Plaza de San Francisco & Calle Sierpes

Site of a market in Muslim times, Plaza de San Francisco has been Seville's main public square since the 16th century. Once the scene of Inquisition burnings, today it's where the city's upper echelons sit on special viewing stands to watch the Semana Santa processions.

The **Ayuntamiento** (City Hall), on the square's western side, is a building of contrasting characters: its southern end is encrusted with lovely Renaissance carving from the 1520s and '30s, while its northern end, a 19th-century extension, is bare.

Pedestrianised Calle Sierpes, which heads north from the square, is Seville's fanciest shopping street. Take a few steps off Sierpes along Calle Jovellanos to the **Capilla de San José** (open 8am-12.30pm & 6.30pm-8.30pm daily). This small 18th-century chapel, created by the city's carpenters' guild, is a world unto itself of breathtakingly intense baroque ornamentation. The altarpieces are absolute riots of gilded, curving, carved wood, and there are cherubim popping out all over the place.

The **Palacio de Lebrija** (☎ 95 421 81 83; Calle de la Cuna 8; admission ground floor only €3, whole building €6.60; open 10.30am-1pm & 4.30pm-7pm Mon-Fri, 10am-1pm Sat), a block east of Calle Sierpes, is a 16th-century noble mansion with a rich collection of art, statuary, furniture and artisanry, and a very beautiful Renaissance/Mudejar courtyard. If you want to see the top floor, you must wait for the guided tour, but it's worth it. The Countess of Lebrija, one of the mansion's now-deceased 20th-century occupants, was an archaeologist who remodelled the house in 1914 and filled many of the rooms with treasures that she collected on her travels. (The countess' nephew lived here until 1999.) Upstairs there are Islamic, Japanese and Chinese rooms. There's also a three-flight staircase, surrounded by 16th- and 17th-century tiles, above which is a Muslim-coffered ceiling imported from another palace. Ancient Rome was the Countess' speciality, so the library is full of books on antiquity. There are also plenty of remains from Itálica, mostly mosaics and mainly on the ground floor. A delightful addition is the sound of birds twittering, right here in the city centre.

Plaza Salvador

A couple of blocks northeast of Plaza de San Francisco, this was the main forum of Roman Hispalis. It's dominated by the **Parroquia del Salvador** (open 8.45am-10am & 6.30pm-9pm Mon-Sat, 10.30am-2pm & 7pm-9pm Sun

CENTRAL SEVILLE

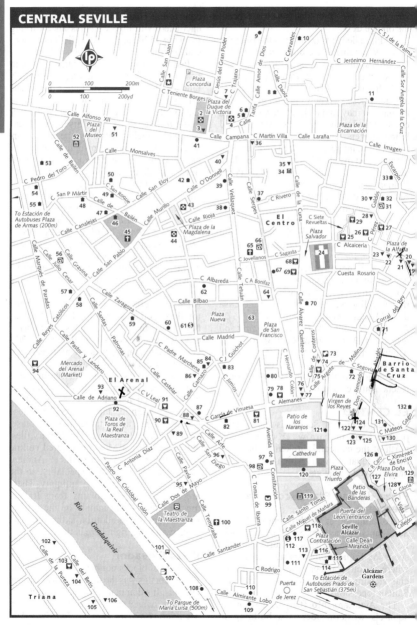

SEVILLA PROVINCE

Oct-June; 5.30pm
Sun July-Sept);
between 167
lim Ishbili
huge, pr
em s
wi

PLACES TO STAY
5 Hostal Pino
6 Hostal Unión
8 Hotel Sevilla
10 Hotel Cervantes
14 Hotel Baco
16 Las Casas del Rey
   de Baeza
17 Hotel Casa Imperial
32 Hostal Sol y Luna
33 Hostal Lis
42 Hostal Lis II
46 Hotel Colón
47 Hotel Plaza Sevilla
48 Hostal Londres
49 Hostal Residencia
   Naranjo
50 Hotel Zaida
53 Hostal Romero
54 Hostal Gravina
55 Hostal Gala
57 Hotel Becquer
58 Hotel Puerta de
   Triana
59 Hostal Central
70 Las Casas de los
   Mercaderes
71 Hostal Sánchez
   Sabariego
72 Hotel Los Seises
82 Hotel Simón
83 Hotel Europa
85 Hotel Maestranza
114 Hotel Arias
115 Pensión Alcázar
116 Hostal Picasso
126 Hostal Monreal
132 Hostal Goya
136 Hostal La Montoreña
139 Huéspedes D
   Sueños/Swe
141 Hostal Bienv
142 Las Casas de
143 Hotel Fernar
144 Hotel Amad
145 Hostal Córd
147 Pensión Fab
148 Pensión San
153 Pensión Cru
155 Pensión Ver
159 Hotel Muril
161 Hostal Tole
167 Hostería de

PLACES TO EAT
3 Café Bar Duque
7 Horno del Duque
12 El Rinconcillo
13 La Giganta
18 Bodega Extremeña
19 La Trastienda
20 Bar Alfalfa
21 La Bodega
22 Horno de San
   Buenaventura
23 Alfalfa 10
28 Habanita
30 Sopa de Ganso
35 Restaurante San Marco
36 Confitería La Campana
40 El Patio San Eloy
51 Bodegón Alfonso XII
64 Bar Laredo
74 Robles Placentines
76 Casa Robles
77 Las Escobas
84 Enrique Becerra
86 Bodega Paco Góngora
88 Mesón Cinco Jotas
89 Mesón Serranito
93 Bar Gloria Bendita;
   Casa Pepe-Hillo
95 Mesón de la Infanta
96 La Infanta
102 O Mamma Mia
104 Mex-Rock
105 Ristorante Cosa Nostra
106 Kiosco de las Flores
113 Restaurante Las Lapas
122 El Giraldillo
124 Cervecería Giralda
125 Café-Bar Campanario
127 Restaurant La Cueva
128 El Rincón de Pepe
130 Bodega Santa Cruz
134 Levíes
140 Restaurante La Judería
149 Carmela; Altamira
   Bar-Café
150 Bar Casa Fernando
151 Restaurante Modesto
156 Restaurante San Marco
157 Café Bar Las Teresas
158 Bar Entrecalles
166 Restaurante La
   Albahaca
168 Corral del Agua

OTHER
1 Police Station (Policía
   Nacional)
2 El Corte Inglés
4 El Corte Inglés
9 Record Sevilla
11 Mercado de la
   Encarnación (Market)
15 Café Lisboa
24 Parroquia del Salvador
25 Bar Europa
   Magdalena
52 Museo de Bellas Artes
56 Cibercenter
60 Renfe Office
61 American Express
62 CLIC
63 Ayuntamiento p.o (City
   Hall)
65 Capilla de San José
66 The E-m@il Place
67 Giacomelli Sport
68 La Sapotales
69 La Antigua Bodeguita
73 Netherlands Consulate
75 Antigüedades;
   La Subasta
78 P Flaherty Irish Pub
79 Librería Beta
80 Halcón Viajes
81 Hijos de E Morales
87 Tintorería Roma
90 Clan Scotsman Pub
91 Arena
92 Empresa Pagés
94 Café Isbiliyya
97 Usit Unlimited
98 Sevilla Internet Center
99 Main Post Office
100 Hospital de la
   Caridad
101 Bus Tours Stop
103 Tequila Connection
107 Jetty; River
   Cruises
108 Torre del Oro &
   Maritime Museum
109 ATA Rent A Car
110 Triana Rent A Car
111 Librería Beta
112 Main Tourist Office
117 Embrujo
118 Rayuela Café
119 Archivo de Indias
120 Cathedral Entrance
121 Giralda
123 Usit Unlimited
129 Hospital de los
   Venerables Sacerdotes
131 Giralda Centre
133 Australian Consulate
135 La Carbonería
137 LTC Map Shop
138 Vera Tintorería
146 Italian Consulate
152 Ciclismo
154 Casa de la Memoria de
   Al-Andalus
160 Casa de Murillo
162 French Consulate
163 El Tamboril
164 Irish Consulate
165 Los Gallos
169 Viajes Asatej; Ciber
   Easytech@
170 Centro de Urgencias
   (Emergency Medical Post)

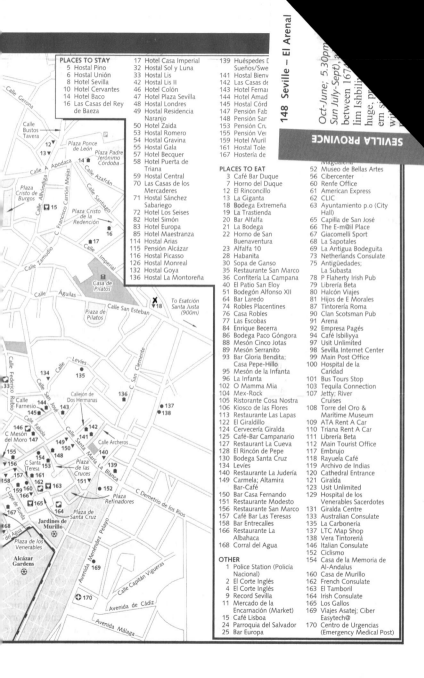

-9pm Mon-Fri, 8am-9pm
big, red baroque church built
and 1712 on the site of Mus-
a's main mosque. Inside are three
fuse baroque retables; on the north-
de, the mosque's small patio remains,
h orange trees, font, and a few half-buried
Roman columns.

Plaza de la Alfalfa

Some 200m east of Plaza Salvador, this was the site of the Muslim silk exchange and a later medieval market. It's an animated place, with many good bars and shops nearby.

Casa de Pilatos

The finest of Seville's noble mansions, still occupied by the ducal Medinaceli family, stands 300m east of Plaza de la Alfalfa along Calle Águilas. The Casa de Pilatos (☎ 95 422 52 98; admission lower floor only €5, whole house €8; open 9am-7pm daily Oct-June, 9am-noon daily July-Sept) is a mixture of Mudejar, Gothic and Renaissance architecture and decoration, with some beautiful tilework and artesonado ceilings. The overall effect is similar to that of the Alcázar. If time or money are short, skip the top floor.

There are rival explanations for the building's name, which means Pilate's House. One is that its 16th-century creator, Don Fadrique Enríquez de Ribera, was trying to imitate Pontius Pilate's palace in Jerusalem, to which city he had made a pilgrimage. Another is that the house served as the first station of a Via Crucis (Way of the Cross) route, in which penitents symbolically retraced Christ's steps to the Crucifixion. The first station would represent Christ's appearance before Pilate.

A plan on your ticket helps you find your way round. From the **Apeadero**, a courtyard for boarding and alighting from carriages, you pass into the **Patio Principal**, which has lots of wonderful 16th-century tiles, intricate Mudejar plasterwork and a Renaissance fountain. The armless statue of Athene, on the far side from the entrance, is Greek, from around the 4th century BC; the statues in the other corners are Roman. Around the walls are busts of Roman historical and mythical figures, plus King Carlos I of Spain.

The names of the rooms off the Patio Principal recall the supposed Pontius Pilate connection. The **Descanso de los Jueces** (Judges' Retiring Room), **Salón Pretorio** (Palace Hall) and **Gabinete de Pilatos** (Pilate's Study) have artesonado ceilings. Beyond the Salón Pretorio are the **Zaquizami**, a corridor with Roman sculptures and inscriptions, and the **Jardín Chico** (Small Garden). The Gabinete de Pilatos leads into the **Jardín Grande** (Big Garden), with Italian-style loggias on three of its sides.

The **staircase** leading from the Patio Principal to the upper floor has the most magnificent tiles in the building, and a great golden artesonado dome above. Visits to the **upper floor** itself, partly inhabited by the Medinacelis, are accompanied by a rather hurried guide. Of interest are the several centuries' worth of Medinaceli portraits and a small Goya bullfight painting, in the Salón Oviedo.

EL ARENAL

A short walk west from Avenida de la Constitución brings you to the bank of the Río Guadalquivir, a pleasant place for a stroll. This district, El Arenal, is home to some of Seville's most interesting sights.

Torre del Oro

The 'Tower of Gold' is a 13th-century Almohad watchtower, on the riverbank just north of the Puente de San Telmo. It once crowned a corner of the city walls that stretched here from the Alcázar, and was supposedly covered in golden tiles. Inside is a small, crowded **maritime museum** (admission €1, free Tues; open 10am-2pm Tues-Fri, 11am-2pm Sat & Sun Sept-July; closed Aug). The collection of models of famous boats merits a visit.

Hospital de la Caridad

A block east of the river, this hospice for the elderly (☎ 95 422 32 32; Calle Temprado 3; admission €3, free Sun; open 9am-1.30pm & 3.30pm-6.30pm Mon-Sat, 9am-1pm Sun & holidays) was founded in the 17th century by Miguel de Mañara – by legend a notorious libertine who changed his ways after experiencing a vision of his own funeral procession. The interest lies in the hospital's church for which, in the 1670s, Mañara commissioned a collection of top-class Sevillan art and sculpture on the theme of death and redemption, by Murillo, Juan de Valdés Leal and Pedro Roldán.

The two masterworks of Valdés Leal, chillingly illustrating the futility of worldly success in the face of death, are at the western end of the church. In *Finis Gloriae Mundi* (The End of Earthly Glory), above the door by which you enter, a bishop, a king and a knight of Calatrava are devoured in their coffins by worms and cockroaches, while Christ's hand weighs their virtues and their sins (represented by animals) in the balance. *In Ictu Oculi* (In the Blink of an Eye), on the opposite wall, shows a skeletal Death figure extinguishing the candle of life while trampling symbols of power, glory, wealth and knowledge. On this same side of the church are Murillo's *San Juan de Dios* (St John of God, caring for an invalid) and *Moises Haciendo Brotar el Agua de la Roca* (Moses Drawing Water from the Rock). These are two of eight large Murillo canvases painted for this church on themes of compassion and mercy – ways of transcending death. (Four of the eight were looted by Napoleonic troops.) To the left of the high altar, steps descend to the crypt where Miguel de Mañara is buried.

The sculpture on the high altar illustrates the ultimate act of compassion – the burial of the dead (in this case Christ). The tableau, with its strong sense of movement, is Pedro Roldán's masterpiece. It was painted by Valdés Leal.

On the southern side of the church are the other two remaining Murillos: *La Multiplicación de Panes y Peces* (The Miracle of the Loaves and Fishes) and *Santa Isabel de Húngria* (St Isabel of Hungary, caring for the diseased and poor), plus another fine Roldán sculpture, of Christ praying before being nailed to the cross.

Plaza de Toros de la Real Maestranza

Seville's bullring (☎ 95 421 03 15; Paseo de Cristóbal Colón 12; open for guided tours 9.30am-2pm & 3pm-7pm daily, 9.30am-3pm *bullfighting days*) is one of the most handsome and important in Spain, and probably the oldest (building began in 1758). It was in this ring and the one at Ronda in Málaga province that bullfighting on foot began in the 18th century. The site was originally a practice ground for Seville's Real Maestranza de Caballería (Royal Cavalry Masterhood) – hence its name today.

You can take a tour of the ring and its museum, and peep into its minihospital for bullfighters who have come off second best. The interesting guided visits, in English and Spanish, happen about every 20 minutes (€3). For more on bullfights in Seville, see Spectator Sports later in this chapter; for general information on bullfighting, see Spectator Sports in the Facts for the Visitor chapter.

Iglesia de la Magdalena

This jewel among Seville's baroque churches (Calle San Pablo; open 8am-11am & 6.30pm-9pm daily) was built between 1691 and 1709. Two paintings by Zurbarán hang in the Capilla Sacramental, and a fine 1612 Crucifixion sculpture, *El Cristo del Calvario* (The Christ of Calvary) by Francisco de Ocampo, is in the chapel to the right of the main altar.

The church is the home of the Quinta Angustia brotherhood, whose 17th-century *Descendimiento* tableau, depicting the taking down of Jesus from the cross, is carried through Seville's streets during Semana Santa. This can usually be seen in the chapel on the left as you enter the church: the Christ is attributed to Pedro Roldán. The church is open at service times.

Museo de Bellas Artes

The Fine Arts Museum (☎ 95 422 07 90; Plaza del Museo 9; admission €1.50, EU citizen free; open 3pm-8pm Tues, 9am-8pm Wed-Sat, 9am-2pm Sun), housed in the beautiful former Convento de la Merced, is Andalucía's best art museum. It does full justice to Seville's leading role in Spain's 17th-century artistic *Siglo de Oro* (Golden Century) – see the boxed text 'The Golden Century in Seville' – and a visit is a big help to understanding the context of much of the other art you see in Seville and Andalucía.

The 17th-century Sevillan masters Murillo, Zurbarán and Valdés Leal are particularly well represented. The museum also holds interesting Sevillan antecedents to the golden age, and some works by artists who worked elsewhere, such as El Greco and José de Ribera.

Room I exemplifies the 15th-century beginnings of the Sevillan school: the best

The Golden Century in Seville

As Spain's richest and most important city for much of the period, Seville played a leading role in the country's artistic *Siglo de Oro* (Golden Century), which ran from roughly the late-16th to late-17th centuries. The great Sevillan artists of this era are well represented in the city's Museo de Bellas Artes.

The 17th century dawned in Seville with artists such as Juan de Roelas (1560–1625) and Francisco Pacheco (1564–1654) adopting an increasingly naturalistic approach to their painting that signalled the move from the stiff, idealised schemes of Mannerism to the flowing curves of baroque. Pacheco's studio was the centre of a humanist circle that influenced most significant Andalucian artists of the century. He advised his pupils to 'go to nature for everything'. Roelas travelled in Italy and his 'two-level' style – depicting heavenly realms in the upper parts of his large canvases and earthly matters below – was also very influential.

The mystically inclined Francisco de Zurbarán (1598–1664), a Basque born in Extremadura, lived most of his life in and around Seville, though he eventually died in poverty in Madrid. Zurbarán's clear, spiritual paintings of saints, churchmen and monastic life often utilise strong light/shadow contrasts comparable with the work of two contemporaries, the Italian Caravaggio and José de Ribera, a Spaniard who spent most of his life in Italy. Notable Zurbarán collections are to be seen in Seville cathedral and the Museo de Cádiz.

Francisco Pacheco's son-in-law, Seville-born Diego Rodríguez de Silva y Velázquez (1599–1660), also showed a strong naturalistic leaning and used masterly light/shadow effects in the early works he painted in Seville –religious scenes (using models drawn from the city's streets), kitchen scenes and portraits. Velázquez left Seville in 1623 to become an official court painter in Madrid and, ultimately, Spain's major artist of the epoch.

Bartolomé Esteban Murillo (1618–82) and his friend Juan de Valdés Leal (1629–90), both Seville-born, led the way to full-blown baroque art. The prolific Murillo, youngest of 14 children, was orphaned at the age of nine. His fine technique and soft-focus beggar images and religious scenes (he did seemingly dozens of versions of the *Concepción Inmaculada*, the Immaculate Conception) were very popular in a time of economic decline and gained him many artistic disciples. He died from injuries received in a fall while painting a retable in Cádiz. The greatest works of the passionate Valdés Leal, who could be both humorous and bitterly pessimistic, can be seen, alongside several Murillos, in Seville's Hospital de la Caridad.

Sevillan sculptor Juan Martínez Montañés (1568–1649) carved such dramatic and lifelike wooden images that contemporaries called him 'El Dios de la Madera' (The God of Wood). His work crops up in many Andalucian churches, and many of the statues still carried by the city's Semana Santa (Holy Week) processional brotherhoods are the work of his hands. Martínez Montañés' Crucifixions, Immaculate Conceptions, infant Christs, and retables with diverse carvings of saints, served as models for generations of sculptors. Among Montañés' many disciples, Juan de Mesa stands out for the pathos of his images, particularly his Crucifixions.

The leading Sevillan sculptor of the second half of the 17th century was Pedro Roldán (1624–99). Some of his work (in wood) was painted by Valdés Leal and, like Leal's, Roldán's best work is in the Hospital de la Caridad. Several of Roldán's children and grandchildren were sculptors too. It was his daughter María Luisa Roldán, or 'La Roldana' (1654–1704), who, according to tradition, created La Macarena, the powerful Virgin image that takes the place of honour in Seville's Semana Santa.

exhibits are Pedro Millán's terracotta sculptures, displaying a realism that was then rare in Spanish art.

Room II was the dining hall of the convent. Displayed here is Renaissance work from Seville and elsewhere, including El Greco's piercing portrait of his son Jorge Manuel and sculptures by Pedro Torrigiano, an Italian who came to Seville in 1522 and was the major artistic figure of the early Renaissance here. His life-size *San Jerónimo Penitente*, with its expressive head and finely studied anatomy, was very influential.

Room III exhibits Sevillan Renaissance retables and early 17th-century baroque Sevillan paintings, including Velázquez's portrait of Don Cristóbal Suárez de Ribera and Alonso Cano's *San Francisco de Borja*. Cano's striking *Las Ánimas del Purgatorio* (Souls in Purgatory) is in the corner between rooms III and IV.

In room IV, which is devoted mainly to Mannerism – a rather stiff transition between Renaissance and baroque art – Alonso Vázquez's large *Sagrada Cena* (Last Supper) stands out. From here you move through the beautiful cloister to room V, the convent church, which is hung with paintings by masters of Sevillan baroque. Zurbarán's masterly *Apoteosis de Santo Tomás de Aquinas* (Apotheosis of St Thomas Aquinas) is here, but the room is dominated by Murillo, whose *Inmaculada Concepción Grande*, depicting the Virgin borne aloft by cherubim, displays all the curving, twisting movement that is so central to baroque art. This painting hangs at the head of the church, along with other works by Murillo, which were, like this, originally painted for other churches.

Upstairs, highlights of room VI include Ribera's very Spanish-looking *Santiago Apóstol* (St James the Apostle) and Zurbarán's small *Cristo Crucificado, Expirante* (Christ Crucified, Expiring), perhaps the most disturbing picture in the whole museum. Room VII is devoted to Murillo and his disciples, room VIII to Valdés Leal, and room IX to baroque art from elsewhere in Europe.

Room X is all Zurbarán: the *Cristo Crucificado* is one of his greatest achievements.

He draws a masterly contrast between the worldly Pope Urban II and the ascetic St Bruno in *Visita de San Bruno a Urbano II*.

Room XI displays Sevillan and Spanish painting of the 18th century, a time when Spain had lost its creative verve. Rooms XII to XIV show 19th- and 20th-century painting, mainly Sevillan, with the works of Romantic Antonio María Esquivel and historical painter Eddo Cano among the most interesting.

There is a Sunday art market outside the museum on Plaza del Museo. Police patrol it to see if stolen artworks are for sale.

SOUTH OF THE CENTRE
Antigua Fábrica de Tabacos
Seville's massive former tobacco factory *(Calle San Fernando; open 8am-9.30pm Mon-Fri, 8am-2pm Sat)* – workplace of Bizet's operatic heroine Carmen – was built in the 18th century and served its original purpose until the mid-20th century. For a long time a cornerstone of the city's economy, the factory had its own jail, stables for 400 mules, 21 fountains, 24 patios and even a nursery, since most of its workers were women. Measuring 250m by 180m, it covers a larger area than any building in Spain except El Escorial, the great palace-monastery near Madrid.

Neoclassical in style, it's an impressive, if rather gloomy building. The main portal sports carvings on the theme of the discovery of the Americas, the original source of tobacco – among them Christopher Columbus, Hernán Cortés (conqueror of the Aztecs) and two native Americans, one of them smoking a pipe. At the top of the portal is Fame blowing a trumpet.

The old tobacco factory is now part of the Universidad de Seville (Seville University). You are free to wander through and take a look.

Parque de María Luisa & Plaza de España
A large area south of the Antigua Fábrica de Tabacos was transformed for the 1929 Exposición Iberoamericana, when architects spattered it with all sorts of fancy and funny

buildings, many of them harking back to Seville's eras of past glory. In their midst, the **Parque de María Luisa** (open 8am-10pm daily), with its maze of paths, flowers, fountains, shaded lawns and 3500 magnificent trees, is a beautiful respite from the hustle of the city. If you're more than one, a fun way to get around the park is by bicycle (with canopy). **Cyclotour** in the northwest corner of the park rents two-/four-seaters for €9/11 per hour.

Facing the northeastern side of the park across Avenida de Isabel la Católica, Plaza de España is one of the city's favourite relaxation spots, with fountains and minicanals. Curving round the square in a semicircle is the most grandiose of the 1929 buildings, a brick-and-tile confection featuring Seville tilework at its gaudiest, with a map and historical scene for each Spanish province. The tilework has recently been renovated.

On Plaza de América at the southern end of the park is a large flock of white pigeons (they'll clamber all over you if you buy a €1.50 bag of seed from vendors), and two interesting museums. Highlights of the big **Museo Arqueológico** (☎ 95 423 24 01; admission €1.50, EU citizen free; open 3pm-8pm Tues, 9am-8pm Wed-Sat, 9am-2pm Sun & holidays) include a room of gold jewellery from the mysterious Tartessos culture and fine collections of Iberian animal sculptures and beautiful Roman mosaics. Among large quantities of Roman sculpture are, in room XX, sculptures of the two emperors from Itálica near Seville, Hadrian (Adriano) and Trajan (Trajano, with the top half of his head missing).

Facing the Museo Arqueológico is the **Museo de Artes y Costumbres Populares** (☎ 95 423 25 76; admission €1.50, EU citizen free; open 3pm-8pm Tues, 9am-8pm Wed-Sat, 9am-2pm Sun & holidays), in the 1929 exhibition's Mudejar pavilion, which appeared as an Arab palace in the film Lawrence of Arabia. Its collection includes mock-up workshops of local crafts such as guitar-making, ceramics and wrought iron, and some really beautiful old bullfight and festival costumes.

NORTH OF THE CENTRE

The more working-class area north of Calle Alfonso XII and Plaza Ponce de León is an interesting contrast to the city centre. A couple of the city's best street markets (see Shopping later in this section) are to be found up here.

Alameda de Hércules

This dusty 350m-long parklike strip was created in the 1570s by draining a marsh. Two columns from a ruined Roman temple were erected at its southern end and topped with statues of Hercules and Julius Caesar by Diego de Pesquera.

Planted with avenues of *álamo* (poplar) trees – hence the name – the Alameda became a fashionable meeting place in the 17th century. By the 1980s, however, the area was little more than a red-light zone. But it has since come back up in the world and is now one of the city's liveliest nightlife areas – with a bohemian, alternative scene. The plaza was dug up for revamping in 2002, which did nothing for its image, but the end result should be worth it.

Basílica de Jesús del Gran Poder

This 1960s church (Plaza de San Lorenzo 13; open 8am-1.45pm & 6pm-9pm daily), behind a large baroque portal in the corner of Plaza de San Lorenzo, houses, above its main altar, a famous and far older sculpture of a cross-bearing Christ (after which it is named). The almost wizened Christ image, sculpted in 1620 by Juan de Mesa, inspires much Sevillan devotion and takes a place of honour in the Semana Santa processions. On either side of the altar are a sculpture of St John the Evangelist, also by de Mesa, and an anonymous *Virgen del Mayor Dolor* (Virgin of the Deepest Grief) of the 18th century or earlier.

Basílica de la Macarena & Around

If you're not in Seville for Semana Santa, you can get an inkling of what it's about at the Basílica de la Macarena (☎ 95 437 01 95; Calle Bécquer 1; open 9am-1pm & 5pm-9pm daily), off Calle San Luis. This 1940s church contains the most adored religious image in Seville, the *Virgen de la Esperanza* (Virgin of Hope), believed to have been sculpted in the mid-17th century. The sculptor's identity is not certain but tradition says it was María Luisa Roldán, 'La Roldana'. Commonly known just as La Macarena, this Virgin is patron of bullfighters and is Seville's supreme representation of the grieving, yet hoping, mother of Christ. She stands in appropriate splendour behind the main altarpiece, adorned with a golden crown, lavish vestments, and five diamond-and-emerald brooches that were donated by a famous early-20th-century matador, Joselito El Gallo.

In front of and below La Macarena stands a beautiful 1654 statue of *El Cristo de la Sentencia* (Christ of the Sentence) by Felipe Morales. Both statues are carried from the church at midnight at the start of every Good Friday: their journey through the city is the climax of Semana Santa in Seville. Their return to the church around 1.30pm is attended by enormous crowds.

The church's **museum** *(admission €2.80; open 9.30am-1pm & 5pm-8pm daily)* displays rich vestments of La Macarena and the lavish Semana Santa platforms *(pasos)* on which both images are carried. The *paso* of El Cristo de la Sentencia is in fact a tableau of the scene of Pontius Pilate washing his hands; that of La Macarena bears 90 silver candlesticks.

Bus Nos C1, C2, C3 and C4 (see Getting Around later in this chapter for details) stop near the Basílica de la Macarena, on Calle Andueza. East of the church extends the longest surviving stretch of Seville's 12th-century **Almohad walls**. On the far side of a small park across the road is the **Parlamento de Andalucía**, Andalucía's regional parliament (not generally open to visitors).

TRIANA

Across the Guadalquivir from the Torre del Oro and Plaza de Toros de la Real Maestranza is Triana, the *barrio* (district) that used to be Seville's *gitano* (Roma people) quarter and was one of the birthplaces of flamenco. The *gitanos* were moved out to new suburban areas in the 1960s and '70s, and Triana is now rather trendified. But the river-front streets Calle del Betis and Paseo de Nuestra Señora de la O make a very pleasant stroll, with views back across the river to the city centre, and some good restaurants and very popular bars and cafés.

ISLA DE LA CARTUJA

North of Triana, this northern part of an island formed by two branches of the Guadalquivir was the site of Expo '92. Since the big year, the area has had a chequered history and expanses of it now lie decaying, victims of political squabbles and lack of funds and purpose. But there's still a bit to see and do. Bus Nos C1 and C2 (see Getting Around later in this chapter for details) go to Isla Mágica and the Conjunto Monumental de La Cartuja.

Conjunto Monumental de La Cartuja

Columbus used to stay in La Cartuja monastery, and after his death his remains lay here from 1509 to 1536. In 1836 the monks were expelled during the Disamortisation (when church property was auctioned off by the state) and the monastery's many art treasures were moved elsewhere. Three years later the complex was bought by a Liverpudlian, Charles Pickman, who turned it into a porcelain factory. Pickman built the five tall bottle-shaped kilns which stand incongruously beside the monastery buildings, and the porcelain factory functioned till 1982.

The complex *(☎ 95 503 70 70; admission €1.80, EU citizen free Tues; open 10am-8pm Tues-Sat, 10am-3pm Sun Oct-Mar; 10am-9pm Mon-Fri, 11am-9pm Sat, 10am-3pm Sun Apr-Sept)* was restored for Expo '92. Today you can visit the main monastery buildings which include the **Centro Andaluz de Arte Contemporáneo** (Andalucian Contemporary Art Centre), a set of exhibition rooms. The entrance is from the monastery's western side on Calle Américo Vespucio, a 1km walk from the monastery's eastern side facing the Puente de la Cartuja footbridge. The monastery also features a now rather bare 15th-century **church**, a pretty Mudejar cloister from the same era, and a roomful of disarmingly realistic 16th-century funerary sculptures of members of the Ribera family. The **Capilla de Santa Ana**, off the church, was built as the Columbus family tomb.

Exhibition Pavilions

Some of the exotic Expo pavilions north and south of the monastery are slowly being turned into a technology industries and trade park. Others are being used by the Universidad de Sevilla, and some are rotting away. Many can only be accessed from the western side (Calle Américo Vespucio), Monday to Friday.

Isla Mágica

The theme park Isla Mágica (☎ 902 16 17 16; admission adult/child or senior €21/14.50 all day, €14.50/11 5pm-closing; open 11am-10pm almost daily May-June; 11am-midnight July–mid-Sept plus some weekends & holidays in Mar, April, Oct & Nov) opened in 1997 as a second attempt to get a post-Expo amusement/theme park going on a site around a lake on the eastern side of the Isla de La Cartuja, near the Puente de la Barqueta. Like its predecessor, Isla Mágica has faced financial problems, and even though about 1.2 million visitors came in 1999, its private-enterprise operators had to be bailed out by the Junta de Andalucía so that it could open for the 2000 season.

The theme is the 16th-century Spanish colonial adventure. Highlight rides include a roller coaster with high-speed 360° turns, and the Iguazú, on which you descend a South American jungle waterfall. At busy times you may have to wait 45 minutes for the big attractions. There are also events such as pirate shows, movies, bird-of-prey displays and lots of entertaining street-theatre-type stuff.

Prices here are for July to mid-September. You can expect to pay less at other times. Child admission costs are for children under 13, and senior prices are for adults over 60. There are plenty of places to eat and drink inside the park.

COURSES
Language

For details of Spanish-language courses at the university, contact Seville University's **Instituto de Idiomas** (☎ 95 455 11 56, fax 95 455 14 50; Universidad de Sevilla, Avenida Reina Mercedes s/n, 41012 Sevilla). The main tourist office can give you a list of about a dozen private language colleges. Three that we have heard good things about are the large and professional **CLIC** (☎ 95 450 21 31; W www.clic.es; Calle Albareda 19), just north of Plaza Nueva, **Lengua Viva** (☎ 95 490 51 31; W www.lenguaviva.es, Calle Viriato 22, Plaza de San Martín), near Alameda de Hércules, and the **Giralda Center** (☎ 95 422 13 46; W www.giraldacenter.com; Calle Mateos Gago 17) near the Giralda. For further information on language courses in Andalucía see Courses in the Facts for the Visitor chapter.

Dance & Guitar

The main tourist office has a list of several dance academies (academias de baile), which you can contact if you're looking for a course in flamenco or other Spanish dance, or guitar. You'll also find adverts in the magazine El Giraldillo (see Entertainment in the Facts for the Visitor chapter).

ORGANISED TOURS

The open-topped double-decker buses and converted trams of **Sevilla Tour** (☎ 902 10 10 81) make several daily city tours of about one hour, with earphone commentary in a choice of several languages. You can board on Paseo de Cristóbal Colón (100m north of the Torre del Oro), or on Avenida de Portugal behind Plaza de España. Frequency of service depends on demand but buses typically leave every 30 minutes from 10am to 8pm. The adult fare is €11. The ticket is valid for 24 hours and you can also get on or off on the Isla de La Cartuja. The route takes in the Puerta de Jerez, Antigua Fábrica de Tabacos, Parque de María Luisa, Plaza de España, Basílica de la Macarena and Plaza de Toros de la Real Maestranza.

Sevirama/Guide Friday (☎ 94 456 06 93) operates similar tours for a similar price from the same stops in open-top double-deckers.

One-hour river cruises by **Cruceros Turísticos Torre del Oro** (☎ 95 456 16 92) go every half-hour from 11am to 10pm from the jetty *(embarcadero)* by the Torre del Oro. Cruises cost €12; children under 12 don't pay.

From around May to September round-trip day cruises sail to Sanlúcar de Barrameda, 100km downriver at the river's mouth. Schedules vary from year to year: early and late in the season, cruises may only go at weekends. Several companies including Cruceros Turísticos Torre del Oro make the trips, from the jetty by the Torre del Oro, for around €23; children under 14 pay €11. It's 4½ hours each way, usually with 4½ hours in Sanlúcar de Barrameda in between.

The **horse-drawn carriages** that hang around near the cathedral and Plaza de España normally charge €25 (up to four people) for a one-hour trot around the Barrio de Santa Cruz and Parque de María Luisa areas. Boards with prices are posted on the street on the east side of the cathedral.

SPECIAL EVENTS

Seville's Holy Week processions (see the boxed text 'Semana Santa in Seville') and its Feria de Abril, the fair which follows a week or two later, are two of Spain's most famous and exciting festivals.

Feria de Abril

The April Fair, in the second half of the month, is a kind of release after the solemnity of Semana Santa. It takes place on a special site *(recinto)*, El Real de la Feria, in the Los Remedios area west of the Guadalquivir. The ceremonial lighting-up of the fairgrounds on the opening Monday night is the starting gun for six nights of eating, drinking, talking, fabulous flouncy dresses, and music and dancing till dawn. Much of the site is taken up by private areas for clubs, associations, families and groups of friends. But there are public areas, too, where much the same fun goes on. There's also a huge fairground.

In the afternoons, from about 1pm, those who have horses and carriages *(enganches)*

parade about the site – and the city at large – in their finery (many of the horses are dressed up too). Seville's major bullfight season also takes place during the *feria*.

Other Festivals

Other Seville events include:

Cabalgata de los Reyes Magos 5 January – a big evening parade of floats in which the Reyes Magos (Three Kings) and their retinues throw some 60,000kg of sweets to the crowds

Corpus Christi late May or June (19 June 2003, 10 June 2004) – an important early-morning procession of the Custodia de Juan de Arfe and accompanying images from the cathedral

Bienal de Flamenco September of even-numbered years – most of the big names of the flamenco world participate in this major flamenco festival, with events most nights for about three weeks, in various Seville locations.

PLACES TO STAY

Just about every room in Seville costs more during Semana Santa and the Feria de Abril. The typical increase is about 50%, but a few places double or even triple their prices. This *temporada extra* (extra season) seems to now last from March to May at some hotels. You should book ahead for rooms in Seville at this time, if you can afford them. Even at normal times accommodation is in demand, so it's always worth ringing ahead.

The summer prices given here can come down significantly between October and March. Some mid-range and top-end places cut prices during July and August. See Accommodation in the Facts for the Visitor chapter for more general information on places to stay.

PLACES TO STAY – BUDGET
Camping

Camping Sevilla (☎ 95 451 43 79; *2 people, tent & car €17; open year-round*) is about 6km out on the N-IV to Córdoba – on the right, just before the airport, if you're approaching from Seville. It runs a shuttle bus (€2) two to three times a day to/from Avenida de Portugal near Plaza de España in the city. The buses to Camping Sevilla from the city centre leave at 6.30pm and 10pm.

Camping Club de Campo (☎ 95 472 02 50) and **Camping Villsom** (☎ 95 472 08 28), slightly more expensive and impractical without your own wheels, are in Dos Hermanas, 15km south of Seville on the N-IV towards Cádiz.

Hostels

Albergue Juvenil Sevilla (☎ 95 461 31 50; Calle Isaac Peral 2; admission under 26/other €12.90/17.25 Mar-Oct & holiday periods; €10.90/15.20 Nov-Feb), the city's HI hostel, was modernised a few years ago and is south of the centre, just off Avenida de la Palmera. It has room for 277 people in twin or triple rooms, over half of which have bathrooms. The hostel is about 10 minutes by bus No 34 from opposite the main tourist office (ask for the *albergue juvenil*).

Hostales & Pensiones

Attractive Barrio de Santa Cruz, close to the cathedral and within walking distance of Prado de San Sebastián bus station, has lots of places, some of them reasonably good value, though many places are creeping up out of the budget range. There are many more budget places north of Plaza Nueva, convenient to Plaza de Armas bus station and still pretty central. Even if every place we mention here turns out to be full, there are plenty more in the same areas of town.

Some places in this price range will give a discount if you stay a few days. Single rooms in this range tend to be very poky.

Barrio de Santa Cruz & Around Towards the eastern edge of the Barrio de

---

Semana Santa in Seville

Every day of the week from Palm Sunday to Easter Sunday, large, richly bedecked images and life-size tableaux of scenes from the Easter story are carried from Seville's churches through the streets to the cathedral. They're accompanied by long processions, which may take more than an hour to pass, and watched by vast crowds. These rites go back to the 14th century but they took their present form in the 17th, when many of the images – some of them supreme works of art – were created.

Semana Santa (Holy Week) in Seville, with its combination of splendour and anguish, spectacle and solemnity, and overriding adoration of the Virgin, can give a special insight into the nature of Spanish Catholicism.

The processions are organised by more than 50 different *hermandades* or *cofradías* (brotherhoods, some of which include women). Each brotherhood normally carries two *pasos*, as the lavishly decorated platforms bearing the images are called. The first *paso* supports a statue of Christ, crucified, bearing the cross, or in a tableau representing a scene from the Passion; the second carries an image of the Virgin. The *pasos* are carried by teams of about 40 bearers called *costaleros*, who work in relays. The *pasos* are heavy – each *costalero* normally carries about 50kg – and they move with a hypnotic swaying motion to the rhythm of their accompanying bands and the commands of their *capataz* (leader), who strikes a bell to start and stop the *paso*.

Each pair of *pasos* has up to 2500 costumed followers, known as *nazarenos*. Many of these wear tall Ku Klux Klan–like capes which cover their heads except for narrow eye slits. The most contrite go barefoot and carry crosses. Membership of an *hermandad* is an honour keenly sought, even by some who normally wouldn't dream of attending mass.

Each day from Palm Sunday to Good Friday, seven or eight *hermandades* leave their churches in the afternoon or early evening and arrive between 5pm and 11pm at Calle Campana at the northern end of Calle Sierpes in the city centre. This is the start of the *carrera oficial* along Calle Sierpes, through Plaza San Francisco and along Avenida de la Constitución to the cathedral. The processions enter the cathedral at its western end and leave at the eastern, emerging on Plaza Virgen de los Reyes. They get back to their churches some time between 10pm and 3am.

Santa Cruz, Calle Santa María La Blanca teems with places to stay and eat.

Hostal Bienvenido (☎ 95 441 36 55; *Calle Archeros 14; singles €18, doubles €30-32, singles/doubles with bathroom €28/60)* is a friendly, 13-room place. There are three more *hostales* on this narrow street off Calle Santa María La Blanca.

Hostal La Montoreña (☎ 95 441 24 07; *Calle San Clemente 12; per person €12)*, a little northeast of Hostal Bienvenido, has eight simple rooms with shared bathrooms.

Pensión San Pancracio (☎ 95 441 31 04; e pensionspancracio@hotmail.com; *Plaza de las Cruces 9; singles/doubles €15/24, doubles with bathroom €36)*, on a small square just west of Calle Santa María La Blanca, has reasonably sized doubles. Run by some friendly women, this place is in a quiet location that gets a bit of a breeze in summer.

Pensión Cruces (☎ 95 422 60 41; *Plaza de las Cruces 10; dorm beds €15, singles €15-20, doubles €37-40)* has some rooms with shower and toilet and one large room adapted for people with disabilities. All rooms in this lovely old Seville house are set around two patios with attractive tiles and lots of greenery; some rooms have balconies and all have fans and winter heating.

Pensión Fabiola (☎ 95 421 83 46; *Calle Fabiola 16; singles €24, doubles €42-48, doubles with bathroom €60)*, with a plant-filled courtyard, has 13 simple, well-kept rooms. We hear that it is cold in autumn.

Hostal Córdoba (☎ 95 422 74 98; *Calle Farnesio 12; singles/doubles €33/51, with small shower-room €45/60)*, which has a

Semana Santa in Seville

The climax of the week is the *madrugada* (early hours) of Good Friday, when some of the most respected and popular *hermandades* file through the city. The first to reach the *carrera oficial*, about 1.30am, is the oldest *hermandad*, El Silencio, which goes in complete silence. At about 2am comes Jesús del Gran Poder, whose 17th-century Christ is one of the masterpieces of Sevillan sculpture. This is followed at about 3am by La Macarena, whose Virgin is the most passionately adored of all. Then come El Calvario from the Iglesia de la Magdalena, Esperanza de Triana, and finally, at about 6am, Los Gitanos, the *gitano* (Roma people) *hermandad*.

On the Saturday evening just four *hermandades* make their way to the cathedral, and finally, on Easter Sunday morning, the Hermandad de la Resurrección. In contrast to their fascination with the Crucifixion and the events leading up to it, Sevillans show relatively little interest in the Resurrection.

The styles of the *hermandades* show marked differences. City-centre brotherhoods, such as El Silencio, are traditionally linked with the bourgeoisie. They're austere, using little or no music, and wearing black tunics, usually without capes. *Hermandades* from the working-class *barrios* (districts) outside the centre, such as La Macarena, have brass and drum bands accompanying more brightly bedecked *pasos*. Their *nazarenos* wear coloured, caped tunics, often of satin, velvet or wool. They also have to come from farther away, and some are on the streets for more than 12 hours.

Programmes showing each *hermandad*'s schedule and route are widely available before and during Semana Santa. *ABC* newspaper prints maps showing the churches, recommended viewing spots (*lugares recomendados*) and other details. It's not too hard to work out which procession will be where and when, so you can pick one up in its own *barrio* or as it leaves or re-enters its church, always an emotional moment.

Crowds along most of the *carrera oficial* make it hard to get much of a view there, unless you manage to get a seat. These are sold for anything from about €10 on Plaza Virgen de los Reyes behind the cathedral to €25 or more on Good Friday morning on Calle Sierpes. But if you arrive early in the evening, you can usually get close enough to the cathedral to see plenty for free.

plant-draped atrium, has 13 nice air-con rooms. No traffic passes on this street.

Pensión Vergara (*☎ 95 421 56 68; Calle Ximénez de Enciso 11; singles/doubles €18/36)* has 12 brightly painted rooms around the upper levels of a 15th-century patio. Plants and skylights add to the cosy atmosphere of this off-beat place.

Hostal Toledo (*☎ 95 421 53 35; Calle Santa Teresa 15; singles/doubles €26/43)* is a friendly, well-kept place that has 10 clean, slightly shabby rooms, all with bath or shower.

Hostal Monreal (*☎ 95 421 41 66; Calle Rodrigo Caro 7; singles/doubles €20/40, doubles with bathroom €60)* is bigger, with 20 varied, clean rooms (a few with views of the Giralda).

Hostal Sánchez Sabariego (*☎ 95 421 44 70; Corral del Rey 23; singles €20-36, doubles €36-52)* is a friendly 14-room place between the Barrio de Santa Cruz and Plaza de la Alfalfa. It has an attractive little courtyard, and individually decorated rooms, most with bathroom.

Hostal Sol y Luna (*☎ 620 557 811; Calle Pérez Galdós 1A; rooms with/without bathroom €18/15)* is in a 19th-century palace just north of Plaza de Alfalfa. Run by a relaxed young couple, it's clean, bright, spacious and a touch quaint. There's a communal lounge room with TV, and a terrace, approached by rickety stairs, with fantastic city views.

Hostal Lis (*☎ 95 421 30 88, Calle Escarpín 10; doubles with shower/bathroom €22/42)*, a seven-room place slightly farther north of Hostal Sol y Luna, has a nice, tiled lobby, and rooms with bathroom, TV and air-con.

Pensión Alcázar (*☎ 95 422 84 57; Calle Deán Miranda 12; doubles with bathroom €37-48)*, on a peaceful little square just west of the Alcázar, has good doubles. There's a little terrace near the top with views of the Giralda.

Hostal Arias (*☎ 95 422 68 40, fax 95 421 83 89; Calle Mariana de Pineda 9; singles/doubles €34/43)*, around the corner from Pensión Alcázar, has 14 decent rooms with shower, TV and air-con. Floral-printed bedspreads lend a cute note to the decor.

North & West of Plaza Nueva A three-minute walk west of Plaza Nueva, **Hostal Central** (*☎ 95 421 76 60; Calle Zaragoza 18; singles €25, doubles €35-45 Mon-Thurs; singles €30, doubles €40-45 Fri-Sun, all with bathroom)*, has well-kept, decent-sized doubles. This place is run by a team of cheerful, semiretired gentlemen and friendly female cleaners. The traffic noise in the rooms on the street-side is significant. Interior rooms are less attractive but quieter.

Hostal Lis II (*☎ 95 456 02 28;* Ⓦ *www .sol.com/hostal-lisII; Calle Olavide 5; singles/ doubles €22.50/35.50, doubles with bathroom €41.80)* is a pretty house on a narrow street off Calle San Eloy. You can use the Internet here (€1.20/1.80 per 30 minutes/ hour). There have been reports of some problems with advance payment by credit card but the rooms are just fine.

Hotel Zaida (*☎ 95 421 11 38, fax 95 421 88 10; Calle San Roque 26; singles/doubles €36.50/54.50)*, a good place, occupies an 18th-century house with a lovely Mudejar-style arched patio. The 27 rooms are plain but decent, with air-con, TV and bathroom. Ground-floor rooms open straight onto the lobby, with its TV, and might be noisy.

Hostal Residencia Naranjo (*☎ 95 422 58 40; Calle San Roque 11; singles/doubles €27/41)*, almost opposite the Zaida, has 27 good rooms with bath, TV, air-con and telephone.

Hostal Londres (*☎ 95 421 28 96, fax 95 450 38 30; Calle San Pedro Mártir 1; singles/ doubles €42.80/57.80)*, a 23-room place, has a pleasant tiled lobby and plain but adequate air-con rooms with bath, TV and, in some cases, little balconies.

Hotel Plaza Sevilla (*☎ 95 421 71 49; Calle Canalejas 2; singles/doubles €39/51.45)*, a pleasant 50-room place neighbouring Hostal Londres, has well-kept if not huge rooms with bathroom and TV.

Hostal Romero (*☎ 95 421 13 53; Calle Gravina 21; singles/doubles €17/24, doubles with bathroom €33)*, a small, friendly place, offers bare but clean rooms around a patio.

Hostal Gravina (*☎ 95 421 64 14; Calle Gravina 46; singles/doubles €10/24)* has 15 adequate rooms with shared bathrooms.

Hostal Gala (✆ 95 421 45 03; Calle Gravina 52; doubles with/without bathroom €33/27) is slightly bigger than Hostal Gravina.

Hostal Unión (✆ 95 421 17 90; Calle Tarifa 4; singles/doubles with bathroom €30/51) is a friendly place near Plaza del Duque de la Victoria, a bustling square surrounded by classy big shops. It has nine good, clean rooms with TV and air-con.

Hostal Pino (✆ 95 421 28 10; Calle Tarifa 6; singles/doubles €21/33, with bathroom €27/42) is next door to Hostal Unión in an old building with a small patio. Rooms are bright and cheerful with lurid colour schemes.

Hotel Sevilla (✆ 95 438 41 61, fax 95 490 21 60; Calle Daoíz 5; singles/doubles €35/55) has around 30 clean, plain, medium-sized rooms with bathroom. Off its large lobby is a small, greenery-filled patio.

PLACES TO STAY – MID-RANGE
Barrio de Santa Cruz & Around
Hostal Picasso (✆/fax 95 421 08 64; e hpicasso@arrakis.es; Calle San Gregorio 1; singles or doubles June-Oct €34.75, Mar-May €86, doubles with bathroom June-Oct €41.40, Mar-May €106), just west of the Alcázar, offers small but pretty rooms with comfortable beds. There are discounts from November to February.

Hostería del Laurel (✆ 95 422 02 95, fax 95 421 04 50; W www.eintec.es/host-laurel; Plaza de los Venerables 5; singles/doubles Mar-June, Sept & Oct €64/90; Jan-Feb, July-Aug & Nov-Dec €45/61), above a characterful old bar in the heart of the Barrio de Santa Cruz, has 21 simple, spacious and attractive air-con rooms with TV and bath or shower.

Hotel Murillo (✆ 95 421 60 95, fax 95 421 96; Calle Lope de Rueda 7; singles/doubles Apr-May €80/104, Mar-June & Aug-Dec €45/60, Jan-Feb & July €35/48), near Hostería del Laurel, has a lobby like an antique showroom, but its 57 rooms are a little tired, if clean.

Huéspedes Dulces Sueños/Sweet Dreams (✆ 95 441 93 93; Calle Santa María La Blanca 21; singles/doubles with bathroom €64.20/85.60 Mar-May, €32.10/42.80

June-Feb), on the eastern edge of the Barrio de Santa Cruz, is friendly and has seven comfortable, clean, air-con rooms.

Hostal Goya (✆ 95 421 11 70; Calle Mateos Gago 31; singles/doubles with bathroom €39/63, doubles with shower €57) is very central and has 20 pleasant, clean rooms and a comfortable downstairs sitting area.

Hotel Amadeus (✆ 95 450 14 43, fax 95 450 00 19; Calle Farnesio 6; doubles €76-88, attic €101, suite €126), on the northern edge of the Barrio de Santa Cruz, is unique in Europe if not the world. The hotel is in an 18th-century mansion and has a music theme which attracts musicians and music lovers. There's a piano in the foyer where classical music concerts are often held. A couple of rooms have pianos and are sound-proofed. Decor is colourful and attractive and there is a terrace with good views.

El Arenal
This is a good, convenient location.

Hotel Simón (✆ 95 422 66 60, fax 95 456 22 41; Calle García de Vinuesa 19; singles/doubles €45.10/67.15),within a fine 18th-century house, has 29 very pleasant rooms with bathroom. It's extremely popular, so book ahead. Breakfast is available.

Hotel Europa (✆ 95 421 43 05, fax 95 421 00 16; W www.HotelEuropaSevilla.com; Calle Jimios 5; singles/doubles €72/91) has 16 decent, quite sizable rooms with TV, air-con, telephone and safety box, all in another fine 18th-century house.

Hotel Maestranza (✆ 95 456 10 70, fax 95 421 44 04; W www.andalunet.com/maestranza; Calle Gamazo 12; singles/doubles €49/87) has 18 rooms with TV, air-con and safes. It's on a quietish street.

North & West of Plaza Nueva
Hotel Corregidor (✆ 95 438 51 11, fax 95 438 42 38; Calle Morgado 17; singles/doubles €80/90), towards Alameda de Hércules, on a quiet little street, is a 77-room place. It has comfortable, clean, moderate-sized, air-con rooms with TV. Downstairs are spacious sitting areas, a bar and a little open-air patio. The hotel has an attractive

tiled lobby with pretty wooden screens. There's parking 200m away

Patio de la Cartuja (☎ 95 490 02 00, fax 95 490 20 56; Calle Lumbreras 8-10; singles/doubles €64/91), just off the northern end of Alameda de Hércules, occupies a former *corral*, a three-storey community of apartments around a patio which was once the typical form of Sevillan lower-middle-class housing. Renovated into 30 cosy apartments each with a double bedroom, kitchen, bathroom and sitting room with double sofa bed, it's a pleasant place to stay if you don't mind being this far north. Occupancy costs a bit less in January, February, July, August, November and December. Garage parking costs €8.40, and there's a café too.

Patio de la Alameda (☎ 95 490 49 99, fax 95 490 02 26; Alameda de Hércules 56; singles/doubles €64/91), near Patio de la Cartuja, is similar, with the same ownership and prices.

PLACES TO STAY – TOP END

Hotel Fernando III (☎ 95 421 73 07; Calle San José 21; singles/doubles €112/142), in the Barrio de Santa Cruz, has 156 comfortable if unimaginative rooms with TV and bathroom. It also has a restaurant, bar, a spacious lounge, garage and rooftop pool.

Las Casas de la Judería (☎ 95 441 51 50, fax 95 442 21 70; w www.casasypalacios .com; Callejón de Dos Hermanas 7; singles/doubles €88/132 Mar-June, Sept–mid-Nov), near Hotel Fernando III, consists of a group of charmingly restored old houses around several patios and fountains, with lots of pretty tiles and plants. Most of the 50-odd cosy rooms cost less during July and August. Breakfast is available, and there's a bar.

Two other similarly sized establishments in the same appealing small group of hotels are located in El Centro: **Las Casas de los Mercaderes** (☎ 95 422 58 58, fax 95 422 98 84; Calle Álvarez Quintero 9-13), centred on an 18th-century patio, with marginally lower rates than Las Casas de la Judería; and the more expensive **Las Casas del Rey de Baeza** (☎ 95 456 14 96, fax 95 456 14 41; Plaza Cristo de la Redención 2). This place has wonderful decor utilising traditional Andalucian features such as exterior blinds, made of esparto grass, as used in the sherry bodegas (traditional wine bars). It also boasts a gorgeous pool.

Hotel Casa Imperial (☎ 95 450 03 00, fax 95 450 03 30; w www.casaimperial.com; Calle Imperial 29; singles/doubles €212/230 Mar-June & Sept-Nov) is another good choice in the same attractive part of town as Las Casas del Rey de Baeza. It's in a 16th-century palace that once had a subterranean passage linking it to nearby Casa de Pilatos. Decoration is sumptuous; there are 24 luxurious rooms.

Hotel Los Seises (☎ 95 422 94 95, fax 95 422 43 34; Calle Segovias 6; singles/doubles €141.50/192.90) is a luxurious, though ageing, place set around the former rear patio of the 16th-century Archbishop's Palace, near the cathedral. The 43 rooms cost less during July and August, December, January and February. The hotel has a good restaurant and a rooftop pool.

Hotel Becquer (☎ 95 422 89 00, fax 95 421 44 00; e hbecquer@arrakis.es; Calle Reyes Católicos 4; singles/doubles €93/118), farther northwest than Hotel Los Seises, has 118 comfortable, modern rooms.

Hotel Puerta de Triana (☎ 95 421 54 04, fax 95 421 54 01; w www.hotelpuertade triana.com; Calle Reyes Católicos 5; singles/doubles €80.25/127.35) is a good 65-room hotel in a well-modernised traditional-style house.

Hotel Colón (☎ 95 422 29 00, fax 95 422 09 38; Calle Canalejas 1; singles/doubles €186/289) is one of the city's top hotels, a 200-room place modernised but with old-fashioned trimmings.

Hotel Baco (☎ 95 456 50 50, fax 95 456 36 54; Plaza Ponce de León 15; singles/doubles €84/129 Mar-June, €48.25/70.75 July-Feb), in the east of El Centro, has 25 recently decorated, quite attractive rooms. You're probably best with an off-street room, because of the bus stop outside.

Hotel Cervantes (☎ 95 490 02 80, fax 95 490 05 36; w www.hotel-cervantes.com; Calle Cervantes 10; singles/doubles €78/111.30) is a charming medium-sized hotel in modern style with 48 rooms that cost less in July, August and December to February. Breakfast is available. Some rooms are off a skylit patio, others are off an external patio with fountain and plants. Hotel Cervantes is on a quiet street in a rather quaint old part of the city, up towards Alameda de Hércules. There's a garage.

Hotel Alfonso XIII (☎ 95 491 70 00, fax 95 491 70 99; ₩ www.starwoodhotels.com; Calle San Fernando 2; singles/doubles €324/ 425), just south of the centre, is a magnificent 1920s confection of old Sevillan styles in mahogany, marble and tiles. You can break the bank in style here. If you're not a guest, wander by for a look and relax in the patio. You might be soothed by classical musicians playing the harp and flute, as we experienced one Sunday afternoon.

PLACES TO EAT

To catch the atmosphere of the city, plunge straight in and follow the winding tapas trail that links scores of spirited bars and bodegas. Classier modern eateries also abound but most give in to their Spanish roots, offering similar tasty titbits with an *alta cocina* (haute cuisine) edge.

Meals

Breakfast is available until about 11am; most restaurants serve lunch between 1pm and 3.30pm and dinner from 8.30pm to 11pm or midnight. If tapas take your fancy but you want more than a quick nibble, you can always opt for a *ración* (a meal-sized serving of a tapas dish) or *media-ración* (half a *ración*).

Barrio de Santa Cruz & Around The interlacing narrow streets and squares just east of the Alcázar make a convenient spot to stop and fill up, though you'll have to cope with the rabble that got there first. Of course, the restaurants are touristy, but thankfully some still have character.

Restaurant La Cueva (☎ 95 421 31 43; Calle Rodrigo Caro 18; menú €9) has a pleasant courtyard, where you can inhale the whiff of orange blossom and sizzling fish. It cooks up a storming paella Valenciana (€17.75 for two people) and the eggs

prepared 'flamenco style' (€9) will get your castanets clicking.

El Rincón de Pepe (☎ 95 456 29 75; Calle Gloria 6; 2-course menú €21.03), located down a shady passage not far from La Cueva, offers a tempting variety of homemade Andalucian dishes, plus fishy favourites such as grilled sole.

Corral del Agua (☎ 95 422 07 14; Callejón del Agua 6; mains €12-16, menú €21.40; closed Sun) has terrific inventive food and its cool, green courtyard is great on a hot day, if you can get a table. It's a good idea to book ahead. Try the lamb stuffed with spinach and pine nuts. Round it off with an Arabic-inspired dessert of orange, carrot and cinnamon!

Restaurante La Albahaca (☎ 95 422 07 14; Plaza de Santa Cruz 12; mains €17-18, 3-course menú €24) doesn't hesitate when it comes to gastronomic inventions and either the dishes or the prices will make you swoon. The flavoursome ragout of salmon and prawns in a sherry sauce (€17) is a tongue-twister in every sense.

El Giraldillo (☎ 95 421 45 25; Plaza Virgen de los Reyes 2; mains €11-15), with its splendid views of the cathedral, does warming chickpea soup (€11) and some great fish dishes, including tuna in onion sauce (€15).

Cervecería Giralda (☎ 95 422 74 35; Calle Mateos Gago 1; breakfast €0.60-3.15) can help conquer the effects of the night before with its recommended breakfasts, which include bacon and a dollop of scrambled eggs (€3.15). Munch on your *tostadas* (toasted rolls; €0.60 to €3.15) and imagine the place in its former guise – a Muslim bathhouse.

Restaurante Las Lapas (☎ 95 421 11 04; Calle San Gregorio 6; menú €8.40; closed Sun) lies in the path of incessant horse-drawn traffic and, it seems, the whole of Seville's student population. With that combination you'll find it rather noisy outside and in, but it's worth coming to try out the *molletes* (soft bread rolls) or the mushroom-and-ham omelette (€5.70).

Restaurante San Marco (☎ 95 421 43 90; Calle Mesón del Moro 6; mains €5.85-6.20; closed Mon) is one of many homogenised, but fairly classy, pizza and pasta places that dot the city. This one has added style because it's in another refurbished Muslim bathhouse. The food, however, doesn't quite match the exotic surrounds.

Hostería del Laurel *(☎ 95 422 02 95; Plaza de los Venerables 5; media-raciones €3.30-9, raciones €5.70-14.70)* brings together two great Spanish qualities: chirpy, affable waiters and an atmosphere that makes dining a pleasure. Hams and herbs drip from the ceiling of the old bar, where you can tuck into top-notch tapas.

Ordinary Calle Santa María La Blanca has a throng of eateries, whose muddle of outdoor seating is invariably crammed with diners.

Carmela *(Calle Santa María La Blanca 6; dish of the day €4)* serves up wholesome fare, such as spinach quiche (€5.20), and has an earthy feel, inspired by the headscarves and aprons donned by the rustic-looking waiting staff.

Altamira Bar-Café *(☎ 95 442 50 30; Calle Santa María La Blanca 4; platos combinados around €8)*, the snazzier place next door, has a medley of choice *media-raciones* (€3.30 to €5.40) and hulking *raciones* (€4.80 to €8.40).

Bar Casa Fernando *(Calle Santa María La Blanca; menú €6)* bustles with punters, most of whom can't resist the charm of the grinning waiter. But the food is pleasing too, with a good-value menu of the day that includes paella and a typical meaty dish.

Leviés *(cnr Calle San José & Calle Leviés; tapas €1.50-2.10, snacks around €3)* revels in the attention of a young and unpretentious Spanish clientele, who indulge in chicken baguettes (€3) and the like. Eat and chill.

Restaurante Modesto *(☎ 95 441 68 11; Calle Cano y Cueto 5; mains around €8)* is a classy place (so don't let the name fool you) that teams up with La Judería to present a full range of fish dishes. Try the mouthwatering tiny white clams in garlic sauce (€7.80).

Restaurante La Judería *(☎ 95 441 20 52; Calle Cano y Cueto 13A; mains around €8)* gives Modesto fans a change of scenery, though the dishes are basically the same.

The dizzily bright lights of the restaurants north of the cathedral function to attract and trap buzzing sightseers, so be prepared.

Las Escobas *(☎ 95 421 94 08; Calle Álvarez Quintero 62; 2-course menú €7.20; open noon-midnight daily)*, meaning 'The Brooms', has a good-value 2-course *menú* including wine.

Casa Robles *(☎ 95 456 32 72; Calle Álvarez Quintero 58; mains €10.80-15)* is more upmarket and splits its menu into dishes 'from the sea' and 'from the mountains'. Surf goodies include swordfish in sherry sauce (€15), while lamb sweetbreads (€11.70) are recommended if you go for turf.

El Arenal Boasting an eye-popping collection of gargantuan bulls' heads that stare down at the diners, **Mesón Serranito** *(☎ 95 421 12 43; Calle Antonia Díaz 9; platos combinados €5.50-6)* does tasty *media-raciones*, including *jamón serrano* (€6.60).

Bodega Paco Góngora *(Calle Padre Marchena 1; media-raciones around €6)* serves a delectable range of seafood at decent prices, including fish *a la plancha* (grilled).

Enrique Becerra *(☎ 95 421 30 49; Calle Gamazo 2; menú around €24; closed Sun)* adds a smart touch to El Arenal and cooks up hearty Andalucían dishes to rave about. The *menú* is a satisfying caboodle of two courses, bread, dessert, coffee and wine.

Bar Gloria Bendita *(Calle de Adriano 24; platos combinados €7.20)* smells of strong coffee and strong cheese, and will happily ply you with both. Share the intimate bar with a few locals or escape with your *bocadillo* (filled roll; €3) to the tables outside.

El Centro The city's most famous bakery, **Confitería La Campana** *(Cnr Calle Sierpes & Calle Martín Villa)*, has been turning out scrumptious cakes and pastries since 1885. Sit outside with your sweet treat and coffee (€1.45), and watch the shoppers flounce by.

Bar Laredo *(Cnr Calle Sierpes & Plaza de San Francisco)* is a popular breakfast stop that slaps together a variety of *bocadillos* (€2.80) for rapid consumption.

Restaurante San Marco (☎ 95 421 24 40; *Calle de la Cuna 6; mains around €7*), in an 18th-century palace, is the grandest of the San Marco batch of eateries. A classic quattro staggioni pizza costs €7.25.

Refresh yourself with a potent Spanish coffee at **Alfalfa 10** or **Horno de San Buenaventura**, both at Plaza de la Alfalfa 10, and perhaps indulge in a Buenaventura cake feast too.

Habanita (☎ 606 71 64 56; *Calle Golfo 3; raciones €5.20-7.80, media-raciones €2.40-4; open 12.30pm-4.30pm & 8pm-12.30am Mon-Sat, 12.30pm-4.30pm Sun*) serves a winning variety of Cuban, Andalucian, vegetarian and vegan food. Wash down specialities, such as mozzarella, tomato and basil salad (*media-ración €3.15*), with a pina colada and chat to the people you met last time.

Bodegón Alfonso XII (☎ 95 421 12 51; *Calle Alfonso XII 33; menú €5.75*) is a convenient breakfast stop for those visiting the Museo de Bellas Artes. Coffee and a delicious bacon *tostada* costs €2.50.

Horno del Duque (☎ 95 421 77 33; *Plaza del Duque de la Victoria; platos combinados €6-9*) throbs with shoppers in search of breakfast or a lunch-time helping of paella (€9).

Café Bar Duque (*Plaza del Duque de la Victoria; platos combinados around €5*) churns out sickly but ambrosial *chocolate y churros* (deep-fried doughnuts to dip in thick hot chocolate; €1.50) and a range of *platos combinados*.

El Corte Inglés, on the western side of Plaza del Duque de la Victoria, has a well-stocked supermarket in the basement.

Mercado del Arenal (*Calle Pastor y Landero*) and the **Mercado de la Encarnación** (*Plaza de la Encarnación*) are central Seville's two food markets. The Encarnación has been in its current 'temporary' quarters, awaiting construction of a new permanent building, since 1973!

South of the Centre Offering a variety of hot baguettes and pizzas (€3.90 to €5.10), **Baguettería La Merienda** (*Calle San Fernando 27; baguettes €1.80-2.85*) pampers the student crowd from the nearby university.

La Raza (☎ 95 423 20 24/38 30; *Avenida de Isabel la Católica 2; mains €11.10-16.20*) spreads its tables out under the trees in leafy Parque de María Luisa, and is a good spot for morning coffee. Peckish patrons may fancy paella too (€11.10 per person; minimum two people).

Restaurante Egaña Oriza (☎ 95 422 72 11; *Calle San Fernando 41; mains €15-35.75*) appeals to a smarter clientele and stakes its claim as the best restaurant in Seville. It does do superb Andalucian–Basque cuisine, including asparagus in fresh tomato vinaigrette (€16.85), though you'll be forgiven for thinking that Oriza's fume-choked position could be better.

Triana Now situated on the river bank, **Kiosco de las Flores** (☎ 95 427 45 76; *Calle del Betis; media-raciones €4.20, raciones €8.80*) has undergone a transformation from a 70-year-old shack to a glam conservatory. It still doles out great *pescaíto frito* (fried fish), including codfish bites and cuttlefish strips.

Restaurante Río Grande (☎ 95 427 39 56/83 71; *Calle del Betis; mains €10.80-15*) wins the prize for most desirable location; many diners spend their mealtime gazing at the Torre del Oro. If the menu does manage to catch your eye, try baked sea bream on a green pepper, tomato and onion layer (€13).

Deprived pizza lovers will be pleased to know that Calle del Betis has three popular parlours to choose from: **Restaurante San Marco** (☎ 95 428 03 10; *Calle del Betis 68; mains around €7*) churns out some functional pizzas in an 18th-century house; the slightly more economical **O Mamma Mia** (☎ 95 427 21 56; *Calle del Betis 33; pizzas €4-6.60*), one of a chain of pizzerias, does a lively trade on its cheese-laden fare; and topping it off is **Ristorante Cosa Nostra** (☎ 95 427 07 52; *Calle del Betis 52; pizzas €3.90-6; closed Mon*), which brims with a chatty crowd who have ventured across the river for the tastiest pizzas around.

Mex-Rock (☎ 95 428 40 12; *Calle del Betis 41*) is a grungy place that serves up a range of authentic Mexican dishes, such as sizzling chicken *fajitas* (€9.90) and vegie enchiladas (€6.30).

Tapas

It's sociable, still in vogue and something that should be done with a few friends in tow. Yes, tapas-hopping in Seville is a way of life that goes on from lunch time till bedtime (whenever that may be). In some bars your account is chalked on the counter in front of you and added up when you leave. For some tapas hints to get you started, see the boxed text 'Put a lid on it – Tapas & Raciones' and under Food in the Facts for the Visitor chapter.

Barrio de Santa Cruz A focal point for tapas pilgrims, **Bodega Santa Cruz** (☎ 95 421 32 46; Calle Mateos Gago; tapas €1.30-1.60), has a wonderful choice of flavoursome bites. Its popularity speaks volumes.

Cervecería Giralda (☎ 95 422 74 35; Calle Mateos Gago 1; tapas €1.50-1.80) merges traditional dishes, such as *pechuga bechamel* (chicken breast in bechamel sauce), with some exotic variations.

Café-Bar Campanario (☎ 95 456 41 89; Calle Mateos Gago 8; tapas €1.50-1.80) cooks up a hotch-potch of tapas favourites, including Spanish omelette, aubergines with cheese and divine croquettes with ham and bechamel. Unlike most of the old bars it has an airy feel.

Café-Bar Las Teresas (☎ 95 421 30 69; Calle Santa Teresa 2; tapas €1.50-3, media-raciones €5-7.50) proudly dangles its hams from the ceiling and keeps its punters amused with plates of authentic tapas, just right for sopping up the beer.

Bar Entrecalles (Calle Ximénez de Enciso; tapas €2) whisks up a fluffy Spanish omelette. If you're not on a date, try the very flavoursome potatoes in *alioli* (garlic mayonnaise).

Hostería del Laurel (☎ 95 422 02 95; Plaza de los Venerables 5; tapas around €1.50) does good tapas at its bar.

El Arenal No-nonsense, quality tapas is served at **Bar Pepe-Hillo** (☎ 95 421 53 90; Calle Adriano 24; tapas €1.65-2.10) in relaxed surroundings.

Mesón Cinco Jotas (☎ 95 421 05 21; Calle Castelar 1; tapas €1.50-2.40) is the place to pig out on succulent Jabugo ham, which

Top Tapas

- Caña de lomo – pork loin
- Cazón en adobo – dogfish marinated in vinegar, salt, lemon and spices, then deep-fried (delicious)
- Espinacas con garbanzos – spinach and chick peas
- Papas aliñás – sliced potatoes and boiled eggs, with vegetable garnish and a vinegar-and-oil dressing
- Pavía – battered fish or seafood
- Puntillitas – baby squid, usually deep-fried

comes from pigs that have snuffled out the finest acorns.

La Infanta (Calle Arfe 36; tapas from €1.50) gets classier tapas-hunters in the swing by sitting them round sherry barrels and indulging them with exquisite tapas. Its sister restaurant **Mesón de la Infanta** (Calle Dos de Mayo 26; tapas €1.50-2.40) cooks up similarly trendy tapas.

Bodega Paco Góngora and **Enrique Becerra** (see El Arenal under Meals, earlier) are prime spots for tapas too.

El Centro Plaza de la Alfalfa is the hub of the tapas scene, with a flush of first-rate bars. Hop from sea-themed **La Trastienda** (Calle Alfalfa; tapas €1.50-2.60), off the eastern end of the plaza, to **La Bodega** (Calle Alfalfa; tapas €1.20-1.80), where you can mix head-spinning quantities of ham and sherry. **Bar Alfalfa** (cnr Calle Alfalfa & Calle Candilejo; tapas €1.50-2.40), perched snugly between the last two, serves authentic tapas in intimate surroundings.

Bodega Extremeña (☎ 95 441 70 60; Calle San Esteban 17; tapas €1.20-1.80), decked out with rustic bits and bobs, flexes its muscles in the meat department and offers mouthwatering *solomillo ibérico* (Iberian pork sirloin).

Sopa de Ganso (Calle Pérez Galdós 8; tapas €1.50-2.70) does some unusual tapas combinations and, unlike most bars, has a few vegetarian options. Fill that last gap with one of its great cakes.

Habanita (☎ 606 71 64 56; Calle Golfo 3; tapas €1.50-2.50) does vegetarian and Cuban tapas. See also El Centro under Meals, earlier, for opening hours.

El Rinconcillo (☎ 95 422 31 83; Calle Gerona 40; tapas €1.20-3.60), founded in 1670, is Seville's oldest bar and is still going strong. The tapas dishes are fairly straightforward but it's had plenty of time to perfect the Spanish omelette with jamón serrano (€3.60).

La Giganta (☎ 95 421 09 75; Calle Alhóndiga 6; tapas €1.50) equals Rinconcillo's talent for tapas, despite being a lot newer (not hard). While you're here, marvel at the weeds sprouting from the roof of the old church of Santa Catalina.

El Patio San Eloy (Calle San Eloy 9; tapas €1.05-1.30) does the usual mix of tapas plus great burguillos (small filled rolls). Its hams hang like stalactites in a cave.

Robles Placentines (☎ 95 421 31 62; Calle Placentines 2; tapas around €1.50), modelled on a Jerez wine cellar, serves up tempting dishes such as white asparagus from the Sierra de Córdoba.

North of the Centre A hip, offbeat place, **La Ilustre Víctima** (Calle Doctor Letamendi 35; tapas €1.80) has just the right atmosphere for some pinchos de pollo (small grilled-chicken kebabs; €3.31). The celebrated vegetarian tapas, including calabacines al roque (courgettes with Roquefort cheese; €1.80), are as tasty as ever. Quit the brooding with a mint tea (€1.05).

Bar-Restaurante Las Columnas (Alameda de Hércules; tapas €1.35-2.10) brings together beefy men and tasty tapas (most come here for the latter). Try something down-to-earth like albondigas (meatballs; €1.50).

Triana A swish, modern place that rustles up delectable food is **La Triana** (☎ 95 433 38 19; Calle de Castilla 36; tapas around €1.65). The hosts are suave and courteous, and while the decor may be minimalist the dishes, even tapas, are not. A variety of tapas, including plump olives, fresh bread, tomato soup and cod in tomato sauce will only set you back around €5.

Las Columnas (Calle San Jacinto 29; tapas €1.05-1.30), brought to us by the inventors of El Patio San Eloy (see under El Centro earlier in this section), purveys more of the same delicious goodies.

Mariscos Emilio (☎ 95 433 25 42; Calle San Jacinto 39; W www.mariscos-emilio.com; tapas around €1.35), the seafood supremo, steams, grills and fries an assortment of aquatic creatures. A few other branches dot the city.

ENTERTAINMENT

Seville proudly presents a feast of night-time delights, from beer-fuelled bopping and thumping live beats to avant-garde theatre and steamy flamenco. Bars usually open 6pm to 2am weekdays, 8pm till 4am at the weekend. Drinking and partying get going at midnight on Friday and Saturday (daily when it's hot) and ups tempo as the night goes on. Pockets of bodegas such as those in Plaza del Salvador give rise to crowds of young boozers, often gathered round bottle-covered cars and scooters. You can find a range of live music most days, except perhaps Monday, and some bars have space for intense bootie-shaking. DJs mix a range of grooves every night, though you'll need to dig deep if hit-and-miss techno pop doesn't appeal.

Get to grips with the latest action by picking up *Welcome & Olé* or *¿Qué Hacer?* (both monthly and free from tourist offices) or logging onto W www.sol.com, W www.sevilla cultural.com and W www.andalunet.com. There's also some information in the newspapers *El Correo*, *ABC* and *El País*.

Bars

Thirst-quenching cerveza (beer) is just as important to Spaniards as tapas. So grab a bar stool in one of the bodegas and make the most of both.

Barrio de Santa Cruz & Around Paddy Flaherty would be proud of **P Flaherty Irish Pub** (☎ 95 421 04 15; Calle Alemanes 7) with its authentic (!) Irish surrounds and buzzing atmosphere. Drench your innards with a Guinness and watch the football (or whatever major sporting event is on). It also has live music, ranging from Celtic folk to upbeat swing, on various days.

Antigüedades *(Calle Argote de Molina 40)* blends mellow beats with weird sack-like effigies and stools that hang upside-down from the ceiling. This is a strange but cool place; wander past and it will suck you in.

La Subasta *(Calle Argote de Molina 36; open 8pm-3am)*, with its smattering of antique paraphernalia, is popular with a slightly older, more conservative crowd.

Bodega Santa Cruz, **Bar Entrecalles** and **Café Bar Las Teresas**, in the heart of the Barrio de Santa Cruz, are a much-loved bunch of beer (and tapas) haunts. See the Tapas section earlier for details.

Rayuela Café *(☎ 95 422 57 62; Calle Miguel de Mañara 9)* is a sophisticated bar located on a quiet pedestrianised street. It's a good place to chill out after visiting the frantic tourist office nearby.

El Arenal With its strip-lighting, **Hijos de E Morales** *(Calle García de Vinuesa 11)*, might look as if it's full of gaunt sherry-pickled locals…and it is. However, this is one of Calle García de Vinuesa's popular bare bodegas, where old wine casks serve as tables.

Calle de Adriano has a couple of bars for drinkers who aren't so fussy. **Clan Scotsman Pub** *(Calle de Adriano 3)* is busy in sporadic bursts and caters to a grungy mob. **Arena** *(Calle de Adriano 10)*, on the other hand, is packed with dizzy young things fluttering around to the latest dance tunes.

Café Isbiliyya *(☎ 95 421 04 60; Paseo de Cristóbal Colón 2)*, near the Puente de Triana, is a busy gay music bar that puts on extravagant drag-queen shows on Thursday and Sunday nights.

Mass open-air gathering spots such as Mercado del Arenal mainly appeal to local youngsters who hang round and glug from booze-filled *litronas* (plastic bottles).

El Centro Plaza del Salvador throbs with drinkers from mid-evening to 1am and is a great place to experience Cruzcampo (the local beer) al fresco. Grab a drink from **La**

Antigua Bodeguita *(☎ 95 456 18 33)* or **La Sapotales** next door and sit on the steps of the Parroquia del Salvador.

Bar Europa *(☎ 95 422 13 54; Calle Siete Revueltas 35)*, with its soothingly colourful tiling, is a pleasant place for a drink and a chat. This place also does tea (€0.90) and croissants (€1.05) if you want a break from alcohol and tapas.

Calle Pérez Galdós, off Plaza de la Alfalfa, has at least five pulsating bars: **Bare Nostrum** *(Calle Pérez Galdós 26)*; **Cabo Loco** *(Calle Pérez Galdós 26)*; **Nao** *(Calle Pérez Galdós 28)*; **La Rebótica** *(Calle Pérez Galdós 11)*; and **Sopa de Ganso** *(☎ 95 421 25 26; Calle Pérez Galdós 8)*. If you're in a party mood, you should find at least one with a scene that takes your fancy.

Alameda de Hércules At first glance, Alameda de Hércules is nothing more than a dusty wasteland with a few seedy characters lurking about. However, it is home to a bohemian and alternative mix of bars and live-music venues.

Bulebar Café *(☎ 95 490 19 54; Alameda de Hércules 83; open 4pm-late daily)* fills up with young sweaty bodies at night, though it is pleasantly chilled in the early evening. Lounge around on the old furniture or sit in the courtyard out front.

El Corto Maltés *(Alameda de Hércules 66)*, the first in a bunch of three good bars clustered at the northeastern end of Alameda, is a laid-back saloon by day and a boisterous drinking den at night.

Café Central *(☎ 95 438 73 12; Alameda de Hércules 64)* must be one of Seville's hippest bars. Sit under the yellow bar lights with a bevy of bright young things.

Habanilla Café *(☎ 95 490 27 18; Alameda de Hércules 63)*, with its attractive display of coffee pots, attracts an arty bunch that seeks the pleasures of Alameda's offbeat atmosphere. The crowd spills out onto the street in summer.

La Ilustre Víctima *(Calle Doctor Letamendi 35)*, a couple of blocks east of Alameda de Hércules, buzzes with an international crowd and plays some good jazzy house music. See also under Tapas earlier.

Triana For a real treat, prop yourself up with a drink by the banks of the Guadalquivir in Triana; the wall along Calle del Betis forms a fantastic makeshift bar. Carry your drink out from one of the following watering holes: **Alambique**, **Big Ben** and **Sirocca**. They are all clustered at Calle del Betis 54 and open from 9pm.

Tequila Connection *(Calle del Betis 41-42)* is half Aztec-themed bar, half Internet café (though the monitors are carefully stowed out of sight). The gushing water feature will cool you off after a few obligatory tequilas.

La Tertulia *(☎ 95 433 32 85; Calle del Betis 13)*, a chilled place at the quieter end of Betis, entertains a snootily hip bunch.

Café de la Prensa *(Calle del Betis 8)* offers weary souls the chance to mellow out with a beer or two. It is also a good spot for coffee the next day.

North of Calle del Betis, Calle de Castilla has more good bars, brimming with a mixed local crowd on weekend nights, including **Casa Cuesta** *(Plaza del Callao 2)* and **Aníbal Café** *(Calle de Castilla 98)*. A couple of passages lead through to the river bank, where you'll find **La Otra Orilla** *(Paseo de Nuestra Señora de la O)*, a buzzing music bar blessed with a great outdoor terrace.

Bohemian Café Bar *(☎ 95 427 53 85; Calle Gonzalo Segovia 2)*, with its comfy chairs and airy atmosphere, is quiet enough to fully contemplate bohemia. Come here for peace.

Madigan's *(☎ 95 427 49 66; Plaza de Cuba 2; open from noon daily)*, another of Seville's raucous Irish pubs, brings Plaza de Cuba to life.

El Tejar *(☎ 95 434 33 40, Calle San Jacinto 68)* might vibrate with the sound of clicking heels when the flamenco gets going but during the day it's a friendly neighbourhood chill-out zone.

Summer Nights by the River
In summer, dozens of temporary open-air late-night bars *(terrazas de verano)*, many of them with live music and plenty of room to dance, spring up along both banks of the river. They change names and ambience from year to year.

As for summer nights *on* the river, swing your thing on the tacky techno riverboat if you've exhausted all the alternatives.

Live Music
Tickets for some major events are sold at the music shop **Sevilla Rock** *(Calle Alfonso XII 1)*. For information on flamenco in Seville, see the boxed text 'Flamenco Haunts of Seville'.

La Imperdible *(☎ 95 438 82 19; Plaza San Antonio de Padua 9;* e *sala@imperdible.org; admission €4.80-6)*, a few blocks west of Alameda de Hércules, is an epicentre of experimental arts in Seville. Its small theatre stages lots of contemporary dance and a bit of drama and music, usually at 9pm. Its bar, the **Almacén** *(☎ 95 490 04 34; admission free)*, hosts varied music events from around 11pm Thursday to Saturday – from soul or blues bands to psychedelic punks to DJs mixing everything from soulful house to industrial breakbeat.

Weekend *(☎ 95 437 88 73; Calle del Torneo 43; admission €4.80-7.20; open 11pm-8am Thurs-Sat)*, just across the road from the Guadalquivir, is one of Seville's top live-music and DJ spots.

Fun Club *(☎ 65 048 98 58; Alameda de Hércules 86;* w *www.funclub.n3.net; admission live-band nights €3-6, other nights free; open around 11.30pm-late Thur-Sun, from 9.30pm live-band nights)* might have a cheesy name but, when it comes to music, this little dance warehouse is deadly serious. With a host of funk, Latino, hip-hop and jazz bands gracing the small stage it's not surprising that it's a music-lovers' favourite. Live bands play Friday and/or Saturday.

Café Jazz Naima *(☎ 95 438 24 85; Calle Trajano 47; admission free; live performances from 10pm)* is an intimate place that sways to the sound of (occasionally live) mellow jazz. Time it right and you might see an entrancing live act.

Blue Moon *(☎ 95 454 08 11;* w *www .bluemoonjazz.com; Calle Juan Antonio Cabestany 10)* puts on great live-jazz performances. Check out its website for a programme of events.

Clubs

Clubs in Seville come and go with amazing rapidity but a few have stood the test of time. The partying starts between 2am and 4am at the weekend, so make the most of your siesta.

Boss *(Calle del Betis 67; open 8pm-7am Tues-Sun)* has two gruff bouncers wedged in the doorway but make it past and you'll find a smashing place to boogie. The music is a total mix and beers cost €4.

Aduana *(☎ 95 423 85 82; W www.aduana.net; Avenida de la Raza s/n; open from midnight)*, 1km south of Parque de María Luisa, is a huge dance venue that plays non-stop grooves for manic party people.

Apandau *(Avenida de María Luisa s/n)*, once called Luna Park, looks more like a palatial greenhouse than a disco. Nonetheless, this is a good spot to shimmy and salsa, with three separate halls.

Café Lisboa *(Calle Alhóndiga 43; admission free)*, in El Centro, offers DJ dance nights with varied electronic music from 10pm Thursday to Saturday.

Theatre & Cinema

The **Teatro de la Maestranza** *(☎ 95 422 65 73; Paseo de Cristóbal Colón 22)*, the ornate-looking **Teatro Lope de Vega** *(☎ 95 459 08 53/54; Avenida de María Luisa s/n)*, and the **Teatro Central** *(☎ 95 446 07 80; Isla de La Cartuja)* and **Auditorio de la Cartuja** *(☎ 95 450 56 56; Isla de La Cartuja)* all stage music, dance and drama. The Maestranza is big on opera and classical music.

Flamenco Haunts of Seville

Seville is one of Spain's flamenco capitals and its Triana *barrio* (district) on the western bank of the Guadalquivir, once the city's *gitano* (Roma people) quarter, was one of flamenco's birthplaces. Though impromptu flamenco in small, smoky bars in Triana or around the Alameda de Hércules is pretty much a thing of the past, there are plenty of spots in the city where you can catch live flamenco song, dance or guitar. Hotels and tourist offices tend to steer you towards *tablaos* (expensive, tourist-oriented flamenco venues), which put on nightly shows, sometimes including dinner. These can be inauthentic and lacking in atmosphere, but **Los Gallos** *(☎ 95 421 69 81; Plaza de Santa Cruz 11; W www.tablaolosgallos.com)* in the Barrio de Santa Cruz is a cut above the average. Some top-notch flamenco artists have trodden Los Gallos' boards in the early stages of their careers. There are two-hour shows at 9pm and 11.30pm nightly for €21 including one drink.

In general, you'll catch a more spontaneous atmosphere in one of the bars that stage regular nights of flamenco, usually with no admission charge. Quality is unpredictable. At the time of writing, these bars offered some good shows:

El Mundo *(Calle Siete Revueltas 5; admission free)* in El Centro – flamenco on Tuesday starting at 11pm

El Tamboril *(Plaza de Santa Cruz; admission free)* in the Barrio de Santa Cruz – jolly crowds pack in to enjoy live *sevillanas* and rumba every night from 10pm

El Tejar *(☎ 95 434 33 40; Calle San Jacinto 68)* – Triana bar with flamenco every Friday night

La Carbonería *(☎ 95 421 44 60; Calle Levíes 18; admission free)* – a converted coal yard in the Barrio de Santa Cruz with two large rooms, each with a bar, that gets thronged nearly every night with locals and visitors alike who come to enjoy the social scene and hear live music – nearly always flamenco – from about 11pm to 4am

La Sonanta *(☎ 95 434 48 54; Calle San Jacinto 31)* – flamenco at 10pm on Thursday in this Triana bar

Big-name flamenco artists make fairly frequent appearances at some theatres, especially the Teatro Central, which runs flamenco seasons under the name Flamenco Viene del Sur. Seville also stages one of Spain's major flamenco festivals, the Bienal de Flamenco (see Special Events earlier in this section), and, if you're present for the Feria de Abril, you'll find plenty going on then.

Cine Nervión Plaza *(☎ 95 442 61 93; Avenida de Luis Morales s/n; tickets €3.90 Mon-Fri, €4.50 Sat & Sun; 3-6 showings per day)* is a massive 20-screen cinema within the Nervión Plaza shopping complex.

SPECTATOR SPORTS

Seville's modern 60,000-seat Estadio Olímpico is at the northern end of the Isla de La Cartuja. Unfortunately, the stadium was not enough to secure the 2008 Olympics but there's word that Seville may try for 2012, although Madrid is also keen!

La Teatral ticket agency *(☎ 95 422 82 29; Calle Velázquez 12)*, in El Centro, sells tickets for bullfights, football matches and some concerts at a mark-up of a few euros. You need to book well in advance for the most popular events.

Bullfights

Fights at Seville's **Plaza de Toros de la Real Maestranza** *(Paseo de Cristóbal Colón 12)* are among the best in Spain. The ring, which holds 14,000 spectators, is one of the country's oldest and most elegant, and its crowds some of the most knowledgeable. The season runs from Easter Sunday to early October, with fights every Sunday, usually at 6.30pm, and every day during the Feria de Abril and the week before it.

From the start of the season until late June/early July, nearly all the fights are by fully fledged matadors (every big star in the bullfighting firmament appears at least once a year in the Maestranza). These are the subscription *(abono)* fights, for which locals buy up the best seats on season tickets. Often only *sol* seats (in the sun at the start of proceedings) are available to non-subscribers attending these fights. They start at about €20. The most expensive tickets, if available, cost a whopping €100. Most of the rest of the season, the fights are novice bullfights *(novilleras)* with young bulls and junior bullfighters. Tickets for these cost from €9 to €42. Tickets are sold in advance at **Empresa Pagés** *(☎ 95 450 13 82; Calle de Adriano 37)*, and from 4.30pm on fight days at the ticket windows *(taquillas)* at the bullring itself.

For more on the Plaza de Toros de la Real Maestranza, see under El Arenal earlier in this section.

Football

Seville has two professional clubs, Real Betis and Sevilla. Betis has had the upper hand in the past decade, though both teams achieved reasonable Primera Liga positions in the 2001–2002 season. Players on Betis' books include Joaquín, whose missed penalty against South Korea eliminated Spain from the 2002 World Cup, and Brazilian midfielder Denilson (who cost a then world record transfer fee of US$35 million in 1997).

Betis plays at the Estadio Manuel Ruiz de Lopera, beside Avenida de Jerez (the Cádiz road) 1.5km south of Parque María Luisa (bus No 34 southbound from opposite the main tourist office). Sevilla's home is the Estadio Sánchez Pizjuán on Calle de Luis Morales, east of the centre.

Except for the biggest games – against Real Madrid or Barcelona, or when the Seville clubs meet each other – you can pay at the gate, from about €15. For the big matches, prices may rise to a minimum of €36 or so, and it's advisable to get tickets in advance.

SHOPPING

Seville has one of the prettiest clusters of pedestrianised shopping streets in Europe. Calles Sierpes, Cuna, Velázquez and Tetuán have retained their charm with a host of small shops selling everything from polkadot flamenco dresses *(trajes de flamenca)* and trendy Camper shoes to diamond rings and antique fans. If stocking up on outdoor gear is more appropriate then head for **Z Zulategui** *(Calle Sierpes 41)* or **Giacomelli Sport** *(Calle Sierpes 81)*. Most shops open between 9am and 9pm but expect ghostly quiet between 2pm and 5pm when they close for siesta.

The large **El Corte Inglés** department store – the best single shop to look for almost anything – occupies four separate buildings a little to the west: two on Plaza de la Magdalena and two on Plaza del Duque de la Victoria. **Sevilla Rock** *(Calle Alfonso XII No 1)*, just off the latter square, is a great music store, and if you fancy mixing flamenco with house then check out **Record Sevilla** *(Calle Amor de Dias 27)*, which has a good collection of vinyl.

You can have an interesting browse along Calle Amor de Dios and Calle Doctor Letamendi, near the hub of the city's alternative scene, Alameda de Hércules. Shops along these two streets specialise in fabrics, jewellery and artefacts from Africa and Asia, rare music recordings, second-hand clothes, and so on.

Tourist-oriented craft shops are dotted all around the Barrio de Santa Cruz, east of the Alcázar. Many sell attractive local tiles and ceramics with colourful Islamic designs, scenes of old rural life, and so on, as well as a lot of gaudy T-shirts.

Nervión Plaza *(☎ 95 498 91 41; Avenida Luis de Morales s/n)* is a large shopping complex, 1.5km east of the Barrio de Santa Cruz, off Avienda de Eduardo Dato.

Street Markets

The Sunday-morning **mercadillo** *(flea market; Alameda de Hércules)*, with clothes, antiques, music, jewellery and so on, is a good browse, with inviting cafés and bars nearby. (At the time of writing, this market had temporarily removed to near the Puente de Alamillo, the first bridge over the Río Guadalquivir beyond Isla Mágica, while work proceeded at Alameda de Hércules.).

The large **Thursday market** *(Calle de la Feria)*, east of Alameda de Hércules, is a colourful event also well worth a visit. Plaza del Duque de la Victoria and Plaza de la Magdalena both stage markets of leather bags and belts, hippie-type necklaces and jewellery, and other clothes, Thursday to Saturday.

GETTING THERE & AWAY
Air

Seville's **Aeropuerto San Pablo** *(☎ 95 444 90 00)* has a fair range of international and domestic flights. Iberia flies daily nonstop between Seville and Valencia/Bilbao/ Madrid/Barcelona. There are also Iberia flights between Seville and London, and Seville and Paris. Spanair flies most days to/from Madrid, and Air Europa flies most days nonstop to/from Barcelona and Palma de Mallorca. All three airlines offer connections to other international and Spanish cities at Madrid and/or Barcelona. Airlines with nonstop international flights include British Airways (to/from London) and LTU (Dusseldorf).

The city office of **Iberia** *(☎ 95 498 82 08; Edificio Cecofar, Avenida de la Buhaira 8)* is just east of the city centre. Iberia also has an **airport office** *(☎ 95 451 06 77)*. Air Europa tickets are sold at **Halcón Viajes** *(☎ 95 421 44 56; Avenida de la Constitución 5)*, near the cathedral. **Spanair** *(☎ 95 444 90 33)* is at the airport.

Bus

Seville has two bus stations. Buses to/from the north of Seville province, Huelva province, Extremadura, Madrid and Portugal use the **Estación de Autobuses Plaza de Armas** *(☎ 95 490 80 40/77 37)* just east of the Puente del Cachorro. Buses to/from most other places in Andalucía and places up the Mediterranean coast use the **Estación de Autobuses Prado de San Sebastián** *(☎ 95 441 71 11; Plaza San Sebastián)*, just southeast of the Barrio de Santa Cruz.

From Plaza de Armas there are frequent buses to Huelva (€7, 1½ hours); a few a day to other places in Huelva province such as La Antilla, Isla Cristina and Ayamonte, Aracena, Minas de Riotinto, El Rocío and Matalascañas; and 14 daily to Madrid (€15.40, six hours). For Extremadura and beyond, about 12 daily go to Mérida (€10.15, 3½ hours), and five or more to Cáceres (€13.70, four hours) and Salamanca (€24.45, eight hours), plus a few to Galicia. For information on buses to/from Portugal, see Land in the Getting There & Away chapter.

Plaza de Armas is also the station for frequent buses to Santiponce (for Itálica), and buses to the Parque Natural Sierra Norte.

From Prado de San Sebastián bus station nine or more daily buses run to Cádiz (€9, 1½ hours), Córdoba (€8.30, 1½ hours), Granada (€15.40, three hours), Málaga (€12.30, 2½ hours), Jerez de la Frontera (€5.60, only two buses on Sunday and holidays) and Sanlúcar de Barrameda (€5.50,

1½ hours); and a few to Arcos de la Frontera and Ronda (€8.40, 2½ hours). This is also the station for frequent buses to Carmona, and a few daily to Osuna, Estepa and Écija in Sevilla province; Tarifa, Algeciras and La Línea, in Cádiz province, one only Monday to Friday to Conil, Barbate and Zahara de los Atunes; Antequera, the Costa del Sol and Nerja in Málaga province; and Jaén, Almería, Valencia and Barcelona.

Train

Seville's **Estación Santa Justa** (☎ 95 454 02 02) is 1.5km northeast of the centre on Avenida Kansas City. There's also a city centre **Renfe information and ticket office** (Calle Zaragoza 29; open 9.30am-2pm & 5.30pm-8pm Mon-Fri, 10am-1.30pm Sat). Luggage lockers at the station cost around €2 to €4.

Four types of train run to/from Madrid. The best and costliest are the 14 daily superfast AVEs, taking as little as 2½ hours. (See The Rest of Spain under Land in the Getting There & Away chapter for fares and other information.)

Other daily trains from Seville include about 20 to Córdoba (€6.75, 45 minutes to 1½ hours); up to 15 to Jerez de la Frontera and Cádiz (€5.65 & €8.05, 1½ to 2½ hours); three or four to Granada (€16.65, three hours); five to Málaga (€13.35, 2½ hours); three to Huelva (€6.30, 1½ hours); three or four north to Cazalla-Constantina (€4.15, 1½ hours); one to Mérida (€10.55, 4½ hours) and Cáceres; and one to Jaén (€14.10, three hours). For Ronda or Algeciras, you have to take a Málaga train and change at Bobadilla. Other destinations include Osuna, Antequera, El Chorro, Valencia and Barcelona. For Lisbon (€43.10 in *turista* class, 16 hours), you must change at Cáceres.

Car & Motorcycle

Some of the cheaper car-rental firms are to be found along Calle Almirante Lobo off the Puerta de Jerez. **Triana Rent A Car** (☎ 95 456 44 39; Calle Almirante Lobo 7) quoted €57.80 a day including IVA and insurance for a small car such as a Renault Clio. **ATA Rent a Car** (☎ 95 422 09 57; Calle Almirante Lobo 1) quoted €70 per day including IVA and insurance for a Renault Twingo. Agencies at the train station include **Avis** (☎ 95 453 78 61), **National/Atesa** (☎ 95 441 26 40) and **Europcar** (☎ 95 453 39 14). Several of them are at the airport too, as is **Hertz** (☎ 95 451 47 20). National/Atesa charges €90.55 all up for daily rental of their smallest car. **Rentamoto** (☎ 95 441 75 00; Calle Méndez Casariego) has 125cc motorbikes for rent from €30 per day.

GETTING AROUND
To/From the Airport

Seville airport is about 7km east of the centre on the N-IV Córdoba road. Buses of **Amarillos Tour** (☎ 902 21 03 17) make the trip between the airport and the Puerta de Jerez (30 to 40 minutes), in front of Hotel Alfonso XIII, at least 15 times daily (€2.10 one way). A taxi costs about €15.

Bus

Bus Nos C1, C2, C3 and C4 do useful circular routes linking the main transport terminals and the city centre. The C1, going east from in front of Santa Justa train station, follows a clockwise circular route via Avenida de Carlos V (close to Prado de San Sebastián bus station and the Barrio de Santa Cruz), Avenida de María Luisa, Triana, Isla Mágica and Calle de Resolana. The C2, heading west from in front of Santa Justa train station, follows the same route in reverse. Bus No 32, from the same stop as No C2, runs to/from Plaza de la Encarnación in the northern part of the city centre.

The clockwise No C3 will take you from Avenida Menéndez Pelayo (near Prado de San Sebastián bus station and the Barrio de Santa Cruz) to the Puerta de Jerez, Triana, Plaza de Armas bus station, Calle del Torneo, Calle de Resolana and Calle de Recaredo. The C4 does the same circuit anticlockwise except that from Plaza de Armas bus station it heads south along Calle de Arjona and Paseo de Cristóbal Colón to the Puerta de Jerez, instead of crossing the river to Triana.

A single bus ride is €0.90. You can pick up a route map, the *Guía del Transporte*

Urbano de Sevilla, from tourist offices or from information booths at major stops including Plaza Nueva, Plaza de la Encarnación, and on the corner of Avenida de Carlos V and Avenida Menéndez Pelayo.

Car
Underground car parks are not very conveniently placed (one of the better locations is Plaza Concordia) and hotels with parking space usually charge as much as a car park, around €9 per day, for its use. If you park illegally on the street you risk having your vehicle towed away, which will cost you more than €150. If you're staying in the Barrio Santa Cruz, you can usually find a parking place 200m or so from the southern edge of the district, east of Avenida Menéndez Pelayo in streets such as Avenida de Cádiz.

Bicycle
Pedalling your way around Seville can be a pleasant way to explore the city. **Embrujo** (☎ 95 456 38 38; Calle Miguel de Mañara 11B), near the main tourist office, rents out decent bikes for €12 per day, Monday to Saturday. **El Ciclismo** (☎ 95 441 19 59; Paseo Catalina de Ribera 29) also charges €12 a day; the price for the weekend (Friday afternoon to Monday morning) is €21.

Taxi
A taxi ride up to 3km should cost €4 to €5. Add about €0.90 per kilometre beyond 3km and 25% from 10pm to 6am and on holidays. Taxis line up outside El Corte Inglés on Plaza del Duque de la Victoria, and by the cathedral.

AROUND SEVILLE
Itálica
Itálica (☎ 95 599 73 76; admission €1.50, EU citizen free; open 8.30am-8.30pm Tues-Sat, 9am-3pm Sun & holidays Apr-Sept; 9am-5.30pm Tues-Sat, 10am-4pm Sun & holidays Oct-Mar), about 8km northwest of Seville on the northwestern edge of the small town of Santiponce, was the first Roman town in Spain. It was founded in 206 BC for soldiers wounded in the Battle of Ilipa, nearby, in which Rome extinguished Carthaginian

ambitions in the Iberian Peninsula. Itálica was also the birthplace of the 2nd-century-AD Roman emperor Trajan, and Trajan's adopted son and successor Hadrian (he of the wall across northern England) received some of his education here.

Most of the Romans' original *vetus urbs* (old town) now lies beneath Santiponce. The partly reconstructed ruins you visit are mainly in the *nova urbs* (new town), which was added by Hadrian. The site is extensive and lacks shade, so time your visit to avoid the hottest hours. It includes one of the biggest of all Roman amphitheatres, able to hold 25,000 spectators; a large public bathhouse, the Termas Mayores; and some lovely mosaics, including one in what was a planetarium. The planetarium's mosaic is the best on site and is easily located – there is a metal viewing platform above it.

To the west, in the old town, you can also visit a restored Roman theatre. Each May this is the location of a European Festival of Greco-Latin Theatre with performances of plays by classical playwrights.

Itálica has been heavily looted over the centuries and parts of its buildings have been used in the construction of buildings in Santiponce, Seville and elsewhere.

A **tourist office** (☎ 95 599 80 28; open 9am-4pm Tues-Fri & Sun) is next to the Roman theatre.

Buses run at least half-hourly (from 6.30am to midnight) to Santiponce from Seville's Plaza de Armas bus station.

La Campiña

This is the rolling area east of Seville and south of the Río Guadalquivir, crossed by the N-IV to Córdoba and the A-92 towards Granada and Málaga. La Campiña is still a land of huge agricultural estates belonging to a few landowners. Today's successors to the rural revolutionaries of the past are led by the communist villagers of **Marinaleda**, between Écija and Estepa, who in the 1980s and early 1990s staged periodic occupations of estates to draw attention to the need for land reform. In 1991 they actually gained

12 sq km of land for their village. Subsequent campaigns have focused on the need for sufficient employment and since the year 2000 the village has had its own vegetable cannery which has contributed to almost full employment. In the last couple of years, the villagers have to some extent aligned themselves with the antiglobalisation movement with whom they share the struggle for basic rights for all, and a concern about degradation of the environment. You can learn more about these feisty villagers at w www.marinaleda.com.

If you're not in a hurry there are four towns (two on the N-IV and two on the A-92) whose surprisingly grand architecture – though clear evidence of the area's long-standing wealth gap – makes them well worthy of a stop: Carmona, Écija, Osuna and Estepa.

CARMONA
postcode 41410 ● pop 25,703
● elevation 250m
Carmona stands on a low hill just off the N-IV, 38km east of Seville. Fortified as early as the 8th century BC, its strategic position was important to the Carthaginians as well as to the Romans. The latter laid out a street plan which survives to this day. Their Via Augusta, which ran from Rome to Cádiz, entered Carmona by the eastern Puerta de Córdoba and left by the western Puerta de Sevilla.

The Muslims built a strong defensive wall around the town but Carmona fell in 1247 to Fernando III (El Santo, the Saint). In the 14th century, Pedro I (El Cruel) turned Carmona's main fortress, the Alcázar, into a splendid residence. The town was later adorned with churches, convents and mansions by Mudejar and Christian artisans.

Orientation & Information
The old part of Carmona stands on the hill at the eastern end of the town: the Puerta de Sevilla marks the western end of the old town. Buses from Seville stop on Paseo del Estatuto, 300m west of the Puerta de Sevilla, though when we visited, the stop had been changed, supposedly temporarily, to Avenida de Jorge Bonsor near the Roman Necropolis.

The helpful **tourist office** (☎ 95 419 09 55; open 10am-6pm Mon-Sat, 10am-3pm Sun & holidays) is in the Puerta de Sevilla. There are banks with ATMs on Paseo del Estatuto and Calle San Pedro, west of the Puerta de Sevilla, and on Plaza de San Fernando, the main square of the old town.

Roman Necropolis
The impressive Roman necropolis (☎ 95 414 08 11; Avenida de Jorge Bonsor 9; admission €1.60, EU citizen free; open 8.30am-2pm Tues-Sat 15 June-15 Sept; 9am-5pm Tues-Fri, 10am-2pm Sat & Sun rest of year, closed holidays) is just over 1km southwest of the Puerta de Sevilla. You can climb down into a dozen or more family tombs, hewn from the rock in the 1st and 2nd centuries AD, some of them elaborate and many-chambered. (A torch would be useful.) Most of the dead were cremated and you can see some of the cremation pits, also hewn from the rock. In the tombs wall niches for the box-like stone urns containing the ashes.

Don't miss the Tumba de Servilia, as big as a temple (it was the tomb of a family of Hispano-Roman bigwigs), or the Tumba del Elefante, with a small elephant statue.

Puerta de Sevilla & Around
This impressive main gate of the old town has been fortified for millennia. Today it also houses the tourist office, which sells tickets (€2) for the interesting upper levels of the structure, the **Alcázar de la Puerta de Sevilla** (open same hours as tourist office, see Orientation & Information earlier for details). This affords fine views and includes an upstairs Almohad patio with traces of a Roman temple. An informative leaflet helps you identify the various Carthaginian, Roman, Muslim and Christian stages of the construction of the Alcázar.

From the Puerta extend lengthy sections of Carmona's mainly Muslim **walls**. If the tower on the **Iglesia de San Pedro** (Calle San Pedro), west of the Puerta de Sevilla, looks familiar, that's because it's an imitation of Seville's La Giralda.

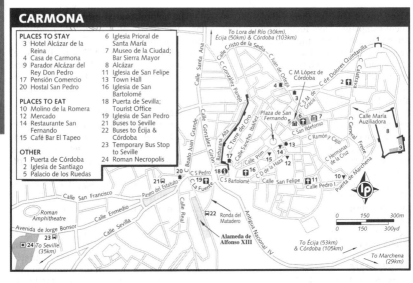

CARMONA

PLACES TO STAY
3 Hotel Alcázar de la Reina
4 Casa de Carmona
9 Parador Alcázar del Rey Don Pedro
17 Pensión Comercio
20 Hostal San Pedro

PLACES TO EAT
10 Molino de la Romera
12 Mercado
14 Restaurante San Fernando
15 Café Bar El Tapeo

OTHER
1 Puerta de Córdoba
2 Iglesia de Santiago
5 Palacio de los Ruedas

6 Iglesia Prioral de Santa María
7 Museo de la Ciudad; Bar Sierra Mayor
8 Alcázar
11 Iglesia de San Felipe
13 Town Hall
16 Iglesia de San Bartolomé
18 Puerta de Sevilla; Tourist Office
19 Iglesia de San Pedro
21 Buses to Seville
22 Buses to Écija & Córdoba
23 Temporary Bus Stop to Seville
24 Roman Necropolis

Old Town Walking Tour

From the **Puerta de Sevilla**, Calle Prim leads up to Plaza de San Fernando (or Plaza Mayor), whose 16th-century buildings are painted a quaint variety of colours. Just off this square on Calle El Salvador, the patio of the 18th-century **Town Hall** (open 8am-3pm Mon-Fri) contains a large, very fine Roman mosaic showing the Gorgon Medusa surrounded by four other heads.

Heading northeast off Plaza de San Fernando, Calle Martín López de Córdoba leads past the noble **Palacio de los Ruedas** to Carmona's most splendid church, the **Iglesia Prioral de Santa María** (admission €2.40; open 9am-2pm Mon-Sat & 6pm-7.30pm Mon-Fri June, July & 1st half of Sept; 10am-2pm Mon-Sat & 5.30pm-7.30pm Mon-Fri mid-Sept–May; closed Aug). Santa María was built, mainly in the 15th and 16th centuries, in a typical Carmona combination of brick and stone on the site of the former main mosque. Especially to be admired inside are the fine Gothic pillars and ceiling tracery, the plateresque main retable, and the Patio de los Naranjos by which you enter (formerly the mosque's ablutions courtyard), with a 6th-century Visigothic calendar carved into one of its pillars.

Behind Santa María is the **Museo de la Ciudad** (City History Museum; ☎ 95 414 01 28; Calle San Ildefonso 1; admission €2, free Tues; open 10.30am-2pm & 6.30pm-9.30pm Wed-Mon, 10.30am-2pm Tues June-Aug; 11am-7pm Wed-Mon, 11am-2pm Tues rest of year), with archaeological and ethnographic displays and an attached restaurant.

From the Iglesia de Santa María, Calle Santa María de Gracia and Calle de Dolores Quintanilla continue to the **Puerta de Córdoba**, an originally Roman gate, with good eastward panoramas.

Moving back uphill and turning southwest down Calle Calatrava you reach the **Iglesia de Santiago**, with a pretty Mudejar tower tiered in red brick and blue tiles. South of here is the **Alcázar**, the Almohad fort that Pedro I turned into a country palace in a Mudejar style, similar to his parts of the Seville Alcázar. Ruined by an earthquake in 1504, the Alcázar was in part restored as a parador in the 1970s. With excellent views and a lovely patio, this is a good place to stop for a drink or (if you can afford it) a meal.

From here, start back along Puerta de Marchena on the southern rim of the town, where there are more good views over the countryside around Carmona. Head into the tangle of streets to see the 14th-century **Iglesia de San Felipe**, with a pretty brick Mudejar tower and Renaissance facade, and the 15th-to-18th-century **Iglesia de San Bartolomé**.

Places to Stay

Prices given are for the summer season (July and August). Expect to pay up to a third more at Semana Santa and during the Seville Feria de Abril.

Pensión Comercio (☎/fax 95 414 00 18; Calle Torre del Oro 56; singles/doubles €18.05/36.05, doubles with bathroom €42 June-Feb; singles/doubles €21/42, doubles with bathroom €48 Mar-May) is in a lovely tiled old building with a Mudejar-style entrance arch and brick-pillared patio. The 14 air-con rooms are well-kept. The *pensión*'s **restaurant** (open Mon-Sat; menú €6.60) has very reasonable prices.

Hostal San Pedro (☎ 95 414 16 06; Calle San Pedro 3; doubles €42) has comfortable doubles with bathroom, TV and air-con. It has recently been refurbished.

Parador Alcázar del Rey Don Pedro (☎ 95 414 10 10, fax 95 414 17 12; e carmona@parador.es; singles/doubles €95.10/121.35) is a big jump in price and quality from the previous places. It's an historic place – the Catholic Monarchs stayed here during part of their siege of Granada – with appropriately luxurious decor. There are 63 rooms and a well-sited swimming pool.

Hotel Alcázar de la Reina (☎ 95 419 62 00, fax 95 414 01 13; w www.alcazardelareina.com; Plaza de Lasso 2; singles/doubles €96/122, €154/193 during Semana Santa & Feria de Abril) is another beautiful old-town hotel with 66 rooms. One of its two patios holds a pool.

Casa de Carmona (☎ 95 419 10 00, fax 95 419 01 89; w www.casadecarmona.com; Plaza de Lasso 1; singles/doubles €195/260), in a 17th-century, 30-room mansion, is yet more luxurious than Hotel Alcázar de la Reina.

Places to Eat

The many bars and cafés around Plaza de San Fernando do *raciones* and tapas; **Café Bar El Tapeo** (☎ 95 414 43 21; Calle Prim 9; menú €7.20) is friendly and popular for both its *menú* and its tapas.

Restaurante San Fernando (☎ 95 414 35 56, Calle Sacramento 3, open for lunch Tues-Sun, dinner from 9pm Tues-Sat; menú €22, fish & meat dishes €11-14), overlooking Plaza de San Fernando, is a much classier place. Its *menú* offers a taste of five or so different dishes, perhaps beginning with cream of green apple soup followed by stuffed salmon pastries, then pears in red wine to finish. One or two other morsels are fitted in along the way. A block south of here you'll find the market, which has a number of other eateries around a central courtyard. **Bar Sierra Mayor** (Calle San Ildefonso 1; tapas €1.20-2.10), with tables on a little interior patio, is attached to the Museo de la Ciudad. The place specialises in meat products and cheeses from the hills of Huelva province. There's at least one related bar in Seville and the cheeses in particular are excellent.

The three top-end hotels (see Places to Stay, earlier) all have fine restaurants. **Casa de Carmona** (fish & meat mains €9.60-16.85, menús €16.83-28.85) offers a choice of three-course *menús*. The Alcázar de la Reina's **Restaurante Ferrara** (starters & stews €5-11.50, meat mains €10-11) offers typical Andalucian fare including ox-tail or pig-cheek stews, and rice dishes.

Molino de la Romera (☎ 95 414 20 00, Puerta de Marchena; 3-course menú including two drinks €15.75), an interesting 15th-century oil mill building, has restaurant, café and bar sections. The restaurant is only open from Monday to Friday but the larger *mesón típico*, another restaurant in the same building, is open all weekend.

Getting There & Away

Eight to 21 daily buses run to Carmona from Seville (Prado de San Sebastián; (one hour) for €2. **Linesur** (☎ 95 441 14 19) and **Alsina Graells** (☎ 95 441 88 11) run a few daily buses to/from Écija and Córdoba, arriving at and departing from Alameda de Alfonso XIII.

ÉCIJA

postcode 41400 • pop 37,771

• elevation 110m

Écija (*ess*-i-ha) stands on the Río Genil, 53km east along the N-IV from Carmona. It's known both as *la ciudad de las torres* (the city of towers), for its many fine baroque church towers studded with colourful tiles, and as *la sartén de Andalucía* (the frying-pan of Andalucía), for its summer temperatures, which have topped 50°C. The town, now quaintly dilapidated, owes its splendours to the 18th century, when the local gentry splashed out on large mansions, and the church towers were rebuilt following a 1757 earthquake.

The **Town Hall** (*Plaza de España; open 8am-3pm Mon-Fri*), on the central square, boasts a Roman mosaic depicting the punishment of Queen Dirce, tied to the horns of a bull. To see the mosaic you need to ask at the **tourist office** (☎ 95 590 29 33; *open 9.30am-3pm & 4pm-7pm Mon-Fri, 9.30am-3pm Sat & Sun*) in the front of the town hall. A staff member will accompany you and give you a spiel about the mosaic and other art treasures housed in the town hall's 19th-century **Sala Capitular** (Chapter House). The tourist office also gives out useful information to help guide you around the town. Additionally, staff operate a **cámara obscura** (*admission €1.80; open 9.30am-3pm Tues-Sun*), which projects live, moving images of the town onto a screen. We found this particularly interesting when we visited because, apart from the wonderful church spires, belfries and old Écija palaces, we could also see a team of archaeologists at work inside the boarded-up main square below us.

A block south along Calle Cintería is the **Palacio de Benamejí** (*Calle Cánovas del Castillo 4*), an impressive 18th-century mansion housing the town's **Museo Histórico Municipal** (☎ 95 590 29 19; *admission free; open 9am-2pm Tues-Sun June-Sept; 9.30am-1.30pm & 4.30pm-6.30pm Tues-Fri, 9am-2pm Sat, Sun & holidays rest of year*) which has another Roman mosaic and recent finds from the archaeological digs in the main square, including the leg of a bronze Roman statue. The museum also

has an equestrian room; Écija is a horse-breeding centre of note.

Two of the most impressive church towers are on the **Iglesia de Santa María**, just off Plaza de España, and the **Iglesia de San Juan Bautista** (*Plaza San Juan*) to the east. Another highlight is the huge **Palacio de Peñaflor** (*Calle Caballeros 26; open 10am-1pm & 4pm-7pm Mon-Fri, 11am-1pm Sat & Sun*), southeast of the main square, with frescoes on its curved facade. You can enter to see the grand staircase and the pretty two-storey patio, which houses the town library and two exhibition halls. It is planned to turn this palace into a luxury hotel.

The **Iglesia Mayor de Santa Cruz** (*Calle Espíritu Santo*), four blocks north of Plaza de España, is Écija's main church and is well worth a look. It was once the town's principal mosque and still has traces of Muslim features and some Arabic inscriptions. There are moss-covered walls, but no roof, of a previous building out front. The effect is romantic.

The **Palacio de Justicia** (*Calle La Marquesa*), five blocks west of the main plaza, has an Alhambra-like patio.

Places to Stay & Eat

The only places to stay in the centre, but both good value, are **Pensión Santa Cruz** (☎ 95 483 02 22; *Calle Practicante Romero Gordillo 8; per person €10, Semana Santa & Aug-Sept €13*), and **Hotel Platería** (☎ 95 590 27 54, e *hotelplateria@retemail.es; Calle Garcilópez 1A; singles/doubles with bathroom €32/55.65, €45/68.50 during Semana Santa & September feria*) with excellent rooms around a central covered courtyard. Both are within two blocks east of Plaza de España. You can park outside the Platería but not the Santa Cruz!

Restaurante Hotel Platería (*see Hotel Platería earlier; salads €4.50-4.80, meat & fish mains €6-11.40*) does terrific food for good prices. We particularly enjoyed the salads and the wild mushrooms *(setas)*. **Las Ninfas** (☎ 95 590 45 92, *Palacio de Benamejí*), beside the history museum and decorated with local art treasures, is a fancier place offering Andalucian and local specialities. The very central **Bisturi** *(Plaza de España 9; menús €9 & €15)* has something for everyone, at reasonable prices. In addition to two- and four-course *menús*, it does *bocadillos* for €2.40 to €4.20 and *platos combinados* for €3.60.

There are more places to stay and eat on and around Avenida de Genil, the main drag into town from the N-IV. **Hotel Ciudad del Sol** and **Restaurante Casa Pirula** *(☎ 95 483 03 00; Avenida Miguel de Cervantes 48)* are recommended.

Getting There & Away

Écija's bus station is on Avenida de Andalucía, six or so blocks south of Plaza de España. Sevibús runs five buses a day between Écija and Seville (Prado de San Sebastián) and there are up to 11 more buses by Linesur. Three or more buses a day go to/from Córdoba.

OSUNA

postcode 41640 • pop 17,221
• elevation 330m

Osuna, 91km southeast of Seville, does not look much from the A-92 but you'll find it a handsome old place with many lovely stone buildings dating from the 16th to 18th centuries. Several of the most impressive were created by the ducal family of Osuna, one of Spain's richest since the 16th century.

The **tourist office** *(☎ 95 481 57 32; open 9am-2pm & 5pm-6pm Mon-Fri)*, next to the town hall on the central Plaza Mayor, hands out useful little guides detailing the town's monuments in various languages. You may find it opens shorter hours in winter. The **Asociación Turístico Cultural Osuna** *(Calle La Torre; open 10.30am-1.30pm & 5pm-8pm Mon-Fri, 10am-2.30pm Sat & Sun)*, a couple of doors from the municipal tourist office, also has tourist information and is open longer hours.

Plaza Mayor

The leafy square has the partly modernised 16th-century town hall on one side, a large market building on the other, and the 16th-century church of the Convento de la Concepción at the end.

Baroque Mansions

You can't go inside most of Osuna's mansions, but the facades of a few are particularly worth hunting out. One is the **Palacio de los Cepeda** *(Calle de la Huerta)*, behind the town hall, with rows of Churrigueresque columns topped by stone halberdiers holding the Cepeda family coat of arms. The 1737 portal of the **Palacio de Puente Hermoso** *(Palacio de Govantes y Herdara; Calle Sevilla 44)*, a couple of blocks west of Plaza Mayor, has twisted pillars encrusted with grapes and vine leaves.

Moving north from Plaza Mayor up Calle Caballos and its continuation Calle Carrera, you pass the **Iglesia de Santo Domingo** (1531) before you reach the corner of Calle San Pedro (marked by an El Monte bank). The **Palacio del Cabildo Colegial** *(Calle San Pedro 16)* bears a sculpted representation of Seville's Giralda, flanked by the Seville martyrs Santa Justa and Santa Rufina. Farther down, the **Palacio de los Marqueses de La Gomera** *(cnr Calle San Pedro & Calle Jesús)* has elaborate clustered pillars, and the family shield at the top of the facade. It's now an upmarket hotel and restaurant (see Places to Stay & Eat, later).

Museo Arqueológico

The Torre del Agua, a 12th-century Almohad tower, just east of the Plaza Mayor, houses Osuna's Archaeological Museum *(☎ 95 481 12 07; Plaza de la Duquesa; admission €1.60; open 11.30am-1.30pm & 4pm-6pm Tues-Sun Oct-Apr; 11.30am-1.30pm & 5pm-7pm Tues-Sun May & Sept; 10am-2pm Tues-Sun June-Aug)*. The mainly Iberian and Roman collection includes copies of local Iberian bronzes and reliefs whose originals are now in the Louvre in Paris and Spain's national archaeological museum in Madrid.

Colegiata de Santa María & Around

Osuna's most impressive monuments overlook the centre from the hill above the Museo Arqueológico. Pre-eminent is the Colegiata de Santa María de la Asunción *(☎ 95 481 04 44; admission by guided tour* only €2; open 10am-1.30pm & 4pm-7pm Tues-Sun, closed Sun afternoon July & Aug), a 16th-century church containing a wealth of fine art collected by the Duques de Osuna.

In the main body of the church are José de Ribera's *Cristo de la Expiración*, a marvellous example of this 17th-century painter's use of light/dark contrast; an elaborate baroque main retable; a contrasting 14th-century retable in the Capilla de la Virgen de los Reyes; and, in the Capilla de la Inmaculada, a Crucifixion sculpture attributed to the 17th-century Sevillan Juan de Mesa. The church's sacristy contains, amid much more religious art, four more Riberas. The tour also includes the lugubrious underground Sepulcro Ducal, created in 1548 with its own chapel as the family vault of the Osunas, who are entombed in wall niches. Art down here includes work by the Seville sculptor Pedro Torrigiano and the painter Luis 'El Divino' Morales from Extremadura, two leading figures of the Renaissance in Spain.

Beside the Colegiata is the **Convento de la Encarnación** *(☎ 95 481 11 21; admission €2; open same hours as Colegiata)*, now a museum with mainly religious art and artefacts, and beautiful old tiles in the cloister. Behind the Colegiata, the **Antigua Universidad** (Old University), a square building with pointed towers, was founded in 1549.

Places to Stay & Eat

Pensión-Residencia Esmeralda *(☎ 95 582 10 73; Calle Tesorero 7; singles/doubles €18/33, with bathroom €21/36)*, located two minutes' walk south of Plaza Mayor, has respectable rooms with air-con.

Hostal 5 Puertas *(☎ 95 481 12 43; Calle Carrera 79; singles/doubles €22/41)*, 200m north of Plaza Mayor, has smallish but decent rooms with shower and toilet, TV, phone and winter heating. There are nine rooms, some of which are let to university students.

Hostal Caballo Blanco *(☎ 95 481 01 84; Calle Granada 1; singles/doubles €25.50/42.45)*, an old coaching inn across the corner from the Hostal 5 Puertas, is slightly more expensive and has rooms with bathroom, TV and courtyard parking. The Caballo Blanco has a restaurant too but it's closed on Sunday.

Hotel Palacio Marqués de la Gomera *(☎ 95 481 22 23; W www.hotelpalaciodel marques.com; Calle San Pedro 20; singles €48.85, doubles €77.15-128.60)* is a luxury hotel in the former Gomera Palace (see Baroque Mansions, earlier), with lovely large rooms and a beautiful arched central patio. Prices include a buffet breakfast. The building houses two restaurants: **La Casa del Marqués** *(fish & meat mains €10.80-15.65)*, where you could try lettuce hearts with fresh white cheese, tomato and anchovies, or salmon stuffed with a fish, prawn and vegetable mousse, and the cheaper **Asador del Palacio** which features a wood oven built in Castilian medieval style and specialises in roasted and grilled meats.

Restaurante Doña Guadalupe *(☎ 95 481 05 58; Plaza Guadalupe 6, Pasaje Calle Quijada-Gordillo; 4-course menú €12.30, meat & fish mains €10-16; closed Tues & 1-15 Aug)* is on a small square between Calle Quijada and Calle Gordillo off Calle Carrera. You can sit in green wicker chairs in the bar area, which has a giant TV screen, in the large restaurant behind, or out in the courtyard.

El Mesón del Duque *(Plaza de la Duquesa 2; cold tapas €0.90-1.35, raciones €7.80-10.20)* has a pleasant terrace overlooking the archaeological museum, and offers a range of choices.

Café Tetuán *(Calle Carrera 62)*, opposite El Monte bank, is a good stop for coffee/ice-cream/cake.

Getting There & Away

The **bus station** *(☎ 95 481 01 46; Avenida de la Constitución)* is about 500m southeast of Plaza Mayor. Half a dozen buses run to/from Seville (Prado de San Sebastián) Monday to Friday, two to four on weekends. Four daily go to/from Estepa and Antequera, and there's also service to/from Málaga.

Three or more trains a day run to/from Seville, Antequera, Granada and Málaga: the **station** *(☎ 95 481 03 08; Avenida de la Estación)* is in the southwest of town, about a kilometre from the centre.

Train is more popular than bus travelling to/from Osuna.

ESTEPA

postcode 41560 • pop 11,831
• elevation 600m

Picturesque Estepa, climbing a hill above the highway 24km east of Osuna, was the scene of a mass suicide back in 207 BC when its inhabitants, who had picked the wrong (Carthaginian) side in the Second Punic War, decided not to throw themselves on the mercy of their Roman conquerors. Today, Estepa is best known for its Christmas sweets, *polverones* and *mantecados*, kinds of softly crumbling biscuit which go down well with a glass of *cava* (Spanish champagne). You can watch them being made at **Don Polverón** (☎ 95 591 34 56). The town has a **tourist office** (☎ 95 591 27 71; *Calle Saladillo 12; open 8am-10pm Mon-Fri)* inside the Casa de la Cultura.

The most impressive buildings in the lower part of town are baroque: the lavish **Iglesia del Carmen** by Plaza del Carmen, and the 18th-century **Palacio de los Cerverales**.

In the upper part of the town – still surrounded by walls and towers constructed by the medieval Knights of Santiago – are the **Torre del Homenaje**, the 14th-century castle keep; the fort-like Gothic **Iglesia de Santa María de la Asunción**, built in the 15th century on the site of a mosque; and, next door to the church, the 16th-century **Convento de Santa Clara**, with a lovely patio. Also up here, the **Balcón de Andalucía** mirador (lookout) has fine views over the countryside and town – including the 18th-century **Torre de la Victoria**, 50m high, which once adorned another convent.

Hostal Balcón de Andalucía (☎ 95 591 26 80; *Avenida de Andalucía 11; doubles €38.50)*, with 18 rooms, is an option for accommodation.

The buses mentioned for Osuna also serve Estepa.

Parque Natural Sierra Norte

This 1648-sq-km natural park, stretching right across the north of Sevilla province, is rolling Sierra Morena country, with no great mountains, but it's attractive, remote and often wild. Much of it is covered in *dehesas*, woodlands of scattered evergreen oaks rising from scrub or pasture. The valleys tend to be more richly vegetated. The spring wildflowers are among the most beautiful you'll see in Andalucía.

Many villages and towns bear a clear Muslim imprint, with forts or castles that go back to Muslim times, part-Mudejar churches and narrow, zig-zagging white streets. The park is good walking territory, especially around Cazalla de la Sierra and in the lovely valley of the Río Huéznar. Most visitors are Sevillans in search of fresh air and rural calm.

The heart of the park is around the two main towns, Cazalla de la Sierra and Constantina, which are 20km apart.

Getting There & Away

There's no public transport between the park and Carmona, or east or west into Córdoba or Huelva provinces.

Bus Linesur runs buses between Seville (Plaza de Armas) and Cazalla de la Sierra, Constantina (€5.25, both 1½ hours), El Pedroso, San Nicolás del Puerto, Alanís and Guadalcanal twice or more daily each way (but at the time of writing there was only one bus back from Cazalla, at 6.30pm on Sunday and holidays). To/from Las Navas de la Concepción there's one bus Monday to Friday.

Train Seven kilometres from Cazalla, 12km from Constantina and 2km from Camping La Fundición (see Places to Stay & Eat under Sierra Norte Villages later for details), **Cazalla-Constantina station** is on the A-455 Cazalla-Constantina road. There are two trains daily to/from Seville (€4.15, 1½ hours), stopping at El Pedroso. Both trains go on to/from Guadalcanal, but only one goes to/from Mérida and Cáceres in Extremadura.

Currently no bus service directly links the station with Cazalla or Constantina, though a couple of buses do pass by (see Getting Around).

Getting Around

Buses between the small towns and villages have complicated, changing schedules. For up-to-date details contact **Linesur** (☎ 95 490 23 68/498 82 22/483 02 39) in Seville or Bar Gregorio (where the buses stop in Constantina, ☎ 95 588 10 43), or try one of the tourist offices. Buses run Monday to Friday between Constantina and San Nicolás del Puerto, Alanís, Guadalcanal and Las Navas de la Concepción. Most buses between Seville and Cazalla de la Sierra or Constantina stop at El Pedroso. One bus leaves Constantina for Cazalla at 9am Monday to Friday. There is a bus from Cazalla to Constantina via El Pedroso at 11.45am Monday to Friday and another direct to Constantina at 2pm on Saturday. None of these appear helpful for train connections.

CAZALLA DE LA SIERRA
postcode 41370 ● pop 5154
● elevation 600m

This pretty little white town, 85km northeast of Seville, is the best geared for visitors to the region. It has a **tourist office** (☎ 95 488 35 62; Paseo del Moro 2; open 10am-2pm Wed-Sat, 11am-2.30pm Sun, also 5pm-7pm or 6-8pm Mon-Sat during Semana Santa & July–mid-Sept), on the road into town from the south. There are plenty of banks with ATMs on Calle Llana, the main road that passes through the northern part of town.

Things to See

The most impressive building in Cazalla de la Sierra's tangle of old-fashioned streets is the enormous fortress-like **Iglesia de Nuestra Señora de la Consolación** (Plaza Mayor), a 14th-century Mudejar and Gothic construction in the typical brick and stone of the region. It was badly damaged in the civil war but has been restored. If its main door on Plaza Mayor is not open, try the one on the other side. **La Cartuja de Cazalla** (adult/child €3/0.60; open 10am-2pm & 5pm-9pm daily) is a large 15th-century monastery in a beautiful, secluded nook of the Sierra Morena, 4km from Cazalla (take the A-455 Constantina road for 2.5km, then turn along a signposted side road). Built on the site of a Muslim mill and mosque, the monastery fell

into ruin in the 19th century. In 1977 it was bought by a redoubtable art lover, Carmen Ladrón de Guevara, who is devotedly restoring it, in part as an arts and cultural centre – there are a ceramics museum and workshop, an exhibition of work by past artists-in-residence, and a concert room – and has opened a guesthouse to help pay for the project (see Places to Stay for details).

Walks

Two tracks lead from Cazalla down to the Huéznar valley and by combining them you can enjoy a round trip of 9km. They pass through typical Sierra Norte evergreen oak woodlands, olive groves and small cultivated plots, and the odd chestnut wood and vineyard. Overhead look for eagles, griffon vultures and the rare black vulture (sometimes the two types of vulture fly together).

One track is the Camino (or Sendero) de las Laderas (also called the Vereda del Valle) which starts at El Chorrillo fountain on the eastern edge of Cazalla at the foot of Calle Parras. The path leads down to the Puente de los Tres Ojos bridge on the Río Huéznar, from where you go up the west bank of the river a short way, then pass under the Puente del Castillejo railway bridge and head back towards Cazalla by the Camino Viejo de la Estación (Old Station Road).

You can also join this walk from Cazalla-Constantina station by following the 'Molino del Corcho' path down the Huéznar for approximately a kilometre to the Puente del Castillejo.

Places to Stay

Hospedaje La Milagrosa (☎ 95 488 42 60; Calle Llana 29; singles/doubles €12/24), on the main road heading north from the town centre, is a homely place with half a dozen small rooms.

Posada del Moro (☎ 95 488 43 26, fax 95 488 48 58; Paseo El Moro s/n; singles/doubles €36/55), near the southern entrance to the town, is much nicer than Hospedaje La Milagrosa and has comfortable rooms with tiled floors, cork-topped furniture and bathroom. The rooms overlook an appealing patio and garden with a pool and lawn area.

Las Navezuelas (☎/fax 95 488 47 64; doubles €51.35/74.90) is 2km south of Cazalla on the Seville road, then 1km east down a dirt road (signposted). This restored 17th-century olive-oil mill has various-sized doubles including bungalows. There's a pool, and a good restaurant. Rates include breakfast.

Hospedería La Cartuja (☎ 95 488 45 16, fax 95 488 47 07; W www.skill.es/cartuja; singles/doubles with bathroom €59/96) is the guesthouse at La Cartuja de Cazalla (see Things to See, earlier). The eight rooms are simple and modern, hung with work by former resident artists. The room rates go down if you stay longer than one night. There are also four suites for up to four people and a small house for family groups with children. Dogs are allowed too. Breakfast is included in the room rates. Dinner is €21 – much of the food is home grown and the dining rooms are in the monastery's old pilgrims' hostel. There's an inviting pool, too.

Places to Eat
For tapas and *raciones*, there are bars on and near the pedestrian street, La Plazuela, which is off Calle Llana. **Cafetería-Bar Gonzalo** (Calle Caridad 3), a few steps off La Plazuela, does inexpensive meals. The **Posada del Moro** (see Places to Stay, earlier) has a good restaurant (*menú* €15) offering local specialities such as wild asparagus, mushrooms, and assorted game. There are a couple of other places to eat on this side of town.

Shopping
Cazalla is known for its *anisados*, aniseed-based liqueurs. Two places you can sample and buy them are **Anís Miura** (Calle Virgen del Monte 54), and **Anís del Clavel** (Calle San Benito 8). Miura's *guinda* (wild cherry) *anisado* is a rich, tasty and heart-warming concoction.

CONSTANTINA
postcode 41450 ● pop 7055
● elevation 555m
The likable valley town of Constantina is the 'capital' of the Sierra Norte. Constantina has a **tourist office** (☎ 95 588 12 96; Avenida de Andalucía s/n; open Jul & Aug only) in a little wooden cabin on the main road just before the petrol station at the southern end of Constantina, or just past the petrol station as you approach the town from El Pedroso. The Parque Natural Sierra Norte's visitor information centre, the **Centro de Interpretación El Robledo** (☎ 95 588 15 97; open 10am-2pm & 4pm-6pm Wed-Sun mid-Oct–April; 6pm-8pm May–mid-Oct) is 1km west along the A-452 El Pedroso road from the petrol station. El Robledo has a botanical garden, a picture in spring, which is well worth strolling through. Inside the centre, the wall displays about the park's flora and fauna are interesting, as is the free 10-minute video you'll be invited to watch.

Buses stop at the Bar Gregorio on Calle El Peso in the centre. There are several banks with ATMs on the pedestrianised main street, Calle Mesones, just north of the bus stop.

Things to See & Do
The western side of Constantina is topped by a **Muslim fort** surrounded by shady gardens. Below are the medieval streets and 18th-century mansions of the **Barrio de la Morería** district. The **Iglesia de Santa María de la Encarnación**, just off Calle El Peso, has a Mudejar tower, topped by a belfry added in 1568 by Hernán Ruiz, who also did the one atop the Giralda in Seville.

The marked walk to **Los Castañares**, northwest from the town's bullring (by the Cazalla road in the north of town), takes you, in about two hours, up through thick chestnut woods to a hilltop viewpoint, then back down to Constantina's fort.

Places to Stay
Albergue Juvenil Constantina (☎ 95 588 15 89; Cuesta Blanca s/n; admission under 26/other €12.90/17.25 holiday periods, €10.90/15.20 June-Sept, €8.50/11.50 Oct-May) has room for 103, mostly in single or twin rooms. Cuesta Blanca leads uphill behind the petrol station at the southern end of town.

Hostal de la Casa (☎ 95 588 01 58; Calle José de la Bastida 25; doubles with/without bathroom €45/36) offers seven good rooms in a modernised old house. It has an attached restaurant and is on the one-way street that heads north through the town.

Hotel San Blas (☎ 95 588 00 77, fax 95 588 19 00; Calle Miraflores 4; singles/ doubles with bathroom €41/58 Aug & Sat all year, €33/46 other times) is well managed and has large, tastefully decorated rooms with big bathrooms. It's up a steep slope off the main road from Cazalla and is clearly signposted. There is ample on-street parking.

Places to Eat

Bodeguita Fali II (Calle Fuente Nueva 21; tapas €1.35, raciones €3.90-12.90) is an excellent little place just around the corner from the Hotel San Blas. You can eat at the bar or at tables outside. Try the scrambled eggs with wild asparagus and a few prawns (€5.70).

There are more options on or near the pedestrianised main street, Calle Mesones. **Cafetería Mesones 39** (Calle Mesones 39) is a decent spot for breakfast.

The local sweet red wine, called mosto, is a good, inexpensive drop.

SIERRA NORTE VILLAGES

The other main settlements in the park are **El Pedroso**, 16km south of Cazalla de la Sierra; **Las Navas de la Concepción**, 22km northeast of Constantina; **San Nicolás del Puerto**, 17km north of Constantina; **Alanís**, 8km northwest of San Nicolás, with a Muslim castle; and **Guadalcanal**, a farther 11km northwest, an ancient mining centre with a castle, medieval walls and Mudejar churches.

Walks

Fourteen walks of a few hours each are marked out in various areas of the park. They're shown on the IGN/Junta de Andalucía 1:100,000 map Parque Natural Sierra Norte, and are described in Spanish in the booklet Cuaderno de Itinerarios del Parque Natural Sierra Norte de Seville. Tourist and information offices in the park should have these for sale, but if you come across them elsewhere, pick them up in case local supplies have run out.

Huéznar Valley The Isla Margarita picnic area, on an island in the Río Huéznar, is about a kilometre up the valley from Cazalla-Constantina station. From Isla Margarita a path (not included in the Cuaderno de Itinerarios) leads up the eastern side of the river all the way to San Nicolás del Puerto: after about 4km it meets the line of a disused railway running to San Nicolás and the old mines of Cerro del Hierro – you can walk along this instead of the path, if you like. Two kilometres before San Nicolás are the impressive Cascada Martinete waterfalls.

Cerro del Hierro The village of this name (meaning Hill of Iron) is a dilapidated ex-mining settlement a short distance east of the SE-163 Constantina-San Nicolás del Puerto road. One kilometre south of the village is a parking area which is the starting point of the marked Sendero de El Cerro del Hierro, a 6.5km loop walk through unusual karstic rock formations and old mining tunnels.

Sendero del Arroyo de las Cañas This 10km triangular marked route, around the country west of El Pedroso, is one of the prettiest in the park. The landscape is notable for its large, curiously shaped, granite rocks.

La Capitana The top of this highest hill in the park (959m) affords tremendous long-distance views over much of the Sierra Norte and north into Extremadura. The 5km walk northwestward to it from Guadalcanal (690m) takes you along the Sierra del Viento, one of the park's most abrupt ranges.

Places to Stay & Eat

Camping La Fundición (☎ 95 595 41 17; San Nicolás del Puerto; camping per person/ tent/car €3.50/2.55/1.65) is a lovely treed site beside the Río Huéznar, 2km up the San Nicolás del Puerto road from the Cazalla-Constantina station.

Camping Cortijo (Camping Batán de las Monjas; ☎ 95 595 41 63; San Nicolás del Puerto; camping per person/tent/car €2.55/ 2.40/2.55), about 5km farther up the same road, has just 20 sites.

Hotel Casa Montehuéznar *(☎ 95 488 90 00; Avenida de la Estación 15, El Pedroso; singles/doubles with bathroom €27.82/ 51.36)* has attractive rooms and a good restaurant when it's up and running.

Restaurante Los Álamos *(☎ 95 488 96 11; Carretera Cantillana Km 29.5; meat raciones €6)* is on the A-432 main road just south of El Pedroso and makes a good lunch stop. You can dine al fresco on a large covered veranda looking out on a treed garden with lots of birds. Meats are a speciality and the local cheese is superb.

Hostal Los Monteros *(☎ 95 588 50 62; doubles with bathroom & TV €30)* is at Las Navas de la Concepción.

Huelva Province

Huelva (**wel**-vah) can seem like the poor, plain relation of Andalucía's more glamorous provinces; but this is a more down-to-earth Andalucía – it mixes stark industrial landscapes with astonishing natural environments, glorious beaches and inspiring heritage sites. The area's connections with Christopher Columbus (known as Cristóbal Colón by the Spaniards) add an irresistible *frisson* of romance. The province includes most of the Parque Nacional de Doñana, the famous wetlands of which are a bird habitat of huge inter-national importance. The *lugares colombinos* (Columbus sites), where Columbus planned his 1492 voyage and from where he set sail, are clustered here, and lining Huelva's coast are some of the best Atlantic beaches of the Costa de la Luz (Coast of Light). The Parque Natural Sierra de Aracena y Picos de Aroche, in the north, is a large area of beautiful, verdant hill country with many good walking routes (and the best *jamón serrano* – mountain ham – in Spain). On the way north, the age-old mining centre of Minas de Riotinto makes an unusual and fascinating stop.

Huelva & Around

HUELVA
postcode 21080 • pop 140,700

The provincial capital of Huelva is a work-worn port lying between the Odiel and Tinto estuaries. Industry dominates the approaches to the city, but central Huelva is a likable place where people are not diminished by the picturesque and where the commercial centre is smart and lively enough. The city was probably founded by the Phoenicians as a trading settlement about 3000 years ago, but much of it was destroyed by the earthquake that devastated Lisbon in 1755. Huelva's subsequent renaissance and relentless industrialisation have produced

a city where fine old buildings and dull modern architecture create a strangely contradictory appeal.

Orientation
Huelva's central area is about 1km square, with the bus station on Calle Doctor Rubio at its western edge, and the train station on Avenida de Italia at its southern edge. Plaza de las Monjas is the central square. From here the main street, Avenida Martín Alonso Pinzón (also called Gran Vía), leads east and becomes Alameda Sundheim. Parallel to Avenida Pinzón, one block south, is a long, narrow, pedestrianised shopping street that runs through several names, from Calle Concepción to Calle Berdigón.

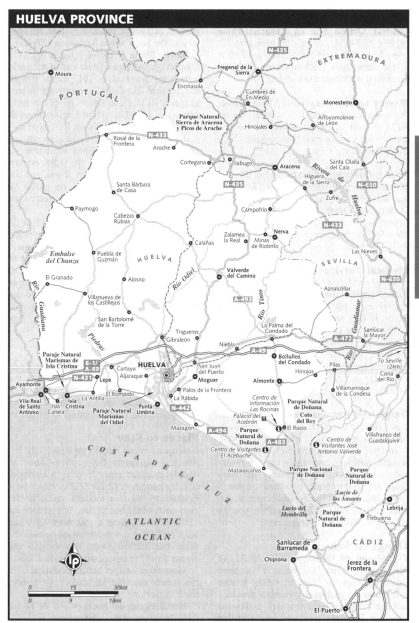

HUELVA PROVINCE

Information

Tourist Office Huelva's **tourist office**
(☎ 959 25 74 03; Avenida de Alemania 12;
open 9am-7pm Mon-Fri, 10am-2pm Sat) is
a few steps from the bus station. It has a
great deal of information and advice.

Money There are banks and ATMs all over
the town centre. The bus station has an
ATM and an exchange booth, where you
can change cash or travellers cheques daily
except Sunday.

Post & Communications The **main post
office** (open 8.30am-8.30pm Mon-Fri,
9.30am-2pm Sat) is on Avenida Tomás
Domínguez. **Cyber Huelva** (Calle Amado de
Lazaro; open 11am-2.30pm & 5pm-10pm
Mon-Sat) is an Internet centre that charges
€1.80 an hour.

Medical Services & Emergency The
main general hospital, **Hospital General
Juan Ramón Jiménez** (☎ 959 20 10 88,
emergency ☎ 959 20 10 00; Ronda Exterior
Norte) is 4km north of the city centre.

The **Policía Local station** (☎ 959 21 02
21; Avenida Tomás Domínguez) is opposite
the main post office. There are two **Policía
Nacional** stations, on Paseo Santa Fé (☎ 959
24 05 92) and Avenida de Italia (☎ 959 24
84 22).

Dangers & Annoyances Like most port
cities Huelva can seem rough and ready at
times, but most people are open and very
friendly. There are a few dodgy characters
around, however, and, again like many sizable ports, there's a seriously unhappy
drugs scene, the results of which are sometimes bleakly visible in off-centre areas.
Take care of belongings wherever you go
and leave nothing in parked cars.

Things to See

The **Museo de Huelva** (☎ 959 25 93 00;
Alameda Sundheim 13; admission free; open
9am-8pm Tues-Sat, 9am-3pm Sun) has an
exhibition on prehistoric Huelva province
and the Tartessos culture which makes the
case that Tartessos was a trading port that

stood where Huelva city stands now (for
more details about Tartessic culture, see History in the Facts about Andalucía chapter).

Barrio Reina Victoria (Queen Victoria
District), just off the eastern end of Alameda
Sundheim, was built in 1917 by the British
mining firm Rio Tinto Company for its em-
ployees. Its straight streets of quaint little
cottages – a kind of hybrid English-Spanish
style – make for a curious stroll. A more surreal stroll, also with Rio Tinto associations,
is along the **Muelle Río Tinto**, an impressive
iron pier curving out into the Odiel estuary
about 500m south of the port. It was built for
the Rio Tinto Company in the 1870s by
George Barclay Bruce, a British disciple of
tower specialist Gustave Eiffel.

The **Santuario de Nuestra Señora de la
Cinta** (admission free), a chapel 2km north
of the city centre off Avenida de Manuel
Siurot, was visited by Columbus – an event
portrayed here in tiles by artist Daniel Zu-
loaga. The chapel's hilltop position affords
good views over the Odiel estuary and the
wetlands to the west. City bus No 6 (€0.90)
from the terminal outside the main bus
station will take you there.

Special Events

Columbus set off for the Americas on 3 August 1492. Each year, Huelva celebrates the
occasion with its Fiestas Colombinas, a week
of music, dancing, sport, cultural events and
bullfighting (normally around 3–9 August).

Places to Stay

Albergue Juvenil Huelva (☎ 959 25 37 93;
Avenida Marchena Colombo 14; bed in
doubles or quads under 26/other July, Aug &
holiday periods €12.90/17.25, rest of year
€10.90/15.20) is a modern youth hostel
2km north of the bus station. It has room for
128. All rooms have a bathroom. City bus
No 6 (€0.90) from the terminal outside the
main bus station stops just around the
corner from the hostel, on Calle JS Elcano.

Most other budget accommodation is in
the streets near the Mercado del Carmen,
the fish market.

Hostal Virgen del Rocío (☎ 959 28 17 16;
Calle Tendaleras 18; singles/doubles €15/30)

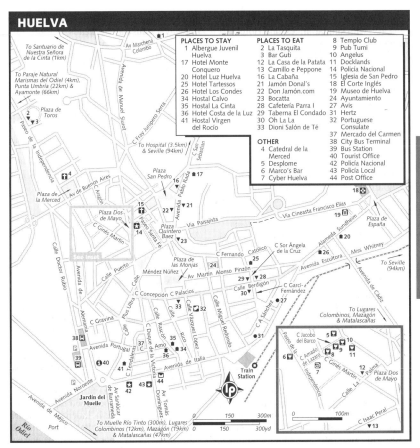

HUELVA

PLACES TO STAY
1 Albergue Juvenil Huelva
17 Hotel Monte Conquero
20 Hotel Luz Huelva
25 Hotel Tartessos
26 Hotel Los Condes
34 Hostal Calvo
35 Hostal La Cinta
36 Hotel Costa de la Luz
41 Hostal Virgen del Rocío

PLACES TO EAT
2 La Tasquita
3 Bar Guti
12 La Casa de la Patata
13 Camillo e Peppone
16 La Cabaña
21 Jamón Donal's
22 Don Jamón.com
23 Bocatta
28 Cafetería Parra I
29 Taberna El Condado
30 Oh La La
33 Dioni Salón de Té

OTHER
4 Catedral de la Merced
5 Desplome
6 Marco's Bar
7 Cyber Huelva
8 Templo Club
9 Pub Tumi
10 Angelus
11 Docklands
14 Policía Nacional
15 Iglesia de San Pedro
18 El Corte Inglés
19 Museo de Huelva
24 Ayuntamiento
27 Avis
31 Hertz
32 Portuguese Consulate
37 Mercado del Carmen
38 City Bus Terminal
39 Bus Station
40 Tourist Office
42 Policía Nacional
43 Policía Local
44 Post Office

HUELVA PROVINCE

---

offers basic rooms. The double rooms have bathrooms.

Hostal Calvo (☎ 959 24 90 16; Calle Rascón 35; singles/doubles €8.50/17) is reached up several flights of grim stairs and has basic rooms, all with shared bathrooms.

Hostal La Cinta (☎ 959 24 85 82; Calle Rascón 31; singles/doubles €8.40/15.70) has the same rather bleak atmosphere as Hostal Calvo and basic rooms, likewise. You'll find it up a couple of flights at the sign for *camas*.

Hotel Costa de la Luz (☎ 959 25 64 22, fax 959 25 32 14; Calle José María Amo 8;

singles/doubles €27/47.60) is near Hostal La Cinta and is a decided step up in spite of its rather functional reception area. It has decent, reasonably comfortable rooms.

Hotel Los Condes (☎ 959 28 24 00, fax 959 28 59 41; Alameda Sundheim 14; singles/doubles €30/56) has 54 air-con rooms with bathroom and TV, and has an economical restaurant.

The three high-end places, each modern and with more than 100 rooms, are: **Hotel Tartessos** (☎ 959 28 27 11, fax 959 25 06 17; Avenida Martín Alonso Pinzón 13; singles/doubles €53/77.80); **Hotel Monte**

Conquero (☎ 959 28 55 00; *Avenida Pablo Rada 10*), with similar prices; and **Hotel Luz Huelva** (☎ 959 25 00 11; *Alameda Sundheim 26; singles/doubles €89.90/106*).

Places to Eat

In the evening, many restaurants and tapas places don't open till after about 8.30pm.

Taberna El Condado (*Calle Sor Ángela de la Cruz 3; tapas from €1.50*), just south of Avenida Martín Alonso Pinzón, is an atmospheric bar for tapas.

Cafetería Parra I (*Calle Sor Ángela de la Cruz 2; platos combinados €4.50-5.40*) is a straightforward place popular for its *platos combinados* (mixed platters), three-course set lunch for €7, and meat and fish *raciones* (meal-sized servings of tapas) and tapas.

Oh La La (*Calle Berdigón 26; pizzas €4.30-5.50*), a few steps away from Cafetería Parra I, is a bright, busy place that also does baguettes and croissants for €2.60 to €4.50. It's one of the few places where you can find a Sunday-morning breakfast.

Dioni Salón de Te (*Calle Palacios 3*), a shiny, almost English-style tearoom, is great to drop into for tea or coffee and a mouth-watering array of cakes and pastries.

Bocatta (*Plaza Quintero Baez; baguettes €2.50-4.50*) serves excellent hot and cold baguettes.

North of Plaza Quintero Baez, Avenida Pablo Rada is lined with popular eateries, many of them with terraces, where you can eat snacks or a sit-down meal. The Avenida is too wide and traffic-bound to lend much character but most places make up for it with lively atmosphere. Busy **Jamón Donal's** offers *montaditos* (small open sandwiches, often toasted) for €0.90 to €1.20 and salads starting at €2.70. Right across the road is **Don Jamón.com**, with much the same food and prices and a limited Internet facility. **La Cabaña** is just up from Jamón Donal's and is a bit fancier, with *montaditos* for €2.10, *revueltos* (scrambled-egg dishes often with ham and vegetables mixed in) from around €9 and grills from €9.

Camillo e Peppone (*Calle Isaac Peral; pasta & pizza €4.50-6.25; open 1pm-4.30pm & 9.30pm-1am Thur-Tues*) serves up excellent dishes in relaxed surroundings. It gets very busy at weekends.

La Casa de la Patata (☎ 959 28 25 75; *Calle Ginés Martín; baked potatoes €1.20-3.30; open Tues-Sun*), a friendly place near Camillo e Peppone, specialises in big baked potatoes with deliciously tasty fillings.

La Tasquita and **Bar Guti**, both on Plaza de Toros, are very popular places that stand side by side in the walls of Huelva's blood-and-sand-coloured bullring at the north end of Paseo de la Independencia. They do a roaring trade in *platos combinados* for €3.60 to €3.90, good tapas at €1.20 and *raciones* of paella for €3.60.

Entertainment

After 9pm some of the tapas bars off Avenida Martín Alonso Pinzón, such as **Taberna El Condado** and **Cafetería Parra I** (see Places to Eat, earlier), get quite lively. Later, crowds flock to the bars and terraces lining Avenida Pablo Rada and, to a lesser extent, the bars around Plaza de la Merced and in the streets to its south, especially Calle Aragón and Calle Jacobo del Barco, where among other spots you'll find the Irish pub **Docklands** and a clutch of bars, including **Desplome**, **Angelus**, **Pub Tumi** and the weirdly decorated **Templo Club**. Just down the road on Paseo de la Independencia, the down-to-earth **Marco's Bar** is a cheerful place that does good tapas. At the north end of Paseo de la Independencia are the bullring bars such as **Bar Guti**. This is a satisfyingly gritty area but it can be uneasy at night, despite the presence of a Guardia Civil station right beside the bullring.

Shopping

There's an **El Corte Inglés** department store on Plaza de España. Many smaller shops are strung along the pedestrianised street running from Calle Concepción to Calle Berdigón.

Getting There & Around

Bus There are buses operated by **Damas** (☎ 959 25 69 00) which run frequently to and from Seville (€5.65, 1¼ hours). For destinations in Huelva province, see those sections later in this chapter. Three or four buses run to Madrid (€21, seven hours) daily, but for other major destinations outside Huelva province, you normally have to change in Seville. For services to Portugal from Huelva, see Bus under Land in the Getting There & Away chapter.

Train From the **train station** (☎ 959 24 56 14) three trains run daily to Seville (€6.15, 1½ hours), an afternoon Talgo 200 goes to Córdoba (€16, two hours) and Madrid (€53, 4¼ hours), and two trains head north to Extremadura (see West of Aracena under The North later in this chapter).

Car & Motorcycle For car hire you can try **Avis** (☎ 959 28 38 36, 607 14 55 55 Avenida de Italia 107), **Hertz** (☎ 959 26 04 60; Avenida de Italia), or **Europcar** (☎ 959 28 53 35) in the train station concourse. Local firms include **Auto Alquiler Huelva** (☎ 959 28 31 38), in the bus station. Driving in Huelva is challenging, to say the least. There is streetside parking around the train and bus stations and at a 500-place secure car park just up from the bus station in Avenida de Italia. The car park charges are €0.75 an hour, €12 for 24 hours. Taxis wait by the bus station, at Plaza de la Merced and Plaza de las Monjas, or call ☎ 959 28 13 13 and ☎ 959 25 00 22.

PARAJE NATURAL MARISMAS DEL ODIEL

This 72-sq-km wetland reserve lies across the Odiel estuary from Huelva. It has a large, varied bird population, including a winter population of up to 1000 greater flamingos. There are about 4000 pairs of spoonbills, and other birds you may see include ospreys, grey herons and purple herons. Some of these birds are easily viewed from a 20km-long road that runs the length of the marshes.

The marshes can be reached by car along the A-497 Punta Umbría road west from Huelva. Cross the bridge over the Río Odiel, then fork right at the sign to 'Ayamonte, Corrales, Dique Juan Carlos I', then go immediately left for Espigón. This curves you back towards Huelva, but in-

stead of re-crossing the bridge take the right turn marked 'Dique Juan Carlos I' to reach the **Centro de Visitantes Calatilla** (☎ 959 50 02 36; open 8am-2.30pm Mon-Fri, closed holidays). You can ask here which of the several paths that strike off from the road farther south are open.

Erebea SL (☎ 959 50 05 12; Centro de Visitantes Calatilla) runs guided trips in the reserve by boat (€25 per person for four hours), by 4WD (€4), on foot (€15) and on horseback (€6 for 1½ hours). If you don't have transport, call to inquire about being collected from Huelva.

LUGARES COLOMBINOS

La Rábida, Palos de la Frontera and Moguer, three of the key sites in the Columbus story, lie along the eastern bank of the Tinto estuary and can all be visited in a fascinating 40km return trip from Huelva. There are accommodation options here too.

La Rábida
postcode 21819 • pop 460
La Rábida is 9km from central Huelva. Just off the main road, and within the entrance to the **Parque Botánico** is a tourist office, the **Centro de Recepción** (☎ 959 53 05 35; open 10am-9pm Tues-Sun Apr-Sept; 10am-7pm Tues-Sun Oct-Mar). You should definitely call here first for information and advice about all the sites in what is an otherwise poorly signed area.

Parque Botánico This pleasant botanical garden (☎ 959 53 05 35; admission €1.50; open 10am-9pm Tues-Sun Apr-Sept; 10am-7pm Tues-Sun Oct-Mar) has an impressive collection that includes plants from the Americas.

Monasterio de La Rábida The 14th-century monastery (☎ 959 35 04 11; admission €2.50, with audio guide €3; open 10am-1pm & 4pm-7pm Tues-Sat Apr-Sept; 4pm-6.15pm Oct-Mar; 4.45pm-8pm Aug; 10.45am-1pm Sun year-round), set amid pine trees, was visited several times by Columbus as he attempted to win royal patronage for his projected voyage. Absorbing

HUELVA PROVINCE

monastery tours are given in simple Spanish every 50 minutes. You can also hire audio guides giving Spanish, English, French and German commentaries. There are several car parks throughout the area. Check at the Centro de Recepción for where, and if, you need to pay a parking fee

Highlights of the tour include a room of 1930s murals portraying the Columbus story by Huelvan artist Daniel Vázquez Díaz; the monastery church, where Martín Alonso Pinzón is buried and which has a lovely *artesonado* ceiling (wooden ceiling with interlaced beams) and a chapel with a 13th-century alabaster Virgin before which Columbus prayed; the peaceful, 15th-century Mudejar cloister, off which are a room where Columbus and Padre Marchena discussed the projected voyage, and the refectory where Columbus ate; and, upstairs, the **Sala Capitular** (Chapter House), where Columbus, the Pinzóns and Abbot Pérez discussed final plans for their voyage.

Muelle de las Carabelas Down on the waterfront below the monastery is a big conference centre and auditorium, the **Foro Iberoamericano**, beyond which is the Muelle de las Carabelas *(Wharf of the Caravels; ☎ 959 53 05 97; admission €3; open 10am-2pm & 5pm-9pm Tues-Fri, 11am-8pm Sat, Sun & holidays Apr-Sept; 10am-7pm Tues-Sun Oct-May)*, where you can board accurate replicas of Columbus' three ships and visit an exhibition on his life. The concept just verges on the kitsch, but there's something quite haunting about the tethered replicas – their small size alone says much about the incredible achievement of the voyages.

Places to Stay Next to the monastery, **Hostería de La Rábida** *(☎ 959 35 03 12; rooms €51.30)* has just five rooms, all with bathrooms. It's a nice place, but is usually booked up well in advance.

Hotel Santamaría *(☎ 959 53 00 01; singles/doubles €30/41.70)*, 1km north on the Palos de la Frontera road, has 18 comfy rooms.

Palos de la Frontera
postcode 21810 • pop 6950

The small town of Palos de la Frontera, 4km northeast of La Rábida, was the port from which Columbus set sail, and which provided two of his ships and more than half his crew. Palos' access to the Tinto estuary is now silted up and there is no momentous atmosphere in what has become a pleasant but everyday country town. But Palos remains justifiably proud of its role in the European discovery of the Americas – especially the part played by the Pinzón cousins as expressed by the statue of Martín Alonso Pinzón in the central square. Moving northeast up Calle Cristóbal Colón, you soon reach the **Casa Museo Martín Alonso Pinzón** *(Calle Cristóbal Colón 24; admission free; open 10.30am-1.30pm & 5pm-7.30pm Mon-Fri)*. It stands, inexplicably, between Nos 32 and 36, but you can't miss the fine old doorway. It was the home of the captain of the *Pinta* and the place where, an inscription proudly claims, the discovery of America was organised.

Farther along Calle Cristóbal Colón, and downhill, is the 14th-century **Iglesia de San Jorge** *(Calle Cristóbal Colón; open 10am-noon & 7pm-8pm Mon-Fri)*, where Columbus and his men took communion before leaving by the Mudejar portal facing the small square to set sail on 3 August 1492. Ten weeks earlier, the royal document ordering Palos to help Columbus had been read out in the square. A monument in the square lists 35 Palos men who sailed with Columbus.

A little farther down the street, now within a small park, is **La Fontanilla** *(Calle Cristóbal Colón)*, a brick well where Columbus' crews drew water for their voyage. A viewing platform above has a plaque marking the site of the jetty from which the three ships sailed.

Places to Stay & Eat Just off Palos' central square, **Pensión Rábida** *(☎ 959 35 01 63; Calle Rábida 9; singles/doubles €9/20)*, is a standard place. It has a **cafeteria** that does *platos combinados* for €5 to €7.

Hotel La Pinta *(☎ 959 35 05 11, fax 959 53 01 64; Calle Rábida 79; singles/doubles*

The Four Voyages of Christopher Columbus

Christopher Columbus (Cristóbal Colón to Spaniards) was born in Genoa, Italy, in 1451, and gained his early sailing experience in the Mediterranean and on trips to Portugal, England, Iceland and Madeira. In 1484 Columbus presented his idea of reaching the spice-rich Orient by sailing west to Portugal's King João II. The notion that the world was round was already widespread, but Columbus' plan was turned down by João.

In 1485 Columbus travelled to the Franciscan monastery of La Rábida, near Huelva, where one of the monks, Antonio de Marchena, encouraged his ambition. Later, the abbot, Juan Pérez, who happened to be a former confessor of Queen Isabel, took up Columbus' cause. In April 1492 Columbus finally won Spanish royal support and was given a *cédula real* (royal document) ordering the port of Palos de la Frontera, near La Rábida, to put two armed caravels at his disposal. The crown also paid for the use of his flagship, the *Santa María*.

Columbus sailed from Palos on 3 August 1492 with about 100 men. His three vessels – none more than 30m long – were the *Santa María*, a *nao* (ship for carrying merchandise) piloted by its owner, Juan de la Cosa from El Puerto de Santa María, near Cádiz; the *Niña*, owned by Juan Niño from Moguer and captained by Vicente Yan ez Pinzón from Palos; and the *Pinta*, captained by Pinzón's cousin, Martín Alonso Pinzón.

After a month in the Canary Islands, Columbus and his crew sailed west in early September. For 31 days they sighted no land and there were mutinous rumblings from the crew. Then, on 12 October, Columbus landed on the island of Guanahaní, Bahamas, which he named San Salvador. The expedition went on to discover Cuba and Hispaniola, where the *Santa María* sank and its timbers were used to build a fort, Fuerte Navidad.

In January 1493 the remaining two ships left for home, leaving 33 Spaniards at Fuerte Navidad. The *Niña* and the *Pinta* reached Palos de la Frontera on 15 March. Columbus, with animals, plants, gold ornaments and six Caribbean Indians, received a hero's welcome from the Catholic monarchs in Barcelona the following month. Everyone was under the impression he had reached the East Indies.

Late in 1493, Columbus sailed from Seville and Cádiz on his second voyage, this time with 17 ships and about 1200 men. The *Niña* was now his flagship. Still in search of Cathay and the Great Khan, he came across Jamaica and other Caribbean islands, but found Fuerte Navidad in ruins, its 33 Spaniards killed. He returned to Cádiz in June 1495.

Columbus sailed west for the third time, with six ships, from Sanlúcar de Barrameda in May 1498. This time he reached Trinidad and the mouth of the Orinoco, but his failings as a colonial administrator led to a revolt by settlers on Hispaniola. Before he could suppress the uprising he was arrested by a royal emissary from Spain in 1500 and sent home a prisoner (though he was released on arrival).

On Columbus' fourth and final voyage, from Sevilla and Cádiz in April 1502, he reached Honduras and Panama, returning to Sanlúcar de Barrameda in November 1503.

Columbus died in 1506 in Valladolid, northern Spain – poor and apparently still believing he had reached Asia. His remains lay at La Cartuja monastery in Seville before being moved to Hispaniola in 1536. They were later transported to Cuba, then in 1899 back again to Seville and their current resting place in the city's cathedral (unless, as some believe, they were mistakenly replaced with someone else's during their Caribbean wanderings).

MICK WELDON

HUELVA PROVINCE

€38.50/64) is a few steps along the same street but is a big, and much pricier, step up, from Pensión Rábida.

Mesón Frenazo *(meat & fish mains €6-9)*, a few doors down the street from Hotel La Pinta, serves good meat and fish main dishes, plus *montaditos* and other tapas.

One kilometre south of the centre on the Mazagón road, amid a very busy built-up area, are **Hostal La Niña** *(☎ 959 53 03 60; Calle Juan de la Cosa 37; doubles with bathroom €28)* and, behind La Niña, **Hostal Los Príncipes** *(☎ 959 35 04 22; Calle Brasil 4; doubles with bathroom €27).*

Getting There & Away Buses leave Huelva daily, every half-hour for Palos (€1, 25 minutes), less frequently on the weekend. There are three turnings into central Palos from the La Rábida–Moguer road; the northernmost is right by La Fontanilla.

Moguer
postcode 21800 • pop 13,370

Moguer is a delightful little town that should charm anyone into lingering for a while. It lies 7km northeast of Palos de la Frontera, with which it has strong historical connections, having provided much of Columbus' crew. Moguer's appeal is enhanced by being the birthplace and longtime home of the 1956 Nobel literature laureate, Juan Ramón Jiménez (1881–1958). The streets are dotted with plaques that bear quotes from Jiménez's *Platero y Yo* (Platero and I; see Generations of '98 and '27 under Literature in the Facts about Andalucía chapter) and his old home is now a museum.

Orientation & Information Finding your way into town can be tricky. If driving in from the south, look for parking signs that will lead you to a good car park that is alongside the tourist office and is handy for the centre. Coming from the northwest it may be best to park when you have a chance, then reconnoitre on foot. Once you have located the central Plaza del Cabildo, with its statue of Juan Ramón Jiménez in a pretty little garden, things are straightforward. There's a helpful **tourist office** *(☎ 959 37 18 50; Calle Castillo;*

open 10am-1.30pm & 6pm-8pm Mon-Fri Apr-Sept; 10.30am-1.30pm & 5pm-7pm Mon-Fri Oct-Mar) in Moguer's old castle, which is being restored. The castle and tourist office are a couple of blocks south of Plaza del Cabildo and are just off Calle Rabida. The surviving walls are medieval, but there are Muslim antecedents and an ancient water cistern has been excavated in the castle yard. The helpful office has lots of information including leaflets for those who wish to follow the Juan Ramón Jiménez trail that wanders the town in the enchanting footsteps of *Platero y Yo*.

Things to See Simply strolling round Moguer's busy morning streets is a pleasure. There are fine buildings everywhere, one of the finest being the 18th-century Italianate **town hall** *(Plaza del Cabildo; open 10.30am-2.30pm Mon-Fri)*, a splendid example of civil architecture at its Andalucian best. It has an arcaded two-storeyed facade in vivid cream and brown colours and inside there is a beautiful patio.

The 14th-century **Monasterio de Santa Clara** *(☎ 959 37 01 07; Plaza de las Monjas)*, near Plaza del Cabildo, is where Columbus kept vigil the night after returning from his first voyage, having vowed to do so if he survived a particularly bad storm off the Azores. It's open for half-hour guided visits (€1.80) at 11am, noon, 1pm, 5pm, 6pm and 7pm, Tuesday to Saturday (except holidays). You'll see a lovely Mudejar cloister, some of the nuns' old quarters, and a collection of religious art.

The **Casa Museo Zenobia y Juan Ramón** *(☎ 959 37 21 48; Calle Juan Ramón Jiménez 10)* is a five-minute walk from Plaza del Cabildo (start along Calle Burgos y Mazo and keep going). It's full of interesting memorabilia of the life and times of Juan Ramón Jiménez and his wife, Zenobia Camprubí. It is open for one-hour guided visits (€1.80) at 10.15am, 11.15am, 12.15pm, 1.15pm, 5.15pm, 6.15pm and 7.15pm Monday to Saturday, and at 10.15am 11.15am, and 12.15pm Sunday.

The 18th-century, baroque **Iglesia de Nuestra Señora de la Granada**, one block southeast of Plaza del Marqués (which is halfway from Plaza del Cabildo to the Casa Museo), has a tower that Jiménez immortalised as resembling Seville cathedral's La Giralda tower from the hazy distance. Close up the comparison stands and the ruby-red stonework of the main walls enhances this fine building even more.

Places to Stay & Eat Moguer has a couple of decent *hostales*.

Hostal Pedro Alonso Niño (☎ 959 37 23 92; Calle Pedro Alonso Niño 13; singles/ doubles with shower €13.85/22) is a friendly place with a tiled patio and comfy rooms. It is 1½ blocks straight on from the northeastern end of Plaza de las Monjas.

Just around the corner, **Hostal Platero** (☎ 959 37 21 59; Calle Aceña 4; singles/ doubles with bathroom & TV €15/25.70) has decent rooms but is less welcoming.

Mesón La Parrala (Plaza de las Monjas 22; mains €4.80-12), in Moguer's finest plaza, serves excellent grills and fish.

Mesón El Lobito (Calle Rábida 31; raciones €4.50-8.40) occupies an old bodega (traditional wine bar) and is an experience even without the food. The smoke-blackened walls are covered in customers' graffiti; huge cobwebs and unimaginable artefacts dangle from the roof, locals occasionally sell fruit and vegetables, the fish and meat *a la brasa* (chargrilled) is good and the house wine too cheap and persuasive to bother with opinions. Tapas start at €1.

Bodeguita de Los Raposo (Calle Fuente 60) is another cracking place, where you order by plate size (€1/1.50/2.20) from a choice of more than 40 fish, meat and salad dishes. There's lots of local wine too. Try the 'Licor de Viagra'; it does wonders, according to numerous locals and the ever-smiling host.

Getting There & Away
At least 10 Damas buses run daily from Huelva bus station to La Rábida and Palos de la Frontera (€1), starting at 7.15am weekdays and 9am on Saturday, Sunday and holidays; some then continue to Mazagón, but most terminate at Moguer. The last daily bus back to Huelva leaves Moguer at 8.15pm.

NIEBLA

Niebla lies 29 miles from Huelva on the A-472 road to Seville. The town's 2km ring of Muslim defensive walls remains complete, its 15th-century Castillo de los Guzmanes is one of Spain's biggest castles, and the Mezquita-Iglesia Santa María de la Granada combines the features of a mosque and a Gothic-Mudejar church in one building.

The municipal **tourist office** (☎ 959 36 22 70; Plaza Santa María), in the centre of the walled area, has information on these and other historic buildings.

Southeast of Huelva

Running 60km southeast from the outskirts of Huelva to the mouth of the Río Guadalquivir is a wide, sandy beach with a wide barrier of pine and shrub-covered dunes between it and the arrow-straight coastal road that runs parallel to the beach for part of the way. Near each end of this road lie the resorts of Mazagón and Matalascañas.

MAZAGÓN
postcode 21130 • pop 130
Mazagón is an unremarkable resort by appearance, but is an engaging place all the same. There's a **tourist office** (☎ 959 37 63 00; open 10am-2pm Mon-Fri) on Carretera de la Playa next to the **police station** and the **theatre**. La Playa is the main street; it runs 1km down from the N-442 to the beach and to a large marina. Residential Mazagón stretches to the east, for three featureless kilometres, along the beachfront Avenida de los Conquistadores. The real off-beach action is around the mid-point of Carretera de la Playa, in the pedestrianised Avenida Hotepiña, where there are good bars and restaurants.

East of Mazagón, you can reach the **beach** easily from beside the Parador de Mazagón, 3km from the town. At Cuesta de Maneli, 9km beyond, a 1.2km boardwalk leads from a car park to the beach through glorious pines and junipers across 100m-high dunes. The Cuesta de Maneli beach has a naturist section.

Places to Stay & Eat

Camping Playa Mazagón (☎ 959 37 62 08; *Cuesta de la Barca s/n; camping per adult/tent/car €4/4/4; open year-round*) is a couple of minutes' walk from the beach at the eastern end of Mazagón. It can get crowded despite its 3000-person capacity.

Camping La Fontanilla (☎ 959 53 62 37; *sites per adult/tent/car €3.50/3.50/3.50; open year-round*) is just above the beach and is accessible from the highway 700m east of Camping Playa Mazagón.

Camping Doñana Playa (☎ 959 53 62 81; *sites per adult/tent/car €4.25/4.25/4.25; open year-round*) is a huge place seven kilometres beyond Camping La Fontanilla.

Mazagón has only a few *hostales*:

Hostal Álvarez Quintero (☎ 959 37 61 69; *Calle Hernández de Soto 174; singles with/without bathroom €10/8, doubles with/without bathroom €30/21*) is a quiet, unassuming place, with fairly monastic rooms. It's just off the seaward end of Carretera de la Playa.

Hostal Hilaria (☎ 959 37 62 06; *Calle Buenos Aires 20; doubles €36*), just off Carretera de la Playa farther up the hill, has a restaurant. You can hire bicycles here.

Hotel Albaida (☎ 959 37 60 29; *singles/doubles €44.40/74*) is a comfortable place on the main road 600m east of the town centre. It has 24 air-conditioned rooms, all with bathroom, and a restaurant.

Parador de Mazagón (☎ 959 53 63 00, fax 959 53 62 28; e mazagon@parador.es; *singles/doubles €99.70/124.60*) is a luxurious 43-room place set in clifftop gardens 3km east of Mazagón, with easy access to the beach below.

Places to eat are mainly on Carretera de la Playa and Avenida Fuentepiña:

El Choco (*Avenida Fuentepiña 47; raciones €7.80-10*) does a roaring local trade and has a great atmosphere. Tapas are €1.50 at the bar, €1.80 at table.

Torre del Loro (☎ 959 53 62 55; *Avenida Fuentepiña 15; mains €6.60-8.40*) is just up from El Choco and is a more sedate place, with good tapas for €1.20 to €1.50, and salads from €1.50 to €4.80, as well as mains.

Bar Caroan (*Avenida Fuentepiña 8; platos combinados €5.40*) is another lively place opposite El Choco. It does good fried fish for €6.50.

Getting There & Away

Six buses run daily from Monday to Friday, from Huelva to Mazagón (€1.44, 35 minutes) via La Rábida and Palos de la Frontera, and vice versa. At weekends and holidays there are three daily, in each direction. There's a bus stop on Carretera de la Playa near the junction with Avenida Fuentpiñã.

MATALASCAÑAS

postcode 21760 • pop 420

This custom-built resort of candy-coloured high-rise hotels and low-rise apartments is a bizarre contrast to the wilderness of the adjoining Doñana natural and national parks. What makes Matalascañas such a favourite of mainly escapees from Seville are its terrific beach and plenty of summertime facilities. Out of season, there's a hollow eeriness about the deserted shopping malls and streets.

Orientation & Information

Matalascañas extends 4km southeast from the junction of the A-494 from Mazagón with the A-483 from El Rocío. From this junction Avenida de las Adelfas heads south straight to the beach, passing the **tourist office** (☎ 959 43 00 86; *open 9am-2.30pm Mon-Sat*). Buses stop by the big roundabout at the beach end of Avenida de las Adelfas, a spot known as Torre Higuera. The east side of the avenida is a wall of shops and restaurants a couple of blocks deep.

Places to Stay & Eat

Camping Rocío Playa (☎ 959 43 02 40; *sites per adult/tent/car €5/5/5; open year-round*), a huge place with room for 4000, is in a fine position just above the beach and is reached down a broad sandy track just before the entry roundabout to Matalascañas as you approach from Mazagon on the A-940.

Hostal Rocío (☎ 959 43 01 41; *Avenida El Greco 60; doubles with bathroom €32*) is just a minute's walk north of the tourist office.

Hostal Los Tamarindos *(☎ 959 43 01 19; Avenida de las Adelfas 31; doubles with bathroom €68)* and **Hostal El Duque** *(☎ 959 43 00 58; Avenida de las Adelfas 34; doubles with bathroom €48.25)* are two more options.

Hotel Flamero *(☎ 959 44 80 20; Ronda Maestro Alonso; doubles €78.50)*, 1km east along the beach, is one of the more appealing of the bigger hotels.

Several restaurants cluster behind the beach near the end of Avenida de las Adelfas and offer a typical three-course *menú del día* (daily set meal) for about €8.40 and *platos combinados* for €5.40.

Getting There & Away

Normally there's one bus daily to/from Huelva (€2.90, 50 minutes) via Mazagón, Monday to Friday, leaving Matalascañas at 7.10am and Huelva at 2.45pm. Extra services may run in summer. Buses also link Matalascañas with El Rocío and Seville (see Getting There & Away under Parque Nacional de Doñana, following).

PARQUE NACIONAL DE DOÑANA

Doñana National Park, which contains some of Europe's most important wetlands, covers 507 sq km in the southeast of Huelva province and neighbouring Sevilla province. The park is a vital refuge for endangered species such as the pardel lynx and Spanish imperial eagle (with populations here of around 50 and 15, respectively), and is a crucial habitat for millions of other birds.

Much of the national park's boundary is bordered by the separate Parque Natural de Doñana, which consists of four distinct zones totalling 540 sq km and forming a buffer for the national park.

There are enduring claims that the area was once the site of fabled Tartessos. In later centuries it was certainly a favourite hunting ground of Spanish nobility and royalty. Doñana was made a national park in 1969, following concern over threats to its wetlands from rice-growing, road and tourism schemes. The World Wide Fund for Nature – then called the World Wildlife Fund – raised much of the cash for the initial purchases of the land. James Michener, in *Iberia*, writes how members of one Danish shooting club were persuaded to dig into their pockets: 'Gentlemen,' they were told, 'if the lakes of Doñana are allowed to disappear, within five years there will be no ducks in Denmark'.

Access to the national park itself is limited. Anyone may walk along the 28km stretch of Atlantic beach between Matalascañas and the mouth of the Guadalquivir (which can be crossed by boats from Sanlúcar de Barrameda), as long they do not stray inland off the beach. To visit the park's interior, you have to book ahead – and pay for – a guided tour. These leave from the Centro de Visitantes El Acebuche, on the western side of the park (see later in this section), and from Sanlúcar de Barrameda (see under The Sherry Triangle in the Cádiz Province chapter). There are, however, several interesting areas bordering the national park which you can visit independently, without paying or booking.

A good base is the village of El Rocío, at the northwestern corner of the park. Another possibility is Matalascañas, 16km southwest of El Rocío (see the preceding Matalascañas section).

The Junta de Andalucía 1:75,000 map *Doñana* (1998) shows the national and natural parks and their surrounds in reasonable detail; it can be bought at the Centro de Visitantes El Acebuche. The IGN's 1:50,000 *Parque Nacional de Doñana* (1992) covers a smaller area in greater detail.

Flora & Fauna

The national park is a refuge for 125 resident and 125 migratory bird species. Six million birds spend at least part of the year here.

Half the national park consists of wetlands, the marshes of the delta of the Guadalquivir, which enters the Atlantic Ocean at the southeastern corner of the park. The park contains only about one-tenth of the Guadalquivir *marismas* (marshlands), but most of those outside it have been drained and/or channelled for agriculture.

The park's marshlands are almost dry from July to October. In autumn they start to fill with water, eventually leaving only a few islets of dry land. Over 500,000 water birds arrive from the north to winter here, including an estimated 80% of Western Europe's wild ducks. As the waters sink in spring, other birds – the greater flamingo, spoonbills, storks, herons, avocets, hoopoes, bee-eaters, stilts – arrive for the summer, many of them to nest. Fledglings flock around shrinking ponds called *lucios* in summer. As the *lucios* dry up in July, herons, storks and kites move in to feast on trapped perch.

Between the marshlands and the park's 28km-long beach is a band of shifting sand dunes, up to 5km wide. Winds move the dunes inland at a rate of up to 6m per year: in shallow valleys called *corrales*, between the dunes, grow pines and other trees favoured as nesting sites by raptors. When dune sand eventually reaches the marshlands, rivers carry it back down to the sea, which

Black Tide

One of the most serious threats to the delicate balance of the Parque Nacional de Doñana came in April 1998, when a dam broke at the Los Frailes heavy-metals mine at Aznalcóllar, 50km north of the park. Nearly seven million cubic metres of mine waste, water and mud loaded with acids and heavy metals flooded into the Río Guadiamar, one of the chief waterways flowing into Doñana's wetlands. Hastily erected dikes prevented the poisonous tide from entering all but a small corner of the national park itself, but up to 100 sq km of wetlands to its northeast were contaminated, and agricultural land bordering about 70km of the river was devastated.

There was no dramatic collapse of the park's ecology, but chronic long-term effects, such as reductions in fertility, were feared. The disaster provoked typical squabbling between national and regional government, but also inspired ambitious environmental improvement plans and saw the emergence of schemes to decontaminate and to protect the area in the future. To date the signs that the area is recovering are encouraging, although threats of pollution caused by human activity remain.

washes it up on the beach where the cycle begins all over again. The beach and moving dunes together make up 102 sq km of the park.

In other parts of the park, stable sand supports 144 sq km of *coto*, the favoured habitat of an abundant mammal population, including red and fallow deer, wild boar, mongoose and a handful of *Homo sapiens*. *Coto* vegetation ranges from heather and scrub through dense wooded thickets to stands of umbrella pine and cork oak.

Centro de Visitantes El Acebuche

El Acebuche (☎ 959 44 87 39; open 8am-8pm daily May-Sept; 8am-7pm daily Oct-Apr) is the national park's main visitor centre and is the starting point for tours into the park. Head 12km south from El Rocío on the A-483, then 1.6km west along an approach road. It includes a café, shop and park exhibition, and can provide maps. Short paths lead to hides overlooking a lagoon with birds. You can reach the centre from Matalscañs by following the A-483 north from its junction with the A-494, for 4km, to reach the entrance to the signed approach road.

National Park Tours Trips from El Acebuche into the national park are run, in all-terrain vehicles holding about 20 people each, by the **Cooperativa Marismas del Rocío** (☎ 959 43 04 32). This is the only way for ordinary folk to get inside the park proper except for guided trips from Sanlúcar de Barrameda (see under The Sherry Triangle in the Cádiz Province chapter). You need to book ahead by telephone – for spring, summer and all holiday times the tours can get booked up more than a month ahead, but otherwise a week, sometimes less, is usually adequate. Bring binoculars if you can and carry plenty of drinking water in summer. Use mosquito repellent, except in winter. The trips go at 8.30am year-round, 3pm in October to April and 5pm in May to September, daily except Monday. They last about four hours and cost €18.20 per person. Most guides speak Spanish only. The route of about 80km normally

The Romería del Rocío

Like most of Spain's holiest images, Nuestra Señora del Rocío – aka La Blanca Paloma (White Dove) – has legendary origins. Back in the 13th century, the story goes, a hunter from the village of Almonte found her in a tree in the *marismas* (marshlands) and started to carry her home. But when he stopped for a rest, the Virgin made her way back to the tree.

Before long, a chapel was built where the tree had stood (El Rocío) and it became a place of pilgrimage. By the 17th century, *hermandades* (brotherhoods) were forming in nearby towns to make pilgrimages to El Rocío at Pentecost, the seventh weekend after Easter (7–9 June in 2003, 29–31 May in 2004). Today, the Romería del Rocío (Pilgrimage to El Rocío) is a vast festive cult that draws people from all over Spain. There are over 90 *hermandades*, some with several thousand members, both men and women, and they still travel to El Rocío on foot, on horseback and in gaily decorated covered wagons pulled by cattle or horses along cross-country tracks.

Solemn is the last word you'd apply to this quintessentially Andalucian event. In an atmosphere similar to Seville's Feria de Abril, participants dress in fine Andalucian costume and sing, dance, drink, laugh and romance their way to El Rocío. The total number of people in the village on this special weekend can reach about a million.

The weekend comes to an ecstatic climax in the very early hours of Monday. Members of the *hermandad* of Almonte, which claims the Virgin for its own, barge into the church and bear her out on a float. Violent struggles ensue as others battle with the Almonte lads for the honour of carrying La Blanca Paloma. The crush and chaos are immense, but somehow good humour survives and the Virgin is carried round to each of the *hermandad* buildings, before finally being returned to the Ermita in the afternoon.

begins with a drive along the beach to the mouth of the Río Guadalquivir, then loops back through the south of the park, taking in moving dunes, marshlands and woods, where you can be pretty certain of seeing a good number of deer and boars. Serious ornithologists may be disappointed by the limited bird-watching opportunities.

From Monday to Saturday, the first morning bus from El Rocío towards Matalascañas, departing at 7am weekdays and 7.15am on Saturday, will get you to El Acebuche in time for the morning tour. However, check current schedules before you go.

Centro de Visitantes José Antonio Valverde

Some of the best bird-watching in the Doñana area is to be had at this visitor centre overlooking a year-round *lucio* on the northern fringe of the national park. Also called the Centro Cerrado Garrido, it's about 30km south of the town of Villamanrique de la Condesa by minor roads and drivable tracks (60km from El Rocío). The

Centro de Visitantes El Acebuche has maps and directions.

El Rocío
postcode 21750 • pop 690
Overlooking the marshlands at the corner of the fenced-off national park, El Rocío has a touch of the Wild West about it. Its sandy streets bear almost as many hoofprints as tyre marks and are lined by rows of verandaed houses – far more than El Rocío's permanent population could ever need and most of them usually standing empty. But this is no ghost town, for the houses are in excellent repair. Most of them belong to the 90-odd *hermandades* (brotherhoods) of pilgrim-revellers who converge on El Rocío every Pentecost (Whitsuntide) in the Romería del Rocío (see the boxed text). Indeed, a fiesta atmosphere pervades the village most weekends of the year as hermandades arrive to carry out lesser rituals.

Information At the time of writing the **tourist office** (☎ 959 44 26 84; *Avenida de la*

HUELVA PROVINCE

Canaliega s/n), just south of the Hotel Puente del Rey at the western end of the village, was closed for major refurbishment. It was expected to reopen by 2003. Some information may be available at the town hall, on the other side of the hotel. National park information is available at the Centro de Información Las Rocinas (see Things to See & Do, following).

An El Monte ATM on the northern side of the Ermita del Rocío takes major cards.

Things to See & Do The heart of the village is the **Ermita del Rocío** *(open 8am-9pm daily)*, a church built in its present form in 1964, which houses the celebrated Nuestra Señora del Rocío – a small wooden image of the Virgin, dressed in long, bejewelled robes, which normally stands above the main altar. People arrive to see the Virgin every day of the year. In the outside, south wall of the church is a special chamber for votive candles. The heat is so ferocious and the fumes so dense that ventilator fans work nonstop to clear the air of what seems more like fire and brimstone than faith.

The **marshlands** at El Rocío contain water all year, thanks to the Río Madre de las Marismas which flows through here, so it's nearly always a good place to spot birds and animals. Deer and horses graze in the shallows and you may be lucky enough to see a flock of flamingos wheeling through the sky in a big pink cloud. The Spanish Ornithological Society's observatory, the **Observatorio Madre del Rocío** *(☎ 959 50 60 93; admission free; open 10am-2pm & 4pm-7pm Tues-Sun)*, is by the water, about 150m east of the Hotel Toruño (see Places to Stay & Eat, following); it has telescopes.

The bridge over the river on the A-483 1km south of the village is another good viewing spot. Just past the bridge is the **Centro de Información Las Rocinas** *(☎ 959 44 23 40; open 9am-3pm & 4pm-7pm daily)*. The centre may stay open until 8pm or 9pm depending on the season. From this national park information centre, short paths lead to bird-watching hides by a year-round creek. Though outside the park itself, this section of the creek is in a special *zona de protección* and has fairly abundant bird life.

Six kilometres west along a road from Las Rocinas in the same *zona de protección*, is the Centro de Visitantes in **Palacio del Acebrón** *(admission free; open 10am-2pm & 4pm-7pm daily)*. It has information and there is a 1.5km walking track through riverbank woodland.

For a longer walk from El Rocío, cross the Puente del Ajolí, at the northeastern edge of the village, and head along the track into the woodland ahead. This is the **Coto del Rey**, a large woodland zone where you can wander freely for hours. It's crossed by numerous tracks which vehicles might manage in dry seasons. In early morning or late evening you may spot deer or boars.

Discovering Doñana *(☎ 959 44 24 66)* runs daily **bird-watching trips** in the Parque Natural de Doñana costing about €20 per person, with binoculars, telescopes and field manuals provided. For more information, ask at Pensión Cristina (see Places to Stay & Eat, following).

You can hire **horses** for hourly or daily trips. Ask at the Hotel Toruño (see Places to Stay & Eat, following) or contact **Doñana Ecuestre** *(☎ 959 44 24 74)*. Charges are around €25 for about two hours or €80 a day. Doñana Ecuestre also arranges 4WD tours of the park.

Places to Stay & Eat During Romería you will never be able to find an empty room. If you want to attend then you need to book well ahead, although hotel rooms are booked often at least a year in advance and prices go sky-high.

Pensión Cristina *(☎ 959 44 24 13; Calle El Real 58; singles/doubles with bathroom €18/30)*, a short distance east of the church, has reasonable rooms as well as a decent restaurant with a *menú* for €9.

Pensión Isidro *(☎ 959 44 22 42; Avenida de los Ánsares 59; singles/doubles €18/36)*, 400m north of the church, and also with a restaurant, is a little better than Pensión Cristina.

Hotel Toruño *(☎ 959 44 23 23, fax 959 44 23 38; e hoteltoruno@terra.es; Plaza Acebuchal 22; singles/doubles €45/64.30)*, just a short distance east of Pensión Cristina, is an attractive, modern place with 30 air-conditioned rooms. All have a bathroom and some have views of the marshlands.

Hotel Puente del Rey (☎ 959 44 25 75; *Avenida de la Canaliega s/n; apartments sleeping 2-3 people €42 per night, €200 per week*) is a vast building at the entrance to El Rocío from the west. Once a hotel, it now houses mainly private apartments, but with a few for general rent on inquiry.

The bars and restaurants of El Rocío do a roaring trade at most times, although the cuisine is geared towards feeding multitudes.

Café Bar El Pocito (*Calle Ermita; tapas €1.50, media-raciones/raciones around €7.50-10, platos combinados €4.25*), just east of the church, does good tapas.

Bar Cafetería El Real (*raciones €8-11*), facing the northern side of the church, is marginally more expensive than Café Bar El Pocito but offers a particularly wide choice, with tapas for €1.50 to €1.80.

Bar-Restaurante Toruño (*Plaza Acebuchal; meat & fish mains €9-17*), overlooking the marshlands and with handsome tile-and-wooden-beam decor, offers lots of meat and fish main dishes.

Getting There & Away
Bus Damas runs three or more daily buses from Seville to El Rocío (€6.30, 1½ hours), Matalascañas (€7.50, 1¾ hours) and back. Three to six Damas buses run daily each way along the A-483 between Almonte and Matalascañas (€2.25, 40 minutes), stopping at El Rocío. All these buses will stop outside the Las Rocinas and El Acebuche national park visitor centres (you may have to request this).

From Huelva, take a Damas bus to Almonte (€3.55, 45 minutes), six daily from Monday to Friday, but few at weekends, then another from Almonte to El Rocío (€1.10, 18 minutes).

West of Huelva

The coast between Huelva and the Portuguese border, 53km to the west, alternates between estuaries, wetlands, good sandy beaches, and small and medium-sized resorts and fishing ports.

PUNTA UMBRÍA
postcode 21100 • pop 10,800
Punta Umbría, on a point of land between the Atlantic and the Paraje Natural Marismas del Odiel, is Huelva's summer playground, 21km from the city by road. It's a modern and pleasant enough resort, though very busy in July and August.

Places to stay include two camping grounds a few kilometres out of town, off the road from Huelva, and the youth hostel, **Albergue Juvenil Punta Umbría** (☎ 959 31 16 50; *Avenida Océano 13*), close to the Atlantic beach.

Hostal Playa (☎ 959 31 01 12, fax 959 65 94 50; *Avenida Océano 95; doubles with bathroom €60.25*), **Hostal Emilio** (☎ 959 31 18 00; *Calle Ancha 21; doubles with bathroom €54.25*) and **Hotel Ayamontino Ría** (☎ 959 31 14 58; *Paseo de la Ría 1; doubles with bathroom €61.25*) are other options. The last two are near the estuary on the eastern side of town.

From Huelva, buses run to Punta Umbría every hour from 7.15am to 9pm (€1.62, 30 minutes). In summer, hourly ferries (€1.80), known as *canoas*, sail from the Muelle de Levante at Huelva port.

EL ROMPIDO
El Rompido, 16km northwest of Punta Umbría, on the Río Piedras estuary, is a fishing and yachting village-cum-minor resort, with several seafood restaurants. The estuary is divided from the ocean by a long spit of land, both sides of which are lined by sandy beaches.

Camping Catapum (☎ 959 39 91 65; e *catapum@terra.es; Careterra El Rompido km3; camping per adult/tent/car €3.85/3.85/3.85*), which can get crowded, is at the eastern end of the village and is handy for good beaches.

Several buses per day travel from Huelva to El Rompido Monday to Friday (€1.80, 30 minutes), but there are only a couple of buses making this trip on Saturday, Sunday and holidays. Drivers continuing west along the coast towards La Antilla must go inland to the N-431 and turn south again at Lepe.

HUELVA PROVINCE

LA ANTILLA
postcode 21449 • pop 520
La Antilla's holiday chalets and apartments now stretch 9km along the fine, wide, sandy beach that runs all the way from the Río Piedras to Isla Cristina, but the place only extends a few blocks inland, although development continues. It's a likable, low-key resort, and out of season is almost empty.

Camping Luz (☎ 959 34 11 42; camping per adult/tent/car €4.30/4.30/4.30) is near the western end of town.

There are two other camping grounds, one at each end of town. At least six hostales are bunched near the beach, on Plaza La Parada, with doubles for between €42 and €54 in summer (but you'd be lucky to get a room in August). For an apartment, try asking at the **Islantilla tourist office** (☎ 959 64 60 13), 1km west of central La Antilla.

Monday to Friday, several Damas buses per day run to La Antilla from Huelva and Isla Cristina, and two from Seville. At weekends and on holidays there's at most one a day from each place.

ISLA CRISTINA
postcode 21410 • pop 17,300
As well as being a beach resort (packed in August), Isla Cristina has a fair-sized fishing fleet. The boats create a lively scene in the morning and evening as they land their catches at the **Puerto Pesquero** (fishing port), a couple of blocks west of the central Plaza de las Flores. From the plaza, Gran Vía Román Pérez heads south for about 1km to the western end of Isla Cristina's beach. The **Oficina Municipal de Turismo** (☎ 959 33 26 94; Avenida Madrid) is 150m east of Gran Vía Román Pérez.

North of town, the road towards the N-431 crosses the **Paraje Natural Marismas de Isla Cristina**, which has a rich bird life, including the greater flamingo and spoonbills. Signs 2km from Isla Cristina indicate the **Sendero de Molino Mareal de Pozo del Camino**, a 1km walking track across the marshlands.

Camping Giralda (☎ 959 34 33 18; camping per adult/tent/car around €4.30 each) among pines by the main road at the eastern edge of town, has room for 2200 people. Playa Central is a stone's throw away.

Camping Playa Taray (☎ 959 34 11 02; e campingtaray@hotmail.com; camping 1 adult, tent & car €11.25) is a cheaper option to the east of town.

Most hotels are in the mid- to top-end range and are around Avenida de la Playa near Playa Central:

Hotel Paraíso Playa (☎ 959 33 02 35; e hparaiso@terra.es; Avenida de la Playa; singles/doubles €48/85) has pleasant rooms and friendly staff. Breakfast is included and there is a restaurant.

Hotel Los Geranios (☎ 959 33 18 00; e geraniosh@yahoo.com; Avenida de la Playa; doubles €89.25) is just along the road and has been imaginatively refurbished; each room has its own colour scheme. Its restaurant does lunch for €12.60.

Hotel Sol y Mar (☎ 959 33 20 50; doubles €60) is right on the seafront.

Acosta Bar-Restaurante (Plaza de las Flores; seafood dishes €5-12) does good fish dishes, or you could head over to the seafood bars and restaurants on the square outside the Puerto Pesquero, such as **Bar-Restaurante Hermanos Moreno**. There are eateries at Playa Central too.

Buses run at least six times daily to/from Huelva (€3.19, one hour), three or more times daily to/from Ayamonte (€1.15, 25 minutes), and one to three times daily to/from Seville (€8.40, two hours).

AYAMONTE
postcode 21400 • pop 176,570
Ayamonte still has a cheerful borderland buzz about it, although you can now pass it by and wheel your way into Portugal, customs-free and toll-free, across the splendid Puente del Guadiana that spans the Río Guadiana, 2km to the north. Romantics can still enjoy the riverwide pace of times past, however, by taking the ferry across the Guadiana between Ayamonte and Vila Real de Santo António.

Plaza de la Coronacíon and Plaza de Ribera are the main centres of activity. Plaza de Ribera has useful tiled seats and cheeky little cupid statues. The inner edges of the plazas are lined with bars and restaurants. Behind, narrow streets full of shops and cafés jostle each other, and lead more quietly inland to some surprising old buildings and fine churches, such as Iglesia de San Francisco and the Parroquia de El Salvador with its leaning columns, a legacy of the Lisbon earthquake of 1755.

Orientation & Information

Ayamonte's heart is the Plaza de la Coronacíon and its seamless neighbour Plaza de Ribera, fronted by the main road Avenida Vila Real de Santo António, which runs alongside the harbour.

The bus station is on Avenida de Andalucía, 700m east of the central plazas. The ferry dock *(muelle transbordador)* is on Avenida Muelle de Portugal, 300m northwest of the plazas.

At the time of writing, Ayamonte's **tourist office** (☎ *959 50 21 21; town hall, Aduana Ayamonte-Portugal)* has no independent location. You can get some information and leaflets from the town hall, at the address above, a block inland from the ferry dock. There is talk of establishing a dedicated tourist office, however; ask at the town hall.

In the pedestrianised streets behind Plaza de la Ribera are several banks with ATMs, open for exchange during banking hours Monday to Friday.

Beach

Ayamonte's beach is at **Isla Canela**, 6km to the south. It's wide, sandy and several kilometres long, with a reasonably undeveloped hinterland apart from low-rise apartments and one big, very expensive hotel. From June to September, buses run every half-hour from Ayamonte. The first bus from Ayamonte (€1.25) is at 9am; the last bus back from Isla Canela is 8.30pm. For the rest of the year the return bus leaves at 2.45pm.

Places to Stay & Eat

Hostal Los Robles (☎ *959 47 09 59; Avenida de Andalucía 121; doubles with/ without bathroom €30.65/24)* is an easygoing place just west of the bus station. Its

bar-restaurant does *plato combinados* and *bocadillos* for €2.40.

Hotel Marqués de Ayamonte (☎ *959 32 01 25; Calle Trajano 14; singles/doubles with bathroom €21/36)*, half a block west of Plaza de la Ribera, has plain but decent rooms.

Parador de Ayamonte (☎ *959 32 07 00;* e *ayamonte@parador.es; El Castillito; singles/doubles low season €60.35/75.45, high season €78.75/98.40)*, on a hill 1.5km north of the town centre, is modern, well-appointed and fairly characterless.

Casino España *(Plaza de la Ribera; raciones €4.90-7.20)* is an old-fashioned members-only meeting place. The bar is open to all, though.

Casa Barberi *(Plaza de la Coronación 12; menú €8.50)* does reasonable meat and fish dishes from €4 to €12.

Mesón La Casona *(Calle Lusitania 2; menú €8)* is a popular place a block northwest of the plazas. Main dishes start at €5.40.

La Palmera *(Pasaeo de los Gavilanes; menú €7.25)* in Isla Canela is a cheerful, down-to-earth bar located just beside the big roundabout at the end of the approach road to Isla Canela from the N-431. It does meat and fish dishes for €5.40 to €9.

Getting There & Around

There are no customs or immigration checks heading in either direction by road or ferry.

Bus Several daily buses run to/from Isla Cristina, Huelva (€3.55, one hour), Seville (€8, two hours) and Madrid (€21, 8½ hours). There are also a few buses along the Algarve and to Lisbon. The **bus station** (☎ *959 32 11 71)* has details.

Boat The ferry (☎ *959 47 06 17)* to/from Vila Real de Santo António runs every half-hour from 9.30am to 9pm from July to September and every 40 minutes from 9.40am to 8pm October to June. One-way fares are €3.50 for a car and driver, €1.80 for a motorcycle and rider, and €1 for adult passengers, €0.50 for children under the age of 10. Fairly frequent buses and trains run through the Algarve from Vila Real de Santo António.

Car & Motorcycle There is parking along the waterfront, opposite Plaza de la Coronacíon, but competition is fierce in the morning and early evening. There's a pay-for car park alongside the eastern end of the harbour.

The North

The rolling hills of Huelva's portion of the Sierra Morena are covered with a thick pelt of cork oaks, pine and chestnut trees, punctuated here and there by dramatic cliffs and by enchanting villages and larger centres such as the area's 'capital', Aracena. These hills – relatively rainy and a little cooler than most of Andalucía in summer – form the 1840-sq-km Parque Natural Sierra de Aracena y Picos de Aroche, Andalucía's second-largest protected area. They draw you in with a persuasive sense of detachment and timelessness. South of the sierra, the landscape has been wrenched apart at the vast mining area of Riotinto to leave a legacy of astonishing industrial landscapes.

MINAS DE RIOTINTO
postcode 21660 • pop 5,200
• elevation 420m

The town of Minas de Riotinto, 68km northeast of Huelva at the heart of one of the world's oldest mining districts, makes a fascinating stop on the way north. You can ride an early-20th-century train, visit a huge opencast mine and take in an excellent mining museum.

The Río Tinto (Coloured River), which rises nearby, takes its name from the hue of the copper and iron oxides washed into it from the ores of the mining zone.

Copper may have been mined in this district as early as 3000 BC, silver was being extracted before the Phoenicians came here in around 1000 BC, and iron was mined at least as early as Roman times. After the Romans, the lodes were largely neglected until 1725. In 1872 the mines were bought by the British-dominated Rio Tinto Company. The company turned the area into one of the world's great copper-mining centres, diverting rivers, digging away an entire metal-rich

hill – Cerro Colorado – and founding the town of Minas de Riotinto to replace a village it had demolished. The mines returned to Spanish control in 1954 and today, mining continues mainly at Cerro Colorado.

Orientation

Minas de Riotinto is 5km east along the A-461 off the N-435 Huelva-Jabugo road. Barrio de Bella Vista (see later in this section) is on the left of the A-461, opposite the turn-off into the town centre. Entering the town, veer right at the first roundabout to reach the Museo Minero, about 400m uphill. Buses stop on Plaza de El Minero, a little beyond the same roundabout.

Museo Minero & Reception Centre

The mining museum (Plaza del Museo s/n), is also the reception centre and main ticket office for visits to the Corta Atalaya opencast mine and rides on the old train, the Ferrocarril Turístico-Minero. All three are run by **Aventura Minaparque** (☎ 959 59 00 25; e aeg1657x@caymasa.es). There are small discounts if you opt for more than one of the three. It's worth ringing ahead to confirm timetables, especially if you plan to ride the train.

The Museo Minero (adult/child under 14 €2.40/1.80; open 10.30am-3pm & 4pm-7pm daily) is a figurative gold mine for devotees of industrial archaeology, but its intriguing displays will also fascinate the nonenthusiast; displays cover the geology, archaeology and history of the mines and the jewellery and statuary of the peoples who lived here. A major feature is a re-creation of a Roman mine through which you are taken by a guide. The convincing tunnels and chambers are a touch claustrophobic. The commentary is in Spanish but the various features tell their own vivid story of a nightmare world. Allow half an hour for the tour. Other features are the big display on the railways that the Rio Tinto Company built to serve the mines. At one time, 143 steam engines, mostly British-built, were puffing up and down these tracks. Pride of place goes to the *Vagón del Maharajah*, a luxurious carriage built in 1892 for a tour of India by Britain's Queen Victoria. That trip never happened, but the carriage was later used for a visit to the mines by Spain's Alfonso XIII.

Barrio de Bella Vista
Barrio de Bella Vista was built in the late 19th century as an exclusive home-from-home for the Rio Tinto Company's mainly British management, with houses, cottages and a Protestant church all in the distinctly suburban English style of the times. There's nothing to stop you wandering around the *barrio* (district), now inhabited by Spaniards.

Corta Atalaya
This enormous and awesome hole in the ground is 1.2km long and 335m deep and is one of the world's biggest opencast mines. It lies 1km west of the town. In its time its terraced walls have yielded huge quantities of copper-bearing iron pyrites. Guided visits (€4.20) depart from the Museo Minero at noon, 1pm, 2pm, 5pm and 6pm daily from mid-April to mid-October; at noon, 1pm, 2pm and 5pm daily during the rest of the year.

Ferrocarril Turístico-Minero
The mine train takes visitors 22km through the scarred landscape of the Río Tinto valley in refurbished early-20th-century carriages pulled by a steam engine of similar vintage. Trips start at Talleres Mina, the old railway repair workshops 2.5km east of Minas de Riotinto, just off the road to Nerva. They depart at 5pm on Saturday, Sunday and public holidays from mid-April to mid-June, at 1.30pm on Saturday, Sunday and public holidays from mid-June to mid-July, at 1.30pm daily mid-July to mid-September, at 5pm on Saturday, Sunday and public holidays from mid-September to mid-October and at 4pm on Saturday, Sunday and public holidays from mid-October to mid-April. Tickets cost €8.40 and are available from the Museo Minero. You have to make your own way to the station and should leave yourself plenty of time to get there, either on foot, by car, or by taxi; ask at the museum about taxis.

Corta Cerro Colorado
About 1km north of Minas de Riotinto, the road towards Aracena passes the Corta Cerro Colorado, a vast opencast mine where nearly all the area's mining activity happens today. There's a viewing platform (the Mirador Cerro Colorado) across the road. A century ago Cerro Colorado was a hill.

Nerva
postcode 21670 • pop 6,300
• elevation 332m
Nerva lies 4km east of Minas de Riotinto and has greater cohesion as a village than the latter. There is a **tourist office** (☎ 959 58 00 73; open 10am-2pm & 5pm-7pm daily) at the north entrance on the Riotinto road alongside a huge reconstructed mine gantry. At the centre of the village, in the pedestrianised Avenida de Andalucía, is the handsome red-brick town hall; the building has a remarkable iron plinth and a fine tower. Across the way is the **Museo Vázquez** (admission free; open 11am-2pm & 5pm-8pm Tues-Sat, 10am-2.30pm Sun & Mon) displaying works by locally born artist Daniel Vázquez Díaz.

Places to Stay & Eat
Hostal Galán (☎ 959 59 08 40; Avenida La Esquila 10; singles/doubles with bathroom €22.25/35.40), around the corner from the Museo Minero, has reasonable rooms and a restaurant with a *menú* for €7.80.

Hotel Los Cantos (☎ 959 59 15 54; Avenida Los Cantos; singles/doubles €22/32) is a short distance beyond Hostal Galán and has decent rooms and a restaurant that does a *menú* for € 5.70.

Hotel Santa Bárbara (☎ 959 59 11 88; Cerro de los Embusteros s/n; doubles with bathroom & air-con €52) is on a hilltop at the eastern end of town; rates include breakfast and its restaurant's *menú* is €9.

Cafetería-Bar Museo Minero (Plaza del Museo; mains €6), the café attached to the museum, does pastas, salads and grills and can do a picnic lunch of *bocadillos*, soft drinks, fruit and chocolate for €4.

La Estación (☎ 959 58 00 34; Carretera Nerva-Riotinto s/n; under 26/other €11.10/14) offers friendly and sparkling hostel-type accommodation in the converted railway station at Nerva. It also does full and half board, can organise various trips and activities and has lots of local information.

Hotel Vázquez Díaz (*☎/fax 959 58 09 27; Calle Cañadilla 51; singles/doubles €17.50/ 32)* is a modern hotel in Nerva with reasonable rooms. Its restaurant does a *menú* for €7.80 and breakfast for €1.80.

Getting There & Away

Three or more Damas buses run daily from Huelva to Minas de Riotinto (€5, 1¼ hours) and Nerva. The last one back leaves Nerva at 4pm and Minas de Riotinto a few minutes later. Casal runs services from Aracena to Minas de Riotinto (€2.20, 40 minutes) and Nerva at 9.55am Monday to Friday and 5.15pm Monday to Saturday, returning from Nerva at 5.45am Monday to Saturday and 12.15pm Monday to Friday, and from Minas de Riotinto five minutes later.

From Seville (Plaza de Armas bus station) there are two or more Casal buses to Nerva and Minas de Riotinto daily.

ARACENA

postcode 21200 • pop 6700
• elevation 730m

Aracena can feel like a virtual metropolis at the heart of remote northern Huelva, but it can also feel very remote out of season, when chill winds slice through its cobbled streets. It's still a hugely appealing place, in a handsome location below a hill crowned by a medieval church and a ruined castle. Below ground is the Gruta de las Maravillas, Aracena's 'Cave of Marvels', the major tourist attraction of the area. Although budget accommodation is limited here, Aracena makes for an ideal centre from which to explore.

Orientation & Information

The town lies between the castle hill, Cerro del Castillo, in the south, and the N-433 Sevilla–Portugal road that skirts it to the north and east. The main square is Plaza del Marqués de Aracena, from which the cobbled main street, Avenida de los Infantes Don Carlos y Doña Luisa (more simply known as Gran Vía), runs west. The Casal

and Damas bus office and stop is a few minutes' walk southeast of Plaza del Marqués de Aracena, on Avenida de Andalucía.

The **Centro de Visitantes Cabildo Viejo** (*☎ 959 12 88 25; Plaza Alta; open daily 10am-2pm & 6pm-8pm Apr-Sept; 10am-2pm & 4pm-6pm rest of year)* is the main information centre of the Parque Natural Sierra de Aracena y Picos de Aroche, but also has information on Aracena town. Located in Aracena's 15th-century former town hall, it has informative displays in the building's handsome brick vaults. The other tourist office is the **Centro de Turismo Rural y Reservas** (*☎ 959 12 82 06; Calle Pozo de la Nieve; open 9am-2pm & 4pm-7pm daily)*, facing the entrance to the Gruta de las Maravillas.

Gruta de las Maravillas

The Cave of Marvels (*☎ 959 12 83 55; Calle Pozo de la Nieve; adult/child under 16 €6.50/4.75; guided visits 10.30am, 11.30am, 12.30pm, 1.30pm, 3pm, 4pm, 5pm, 6pm Mon-Fri; 10.30am then every half-hour to 1.30pm & 3pm then every half-hour to 6pm Sat, Sun, public holidays)* is remarkable, if rather theatrical. The system of chambers and tunnels was carved out of the limestone beneath Cerro del Castillo by millennia of water action and ranks among the most spectacular in Spain; it attracts 150,000 visitors each year. The 1.2km route open to visitors features 12 chambers and six lakes, and has all sorts of weird and beautiful stalactites, stalagmites and rock formations. It culminates at the aptly named **Sala de los Culos** (Chamber of the Backsides), usually heralded by roars of laughter from elderly Spanish ladies and a bashful silence from their husbands. Coloured lighting and piped music heighten the romantic-cum-kitsch effect. Keep to the back of the group for a chance to look around, but note that the lights switch off once the group moves on.

The tours go when there are 25 people: this is no problem in summer, but on a wet Monday in November you might wait all day.

Plaza Alta

This handsome, cobbled square on the slopes of Cerro del Castillo was once the

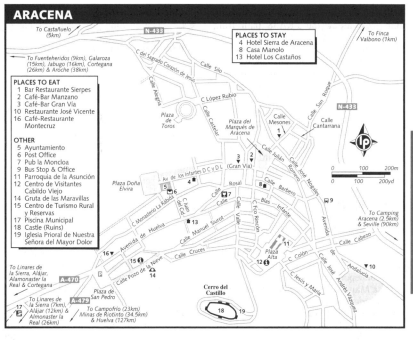

ARACENA

To Castañuelo
(5km)

N-433

To Finca
Valbono (1km)

PLACES TO STAY
4 Hotel Sierra de Aracena
8 Casa Manolo
13 Hotel Los Castaños

To Fuenteheridos (9km), Galaroza
(15km), Jabugo (16km), Cortegana
(26km) & Aroche (38km)

C del Sagrado Corazón de Jesús

Calle Silo

N-433

Calle San Roque

PLACES TO EAT
1 Bar Restaurante Sierpes
2 Café-Bar Manzano
3 Café-Bar Gran Vía
10 Restaurante José Vicente
16 Café-Restaurante
    Montecruz

OTHER
5 Ayuntamiento
6 Post Office
7 Pub la Moncloa
9 Bus Stop & Office
11 Parroquia de la Asunción
12 Centro de Visitantes
    Cabildo Viejo
14 Gruta de las Maravillas
15 Centro de Turismo Rural
    y Reservas
17 Piscina Municipal
18 Castle (Ruins)
19 Iglesia Prioral de Nuestra
    Señora del Mayor Dolor

Calle Alegría

C López Rubio

Plaza
de
Toros

Calle Castelar

Plaza del
Marqués de
Aracena

Calle
Mesones

Calle
Cantarrana

Calle Julián
Romero

Calle José Noñales

LP

Av de los Infantes D C y D L
(Gran Vía)

Rosal

Calle
Barbero

0   100   200m
0   100   200yd

Plaza Doña
Elvira

C Monasterio La Rábida

C Juan
del Cid

Calle

C Blas
Infante

C Fco Rincón

To Camping
Aracena (2.5km)
& Seville (90km)

Avenida de Huelva

Calle Manuel Siurot

Calle
Valle

Calle Cabezo

To Linares de
la Sierra, Alájar,
Alamonaster la
Real & Cortegana

A-470

Calle Pozo de la Nieve

Calle Cruces

Plaza
Alta

C Colón

C Andrés Vázquez

To Linares de
la Sierra (7km),
Alájar (12km) &
Almonaster la
Real (26km)

A-479

Plaza de
San Pedro

To Campofrío (23km),
Minas de Riotinto (34.5km)
& Huelva (127km)

Cerro del
Castillo

C Jesús y María

C José
Andalucía

HUELVA PROVINCE

---

centre of town. On one side stands the 15th-century **Cabildo Viejo** (Old Town Hall; see Orientation & Information, earlier). The huge, Renaissance **Parroquia de la Asunción** *(open for Mass at noon Sun, 7.30pm Mon-Fri in winter, 8.30pm Mon-Fri rest of year)*, at the foot of the square, is built in stone with the brick string-courses typical of the area's churches. Building of the church began in 1528 but was never completed.

Cerro del Castillo

A small Muslim fort atop the castle hill was conquered in the 13th century by the Portuguese, who built their own **castle** before being evicted from the area by Castile's Fernando III. It was around 1300 that the hilltop **Iglesia Prioral de Nuestra Señora del Mayor Dolor** *(admission free; open 11am-7pm)* was built, and the castle rebuilt – probably by the Knights of Santiago.

An initially steep road from Plaza Alta runs up to the beautiful Gothic-Mudejar

stone-and-brick church, which has a tower with brick tracery and, inside, three rib-vaulted naves. The ruins of the castle stretch along the hilltop beside the church.

Linares de la Sierra & Alájar Walk

Many walking routes start from Aracena. A good round trip of about 12km can be made by leaving Aracena between the Piscina Municipal (municipal swimming pool) and the A-470 road at the western end of town. This path descends a verdant valley to Linares de la Sierra (see West of Aracena later in this chapter).

To return by the more southerly PRA39 path, find a small stone bridge over the river below Linares, beyond which the path goes round Cerro de la Molinilla, passing old iron mines, and then crosses a stream for a stony ascent to Aracena, bringing you out on the A-479 in the southwest of town.

You could extend the walk by continuing 4km west along the PRA38 path from Linares to Alájar, via the hamlet of Los Madroñeros. There are fine views on this stretch. From Alájar you can walk back the way you came or catch the afternoon bus, daily except Sunday, to Aracena (see Getting There & Away under West of Aracena for bus information).

Special Events

Aracena's main summer *feria* (fair), with fireworks, music, dancing, funfairs, bullfights and more, happens in the third week of August.

Places to Stay

Camping Aracena (☎ 959 50 10 04; *camping per adult/tent/car* €3.70/3.50/3.50; *open year-round*) has room for about 270 people, and is in a valley 500m north of the N-433, 2km east of Aracena. Take the Corteconcepción turning.

Casa Manolo (☎ 959 12 80 14; *Calle Barbero 6; singles/doubles €12.85/23.50*), just south of Plaza del Marqués de Aracena, has Aracena's only budget beds. There are seven basic but adequate rooms.

Hotel Sierra de Aracena (☎ 959 12 61 75; *Gran Vía 21; singles/doubles €34.25/47*) has comfy rooms, each with TV and bathroom.

Hotel Los Castaños (☎ 959 12 63 00; *Avenida de Huelva 5; singles/doubles €25.70/51*) is a 33-room place with a restaurant *menú* for €12.

Finca Valbono (☎ 959 12 77 11, fax 959 12 76 79; *Carretera de Carboneras km1; doubles €64.30, 4-person apartments €109.30*), a converted farmhouse 1km north of Aracena, is easily the most charming and comfortable place in the area. Facilities include a bar, a pool, riding stables and a good, medium-priced restaurant.

Places to Eat

Café-Bar Manzano (*Plaza del Marqués de Aracena; tapas €1.20-1.80, platos combinados €4.80-9*) is a fine spot for varied tapas, *raciones* and *platos combinados*. Steak, egg and chips will set you back €8.50. Add 20% for table service.

Café-Bar Gran Vía (*Gran Vía s/n; raciones €4.80*) is a bustling place that has tons of tapas and *raciones* – tapas cost €1.20.

Café Restaurante Montecruz (*Plaza de San Pedro; platos combinados €6-7*) also does salads for €4 to €6.

Several tourist-oriented restaurants, many of them with *platos combinados* for €7 to €9, line Plaza San Pedro and Calle Pozo de la Nieve near the Gruta de las Maravillas.

Bar-Restaurant Sierpes (*Calle Mesones 13; raciones €4.85*) is a pleasant bar with a sumptuous adjoining restaurant, just up from the central Plaza del Marqués de Aracena. It does tapas for under €1 and has a restaurant *menú* for around €10.

Restaurante José Vicente (☎ 959 12 84 55; *Avenida de Andalucía 53; 3-course menú €15*) is a good place to enjoy the area's famous ham and pork. There is an excellent *menú* (including a drink), or you could choose to indulge in a *ración* of *jamón Jabugo* (Jabugo ham) at €14.40.

Entertainment

Nightlife in Aracena is limited to the main bars, but for cool company and late-night drinking try the excellent **Pub La Moncloa** (*Calle Rosal*), tucked away in a quiet side street and with a 16th-century *pozo* (deep well), preserved in one corner. It opens from about 10pm to 4am most nights in summer.

Getting There & Away

Casal (☎ 959 12 81 96) runs three daily buses to/from Seville's Plaza de Armas (€4.93, 1¼ hours), plus buses to Minas de Riotinto (see earlier in this chapter), to villages around northern Huelva province (see West of Aracena, following) and one daily bus at 10.30am to the Portuguese border (just beyond Rosal de la Frontera), where you can change to onward Portuguese buses. From the same Avenida de Andalucía stop, Damas runs daily buses to/from Huelva (€6.70, two hours). Damas also has a new service direct to Beja (Portugal) and Lisbon (3½ hours), that departs from the same bus stop at 10.30am Monday, Wednesday and Friday.

WEST OF ARACENA

West of Aracena stretches one of Andalucía's most unexpectedly beautiful landscapes, a sometimes lush, sometimes severe hill-country region dotted with old stone villages where time seems to have proceeded very slowly. Many of the valleys are full of woodlands, while elsewhere are expanses of *dehesa* – evergreen oak groves where the region's famed black or dark-brown Iberian pigs, raw material of the best ham in Spain, forage for acorns.

Some of the villages date back a long, long time, but others owe their existence to a Castilian repopulation drive after Castile had pushed out Portugal (which had driven out the Muslims) in the 13th century. Most villages grew up around fortress-like churches, or hilltop castles, constructed to deter the Portuguese.

There's an extensive network of marked walking trails throughout the Parque Natural Sierra de Aracena y Picos de Aroche, and particularly between Aracena and Aroche. Most villages are served by buses and many have accommodation, so you can make day hikes or string together a route of several days. It's advisable to phone ahead for rooms.

The N-433 from Aracena to Aroche passes through Galaroza, and close to Fuenteheridos, Cortegana and Jabugo. A more scenic route as far as Cortegana is the A-470 through Santa Ana la Real and Almonaster la Real (passing close to Linares de la Sierra and Alájar). Several roads and paths cut across the hills to link these two roads.

Walking

Information The best information on walking routes in the Aracena area is a leaflet, *Footpaths of the Sierra de Aracena and Picos de Aroche* (in Spanish *Senderos de la Sierra de Aracena y Picos de Aroche*), which gives fairly good descriptions and directions to a number of linear and circular walks in the area, with information on the wayside flora and fauna. Ask at the Centro de Turismo Rural y Reservas in Aracena, or at Huelva city's tourist office before heading north. The map *Parque Natural Sierra de Aracena y Picos de Aroche* (1:75,000), published by the Junta de Andalucía, and the SGE 1:50,000 sheets *Aracena*, *Aroche* and *Santa Olalla del Cala* give good overviews of the topography of the area but are not

HUELVA PROVINCE

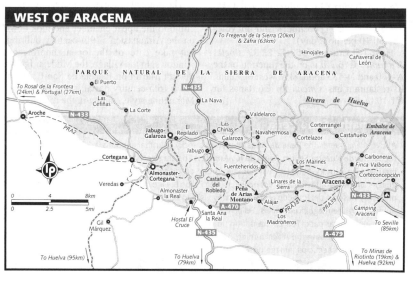

WEST OF ARACENA

entirely helpful for route-finding. The former should be available locally, but SGE maps are usually only available at city outlets (see Facts for the Visitor).

Linares de la Sierra
postcode 21350 • pop 307
• elevation 505m

Seven kilometres west of Aracena on the A-470, a 1km side road leads down to this poor but pretty little village, surrounded by stone-walled fields in a verdant river valley. The street cobbles are set in patterns in front of many doors – rather like stone doormats. The central square has a channelled *fuente* (fountain). The bar on the square next to the church serves food.

Alájar
postcode 21340 • pop 799
• elevation 574m

Five kilometres west of Linares de la Sierra, and also off the A-470 in a river valley, Alájar is a bigger cobblestoned village, clustered around a typical large sierra church.

La Posada (☎ 959 12 57 12; Calle Médico Emilio González 2; singles/doubles €40.50/51.50), a cosy place near Alájar's church, has eight rooms with bathrooms, and a **restaurant** (menú €9.60). La Posada also hires out horses (€7 per hour) and bicycles (€3.50/10 per hour/day).

Hostal El Cruce (☎ 959 12 23 33; singles & doubles €15.30) is on the junction of the A-470 and N-435 about 8km west of Alájar. Its restaurant has a *menú* for €6, tapas for €1.10 to €2.

Almonaster la Real
postcode 21350 • pop 2000
• elevation 613m

This picturesque village, 7km west of Santa Ana la Real, is home to one of the most perfect little gems of Islamic architecture in Spain. The **mezquita** *(mosque; open 9.30am-8pm daily)* stands on a hilltop five minutes' walk up from the main square. It's normally open until 6pm or 7pm in winter. If you find it shut, ask for the key at the town hall on the square.

The *mezquita* was built in the 10th century. In the 13th century the conquering Castilians turned it into a church, but left the Islamic structure largely intact. You enter beneath an original Muslim horseshoe arch and a Visigothic lintel carved with a cross and two fleurs-de-lis. The inside is like a miniature version of the great Mezquita in Córdoba, with rows of brick arches supported by varied columns. At the eastern end is the semicircular mihrab (prayer niche), indicating the direction of Mecca. The Christians added a Romanesque apse on the northern side, where parts of a broken Visigothic altar, carved with a dove and angels' wings, have been reassembled.

The original minaret, a square, three-level tower, adjoins the main building. You can climb to the upper chamber and look down on the Almonaster's 19th-century bullring, but take care of the open, unprotected windows. In the village, the Mudejar **Iglesia de San Martín** on Placeta de San Cristóbal has a 16th-century portal in the Portuguese Manueline style, unique in the region.

Polymath of the Peña

Above Alájar stands the **Peña de Arias Montano**, a rocky spur that supports a 16th-century chapel, the **Ermita de Nuestra Señora Reina de los Ángeles**. The crag gets its name from Benito Arias Montano, a 16th-century polymath who produced one of the first maps of the world, learned 11 languages and was confessor, adviser and librarian to Felipe II. Late in life Montano became parish priest of nearby Castaño del Robledo and made many visits to this spot for retreat and meditation, inspired no doubt by the magnificent views. Felipe II is said to have visited him here and prayed in the cave just below the car park. The Ermita is 1km up the side road towards Fuenteheridos that leaves the A-470 almost opposite the Alájar turning. The church has a 13th-century carving of the Virgin and is the focus of a hectic pilgrimage on 7 September, when Alájar villagers race up on horseback.

Casa García (☎ *959 14 31 09, fax 959 14 31 43; Avenida San Martín 2; doubles €45-96.50)*, at the entrance to the village from the A-470, is a plush, stylish hotel; its good restaurant specialises in local meat dishes, with mains between €8.70 and €12.

Hostal La Cruz (☎ *959 14 31 35; Plaza El Llano 8; singles/doubles €24/30)* has a few rooms. It has a bar-restaurant with *raciones* for around €5.

Cortegana

postcode 21230 • pop 5075
• elevation 673m
Cortegana, 6km northwest of Almonaster la Real, is a sizable town overlooked by a 13th-century **castle** that contains an exhibition on medieval fortifications in northern Huelva, which was an important frontier zone between Sevilla province and Portugal. Also worth a look are the 16th-century **Capilla de Nuestra Señora de la Piedad** next to the castle and the Gothic/Mudejar **Iglesia del Divino Salvador** *(Plaza del Divino Salvador)*.

Pensión Cervantes (☎ *959 13 15 92; Calle Cervantes 27B; doubles with/without bathroom €24/18)*, is just off Plaza de la Constitución.

Aroche

postcode 21241 • pop 3500
• elevation 406m
From Cortegana, the N-433 and the PRA2 footpath run 12km west along a broad, open valley to the little hilltop town of Aroche, 27km from the Portuguese border. Aroche is a cheerful, friendly place and is full of narrow, pebbled streets. There's a useful car park in Calle Dolores Losado beside the bus stop as you enter the town.

Aroche's **castle** *(admission free; open 10am-2pm & 5pm-7pm Sat, Sun & holidays)*, at the top of the village, was originally built by the Almoravids in the 12th century and has more recently been converted into a bullring. Outside the official opening hours you can ask at the **Casa Consistorial** *(town hall; Plaza de Juan Carlos I)*, on the central plaza, or at the Cafetería Lalo, up the steps beside the Casa Consistorial, for a guide to take you up.

Just below the castle is the large **Iglesia de Nuestra Señora de la Asunción**. It is Gothic/Mudejar in style, but it has a 16th-century Renaissance portal. The **Museo del Santo Rosario** *(Paseo Ordoñez Valdéz)* just before the car park, has a collection of more than 1000 rosaries from around the world, some donated by the rich and famous.

Hostal Picos de Aroche (☎ *959 14 04 75; Carretera de Aracena 12; singles/doubles €18/30)* is on the road up into town from the N-433 and is a spotless, comfortable place; it's wise to book ahead.

Centro Cultural Las Peñas *(Calle Real; tapas €1.20-1.50)* has a great local atmosphere and does good tapas, and also *raciones* for €8 to €11.

Restaurante Mirasierra *(raciones €6-9)* is a roadside restaurant on the road to Portugal just west of Aroche. It does tapas for €1.20.

Jabugo

pop 2600
Just south of the N-433, 10km east of Cortegana, Jabugo is famous throughout Spain for its *jamón ibérico* (ham from the Iberian breed of pig; see the boxed text 'From Little Acorns, Great Hams Grow' under Food in the Facts for the Visitor chapter). If you're not a fan of ham, Jabugo is fairly unexciting.

The village is the main processing centre for hams from the Huelva sierras, and a line of bars and restaurants along Carretera San Juan del Puerto, on the eastern side of the village, wait for you to sample what's acclaimed as the best *jamón* in the country. At **Mesón Cinco Jotas**, run by the biggest producer, Sánchez Romero Carvajal, a serving of the best ham, *cinco jotas* (5 Js), will set you back €7, or you could really 'pig out' on *cinco jotas* and fried eggs for about €10. In the bars a *bocadillo* of fine *jamón* costs about €5. Shops such as **de Jabugo la Cañada** (☎ *959 12 12 07; Carretera San Juan del Puerto 2)* sell a huge selection of products. *Jamón* to take away costs about €20 per kilogram. The best is *jamón ibérico de bellota* (ham from acorn-fed Iberian pigs) and a seven-kilogram whole ham costs around €252.

Other Villages

Between Jabugo and Aracena several attractive little villages can be reached from the N-433. Worth a visit, if you have time, are Galaroza, Fuenteheridos and especially Castaño del Robledo.

This small, impoverished village, on a minor road between Fuenteheridos and the N-435, has a positively medieval feel, with two large churches in states of advanced disrepair and the tiled roofs of houses bending under the weight of the years.

You'll find a couple of bars on Plaza del Álamo, behind the Iglesia de Santiago el Mayor (the church with the pointier tower).

Getting There & Away

Bus Many of the villages are served by Casal (☎ 959 12 81 96) buses from Seville (Plaza de Armas) and Aracena. Two buses run daily, except Sunday, from Aracena to Cortegana (€2.16, 50 minutes), and two back, via Linares de la Sierra (€0.65, 15 minutes), Alájar (€0.75, 20 minutes) and Almonaster la Real (€1.50, 40 minutes), with one of them continuing to/from Aroche (€2.90, 1¼ hours) and the other to/from Seville. Four buses run daily each way between Aracena and Cortegana via Fuenteheridos, Galaroza and Jabugo, with two or three continuing to/from Aroche and Rosal de la Frontera and two to/from Seville.

Damas buses run each way between Huelva and Almonaster la Real, Cortegana and Aroche (€7.10, 2½ hours), twice a day Monday to Friday and once on Saturday.

Train Two trains run daily between Huelva and Almonaster-Cortegana (€4.80, 1¾ hours) and Jabugo-Galaroza (€5.25, 2 hours) stations. At the time of writing they leave Huelva at 9.35am and 1pm. Only one stops on a return trip, at Jabugo-Galaroza (5.04pm), and at Almonaster-Cortegana (5.15pm). Both of the outbound trains from Huelva terminate in Extremadura: one at Fregenal de la Sierra, the other at Zafra. Almonaster-Cortegana station is 1km off the Almonaster-Cortegana road, about halfway between the two villages. Jabugo-Galaroza station is in El Repilado, on the N-433, 4km west of Jabugo.

Cádiz Province

The province of Cádiz (**cad**-i, or just **ca**-i) stretches from the mouth of the Río Guadalquivir to the Strait of Gibraltar and inland to the rainy Sierra de Grazalema. Its attractions include the historic port of Cádiz, the triangle of sherry-making towns (Jerez de la Frontera, Sanlúcar de Barrameda and El Puerto de Santa María), the long, sandy and little-developed Atlantic beaches along the Costa de la Luz (Coast of Light) and the beautiful, green sierras (mountain ranges), with their remote white towns and villages.

The proliferation of 'de la Frontera' place names here dates from the days of the Reconquista (Reconquest). Castile took most of what's now Cádiz province from the Muslims in the 13th century, but the south was then raided repeatedly by the Merenids of Morocco, while to the east lay the Emirate of Granada. Hence for over 200 years this region was a frontier *(frontera)* of Christian territory. In the mid-14th century King Alfonso XI offered a free pardon to murderers and criminals who would come here and serve a year and a day in his army. The region still has an untamed feel today, with windy coasts, large tracts of sparsely inhabited hill country and big lowland ranches that breed famous fighting bulls.

Developers are starting to foul up some bits of the coastline but, happily, the Costa de la Luz is still a very far cry from the Costa del Sol.

Highlights

- Savour the surf and beach scene at Tarifa, an old Muslim town on Spain's southern tip, and one of Europe's top windsurfing and kitesurfing spots
- Enjoy the fun-loving, historic port city of Cádiz
- Visit Jerez de la Frontera, famous for its sherry, horses and flamenco
- Tour the tasty tapas bars of El Puerto de Santa María or enjoy a succulent seafood dinner at Sanlúcar de Barrameda
- Explore the white villages and craggy mountains of the Sierra de Grazalema
- Unwind on the Costa de la Luz – long sandy beaches, laid-back coastal villages

CÁDIZ PROVINCE

Cádiz

postcode 11080 • pop 138,000

Few people remember Cádiz when they list the great cities of Andalucía, yet this port is as famous and historic as almost any of them. It's just that it's out on a limb, almost as intimate with the oceans and distant continents as with its own land, and with no Muslim or Reconquista heritage whatsoever.

Once past the coastal marshes and industrial sprawl around Cádiz, you emerge into an 18th-century city of decayed grandeur, now being restored, crammed onto the head of a long peninsula like some huge, overcrowded, ocean-going ship. The people of Cádiz, called *gaditanos*, are mostly an unassuming and tolerant lot, whose main concern is to make the best of life – whether staying out late to enjoy the after-dark cool in the sweltering summer months, or indulging in Spain's most riotous *carnaval* (carnival) in spring. Cádiz has one of the highest levels of unemployment in Spain, partly due to the decline of its shipbuilding and fishing industries.

HISTORY

Cádiz may be the oldest city in Europe. It was founded, tradition says, in 1100 BC by the Phoenicians, who called it Gadir and came here to trade Baltic amber and British tin for Spanish silver. Later, it became a naval base for the Romans, who heaped praise on its culinary, sexual and musical delights. It then faded into obscurity until 1262, when it was taken from the Muslims by Alfonso X.

Cádiz began to boom with the discovery of America. Christopher Columbus sailed from this port on his second and fourth voyages. It attracted Spain's enemies too: in 1587 England's Sir Francis Drake 'singed the king of Spain's beard' with a raid on the harbour, delaying the imminent Spanish Armada. Then, in 1596, Anglo-Dutch attackers burnt almost the entire city.

Cádiz's golden age was during the 18th century, when it enjoyed 75% of Spanish trade with the Americas. It grew into the richest and most cosmopolitan city in Spain and gave birth to the country's first middle class of progressive, liberal inclinations. Most of the city's fine buildings date from this era.

The Napoleonic Wars brought British warships back to blockade and bombard the

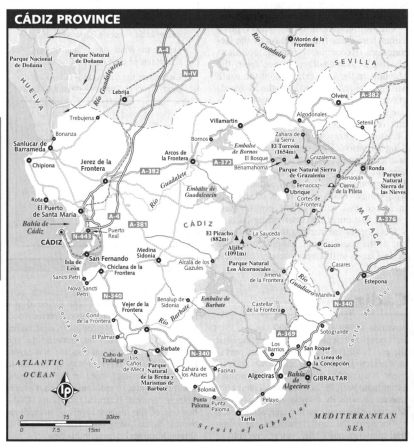

CÁDIZ PROVINCE

city and shatter the Spanish fleet at the Battle of Trafalgar, nearby, in 1805. After Spain turned against Napoleon in 1808, Cádiz was one of the few cities not to fall to the French, withstanding a two-year siege from 1810. During this time a national parliament convened here. It was a lopsidedly liberal gathering which adopted Spain's 1812 constitution, proclaiming sovereignty of the people and setting the scene for a century of struggle between liberals and conservatives.

The loss of the American colonies in the 19th century plunged Cádiz into a decline from which it is still emerging.

ORIENTATION

Breathing space between the huddled streets of the old city is provided by numerous squares. From Plaza de San Juan de Dios, towards the eastern end of the old city, Calle Nueva, which becomes Calle San Francisco, leads northwest towards another important square, Plaza de Mina.

The train station is in the east of the old city, just off Plaza de Sevilla, with the main bus station of the Comes line 800m to the north on Plaza de la Hispanidad. The main harbour lies between the two.

The 18th-century Puertas de Tierra (Land Gates) mark the eastern boundary of the old city. Modern Cádiz extends back along the peninsula.

INFORMATION

The **municipal tourist office** (☎ 956 24 10 01; Plaza de San Juan de Dios 11; open 9am-2pm & 5pm-8pm Mon-Fri) has vibrant staff. A **tourist information kiosk** (open 10am-1.30pm & 5pm-7.30pm Sat & Sun at least July & Aug; 10am-1.30pm & 4pm-6.30pm Sat & Sun rest of year) opens on the square at weekends. The **regional tourist office** (☎ 956 25 86 46; Avenida Ramón de Carranza s/n; open 9am-7pm Tues-Fri, 9am-2pm Sat & Mon) is well stocked.

Banks with ATMs are on Avenida Ramón de Carranza and Calle San Francisco, northwest of Plaza de San Juan de Dios. The main **post office** (Plaza de Topete) is by the market.

Internet (cnr Calle Isabel la Católica & Calle Antonio López; open 11am-11pm Mon-Sat) is fairly central in the old town. It charges €1.80 per hour.

The **Policía Local** (emergency ☎ 092; Avenida Cayetano del Toro) are 2km southeast of the centre. The main hospital is the **Puerta del Mar** (☎ 956 00 21 00; Avenida Ana de Viya 21), 2.25km southeast of the Puertas de Tierra.

TORRE TAVIRA

The Torre Tavira (☎ 956 21 29 10; Calle Marqués del Real Tesoro 10; admission €3.50; open 10am-8pm daily mid-June–mid-Sept; 10am-6pm daily mid-Sept–mid-June) is the highest and most important of the city's old watchtowers, and is a fine place to get your bearings and a dramatic panorama of Cádiz. Its camera obscura projects moving images of the city onto a screen (sessions start at half-hourly intervals). Back in the 18th century, Cádiz had no less than 160 towers to watch over its harbours.

PLAZA DE TOPETE

A couple of blocks southeast of the Torre Tavira, this square is one of Cádiz's liveliest, bright with flower stalls and adjoining the large Mercado Central (central market). It's still commonly known by its old name, **Plaza de las Flores** (Square of the Flowers).

HOSPITAL DE MUJERES

The real attraction of this 18th-century former women's hospital (Calle Hospital de Mujeres) is the **Capilla** (Chapel; admission €0.60; open 10am-1pm Mon-Fri). One of the many profusely decorated churches from Cádiz's golden century, this one contains El Greco's Extasis de San Francisco (Ecstasy of St Francis), depicting the grey-cloaked saint experiencing a mystical vision.

MUSEO HISTÓRICO MUNICIPAL

The City History Museum (Calle Santa Inés 9; admission free; open 9am-1pm & 4pm-7pm Tues-Fri Oct-May, 9am-1pm & 5pm-7pm Tues-Fri June-Sept, 9am-1pm Sat & Sun) contains a large, detailed 18th-century model of the city, made in mahogany and ivory for Carlos III, which would merit a visit even if nothing else was there.

CÁDIZ PROVINCE

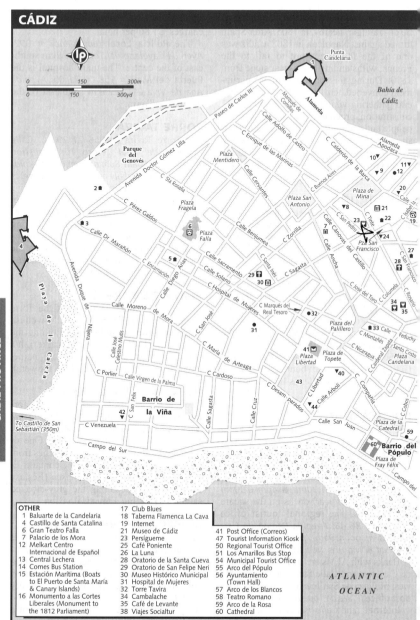

CÁDIZ

Punta Candelaria

Bahía de Cádiz

Parque del Genovés

Plaza Mentidero

Plaza Fragela

Plaza Falla

Plaza San Antonio

Plaza de Mina

Plaza San Francisco

Playa de la Caleta

To Castillo de San Sebastián (350m)

Barrio de la Viña

Plaza del Palillero

Plaza de Topete

Plaza Libertad

Plaza Candelaria

Plaza de la Catedral

Barrio del Pópulo

Plaza de Fray Félix

ATLANTIC OCEAN

OTHER
1 Baluarte de la Candelaria
4 Castillo de Santa Catalina
6 Gran Teatro Falla
7 Palacio de los Mora
12 Melkart Centro Internacional de Español
13 Central Lechera
14 Comes Bus Station
15 Estación Marítima (Boats to El Puerto de Santa María & Canary Islands)
16 Monumento a las Cortes Liberales (Monument to the 1812 Parliament)

17 Club Blues
18 Taberna Flamenca La Cava
19 Internet
21 Museo de Cádiz
23 Persígueme
25 Café Poniente
26 La Luna
28 Oratorio de la Santa Cueva
29 Oratorio de San Felipe Neri
30 Museo Histórico Municipal
31 Hospital de Mujeres
32 Torre Tavira
34 Cambalache
35 Café de Levante
38 Viajes Socialtur

41 Post Office (Correos)
47 Tourist Information Kiosk
50 Regional Tourist Office
51 Los Amarillos Bus Stop
54 Municipal Tourist Office
55 Arco del Pópulo
56 Ayuntamiento (Town Hall)
57 Arco de los Blancos
58 Teatro Romano
59 Arco de la Rosa
60 Cathedral

CÁDIZ PROVINCE

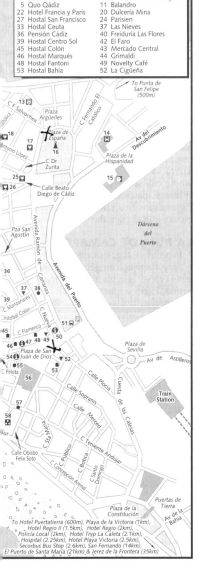

PLACES TO STAY	PLACES TO EAT
2 Hotel Atlántico	8 Café Bar Madrileño
3 Residencia Universitaria La Sal	9 Cervecería Aurelio
5 Quo Qádiz	10 Mesón Cumbres Mayores
22 Hotel Francia y París	11 Balandro
27 Hostal San Francisco	20 Dulcería Mina
33 Hostal Ceuta	24 Parisien
36 Pensión Cádiz	37 Las Nieves
39 Hostal Centro Sol	40 Freiduría Las Flores
45 Hostal Colón	42 El Faro
46 Hostal Marqués	43 Mercado Central
48 Hostal Fantoni	44 Grimaldi
53 Hostal Bahía	49 Novelty Café
	52 La Cigüeña

To Punta de San Felipe (500m)

To Hotel Puertatierra (600m), Playa de la Victoria (1km), Hotel Regio II (1.5km), Hotel Regio (2km), Policía Local (2km), Hotel Tryp La Caleta (2.1km), Hospital (2.25km), Hotel Playa Victoria (2.5km), Secorbus Bus Stop (2.6km), San Fernando (14km), El Puerto de Santa María (21km) & Jerez de la Frontera (35km)

ORA[...]

This [...]
€1.2[...]
Cádi[...]
also [...]
men[...]
and [...]
terp[...]
plac[...]

COASTAL WALK

Head one block north [...]
emerge on the city's [...]
views across the B[...]
de Santa María [...]
west along the [...]
arte de la [...]
west bes[...]
Geno[...]
Ala[...]

CA[...]

A c[...]
San [...]
street of late-18th- and early-19th century
Cádiz. Its cafés and bars were the unofficial
gathering and debating places for members
of the 1812 parliament. The **Palacio de los
Mora** *(Calle Ancha 28-30; open 11am-1pm
Sat)* is one of the most sumptuous of
Cádiz's urban mansions, built in the eclec-
tic Isabelline style of the mid-19th century.

ORATORIO DE LA SANTA CUEVA

This 1780s neoclassical church *(Calle
Rosario; admission €1.50; open 10am-1pm
Tues-Sat, 4.30pm-7.30pm Sat & Sun)*, attached to the Iglesia del Rosario, is a two-in-
one affair, with the austere underground
Capilla Baja contrasting sharply with the
richly decorated oval-shaped upper Capilla
Alta. Framed by three of the Capilla Alta's
eight arches are paintings by Goya depicting
the Miracle of the Loaves and Fishes, the
Guest at the Wedding, and the Last Supper.

MUSEO DE CÁDIZ

The city's excellent major museum *(☎ 956 21
22 81; Plaza de Mina; admission €1.50, EU
citizen free; open 2.30pm-8pm Tues, 9am-
8pm Wed-Sat, 9.30am-2.30pm Sun)* is on one
of its most attractive squares. Pride of the
ground-floor archaeology section is a pair of
Phoenician white-stone sarcophagi carved in
human likeness. There's also some beautiful
Phoenician jewellery and Roman glassware,
and lots of Roman statues – plus Emperor
Trajan, with head, from Baelo Claudia (see
the Bolonia section later in this chapter).

A highlight of the 2nd-floor fine arts collection is a group of 21 superb canvases of
saints, angels and monks by Zurbarán.

...f Plaza de Mina to ...northern seafront, with ...hía de Cádiz to El Puerto ...From here you could head ... **Alameda** garden to the **Balu-...Candelaria** bastion, then south-...de the sea wall to the **Parque del ...és**, which was laid out, like the ...meda, in the 19th century. From the park, ...venida Duque de Nájera leads south to **Playa de la Caleta** (very crowded and dirty in the summer), on a bay between two forts. The star-shaped **Castillo de Santa Catalina**, built in 1598, at the northern end of the beach, was for a long time Cádiz's main citadel. The **Castillo de San Sebastián**, far out on the southern side of the bay, is in military use. From Playa de la Caleta you can follow the coast eastwards to the cathedral.

CATHEDRAL & AROUND

The story of Cádiz's yellow-domed cathedral *(Plaza de la Catedral; admission €3; open 10am-1pm Tues-Sun & 4.30pm-7pm Tues-Fri)* reflects that of the whole city in the 18th and 19th centuries. The decision to build it was taken in 1716 on the strength of the imminent transfer from Seville to Cádiz of the Casa de la Contratación, which controlled Spanish trade with the Americas. But the cathedral wasn't finished till 1838, by which time not only had neoclassical elements diluted Vicente Arturo's original baroque design, but also funds had dried up, forcing cutbacks in size and quality. It's still a large and impressive construction, with little ornamentation to distract from the grandeur of the marble and stone interior, lit from the 50m-high main dome. The Cádiz-born composer Manuel de Falla is buried in the crypt.

A short distance east along Campo del Sur are the excavated remains of a Roman theatre, the **Teatro Romano** *(admission free; open 11am-1.30pm Tues-Sun)*.

PLAZA DE SAN JUAN DE DIOS & AROUND

The shabby **Barrio del Pópulo** district between the Teatro Romano and Plaza de San Juan de Dios was the kernel of medieval Cádiz, a fortified enclosure wrecked in 1596. Its three 13th-century gates, the Arco de los Blancos, Arco de la Rosa and Arco del Pópulo, however, remain. Plaza de San Juan de Dios is dominated by the imposing neoclassical **town hall** *(ayuntamiento)* built around 1800.

If by now you're in need of a cool, quiet and leafy resting spot, the bougainvillea-shaded benches in **Plaza Candelaria**, 250m northwest of Plaza de San Juan de Dios, fit the bill nicely.

PLAYA DE LA VICTORIA

This wide beach stretches many kilometres back down the ocean side of the peninsula, beginning about 1km beyond the Puertas de Tierra. On hot summer weekends almost the whole city seems to be out here. Bus No 1 'Plaza España–Cortadura' from Plaza de España runs along the peninsula one or two blocks inland from the beach.

LA RUTA DE CAMARÓN

A handful of sites associated with the legendary flamenco singer El Camarón de la Isla (1950–92) in his home town of San Fernando, 13km southeast of Cádiz, are linked together in the self-guided Ruta de Camarón. You can pick up a leaflet with a description and map of the route at Cádiz's regional tourist office.

LANGUAGE COURSES

Cádiz's most popular language school is **Gadir Escuela Internacional de Español** *(☎/fax 956 26 05 57;* **W** *www.gadir.net; Calle Pérgolas 5)*. Two weeks' intensive classes in a small group cost €316.80 from July to September. **Melkart Centro Internacional de Español** *(☎/fax 956 22 22 13;* **W** *www.centromelkart.com; Calle General Menacho 7)*, in the old town, is similarly professional but cheaper.

SPECIAL EVENTS

No other Spanish city celebrates Carnaval with the verve of Cádiz, where it turns into a 10-day singing, dancing and drinking fancy-dress party that continues until the weekend after the normal Shrove Tuesday close. Everybody – locals and visitors alike – dresses up, and the fun, abetted by enormous quantities of alcohol, is infectious. Costumed groups called *murgas* tour the city on foot or on floats, singing witty satirical ditties, dancing or performing sketches. In addition to the 300 or so officially recognised *murgas*, who are judged by a panel in the Gran Teatro Falla, there are also the *ilegales* – any group that fancies taking to the streets and trying to play or sing.

Some of the liveliest scenes are in the working-class Barrio de la Viña, between the Mercado Central and Playa de la Caleta, and on Calle Ancha and Calle Columela where *ilegales* tend to congregate.

Rooms in Cádiz are all booked months in advance for Carnaval. Assuming you haven't managed this, you could just go for the night from Seville or anywhere else within striking distance. Plenty of people do this – many in fancy dress.

PLACES TO STAY – BUDGET
Hostels

Quo Qádiz (π/fax 956 22 19 39; Calle Diego Arias 1; dorm beds €6-12, singles/doubles €12.50/24), Cádiz's excellent independent youth hostel, is in a revamped old house just a block south of the Gran Teatro Falla. Cheerful dorms and private singles and doubles occupy several floors topped by an extensive roof terrace. Breakfast is included and vegetarian food is served for lunch or dinner. The dynamic owners are bicycle fanatics who organise trips to beaches up and down the coast, the mountain ranges of Cádiz province and even Morocco.

Hostales & Pensiones

Cheaper places cluster just northwest of Plaza de San Juan de Dios.

Hostal Fantoni (π 956 28 27 04; Calle Flamenco 5; singles/doubles €18/25, doubles with bathroom €36), a friendly, family-run place in an old house, is a good choice. It has 16 spotless, renovated rooms and a rooftop terrace catching a breeze in summer.

Hostal Marqués (π 956 28 58 54; Calle Marqués de Cádiz 1; singles/doubles €18/30, doubles with bathroom €30-36) has 15 slightly ageing but clean rooms, all with balconies.

Hostal Colón (π 956 28 53 51; Calle Marqués de Cádiz 6; singles/doubles €21/ 24, doubles with bathroom €30) is more modern than Hostal Marqués.

Pensión Cádiz (π 956 28 58 01; Calle Feduchy 20; singles/doubles €20/30), north from Hostal Colón, is a popular little place.

Hostal Ceuta (π 956 22 16 54; Calle Montañés 7; doubles with bathroom €30), close to Pensión Cádiz, is clean and friendly.

Hostal San Francisco (π/fax 956 22 18 42; Calle San Francisco 12; singles/doubles €17/28, doubles with bathroom €37.50) is a clean but basic place further into the old city.

Residencia Universitaria La Sal (π 956 21 15 39; Calle Doctor Marañón 14; singles/ doubles €21/33) has good rooms and Internet access. Rates include breakfast.

PLACES TO STAY – MID-RANGE

Hostal Bahía (π 956 25 90 61, fax 956 25 42 08; Calle Plocia 5; singles/doubles with TV & air-con €52.50/63), just off Plaza de San Juan de Dios, has comfortable rooms available.

Hostal Centro Sol (π 956 28 62 41, fax 956 28 31 03; Calle Manzanares 7; singles/ doubles with bathroom €35.50/45), is efficient, clean and friendly. It has 19 smallish rooms, with cable TV. The owners speak French.

Hotel Francia y París (π 956 21 23 18, fax 956 22 23 48; Plaza San Francisco 2; singles/ doubles €54/72) is bigger (57 rooms) and more luxurious.

Other mid-range options are mostly outside the old city. **Hotel Regio II** (π 956 25 30 08, fax 956 25 30 09; Avenida de Andalucía 79; doubles €77) and **Hotel Regio** (π 956 27 93 31, fax 956 27 91 13; Avenida Ana de Viya 11; doubles €77) are both on the main road down the peninsula, respectively 1.5km and 2km from the Puertas de Tierra.

CÁDIZ PROVINCE

PLACES TO STAY – TOP END

Hotel Atlántico (*☎ 956 22 69 05, fax 956 21 45 82; Avenida Duque de Nájera 9; singles/ doubles €87.50/116*), on the seafront by Parque del Genovés, is a modern parador.

Hotel Puertatierra (*☎ 956 27 21 11, fax 956 25 03 11; Avenida de Andalucía 34; doubles €128.50*), outside the old city 750m southeast of the Puertas de Tierra, is large and stylish.

Hotel Tryp La Caleta (*☎ 956 27 94 11, fax 956 25 93 22; Avenida Amilcar Barca s/n; doubles €145*) is on the beachfront, 1.5km further southeast.

Hotel Playa Victoria (*☎ 956 27 54 11, fax 956 26 33 00; Glorieta Ingeniero La Cierva 4; doubles €148*), 400m beyond Hotel Tryp La Caleta, is the biggest and best in town, with 188 rooms.

PLACES TO EAT
Barrio de la Viña

El Faro (*☎ 956 22 99 16; Calle San Felix 15; open noon-4.30pm & 8pm-midnight daily*), in the old fishermen's district, is Cádiz's most famous seafood restaurant with a fancy menu and prices to match. Its attached **bar** (*tapas €1.50-1.80, raciones €6*) has more moderately priced yet exquisite seafood tapas. We enjoyed the *hojaldre de salmon y queso* (pastry with salmon and cheese).

Nearby, orange-tree-lined Calle Virgen de las Palmas has several cheap restaurants and bars for fish and seafood. Stroll by at night!

Grimaldi (*☎ 956 22 83 16; Calle Libertad 9; mains €5.50-13.50*), between the market and seafront, is another good seafood place. It's decorated with old photos of Cádiz and offers a range of unusual fishy things.

Plaza de San Juan de Dios & Around

This central square offers plenty of choice.

Novelty Café (*Calle Nueva 9*), on the northwest corner of the plaza, is a fine place to go for a light breakfast, cakes or snacks.

La Cigueña (*☎ 956 25 01 79; Calle Plocia 2; mains €10.75-15; closed Mon*), one block off the square, has a Dutch chef and an international, experimental menu. You could start with prawn tempura and soy dipping sauce, then move on to roast lamb with lavender sauce, or sea bass baked with wine and vegies.

Las Nieves (*Plaza Mendizábal; menú €6*), a couple of blocks into the old town from Plaza de San Juan de Dios, is a slightly sophisticated spot for your morning *tostada* (toasted roll or slice of bread), a snack, or Monday to Friday lunch-time *menú*.

Plaza de Mina

Café Bar Madrileño (*Plaza de Mina s/n; tapas €1.20, seafood raciones from €5.50, menú €6*) has a wide choice of food at a reasonable price.

Dulcería Mina (*Calle Antonio López 2; breakfast from €2.50*) does good pastries and excellent filled baguettes. Locals love this little place for breakfast. You can have tea or coffee, juice and a *tostada*, or pay more for a bacon and eggs option.

Cervecería Aurelio (*Calle Zorrilla 1; tapas/raciones €1.20/6*), off the northern side of the square, is hard to pass by due to its mouthwatering fresh seafood tapas. Try the *cazón en adobo* (marinated, deep-fried dogfish).

Mesón Cumbres Mayores (*☎ 956 21 32 70; Calle Zorrilla; mains €8-9*) has a popular bar, but out the back is a more formal dining area where you can eat very well and economically. The salad starter of endive and avocado with a roquefort dressing is a meal in itself. If you have room, you can follow up with *guisos* (stews), soups, fish, seafood and barbecued meats.

Balandro (*☎ 956 22 09 92; Alameda Apodaca 22; meat & fish raciones €6-7.50; open Tues-Sun*) has sea views from its terrace and an upstairs dining room. It's popular year-round for its good food, cheap prices and attractive old crockery. Try the pizza-like *pan horneado* with a smoked salmon, anchovy and cream cheese topping.

Plaza de Topete

The **Mercado Central** sells, among other things, *churros* (long, deep-fried doughnuts), which you can take to nearby cafés to enjoy with a hot chocolate for breakfast.

CÁDIZ PROVINCE

Freiduría Las Flores *(Plaza de Topete 4; mixed seafood platter €6)*, is like a fancy fish and chip shop. To try it all, order a *surtido*, a mixed fry-up.

Plaza San Francisco

Parisien *(breakfast from €1.80)*, with tables on the square opposite the church, is good for a drink at any time of day and has breakfast deals.

ENTERTAINMENT

There's a great atmosphere in old-city squares like **Plaza de Mina** on hot summer nights, with bars and cafés busy till well after midnight, and kids playing football or cruising on bikes or skates.

From midnight in summer the real scene migrates to the **Paseo Marítimo** along Playa de la Victoria – about 3km down the peninsula from the Puertas de Tierra. Here, 300m to 600m past the big Hotel Playa Victoria, you'll find lively music bars and throngs of people standing in the street drinking. Others simply hang out at the beach. A taxi from the old city (try Plaza de España) to this area costs around €5. Up to about 1.30am you can use bus No 1 to get here (see under Playa de la Victoria earlier in this chapter).

In winter, the bars in the streets west of **Plaza de España**, such as **Calle Dr Zurita**, are among the liveliest, and the square itself and Plaza de Mina are the setting for the Saturday night teenager scene. **Club Blues** *(Plaza de España 12; open until late Thur-Sun)* is a popular hangout. **Café Poniente** *(Calle Beato Diego de Cádiz 18)* is a good gay bar. **La Luna** *(Calle Doctor Zurita s/n)* is another. A little further east is **Punta de San Felipe**, the real late, late night zone, with a row of dance bars. Here, **El Malecón** *(☎ 956 22 45 19; Paseo Pascual Pery)*, is Cádiz's most famous Latin dance spot.

In the centre **Persígueme** *(cnr Calle Tinte & Calle Sagasta; open from 4.30pm daily)* is a cool place for a drink. The hip **Cambalache** *(Calle José del Toro 20)* is the place to hear good jazz. Or stop by the laid-back **Café de Levante** *(Calle Rosario 35)*.

Taberna Flamenca La Cava *(☎ 956 21 18 66; Calle Antonio López 16; drink & show €21.40)*, between Plaza de la Mina and Plaza de España, has a flamenco show at 9pm on Tuesday and Saturday.

The **Gran Teatro Falla**, in the northwest of the old town, is the main venue for cultural events, including music, dance (sometimes flamenco), film and theatre. The ageing **Central Lechera** *(Plaza de Argüelles s/n)* also hosts theatre and music concerts.

GETTING THERE & AWAY

Bus

Most buses are run by **Comes** *(☎ 956 21 17 63)* from Plaza de la Hispanidad. These include at least 10 daily each to Seville (€9, 1¾ hours), El Puerto de Santa María (€2.40, 40 minutes), Jerez de la Frontera (€2.50, 40 minutes), and Algeciras (€7.90, two hours), seven to Tarifa (1½ hours), six to Barbate (1¼ hours) and Vejer (one hour), three or more to Arcos de la Frontera (€4.30, 1¼ hours), Ronda (3¾ hours), Málaga and Zahara de los Atunes, two to Granada and one to Córdoba.

Los Amarillos runs up to 10 buses daily to El Puerto de Santa María (€1.50) and Sanlúcar de Barrameda (€2.50, 1¼ hours), and two or three daily to Arcos de la Frontera (€2.50, 1¼ hours), El Bosque (€6) and Ubrique (€7), from its stop by the southern end of Avenida Ramón de Carranza. Tickets and information are available from **Viajes Socialtur** *(☎ 956 28 58 52; Avenida Ramón de Carranza 31)*.

Secorbus *(☎ 956 25 74 15)* operates six buses daily to Madrid (€21.50, six hours) from Plaza Elios by the Estadio Ramón de Carranza football ground, about 2.7km southeast of the old city.

Train

The **station** *(☎ 956 25 43 01)* is just off Plaza de Sevilla, near the port. Up to 20 suburban trains *(cercanías)* run daily to/from El Puerto de Santa María (€2, 30 minutes) and Jerez de la Frontera (€2.40, 40 minutes), and up to 12 regional trains *(regionales)* to/from Seville (€8, two hours) via the same places.

There are three trains daily to/from Córdoba (€14.10 to €25.50, three hours) and two for Madrid (€49.50 to €69).

Car & Motorcycle

The A-4 motorway from Seville to Puerto Real on the eastern side of the Bahía de Cádiz carries a toll of €5.50. The toll-free alternative, the N-IV, is a lot busier and slower. From Puerto Real, the N-443 crosses a bridge over the narrowest part of the bay to join the southern road into Cádiz, about 4km short of the old city.

Boat

See the El Puerto de Santa María section later in this chapter for details of services from Cádiz to that town.

Trasmediterránea (☎ 902 45 46 45; W www.trasmediterranea.es) at the Estación Marítima operates a passenger and vehicle ferry to the Canary Islands, leaving Cádiz on Saturday and arriving in Santa Cruz de Tenerife, Las Palmas (Gran Canaria) and Santa Cruz de la Palma (La Palma) respectively, 1½, two and three days later. One-way passenger fares start at €200. It can be bumpy!

The Sherry Triangle

North of Cádiz, the towns of Jerez de la Frontera, Sanlúcar de Barrameda and El Puerto de Santa María are best known for being the homes of sherry. But there's a wealth of other good reasons to visit: beaches, music, horses, history, and visits to the Parque Nacional de Doñana.

EL PUERTO DE SANTA MARÍA
postcode 11500 • pop 76,500

El Puerto, 10km northwest of Cádiz across the Bahía de Cádiz (22km by road), is easily and enjoyably reached by ferry. It was here that Christopher Columbus met Juan de la Cosa, the owner of his 1492 flagship, the *Santa María*, and Columbus' pilot on the great voyage. From the 16th to 18th centuries it was the base of the Spanish royal galleys. Its heyday came in the 18th century, when El Puerto flourished on American trade and earned the name 'Ciudad de los Cien Palacios' (City of the Hundred Palaces). Today its beaches, sherry bodegas (wineries) and tapas bars make it a favourite

outing for *gaditanos*, *jerezanos* and others looking for a change of scenery. In summer it's a very lively town.

Orientation & Information

The heart of the town is on the northwest bank of the Río Guadalete, just upstream from its mouth, though development spreads along the beaches to the east and west. The ferry *El Vapor* arrives dead centre at the Muelle (jetty) del Vapor on Plaza de las Galeras Reales. Calle Luna, one of the main streets, runs straight inland from Plaza de las Galeras Reales. The excellent **tourist office** (☎ 956 54 24 13; Calle Luna 22; open 10am-2pm & 6pm-8pm daily May-Sept; 10am-2pm & 5.30pm-7.30pm daily Oct-Apr) is 2½ blocks along.

The train station is a 10-minute walk northeast of the centre, beside the Jerez road. Some buses stop at the train station, others at the Plaza de Toros (Bullring), five blocks south of Calle Luna.

You can check your email and make cheap international phone calls at **Keur Khadim** (Calle Palacios 39).

Walking Tour

Start your explorations at the historic four-spouted **Fuente de las Galeras Reales** (Fountain of the Royal Galleys), on Plaza de las Galeras Reales. America-bound ships drew their water here. Two blocks southwest, then a block inland, stands the **Castillo San Marcos** (Plaza Alfonso El Sabio 3; admission €1.80, free Tues; open 10am-1.30pm Tues-Sat July-Sept, 11am-2pm Tues, Thur & Sat Oct-June). It incorporates a mosque and was built by Alfonso X after he took the town in 1260. Visits are by half-hour guided tour of the ground floor only: the highlight is the mosque itself, converted to a church.

Three blocks further inland is the **Fundación Rafael Alberti** (☎ 956 85 07 11; Calle Santo Domingo 25; due to reopen late 2002 after extension works), with interesting exhibits on one of El Puerto's famous son Rafael Alberti (1902–99). A poet, painter and communist politician of the Generation of '27 (see Literature in the Facts about Andalucía chapter), Alberti lived in this house as a child.

Sacred Bulls

Roaming the highways of Spain, every now and then you catch sight of the silhouette of a truly gigantic black bull on the horizon. When you get closer to the creature you'll realise it's made of metal and held up by bits of scaffolding. What's it for?

It's not a silent homage to bullfighting erected by the local folk, nor a sign that you're entering a notable bull-breeding area. It's a sherry and brandy advertisement for the Osborne company of El Puerto de Santa María. At the last count there were 92 *toros de Osborne*, each weighing up to four tonnes, looming beside roads all over the country. And over the years they have raised as much dust as a champion bull trying to stay alive on a hot Sunday afternoon.

Why doesn't Osborne put its name on the bulls if it's trying to advertise, you might ask? From 1957, when the first bull was erected on the Madrid-Burgos road, until 1988, it did. Then a new law banned advertising hoardings beside main roads, to prevent drivers being distracted. Osborne left the bulls standing but removed its name, which seemed to pacify the authorities, until 1994 when word got about that the law was going to be enforced strictly, meaning no more bulls. This provoked an enormous furore, with intellectuals writing to newspapers about the national heritage, the Andalucian regional government declaring the 21 bulls in Andalucía protected monuments, and Osborne taking the fight to the courts. In 1997 Spain's supreme court decided that the bulls had transcended their original advertising purpose and were now part of the landscape. They still are.

Nearby, the little **Museo Municipal** (*Calle Pagador 1; admission free; open 10am-2pm Tues-Fri, 10.45am-2pm Sat & Sun*) has interesting archaeological and fine arts sections. The impressive sandstone **Iglesia Mayor Prioral** (*open 8.30pm-12.45pm Sun-Fri, 8.30am-noon Sat, 6.30pm-8.30pm daily*) dominates Plaza de España. Built between the 15th and 18th centuries, it boasts a lavish plateresque/baroque portal facing the plaza and a huge 17th-century Mexican-made silver retable in the Capilla del Sagrario (to the right of the main altar). If you're interested in bullfighting, detour four blocks southwest from Plaza de España to El Puerto's 19th-century **Plaza de Toros** (*admission free; open 11am-1.30pm & 6pm-7.30pm Tues-Sun*). This is one of Andalucía's most important bullrings, with room for 15,000 spectators. It's closed on days before and after bullfights. See Spectator Sports later in this section for details of when bullfights are held.

A short walk northeast from Plaza de España is the **Casa de los Leones** (*House of the Lions; Calle La Placilla 2; admission free; open 10am-2pm & 6pm-8pm daily*), one of the finest of the many baroque mansions built in El Puerto's 18th-century heyday.

This house was recently restored as holiday apartments: most impressive is its facade but there are interesting information panels in the interior patio.

Sherry Bodegas

Phone a day or more ahead to visit either of the best-known sherry wineries, **Osborne** (☎ 956 86 91 00; Calle Los Moros) and **Terry** (☎ 956 85 77 00; Calle Toneleros s/n). These bodegas offer tours (€3) Monday to Friday; Terry includes a visit to its carriage museum.

You can visit three other sherry houses without booking: **Bodegas 501** (☎ 956 85 55 11; Calle Valdés 9; admission €3; open 9am-2pm Mon-Fri), **Grant** (☎ 956 87 04 06; Calle Los Bolos 1; admission €2.10; tours 12.30pm Sat) and **Gutiérrez Colosía** (☎ 956 85 28 52; Avenida de la Bajamar; admission €3; tours 1.30pm Sat).

Beaches

Pine-flanked **Playa de la Puntilla** is a half-hour walk southwest of the town centre, or you can get there by bus No 26 (€0.60) heading southwest on Avenida Aramburu de Mora. **Playa Fuentebravía**, further out west, is accessible by bus No 35 (€0.60) from the same stop. Between the two beaches is a swish marina development called, of course, **Puerto Sherry**.

Boat Trips
From about mid-July to early September **El Vapor** (☎ 956 85 59 06) does 1½-hour night cruises around the bay at 9.45pm on Tuesday, Thursday and Saturday for €4.

Organised Tours
Free guided tours of the town set off at 11am Saturday (and Tuesday in July and August) from the tourist office.

Special Events
El Puerto's Feria de la Primavera (Spring Fair), over a few days in late April or early May, is deeply influenced by sherry, with around 200,000 half-bottles being drunk. An unofficial motorbike fiesta takes over central El Puerto over the weekend of the Jerez motorcycle grand prix in May, when vast numbers of bikers gather here.

Places to Stay
Camping Las Dunas (☎ 956 87 22 10; camping per adult/tent/car €4/4/3.50) is a good, shady site just behind Playa de la Puntilla.

Hostal Santamaría (☎ 956 85 36 31; Calle Pedro Muñoz Seca 38; singles/doubles €12/24, with bathroom €13/26) is friendly, with good, clean, simple rooms. Its signs simply say 'CH' and 'Camas'.

Hostal Manolo (☎ 956 85 75 25; Calle Jesús de los Milagros 18; singles/doubles with bathroom €18/31), a block inland from Plaza de las Galeras Reales, has slightly better rooms than the Santamaría; many have little balconies. Prices go up a few euros in August.

Hostal Loreto (☎/fax 956 54 24 10; Calle Ganado 17; singles/doubles/triples €21/36/60, doubles/triples with bathroom €42/72) is set around a leafy courtyard; all 20 rooms have windows on the street or courtyard.

Casa No 6 (☎ 956 87 70 84; w www .casano6.com; Calle San Bartolomé 14; singles or doubles with bathroom €60, family rooms €90) is an early-19th-century house beautifully renovated by its English owners to provide charming, spacious and spotless rooms with high, wood-beamed ceilings, comfy beds and old-fashioned tiling, all around a lovely pillared patio open to the sky. Prices include breakfast and dip deeply outside the high season.

Hotel Los Cántaros (☎ 956 54 02 40; w www.hotelloscantaros.com; Calle Curva 6; singles/doubles first half May & mid-July–mid-Sept €76/98, other times up to €47.50/68) is a classy hotel with 39 comfortable, well equipped rooms and its own café.

Hotel Monasterio San Miguel (☎ 956 54 04 40; w www.jale.com/monasterio; Calle Virgen de los Milagros 27; singles/doubles from €133/166) is a stylish and luxurious hotel in a converted 18th-century monastery. Tropical garden, pool, valuable artworks and gourmet restaurant await your pleasure if your pockets are deep enough. Rates rise €33.70 for Semana Santa, the *feria* and the motorbike grand prix.

Places to Eat
El Puerto is an excellent place to sample seafood and has some terrific tapas bars.

Romerijo (Ribera del Marisco s/n; seafood from €2 per 250g) is a huge El Puerto institution, with crowds flocking to its two facing buildings. One building boils the seafood, the other fries it, and you buy portions in paper cones to take away or eat at the many tables. Everything's on display and you just take your pick and buy by the quarter-kilogram: €2.40 for fried *boquerones* (sprats) or €4.20 to €12.90 for various types of boiled prawns, for example.

For a fancier sit-down meal, it's hard to go wrong at **Los Portales** (Ribera del Río 13; mains €8.50-17) for fish and seafood, or the wider-ranging **Casa Flores** (Ribera del Río 9; mains €8-14). A local speciality well worth trying at either place is *urta roteña* (sea bream cooked in white wine, tomatoes, peppers and thyme).

Mesón del Asador (Calle Misericordia; mains €6-9) is popular for its moderately priced grilled meats.

Calle Misericordia also sports half a dozen varied tapas bars dishing up some of the tastiest morsels in the region.

EL PUERTO DE SANTA MARÍA

PLACES TO STAY
- 3 Hotel Monasterio San Miguel
- 9 Hostal Loreto
- 10 Hotel Los Cántaros
- 19 Casa No 6
- 22 Hostal Santamaría
- 24 Hostal Manolo

PLACES TO EAT
- 6 Mercado de la Concepción
- 11 Casa Luis
- 12 Casa Flores
- 13 Los Portales
- 14 Romerijo
- 15 Romerijo
- 16 Mesón del Asador
- 17 Bodeguita La Antigua
- 28 La Abuela María
- 34 La Dorada

OTHER
- 1 Bodegas Terry
- 2 Monasterio de la Victoria
- 4 Peña Flamenca El Nitri
- 5 Peña Flamenca El Chumi
- 7 Casa de los Leones
- 8 Iglesia Mayor Prioral
- 18 Tourist Office
- 20 Museo Municipal
- 21 Fundación Rafael Alberti
- 23 Keur Khadim
- 25 Fuente de las Galeras Reales
- 26 Muelle Vapor
- 27 Bus Stop to Playa Puntilla; Plata Fuentebravía
- 29 Castillo San Marcos
- 30 Post Office
- 31 Bodegas Grant
- 32 Bodegas Osborne
- 33 Bodegas 501
- 34 La Pescadería
- 36 Bodegas Gutiérrez Colosía

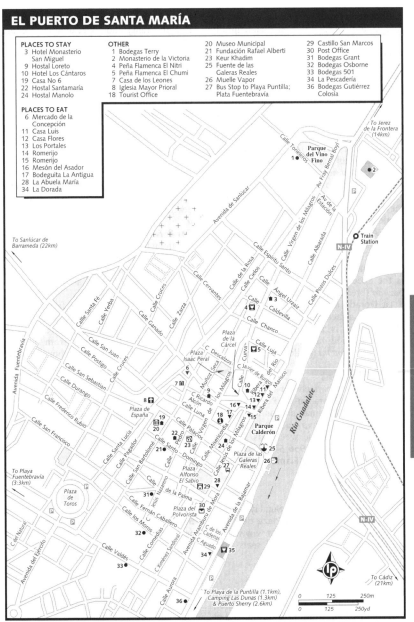

CÁDIZ PROVINCE

Bodeguita La Antigua *(Calle Misericordia 8; tapas around €2.40)* is one that helpfully provides tapas menus in English and German as well as Spanish. The *serranito*, a bread roll with ham, pork, fried green pepper and a few chips, makes many people happy.

Casa Luis *(Ribera del Marisco s/n; tapas €2.10, raciones €6; closed Mon)* is a tightly packed little den with just a few tables inside and out, and a bar you can only elbow towards. They come for Luis' innovative tapas, such as *paté de cabracho* (scorpionfish pate) or *hojaldres* (puff pastries) with cheese and anchovy filling.

Crowds also flock to the tapas bars along the streets south of Plaza de las Galeras Reales.

La Abuela María *(Avenida Aramburu de Mora s/n; tapas/media-raciones/raciones €1.80/3.60/6.60)* is neat and relatively spacious, with interesting sculptures. Seafood is the speciality: go for the *bacalao rebozado* (breadcrumbed salted cod).

La Dorada *(Avenida de la Bajamar 26; tapas/media-raciones around €1.50/4.50; closed Mon)* is a slightly rougher-and-readier seafood haunt: the speciality is *choco a la plancha* (grilled cuttlefish).

Entertainment

Youthful music bars cluster down Avenida Aramburu de Mora, in **La Pescadería** on Avenida de la Bajamar, and on the eastern side of town at Playa Valdelagrana. Flamenco happens some weekends at **Peña Flamenca El Nitri** *(☎ 956 54 32 37; Calle Diego Niño 1)* and **Peña Flamenca El Chumi** *(Calle Luja 15)*.

Spectator Sports

Top matadors fight every Sunday in July and August at El Puerto's **Plaza de Toros** *(Bullring; ☎ 902 15 78 70; ⓦ www.justo -ojeda.com; Plaza Elías Ahuja; seats from €10)*.

Getting There & Away

Bus Monday to Friday, buses to Cádiz *(€2.40, 40 minutes)* go about half-hourly, 6.45am to 10pm, from the bullring, and at least 12 times between 9.30am and 8.45pm from the train station. Weekend services are about half as frequent. For Jerez de la Frontera *(€1.20, 20 minutes)* there are eight to 12 buses daily from the train station and eight from the bullring Monday to Friday (but only two on other days). For Sanlúcar de Barrameda *(€1.35, 30 minutes)* and Chipiona *(30 minutes)*, five to 11 buses daily go from the bullring. For Seville *(€6.25, 1½ hours)*, four buses go daily from the train station.

Train Up to 33 trains daily travel to/from Jerez *(from €1.10, 12 minutes)* and Cádiz *(from €2, 30 minutes)*, and up to 15 to/from Seville *(from €6, 1½ hours)*.

Car & Motorcycle There's plenty of parking along the riverfront, especially south of Plaza de las Galeras Reales. Most of it is free, but the semisupervised area next to the plaza costs €1.20 for 24 hours.

Boat The small passenger ferry *Adriano III*, better known as *El Vapor* or **El Vaporcito** *(The Little Steamship; ☎ 956 85 59 06)* sails for El Puerto from Cádiz's Estación Marítima at 10am, noon, 2pm and 6.30pm daily (except non-holiday Mondays) from approximately February to November, with an extra trip at 4.30pm on Sunday and at 8.30pm daily in summer (approximately early July to mid-September). Trips back from El Puerto are at 9am, 11am, 1pm and 3.30pm, plus 5.30pm on Sunday and 7.30pm daily in summer. The crossing *(€2)* takes 45 minutes. The *Adriano III* and its predecessors *Adriano I* and *Adriano II* have provided this vital link between the two cities since 1929.

SANLÚCAR DE BARRAMEDA
postcode 11540 • pop 62,000

The northern tip of the sherry triangle and a flourishing summer resort, Sanlúcar is 23km northwest of El Puerto de Santa María. It has a likable atmosphere and a fine location on the Guadalquivir estuary looking across to the Parque Nacional de Doñana.

Sanlúcar to Sanlúcar via Tierra del Fuego

Columbus set sail from Sanlúcar on his third voyage to the Caribbean in 1498. So, on 20 September 1519, did another foreigner sailing under the Castilian flag – the Portuguese Ferdinand Magellan, who set off with five ships and a crew of 265 seeking, like Columbus, a westerly route to the spice islands of Indonesia.

Magellan made the first known voyage through the strait between Tierra del Fuego and the South American mainland (now the Magellan Strait), but was killed in a battle in the Philippines. By the time his Basque pilot Juan Sebastián Elcano completed the first circumnavigation of the globe by returning to Sanlúcar via the Cape of Good Hope in 1522, just 17 crew members and one ship, the *Victoria*, were left.

Orientation & Information

Sanlúcar stretches along the southeast side of the Guadalquivir estuary. Calzada del Ejército, running 600m inland from the seafront Paseo Marítimo, is the main avenue – often just called La Calzada. A block beyond its inland end is Plaza del Cabildo, the central square. A new bus station was due to open by the end of 2002 on Avenida de la Estación, 100m southwest of the middle of La Calzada.

The old fishing quarter, Bajo de Guía, site of Sanlúcar's best restaurants and Doñana boat departures, is 750m northeast along the riverfront from La Calzada.

The very helpful **tourist office** (☎ 956 36 61 10; Calzada del Ejército s/n; open 10am-2pm daily & 5pm-7pm Mon-Fri, 6pm-8pm Sat & Sun Nov-June; 10am-2pm & 6pm-8.30pm daily July-Oct) is towards the inland end of La Calzada.

The **Centro de Visitantes Fábrica de Hielo** (☎ 956 38 16 35; Bajo de Guía s/n; open 9am-7pm or 8pm daily) has interesting displays and information on the Parque Nacional de Doñana and related topics.

Haif@ (Calle Tartaneros), in a street off Plaza Cabildo, offers Internet access for €1/2 per 30/60 minutes. This is a genuine cybercafé with good coffee!

Walking Tour

From Plaza del Cabildo, cross Calle Ancha to Plaza San Roque and head up Calle Bretones to admire the elaborate Gothic facade of **Las Covachas**, a set of 15th-century wine cellars in an outer wall of the Palacio Medina Sidonia (see the next paragraph). Here, the street becomes Calle Cuesta de Belén and dog-legs up to the entrance to the **Palacio de Orleans y Borbon** (admission free; open 10am-1.30pm Mon-Fri). The creation of this beautiful neo-Mudejar palace as a summer home for the aristocratic Montpensier family in the 19th century was what started Sanlúcar's growth as a resort. Today it's Sanlúcar's town hall.

From the town hall entrance at the top of Calle Cuesta de Belén, a block to the left along Calle Caballero is the 15th-century **Iglesia de Nuestra Señora de la O** (Plaza de la Paz; open 7.30pm-8pm Sun-Fri), with a Mudejar facade and ceiling. Next door is the **Palacio de los Duques de Medina Sidonia** (☎ 956 36 01 61; Plaza Condes de Niebla 1; admission free; open 10.30am-1.30pm Sun, closed 1-21 July), a large and rambling stately home that dates all the way back to the time of the original 13th-century Duque de Medina Sidonia, Guzmán El Bueno (see the Tarifa section later in this chapter for more on him). This powerful aristocratic family once owned more of Spain than anyone else. The current incumbent, Luisa Isabel Álvarez de Toledo, has fought long and hard to keep the priceless Medina Sidonia archive in Sanlúcar. Some 200m further along the street is the 15th-century **Castillo de Santiago** (Plaza del Castillo; not open), amid buildings of Sanlúcar's biggest sherry company, Barbadillo. From the castle you can return directly downhill to the town centre.

Beach

Sanlúcar's good sandy beach runs all along the riverfront and for several kilometres beyond to the southwest.

Bodegas

Sanlúcar produces a distinctive sherry-like wine, manzanilla. Three bodegas give tours for which you don't need to book ahead: **La Cigarrera** (*Plaza Madre de Dios; tour €2; 10am-2pm Mon-Sat*); **Barbadillo** (*Calle Luis de Eguilaz 11, near the castle; tour €3; noon & 1pm Mon-Sat*); **Pedro Romero** (*Calle Trasbolsa 84; tour €1.80; 12.30pm Fri & Sat*).

Parque Nacional de Doñana

Viajes Doñana (☎ 956 36 25 40; *Calle San Juan 20*) operates 3½-hour guided tours (€30 per person) into the national park from Bajo de Guía at 8.30am and 2.30pm (8.30am and 4.30pm from May to mid-September) on Tuesdays and Fridays. After the river crossing, the trip is by 4WD vehicle holding about 20 people, visiting much the same spots as the tours from El Acebuche (see Parque Nacional de Doñana in the Huelva Province chapter). Book as far ahead as you can.

The boat *Real Fernando* makes one or two 3½-hour trips daily on the Guadalquivir from Bajo de Guía. Despite stops in the national park and the Parque Natural de Doñana, these trips are not designed for serious nature enthusiasts. Tickets are sold at the **Centro de Visitantes Fábrica de Hielo** (☎ 956 36 38 13, fax 956 36 21 96); the adult fare is €14.20. Book two or three days ahead, and a week or more ahead in summer and during holiday periods.

On any of these trips, take mosquito repellent, or wear clothes that cover your skin.

Special Events

The Sanlúcar summer gets going with a big spring fair, the Feria de la Manzanilla, in late May or early June, and blossoms in July and August with jazz, flamenco and classical music festivals, one-off concerts by top Spanish bands, and Sanlúcar's unique horse races (see the boxed text 'Horsing Around with the Tides').

CÁDIZ PROVINCE

Horsing Around with the Tides

Sanlúcar's *carreras de caballos* (horse races), held every year since 1845 (bar a couple of interruptions for war), may be the only sporting event in the world where police crowd control involves gently persuading spectators to take off their shoes and stand in the sea. It's an exciting spectacle in which thoroughbred racehorses thunder along Sanlúcar beach watched by large crowds.

Two meetings of three or four days are held every August, one in the first half or middle of the month, the other in the second half, usually with four races each day. Exact starting times depend on the tides, but the first race normally begins around 6pm. Most races start at Bajo de Guía and the finish is about 1km southwest of Calzada del Ejército. Prize money per race ranges from €4000 to €16,000.

Serious racegoers make for the area with spectator stands, bookmakers, paddock and winner's enclosure, up by the finishing post. The rest of the crowd strings itself back along the course. Here the only bookies, it seems, are children who set up little cardboard-box booths and scrape a line across the track in front, then take money on which horse will cross their 'finish' first!

For dates and much more detail about the races, check Ⓦ www.carrerassanlucar.com.

Places to Stay

Book well ahead for a room at holiday times. Budget accommodation is scarce.

Hostal La Blanca Paloma (☎ 956 36 36 44; ⓔ hostalblancapaloma@mcn.co; *Plaza San Roque 9; singles/doubles €15/27*) has eight adequate rooms.

Hostal La Bohemia (☎ 956 36 95 99; *Calle Don Claudio 1; singles €18, doubles with bathroom €37.50*), off Calle Ancha, 300m northeast of Plaza del Cabildo, is a bit better than the Blanca Paloma.

Hotel Los Helechos (☎ 956 36 13 49; Ⓦ www.hotelloshelechos.com; *Plaza Madre de Dios 9; singles/doubles with bathroom €43.50/58*), off Calle San Juan 200m from

Plaza del Cabildo, has air-con rooms, two pretty courtyards and a cosy bar. However, rooms on the courtyards can be noisy.

Hotel Posada de Palacio (☎ 956 36 48 40, e posadadepalacio@terra.es; Calle Caballeros 11; singles €51.50-90, doubles €64.50-103, quads €122; closed Dec-Feb), in the upper part of town, is Sanlúcar's most charming lodging: an 18th-century mansion with 16 good-sized rooms and at least three pretty patios. A pool is being added.

Hotel Tartaneros (☎ 956 38 53 78, fax 956 38 53 94; Calle Tartaneros 8; singles/doubles €77/96.50), at the inland end of Calzada del Ejército, is a century-old industrialist's mansion with solidly comfortable rooms. Prices come down 50% for most of January and February.

Hotel Guadalquivir (☎ 956 36 07 42; w www.hotelguadalquivir.com; Calzada del Ejército 10; singles/doubles €71/89) is a much bigger, modern place near Hotel Tartaneros. Prices nearly halve between mid-October and late March.

Places to Eat

The line of seafood restaurants facing the river at Bajo de Guía are a reason in themselves for visiting Sanlúcar. It's an idyllic experience to watch the sun go down over the Guadalquivir while tucking into the succulent fresh fare here and washing it down with a drop of manzanilla. Just wander along and pick a restaurant that suits your pocket. **Restaurante Virgen del Carmen** (fish mains €6-10) is one that's good but not excessively expensive. Decide whether you want your fish plancha (grilled) or frito (fried), and don't skip the starters: langostinos (king prawns) and the juicy coquines al ajillo (clams in garlic), both €6, are specialities. A half-bottle of manzanilla costs €4. Other popular places along here include **Restaurante Poma**, **Casa Bigote**, **Casa Juan** and **Bar Joselito Huerta**.

Lots of cafés and bars, many serving manzanilla from the barrel, surround Plaza del Cabildo.

Casa Balbino (Plaza del Cabildo 11, tapas/raciones €1.50/9) has wonderful seafood and other snacks – try the tortillas de camarones (crisp shrimp fritters) or solomillo a la cerveza (pork cooked in beer).

Bar El Cura (Calle Amargura 2; platos combinados €5), in an alley between Calle San Juan and Plaza San Roque, does economical platters.

Café Tartaneros (Calle Tartaneros 8) is inside Hotel Tartaneros (see Places to Stay). Sink into a comfortable chair and enjoy a pot of tea and chocolate cake (€4).

Entertainment

There are some lively music bars on and around Calzada del Ejército and Plaza del Cabildo. Lots of concerts are held here during the summer months.

Getting There & Away

Bus Up to 11 **Los Amarillos** (☎ 956 38 50 60) buses run daily to/from El Puerto de Santa María (€1.35) and Cádiz (€2.50) and up to nine to/from Seville (€5.50), plus buses to Chipiona, Arcos de la Frontera and El Bosque. Until the new bus station on Avenida de la Estación opens, Amarillos buses go from Plaza del Pradillo, 500m southwest of Plaza del Cabildo along Calle San Juan. **Linesur** runs at least seven buses daily to/from Jerez de la Frontera (€1.35): until the new bus station opens, the stop is at Bar La Jaula behind the tourist office.

Boat Though you can visit Sanlúcar on day-trip boats from Seville (see Organised Tours under Seville in the Sevilla Province chapter), you can't take a one-way ride upriver from Sanlúcar to Seville.

CHIPIONA

postcode 11550 • pop 17,000

Chipiona, 9km west of Sanlúcar, has long sandy beaches, about 30 hostales and hotels, and Spain's tallest lighthouse (69m). The **tourist office** (☎ 956 37 71 50; Calle Larga 74) is in the older part of town.

Hotel La Española (☎ 956 37 37 71; Calle Isaac Peral 4; singles/doubles high season €29.40/51.50), a few steps back from Chipiona's northern seafront, has good rooms and a reasonable restaurant.

The Solera Process

Once sherry grapes have been harvested, they are pressed and the resulting must is left to ferment. Within a few months a frothy veil of yeast called *flor* appears on the surface. The wine is then transferred to the *bodegas* in big barrels of American oak.

The wine enters the *solera* process when it is a year old. The barrels, about five-sixths full, are lined up in rows, called *escalas*, at least three barrels high. The barrels on the bottom layer, called the *solera* (from *suelo*, meaning floor), contain the oldest wine. From these, around three times a year, 10% of the wine is drawn off. This is replaced with the same amount from the barrels in the layer above, which is in turn replaced from the next layer. The wines are left to age for between three and seven years. A small amount of brandy is added to stabilise the wine before bottling, bringing the alcohol content to 16-18%, which stops fermentation. (This constitutes the 'fortification' of the wine.)

Sherry houses are often beautiful buildings in attractive gardens. A tour will take you through the cellars where the wine is stored and aged, inform you about the process and the history of the sherry producers, and allow you a tasting.

See Drinks in the Facts for the Visitor chapter for more on the subject of sherry.

JEREX DE LA FRONTERA

postcode 11480 • pop 185,000

• elevation 55m

The city of Jerez, spread over a low rise in the rolling countryside 36km northeast of Cádiz, is world-famous for its wine – sherry – made from grapes grown on the chalky soil surrounding the town. Many people come here to visit its bodegas, but Jerez (heh-**reth** or, in the Andalucian accent, just heh-**reh**) is also Andalucía's horse capital and, alongside its affluent uppercrust society, is home to a *gitano* (Roma) community that is one of the hotbeds of flamenco.

The British have for centuries had a taste for sherry, and British money was largely responsible for the development of wineries from the 1830s. Today, Jerez high society is a mixture of Andalucian and British, due to intermarriage among families of wine traders over the past 150 years. Since the 1980s most of the wineries, previously owned by about 15 families, have been bought out by multinational companies. Jerez reeks of money, with fancy shops, well-heeled residents, and old mansions and beautiful churches in its old quarter. It stages fantastic fiestas with sleek horses, beautiful people and flamenco.

History

The Muslims called the town 'Scheris', from which 'Jerez' and 'sherry' are both derived.

The drink was already famed in England in William Shakespeare's time. Jerez had its share of strife during the late 19th century, when anarchism gained ground in Andalucía. One day in 1891, thousands of peasants armed with scythes and sticks marched in and occupied the town for a few hours, succeeding only in bringing about further repression. The sherry industry has provided greater prosperity in more recent times. Jerez brandy, widely drunk in Spain, is also a profitable product.

Orientation & Information

The centre of Jerez is between the Alameda Cristina and Plaza del Arenal, which are connected by the north–south Calle Larga and its continuation, Calle Lancería (both pedestrianised). The old quarter is west of Calle Larga. Most budget accommodation clusters around Avenida de Arcos and Calle Medina, east of Calle Larga.

The **tourist office** (☎ 956 35 96 54; *Plaza del Arenal* • ☎ 956 33 11 50; *Alameda Cristina; both branches open 10am-2pm & 5pm-7pm Mon-Fri, 10am-3pm Sat & Sun 16 June-14 Sept; 9.30am-2.30pm & 4.30pm-6.30pm Mon-Fri, 9.30am-3.30pm Sat & Sun rest of year*) has energetic multilingual staff with mountains of information.

There are plenty of banks and ATMs on and around Calle Larga. The **post office**

CÁDIZ PROVINCE

(cnr Calle Cerrón & Calle Medina) is just east of Calle Larga.

Info Jerez *(Calle San Agustín; open 10am-10pm Mon-Sat, 3pm-10pm Sun)*, provides Internet access for €1.50 an hour (minimum €0.20). **Centernet** *(Avenida de Arcos)* charges €1.80 per hour but opens all day at weekends.

You'll find a lot of useful Jerez information on the city hall's website, W www.web jerez.com.

Old Quarter

The obvious place to start a tour of the old town, parts of whose walls survive, is the 11th- and 12th-century Muslim fortress southwest of Plaza del Arenal, the **Alcázar** *(☎ 956 31 97 98; Alameda Vieja; admission including/excluding camera obscura €3.25/1.50; open 10am-8pm Mon-Sat, 10am-3pm Sun mid-June–mid-Sept; 10am-6pm daily mid-Sept–Apr; 10am-8pm daily May–mid-June)*. Inside the Alcázar are the beautiful **mezquita** (mosque), converted to a chapel by Alfonso X in 1264; an impressive set of **Baños Árabes** (Arab Baths) and the 18th-century **Palacio Villavicencio**. A camera obscura in the palace's tower provides a picturesque live panorama of Jerez accompanied by an interesting 15-minute commentary in Spanish, English, French and German (see the Torre Tavira section under Cádiz for information about cameras obscura). Camera obscura sessions begin every half-hour until 30 minutes before closing time.

The orange-tree-lined promenade around the Alcázar has good vistas to the west. In the foreground stands a large **statue of Manuel María González Ángel** (1812–87), the founder of Bodegas González Byass. It was this man's uncle, José Ángel, who gave his name to González Byass' famous dry sherry Tio Pepe *(tío* meaning uncle and Pepe being a nickname for José). Behind Sr González is Jerez's mainly 18th-century **cathedral** *(admission free; open 11am-1pm daily, 6pm-8pm Mon-Sat)*, which has Gothic, baroque and neoclassical features, and was built on the site of the Muslim town's main mosque. Note the 15th-century Mudejar/Gothic belfry, set slightly apart.

A couple of blocks northeast of the cathedral is Plaza de la Asunción, with a handsome 16th-century **former town hall** and the lovely 15th-century Mudejar **Iglesia de San Dionisio**, named after the town's patron saint.

North and west of here is the **Barrio de Santiago**, a quarter with a sizable *gitano* population and one of the centres of flamenco. This district has churches dedicated to all four evangelists: the Gothic **Iglesia de San Mateo**, with Mudejar chapels, is on Plaza del Mercado, where you'll also find the excellent **Museo Arqueológico** *(☎ 956 33 33 16; admission €1.50; open 10am-2.30pm Tues-Sun 15 June-31 Aug; 10am-2pm & 4pm-7pm Tues-Fri, 10am-2.30pm Sat, Sun & holidays rest of year)*. The pride of the museum's collection is a 7th-century-BC Greek helmet found in the Río Guadalete.

Also in this area is the **Centro Andaluz de Flamenco** *(Andalucian Flamenco Centre; ☎ 956 34 92 65; W caf.cica.es; Plaza de San Juan 1; open 9am-2pm Mon-Fri)*. Jerez is at the heart of the Seville-Cádiz axis, where flamenco began and which remains its heartland today. The centre is a kind of museum and school dedicated to the preservation and promotion of the flamenco arts, with print and music libraries holding thousands of works. Several flamenco videos are screened each morning that it's open.

Just southeast of Plaza del Arenal is one of Jerez's loveliest churches, the 16th-century **Iglesia de San Miguel** *(Plaza San Miguel; admission €1.80; open 3.30pm-6.30pm Mon, 10am-1.30pm Tues-Sat)*, built in Isabelline Gothic style but with a later, baroque main facade, and featuring superb stone carving, beautiful stained glass windows and an elaborate retable by Juan Martínez Montañés.

Sherry Bodegas

For most bodegas, you need to phone ahead to book your visit. But a few offer tours where you can just turn up. It's advisable to confirm hours and arrangements in advance with the wineries or tourist offices, which have full details on bodega visits. Most of the wineries do tours in English, and often German, as well as Spanish.

Wineries where you can turn up without booking include: **González Byass** (☎ *956 35 70 00;* Ⓦ *www.gonzalezbyass.es; Calle Manuel María González 12; tours €7; in English 11.30am-2.30pm daily, 3.30pm-6.30pm Mon-Sat),* one of the biggest sherry houses and handily located just west of the Alcázar; and **Sandeman** (☎ *956 15 17 00;* Ⓦ *www.sandeman.com; Calle Pizarro 10; tours €4; in English 10.30am-2.30pm Mon-Fri, 11.30am & 1.30pm Sat mid-Mar-mid-Oct, 10.30am, 12.30pm & 1.30pm Mon-Wed & Fri rest of year),* whose sherries carry the black-caped 'Don' logo.

Other Things to See

One of Jerez's great attractions is the **Real Escuela Andaluza del Arte Ecuestre** *(Royal Andalucian School of Equestrian Art;* ☎ *956 31 80 08;* Ⓦ *www.realescuela.org; Avenida Duque de Abrantes),* in the north of town. The school trains horses and riders in dressage and you can watch them being put through their paces in **training sessions** *(admission €6; open 10am-1pm Mon, Wed & Fri).* At noon on Thursday year-round (except holidays) and noon on Tuesday from March to October (except holidays) there's an official **espectáculo** *(show; admission €12-18)* where the handsome white horses show off their tricks to classical music.

Close to the equestrian school, the **Palacio del Tiempo & El Misterio de Jerez** *(Palace of Time & The Mystery of Jerez; Centro Temático La Atalaya;* ☎ *956 18 21 00; Calle Cervantes 3),* due to open in late 2002, combines Jerez's clocks-and-watches museum, revamped with multiple special effects, with a new sherry museum incorporating actors and wraparound images on giant screens. Pre-opening publicity *sounded* fun.

A couple of kilometres west of the centre is the **Parque Zoológico** *(Zoo Jerez;* ☎ *956 18 23 97; Calle Taxdirt s/n; adult/child €4/2.50; open 10am-8pm Tues-Sun June & Sept; 10am-8pm daily July & Aug; 10am-6pm Tues-Sun rest of year)* with 1300 beasts, nice gardens and a recuperation centre for wild animals.

Organised Tours

The popular **Tour por Jerez** (☎ *615 35 45 09; €8)* takes you round the sights in an open-topped double-decker bus, with live commentary in several languages. Get off and on as many times as you please in 24 hours. Buses go about every half-hour in summer, every hour at other times. One convenient central stop is outside the tourist office on Plaza del Arenal.

Special Events

Jerez's **Feria del Caballo** (Horse Fair), one week in the first half of May, is one of Andalucía's biggest festivals, with music, dancing and bullfights, as well as all kinds of horse competitions. Colourful parades of horses pass through the Parque González Hontoria fairgrounds in the north of town, the aristocratic-looking male riders decked out in flat-topped hats, frilly white shirts, black trousers and leather chaps, their female *crupera* (sideways pillion) partners in long, frilly, spotted dresses. The Jerez motorcycle grand prix (see Spectator Sports, later) often coincides with the Feria del Caballo.

Earlier in the year, the **Festival de Jerez** is a two-week event dedicated to music and dance, particularly flamenco; this is a good opportunity to see big flamenco names in action. The **Teatro Villamarta** (see Entertainment, later) is the main venue.

The **Fiestas de Otoño** *(Autumn Festivals),* celebrating the grape harvest for three weeks or so in September, range from flamenco and horse events to the traditional treading of the first grapes on Plaza de la Asunción. They conclude with a massive parade of horses, riders and horse-drawn carriages.

Jerez also hosts one of Spain's major indie music festivals, **Espárrago Rock**. In recent years it has happened over a weekend in mid-July, out at the Circuito Permanente de Velocidad – see Spectator Sports, later.

Places to Stay

Room rates go sky-high during the Feria del Caballo and you need to book well ahead.

Albergue Juvenil Jerez (☎ *956 14 39 01; Avenida Carrero Blanco 30; under 26/other public holidays €13/17.50, €11/15.20*

JEREZ DE LA FRONTERA

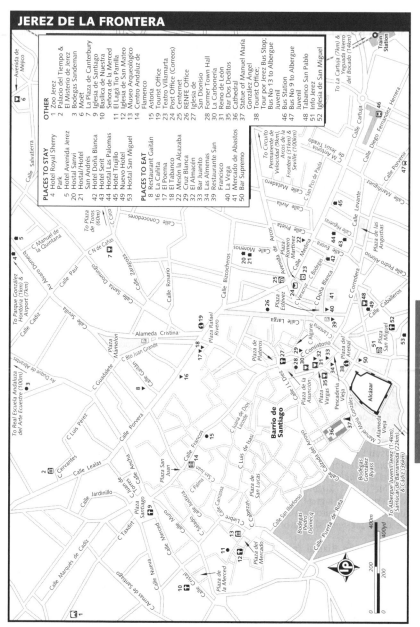

PLACES TO STAY
4 Hotel Royal Sherry Park
5 Hotel Avenida Jerez
20 Hostal Sanvi
21 Hostal/Hotel San Andrés
42 Hostal Doña Blanca
43 Hotel Serit
44 Hostal Las Palomas
45 Hotel Trujillo
49 Nuevo Hotel
53 Hostal San Miguel

PLACES TO EAT
8 Restaurant Gaitán
16 La Cañita
17 El Poema
18 El Tabanco
22 Mesón la Alcazaba
29 Cruz Blanca
32 El Almacén
33 Bar Juanito
34 Las Almenas
39 Restaurante San Francisco
40 La Vega
41 Mercado de Abastos
50 Bar Supremo

OTHER
1 Zoo Jerez
2 Palacio del Tiempo & El Misterio de Jerez
3 Bodegas Sandeman
6 Moët
7 La Plaza de Canterbury
9 Iglesia de Santiago
10 Basílica de Nuestra Señora de la Merced
11 El Lagá Tío Parrilla
12 Iglesia de San Mateo
14 Museo Arqueológico de Centro Andaluz de Flamenco
15 Astoria
19 Tourist Office
23 Teatro Villamarta
24 Post Office (Correos)
25 Centemet
26 RENFE Office
27 Iglesia de San Dionisio
28 Former Town Hall
30 La Carbonería
31 Reino de León
35 Bar Dos Deditos
36 Cathedral
37 Statue of Manuel María González Ángel
38 Tourist Office; Tour por Jerez Bus Stop; Bus No 13 to Albergue Juvenil
46 Bus Station
47 Bus No 9 to Albergue Juvenil
48 Tabanco San Pablo
51 Info Jerez
52 Iglesia de San Miguel

CÁDIZ PROVINCE

June-Sept , €8.50/11.50 Oct-May), a modern youth hostel 1.5km south of the centre, has 120 places in singles, doubles and triples, with shared bathrooms, and a good pool. Bus No 13 from Plaza del Arenal, or bus No 9 from Calle Porvenir, one block south of the bus station, will take you there. Get off at the Campo Juventud stop. Jerez buses (€0.70) are painted an eye-catching fluorescent lilac.

Hostal Sanvi (☎ 956 34 56 24; Calle Morenos 10; singles/doubles €21/30) is simple, friendly and very clean. Rooms sport blue tiles, salmon-pink walls and air-con. There's a large garage (€5 per day).

Hostal/Hotel San Andrés (☎ 956 34 09 83, fax 956 34 31 96; Calle Morenos 12; singles/doubles €20/24, with bathroom €24/38), next door to Hostal Sanvi with three plant-filled patios, is another reasonable choice. It's clean, with winter heating.

Hostal Las Palomas (☎ 956 34 37 73; Calle Higueras 17; singles/doubles €20/30) provides spacious, nicely furnished rooms, some with private bathroom at no extra cost.

Nuevo Hotel (☎ 956 33 16 00; W www .nuevohotel.com; Calle Caballeros 23; singles/doubles €19.50/32), located in a modernised mansion, provides spacious rooms with bathroom, TV and winter heating. Rates rise a few euros during August and the major festivals.

Hotel Trujillo (☎/fax 956 34 24 38; Calle Medina 36; singles/doubles €23.50/35.50), in a 19th-century house, has 26 modern-ish rooms with bathroom and, in most cases, air-con.

Hostal San Miguel (☎/fax 956 34 85 62; e sanmiguelhostal@terra.es; Plaza San Miguel 4; singles/doubles €25/40) has an amiable owner, 20 pleasant rooms and a roof terrace with a great view of the beautiful San Miguel church tower in front. Prices are the same with shared or private bathroom.

Hotel Doña Blanca (☎ 956 34 87 61; W www.hoteldonablanca.com; Calle Bodegas 11; singles/doubles €59/71), on a quiet side street, is an excellent 30-room hotel with parquet floors and soothing light-blue paintwork. There's parking in the same building and buffet breakfast is €5.70.

Hotel Serit (☎ 956 34 07 00; Calle Higueras 7; W www.hotelserit.com; singles/ doubles €49/70.50) provides 35 straightforwardly comfortable rooms with air-con and satellite TV. A few ground-floor rooms are adapted for wheelchair users. Breakfast is €6 and parking €7 per day.

Jerez's top hotels tend to be found in the north of town along Avenida Álvaro Domecq and the parallel Avenida Duque de Abrantes.

Hotel Avenida Jerez (☎ 956 34 74 11; W www.nh-hoteles.com; Avenida Álvaro Domecq 10; singles/doubles mid-week €92/102.50, weekends €71.50/86.50) is a solidly comfortable 90-room option.

Hotel Royal Sherry Park (☎ 956 31 76 14; W www.sherryparkhotel.com; Avenida Álvaro Domecq 11; singles/doubles €106/132.50) boasts 170 air-con and soundproofed rooms, excellent indoor and outdoor pools, verdant park-like grounds and a restaurant, café and banquet hall.

Places to Eat

Jerez food combines a Muslim heritage and maritime influences with English and French touches. Not surprisingly, sherry flavours many local dishes, such as *riñones al jerez* (kidneys in gravy), and *rabo de toro* (oxtail or bull's tail stew). **Bar Supremo** (Plaza del Arenal 16; meat & seafood mains €5-8) has tables outside on this central plaza and is a convenient place for a straightforward feed.

The restaurants on Pescadería Vieja, a little alley off Plaza del Arenal, are moderate to expensive but the alley catches a refreshing breeze on a hot day.

Las Almenas (Pescadería Vieja; tapas from €1.80, fish/revueltos raciones €8/10.80) serves up good food but service can be *very* unenthusiastic.

Restaurante San Francisco (Plaza Estévez 2; menú €7.20) does a reliable three-course lunch with wine and bread.

La Vega (Plaza Estévez s/n; raciones €7.50) is a bustling café with good service. It's a fine spot for breakfast: you can buy *churros* (€1.50 per 250g) at a kiosk by the adjacent market and bring them here to eat with a coffee or hot chocolate.

Méson la Alcazaba *(Calle Medina 19; menú €5-7)*, with a covered patio, has cheap, filling food; the *menús* offer plenty of choice and include two courses, a drink and fruit.

Restaurant Gaitán *(Calle Gaitán 3; menú turístico €17)*, with fancy decor of antlers and past clients' photos, is a place to try for a splash-out meal. A la carte, you might pay €7 for a starter of anchovies stuffed with spinach and ham, and €13 to €17 for main courses such as lamb in honey-and-brandy sauce.

Tapas Two fine spots to sample tapas (€1.50 to €2.50) with a sherry are **Bar Juanito** *(Pescadería Vieja 8-10)* and **El Almacén** *(Calle Ferros 8)* round the corner. Get a table in El Almacén's bodega-like back room, put together a *tabla* (board) of patés and cheeses, and soak up the atmosphere.

Cruz Blanca *(Calle Consistorio 16; seafood tapas €1.25-2)*, a short walk away, has tables under the tall jacarandas on Plaza de la Yerba. The sushi-style *bacalao* (salted cod) and *chocos a la plancha* (grilled cuttlefish) are sensational!

Further brilliant tapas bars surround quiet little Plaza Rafael Rivero, about 500m north, with tables out under the sky. Don't miss a *montadito* (€1.35 to €1.80) at **El Poema**. Then move a couple of tables away for a bite of ham at **El Tabanco**.

La Cañita *(Calle Porvera 11; montaditos €1.35)* is the best of another string of tapas spots just a short walk from Plaza Rafael Rivero – if you've still got room! The *montaditos* (again) are small but delicious: try brie and anchovies.

Entertainment

Check at the tourist office, visit ⓦ www .webjerez.com and watch for posters advertising upcoming events. *Diario de Jerez* and *Jerez Información* newspapers have some what's-on information and the **Teatro Villamarta** *(☎ 956 32 95 07; Plaza Romero Martínez)* puts out a monthly programme. Varied live music happens at **Astoria** *(Calle Francos)*, an outdoor concert area; there are sometimes concerts in the bullring too.

A small cluster of bars in the narrow streets north of Plaza del Arenal can get lively with a twenties-ish crowd late in the evening: try **Bar Dos Deditos** *(Plaza Vargas 1)*, **Reino de León** *(Calle Ferros)* and **La Carbonería** *(Calle Letrados 7)*. You might run across some live music at one of these places. On the other side of Plaza del Arenal, the neighbourhood bars along pedestrianised Calle San Pablo can keep going till 2am or so: **Tabanco San Pablo** *(Calle San Pablo 12; closed Sun)* is a lively, tavern-like spot with big sherry barrels.

Northeast of the centre, **La Plaza de Canterbury**, with lots of bars around a central courtyard, attracts a young crowd. For music bars and a spot of dancing, head a little further northeast to Avenida de Méjico and places such as **Moët**. The crowd is young, and hundreds more teenagers prefer to just hang out and drink on the street after midnight here and on nearby Calle Salvatierra (and on Plaza del Arenal).

There are several active *peñas flamencas* (flamenco clubs) in the Barrio de Santiago and elsewhere. They generally welcome genuinely interested visitors: ask at the tourist office about upcoming events. The **Viernes Flamencos** season sees open-air flamenco performances on August Friday nights at the Astoria: the season culminates in the **Fiesta de la Bulería**, a festival of flamenco song and dance in the Plaza de Toros, one Saturday in September. **El Lagá Tio Parrilla** *(☎ 956 33 83 34; Plaza del Mercado)* has flamenco performances at 10.30pm and 12.30am Monday to Saturday: it's more tourist-oriented but it can still be pretty gutsy.

Spectator Sports

Jerez's **Circuito Permanente de Velocidad** *(☎ 956 15 11 00; ⓦ www.circuitodejerez .com; Carretera de Arcos Km 10)*, on the A-382 10km east of town, hosts several motorcycle and car race events through the year including – in April or May – one of the Grand Prix races of the World Motorcycle Championship. This is one of Spain's biggest sporting events, with around 150,000 spectators, and Jerez and other nearby towns are swamped by fans and their bikes. Occasionally one of the motor-racing events is a Formula 1 Grand Prix.

CÁDIZ PROVINCE

Getting There & Away

Air Jerez airport (☎ 956 15 00 83), the only one serving Cádiz province, is 7km northeast of town on the N-IV. **Iberia** has several direct flights daily to/from Madrid and one daily to/from Barcelona. The budget airline **Buzz** flies to/from London Stansted on Saturdays.

Bus The **bus station** (☎ 956 34 52 07; Calle Diego Fernández Herrera) is 1km southeast of the centre. **Comes** (☎ 956 34 21 74) has buses for Cádiz (€2.50, 40 minutes, up to 20 daily), El Puerto de Santa María (€1.25, 20 minutes, up to 12 daily), Barbate (€6, 1½ hours, one daily except Sunday; via Vejer de la Frontera Monday to Friday, via Los Caños de Meca Saturday), Ronda (€8.20, three hours, four daily) via Arcos de la Frontera (€1.90, 45 minutes) with one continuing to Málaga (€16.50, five hours), and Algeciras via Tarifa. **Los Amarillos** (☎ 956 32 93 47) has more frequent buses to Arcos and also runs twice or more daily to El Bosque (€5, 1½ hours) and Ubrique (€7, two hours). There are plenty of buses to Seville (€5.50, 1¼ hours) by **Linesur** (☎ 956 34 10 63) and a few by Comes. Linesur also runs to Sanlúcar de Barrameda (€1.35, 30 minutes) at least seven times daily, and to Algeciras (three hours).

Train The **train station** (☎ 956 34 23 19; Plaza de la Estación) is a block southeast of the bus station. A taxi from the town centre costs about €3. Jerez is on the Cádiz–El Puerto de Santa María–Seville line, with plenty of trains in both directions. You can buy train tickets at the **Renfe office** (☎ 956 33 48 13; Calle Larga 34).

Car & Motorcycle There is meter parking on many streets, indicated by blue lines on the road. You only have to pay for parking from 9am to 1.30pm and 5pm to 8pm Monday to Friday, and 9am to 2pm Saturday, but there is a two-hour maximum (€1.30) during these periods. The underground **Parking Plaza Estévez** costs €1 an hour or €11 for 24 hours.

AROUND JEREZ
La Cartuja & Yeguada del Hierro del Bocado

La Cartuja monastery (☎ 956 15 64 65; gardens open 9.30am-11.15am & 12.45pm-6.30pm Mon-Sat), founded in the 15th century, is an architectural gem amid lovely gardens beside the A-381 towards Medina Sidonia, 9km from central Jerez. The early monks here are credited with breeding the much-prized Spanish thoroughbred horse, also called the Cartujano or Andaluz, particularly admired for its grace and gentle temperament. Around 1950, the former monastery was returned to the Carthusian monks, a closed religious order. At the time of research its buildings were closed for restoration, with no reopening date in sight, but you can look round the gardens and admire the church's impressive baroque facade.

The Yeguada del Hierro del Bocado (☎ 956 16 28 09; ⓦ www.yeguadacartuja.com; Finca Fuente del Suero; adult/child €9/5), a stud farm dedicated to improving the Cartujano stock, is open for two-hour tours at 11am on Saturdays. It's best to book ahead. To get there, turn off the A-381 at the 'La Yeguada' sign 5km after La Cartuja, and follow the side-road for 1.6km to the entrance.

Arcos & the Sierra

The mountainous Parque Natural Sierra de Grazalema in the northeast of Cádiz province is one of Andalucía's most beautiful and greenest areas. Between the park and Jerez de la Frontera is the spectacular old town of Arcos de la Frontera.

ARCOS DE LA FRONTERA
postcode 11630 • pop 28,000
• elevation 185m

Arcos is 30km east of Jerez along the A-382, across pretty wheat and sunflower fields, vineyards and fruit orchards. The old town could not be more dramatically sited: it stands on a high ridge with sheer precipices dropping away on both sides. Arcos is said to have a dark, sinister side; there are tales of madness, interbreeding, covens and witchcraft. Whatever the truth, it is well worth visiting to explore its old town, whose street plan has changed little since medieval times. There are a number of lovely post-Reconquista buildings, including Renaissance palaces and two beautiful churches.

History

Arcos has always been prized for its strategic location. In Muslim times it was, for a while during the 11th century, an independent kingdom, until being absorbed by Seville. In 1255 Alfonso X took the town and repopulated it with Castilians and Leonese. Some Muslims stayed, but rebelled in 1261 and were evicted by 1264. In 1440 the town passed to the Ponce de León family, Duques de Arcos, who were active in the conquest of Granada. When the last Duque de Arcos died heirless in 1780, his cousin, the Duquesa de Benavente, took over his land. She was partly responsible for replacing sheep farming with cereals, olives, vines and horse breeding as the dominant economic activities around Arcos.

Orientation & Information

From the bus station on Calle Corregidores in the new town (see the inset on the Arcos map), it's a kilometre walk uphill to the old town, via the leafy Paseo de Andalucía. From Plaza España at the top of Paseo de Andalucía, Paseo de los Boliches and Calle Debajo del Corral (becoming Calle Corredera) both head east up to the old town's main square, Plaza del Cabildo.

The **tourist office** (☎ 956 70 22 64; Plaza del Cabildo; open 10am-2pm Mon-Sat year-round & 4pm-8pm Mon-Sat 15 Mar-15 Oct, 3.30pm-7.30pm Mon-Sat 16 Oct-14 Mar) is on the old town's main square. There's also a **tourist information kiosk** (Paseo de Andalucía; open 10.30am-1.30pm Mon-Sat year-round & 5.30pm-7pm Mon-Fri 15 Mar-15 Oct, 5pm-6.30pm Mon-Fri 16 Oct-14 Mar) in the new town.

Banks and ATMs, on Calle Debajo del Corral and Calle Corredera, and the **post office** (Paseo de los Boliches 24) are down to the west of the old town.

Things to See

The thing to do in Arcos is simply to wander around the old town with its narrow cobbled lanes, Renaissance mansions, whitewashed houses and spectacular vistas. **Plaza del Cabildo** is surrounded by fine old buildings and has a vertiginous **mirador** with panoramic views over the river and countryside. On the west side of the square, Arcos' crowning glory, the **Castillo de los Duques**, dating from the 11th century, is privately owned and not open to the public. On the northern side, the **Basílica-Parroquia de Santa María** (admission €1; open 10am-1pm & 4pm-7pm Mon-Fri, 10am-2pm Sat) was begun on the site of a mosque in the 13th century but not completed until the 18th century. Its western facade is in Gothic style but the tower, built later, is baroque. On the eastern side of the square, the **parador** hotel is a 1960s reconstruction of a 16th-century magistrate's house, the Casa del Corregidor.

Explore the streets east of here, passing lovely buildings such as the 16th-century **Convento de la Encarnación** (Calle Marqués de Torresoto), which has a Gothic facade. The **Iglesia de San Pedro** (Calle Núñez de Prado; admission €1; open 10am-1pm & 4pm-7pm Mon-Sat, 10am-1.30pm Sun) is in 15th-century Gothic style but with an impressive baroque facade and bell tower. Inside is a large collection of religious paintings. Nearby, the 17th-century **Palacio Mayorazgo** (admission free; open 10am-2pm & 5pm-8pm Mon-Sat, 11am-2pm Sun), with a Renaissance facade and pretty patios, is now a senior citizens' centre.

Organised Tours

Guided tours of the old town's monuments start from the tourist office at 10.30am Monday to Saturday and 5pm Monday to Friday. Tours of Arcos' pretty patios start from the tourist office at noon Monday to Saturday and 6.30pm Monday to Friday. Both types of tour cost €3 and last about one hour.

Special Events

Easter processions through the town's narrow streets are dramatic, and on Easter Sunday there's a hair-raising running of the bulls. The

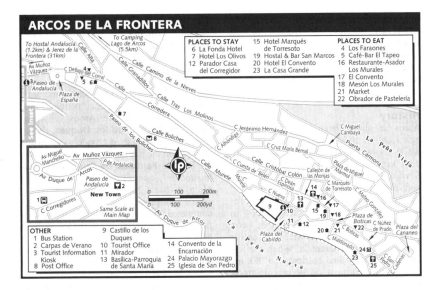

ARCOS DE LA FRONTERA

PLACES TO STAY
6 La Fonda Hotel
7 Hotel Los Olivos
12 Parador Casa del Corregidor
15 Hotel Marqués de Torresoto
19 Hostal & Bar San Marcos
20 Hotel El Convento
23 La Casa Grande

PLACES TO EAT
4 Los Faraones
5 Café-Bar El Tapeo
16 Restaurante-Asador Los Murales
17 El Convento
18 Mesón Los Murales
21 Market
22 Obrador de Pastelería

OTHER
1 Bus Station
2 Carpas de Verano
3 Tourist Information Kiosk
8 Post Office
9 Castillo de los Duques
10 Tourist Office
11 Mirador
13 Basílica-Parroquia de Santa María
14 Convento de la Encarnación
24 Palacio Mayorazgo
25 Iglesia de San Pedro

three-day Fiesta de la Virgen de las Nieves in early August includes a top-class flamenco night in Plaza del Cabildo, usually on the 5th. Arcos celebrates its patron saint San Miguel with a four-day *feria* at the end of September.

Places to Stay

Camping Lago de Arcos (☎ 956 70 83 33; *Santiscal s/n; camping per adult/tent/car €3/3/2.50; open year-round*) is a first-rate camping ground, with a good swimming pool, in El Santiscal near the Lago de Arcos reservoir northeast of town. The easiest route from the old town is by the A-382 and the Carretera El Bosque y Ubrique (A-372). Turn left after the bridge across the dam. A local bus runs out here from Arcos.

There's little budget accommodation up in the old town.

Hostal San Marcos (☎ 956 70 07 21; *Calle Marqués de Torresoto 6; singles/doubles/triples €20/30/45*), a short walk east of Plaza del Cabildo, has four pretty little rooms with bathroom and either fan or air-con. There's a roof terrace and an economical café downstairs (see Places to Eat).

Hostal Andalucía (☎ 956 70 48 96; *Polígono El Retiro; singles/doubles €16/30*), on

the A-382, 750m southwest of the bus station, offers one of the best deals, even though it's above a car showroom and backed by workshops. The rooms are large, with bathroom, fan and TV.

Arcos has some charming mid-range and top end places to stay.

La Fonda Hotel (☎ 956 70 00 57; *Calle Corredera 83; singles/doubles €32/51*), a renovated 19th-century inn, has good-sized rooms with bathroom, heating, air-con and TV. The street is noisy, though.

Hotel El Convento (☎ 956 70 23 33, fax 956 70 41 28; *Calle Maldonado 2; singles/ doubles €48/60, doubles with terrace €72*), in a beautiful 17th-century convent just east of Plaza del Cabildo, has 11 tasteful and varied rooms: try for one with a view.

Hotel Marqués de Torresoto (☎ 956 70 07 17, fax 956 70 42 05; *Calle Marqués de Torresoto 4; singles/doubles/triples €45.60/ 61.40/75.20*) is a converted old-town mansion with 15 large, very comfy rooms. Check out the fascinating little 17th-century retable in the courtyard restaurant.

Hotel Los Olivos (☎ 956 70 08 11, fax 956 70 20 18; *Paseo de los Boliches 30; singles/ doubles/triples €41/67/79*) is a friendly, attractive, 19-room hotel situated down the hill towards Paseo de Andalucía.

La Casa Grande (☎/fax 956 70 39 30; W www.lacasagrande.net; Calle Maldonado 10; doubles €70.50-90) occupies a gorgeous 18th-century cliffside mansion that once belonged to flamenco dancer Antonio Ruiz Soler. It has just four very individual rooms and suites.

Parador Casa del Corregidor (☎ 956 70 05 00; e arcos@parador.es; Plaza del Cabildo; singles/doubles €92/115) provides typical parador luxury, with magnificent views.

Places to Eat

Bar San Marcos (Calle Marqués de Torresoto 6; tapas & montaditos €1.20-2, platos combinados €4-5, menú €6) is a friendly and reliable little place up in the old town.

Mesón Los Murales (Calle Boticas 1; mains €4.80-8.40, menú €6), another inexpensive old-town option, has tables outside on Plaza Boticas.

Restaurante-Asador Los Murales (☎ 956 71 79 53; Calle Marqués de Torresoto; menú €15) is a classier spot specialising in meat and fish grilled a la brasa (€8 to €11).

El Convento (☎ 956 70 32 33; Calle Marqués de Torresoto 7; mains €8-15), in the pillared patio of a 17th-century palace, is a fancy restaurant turning out old-country dishes including venison steak and wild asparagus with ibérico ham.

The **market** (mercado) is opposite Mesón Los Murales. A little further east is the good bakery **Obrador de Pastelería** (Calle Boticas). **Los Faraones** (Calle Debajo del Corral 8; vegetarian/nonvegetarian menú €9/10), the 'only Egyptian restaurant in Andalucía', down towards the new town, serves up reliable if not exactly gourmet fare with a Middle Eastern touch. The set menus are available for lunch and dinner.

Café-Bar El Tapeo (Calle Debajo del Corral) is good for an inexpensive (€1.50) breakfast of café con leche and mollete (soft bread roll) with butter and jam.

Entertainment

Arcos' **Jueves Flamencos** are a series of weekly flamenco nights on Thursdays throughout July and August, at the small but atmospheric Plaza del Cananeo in the old town. From mid-June to late August, free concerts of pop, salsa, rock etc happen on Friday nights at the **Carpas de Verano**, an open-air entertainment area on Avenida Duque de Arcos.

Getting There & Away

Daily buses from the **bus station** (☎ 956 70 49 77) by Los Amarillos and/or Comes from Monday to Friday include 26 to Jerez (€1.90, one hour), nine to Cádiz (€4.30, 1¼ hours), six to El Puerto de Santa María (€3, 1¼ hours), five to El Bosque (€2.35, 45 minutes), four to Ronda (€6.30, two hours) and two each to Seville and Málaga. At weekends most services are far less frequent.

You can park on Plaza del Cabildo in the old town and around Paseo de Andalucía in the new town.

PARQUE NATURAL SIERRA DE GRAZALEMA

The Cordillera Bética, the band of rugged mountain ranges that stretches across much of Andalucía, has beautiful beginnings in the Sierra de Grazalema – actually a group name for several small ranges – in northeast Cádiz province. The landscape, dotted with white villages, ranges from pastoral river valleys to precipitous gorges and rocky summits. It's one of the greenest parts of Andalucía: Grazalema town has the highest measured rainfall in all Spain at an average 2153mm a year. Snow is common on the mountains in late January or February.

This is excellent walking country (the best months are May, June, September and October) and there are opportunities for other activities, from rock climbing and caving to paragliding and trout fishing.

A fairly good map of the 517 sq km Parque Natural Sierra de Grazalema, which with luck you'll find in shops and tourist offices locally, is the IGN/Junta de Andalucía Sierra de Grazalema (1:50,000). The park extends into northwestern Málaga province, where it includes the Cueva de la Pileta near Ronda.

CÁDIZ PROVINCE

Flora & Fauna

Much of the area is covered in beautiful Mediterranean woodland of evergreen oaks, wild olive *(acebuche)* and carob *(algarrobo)*. In autumn, broom adds splashes of yellow. The northern flank of the Sierra del Pinar between Grazalema and Benamahoma supports a 3 sq km *pinsapar* (woodland of Spanish firs), the best preserved of all stands of this rare tree (*pinsapo* in Spanish). Over 500 ibex live in the park: you may see some if you climb El Torreón. You *will* see a lot of domesticated animals grazing in semi-liberty, among them plenty of Iberian pigs. Around 100 pairs of griffon vultures live in the Garganta Verde and Garganta Seca gorges, 2km apart.

Getting There & Away

Bus schedules are subject to change. To confirm schedules of **Los Amarillos**, you can ring their offices in Cádiz or Jerez (see those city sections) or Ubrique (☎ 956 46 80 11), Málaga (☎ 95 235 00 61), Ronda (☎ 95 218 70 61) or Seville (☎ 95 441 71 11).

Los Amarillos runs up to six buses a day to El Bosque and Ubrique from Jerez and Arcos de la Frontera, and two each from Cádiz and Seville (Prado de San Sebastián bus station). Fares to El Bosque are €5.80 from Cádiz, €5 from Jerez, €2.35 from Arcos and €6 from Seville. From El Bosque, except on Sunday, there's a 3pm Los Amarillos bus to Grazalema (€1.75). The Grazalema–El Bosque bus departs at 5.30am Monday to Saturday.

Los Amarillos also runs from Málaga to Ubrique via Ronda, Grazalema and Benaocaz. At the time of writing, buses leave Málaga at 10.30am daily, 4pm Monday to Friday, and 3pm Saturday, Sunday and holidays. They leave Ronda two to 2½ hours later. The return buses leave Ubrique at 7.30am and 3pm Monday to Friday, 8.30am and 3.30pm Saturday, Sunday and holidays, stopping in Benaocaz after about five minutes and Grazalema after half an hour. Fares to Grazalema are €1.95 from Ronda and €8.75 from Málaga.

Comes (☎ 95 287 19 92) operates two buses each way Monday to Friday between Ronda and Zahara de la Sierra (€3), via Algodonales. Departures from Ronda are at 7am and 1pm, and from Zahara at 8.15am and 2pm. To travel between Zahara and Seville, Arcos, Jerez or Cádiz, you need to change buses at Algodonales. There's no bus service between Zahara and Grazalema.

El Bosque
postcode 11670 ● pop 1900
● elevation 385m

El Bosque, 33km east of Arcos across rolling countryside, is prettily situated below the wooded Sierra de Albarracín to the southeast. There's a take-off point for hang-gliders and paragliders in the Sierra de Albarracín, and trout to be fished in local streams. A pleasant 5km path up the Río El Bosque to Benamahoma starts beside El Bosque's youth hostel.

The natural park's main information office, the **Punto de Información El Bosque** (☎ 956 72 70 29; *Avenida de la Diputación s/n; open 10am-2pm daily year-round & 6pm-8pm Fri, Sat & holidays Apr-Sept, 4pm-6pm Fri, Sat & holidays Oct-Mar*) is down a lane off the A-372 at the western end of the village, opposite Hotel Las Truchas.

Camping La Torrecilla (☎/fax 956 71 60 95; *camping per adult/tent/car €2.85/2.10/1.80; open 1 Feb-15 Dec*) is 1km south of the village centre on the old road to Ubrique.

Albergue Campamento Juvenil El Bosque (☎ 956 71 62 12; *Molino de Enmedio s/n; camping per person €6, under 26/other during holiday periods €12.90/17.25, June-Sept €10.90/15.20, rest of year €8.50/11.50*), the youth hostel, is pleasantly sited 800m up a side-road from Hotel Las Truchas. It has a swimming pool and shady camping area as well as double and triple rooms, most with bathroom. At the time of writing it was under renovation: check in advance that it's open.

Hostal Enrique Calvillo (☎ 956 71 61 05; *Avenida Diputación 5; singles/doubles with bathroom €18/30*), near the park information office, provides decent, plain rooms with bathroom and air-con.

Hotel Las Truchas (☎ 956 71 60 61; *Avenida Diputación 1; singles/doubles €31/50.50*) has comfy rooms, many with

Visiting the Grazalema Reserve Area

Much of the Grazalema natural park's most spectacular scenery, and its three major highlight walks, are within a 30 sq km *área de reserva* (reserve area) between Grazalema, Benamahoma and Zahara de la Sierra.

Rules for entering the reserve area change from time to time, so it's well worth seeking advance information from one of the park information offices or local tourist offices, such as in El Bosque, Grazalema and Zahara de la Sierra. Non-Spanish language skills are highest in the Grazalema office.

For any of the walks in the reserve area you need a permit (free) from the El Bosque park office. You can call or visit El Bosque up to 15 days in advance for this, and it's advisable to do so, as the number of people allowed on each route per day is limited; you can arrange to collect permits at the Zahara visitor centre or Grazalema tourist office instead of El Bosque.

In July, August and September, when fire risk is high, some routes are closed wholly or partly, or you may be required to go with a guide from an authorised local company. Such companies – which offer guided walks year-round – include Horizon, Ocio Natural and Pinzapo (see the Grazalema section) and Al-qutun (see Zahara de la Sierra). Horizon charges €11/17 per person for a half/whole day.

Ascent of El Torreón

The usual route up El Torreón (1654m), the highest peak in Cádiz province, starts 100m east of the Km 40 marker on the Grazalema–Benamahoma road, about 8km from Grazalema. From this point (about 850m high), it takes about 2½ hours of walking to reach the summit and 1½ hours to get back down. From the summit on a very clear day you can see Gibraltar, the Sierra Nevada and the Rif Mountains of Morocco.

Grazalema–Benamahoma via the Pinsapar

This 14km walk takes around six hours. Going from east to west, after a couple of steepish ascents in the first third of the walk, it's downhill most of the way.

You walk about 40 minutes up from Grazalema to a point on the Zahara road where a footpath heads off across the northern slopes of the Sierra del Pinar. After an initial ascent of some 300m, the path sticks close to the 1300m contour, passing below Pico San Cristóbal, whose pointed summit has long provided the first glimpse of home for Spanish sailors crossing the Atlantic.

The thickest part of the *pinsapar* (woodland of rare Spanish firs) comes in the middle third of the walk, below the range's precipitous upper slopes. The dark green Spanish fir survives in significant numbers only in isolated pockets in southwest Andalucía and northern Morocco. Growing up to 30m high, it's a relic of the extensive Mediterranean fir forests of the Tertiary Period, which ended about 2.5 million years ago.

Garganta Verde

The path into the 'Green Gorge' – a lushly vegetated ravine, more than 100m deep – starts 3.5km from Zahara de la Sierra on the Grazalema road. It passes a viewpoint overlooking a large colony of enormous griffon vultures before the 300m descent to the bottom of the gorge. Then you come back up! It's a beautiful walk. Allow three to four hours if you drive to the start, five or six if you walk from Zahara.

An adventurous alternative to coming back up is to carry on down the gorge till it emerges on a country road southwest of Zahara. This involves abseiling down a few 10m drops and qualifies as 'canyoning': local adventure firms such as Al-qutun will guide you.

balconies, and a restaurant terrace overlooking the village and countryside. Try the trout, the local speciality.

El Tabanco (*Calle La Fuente 3*), up in the village centre, just off the square, serves excellent meat and tapas at reasonable prices.

Benamahoma
postcode 11679 • elevation 450m

The small village of Benamahoma, 4km east of El Bosque on the A-372 to Grazalema, is known for its market gardens, trout farm and a cottage industry of rush-backed chairs. You can walk to Zahara de la Sierra from here on dirt roads via the Puerto de Albarranes, Laguna del Perezoso and Puerto de Breña – a beautiful trip of 16km (five hours plus stops). Benamahoma remembers its past in its Fiestas de Moros y Cristianos (Festival of Moors and Christians), on the first Sunday of August.

Camping Los Linares (*☎ 956 71 62 75; camping per adult/tent/car €4/4/3.25, cabins for up to 4 €69; open daily June-Sept, weekends Oct-May*) is 600m up Camino del Nacimiento at the back of the village.

Grazalema
postcode 11610 • pop 2250
• elevation 825m

From Benamahoma the A-372 winds east over the Puerto del Boyar (1103m) to Grazalema. Take care driving on this road when the mist comes down.

Grazalema is a neat, pretty, picture-postcard village, especially when dusted with snow. Its steep cobbled streets, lined by white houses with flowery window boxes, nestle into a corner of beautiful mountain country beneath the rock climbers' crag Peñón Grande. Local products include pure wool blankets and rugs – a centuries-old tradition.

The village centre is the charming Plaza de España, where you'll find the **tourist office** (*☎ 956 13 22 25; open 10am-2pm & 5pm-8pm Tues-Sun Semana Santa–Oct; 10am-2pm & 4pm-6pm Tues-Sun rest of year*), with an upstairs shop selling local wool products and other crafts (blankets and rugs start around €55). Unicaja bank, right by Plaza de España, has an ATM.

Things to See & Do Grazalema has a couple of lovely 17th-century churches, the **Iglesia de la Aurora** (*Plaza de España*) and the nearby **Iglesia de la Encarnación**.

Horizon (*☎ 956 13 23 63; Calle Corrales Terceros 29*), a block off Plaza de España, offers a range of activities such as climbing, bridge-jumping, caving, canyoning and walking, with English-speaking guides. Prices per person range from around €11 for a half-day walk to over €40 for some caving and canyoning trips. **Pinzapo** (*☎ 956 13 24 36; e pinzapo@wanadoo.es*) and **Ocio Natural** (*☎ 956 13 23 55*) offer some similar activities.

Grazalema's large, open-air, public swimming pool, with good views, is by the El Bosque road up at the eastern end of the village.

Special Events Grazalema's Fiestas del Carmen, with plenty of late-night music and dance performances, fill several days in mid-July, ending on a Monday with a bull-running through the streets.

Places to Stay & Eat At the top of the village beside the A-372 to El Bosque you'll find **Camping Tajo Rodillo** (*☎ 956 71 62 75; camping per adult/tent €3.60/3.60, free car park at site entrance*). In winter you may only find it open at weekends.

Casa de las Piedras (*☎ 956 13 20 14; Calle Las Piedras 32; singles/doubles €9.50/19, with bathroom €27/39.50*) is a good-value *hostal* with a couple of patios and a lounge with a log fire in winter. Its restaurant serves hearty medium-priced breakfasts and meals.

Hotel Peñón Grande (*☎/fax 956 13 24 35; Plaza Pequeña 7; singles/doubles €35/50*) is a good, recently-opened small hotel just off Plaza de España, in rustic style, with yellow walls, blue tiles and big wooden bedheads. Bicycles rent for €8/12 per half/whole day.

Hotel Puerta de la Villa (*☎ 956 13 23 76; w www.grazhotel.com/hotelpuertadelavilla; Plaza Pequeña 8; singles/doubles €93.50/ 116.50; 4-course menú €19*), also recently opened, is stylish, with pool, sauna, gym and classy restaurant.

Villa Turística (*☎ 956 13 21 36, fax 956 13 22 13; El Olivar s/n; singles/doubles*

€31/50.50, apartment for 2 €64.50), with great views over the village from a hillside to the north, is comfortable, with 24 rooms, 38 apartments, lawns, pool and restaurant.

There are plenty of places to eat and drink on Calle Agua, off Plaza de España, among them the good-value **Bar La Posadilla** (Calle Agua 19; platos combinados €2-4).

Restaurante Càdiz El Chico (Plaza de España 8; mains €6-13) is good for a more expensive meal, from fish or carnes a la plancha (grilled meat) starting around €6, to venison, lamb or pork (€9 to €13).

Zahara de la Sierra
postcode 11688 • pop 1550
• elevation 550m

Topped by a crag with a ruined castle, Zahara de la Sierra is the most northerly and most dramatically sited of the natural park's villages. It feels quite otherworldly if you've driven the 18km from Grazalema through heavy mist via the vertiginous 1331m Puerto de los Palomas (Doves' Pass, but with more vultures than doves). There's a large reservoir below the village, to the north and east.

Founded by Muslims in the 8th century, Zahara fell in 1407 to the Castilian prince Fernando de Antequera. Its brief recapture by Abu al-Hasan of Granada in a daring night raid in 1481 sparked the last phase of the Reconquista, which ended in the fall of Granada. In the late 19th century Zahara was a noted hotbed of anarchism.

The village centres on Calle San Juan, with a church at each end. Near one end is the Sierra de Grazalema natural park's **Centro de Visitantes Zahara de la Sierra** (☎ 956 12 30 14; Plaza del Rey 3; open 9am-2pm daily, 4pm-7pm Mon-Sat). If you have a car to park, follow the one-way street beyond here for 150m.

Things to See & Do There's a **mirador** at one end of Calle San Juan, in front of the baroque **Iglesia de Santa María de la Mesa**. To climb to the 12th-century **castle**, of which only the keep survives intact, take the path almost opposite the entrance to Hotel Arco de la Villa – it's a steady 10- to 20-minute climb. Zahara's streets invite investigation, with vistas framed by tall palms or hot-pink bougainvillea in summer, and fruited orange trees in winter.

Al-qutun (☎ 956 13 78 82; w www .al-qutun.com; Calle Zahara de la Sierra) in Algodonales, 7km north of Zahara, organises activities, from canyoning in the Garganta Verde, to paragliding, hang-gliding, walking, caving and climbing.

Places to Stay & Eat Down towards the municipal swimming pool on the southwestern edge of the village, **Hostal Los Tadeos** (☎ 956 12 30 86; Paseo de la Fuente s/n; singles/doubles/triples €24/37/50) is friendly, with 11 good, new rooms with bathroom, nice tiled floors and wooden furniture, and a small restaurant.

Hostal Marqués de Zahara (☎/fax 956 12 30 61; Calle San Juan 3; singles/doubles €28/40), a converted mansion in the village centre, has 10 comfy rooms with bathroom and winter heating, and a restaurant.

Hotel Arco de la Villa (☎ 956 12 32 30; Paseo Nazarí s/n; singles/doubles €31/ 50.50) provides 17 air-con rooms with TV and spectacular views, and a restaurant.

You won't go wrong eating at either of two neighbouring establishments on Calle San Juan: **Restaurante Los Naranjos** (meat & fish mains €5.50-11) or the economical **Bar Nuevo** (menú €8), which serves homestyle food such as venison stew.

Benaocaz
postcode 11612 • pop 660 • elevation 790m

The pretty village of Benaocaz, on the A-374 Ubrique–Grazalema road amid limestone country in the south of the park, has a couple of reasonable accommodation options and is a starting point for some good walks. The seven-room **Museo Histórico de Benaocaz** (Calle Jabonería 7; normally open weekends only) surveys the district's history from the early Stone Age to the 20th century.

Walks It's about 1¼ hours' walk north to the **Salto del Cabrero**, a dramatic fissure in the earth's surface 500m long, 100m wide and 100m deep; or 1½ hours northeast to the **Casa del Dornajo**, a ruined farmstead high in a beautiful valley. From either of these you can continue to Grazalema in about two hours via the Puerto del Boyar pass on the A-372. A 3km stretch of **Roman road** heads southwest down from Benaocaz to the town of Ubrique, and the GR-7 long-distance path comes through here en route between Ubrique and Ronda. Ubrique (population: 17,000) is a busy working town: if you need a smart leather bag, briefcase, wallet, jacket or belt, in almost any conceivable colour, take a walk along its main street, Avenida Solís Pascual, which is lined with shops selling these goods, all made in Ubrique.

Places to Stay & Eat Up at the northern end of Benaocaz, **Hostal San Antón** (☎ 956 12 55 77; Plaza de San Antón s/n; singles/doubles/quads €18/30/60) has five pretty rooms with bathroom, kitchenette and fireplace. Those upstairs have breezy terraces.

Hotel Los Chozos (☎ 956 23 41 63; w www.sierradecadiz.com/loschozos; doubles/quads €84/97, weekends €97/125) offers accommodation in comfy two-storey thatched stone huts, in imitation of traditional local buildings. It has a restaurant. Turn off the A-374, 1km below the village and go 800m.

Las Vegas (Plaza de las Libertades; tapas/media-raciones €1.20/4.50) is the most dependable place to eat in the village.

Costa de la Luz

The 90km coast between Cádiz and Tarifa can be windy, and its Atlantic waters are a shade cooler than those of the Mediterranean. But these are small prices to pay for an unspoiled, often wild shore, strung with long, clean, white-sand beaches and just a few small towns and villages. Andalucians are well aware of its attractions and flock down here in their thousands during July and August, bringing a vibrant fiesta atmosphere to the normally quiet coastal settlements. Ring ahead for rooms in these months.

From before Roman times until the advent of 20th-century tourism, this coast was mainly devoted to tuna fishing. Shoals of big tuna, some weighing 300kg, are still intercepted by walls of net several kilometres long as the fish head in from the Atlantic towards their Mediterranean spawning grounds in spring, and again as they head out in July and August. Barbate has the main tuna fleet today.

VEJER DE LA FRONTERA
postcode 11150 ● pop 12,300
● elevation 190m

This old-fashioned white town looms mysteriously atop a rocky hill above the busy N-340, 50km from Cádiz and 10km inland. It's well worth a wander.

Orientation & Information

The oldest area of town, still partly walled and with narrow winding streets clearly signifying its Muslim origins, spreads over the highest part of the hill. Just below is the small Plazuela, more or less the heart of town, with the Hotel Convento de San Francisco and, nearby, the **tourist office** (☎ 956 45 01 91; Calle Marqués de Tamarón 10; open 8am-3pm & 5pm-8pm Mon-Fri mid-Sept–mid-June; 8am-3pm & 6pm-10pm Mon-Fri mid-June–mid-Sept, 11am-2pm Sat & Sun July & Aug). Buses stop on Avenida Los Remedios, the road up from the N-340, about 500m below the Plazuela. You'll find cybercafés on Calle San Francisco and on Calle Altozano, both near the market.

Things to See

Vejer's walls date from the 15th century. Four gateways and a couple of towers survive. Within the 40,000 sq metre walled area, seek out the **Iglesia del Divino Salvador**, whose interior is Mudejar at the altar end and Gothic at the other; and the much-reworked **castle** (open Semana Santa & mid-June–mid-Sept), with great views from its battlements and a small museum that preserves one of the black cloaks, covering everything but the eyes, that Vejer women wore until just a couple of decades ago. Don't miss pretty palm-filled **Plaza de España** and its attractive Seville-tiled fountain, a 10-minute stroll along Calle Marqués de Tamarón from the tourist office.

Activities

You can rent good mountain bikes (€12 per day) and surf boards (€10 per day) from **Discover Andalucía** (☎ 956 44 75 75; *Avenida Los Remedios 45)*, opposite the bus stop. Paragliding is possible with **Lijar Sur** (☎ 617 49 05 00).

Special Events

There's a running of the bulls on Easter Sunday. The *feria*, from 10 to 24 August, features music and dancing nightly in Plaza de España. At least one night is devoted entirely to flamenco.

Places to Stay & Eat

Hostal La Janda (☎ 956 45 01 42; *Calle Machado s/n; doubles with bathroom €36)* is a friendly place across town from the old walled area.

Hostal Buena Vista (☎ 956 45 09 69; *Calle Manuel Machado 4; doubles with bathroom €36)*, situated down a side street near Hostal La Janda, has spotless, spacious doubles, some with fine views across to the old part of town.

Hotel Convento de San Francisco (☎ 956 45 10 01; w *www.tugasa.com; Plazuela s/n; singles/doubles €43.50/61.50)* has 25 simple but charming rooms in a restored 17th-century convent.

Hotel La Casa del Califa (☎ 956 44 77 30; w *www.vejer.com/califa; Plaza de España 16; singles/doubles from €47.50/59)* has 19 comfortable rooms with Islamic-influenced decor. Rates include breakfast.

Casablanca (☎ 956 44 75 69; w *www .andaluciacasablanca.com; Calle Canalejas 8; doubles €43)* has four self-catering apartments set around a pretty traditional patio.

La Bodeguita (☎ 956 45 15 82, *Calle Marqués de Tamarón 9)*, near the tourist office and with a small terrace, has excellent tapas and meals. Across the street, **Bar Joplin** is a laid-back place for a drink, best late at weekends. **Restaurante Trafalgar** (☎ 956 44 76 38; *Plaza de España 31; 2-course meal with wine €24-30)*, owned by the same folk as the Casablanca, provides more formal dining. Specialties are local fish and seafood and rice dishes.

Getting There & Away

The small office of **Comes** (☎ 956 44 71 46; *Plazuela)* has bus information. Buses run to/from Cádiz (€3.50, 50 minutes) and Barbate (€0.90, 10 minutes) up to 10 times a day. More buses for the same places, plus Tarifa (50 minutes) and Algeciras (about 10 daily), La Línea (eight daily, 1¼ hours), Málaga (two daily) and Seville (five daily) stop at La Barca de Vejer, on the N-340 at the bottom of the hill. By road it's 4km uphill from La Barca to the town; on foot, there's an obvious 15-minute shortcut.

EL PALMAR

postcode 11159

Ten kilometres out of Vejer, sleepy El Palmar has a lovely 4.8km sweep of beach, good for body surfing, and for board surfing from October to March. It livens up during Semana Santa and high summer. The well-equipped **Camping El Palmar** (☎ 956 23 21 61; *2 adults, tent & car €39)* is 900m from the beach. **Hostal Francisco** (☎ 956 23 28 61; *doubles €42; menú €7.25)*, right in front of the beach and with a good restaurant, is the best of a handful of *hostales* and is open for most of the year. One bus runs daily to/from Seville.

LOS CAÑOS DE MECA

postcode 11159

Los Caños, once a hippy hideaway, straggles untidily along a series of sandy coves beneath a pine-clad hill about 7km southeast of El Palmar and 12km west of Barbate. It maintains its laid-back, off-beat air even during the height of summer.

Coming from El Palmar or Vejer, you pass through the separate settlement of Zahora a couple of kilometres short of Los Caños. Then, at the western end of the Los Caños, a side-road leads out to a lighthouse on a low spit of land with a famous name – Cabo de Trafalgar. It was off this cape that Spanish naval power was terminated in a few hours one day in 1805 by a British fleet under Admiral Nelson. Decent beaches stretch either side of Cabo de Trafalgar. Towards the eastern end of Los Caños, the main street, which is mostly called Avenida Trafalgar, is met by the road from Barbate. The main beach is straight in front of this junction. Those who want to swim nude do so around the small headland at its eastern end. At the western end there are surfable waves in winter. **La Pequeña Lulu** *(Avenida Trafalgar)*, at the far eastern end of the village, offers Internet connection from 1pm until late daily.

The coast between Los Caños and Barbate is mostly cliffs up to 100m high. The road between the two places runs inland through La Breña umbrella pine forest. These cliffs and forest, along with wetlands east and north of Barbate, form the **Parque Natural de La Breña y Marismas de Barbate**. A couple of walking paths start from the road: one goes to Playa de la Hierbabuena beach just west of Barbate, the other to the Torre del Tajo, a 16th-century clifftop lookout tower. Another tower, the Torre de Meca on the hill behind Los Caños, can be reached from this road.

Places to Stay

Three medium-sized camping grounds open from April to September and get pretty crowded and noisy in high summer.

Camping Caños de Meca *(☎ 956 43 71 20; 2 adults, tent & car €17.90)* is in Zahora.

Camping Faro de Trafalgar *(☎ 956 43 70 17; 2 adults, tent & car €16)* is 1.7km west from the Barbate road corner in Los Caños village.

Camping Camaleón *(☎ 956 43 71 54; Avenida Trafalgar s/n; 2 adults, tent & car €17.50)* is nearest the centre, about 1km west from the Barbate road corner. Sites are shady.

There are several *hostales* out at Zahora and about 10 more strung along Avenida Trafalgar in Los Caños. Most are pretty similar and have decent rooms with bathroom. The quieter end of Los Caños village is east from the Barbate road corner. What follows is set out in west-to-east order, starting at Zahora.

Hostal Alhambra *(☎ 956 43 72 16; Carretera Caños de Meca Km 9.5; doubles with bathroom €38.50; closed 25 Dec-14 Jan)*, at Zahora, opposite Camping Caños de Meca, has Alhambra-esque trimmings, a restaurant, and pleasant rooms with attractive furniture and little verandas.

Casa Meca *(☎ 956 43 14 50, 639 61 34 02; ⓦ www.casameca.com; Avenida Trafalgar s/n; studio for 2 from €51.50, 2-bedroom apartments €510-590 per week)* is on the main road, 100m east of the Cabo de Trafalgar turning. This friendly place has three bright apartments with kitchen, bathroom, salon, views and outdoor sitting areas.

Casas Karen *(Fuente del Madroño; ☎ 956 43 70 67, fax 956 43 72 33; ⓦ www.casaskaren.com; Fuente del Madroño 6; doubles €40-80, traditional hut for 2 €220-430 per week)* is accessed from the main road, 500m east of the Cabo de Trafalgar turning. Look for a whitewashed wall with 'Apartamentos y Bungalows' tiled into it. Follow the road next to the sign for six blocks, then turn right for one block and you'll reach the accommodation set on a large, pretty mimosa-covered plot. It's owned by a warm and dynamic Englishwoman. The eclectic buildings, all with kitchen, bathroom, lounge and outdoor sitting areas and hammock, range from a converted farmhouse to an exotic, thatch-roofed, traditional hut *(choza)*, built of local materials. Individuals and short stays are welcome, but the place caters more for weekly rentals.

Hostal El Ancla *(☎ 956 43 71 00; Avenida Trafalgar 148; doubles or triples €36-42; open July-Sept)*, past the 'Apartamentos y Bungalows' turning, has simple rooms with bathroom, fridge and TV.

Hostal Miramar *(☎ 956 43 70 24, fax 956 43 70 33; Avenida Trafalgar 112; doubles with bathroom €42; open Semana Santa–end Sept)*, past the Camping Camaleón turning, boasts a pool and restaurant.

Hostal Madreselva *(formerly Hostal Mar y Sol; ☎ 956 43 72 55; Avenida Trafalgar 102; doubles with bathroom €49-67; open Semana Santa–Oct)* has been tastefully remodelled by the owners of the Hurricane Hotel near Tarifa. Some of the 18 rooms have small gardens. There's a bar and a pool, a branch of Club Mistral (see the Tarifa section) for windsurfing and kitesurfing, plus mountain bike and horse rental.

Hostal Fortuna *(☎ 956 43 70 75; Avenida Trafalgar s/n; doubles Aug €64.50, rest of year €39.50-51.50)*, located a couple of hundred metres east of the Barbate corner, has excellent rooms. It's sometimes open throughout winter.

Hostal Castillejos *(☎ 956 43 70 19; Avenida Trafalgar s/n; doubles with bathroom €48; open at least June-Sept)* is a quaint turreted little place with lingering hippy vibes and only three rooms.

Places to Eat

Bar-Restaurante El Caña *(Avenida Trafalgar s/n; seafood dishes from €8.50)* has a fine position atop the small cliff above the beach. It's a short distance east from the Barbate road corner, but only open in tourist seasons.

El Pirata *(Avenida Trafalgar s/n; seafood media-raciones €5)*, overlooking the beach a couple of hundred metres west of El Caña, is a good bet whenever the weather is fine. The excellent *revuelto de gambas* (scrambled eggs with shrimps) costs €6.60. It's a cosy place for a drink on winter weekend nights when there's an open fire and good music.

In winter, when no eatery is open in the village, try **Restaurante El Capi** *(homemade fish croquettes €6 per media-ración)* attached to the *hostal* of the same name on the main road at Zahora, which serves decent tapas and good fish dishes and has a welcoming open fire.

Entertainment

Out of season, head for **La Pequeña Lulu**, at the far eastern end of the village. It has live music and vegetarian food on at least Friday and some Saturday nights. In the main tourist season, good bars include the cool **Los Castillejos** near Hostal Castillejos (see Places to Stay), **Café-Bar Ketama** across the street from El Pirata, and a couple of livelier places with music on the road out to Cabo de Trafalgar such as **Las Dunas** *(open year-round)*. **La Jaima**, in a Moroccan tent *(carpa)* with plush red seats, overlooking the beach just east of the Barbate road corner, sometimes has entertainment. The bar at **Hostal Madreselva** (see Places to Stay) will probably become a bit of a Meca mecca.

Getting There & Away

Monday to Friday, two buses each run to/from Barbate and Cádiz. There is one bus to/from Seville (Prado de San Sebastián) daily and another to/from Zahara de los Atunes. From mid-June to early September, there's usually a daily bus leaving Seville at 9am for Los Caños (€12), Barbate and Zahara, returning from Los Caños at 7pm.

BARBATE

postcode 11160 • pop 20,000

A fishing and canning town with a long sandy beach and a big harbour, Barbate becomes a fairly lively resort in summer, but it's mostly a drab place. You might need to use Barbate as a staging post if you're travelling by bus. The **Comes bus station** *(☎ 956 43 05 94; Avenida del Generalísimo)* is more than 1km back from the beach at the northern end of the long main street. Barbate's **tourist office** *(☎ 956 43 39 62; Calle Vázquez Mella s/n; open 8am-3pm Mon-Fri; 8am-2pm & 5pm-8pm daily mid-June–mid-Sept)* is the only one in the Los Caños-Barbate-Zahara de los Atunes area. Coming from the bus station along Avenida del Generalísimo towards the beach, turn left into Calle Agustín Varo about half-way, and follow it nine blocks to Calle Vázquez Mella. The tourist office is one block south of here.

Hotel Galia *(☎ 956 43 04 82; Calle Doctor Valencia 5; singles €24-36, doubles €30-54)*, a few blocks towards the sea from the bus station, is fine and open year-round.

Hotel Nuro *(☎ 956 43 48 84; Avenida José Antonio s/n; doubles with bathroom, air-con & TV €30-54)* is simple but comfy and only 100m from the intersection of Avenida José Antonio with Avenida del Generalísimo and the bus station.

Hotel Madreselva *(☎ 956 45 40 33, ℮ barbate@madreselvahotel.com; Calle Real 1, cnr Avenida José Antonio; singles/doubles €55/67)* is about 1km beyond the Hotel Nuro. Tastefully refurbished by the owners of Tarifa's lovely Hurricane Hotel, the Madreselva has Moroccan flourishes and an attractive bar.

There are plenty of seafood eateries with lots of local specialities on Paseo Marítimo. **Bar Nani** is recommended for sea bass and prawns. Away from the beach, **Café-Bar Estrella Polar** *(Avenida del Generalísimo*

CÁDIZ PROVINCE

106; mains €4-7.50, salads €2.70) offers good portions at fair prices. Try the swordfish, or a platter of mixed fried fish.

Buses run to/from La Barca de Vejer (see the Vejer de la Frontera section, earlier) and Cádiz up to 15 times daily, Vejer de la Frontera up to nine times daily, and Tarifa and Algeciras once daily. There's one bus Monday to Friday to/from Seville. Three buses run daily Monday to Friday (two on Saturday and Sunday) to/from Zahara de los Atunes.

ZAHARA DE LOS ATUNES
postcode 11393
Plonked in the middle of nothing except a broad, 12km-long, west-facing sandy beach, Zahara is an elemental sort of place. At the heart of the village stand the crumbling walls of the old Almadraba, once a depot and refuge for the local tuna fishers, who were an infamously rugged lot. Cervantes, in *La Ilustre Fregona*, wrote that no one deserved the name *pícaro* (low-life scoundrel) unless they had spent two seasons at Zahara fishing for tuna. The pícaros were evidently good at their job, for records state that in 1541 no fewer than 140,000 tuna were brought into Zahara's Almadraba. Today the tuna industry has dwindled out of sight but Zahara is an increasingly popular, almost fashionable, Spanish summer resort. With a little old-fashioned core of narrow streets, it's altogether a fine spot to let the sun, sea, wind – and, in summer, a spot of lively nightlife – batter your senses.

Unicaja *(Paseo del Pradillo)*, near the heart of Zahara, and **Caja Rural** *(Calle María Luisa opposite Plaza de Tamarón)* both have ATMs.

Places to Stay
Camping Bahía de la Plata *(☎ 956 43 90 40; 2 adults, tent & car €16.50; open year-round)* is near the beach at the southern end of Zahara.

Hostal Monte Mar *(☎ 956 43 90 47; Calle Peñón 12; doubles with bathroom €42)*, at the northern tip of the village, is otherwise the cheapest place, and the most likely to have a room when everywhere else is full in July/August.

Hotel Nicolás *(☎ 956 43 92 74,* W *www .hotel-nicolas.tuweb.net; Calle María Luisa 13; singles/doubles €35.50/48, with half-board €47.50/72.50)* is friendly with just 11 simple but attractive rooms with TV, bathroom, heating and air-con, and a restaurant. Half-board is obligatory in high season.

Hotel Gran Sol *(☎ 956 43 93 09,* W *www .hotelgransol.com; Calle Sánchez Rodríguez s/n; doubles €84, sea view €12 extra)* occupies the prime beach spot right by the sands and facing the old Almadraba walls. It has large, comfortable doubles.

Hotel Doña Lola *(☎ 956 43 90 09; Plaza Thompson 1; singles/doubles €90/100)*, near the entrance to Zahara, is a modern place in an attractive old-fashioned style, with good doubles.

Places to Eat
Most restaurants are on or near Plaza de Tamarón near the Hotel Doña Lola, and most offer similar lists of fish, seafood, salads, meat and sometimes pizzas.

Patio la Plazoleta *(Plaza de Tamarón; fish dishes €7.20, pizzas €8.50)* is a good choice, open to the air: try the *pez limón a la plancha* (grilled tuna with vegetables and lemon), or a pizza.

Café-Bar Casa Juanita *(Calle Sagasta)*, off the main drag near Plaza de Tamarón, is another pleasant place, with similar fare and prices to Patio la Plazoleta. It's not a bad spot for your morning coffee and *tostada*.

La Dulce Campesina *(Calle María Luisa)* is a good bakery-cum-eatery, with a cheap *menú del día*.

Entertainment
In July and August a line of tents and makeshift shacks along the beach south of the Almadraba serve as bars, discos and *teterías* (Islamic-style tearooms). They get busy from about midnight, and some have live flamenco or other music.

Getting There & Away
The Comes line runs three buses daily to/from Cádiz (€5.50) via Barbate, and one each Monday to Friday to/from Tarifa (€2.50) and to/from Seville via Los Caños

de Meca (€12.50). There are more buses from mid-June to September.

BOLONIA
postcode 11391

This tiny village, 10km down the coast from Zahara and about 20km from Tarifa, has a fine white sand beach good for windsurfing, several restaurants and small *hostales*, lots of cockerels, and the ruins of the Roman town of **Baelo Claudia** (☎ 956 68 85 30; admission €1.50, EU citizen free; 10am-7pm Tues-Sat Mar-May & Oct; 10am-8pm Tues-Sat June-Sept; 10am-6pm Tues-Sat Nov-Feb; 10am-2pm Sun year-round). The ruins include substantial remains of a theatre, a paved forum surrounded by remains of temples and other buildings, and the remains of the workshops that turned out the products which made Baelo Claudia famous in the Roman world: salted fish and *garum* paste (a spicy seasoning derived from fish). The place flourished under Claudius from AD 41 to AD 54 but went into economic decline after an earthquake in the 2nd century AD.

Bolonia is destined to be the Spanish end of a tunnel under the Strait of Gibraltar to Tangier, Morocco. The 38km tunnel, for vehicle-carrying trains, is projected by the Spanish and Moroccan governments but won't happen until sufficient funds are found and technical problems ironed out. It will actually begin a couple of kilometres inland and cross under the coastline between Bolonia and Punta Paloma.

Places to Stay

The following places are open year-round. **Hostal Bellavista** (☎ 956 68 85 53; singles/doubles with bathroom €40/48) is in the centre of the village.

Hostal Miramar (☎ 956 68 42 04; doubles with bathroom €60, 2-bedroom quads €72) is run by friendly folk from Tarifa.

Hostal Lola (☎ 956 68 85 36, W www.cherrytel.com/hostallola; El Lentiscal 26; doubles/triples with bathroom €40/46), with a pretty garden, has simple but attractive rooms. There's a little Moroccan-inspired sitting area too, all overseen by the likable Loli and family. Follow the signs on giant surfboards to beyond and behind Hostal Miramar.

Places to Eat

In summer there are three or four open-air restaurants on the beach at the eastern end of the village. In the village, **Restaurante Bellavista** (fish mains €7, salad €4), attached to the Hostal Bellavista, does straightforward Spanish fare very nicely and has a terrace. Also on the main drag, try the seafood at **Restaurante Marisma** (mains €4.50-8, open daily Semana Santa–Oct, weekends year-round) with tables outside, or at popular **Bar Restaurante Las Rejas** (fish mains €5.50-10.25, open year-round) where the waiters will suggest which tasty options are best on the day. The friendly and relaxed **Rincón Beatriz** (fish dishes €4.50-5.50, open Semana Santa–Oct) is near Hostal Lola.

Getting There & Away

The only road to Bolonia heads west off the N-340, 15km from Tarifa. Without wheels it would be a 7km hilly walk from the main road, as there's no regular bus service. You could also walk 8km along the coast from Ensenada de Valdevaqueros via Punta Paloma (see the Beaches entry in the Tarifa section) or 3km from Zahara de los Atunes.

TARIFA
postcode 11380 • pop 15,000

Even at peak times Tarifa is an attractive, laid-back town. Two decades ago it was relatively unknown, but it has since become a mecca for windsurfers, and more recently, kitesurfers. It's strange to see the international surf scene transported to this European setting with a strong Arabic feel. The beaches have clean, white sand and good waves, and inland the country is green and rolling, though it can be chilly and wet in winter. Then there's the old town to explore with its pretty, narrow streets, whitewashed houses and flowers cascading from balconies and window boxes. Tarifa's castle is striking too. The only negative – though not for windsurfers and kitesurfers or the hundreds of modern windmills on the hilltops inland – is the wind on which Tarifa's new prosperity is based. For much of the year, either the *levante* (easterly) or *poniente* (westerly) is blowing, ruinous for a relaxed sit on the beach and tiring if you're simply wandering around. August can be blessedly still, hot but not too hot, crowded but not overly so. The windmills are a mainly EU-funded experiment, recently expanded, feeding power into Spain's national grid.

History

Tarifa may be as old as Phoenician Cádiz and was definitely a Roman settlement, but it takes its name from Tarif ibn Malik who led a Muslim raid in 710, the year before the main Islamic invasion of the peninsula. Muslims built the castle in the 10th century as fortification against Norse and African raids. Pirates in the area at this time are said to have extracted a fee from ships wishing to pass safely from the Atlantic through the Strait of Gibraltar to the Mediterranean. This may be the origin of the Spanish word *tarifa* and its English equivalent, tariff. Christians took Tarifa in 1292 but it was not secure until Algeciras was won in 1344. Later, Tarifa was active in the colonisation of the Americas: many of its people left for Peru in the 16th and 17th centuries.

Orientation & Information

Two roads lead into Tarifa from the N-340. The one from the northwest becomes Calle Batalla del Salado, which ends at east–west Avenida de Andalucía, where the Puerta de Jerez leads through the walls into the old town. The one from the east becomes Calle Amador de los Ríos, which also meets Avenida de Andalucía at the Puerta de Jerez.

The main street of the old town is Calle Sancho IV El Bravo, with the Iglesia de San Mateo at its eastern end. To the southwest of the town protrudes the Punta de Tarifa, a military-occupied promontory that is the southernmost point of continental Europe, with the Strait of Gibraltar to the south and east and the Atlantic Ocean to the west. Africa is only 14km across the strait.

The **tourist office** (☎ 956 68 09 93; open 10am-2pm & 5pm-7pm Mon-Sat) is near the top end of the palm-lined Paseo de la Alameda.

There are banks and ATMs on Calle Sancho IV El Bravo and Calle Batalla del Salado. The **post office** (Calle Coronel Moscardó 9) is south from the Iglesia de San Mateo. The **Policía Local** (☎ 956 61 41 86) are in the town hall. Tarifa has a **Centro de Salud** (Health Centre; ☎ 956 68 15 15/35; Calle Amador de los Ríos).

International newspapers are sold at the **News Stand** (Calle Batalla del Salado). Internet access is available at **Pandora's Papelería** (Calle Sancho IV El Bravo; open 10am-2pm & 5pm-10pm daily), diagonally opposite Café Central. Cost for 10/30/60 minutes is €0.90/2.40/4.80. For laundry, head to **Lavandería Acuario** (Calle Colón 14; open 10am-1.45pm & 5.45pm-8pm Mon-Sat), which charges €4 to wash 5kg, €9 to wash, dry and fold 5kg.

Things to See

Tarifa is best enjoyed by strolling through the tangled streets of the old town to the castle walls, checking out the castle, stopping in at the busy port and sampling the beaches.

The Mudejar **Puerta de Jerez** was built after the Reconquista. Look in at the bustling, neo-Mudejar **market** (Calle Colón) before winding your way to the heart of the old town and the mainly 15th-century **Iglesia de San Mateo**. The streets south of the church are little-changed since Islamic times. Climb the stairs at the end of Calle Coronel Moscardó and go left on Calle Aljaranda to reach the **Mirador El Estrecho** atop part of the castle walls, with spectacular views across to Africa. Nearby is the small **Museo Municipal** (Plaza de Santa María; admission free; open 10am-1.30pm Mon-Fri).

The **Castillo de Guzmán** (Calle Guzmán; admission €1.80; open 11am-2pm & 6pm-8pm Tues-Sat summer; 11am-2pm & 4pm-6pm rest of year) extends west from here but is entered at its far end on Calle Guzmán. Tickets are sold in the stationery shop across the street from the castle entrance. The castle is named after the Reconquista hero Guzmán El Bueno, who in 1294, when Merenid attackers from Morocco threatened to kill his

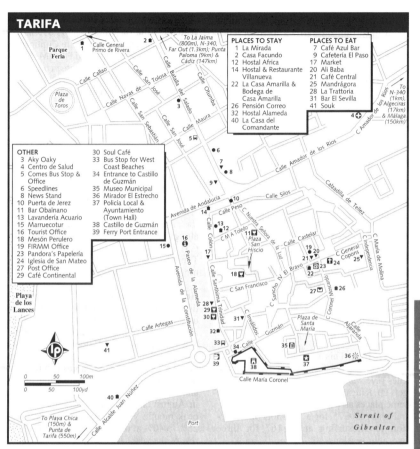

TARIFA

PLACES TO STAY
1 La Mirada
2 Casa Facundo
12 Hostal Africa
14 Hostal & Restaurante Villanueva
22 La Casa Amarilla & Bodega de Casa Amarilla
26 Pensión Correo
32 Hostal Alameda
40 La Casa del Comandante

PLACES TO EAT
7 Café Azul Bar
9 Cafetería El Paso
17 Market
20 Ali Baba
21 Café Central
25 Mandrágora
28 La Trattoria
31 Bar El Sevilla
41 Souk

OTHER
3 Aky Oaky
4 Centro de Salud
5 Comes Bus Stop & Office
6 Speedlines
8 News Stand
10 Puerta de Jerez
11 Bar Obaïnano
13 Lavandería Acuario
15 Marruecotur
16 Tourist Office
18 Mesón Perulero
19 FIRMM Office
23 Pandora's Papelería
24 Iglesia de San Mateo
27 Post Office
29 Café Continental
30 Soul Café
33 Bus Stop for West Coast Beaches
34 Entrance to Castillo de Guzmán
35 Museo Municipal
36 Mirador El Estrecho
37 Policía Local & Ayuntamiento (Town Hall)
38 Castillo de Guzmán
39 Ferry Port Entrance

CÁDIZ PROVINCE

kidnapped son unless he relinquished this castle to them, threw down his dagger for his son to be killed. Guzmán's descendants became the Duques de Medina Sidonia, who ran much of Cádiz province as a private fiefdom for a long time and remained Spain's largest landowners well into the 20th century.

The imposing fortress was originally built in 960 under the orders of the Cordoban Caliph, Abd ar-Rahman III. You can walk along the parapets and stand atop the 13th-century Torre de Guzmán El Bueno for 360° views out to sea and Africa and back across the town to the windmills on the hills behind.

Beaches

The popular town beach is the sheltered but extremely small **Playa Chica**, on the isthmus leading out to the Punta de Tarifa. From here **Playa de los Lances** stretches 10km northwest to the huge sand dune at Punta Paloma.

Activities

Aky Oaky (☎ 956 68 53 56; *Calle Batalla del Salado 37*) offers a range of organised activities (costing €24 to €42) including walking, caving, rock climbing, mountain biking in Parque Natural Los Alcornocales and horse riding.

Windsurfing Conditions are often right for windsurfing on Tarifa's town beaches but most of the action occurs along the coast between Tarifa and Punta Paloma, 10km northwest. The best spots, of course, depend on wind and tide conditions. El Porro, on Ensenada de Valdevaqueros, the bay formed by Punta Paloma, is one of the most popular, as it has easy parking and plenty of space to set up. Other popular take-off points are the Río Jara, about 3km from Tarifa, and Arte-Vida and Hurricane, in front of the respective hotels.

You can buy new and second-hand windsurf gear in Tarifa at the surf shops along Calle Batalla del Salado. For board rental and classes you need to try places up the coast such as **Club Mistral** (*☎ 956 68 90 98; Hurricane Hotel • ☎ 619 34 09 13; Cortijo Valdevaqueros*) or **Spin Out** on the beach in front of Camping Torre de la Peña II, near El Porro. At Club Mistral board rental costs €20/52 per hour/day, and a six-hour beginner's course is €121.

Competitions are held year-round with at least one international event in summer, the World Cup (Formula 42) in July or August.

Kitesurfing This exciting and colourful sport is taking the Tarifa coast by storm, but kites give way to sails when the wind really gets up. Kitesurf rental is available from the same places as windsurfing gear. Club Mistral charges €75 for a two-hour introduction to kitesurfing and €167 for three two-hour sessions.

Tarifa hosted an international kitesurfing competition with 100 competitors in April 2002.

Horse Riding On Playa de los Lances, both the Hotel Dos Mares' **Aventura Ecuestre** (*☎ 956 23 66 32*) and the Hurricane Hotel's **Club Hípica** (*☎ 956 68 90 92*) rent horses with excellent guides. An hour's ride along the beach costs €25. Four- to five-hour rides, incorporating both beach and inland routes, cost €60 to €70.

Whale Watching Three-hour boat trips to track and watch dolphins and whales

(€27/18 for over/under 14) are run by **Whale Watch España** (*☎ 956 68 22 47, 639 47 65 44*), which operates out of Cafe Continental on Paseo de la Alameda, and **FIRMM** *(Foundation for Information and Research on Marine Animals; ☎ 956 62 70 08, 619 45 94 41; Calle Pedro Cortés 4)*, next to Café Central.

Bird-Watching The Tarifa area is one of the best places in Andalucía for bird-watching (see the boxed text 'High-Fliers over the Strait of Gibraltar', later).

Places to Stay

Camping There are six year-round **camping grounds**, with room for more than 4000 campers, on or near the beach between Tarifa and Punta Paloma, 10km northwest along the N-340. They charge €19.80 to €31.25 for two people with a tent and a car. The two Torre de la Peña sites are more modern than the others.

Hostales & Hotels There are several options in the old town and plenty of choice on and around Calle Batalla del Salado. At least nine more places are dotted along the beach and the inland side of the N-340 within 10km northwest from Tarifa, but none of these is cheap. Rooms can be tight in summer and when there are windsurfing and kitesurfing competitions. Phone ahead in August. Prices given here are for this peak month: you can expect reductions of 25% to 40% at most places for much of the rest of the year.

In Town Located in the old post office, **Pensión Correo** (*☎ 956 68 02 06; Calle Coronel Moscardó 9; €15-20 per person*) is a good budget choice. The brightly painted rooms, some with bathroom, are not flash, but comfy enough. The best double (with gorgeous views and its own terrace) costs €43.

La Casa Amarilla (*☎ 956 68 19 93, W www .tarifa.net/lacasamarilla; Calle Sancho IV El Bravo 9; doubles €58*) is in an imaginatively restored, tastefully decorated 19th-century building. Most of the rooms have a kitchenette with a small cooker and fridge: all have private bathroom, heating and satellite TV.

Hostal Villanueva (☎ 956 68 41 49; Avenida de Andalucía 11; singles/doubles €27/60.10) is built into the old city walls a few doors west of the Puerta de Jerez. This friendly *hostal* has good clean rooms, all with bathroom, some with TV and some with views to the castle. The owner speaks French and there's a terrace.

Hostal Africa (☎ 956 68 02 20, 606 91 42 94; Calle María Antonia Toledo 12; singles/doubles €16/25, with bathroom €25/37), close to the market, has lively, well-travelled young owners who have revamped an old house to make bright, attractive rooms. There's a large roof terrace. You can store boards and bicycles here.

Hostal Alameda (☎ 956 68 11 81, W www.hostalalameda.com; Paseo de la Alameda 4; doubles with bathroom €60) is on the edge of the old town in front of the port. Rooms are cosy, with heating and air-con, and some have views.

La Casa del Comandante (☎/fax 956 68 19 25, W www.tarifaweb.com/casadel comandante/; Calle Alcalde Juan Núñez 8; singles/doubles €42/60.10, doubles with view €72, cabañas for 2 €36), opposite the port, is bright and new with a distinctive glassed-in terrace restaurant. It has nine smart rooms, all with bathroom.

Casa Facundo (☎ 956 68 42 98; Calle Batalla del Salado 47; doubles with/without bathroom & TV €49/37) is geared to windsurfers, with storage place boards, and is popular because it's relatively cheap. Rooms are variable: the best are actually those opening right on to the street on Calle Callao and Calle San Luis. The rooms opening onto a back street on the east side of Calle Batalla del Salado are grungy.

La Mirada (☎ 956 68 06 26; Calle San Sebastián 41; singles/doubles €42/66) is a good place if you're after sea views, as 14 of the 24 good rooms have them.

Along the Coast All these places have rooms with private bathrooms and are on the N-340.

Hotel Dos Mares (☎ 956 68 40 35; e dosmares@cherrytel.com; singles/doubles interior €88/110, in bungalows & cabañas from €68/85) is right on the beach about 4.5km from Tarifa. Prices include breakfast. Its architecture has a basically Islamic theme. You can stay in the main building, or go for a bungalow in the gardens or on the beachfront. The smoky bar with tremendous views out to Africa is a popular hangout. The hotel has its own stables, too.

Hostal Arte-Vida (☎ 956 68 52 46; W www.hotelartevida.com; singles/doubles €115.75/128.50), 5km from the town centre, has a nice little garden opening onto the beach, its own restaurant, and attractive, medium-sized rooms. Decor is oriental minimalist (white features, lots of cane and bamboo). Prices include a buffet breakfast.

Hurricane Hotel (☎ 956 68 49 19; W www.hurricanehotel.com; doubles land-/ocean-side €113.50/133.75), 6km out, is the place to go if money is no object. Set in beachside semitropical gardens, this gorgeous hotel has around 30 large, comfy rooms, two pools (one heated), a health club and a windsurfing/kitesurfing school with board rental next door. Rates include a scrumptious and, if you like, enormous buffet breakfast.

Hostal Oasis (☎ 956 68 50 65; doubles €36-60, bungalows for 2 €48-75) and **Hotel La Ensenada** (☎ 956 68 06 37; doubles €60), both about 8km out, are two of the less pricey places along here. Hostal Oasis's 11 clean, spacious bungalows, set around a large lawn area, have equipped kitchens.

100% Fun (☎ 956 68 03 30, fax 956 68 00 13; singles €72, doubles €81-90) is on the N-340 just short of Punta Paloma. The restaurant and some of the rooms are set in pretty tropical-style gardens adorned with totem poles. Eleven rooms share a large patio, each room with its own flower-shaded veranda. There's a swimming pool and an excellent surf-shop and breakfast is included.

Cortijo Valdevaqueros (☎ 956 23 67 05; rooms with bathroom around €78, apartment for 3 or 4 €102; open Mar-Nov), across the N-340 from 100% Fun, almost on the beach, is an attractive place (same owners as the Hurricane Hotel) with a handful of rooms. You'll recognise the entrance by the metallic sign with two horse heads above the beginning of a long, bumpy driveway.

Places to Eat

Thanks to Tarifa's many international visitors, you're guaranteed some variation from regular Spanish fare.

In Town Calle Sancho IV El Bravo has all manner of takeaway options. **Ali Baba** (*Calle Sancho IV El Bravo*), a popular place with benches and stand-up tables outside, serves up cheap, filling and tasty Arabic food made with lovely fresh ingredients by a German-speaking Syrian. Vegetarians can enjoy excellent falafel for €2.40; carnivores pay €2.70 for the kebabs. You can try the lot (*plato Ali Baba*) for €6. **Café Central** (*Calle Sancho IV El Bravo 8; breakfast €2.40-3.90*) has delicious *churros y chocolate* and a large range of breakfasts.

Mandrágora (☎ 956 68 12 91; *Calle Independencia 3; main dishes €7-11; closed Sun*), behind Iglesia San Mateo, is an intimate place with Andalucian/Arabic food. Delicious options include lamb with plums and almonds, couscous and falafel.

Bar El Sevilla (*Calle Inválidos 34*) has the best-value seafood in town. There's no name outside. Mixed fish and seafood fry-ups cost €1.35 for a generous tapa or €9.60 for a ración.

Restaurante Villanueva (*Avenida de Andalucía 11; lunch menú €6*), attached to the *hostal*, does a brisk trade with its lunch *menú*.

La Trattoría (☎ 956 68 22 25; *Paseo de la Alameda; pasta €6-7.50; meat mains from €10, pizzas €4.50-7.50*) is our current Tarifa Italian favourite. The food is great and the service excellent.

Souk (*Huerta del Rey 11; starters €4-6, mains €8-11*), dripping with Moroccan decorations, has terrific Moroccan-/Asian-inspired food. We enjoyed the *hojaldre de espinacas* (spinach pastry with feta cheese and spices) and the *Thai Rojo de verduras* (Thai vegetables in coconut).

Café Azul Bar (*Calle Batalla del Salado; breakfasts €3-6; open Semana Santa–Oct*) prepares the best breakfasts in town. We recommend the large muesli, fruit salad and yoghurt. There's good coffee, excellent juices and often Thai food at lunch time.

Cafetería El Paso (*Calle Batalla de Salado, breakfasts €2.25-4.20*) is a bakery-cum-cafeteria open long hours year-round. Toast, orange juice and coffee cost €3.30 but you can have something more substantial.

Along the Coast Most hotels and *hostales* up here have restaurants. The restaurant at **Hostal Arte-Vida** does a range of slightly fancy meat and fish dishes from €12 and there's always a vegetarian plate. Visit to sample the lovely ocean and Morocco views. The Hurricane Hotel's **Terrace Restaurant**, with the same views, is good for a medium-priced lunch (various salads, chicken, local fish and seafood, main dishes €6 to €8) or drinks. In the evenings the hotel's interior restaurant prepares creative meals, including very good salads (€6 to €8) such as salmon, avocado and grapefruit, and main dishes (€10 to €18) such as monkfish brochette with oregano or duck with raisins and port. **Cortijo Valdevaqueros** fills windsurfer stomachs with plates of chicken, salad, bread and condiments (€10). We like the cakes, perfect with tea or coffee!

Entertainment

Bodega de Casa Amarilla (*Calle Sancho IV El Bravo 9; open from 7.30pm daily, 1pm-4.30pm Thurs-Sun*) is a convivial bar/restaurant run by the Café Central family; it sometimes has live flamenco.

Bar Obaïnano (*Calle Nuestra Señora de la Luz*) serves fresh juices and exotic cocktails to cheerful background music.

Café Continental (*Paseo de la Alameda*) has low-key local live music on summer weekend nights and is a good tapas, drinks or coffee stop at any time.

Soul Café (*Calle Santísima Trinidad 9*), nearby, is a hip and popular bar run by travel-loving Italians. Stop by after 11pm, but not in winter when the owners are travelling.

In summer, a big Moroccan tent known as **La Jaima** (*Playa de los Lances; cover €9*) pops up on the beach near the edge of town. From 7pm to 10pm it's an Islamic-style tearoom (try the mint tea at sunset!) but, come midnight, it's a popular disco.

Far Out *(Carretera N-340; admission €6)*, just out of town, is a huge barn with a couple of bars, pool table, and raised platforms for dancers. The whole place jumps from 2am nightly throughout summer. Otherwise, it's open from midnight to 8am on Friday and Saturday nights.

Mesón Perulero *(Plaza San Hiscio 2)* has live flamenco from 10pm on Thursdays.

Getting There & Away

Bus From its base, 1½ blocks north of Avenida de Andalucía, **Comes** *(☎ 956 68 40 38; Calle Batalla del Salado)*, runs nine or more buses daily to Cádiz (1 hour 40 minutes) and Algeciras (30 minutes), seven to La Línea (40 minutes), three to Jerez de la Frontera (2½ hours), four to Seville (3½ hours) and two to Málaga (two hours). Two buses run to Facinas (except Sunday), and one to Barbate (40 minutes), Zahara de los Atunes (30 minutes) and Los Caños de Meca (except Saturday and Sunday; 50 minutes).

Car & Motorcycle Stop at the Mirador del Estrecho, about 7km out of Tarifa on the N-340 towards Algeciras, to take in magnificent views of the Strait of Gibraltar, the Mediterranean, the Atlantic and two continents. Beware of the frequent police speed trap in the 50km/h zone at Pelayo, a few kilometres further east.

Boat A fast ferry operated by **FRS** *(☎ 956 68 18 30; w www.frs.es)* runs between Tarifa and Tangier (passenger/car/motorcycle €21/69/21; 35 minutes one-way) from one to three times daily, with possibly more sailings in July and August. There is a daily sailing from Tarifa at 9am or 11.30am and from Tangier at 5pm or 6pm (Moroccan time). You can get details of the service at the harbour or at **Marruecotur** *(☎ 956 68 47 51; Avenida de la Constitución 5/6)*.

Warning: at the time of writing only travellers with EU passports or residence documents could board this ferry. So, if you're American, Australian and even Moroccan, without the right to live in Europe, you need to depart for Morocco from Algeciras or another port.

Getting Around

From March to October local buses run every 90 minutes from Tarifa up the coast to Punta Paloma. The travel agency **Speedlines** *(☎ 956 62 70 48; Calle Batalla del Salado 10)* will have the bus timetable. There's a stop at the bottom of the Paseo de la Alameda. Taxis (around €10) line up on Avenida de Andalucía near the Puerta de Jerez. You can hire bicycles from the Hurricane Hotel for €18 per day or from Speedlines for €12 per day.

The Southeast

PARQUE NATURAL LOS ALCORNOCALES

This large (1700 sq km) and beautiful natural park stretches 75km north from the Strait of Gibraltar to the border of the Parque Natural Sierra de Grazalema. It's a jumble of sometimes rolling, sometimes rugged hills of medium height, lying on major bird migration routes and much of it covered in Spain's most extensive cork oak woodlands *(alcornocales)*. The northern half of the park is generally more rugged.

Los Alcornocales is rich in natural, archaeological and historical interest, but little visited because it's hard to access and it lacks any major 'must-see' attractions – which makes it all the more appealing to travellers with the time and inclination to get away from the crowds and do a little exploring. There are plenty of walks and opportunities for other activities in the park, but you need your own wheels to make the most of it, as it's sparsely populated and public transport runs mostly along its fringes.

The best source of information on the park is the **Oficina del Parque** *(Park Office; ☎ 956 41 33 07 Mon-Fri, 956 41 32 28 Sat, Sun & holidays; e pn.lalcornocales@cma.junta -andalucia.es; Plaza San Jorge 1; open 9am-2pm Mon-Fri, 10am-1.30pm Sat & Sun)*, at the top of the remote white hill town of Alcalá de los Gazules on the western boundary of the park. If you should need a room in Alcalá, head down to **Hostal Pizarro** *(☎ 956 42 01 03; Paseo de la Playa s/n; singles/doubles with bathroom €15/27)*.

CÁDIZ PROVINCE

High-Fliers over the Strait of Gibraltar

At some point, keen bird-watchers in Andalucía will want to head for the Strait of Gibraltar, a key point of passage for raptors, storks and other migrators between Africa and Europe. In general, northward migrations occur between mid-February and early June, and southbound flights happen between late July and early November. When a westerly wind is blowing, Gibraltar itself is usually a good spot for seeing the birds. When the wind is calm or easterly, the Tarifa area (including the Mirador del Estrecho 7km east of the town) is usually better.

Soaring birds such as raptors, storks and vultures cross at the Strait of Gibraltar because they rely on thermals and updrafts, which don't happen over wider expanses of water. White storks sometimes congregate in flocks of up to 3000 to cross the strait (January and February northbound, July and August southbound).

The park also has two visitor centres, the **Centro de Visitantes Huerta Grande** (☎ 956 67 91 61), at Pelayo on the Tarifa–Algeciras road, and **Centro de Visitantes Cortes de la Frontera** (☎ 95 215 45 99; *Avenida de la Democracia s/n*) in the appealing village of Cortes de la Frontera, about 25km southwest of Ronda; and **information offices** at Benalup-Casas Viejas (☎ 956 42 41 29; *Calle Conciliar s/n*) and Medina Sidonia (☎ 956 41 24 04; *Plaza Iglesia Mayor*).

Towns such as Tarifa, Medina Sidonia, Vejer de la Frontera, Arcos de la Frontera and Grazalema are all possible bases for visiting the park. Another is **Jimena de la Frontera**, on the A-369 Algeciras-Ronda road on the park's eastern boundary. Jimena is a small town crowned by a fine **Muslim castle**, with a handful of **hostales**, and is served by train and bus from Algeciras and Ronda. The CA-3331 heading northwest from here will take you to **La Sauceda**, an abandoned village that's now the site of a recreational area and field education centre.

The La Sauceda area, actually a finger of Málaga province jutting into Cádiz, is beautiful country covered in cork and gall oaks, laurel, wild olives, rhododendrons and ferns. It was once a den of bandits and smugglers, and even guerrillas during the Spanish Civil War (during which the village was bombed by Franco's planes). Walking possibilities from here include the ascent of Aljibe (1091m), the park's highest peak, and nearby El Picacho (882m).

ALGECIRAS

postcode 11280 • pop 105,000

Algeciras, the major port linking Spain with Africa, is also an industrial town, a big fishing port and a centre for drug smuggling. Overall, it's unattractive and polluted but it's not without interest. Its proximity to Africa gives the port an air of excitement and the beautifying of the town centre with pedestrian streets and smart shops makes it now quite pleasant to walk around. A few pretty old buildings with wrought iron balconies remain and there are some good places to eat. During the summer the port is hectic with hundreds of thousands of Moroccans working in Europe who return home for summer holidays.

History

Algeciras was an important Roman port. Alfonso XI of Castile wrested it from the Merenids of Morocco in 1344 but later Mohammed V of Granada razed it to the ground. In 1704, Algeciras was repopulated by many of those who left Gibraltar after the British took it. During the Franco era, industry was developed.

Orientation

Algeciras is on the western side of the Bahía de Algeciras, opposite Gibraltar. Avenida Virgen del Carmen runs north to south along the seafront, becoming Avenida de la Marina around the entrance to the port. From here Calle Juan de la Cierva (becoming Calle San Bernardo) runs inland beside

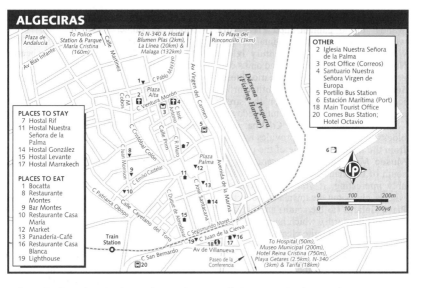

ALGECIRAS

Plaza de Andalucía

To Police Station & Parque María Cristina (160m)

To N-340 & Hostal Blumen Plas (2km), La Línea (20km) & Malaga (132km)

To Playa del Rinconcillo (3km)

Av Blas Infante

Calle Martínez

Av Virgen del Carmen

Dársena Pesquera (Fishing Harbour)

OTHER
2 Iglesia Nuestra Señora de la Palma
3 Post Office (Correos)
4 Santuario Nuestra Señora Virgen de Europa
5 Portillo Bus Station
6 Estación Marítima (Port)
18 Main Tourist Office
20 Comes Bus Station; Hotel Octavio

C Pablo

C M Cobos

Plaza Alta

C Ventura Morón

C José Antonio

PLACES TO STAY
7 Hostal Rif
11 Hostal Nuestra Señora de la Palma
14 Hostal González
15 Hostal Levante
17 Hostal Marrakech

PLACES TO EAT
1 Bocatta
8 Restaurante Montes
9 Bar Montes
10 Restaurante Casa María
12 Market
13 Panadería-Café
16 Restaurante Casa Blanca
19 Lighthouse

C Cristóbal Colón

C Juan Morrison

C Emilio Castelar

C Patrocio Obispo

Calle Cayetano del Toro

Duque de Almodóvar

C R Muro

Calle Prim

Plaza Palma

C José Santacana

Avenida de la Marina

Plaza de la Cierva

C Segismundo Moret

Train Station

C San Bernardo

Av de Villanueva

Paseo de la Conferencia

To Hospital (50m), Museo Municipal (200m), Hotel Reina Cristina (750m), Playa Getares (2.5km), N-340 (3km) & Tarifa (18km)

0   100   200m
0   100   200yd

a disused rail track to the Comes bus station (about 350m) and the train station (400m). The central square, Plaza Alta, is a couple of blocks inland from Avenida Virgen del Carmen. Plaza Palma, with a bustling daily market (except Sunday), is one block west of Avenida de la Marina.

Information
Tourist Office The English-speaking main tourist office (☎ 956 57 26 36; Calle Juan de la Cierva s/n; open 9am-2pm Mon-Fri) is a block inland from Avenida de la Marina. Inside there's a useful message board.

Money If you're travelling to Morocco and arriving late at night you should have some dirham with you. Exchange rates for buying dirham are better at the banks than at travel agencies. There are banks and ATMs on Avenida Virgen del Carmen and around Plaza Alta, plus a couple of ATMs inside the port.

Post & Communications The post office (Calle José Antonio) is just south of Plaza Alta. There are telephones in the port, on Avenida de la Marina, near the market and at the train station.

Left Luggage In the port, luggage storage (€1.20 to €1.80) is available from 7am to 9.30pm. Bags need to be secured. If you have valuables there are lockers nearby (€2.40). Both the Comes and the smaller Portillo/Alsina Graells bus stations have luggage storage.

Medical Services & Emergency The Hospital Cruz Roja (☎ 956 65 37 57; Paseo de la Conferencia s/n) is central, located on the southern extension of Avenida de la Marina.

The Policía Nacional (☎ 956 66 04 00; Avenida de las Fuerzas Armadas 6) are next to Parque de María Cristina, northwest of the town centre. For an ambulance you can dial ☎ 956 66 41 51.

Dangers & Annoyances Keep your wits about you in the port, bus terminal and market and walk purposefully when moving between the Comes and Portillo bus stations in the evening. If you arrive by car and want to leave your vehicle in Algeciras, your most secure bet is the multistorey car park inside the port (€12 per 24 hours).

Things to See & Do

Wander up to palm-fringed **Plaza Alta**, which has a lovely tiled fountain. On its western side is the 18th-century **Iglesia Nuestra Señora de la Palma** and on its eastern side the 17th-century **Santuario Nuestra Señora Virgen de Europa**, both worth a look. Some of the houses on the streets around here are delightfully tumbledown.

Leafy **Parque de María Cristina**, a few blocks to the north, also provides a change from the hustle and bustle of the port. The **Museo Municipal** (*Calle Nicaragua*), just south of the main tourist office, is reasonably interesting. If you've got your own wheels, check out the town's two beaches – **Playa Getares** (to the south) and **Playa del Rinconcillo** (north), which have reasonable sand and are kept quite clean.

Special Events

The *feria* happens in the last week of June. On 15 August the town honours its patroness in the Fiesta del Virgen de la Palma.

Places to Stay

There's loads of budget accommodation in the streets behind Avenida de la Marina, but market traffic in the small hours makes sleep difficult. If it's not too hot, try for an interior room.

Hostal Rif (☎ 956 65 49 53; *Calle Rafael de Muro 11; per person €8.50*) has simple rooms with shared bathrooms in an old house with beautiful tilework. There's a rooftop for relaxing.

Hostal González (☎ 956 65 28 43; *Calle José Santacana 7; singles/doubles with bathroom €15/24*) has good, clean rooms.

Hostal Nuestra Señora de la Palma (☎ 956 63 24 81; *Plaza Palma 12; €14 per person*), near the market, has 25 comfortable rooms with bathroom and TV.

Hostal Levante (☎ 956 65 15 05; *Calle Duque de Almodóvar 21; singles/doubles with shower €10/17*) is a little removed from the thick of things; rooms are reasonable, though the corridors are a bit musty and management offhand.

Hostal Marrakech (☎ 956 57 34 74; *Calle Juan de la Cierva 5; singles/doubles €18/24*)

is a clean and secure place run by a helpful Moroccan couple.

Hostal Blumen Plas (☎ 956 63 16 75; *N-340 Km 108; doubles €39*), a cheerful place on the main road in the northwest of town, is a good choice if you want to stay out of the town centre.

Hotel Octavio (☎ 956 65 27 00; *Calle San Bernardo 1; singles/doubles €58/77*) is a big step up in price, despite its unsalubrious location above the Comes bus station.

Hotel Reina Cristina (☎ 956 60 26 22; *Paseo de la Conferencia s/n; doubles €155*), a 10-minute walk south of the port, is an old colonial-style hotel with 160 rooms set amid tropical gardens. This hotel, a suitable place to observe sea traffic in the Strait of Gibraltar, was a haunt of spies in WWII.

Places to Eat

The city **market** has a wonderful array of fresh fruit, vegetables, hams and cheese – perfect for packing a picnic lunch. The excellent **Panadería-Café** (*Calle José Santacana*), situated near the market, is good for breakfast.

Plaza Alta has a couple of sidewalk cafés and restaurants. **Bocatta** (*Plaza Alta 5; bocadillos €2.40*) is part of a reliable chain specialising in good fresh snacks. English-speaking Christians run the friendly little **Lighthouse** (*Calle Juan de la Cierva*), 200m east of the railway station, with decent breakfasts and helpful tourist advice.

Restaurante Casa Blanca (*Calle Juan de la Cierva 1; menú €6*), near the tourist office, has a *menú* of three courses, bread and soft drink; other options, including Moroccan food, are moderately priced and the tapas are good and fresh.

Bar Montes (*Calle Emilio Castelar 36*), several blocks northwest of the main tourist office, is a good tapas bar.

Restaurante Montes (☎ 956 65 42 07; *Calle Juan Morrison 27; menú €7.20*), around the corner from Bar Montes and slightly flashier, has a hugely popular lunch *menú* of three courses, bread and wine, and an à la carte seafood list.

Restaurante Casa María (☎ 956 65 47 02; *Calle Emilio Castelar 53; lunch menú €7,*

Benaocaz, perched amid limestone country in the Parque Natural Sierra de Grazalema, Cádiz province

Jerez de la Frontera is a hotbed of flamenco

The running of the pigs, Huelva province

Three-hundred-year-old barrels at González Byass, one of the biggest sherry bodegas in Cádiz province

Cathedral, Jerez de la Frontera, Cádiz

A warm Andalucian smile

The old town of Arcos de la Frontera, Cádiz

The Rock of Gibraltar looms over Spain's most southerly coast

mains €6.20-14.10), diagonally opposite Bar Montes, is another popular lunch place, with more choice. À la carte choices are slightly elaborate: fish dishes come with various sauces and there are steaks and roast lamb.

Tea on the terrace at the Hotel Reina Cristina is pleasant.

Entertainment
In the summer, flamenco, rock and other concerts happen at some of the more attractive spots in town – Parque de María Cristina, Plaza de Andalucía, the Plaza de Toros and Playa Rinconcillo. The tourist office has a list of events.

Getting There & Away
The daily paper *Europa Sur* has up-to-date transport arrival and departure details.

Bus There are **Comes** (☎ 956 65 34 56; *Calle San Bernardo)* buses for La Línea every 45 minutes from 7am to 9.30pm Monday to Saturday, but only eight on Sundays. Other daily buses include seven to Tarifa (30 minutes), at least 10 to Cádiz (€7.90, 2¼ hours), five to Seville (€13.20, 3¼ hours), two to Jimena de la Frontera (except Sunday; 30 minutes), and four to Madrid (€21.20, six to seven hours). There's one bus daily (except Sunday) to Zahara de los Atunes (one hour) and Barbate (€4, one hour 10 minutes), and one bus to Ronda (two to three hours) Monday to Friday.

Portillo & Alsina Graells (☎ 956 65 10 55; *Avenida Virgen del Carmen 15)* operates six direct buses daily to Málaga (€8.70, 1¾ hours), four to Granada (€16.25, 3½ hours) and two to Jaén (€21.70, five hours). Several more buses daily to Málaga (three hours) stop at Estepona, Marbella, Fuengirola and Torremolinos.

Bacoma/Alsa/Enatcar (☎ 902 42 22 42), inside the port, runs up to four services daily to Murcia, Alicante, Valencia and Barcelona. This company also runs buses to Portugal, France, Germany and Holland.

Train From the **station** (☎ 956 63 02 02), adjacent to Calle San Bernardo, two direct trains run daily to/from Madrid (€32 to €58, six or 11 hours) and three to/from Granada (€15.10, four hours). All trains pass through Ronda (€5.65 to €10.50, 1¾ hours) and Bobadilla, taking in some spectacular scenery en route. At Bobadilla you can change for Málaga, Córdoba and Seville plus more trains to Granada and Madrid.

Boat Trasmediterránea (☎ 956 58 34 00, 902 45 46 45; ⓦ *www.trasmediterranea.es)*, **EuroFerrys** (☎ 956 65 11 78; ⓦ *www.euro ferrys.com)* and other companies operate frequent daily passenger and vehicle ferries to/from Tangier and Ceuta, the Spanish enclave on the Moroccan coast. Usually at least 20 to 25 sailings per day go to Tangier and 15 to 20 to Ceuta. From mid-June to September there are ferries almost round the clock to cater for the Moroccan migration – you may have to queue for up to three hours. Buy your ticket in the port or at the agencies on Avenida de la Marina: prices are the same everywhere.

To Tangier, on a ferry taking 2½ hours, one-way fares for passenger/car/motorcycle over 500cc are €23.30/72/22.20.

To Ceuta, a fast ferry takes 35 minutes. One-way fares for passenger/car/motorcycle over 500cc are €21/60.70/16.60. **Buquebus** (☎ 902 41 42 42) also does Algeciras–Ceuta in 35 minutes, six times daily. One-way fares for passenger/car/motorcycle are €23.50/59.50/15.50. A return passenger fare is €42.

LA LÍNEA DE LA CONCEPCIÓN
postcode 11300 • pop 60,500
La Línea, 20km east of Algeciras, round the bay, is the unavoidable stepping stone to Gibraltar. The city was built in 1870 in response to the British expansion around the rock of Gibraltar. A left turn as you exit La Línea's bus station will bring you out on Avenida 20 de Abril, which runs the 300m or so between the town's main square, Plaza de la Constitución, and the Gibraltar border. There's a **regional tourist office** (☎ 956 76 99 50; *open 9am-7pm Mon-Sat May-Sept; 9am-3pm Oct-Apr)* on the corner of the square. At the opposite end of Avenida 20 de Abril facing the border is the **municipal tourist office** (☎ 956 17 19 98; *Avenida Príncipe Felipe s/n)*.

CÁDIZ PROVINCE

Things to See & Do

La Línea's city centre is being improved and it has a couple of museums worth looking at. The **Museo del Istmo** *(Plaza de la Constitución)* has archaeological finds, paintings, sculptures and changing exhibitions. **Museo Cruz Herrera** *(Calle Doctor Villar)*, opposite the palm-lined Plaza Fariñas, exhibits the work of José Cruz Herrera, a successful early-20th-century painter from La Línea. His subjects were often beautiful Andalucian women and he lived and worked for a time in Morocco, both reflected in the paintings on display.

You can also visit bunkers opposite Gibraltar dating from WWII.

Places to Stay & Eat

Pensión La Perla *(☎ 956 76 95 13; Calle Clavel 10; singles/doubles €12/21)*, two blocks north of Plaza de la Constitución, has nine clean, spacious yellow and white-trimmed rooms.

Hostal La Campana *(☎ 956 17 30 59; Calle Carboneros 3; singles/doubles €36/42)*, just off the western side of Plaza de la Constitución, has decent rooms with bathroom and TV. Its **restaurant** does a three-course *menú* for €5.75.

Hostal La Esteponera *(☎ 956 17 66 68; Calle Carteya 10; doubles with/without bathroom €21/15)* is located five blocks west of La Perla.

Cafetería Okay *(Calle Real 23)*, just off the northwestern corner of Plaza de la Constitución, has a good bakery and does breakfasts. Later in the day, check out Plaza del Pintor Cruz Herrera, with a pretty tiled fountain and orange trees, where there are more places to eat and drink.

Getting There & Away

Bus Buses run about every 30 minutes to/from Algeciras (€1.50, 30 minutes). Four buses daily go to Málaga (€8, 2½ hours), stopping in Marbella, Fuengirola and Torremolinos; five to Tarifa (€2.85, 45 minutes) and Cádiz (€10, 2½ hours); three to Seville (€16.50, four hours); and two to Granada (€16, four hours). Eight buses daily run to Estepona (€2.80). There's a bus at 1.30pm Monday to Friday for Jimena de la Frontera (€3.25).

Car & Motorcycle Owing to the usually long vehicle queues at the Gibraltar border, many visitors to Gibraltar opt to park in La Línea then walk across the border. Parking meters in La Línea cost €0.90 for one hour or €4.50 for six hours and are free from 10.30pm until 9am Monday to Friday and from 2pm Saturday until 9am Monday. Meters are plentiful on Avenida Príncipe Felipe opposite the frontier. The underground Parking Fo Cona, just off Avenida 20 de Abril, charges €1/6.30 per hour/day.

Gibraltar

Looming like some great ship off Spain's most southerly coast, the British colony of Gibraltar is such a fascinating mix of curiosities that a visit here can hardly fail to interest even the most jaded traveller.

The mere sight of the Rock's awesome northeastern face is compelling. A vast limestone ridge that rises to 426m, with sheer cliffs on its northern and eastern sides, Gibraltar is 5km long, and 1.6km across at its widest point. To the ancient Greeks and Romans, Gibraltar was one of the two Pillars of Hercules, set up by the mythical hero to mark the edge of the known world. (The other pillar is the coastal mountain Jebel Musa in Morocco, 25km south across the stormy waters of the Strait of Gibraltar.)

History

About 50,000 years ago Gibraltar was home to Neanderthal *Homo sapiens*, as skulls found there in 1848 and 1928 testify. The skull discovered in 1848 was that of a female; this find predated the discovery of a male skull in Germany's Neander Valley by eight years. (The latter discovery inspired the anthropological term 'Neanderthal Man', although 'Gibraltar Woman' surely had the fairer claim.)

Phoenicians and ancient Greeks left traces here, but Gibraltar really entered the history books in AD 711 when Tariq ibn Ziyad, the Muslim governor of Tangier, made it the initial bridgehead for the Islamic invasion of the Iberian Peninsula, landing with an army of some 10,000 men. The name Gibraltar is derived from Jebel Tariq (Tariq's Mountain).

The Almohad Muslims founded a town here in 1159 and Muslims held it most of the time until Castile (Castilla in Spanish) wrested it from them in 1462. Then in 1704 an Anglo-Dutch fleet captured Gibraltar during the War of the Spanish Succession. Spain ceded the Rock of Gibraltar to Britain by the Treaty of Utrecht in 1713, but didn't finally give up military attempts to regain it

Highlights

- Go on a dolphin-watching trip on the Bahía de Algeciras
- Explore the caves, paths and old military installations of the Upper Rock Nature Reserve and meet the Gibraltar apes along the way
- Take a trip on the cable car for a bird's eye view of the Bahía de Algeciras
- Relax in the leafy quiet of the Alameda Botanical Gardens
- Branch out from Main St and explore Gibraltar town's hidden corners

until the failure of the Great Siege of 1779–83. Britain developed it into an important naval base, and during WWII, when much of the local population was evacuated to Britain, Madeira and Jamaica, Gibraltar became a base for allied landings in North Africa. The British garrison was withdrawn in the early 1990s but the British navy continues to use Gibraltar's facilities.

Spain wants Gibraltar back. During the Franco period Gibraltar was a constant point of contention between Spain and Britain. Franco closed the Spain-Gibraltar border in 1967 and it was not reopened until 1985, 10 years after his death. The result was the complete severing of cross-border relationships and the seemingly irrevocable polarisation of attitudes and sentiments in Gibraltar and Spain. In a 1969 referendum, Gibraltarians voted 12,138 to 44 in favour of British rather than Spanish sovereignty. That year a new constitution committed Britain to respecting Gibraltarians' wishes over sovereignty, and gave Gibraltar domestic self-government and its own parliament, the House of Assembly.

Government & Politics

Gibraltar's last two elections (1996 and 2000) have been won by the centre-right Gibraltar Social Democrat Party, led by Peter Caruana. The main opposition is the Gibraltar Socialist Labour Party, led by Joe Bossano. Caruana has shown himself willing to talk with Spain about Gibraltar's future but fiercely opposes any concessions over sovereignty.

When Spain wants to exert pressure on Gibraltar, it employs such methods as extra-thorough customs and immigration procedures, which cause hours-long delays at the border. Spain has proposed a period of joint British-Spanish sovereignty leading to Gibraltar eventually becoming the 18th Spanish region, with greater autonomy than any of the others.

Tourism, the port and financial services are the mainstays of Gibraltar's economy. Spanish police complain that Gibraltar, with more than 70,000 domiciled companies, is a centre for the laundering of illicit money from organised crime and tax evasion elsewhere in Europe. Much of this money, it's said, is invested in property in southern Spain. Caruana does not deny that Gibraltar is a tax haven but says it is a well-supervised one. Another problem, cigarette smuggling from Gibraltar into Spain, seems to have diminished under the Caruana government.

Successive British governments have refused to give way over Gibraltar's sovereignty, but at the European Council's Barcelona Summit of March 2002, the 15 member states of the European Union (EU) backed Britain and Spain's agreement to share sovereignty over Gibraltar. Gibraltar reacted angrily at what it saw as Europe-wide support for a nonrepresentative deal over the Rock allegedly being set up by Britain's Prime Minister Tony Blair and his Spanish counterpart José María Aznar. Gibraltarians saw the deal as Britain offering Spain 'in-principle' sovereignty concessions over the colony that breached the 1969 constitutional commitment.

In response, an estimated 20,000 Gibraltarians answered Peter Caruana's call to take to the streets on 18 March 2002 in a peaceful but passionate demonstration of their fierce commitment to retaining their British nationality. The rallying cry was: 'No in-principle concessions against our wishes. Yes to reasonable dialogue'. Gibraltarians rejected, with contempt, any suggestion that they might be bought off with a suggested £35 million cash sweetener aimed at regenerating the Rock and the La Línea hinterland as a joint economic area. Gibraltar subsequently gave a hostile reception to British Foreign Secretary Jack Straw and a warm one to anti-shared-sovereignty UK Conservative Party leader Iain Duncan Smith. By mid-2002 it appeared that a UK-Spain deal was foundering in any case, over the issue of control of Gibraltar's naval base and military airfield.

In early September 2002 the government of Gibraltar announced the staging, on 7 November 2002, of a referendum that would ask its people whether or not Britain should share sovereignty with Spain over Gibraltar. The result of the referendum was expected to be a resounding rejection of the idea by the people of Gibraltar.

Britain and Spain both said that they would not recognise the referendum. The British government reiterated its position that it would not relinquish Gibraltar's status against local wishes, but insisted that it would not recognise, as legitimate, any referendum not called by the UK government.

Yet the resolution of this remarkable territorial anomaly probably lies in a political-economic compromise; one that brings mutual benefits to Gibraltar and Spain while satisfying the passionate desire of Gibraltarians to retain British citizenship under British sovereignty, and the territorial sensitivity of the Spanish.

Population & People
Of Gibraltar's 27,000 civilian population, about 77% are classed as Gibraltarians, 14% British and 9% are of other nationalities. The Gibraltarians are of mixed Genoese, Jewish, Spanish and British ancestry, the Genoese element coming from Genoese ship repairers brought here by the British in the 18th century. A substantial percentage of those of other nationalities are Moroccans, many of whom are on short-term work contracts.

Language
Gibraltarians speak English, Spanish and a curiously accented, sing-song mix of the two, slipping back and forth from one to the other, often in mid-sentence. Signs are in English.

Orientation & Information
To reach Gibraltar by land you must pass through the Spanish frontier town of La Línea de la Concepción (see the Cádiz Province chapter). Just south of the border, the road crosses the runway of Gibraltar airport, which stretches east to west across the neck of the peninsula. The town and harbours of Gibraltar lie along the Rock's less-steep western side, facing the Bahía de Algeciras (or the Bay of Gibraltar).

Tourist Offices The **Gibraltar Tourist Board** has several very helpful information offices with plenty of free information sheets and brochures. The main office (☎ 45000, 74950; ⓦ www.gibraltar.gov.uk; open 9am-5.30pm Mon-Fri) is in Duke of Kent House, Cathedral Square. Others are at Grand Casemates Square (☎ 50762; open 9am-5.30pm Mon-Fri, 10am-4pm Sat, Sun & public holidays); in the airport arrivals hall (☎ 73026; open Mon-Fri, for lunch-time flights only); and at the cruise-ship terminal (☎ 47670; open only when a cruise liner is in port). Another office (☎ 78198; open 9am-4.30pm Mon-Fri, 10am-3pm Sat) is at the coach terminus on Waterport Wharf Rd. A new office at the border was due to open in 2002.

Foreign Consulates Eleven countries, mostly European, have consulates in Gibraltar. Tourist offices have lists of these.

Visas & Documents To enter Gibraltar you need a passport or, for those EU nationalities that possess them, an identity card. Australia, Canada, EU, Israel, New Zealand, Singapore, South Africa and USA passport-holders are among those who do not need visas for Gibraltar. For further information you can contact Gibraltar's **Immigration Department** (☎ 71543).

Those who need visas for Spain should have at least a double-entry Spanish visa so that they can return to Spain from Gibraltar. Passports are not always checked when you enter Spain from Gibraltar but you should be prepared for such checks.

Money The currencies in Gibraltar are the Gibraltar pound and the pound sterling, which are interchangeable. You can use euros (except in pay phones and post offices) but you'll get a better value if you convert them into pounds. Exchange rates for buying euros are a bit better than in Spain. You can't use Gibraltar money outside Gibraltar, so it's worth requesting change in British coins and changing any unspent Gibraltar pounds before you leave.

Banks are generally open between 9am and 3.30pm Monday to Friday. There are several on Main St. There are also exchange offices, which are open longer hours. American Express (AmEx) is represented by **Bland Travel** (☎ 77012; ⓔ henry@bland.gi; 81 Irish Town).

Post & Communications The main **post office** (☎ 75714; 104 Main St) is open from 9am to 2.15pm Monday to Friday and from 10am to 1pm Saturday mid-June to mid-September. For the rest of the year, it's open from 9am to 4.30pm Monday to Friday and 10am to 1pm Saturday.

To phone Gibraltar from Spain, precede the five-digit local number with the code ☎ 9567; from other countries dial the international access code, then ☎ 350 (Gibraltar's country code) and the local number.

In Gibraltar you can make international as well as local calls from street pay phones. To phone Spain, just dial the nine-digit number. To phone other countries dial the

GIBRALTAR

international access code (☎ 00), then the country code, area code and number.

The **General Internet Business Centre** (☎ *44227; 36 Governor's St; open 10am-10pm Tues-Sat, noon-9pm Sun & Mon)* is an Internet place that charges £3 an hour, although you can spread the time over 15 days.

Digital Resources A useful Gibraltar-specific website is the Gibraltar government–maintained site, W www.gibraltar.gov.uk, and W www.gibraltar.gi.

Bookshops Two good places to stock up on English-language reading material are **Bell Books** *(11 Bell Lane)* and **Gibraltar Bookshop** *(300 Main St)*.

Medical Services & Emergency There are 24-hour emergency facilities at **St Bernard's Hospital** *(☎ 79700; Hospital Hill)*. There's also a **health centre** *(☎ 72355, 77003; Grand Casemates Square)*. The **police station** *(☎ 72500; Rosia Rd)* is in the south of the town at New Mole House, but there's a more central station *(☎ 120 Irish Town)*. The police wear British uniforms. In an emergency you can call ☎ 199 for the police or an ambulance.

Electricity Electric current is the same as in Britain, 220V or 240V, with plugs of three flat pins.

Public Holidays Gibraltar observes the following public holidays:

New Year's Day 1 January
Commonwealth Day March – second Monday
Good Friday 18 April 2003, 9 April 2004
Easter Monday 21 April 2003, 12 April 2004
May Day 1 May
Spring Bank Holiday May – last Monday
Queen's Birthday June – Monday after the second Saturday
Late Summer Bank Holiday August – last Monday
Gibraltar National Day 10 September
Christmas/Boxing Day 25/26 December

Work Casual work is not easy to find in Gibraltar, but information on job opportunities can be obtained from the **Employment**

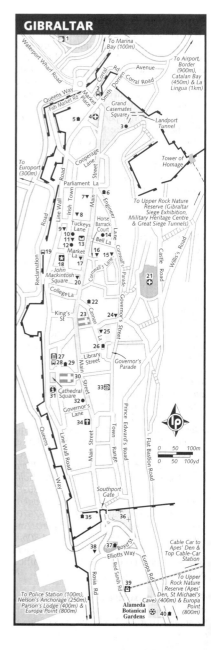

GIBRALTAR

PLACES TO STAY		16	Viceroy of India	18	Police Station
5	Emile Youth Hostel	17	The English Tea Room	19	Bus No 10
6	Continental Hotel	20	The Piazza	21	St Bernard's Hospital
22	Cannon Hotel	24	Three Roses Bar	23	Cathedral of St Mary the
26	Eliott Hotel	25	Cannon Bar		Crowned
29	Bristol Hotel	38	Piccadilly Gardens Bar	27	Gibraltar Museum
35	Toc H Hostel			28	Bus No 3
37	Queen's Hotel	**OTHER**		30	Cathedral of the Holy Trinity
40	Rock Hotel	1	Watergardens Quay	31	Gibraltar Tourist Board Main
		2	Bus No 9		Office
PLACES TO EAT		3	Gibraltar Crystal	32	Gibraltar Bookshop
7	Maxi Manger	4	Health Centre	33	General Internet Business
8	House of Sacarello	10	Tower & Co		Centre
9	The Clipper	12	Bland Travel	34	King's Chapel
11	Corks Wine Bar	13	Main Post Office	36	Trafalgar Cemetery
15	Kerry's Restaurant	14	Bell Books	39	Lower Cable-Car Station

and Training Board (☎ 74999; Rosia Rd). Except for Palma de Mallorca, Gibraltar is better than anywhere in Spain for picking up unpaid yacht berths. Ask around at Marina Bay harbour.

The Town

Gibraltar's town centre generates an engaging mid-morning Mediterranean buzz, although there is an emphatically British flavour about the shops, pubs and restaurants that line either side of the pedestrianised Main St. A Spanish lilt in the air and the fairly regular sight of Moroccans in traditional dress are reminders also that this is still Mediterranean Europe and that the Rock was a Muslim stronghold for over seven centuries and a Spanish one for 240 years. Most Islamic and Spanish buildings were destroyed in 18th-century sieges and street names reflect 300 years of British military and bureaucratic presence. The entire Rock bristles with the often antique remnants of British fortifications, gates and gun emplacements; the *Guided Tour of Gibraltar* booklet by TJ Finlayson is rewarding if you want to delve into details of the British heritage.

The **Gibraltar Museum** (Bomb House Lane; adult/child under 12 £2/1; open 10am-6pm Mon-Fri, 10am-2pm Sat) contains very worthwhile historical, architectural and military displays and goes back to prehistoric times. Highlights include a well-preserved Muslim bathhouse, and a detailed model of the Rock made in the 1860s by British officers.

The nearby Anglican **Cathedral of the Holy Trinity** was built in the 1820s and 1830s. The Catholic **Cathedral of St Mary the Crowned** (Main St) stands on the site of Muslim Gibraltar's chief mosque. The **King's Chapel** (Main St) is part of a 16th-century Franciscan convent, which is now the governor's residence. Admission to all three of these places is free. Donations are appreciated.

Many of the graves in the **Trafalgar Cemetery**, just south of Southport Gate, are of British sailors who died at Gibraltar after the Battle of Trafalgar (1805). Located a short distance south of here are the **Alameda Botanical Gardens** (admission free; open 8am-sunset daily), entered from Europa Rd. Just over 250m farther south, **Nelson's Anchorage** (Rosia Rd; admission free; open 9.30am-5pm Mon-Sat) contains a 100-ton Victorian supergun, made in Britain in 1870, and overlooks Rosia Bay, where Nelson's body was brought ashore from HMS *Victory* – in a rum barrel, legend has it – after the Battle of Trafalgar. A little farther south on Rosia Rd is **Parson's Lodge** (adult/child £1/50p; open 10am-6pm Mon-Fri), a gun battery, atop a 40m cliff. Beneath the gun emplacements is a labyrinth of tunnels with former ammunition stores and living quarters.

GIBRALTAR

Europa Point

The southern tip of Gibraltar is known as Europa Point. It has a lighthouse, the Christian Shrine of Our Lady of Europe and the Mosque of the Custodian of the Two Holy Mosques. The latter was opened in 1997 and is said to be the largest mosque to be located in a non-Islamic country. Call ☎ 47693 for information on current opening hours.

Upper Rock Nature Reserve

Most of the upper parts of the Rock, starting just above the town, are a nature reserve with spectacular views, a web of quiet roads and pathways, and several interesting spots to visit. Tickets for the Upper Rock Nature Reserve *(adult/child/vehicle £7/4/1.50, pedestrians excluding attractions £2; open 9.30am-7pm daily, last visit 6.30pm)* include entry to St Michael's Cave, the Apes' Den, the Great Siege Tunnels, the Military Heritage Centre, the Tower of Homage and the 'Gibraltar: A City Under Siege' exhibition. The upper Rock is home to 600 plant species and is ideal for observing the migrations of birds between Europe and Africa (see the boxed text 'High-Fliers over the Strait of Gibraltar' in the Cádiz Province chapter).

The upper Rock's most famous inhabitants are Gibraltar's colony of Barbary macaques, the only wild primates (apart from *Homo sapiens*) in Europe. Some of these hang around the **Apes' Den** near the middle cable-car station; others can often be seen at the top cable-car station and Great Siege Tunnels. Legend has it that when the monkeys (which may have been introduced from North Africa in the 18th century) disappear from Gibraltar, so will the British. When numbers were at a low ebb during WWII, the British brought in simian reinforcements from Africa. Recently their numbers have been increasing rapidly and a range of control measures from contraceptive implants to 'repatriation' to North Africa have been considered.

The cable car provides fine views over the Bahía de Algeciras. From the top cable-car station, there are views as far as Morocco in decent weather. You can also look down the sheer precipices of the Rock's eastern side to the biggest of the old water catchments, which channelled rain into underground reservoirs. Today these have been replaced by desalination plants.

About 15 minutes' walk south down St Michael's Rd from the top cable-car station, O'Hara's Rd leads up to the left to **O'Hara's Battery**, an emplacement of big guns on the Rock's summit. Just by the gate is the top of the Mediterranean Steps (see the boxed text).

St Michael's Cave, a few minutes farther down St Michael's Rd (or 20 minutes up from the Apes' Den), is a big natural grotto with fine stalagmites and stalactites. It was once home to Neolithic inhabitants of the Rock. Today, apart from attracting tourists in droves, it's used for concerts, plays and even fashion shows. There's a café just above the entrance.

About 30 minutes' walk north (downhill) from the top cable-car station is Princess Caroline's Battery, housing the **Military Heritage Centre**. From here one road leads down to the Princess Royal Battery – more gun emplacements – while another leads up to the **Great Siege Tunnels** (or Upper Galleries). These impressive galleries were hewn out of the Rock by the British during the siege of 1779–83 to provide gun emplacements. They constitute only a tiny proportion of more than 70km of tunnels and galleries in the Rock, most of which are off limits to the public. General Eisenhower had an office in one such tunnel during WWII.

On Willis's Rd, the way down to the town from Princess Caroline's Battery, you'll find the **'Gibraltar: A City Under Siege' exhibition**, in the first British building on the Rock (originally an ammunition store), and the **Tower of Homage**, the remains of Gibraltar's Muslim castle built in 1333.

Dolphins

The Bahía de Algeciras has a sizable year-round population of dolphins and at least six boats run dolphin-spotting trips. From about April to September most boats make two or more daily trips; at other times of year there's usually at least one in daily operation. Most of the boats go from Watergardens Quay or

The Mediterranean Steps

For the fit and agile, one of the best ways to climb the upper Rock is via the Mediterranean Steps, a terrific two-hour clamber up the Rock's eastern face along paths that zig-zag between limestone cliffs and through a lushly vegetated landscape that smacks of a semi-wild Muslim garden, and a bird reserve. The views are stupendous. The paths are linked by sections of steps and the final, upper section leads to O'Hara's Battery, the Rock's highest point. The Mediterranean Steps date from the late-18th century and connect a series of now-ruined gun placements. The intermittent flights of steps are broken in places, but not dangerously so, although a descent of the route from O'Hara's Battery can be uncomfortable and is not recommended. The way up is the better option; it is more strenuous, but it is not daunting for an average fit person and nowhere is the route exposed, nor does it traverse dangerous ground. The Mediterranean Steps path start at Jew's Gate, the entranceway to the Upper Rock Nature Reserve. Jew's Gate can be reached on foot, or by taxi, up Engineer Rd. There is a tumbledown sign, indicating the start of the path, down to the left of the single-storey building behind Jew's Gate. The route is not overly difficult to follow, but you'd be advised to obtain from the tourist office a print-out that gives simple directions and that describes some of the wildlife along the way.

the adjacent Marina Bay, northwest of the town centre. Trips last about 2½ hours and the cost per adult ranges from £15 to £20. Children can go for about half price. You'll be unlucky if you don't get plenty of close-up dolphin contact, and you may even come across whales.

Two possibilities for trips are **Dolphin World** (☎ 54481000; Admiral's Walk; adult/child under 12 £16/8) and **Dolphin Safari** (☎ 71914; Marina Bay; adult/child under 12 £20/10; bookings by prior arrangement).

Organised Tours

Taxi drivers will take you on a 1½-hour 'Official Rock Tour' of Gibraltar's main sights for £7 per person (minimum four people) plus the cost of admission to the Upper Rock Nature Reserve. Most drivers are knowledgeable. Many travel agents run tours of the same sights for £11 to £12.50.

Bland Travel (☎ 77012), **Parodytur** (☎ 76070) and **Exchange Travel** (☎ 71101) offer guided day trips to Tangier for £45 including lunch (children £35).

Places to Stay

Emile Youth Hostel (☎/fax 51106, 57686000; Montagu Bastion, Line Wall Rd; dorm beds/singles/doubles £12/15/25) is a hostel with 43 places in single- to eight-

person rooms. Conditions are basic, and the eight-person dorms are a bit cramped. The breakfast, which is included in the price, is basic also. There are showers, a good-sized TV/sitting room and an outside patio.

Toc H Hostel (☎ 73431; dorm beds per night/week £6.50/25), a ramshackle, rather musty old place tucked into the city walls at the southern end of Line Wall Rd, is the cheapest place in town. The showers are cold, but you'll receive an old-fashioned, warm welcome.

Queen's Hotel (☎ 74000, fax 40030; e queenshotel@gibnynex.gi; 1 Boyd St; singles/doubles with shared bathroom £26/40, with bathroom or shower £40/50) has a restaurant, bar and games room. Discounts of 20% are offered to students and travellers under the age of 25. All rates include breakfast. Free parking is available.

Cannon Hotel (☎ 51711, fax 51789; e cannon@gibnet.gi; 9 Cannon Lane; singles/ doubles with shared bathroom £22.50/ 34.50, doubles with bathroom £42) also has decent rooms, each sharing a bathroom with one other room. Rates include an English breakfast.

Bristol Hotel (☎ 76800, fax 77613; e bristhtl@gibnet.gi; 10 Cathedral Square; singles/doubles without sea views £49/64, with sea views £53/69) has good-sized

GIBRALTAR

rooms, with TV and bathroom. Free parking is available.

Continental Hotel (☎ 76900, fax 41702; 1 Engineer Lane; singles/doubles with air-con £42/55) is cosier than the Bristol and rates include a continental breakfast.

Gibraltar has two luxury hotels with over 100 rooms each:

Eliott Hotel (☎ 70500, fax 70243; e eliott@gibnet.gi; 2 Governor's Parade; rooms £165-220, suites £200-420) is centrally placed, but is in a leafy square, and has a good restaurant and pool. Free parking is available.

Rock Hotel (☎ 73000, fax 73513; e rock hotel@gibnynex.gi; 3 Europa Rd; singles & doubles with/without balcony £165/160) is higher up the west side of the Rock and boasts such past guests as Winston Churchill and Noel Coward. The lavish service includes bathrobes, CD players and free parking.

If you feel daunted by Gibraltar's prices, there are some economical options in the Spanish frontier town of La Línea (see the Cádiz Province chapter for details).

Places to Eat

Most of the many pubs in town do typical British pub meals.

The Clipper (☎ 79791; 78B Irish Town; mains £4.50-5.25) is one of the best and busiest; it has a varied menu, with generous servings of fish and chips and lasagne, and Sunday roast dinner for £5.95. Weekend live-music sessions are promised for 2003.

Corks Wine Bar (☎ 75566; 79 Irish Town; lunch £5.50) is another big, lively place that does tasty baguettes for £2.95 to £3.75.

Three Roses Bar (☎ 51614; 60 Governor's St; breakfast £3.50) does a hefty breakfast of two eggs, sausage, bacon, fried bread, beans, tomato and mushrooms – but it's not for early risers, as it opens at 11am. This is Gibraltar's unofficial 'Scottish Embassy', with Scottish dishes a speciality.

Cannon Bar (☎ 77288; 27 Cannon Lane; mains around £4.75) is justifiably famous for some of the best fish and chips in town, and in big portions. It also does steak-and-kidney pie and salads for about the same price.

Piccadilly Gardens Bar (☎ 75758; Rosia Rd; mains around £8, 3-course dinner £10) has garden seating just far enough back from the busy street.

Maxi Manger (☎ 43840; 24 Main St; sandwiches & baguettes £1.50-2.20) is an excellent place for snacks.

House of Sacarello (☎ 70625; 57 Irish Town; daily specials £5.50-6.10) is a chic place and a good bet for a meal, with tasty soups for around £2 and some excellent daily specials for £4.50 to £5.95, including delicious steak-and-mushroom Guinness pie. You can linger over a £7.75 afternoon tea for two between 3pm and 7.30pm.

Viceroy of India (☎ 70381; 9/11 Horse Barrack Court; 3-course lunch special £6.95) is tucked away off Main St and has Indian food that is usually pretty good. There are vegetarian dishes for £3.50 to £4.50.

The Piazza (☎ 47780; 156 Main St; fish & meat mains £4.75-8.25) does decent burgers and pizzas for £3.95 to £6.35. There are occasional live-music sessions on Friday and Saturday nights.

Kerry's Restaurant (☎ 44195; 5 Cornwall's Centre; mains £8.95-11.50) has a stylish ambience and offers imaginative meat and fish dishes.

The English Tea Room (9 Market Lane) rather neatly hedges its bets with the dual name of Le Rendez-Vous. Its scones, jam and cream are great, and it does lunch-time specials too.

At Marina Bay, a little out of the centre, there's a line of pleasant waterside cafés and restaurants.

Entertainment

Several of Gibraltar's pubs put on live music from pop to rock, jazz to folk (see entries for The Piazza and The Clipper under Places to Eat). Concerts and other performances are staged in the atmospheric venue of **St Michael's Cave** (check with the tourist offices for details). The **Ladbroke International Casino** (☎ 76666; 7 Europa Rd) offers casino gaming and slot machines, and also has live entertainment, a disco and restaurant. No membership or passport is needed and smart casual wear is accepted.

Shopping

Gibraltar has lots of British high-street chain stores, such as **Marks & Spencer**, **Mothercare** and **The Body Shop** (all on Main St) and **Safeway** (in the Europort development at the northern end of the main harbour). **Gibraltar Crystal** *(☎ 50136, fax 79980; Grand Casemates Square)* produces fine glassware on its premises and there are free demonstrations. Shops are normally open 9am to 7.30pm Monday to Friday and until 1pm Saturday.

Getting There & Away

The border is open 24 hours daily. Give yourself ample time if you are heading out of Gibraltar to catch a bus from La Línea. Vehicles and pedestrians are delayed from crossing the airport runway for a minimum of five minutes when flights are landing or taking off. There are two to three flights a day. You may also be delayed passing through Spanish customs, where bag searches are usually perfunctory, but may be time-consuming.

Air At the time of writing, the only flights into and out of Gibraltar are from/to the UK.

GB Airways *(☎ 79300, fax 76189)* flies daily to/from London. Return fares from London range between UK£129 and UK£189, depending on the season and special offers.

Monarch Airlines *(☎ 47477, fax 70154)* flies daily to/from Luton. Return fares range between UK£89 and UK£174.

At the time of writing, both carriers were offering cut-price one-way flights to London for £45.

In Gibraltar the airline offices are at the airport; alternatively, book through travel agents.

Bus Buses from Spain do not terminate within Gibraltar itself, but the bus station in La Línea (see the Cádiz Province chapter) is only a short walk from the border, from where there are frequent buses into Gibraltar town centre (see Getting Around, later).

Boat At the time of writing there is only one ferry a week between Gibraltar and Tangier, departing Gibraltar at 6pm on Friday. One-way/return fares are: adult £18/30, child £9/15 and car £46/92. The ferry takes 80 minutes. The ferry leaves from the terminal in front of the coach park. In Gibraltar, you can buy tickets for the ferry at **Turner & Co** *(☎ 78305; e turner@gibnynex.gi; 65 Irish Town)*. Booking ahead is advised. Ferries to and from Tangier are more frequent from Algeciras (see the Cádiz Province chapter).

For information on Gibraltar–Tangier and Algeciras–Tangier ferries, see the website **w** www.frs.es.

Getting Around

The 1.5km walk from the border to the town centre is entertaining, not least because it crosses the airport runway. A left turn (south) off Corral Rd will take you through the pedestrian-only Landport Tunnel (once the only land entry through Gibraltar's walls) into Grand Casemates Square and on to Main St.

Alternatively, buses No 3, 9 and 10 go from the border into town about every 15 minutes on weekdays, and every 30 minutes on Saturday and Sunday. Bus No 9 goes to Market Place (Grand Casemates Gate). It runs between 8am and 8.30pm Monday to Saturday and from 10am to 8pm on Sunday. Bus No 3 goes to Cathedral Square and the lower cable-car station, then goes up Europa Rd and on to Europa Point at the southern end of the Rock. It runs between 6.30am and 8.30pm Monday to Friday and from 7.30am to 9pm on Saturday and Sunday. Bus No 10 goes from the border to Europort (with a stop at the Safeway supermarket), then via Queens Way to Reclamation Rd near the town centre. Bus No 4 connects Catalan Bay on the Rock's eastern side with the centre and Europort. All buses cost 60p or €1 per trip.

All of Gibraltar can be covered on foot and much of it (including the upper Rock) by car or motorcycle, but there are other options worth considering. Most obvious is the **cable car** *(Red Sands Rd; adult one way/return £6/7, child one way/return £1.80/2.45; open 9.30am-5.15pm Mon-Sat; every few minutes; last cable down 4.45pm)*. Tickets at the prices shown also include admission to all the attractions on the upper Rock. You can also buy an adult one-way/return ticket for £4/5 without access to any of the attractions. For the Apes' Den, disembark at the middle station. You can get back on to go up to the top station. The operation of the cable car may be halted during periods of bad weather, especially if wind speeds are very high.

Car & Motorcycle Gibraltar's streets are congested and parking can be difficult. Vehicle queues at the border often make it less time-consuming to park in La Línea, then walk across the border. To take a car into Gibraltar you need an insurance certificate, registration document, nationality plate and driving licence. You do not have to pay any fee: some people driving into Gibraltar have been cheated of a dozen or so euros by con artists claiming you need to pay to take a vehicle across the border. In Gibraltar, driving is on the right, as in Spain. At the time of writing petrol in Gibraltar was around 10% cheaper than in Spain. There are car parks on Line Wall Rd, Reclamation Rd, and at the Airport Car Park on Winston Churchill Ave; the hourly charge at these car parks is about 60p.

Málaga Province

This southern province – the point of entry into Andalucía for many visitors – is much more than just the Costa del Sol, Spain's most densely packed holiday coast. Málaga city is Andalucía's second biggest and one of its most vibrant and self-confident. Inland are intriguing old towns – such as Ronda and Antequera – and a fascinating scatter of white-walled villages in some spectacular locations. The dramatic mountains of the interior offer every kind of outdoor activity including walking, cycling, horse riding and rock climbing.

Málaga

postcode 29080 • pop 534,000
Compared with the adjoining Costa del Sol, Málaga is a world apart. It's a briskly modern, yet historic city that still retains the atmosphere and swagger of a Mediterranean port. Forget the concrete and commonplace of the city's peripheries and you'll find that the centre pulses with colourful life; even the ceaseless torrent of traffic along the main throughway, the Alameda Principal, adds its own exciting rhythm. The city, with its backdrop of the blue Mediterranean, offers a seductive mix of wide, leafy boulevards, beautiful gardens, a handful of impressive monuments, some charmingly dilapidated old streets, plenty of fashionable shops and terrific bars. Málaga is a late-starter to the idea of sprucing itself up to attract tourists, but things are changing; a major new museum devoted to Málaga-born Pablo Picasso is due to open in 2003 – or later, as is the way in Málaga. The city stays open very late; plenty of the bars have happy hours that don't start until midnight, and things are up and running fairly early in the mornings.

HISTORY
Early Phoenician traders are credited with planting the area's first vineyards. In Muslim times, Málaga flourished under the

Highlights

- Soak up the vibrant, street life of Málaga and catch the city's exuberant August *feria* or its passionate Semana Santa
- Wander through the fascinating gorge-side town of Ronda
- Unravel the spectacular limestone mountains of El Chorro and El Torcal
- Explore the white villages of La Axarquía
- Spend time in the untainted Sierra de las Nieves
- Sample the unashamed good-time resorts of the Costa del Sol

11th-century Granada *taifa* (small kingdom) and the later Emirate of Granada. Its fall to the Christians in 1487 was a big nail in the emirate's coffin.

The expulsion of the Moriscos, who had been active in agriculture, contributed to famine in the 17th century, but some prosperity emerged in the 19th century with a dynamic middle class that founded textile factories, sugar mills, shipyards and steel mills. Málaga dessert wine, popular in Victorian England, was profitable until a bug devastated the vineyards around the city. Early tourism helped compensate: the city had been popularised by the Romantic movement and

MÁLAGA PROVINCE

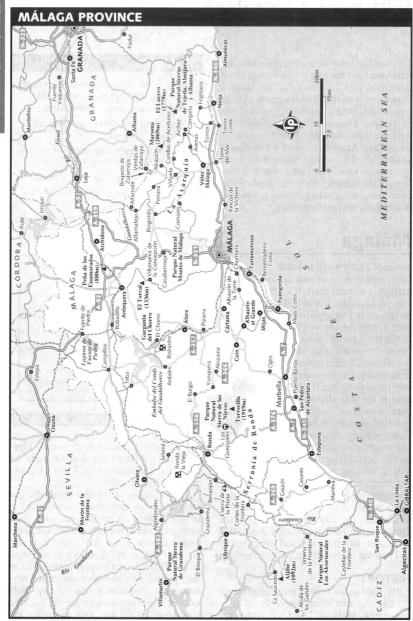

in the 1920s it became the favourite winter resort of rich people from Madrid.

In the civil war, Málaga was initially a Republican stronghold. Hundreds of Nationalist sympathisers were killed and churches and convents burnt. The city was then bombed by Italian planes before falling to the Nationalists in February 1937. Particularly vicious reprisals followed.

Málaga's economy has enjoyed plenty of spin-offs from tourism on the Costa del Sol since the 1960s, but youth unemployment is high.

ORIENTATION

The central axis comprises Paseo del Parque, Alameda Principal and Avenida de Andalucía. The city is dominated by the Gibralfaro, the hill rising above the eastern half of Paseo del Parque and supporting the Alcazaba and Castillo de Gibralfaro. The old heart of the city, with narrow, winding streets, spreads north from the western half of Paseo del Parque and the Alameda Principal. The main streets leading north into the old town are Calle Marqués de Larios, ending at Plaza de la Constitución, and Calle Molina Lario. The modern shopping district stretches between Calle Marqués de Larios and Calle Puerta del Mar.

INFORMATION
Tourist Offices

The helpful **Junta de Andalucía tourist office** (☎ 95 221 34 45; *Pasaje de Chinitas 4; open 9am-7pm Mon-Fri, 10am-2pm Sat & Sun*) is on an alley off Plaza de la Constitución. The **municipal tourist office** (☎ 95 260 44 10; *Avenida de Cervantes 1; open 8am-2.30pm & 4pm-7pm Mon-Fri, 9.30am-1.30pm Sat & Sun*), also helpful, is just off Paseo del Parque. There are smaller tourist offices at the airport and bus station, and information kiosks on Plaza de la Merced and outside the post office.

Money

There are plenty of banks with ATMs on Calle Puerta del Mar and Calle Marqués de Larios. ATMs can be found in the airport arrivals hall.

Post & Communications

The main **post office** (*Avenida de Andalucía 1; open 8am-8.30pm Mon-Fri, 9.30am-2pm Sat*) is fairly centrally located.

The large **Internet Meeting Point** (*Plaza de la Merced 20; open 10am-11pm daily*) has plenty of computers, a café and friendly staff. Charges are €0.90 per hour until noon and €0.90 per half-hour from noon to 11pm.

Bookshops

Librería Alameda (*Alameda Principal 16*) is a big Spanish bookshop that stocks some English and French titles as well as Lonely Planet titles. Another well-stocked place is **Promoto y Proteo** (*Calle Puerta Buenaventura 3-6*) where you'll find a good range of books and a selection of CDs and tapes.

Medical Services & Emergency

The main hospital is **Hospital Carlos Haya** (☎ 95 239 04 00; *Avenida de Carlos Haya*), 2km west of the city centre. The **Policía Nacional** (☎ 95 204 62 00) station is at Plaza de la Aduana 1, and the **Policía Local** (☎ 95 212 65 00) at Avenida de la Rosaleda 19.

Dangers & Annoyances

Take care of your valuables at all times and watch bags, especially when you're seated at café terraces and the bus station; there are some sharp teams of snatchers around. Night-time Málaga is generally safe, but avoid the darker and quieter side streets. The teenage craze for El Botellon (see 'The Big Bottle' boxed text in the Facts for the Visitor chapter) parties hit Málaga in locations like Plaza de la Merced. The downside is more mess than mayhem.

ALCAZABA

The Alcazaba (☎ 95 221 60 05; *Calle Alcazabilla; admission free; open 9am-8pm Tues-Sun, 9am-7pm Oct-Mar*), at the lower, western end of the Gibralfaro, was the palace-fortress of Málaga's Muslim governors. Begun in 1057 by the fearsome Granada *taifa* ruler Badis, the Alcazaba has two rings of walls, a large number of defensive towers, and staggered entrance passages to impede attackers. It was heavily reconstructed in

MÁLAGA

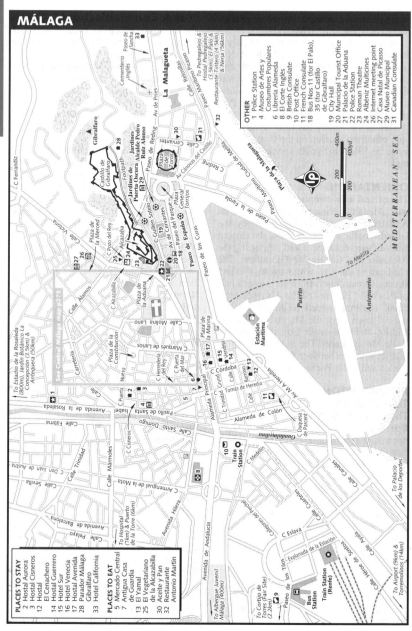

La Malagueta

OTHER
1 Police Station
4 Museo de Artes y
   Costumbres Populares
6 Librería Alameda
8 El Corte Inglés
9 British Consulate
10 Post Office
11 French Consulate
18 Bus Nos 11 (for El Palo),
    35 (for Castillo
    de Gibralfaro)
19 City Hall
20 Municipal Tourist Office
21 Palacio de la Aduana
22 Police Station
23 Roman Theatre
24 Albéniz Multicines
26 Internet meeting point
27 Casa Natal de Picasso
29 Museo Municipal
31 Canadian Consulate

MEDITERRANEAN SEA

See Central Málaga (map p274)

PLACES TO STAY
2 Hostal Aurora
3 Hostal Cisneros
12 Hostal
    El Cenachero
14 Hostal Guerrero
15 Hotel Sur
16 Hotel Venecia
17 Hostal Avenida
28 Parador Málaga
    Gibralfaro
33 Hotel California

PLACES TO EAT
5 Mercado Central
7 Antigua Casa
   de Guardia
13 El Yamal
25 El Vegetariano
    de la Alcazabilla
30 Aceite y Pan
32 Restaurante
    Antonio Martín

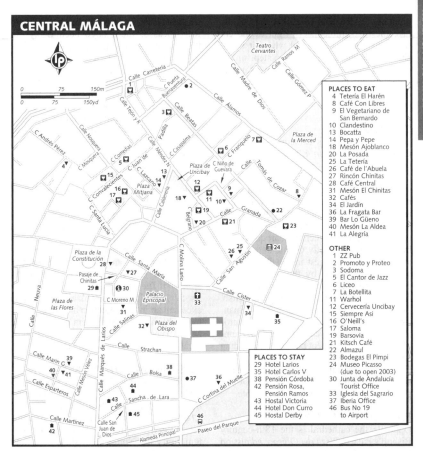

CENTRAL MÁLAGA

PLACES TO EAT
4 Tetería El Harén
8 Café Con Libres
9 El Vegetariano de San Bernardo
10 Clandestino
13 Bocatta
14 Pepa y Pepe
18 Mesón Ajoblanco
20 La Posada
25 La Tetería
26 Café de l'Abuela
27 Rincón Chinitas
28 Café Central
31 Mesón El Chinitas
32 Cafés
34 El Jardín
36 La Fragata Bar
39 Bar Lo Güeno
40 Mesón La Aldea
41 La Alegría

OTHER
1 ZZ Pub
2 Promoto y Proteo
3 Sodoma
5 El Cantor de Jazz
6 Liceo
7 La Botellita
11 Warhol
12 Cervecería Uncibay
15 Siempre Así
16 O'Neill's
17 Saloma
19 Barsovia
21 Kitsch Café
22 Almazul
23 Bodegas El Pimpi
24 Museo Picasso (due to open 2003)
30 Junta de Andalucía Tourist Office
33 Iglesia del Sagrario
37 Iberia Office
46 Bus No 19 to Airport

PLACES TO STAY
29 Hotel Larios
35 Hotel Carlos V
38 Pensión Córdoba
42 Pensión Rosa, Pensión Ramos
43 Hostal Victoria
44 Hotel Don Curro
45 Hostal Derby

1930, but the first of its three patios contains an original arch. Work continues on refurbishing the site, but most of it is now open. There are some scant explanatory displays, but information apart, the Alcazaba's multi-faceted construction, its jacarandas and flowerbeds, its cobbled ramps and archways and its leafy terraces with their rising sequence of viewpoints, are pleasure enough. Roman columns and capitals are embedded everywhere in the rich red stonework of the building, and below the new entrance foyer the remains of a **Roman theatre** have been excavated.

CASTILLO DE GIBRALFARO

Above the Alcazaba rises the older Castillo de Gibralfaro (admission free; open 9am-8pm daily Apr-Sept, 9am-7pm Oct-Mar), built by Abd ar-Rahman I, the 8th-century Cordoban emir. It was rebuilt in the 14th and 15th centuries, when Málaga was the Emirate of Granada's main port. The views from up here are exhilarating. The fortress includes an airy walkway round the top of its walls and there is a small museum.

The Alcazaba and Castillo are connected by a curtain wall called La Coracha, but you cannot reach the Castillo from the highest point of the Alcazaba. To walk to the Castillo take the road immediately right of the entrance to the Alcazaba and where it bends sharply left into a tunnel, go up steps on the right and follow the surfaced pathway uphill. Alternatively, take bus No 35 from Avenida de Cervantes (roughly every 45 minutes) and stroll back down.

CATHEDRAL

Building of Málaga's cathedral *(enter from Calle Cister; admission €2; cathedral & museum open 10am-6.45pm Mon-Sat, closed holidays)* began in the 16th century on the site of the former main mosque and continued for two centuries. The cathedral is known locally as La Manquita (the One-Armed) because the southern tower was never completed. The cathedral has an 18th-century baroque facade but the inside is chiefly Gothic and Renaissance. Of special interest are the finely carved wooden choir stalls by the popular 17th-century Andalucian sculptor Pedro de Mena. There are explanatory panels in English, French and Spanish inside. In 2002 the Spanish government allocated over a million euros for restoration of the cathedral and its crumbling facades, so expect possible scaffolding and disruption for some time.

On the cathedral's northern side, the **Iglesia del Sagrario** has a splendid late-Gothic portal and a gilded Renaissance retable.

PALACIO EPISCOPAL

Opposite the cathedral is the 18th-century Bishop's Palace *(Plaza del Obispo; admission free; open 10am-2pm & 7pm-10pm in summer, 10am-2pm & 6pm-9pm in winter)*. Set in a handsome square and now used as an exhibition hall, this building has one of the most impressive facades in the city and a beautiful patio with an imperial-type staircase.

MUSEO PICASSO & MUSEO DE MÁLAGA

The 16th-century Palacio de los Condes de Buenavista *(Calle San Agustín)*, in what was Málaga's Judería *(Jewish Quarter)* in Muslim times, is being converted into a major new Picasso museum. Based on 186 Picasso works donated or lent by his daughter-in-law

Christine Ruiz-Picasso and grandson Bernard Ruiz-Picasso, there have been delays to the opening of the museum. At the time of writing, the estimate was October 25, 2003 – the 122nd anniversary of Picasso's birth. The delays have resulted, in part, from enthusiastic expansion of the original plans as the Picasso family donated more paintings, and from the serendipitous discovery of Phoenician, Roman and Muslim features within the Palacio's foundations during building work.

The Picasso donation means that the Museo de Málaga, a fine arts and archaeological museum which occupied the Buenavista palace from 1961, has had to move out. Debate about where it should reopen has raged in the city and at the time of writing this has not been resolved. Meanwhile, selections from the art collection are usually on temporary display in the **Palacio de la Aduana** *(Paseo del Parque; admission free; open 3pm-8pm Tue, 9am-8pm Wed-Fri, 9am-3pm Sat-Sun)* – well worth a look as there's some excellent art in the collection including works by Zurbarán, Murillo, Ribera and Pedro de Mena. Theres also a tantalising selection of local artists' work, including Picasso.

CASA NATAL DE PICASSO

The house where Picasso was born *(☎ 95 206 02 15; Plaza de la Merced 15; admission free; open 11am-2pm & 5pm-8pm Mon-Sat, 11am-2pm Sun)* in 1881 is a centre of exhibitions and research on Picasso and contemporary art. Some good shows are held here and the Picasso memorabilia, including photographs is compelling.

ALAMEDA PRINCIPAL & PASEO DEL PARQUE

The Alameda Principal, now a busy thoroughfare, was created in the late 18th century as a boulevard on what were then the sands of the Guadalmedina estuary. It's adorned with old trees from the Americas and lined with 18th- and 19th-century buildings.

In the 1890s the palm-lined Paseo del Parque, an extension of the Alameda, was built on land reclaimed from the sea. The garden along its southern side, Paseo de España, is

MICK WELDON

The life and work of Andalucía's most famous son, Pablo Picasso, is celebrated in Málaga

full of exotic tropical plants, making a pleasant refuge from the bustle of the city.

MUSEO DE ARTES Y COSTUMBRES POPULARES

The Museum of Popular Arts & Customs *(☎ 95 221 71 37; Pasillo de Santa Isabel 10; adult/child under 16 €1.20/free; open 10am-1pm & 5pm-8pm Sun-Fri 15 June–1 Oct, 10am-1.30pm & 4pm-7pm Sun-Fri 1 Oct–15 June)*, housed in a 17th-century inn, is a fun place to visit, especially for children. The collection focuses on everyday life and includes items connected with farming and fishing. Note the glass cabinets containing painted clay figures *(barros)* of the highwayman, the couple dancing, the rider from Ronda and other characters from local folklore.

MUSEO MUNICIPAL

This modern exhibition space *(Paseo de Reding 1; admission free; open 10am-8pm daily Oct-Mar, 11am-9pm Apr-Sept)*, opened in 1999, exhibits visiting art shows and will eventually have a permanent collection of its own.

PLAZA DE TOROS & CEMENTERIO INGLÉS

Visit Málaga's bullring *(Paseo de Reding; admission €1.80; open 10am-1pm Mon-Fri Oct-Mar, 10am-8pm Mon-Fri Apr-Sept)* and then ring the changes by visiting the tranquil English cemetery *(Avenida de Príes; open 9am-1pm & 3pm-5pm Mon-Fri, 9am-11am Sat & Sun)*, a couple of hundred metres east of the bullring along Paseo de Reding. Before the cemetery was founded in 1829, non-Catholic bodies were buried at night, upright in the sand at the foot of the beach – dogs and rough seas tended to recycle them. It is a peaceful, reflective place, although its charm has been slightly eroded by the construction of featureless apartments that now overlook it. The original walled inner cemetery, in the far corner, contains many graves covered in cockle shells. St George's Anglican church here holds regular Sunday services.

JARDÍN BOTÁNICO LA CONCEPCIÓN

Four kilometres north of the city centre are the largely tropical La Concepción gardens *(☎ 95 225 21 48; adult/child €2.80/1.40; open from 10am Tues-Sun)* featuring plants from all over the world. It is closed 25 December and 1 January. Visits are by 1½-hour guided tour, with the last starting at 7.30pm from 21 June to 10 September, at 4pm from 11 December to 31 March, and at varying intermediate hours in other seasons.

By car, take the N-331 Antequera road north from the Málaga ring road (N-340) to Km 166 and follow the signs. On Saturday, Sunday and holidays the No 61 bus leaves Málaga's Alameda Principal for La Concepción hourly from 11am.

BEACHES

Sandy beaches line most of the waterfront for several kilometres in each direction from the port. Playa de la Malagueta is handiest from the centre, and has several places to eat and drink close by. In recent years there has been a public outcry against alleged pollution of the sea along the beachfronts. In 2002 the city authorities started operating two vessels to try and clear up

MÁLAGA PROVINCE

surface scum and other detritus. For unbiased advice concerning possible pollution, if you fancy a dip, it's probably best to consult locals on the beaches; or cool off under the beach showers like everyone else.

LANGUAGE COURSES

Foreigners' courses run by the **Universidad de Málaga** (☎ 95 227 82 11, fax 95 227 97 12) are very popular. Four-week intensive Spanish language courses cost €508, and there is the option of staying with a host family (singles/doubles €170/145 a week per person) or sharing an apartment (singles/doubles €72/60 per person). For information, you can write to Universidad de Málaga Cursos de Español para Extranjeros, Inés Carrasco Cantos (Directora), Avenida de Andalucía 24, 29007 Málaga.

There are at least 20 private language schools in Málaga; the main tourist offices have contact lists.

SPECIAL EVENTS

Málaga's big annual festivals are as follows:

Semana Santa Holy Week (the week before Easter) in Málaga is second only to Seville in splendour and solemnity. Each night from Palm Sunday to Good Friday, six or seven *cofradías* (lay brotherhoods) bear their holy images for several hours through the city, watched by big crowds. Málaga's *tronos* (floats) are large and heavy and are borne on long poles by teams of up to 150 carriers. Events climax on Good Friday. A good place to watch from is the Alameda Principal, where the processions pass through between about 7pm and midnight.

Costa Pop Previously called World Dance Costa del Sol (one night in late May), this massive all-night concert is attended by 100,000 or more fans and performed by top Spanish and Latin pop stars.

Feria de Málaga Málaga's nine-day mid-August fair, launched by a huge midnight firework display on the opening Friday, is the biggest and most ebullient of Andalucía's summer *ferias*. During daytime, especially on the two Saturdays, the city centre thrives with music and dancing in the packed streets and bars, and horses and riders in their finery parading round a circuit of streets. Head for Plaza Uncibay, Plaza de la Constitución, Plaza Mitjana or Calle Marqués de Larios to be in the thick of it. At night the fun switches to the large fairgrounds and

nightly rock and flamenco shows at Cortijo de Torres, 4km southwest of the city centre. Special buses run from all over the city. Málaga also stages its main bullfight season during the *feria*; tourist offices have programmes of events.

Fiesta Mayor de Verdiales On 28 December thousands congregate at Puerto de la Torre on the Almogía road on the northwestern outskirts of the city, for a grand gathering of verdiales groups, who perform an exhilarating type of folk music and dance unique to the Málaga area – a kind of Celtic/*gitano* mix, with lots of high-pitched fiddle and tambourine-type percussion. It accompanies intricate, flag-waving dances and participants wear colourful, flowery hats. Bus No 21 from the Alameda Principal goes to Puerto de la Torre.

PLACES TO STAY

Outside the July-to-September peak season, many places, especially in the mid-range and top end, reduce prices significantly, and some places that don't have single-occupancy rates in the peak season introduce them.

PLACES TO STAY – BUDGET
Hostels

Albergue Juvenil Málaga (☎ 95 230 85 00, fax 95 230 85 04; Plaza Pío XII No 6; under 26/other mid-Jun–mid-Sept & holiday periods €12.90/17.25, rest of year €10.90/15.20), 1.5km west of the centre and a couple of blocks north of Avenida de Andalucía, has 110 places, most in double rooms and many with bathroom. Bus No 18 along Avenida de Andalucía from the Alameda Principal goes most of the way.

Hostales & Pensiones

True budget rooms are, on the whole, not particularly appealing.

North of the Alameda The friendly **Pensión Córdoba** (☎ 95 221 44 69; Calle Bolsa 9; singles/doubles €14/25) is not a bad choice.

Hostal Derby (☎ 95 222 13 01; Calle San Juan de Dios 1; singles/doubles €27/36) has spacious rooms with bathrooms and big windows. It shares a building with various offices; find its bell beside the big studded door.

Pensión Rosa (☎ 95 221 27 16; Calle Martínez 10; singles/doubles €23/30) and

Pensión Ramos (☎ 95 222 72 68; Calle Martínez 8; singles/doubles €20/30), are neighbours southwest of Plaza de la Constitución. Both have adequate rooms with shared bathrooms. You can't miss their flowery balconies.

Hostal Aurora (☎ 95 222 40 04; Calle Muro de Puerta Nueva 1; singles/doubles €20/36), off Calle Puerta Nueva, has six clean, attractive rooms, despite the dingy entrance.

Hostal Cisneros (☎ 95 221 26 33; Calle Cisneros 7; singles/doubles €24/42, doubles with bathroom €48) is spotless and friendly.

South of the Alameda The basic **Hostal Avenida** (☎ 95 221 77 28; Alameda Principal 5; singles/doubles €12.60/21, doubles with bathroom €30) has clean rooms.

Hostal El Cenachero (☎ 95 222 40 88; Calle Barroso 5; doubles €34, singles/doubles with bathroom €25/38) is a cheerful place with pleasant rooms.

Hostal Guerrero (☎ 95 221 86 35; Calle Córdoba 7; singles/doubles €22/31, with bathroom €28/38) is a spick-and-span place up a couple of flights.

PLACES TO STAY – MID-RANGE
In this range, bathroom, TV (often cable) and air-con are standard.

Hotel Carlos V (☎ 95 221 51 20, fax 95 221 51 29; Calle Císter 10; singles/doubles €41.50/52.90), just east of the cathedral, is a bit gloomy inside, but has reasonable rooms.

Hostal Victoria (☎ 95 222 42 24, fax 95 222 42 23; Calle Sancha de Lara 3; singles/doubles €50/60) has good modern rooms in a handy location.

Hotel Venecia (☎ 95 221 36 36; Alameda Principal 9; singles/doubles €58/72), on the southern side of the Alameda, has 40 very comfortable rooms.

Hotel Sur (☎ 95 222 48 03, fax 95 221 24 16; Calle Trinidad Grund 13; singles/doubles €52/60) is another reasonable option. Its rooms and decor are beginning to look a bit worn, but it's relaxed and quiet.

Hotel California (☎ 95 221 51 65; e hcalifornia@spa.es; Paseo de Sancha 17; singles/doubles €63/78), 1km east of the city

centre and close to the beach, has 28 comfy, good-sized rooms. Breakfast is available.

Hostal Pedregalejo (☎ 95 229 32 18; e hosped@spa.es; Calle Conde de las Navas 9; singles/doubles €32/47.50), about 4km east of the city centre and again near the beach, has attractive rooms.

Hotel Don Curro (☎ 95 222 72 00, fax 95 221 59 46; e doncurro@infonegocio.com; Calle Sancha de Lara 7; singles/doubles €63/72.75) is in the city centre. Rooms here cost €6 to €9 more in August.

PLACES TO STAY – TOP END
Parador Málaga Gibralfaro (☎ 95 222 19 02; e gibralfaro@parador.es; singles/doubles €100/124.65), with an unbeatable location up on the Gibralfaro, was refurbished not long ago and has a pool and a good restaurant.

Hotel Larios (☎ 95 222 22 00; e info@hotel-larios.com; Calle Marqués de Larios 2; doubles €138) is a centrally located 40-room place with smart rooms and services. Room prices rocket to €388 during Semana Santa.

PLACES TO EAT
A speciality of Málaga is fish fried quickly in olive oil. Fritura malagueño consists of fried fish, anchovies and squid. Cold soups are popular: as well as gazpacho, in the tomato season, and sopa de ajo (garlic soup), try sopa de almendra con uvas (almond soup with grapes). Ham is requisite for most tapas combinations and you'll see air-dried hindquarters hanging around everywhere.

Seafood
Rincón Chinitas (Pasaje de Chinitas; tapas €2.10, raciones €4.50) is little more than a hole in the wall but it manages to fry up hefty raciones (meal-sized servings of tapas). The delectable shrimp fritters are worth nudging your way in for.

Aceite y Pan (☎ 95 236 18 18; Calle Cervantes 5; 2-course meal around €21; open 1.30pm-5pm & 9pm-12.30am Tues-Sun) is a classy place in the well-heeled La Malagueta area. It does a range of classic Mediterranean seafood dishes including tasty patas de cangrejo (crab claws).

Restaurante Antonio Martín (☎ 95 222 73 98; Playa de la Malagueta; mains €7-14), located right on the beach, rustles up a range of fish and seafood dishes. Celebrities are rumoured to hang out here, so keep your eyes open for Antonio Banderas.

The seafront eateries at Pedregalejo, 4.5km east of the city centre, serve plenty more fish, or you could continue a farther kilometre east to the seafront **Restaurante Tintero** in El Palo, where plates of fish and seafood (around €4) are brought out by the waiters and you shout for what you want. The food is not exquisite (get it hot) but the place is fun.

Around Plaza de la Constitución

Café Central (Plaza de la Constitución; menú €7.25; 9am to mid-evening) vibrates with the sound of happy chatting and plastic chairs scraping against the floor. Yes, it's a noisy local favourite, with reasonably priced food and strong coffee to perk you up.

Mesón El Chinitas (☎ 95 221 09 72/95 222 64 40; Calle de Moreno Monroy 4-6; dishes €8.40-15, menú €13.20) appeals to classy diners who don't mind being eyeballed by cheesy portraits. The menú offers a range of mainly fish dishes, including the sweet Picasso sole (€11.50), sprinkled with cubed fruit, and chunky fish kebabs (€12).

Pepa y Pepe (Calle Caldería; tapas €1.10-1.50, raciones €3.60-4.10) is a snug tapas bar that brims with diners chomping their way through calamares (battered squid) and fried green peppers, which are greased beyond recognition.

For a reasonably priced sit-down meal at a pavement table, head for pedestrian Calle Marín García and Calle Esparteros, just west of Calle Marqués de Larios. **La Alegría**, **Bar Lo Güeno** and **Mesón La Aldea**, all in this area, serve plenty of fish and other dishes costing between €6 and €11.

Mesón Ajoblanco (Plaza de Uncibay 2; baguettes €2.55-3), with its usual gathering of young men at the bar, offers cheese, meat or ahumados (smoked fish) boards for €7.20 to €10.80. It also does a range of tasty baguettes.

La Posada (Calle Granada 33; tapas €1.80, mains around €8-16) is a barn-like place, great for greasy meat in tremendous proportions; the filling paletilla cordero (shoulder of lamb) will set you back €12.60.

Bocatta (Calle Calderería 11; baguettes €3.10-3.90), one of a chain of baguette places, is good for manic sightseers who want to eat on the hoof.

Clandestino (☎ 95 221 93 90; Calle Niño de Guevara 3; menú €7.50; open 1pm-1am), a trendy backstreet joint, serves up top meals to hip, house beats. Hedonistic diners can finish up with a dreamy Doña Blanca ice cream (€2.70).

Tetería El Harén (Calle Andrés Pérez 3; open 6pm-late) is a teahouse with a real caravanserai atmosphere – wooden balcony and beams, a small patio open to the sky, candlelit tables in several nooks and rooms. Heaps of aromatic and classic teas, herbal infusions, coffees, juices, liqueurs and crepes are on offer for around €1.70. It also has live music, card or tea-leaf readings, and storytelling on various nights.

Near the Cathedral

The **cafés** on Plaza del Obispo have a breathtaking view of the cathedral facade.

El Jardín (☎ 95 222 04 19; Calle Cañón 1; platos combinados €4.20-7.50; open 9am-midnight Mon-Thur, 9am-2pm & 5pm-midnight Fri & Sat, 5pm-midnight Sun), next to the palm-filled gardens of the cathedral, has a rather fetching interior with mock-gold leaf frames and fancy furniture. The food is grand too, though it's an equally pleasant spot to relax with a morning coffee (€1.10).

La Fragata Bar (Calle Cortina del Muelle; open 7am-4pm daily; pitufos €1) is an unassuming place that does tempting ham and cheese pitufos (small filled rolls) for a snip; a pitufo and coffee costs just €1.80. Gape at the backside of an ibérico pig while you get stuck in.

Café de l'Abuela (Cnr Calle San Agustín & Calle Echegaray; breakfasts €2.20, crepes €1.65-3) woos its customers with good-value breakfasts (coffee, juice and croissant) and sumptuous crepes later in the day.

La Tetería (Calle San Agustín 9; normal tea €1.70, special tea €1.85; open 4pm-midnight) offers a connoisseur's range of teas from peppermint to *'antidepresivo'* depending on how you feel. Sit outside and marvel at the beautiful church opposite.

Café Con Libres *(Cnr Tomás de Cozar & Calle San Agustín)* seats its patrons between bookshelves. Grab a tome and look intellectual while you sip your coffee (€1.50).

Around the Alameda

Stock up on an eye-widening array of regional gastronomy at the colourful **Mercado Central** *(open early-1pm)*, north of the Alameda Principal. It buzzes with people unearthing the best meat cuts and plumpest fruit. The building itself was constructed in the 19th century in a Mudejar-influenced style and it retains a 14th-century arch. Nearby are plenty of **cafés** on pedestrian Calle Herrerería del Rey.

Antigua Casa de Guardia *(☎ 95 221 46 80; Alameda Central 18; tapas €1-1.50, raciones €4-6)* has been going strong since 1840 and is a particularly atmospheric bar. Málagan wine from the barrel starts at €0.70 per glass, and it serves good seafood tapas.

El Yamal *(☎ 95 221 20 46; Calle Blasco de Garay 7; mains €8-9; open lunch time Mon-Sun)* rustles up excellent Moroccan food in traditional *tajines* (earthenware dishes with pointed lids). Choose from fish, chicken or couscous with vegetables and soak up the relaxed atmosphere.

Vegetarian

El Vegetariano de la Alcazabilla *(☎ 95 221 48 58; Calle Pozo del Rey 5; mains €6-8; open 1.30pm-4pm & 9pm-11pm Mon-Sat)* manages to juggle friendly service and spectacular food, while keeping a laid-back vibe. Good-value dishes include *pancerottis* (filled wholemeal pasta with a creamy cheese sauce; €8) and zucchini-filled croquettes (€6). Leave your mark: graffiti on the yellow walls like the diners before you.

El Vegetariano de San Bernardo *(☎ 95 222 95 87; Calle Niño de Guevara; mains €6-8; open 1.30pm-4pm & 9pm-11pm Mon-Sat)*, the more central sibling of El Vegetariano de la Alcazabilla, has a similar menu.

ENTERTAINMENT

Party-seeking holidaymakers generally ignore Málaga and head along the coast, which means the bars, cafés and clubs in Malaga are left for discerning locals. Thankfully, this has created a flourishing scene of hip, welcoming joints where you can experience Spanish nightlife for real.

The back pages of *Sur* newspaper, and its Friday *Evasión* section, are useful for what's-on information, as is monthly *¿Qué Hacer?* (free from tourist offices).

Bars & Clubs

On hot weekends, the web of narrow old streets north of Plaza de la Constitución come alive with people having a fabulous time; midweek the place is dead. The best places to look for bars are Plaza de la Merced in the northeast to Calle Carretería in the northwest, Plaza Mitjana (officially called Plaza del Marqués Vado Maestre) and Plaza de Uncibay.

Kitsch Café *(☎ 95 260 83 78; Calle Granada 24)* has a great lounge feel and plays deep house to get you in the mood. Guzzle your pre-club drinks here.

Bodegas El Pimpi *(Calle Granada 62)*, a minor warren of rooms and mini-patios, has traditional decor of casks and bullfight posters that attracts a fun-loving crowd with its sweet wine and thumping music.

Cervecería Uncibay *(Plaza de Uncibay 5)* is a functional bar that's good for pub-crawlers in need of a top up; it's not the place you'd settle into for the night.

El Cantor de Jazz *(☎ 95 222 28 54; Calle Lazcano 7)* has buffed wooden floors, great jazz portraits and a piano that's longing to be played (although there's occasional jazz on Thursday nights). However, after a few gin fizzes (€4) at this *coctelería* (cocktail bar) it probably won't matter.

La Botellita *(Calle Álamos 36; open 7pm-3am)*, just off Plaza de la Merced, is chock-a-block with miniature bottles filled with an assortment of spirits. The crowd is young and invariably tipsy.

ZZ Pub *(☎ 95 230 84 09; Calle Tejón y Rodríguez 6; open 10pm-3am Mon-Thur, 10pm-5am Fri & Sat)* keeps its faithful fans happy by continuing to host live bands Monday and Thursday. It's intimate, grungy and the acts mainly play guitar-twanging rock.

O'Neill's (☎ 95 260 14 60; Calle Luis de Velázquez 3) likes to prove how Irish it is by playing nonstop U2. Happily, the bar staff have never heard of optics so you'll get good spirit measures to help you cope. This is one of the few places that's crammed midweek regardless of the weather.

Saloma (☎ 95 222 05 03; Calle Luis de Velázquez 5) is a place with low lighting and high prices befitting a classier clientele. There's space for a quick shimmy on the dance floor too.

Siempre Asi (Calle Convalecientes 5) plays flamenco, rumba and rocky Latino to a 25-to-40-year-old crowd from 9.30pm Thursday to Saturday.

Liceo (Calle Beatas 21), a grand old mansion turned young music bar, buzzes with a student crowd after midnight. Go up the winding staircase and you'll find more rooms to duck into.

Barsovia (Calle Belgrano 6) might be stuck in a music timewarp but that doesn't stop it filling up with groovers. Yes, people still listen to '80s pop.

Sodoma (Calle Juan de Padilla 15) whips up a house-music storm from 11pm Thursday to Saturday.

Warhol (Calle Niño de Guevara; open 11pm-late) is a new haunt for choosy clubbers who want funky house beats all night. Dreadlocked DJs smoothly mix tunes to a mainly gay crowd but everyone who loves to dance is welcome.

Theatre & Cinema

Teatro Cervantes (tickets ☎ 95 222 41 00 or information ☎ 95 222 41 09; Calle Ramos Marín s/n; W www.teatrocervantes.com), housed in a palatial building, has a good programme of music, dance and theatre.

Posters and Sur newspaper list the current movies at Málaga's cinemas. **Albéniz Multicines** (☎ 95 221 58 98; W www.cineciudad .com; Calle Alcazabilla 4) is the home of the Cinemateca Municipal, showing international films with Spanish subtitles at 10pm most nights.

SPECTATOR SPORTS

Málaga football club went bankrupt and ceased to exist around 1990 but, after being reborn in the early '90s, it now occupies a fair mid-table position in Spain's Primera Liga. The club plays at the Estadio de la Rosaleda, beside the Río Guadalmedina, 2km north of the city centre.

Málaga's Unicaja basketball team does quite well in the national league and plays at the Palacio de los Deportes, in the city's southwest.

SHOPPING

Málaga's branch of **El Corte Inglés** (Avenida de Andalucía), situated on the western continuation of the Alameda Principal, is chock full of goodies ranging from chocolate spread to tailored suits.

Almazul (off Calle San Agustín) has a range of hand-crafted Andalucian ceramics, including chunky teapots and colourful plates.

There is a Sunday morning **market** near the Estadio de la Rosaleda.

GETTING THERE & AWAY
Air

Málaga's busy **airport** (☎ 95 204 88 38), the main international gateway to Andalucía, is 9km southwest of the city centre. See the introductory Getting There & Away chapter for information on international and domestic flights. Most airline offices are at the airport but **Iberia** (☎ 902 40 05 00; Calle Molina Lario 13) has one in the city centre.

Bus

The **bus station** (☎ 95 235 00 61; Paseo de los Tilos) is 1km west of the centre. Frequent buses run along the coast and several go daily to inland towns including Antequera (€3) and Ronda (€7.70). Other destinations include Seville (€12, 2½ hours, 10 buses daily), Córdoba (€9.50, 2½ hours, five daily), Granada (€7.25, 1½ to two hours, 16 daily), Cádiz, Jaén, Valencia, Barcelona (€52, 15 hours), and Madrid (€16.30, six hours, seven or more daily). There are also buses to Germany, England, Portugal, France, Belgium, the Netherlands and Morocco.

Train

The **train station** (☎ 95 236 02 02; Explanada de la Estación) is round the corner from the bus station.

Nine or more trains run daily to/from Córdoba (€12 to €24, two to 2½ hours). To/from Seville (€13.35, 2½ hours) there are five regional Trenes Regionales Diésel (TRDs) daily. For Granada there are no direct trains, but you can get there in 2½ hours for €11.50 with a transfer at Bobadilla. For Ronda, too, you usually change at Bobadilla: the best connections give a 1½-hour journey (€7.75).

Four or more daily Talgo 200s go to/from Madrid (€44 to €52, four to 4½ hours). A slower daily train leaves late morning for Madrid (€31, 6½ hours). For Valencia and Barcelona (€42 to €47, 9½ to 13 hours) there are two trains daily, one overnight.

Car

Numerous international and local agencies have desks at the airport. You'll find them down a ramp in the luggage-carousel hall, and out the side of the arrivals hall.

Boat

Trasmediterránea (☎ 95 206 12 18, 902 45 46 45; Estación Marítima, Local E1) operates one ferry daily (except Sunday mid-September to mid-June) to/from Melilla. The trip takes about 7½ hours, with passenger fares starting at €26.30 one way; a car costs €112.

GETTING AROUND
To/From the Airport

A taxi from the airport to the city centre costs around €9.40 from 10pm to 6am.

Bus No 19 to the city centre (€1) leaves from the 'City Bus' stop outside the arrivals hall, about every half-hour from 7am to midnight, stopping at Málaga's main train and bus stations en route. Going out to the airport, you can catch it at the western end of Paseo del Parque, and outside the stations, about every half-hour from 6.30am to 11.30pm. The journey takes around 20 minutes.

The Aeropuerto train station, on the Málaga-Fuengirola line, is a five-minute walk from the airport terminal: follow signs from the departures hall. Trains run about every half-hour from 7am to 11.45pm to Málaga's Renfe station (€0.90, 11 minutes) and the Centro-Alameda station beside the Río Guadalmedina. Departures from the city to the airport and beyond are about every half-hour from 5.45am to 10.30pm. Fares are €1 at the weekend and holidays.

Bus

Useful buses around town (€0.90) include No 11 to Pedregalejo and El Palo from Avenida de Cervantes.

Taxi

Fares within the city centre, including to the train and bus stations, are around €3.50. Expect to pay €5 to the Castillo de Gibralfaro.

Parking

Convenient car parks such as on Plaza de la Marina tend to be expensive (about €1.25 an hour, €17.20 for 12 to 24 hours). Side-street parking, off the south side of the Alameda for example, is metered (€1.50 per hour, €14.70 for 12 to 24 hours). Vacant lots are much cheaper (€1 to attendant); there is a large one behind El Corte Inglés, which is free overnight, but it is not secure and is prone to break-ins of vehicles.

Costa del Sol

Strewn along the Málaga seaboard, the Costa del Sol stretches like a wall of wedding cakes. Its recipe for success is the certainty (more or less) of sunshine, convenient beaches, warm sea, cheap package deals and plenty of nightlife and entertainment.

The resorts were fishing villages until the 1950s or '60s, but there's little to show for that now. Launched as a Francoist development drive for impoverished Andalucía, the Costa del Sol is an eye-stinging example of how to fill all open spaces without exception. What contains it all, both physically and aesthetically, are Andalucía's coastal mountains. Yet, seamless though the Costa may appear, each of its honey-pot resorts has a distinctive character and appeal; they are all fun places in which to spend a bit of time.

Activities

The Costa del Sol is good for leisure-sport lovers, with nearly 40 golf clubs, several busy marinas, tennis and squash courts, riding schools, swimming pools and gyms. Many of the beaches offer water sports such as windsurfing, water-skiing and parasailing.

Places to Stay

There are a huge numbers of rooms at almost every price, but even so, to avoid a weary trudge from one *completo* (full) sign to another, you are strongly advised to book ahead during the high season of July, August and, in some places, September. Outside these peak months, room rates often drop sharply.

The Costa has about 15 camp sites.

Getting There & Around

A convenient train service links Málaga and its airport with Torremolinos (€0.90 Monday to Friday, €1 Saturday and Sunday) Arroyo de la Miel (Benalmádena; Monday to Friday €0.90, €1 Saturday and Sunday) and Fuengirola (€1.50 Monday to Friday,

€1.65 Saturday and Sunday). Plenty of buses link coastal towns.

The A-7 Autopista del Sol, bypassing Fuengirola, Marbella, San Pedro de Alcántara and Estepona, makes moving along the Costa del Sol a lot easier for those willing to pay its tolls (€4.85 Málaga–Marbella, €3.30 Marbella-Estepona during Easter and June to September; €3 October to May). Many places use Km numbers to pinpoint their location. These numbers rise from west to east. Estepona is at Km 155 and central Marbella at Km 181. Km markers aside, undoubtedly the most useful sign on the N-340 is 'Cambio de Sentido', indicating that you can change direction to get back to a turning you might have missed. Do not be pushed by impatient drivers behind you into going too fast for comfort. Go steadily and you should not have any problems, but in general, beware of other motorists and watch out for cats, dogs and footloose drunks who may be roaming.

Bargain rental cars (€136 to €150 a week, all inclusive) are available from local firms in all the resorts.

Costa del Crime

Andalucía's mountains sheltered ruthless bandits during the 19th century, as Ronda's Museo del Bandolero reveals. But modern 'bandits' have also fuelled the Costa del Crime image that clings to Málaga's sunshine coast. For many years cumbersome extradition agreements between Spain and Britain, meant that crooks from the UK found secure bolt holes on the Mediterranean, when things got too hot for them on their native turf. The extradition system improved after Spain and Britain signed a 'Fast Track Judicial Surrender' treaty in 2001, but the image of the Costa being awash with crooks is still eagerly fostered by tabloid newspapers. It becomes less convincing once you spend time in Marbella and Torremolinos amid law-abiding Andalucians and the crowds of guiltless holiday-makers and long-term foreign residents. The latter are more likely to have a golf club than a shot-gun slung over their shoulders.

One of Britain's most notorious criminals, Kenneth Noye took off for Spain in 1996 after stabbing to death another motorist during a violent road-rage incident. Noye was eventually pounced on by British and Spanish undercover cops in 1998 at a *taberna* in Barbate, a coastal town on the Costa de la Luz, south of Cádiz. He was imprisoned in El Puerto de María's high security jail where the 'last' Ronda bandit Juan Mingolla Gallardo had languished in 1932. Noye was extradited to Britain in 1999. He was tried and found guilty and was sentenced to life imprisonment.

In spite of tougher extradition agreements, crooks on the run still flit in and out of the Costa del Sol. In half-finished haciendas in the hills above Marbella, or on soap-dish cruisers that never go to sea, they sweat away the time behind dark glasses, dreaming of happier days in the chillier north.

TORREMOLINOS & BENALMÁDENA

(Torremolinos) postcode 29620
• pop 35,500

Britain's Blackpool would kill for what Torremolinos has got, as far as sunshine goes. This concrete high-rise jungle, beginning 5km southwest of Málaga airport, is designed to squeeze as many paying customers as possible into the smallest available space. Even in winter, pedestrian traffic jams the narrow lanes behind the main beach. One of the few legacies of Torremolinos' past is an Islamic watchtower at the foot of Calle San Miguel, once known as the Torre de los Molinos (Tower of the Mills). After leading the Costa del Sol's mass tourist boom of the 1950s and '60s, 'Torrie' lost ground to other resorts but spruced up in the '90s. A pleasant seafront walk, the Paseo Marítimo, now extends for nearly 7km and has given a degree of cohesion and character to the resort.

Orientation

The main road through Torremolinos from the northeast (the direction of the airport and Málaga) is called Calle Hoyo, becoming Avenida Palma de Mallorca after it passes through Plaza Costa del Sol. Calle San Miguel runs most of the 500m from Plaza Costa del Sol down to the central beach; Playa del Bajondillo is the main pedestrian artery. The bus station is on Calle Hoyo and the train station is on Avenida Jesús Santos Rein, a pedestrian street intersecting Calle San Miguel 200m from Plaza Costa del Sol. Southwest of Playa del Bajondillo, around a small point, is Playa de la Carihuela, once the fishing quarter, backed by generally lower-rise buildings.

The southwestern end of Torremolinos merges with Benalmádena Costa, the seafront area of Benalmádena. About 2km uphill from here is the part of Benalmádena called Arroyo de la Miel, with the original, surprisingly unspoiled village, Benalmádena Pueblo, to its west.

Information

Torremolinos has **tourist offices** on Playa del Bajondillo (☎ 95 237 19 09; open 9.30am-2.30pm Mon-Fri Oct-May, 10am-2pm & 5pm-8pm daily June-Sept) near Plaza de las Comunidades Autónomas, at the eastern end of Playa del Bajondillo; Calle Borbollón Bajo (☎ 95 237 29 56; open 9.30am-2.30pm Mon-Fri Oct-May, 10am-2pm & 5pm-8pm daily June-Sept); Plaza de la Independencia (☎ 95 237 42 31; open 9.30am-1.30pm Mon-Fri), a block inland from Plaza Costa del Sol; and in the town hall (☎ 95 237 9511; Plaza de Blas Infante; open 9.30am-1.30pm Mon-Fri), farther inland.

Benalmádena's **main tourist office** (☎ 95 244 24 94; Avenida Antonio Machado 10) is on the main road from Torremolinos.

Beaches

Torremolinos' beaches are wider, longer and a paler shade of grey-brown than most on the Costa del Sol. They get crowded, to say the least.

Aquapark

This park (☎ 95 238 88 88; Calle Cuba 10; adult/child €12.60/8.40; open 10am-6pm May-June & Sept, 10am-7pm July-Aug) has varied water slides and a wave pool in the typical water-fun-park mould.

Sea Life

In Benalmádena Costa's swish Puerto Deportivo (marina), Sea Life (☎ 95 256 01 50; adult/child €7/5; open 10am-6pm) is a good modernistic aquarium of mainly Mediterranean marine creatures. Highlights include touch pools where you can handle specimens, the walk-through shark and stingray tunnel and a re-creation of Atlantis.

Tivoli World

This is the Costa's biggest amusement park, located at Arroyo de la Miel. As well as multifarious rides and slides, Tivoli World (☎ 95 257 70 16; admission €4; open 4pm-1am Mon-Fri Apr-May & mid-Sept–Oct; 5pm-2am 1 June–mid-June; 6pm-3am July-Aug; & 1pm-10pm Sat & Sun Nov-Mar) stages daily dance, musical and children's events. It's five minutes walk from Benalmádena-Arroyo de la Miel train station. Apart from the entry fee, there are additional fees for rides.

For children, consider the 'Supertivolino' ticket for €15, which allows unlimited use on more than 35 rides.

Museo Arqueológico

The Archaeological Museum (☎ 95 244 85 93; Avenida Juan Peralta 49; admission free; open 10am-2pm & 5pm-7pm Mon-Fri July-Aug, 10am-2pm & 4pm-7pm Mon-Fri Sept-June), in Benalmádena Pueblo, exhibits an interesting collection of pre-Columbian sculpture and ceramics from Mexico and Central America.

Places to Stay

Torremolinos has more than 50,000 hotel and apartment beds.

Hostal Micaela (☎ 95 238 33 10, fax 95 237 68 42; Calle Bajondillo 4; doubles with bathroom €36), a pleasant, 17-room place, is close to Playa del Bajondillo.

Hostal Guillot (☎ 95 238 01 44; Pasaje Río Mundo 4; doubles €30), off Pasaje de Pizarro near Plaza Costa del Sol, is fairly ordinary, but adequate.

Hostal Guadalupe (☎ 95 238 19 37; Calle del Peligro 15; singles/doubles with bathroom €33/40) is a small place just across the Paseo Marítimo from Playa del Bajondillo.

Hotel El Pozo (☎ 95 238 06 22; Calle Casablanca 2; doubles €53) is a 28-room place in central Torremolinos.

Hostal Flor Blanco (☎ 95 238 20 71; Pasaje de la Carihuela 4; doubles with bathroom €40.40), in La Carihuela, about 1.5km southwest of central Torremolinos, is almost on the beach and several of its 12 rooms have sea views.

Hotel Miami (☎ 95 238 52 55; Calle Aladino 14; doubles €50.60), a few blocks back from La Carihuela beach, is a quaint 1940s villa turned into a small hotel with nice gardens and a pool.

La Fonda (☎/fax 95 256 82 73; Calle Santo Domingo 7; singles/doubles €54/73.50), a charming place in Benalmádena Pueblo, has large rooms built around patios with fountains, and a restaurant that forms part of a catering school serving excellent but very well-priced food.

Places to Eat

British pit stops pop up everywhere, but if you want to savour the fish flavours of the Costa del Sol head for the beach. An abundance of seafood eateries are strewn along palm-lined Playa del Bajondillo.

Restaurante Los Pescadores Playa (☎ 95 237 01 95; Playa del Bajondillo) does a fantastic plate of grilled and fried fish, fritura malagueña, for €8.50.

Bodega Quitapeñas (Cuesta del Tajo), tucked away near the tower, and **Bar La Bodega** (Calle San Miguel 40) are popular with Spaniards for their seafood raciones (€4.50 to €6) and tapas (€1.10 to €1.80). They are both convenient after that long hike up from the beach.

Restaurante Miramar (☎ 95 205 03 48; Calle San Miguel 69; menú €4.50) rustles up Chinese food for its touristy clientele. Go for the good-value menú if you hanker for noodles.

Casa Juan (☎ 95 238 41 06; Calle San Gine's 20; mains €4.50-15) is one of a string of first-rate seafood eateries in La Carihuela and does fantastic fish Malagueña style. Crack apart a plump lobster or go for fish with rice.

Casa Gauquín (☎ 95 238 45 30; Calle Carmen 37; mains €4.50-15), a relative of Casa Juan, concocts more good fish dishes from Costa's abundant supply.

El Roqueo (☎ 95 238 49 46; Calle Carmen 35; 2 courses around €18) still retains the atmosphere of a beach-side diner, though it's much classier. Splash out on a tempting range of aquatic fare.

Entertainment

Torremolinos' clubbing vibe has started to wane, with the thrust of the action moving westwards to Benalmádena Costa's Puerto Deportivo (marina) area. However, Torrie still has some big venues.

Fun Beach (☎ 95 205 23 97; Avenida Palma de Mallorca 7; open 8pm-6am), previously known as Piper's, is reputed to be the largest club in Europe. Lose yourself on one of the seven dance floors.

Discoteca Palladium (☎ 95 238 42 89; Avenida Palma de Mallorca 36; open 10pm-

7am), with its fancy swimming pool, spins some brain-bashing tunes to twirl around to.

There are a number of gay bars on Calle Nogalera, off Avenida Jesús Santos Rein.

Benalmádena Costa has some classy (and touristy) bars around the marina area. At night try **Disco Kiu** *(Plaza Sol y Mar)*, the popular giant, which has foam parties for added excitement. Dress codes aren't strict but men generally wear collared shirts.

Getting There & Away

From a stop on Avenida Palma de Mallorca at the corner of Calle Antonio Girón, 200m southwest of Plaza Costa del Sol, buses run to/from Benalmádena Costa (€0.80, 15 minutes, about every 15 minutes from 7am to 1.30am); Málaga (€87, 30 minutes, about every 15 minutes from 7am to 2.10am); Benalmádena Pueblo (€0.80, 40 minutes, every 30 minutes); Fuengirola (€1, 30 minutes, every 20 or 30 minutes from 7am to 10pm); and Mijas (hourly from 7am to 10pm).

From the **bus station** *(☎ 95 238 24 19; Calle Hoyo)*, buses run to Marbella (€2.90, one hour, 14 or more times daily) and to Ronda, Estepona, La Línea, Algeciras, Tarifa, Cádiz and Granada a few times a day.

Trains run to Torremolinos, about every half-hour, 5.30am to 10.30pm, from Málaga city (€1, 20 minutes) and the airport (€0.85, 10 minutes), then continue on to Benalmádena-Arroyo de la Miel and then Fuengirola (€1, 20 minutes).

FUENGIROLA

postcode 29640 • pop 43,000

Fuengirola, another beach resort 18km down the coast from Torremolinos, has more of a family-holiday scene but is even more densely packed; its sometimes drab buildings rather overpower the waterfront and beaches.

Orientation & Information

The narrow streets in the few blocks between the beach and Avenida Matías Sáenz de Tejada (the street the bus station is on) constitute what's left of the old town, with Plaza de la Constitución at its heart. The train station is a block inland from the bus station, on Avenida Jesús Santos Rein.

The **tourist office** *(☎ 95 246 74 57; Avenida Jesús Santos Rein 6; open 9.30am-2pm & 4.30pm-7pm Mon-Fri, 10am-1pm Sat)* is just along from the train station.

Things to See & Do

The **Parque Acuático Mijas** *(☎ 95 246 04 09; adult/child €11.50/7; open May-Sept)*, beside the N-340 Fuengirola bypass, is like Torremolinos' Aquapark but is slightly cheaper. Child admission is for children aged four to 12 years. The **Castillo de Sohail** *(admission €1.30; open 10am-2.30pm & 4pm-6pm Tues-Sun)*, at the southwestern end of Fuengirola beach, dates from the 10th century. Recently restored, it has an auditorium in its central courtyard.

The **Hipódromo Costa del Sol** *(☎ 95 259 27 00)*, Andalucía's leading horse race track, opened in 2000 at Urbanización El Chaparral, off the N-340 at the southwestern end of Fuengirola. Floodlit races in summer run between 11pm and 2am every Saturday. Winter races are held at noon on Sunday.

Special Events

The 16 July **Virgen del Carmen** celebrations in Los Boliches, a former fishing village that's now an eastern suburb of Fuengirola, are famous. In a two-hour procession 120 bearers carry a heavy platform, supporting the image of the virgin, from Los Boliches church into the sea.

Places to Stay

Hostal Italia *(☎ 95 247 41 93, fax 95 246 19 09; Calle de la Cruz 1; singles/doubles with bathroom, air-con & TV €40/53)*, a friendly 35-room place, is in the heart of things – a couple of blocks from the beach.

Hostal Cuevas *(☎ 95 246 06 06; Calle Capitán 7; doubles €28/41.50)*, along the street, is a decent smaller place.

Hostal Marbella *(☎/fax 95 266 45 03; Calle Marbella 34; singles/doubles €39/48)*, just southwest of Plaza de la Constitución, is Swedish-owned, friendly and clean.

Places to Eat

Calle Moncayo and Calle de la Cruz, a block back from the Paseo Marítimo, are awash with eateries. Choose from Italian, Belgian, Cypriot, Chinese, Indonesian and even Spanish fare and then quench your thirst in a nearby bar. The Paseo Marítimo itself and the Puerto Deportivo (marina) have further strings of bargain eateries: some places do *menús* for €5 to €6.

Méson El Castellano (☎ 95 246 27 36; *Camino de Coín 5; mains €4-10)* is a hospitable place that cooks great meaty dishes, as well as the fluffiest Spanish omelette around (half a large one costs €4.40).

Restaurante Portofino (☎ 95 247 06 43; *Paseo Marítimo 29; mains €10.50-30)* is the place to go for a splurge. It has great sea views and an international menu that includes a host of classic fish dishes.

Cafeteria Costa del Sol (☎ 95 247 17 09; *Calle Marbella 3; rosquillas €2.10)*, with its stripey awning, does excellent breakfasts. Their hot ham and cheese *rosquillas* (toasted rolls) are out-of-this-world, so too is the potent coffee (€1.05).

Entertainment

Plenty of tacky disco-pubs line Paseo Marítimo and a cluster of music bars and discos can be found opposite the Puerto Deportivo. A few hip bars dot the town too.

Cotton Club (*Avenida Condes San Isidro 9)* attracts a chilled bunch who are wised-up to the laid-back vibe of this excellent bar. It has jam sessions on Thursday nights and some comedy evenings too.

Irish Times and **Cafetería La Plaza** are bars at opposite ends of Plaza de la Constitución. Both fill up with lively, mainly Spanish crowds in the evening. The Irish Times' patio is great on a hot night.

Moochers (☎ 95 247 71 54; *Calle de la Cruz 17)* is a jazz café and restaurant that has live music every night. OK, so it's not Ronnie Scott's but it'll keep you amused.

Getting There & Away

From the **bus station** (☎ 95 247 50 66) frequent buses run to Torremolinos (€1, 30 minutes), Málaga (€1.95, one hour) and Marbella (€1.95, one hour), plus a few a day to Ronda, Seville, Granada and elsewhere.

Fuengirola is served by the same trains as Torremolinos, costing €1.50 from Málaga and €1.40 from the airport.

MIJAS

postcode 29650 • pop 12,000
• elevation 428m

Mijas, a village of Muslim origin looking down on Fuengirola from the hillside 8km north, was where foreign artist and writer types settled in the 1950s and '60s when their package-tour compatriots were pouring into the beach towns below. Since then villas and suburbs have sprawled across the surrounding hills. Mijas remains a pretty place but it's full of souvenir and craft shops besieged by busloads up from the Costa. It has a few *hostales* and hotels and a gamut of restaurants and cafés, if the mood takes you. Frequent buses run from Fuengirola (€0.80, 25 minutes).

MARBELLA

postcode 29600 • pop 98,823

Marbella is the supermodel on the Costa cat walk, always on show, but still managing to strut with style. Its looks are flattered even more by the backdrop of the shapely Sierra Blanca.

It was the building in the 1950s of the exclusive Marbella Club Hotel, just west of town, by Alfonso von Hohenlohe, a part-Mexican, part-Austrian aristocrat with strong Spanish connections, that turned Marbella into a playground for international players. For three decades oil-rich Arabs, film and fashion followers, brokers, barons, and the bankable flocked to build luxury pieds-a-terre and to mirror each other and be seen amid shoals of glamour groupies.

In the 1980s, an economic slump and the rapid growth of suburbs with their own bars and restaurants took the shine off the 'rich and famous' tag. Marbella drifted into decline, until the beginning of the 1990s when Jesús Gil y Gil, a flamboyant right-wing businessman, won a landslide election victory and become mayor. Gil, whose motto at election times seems to be '*my* picture on every

MARBELLA

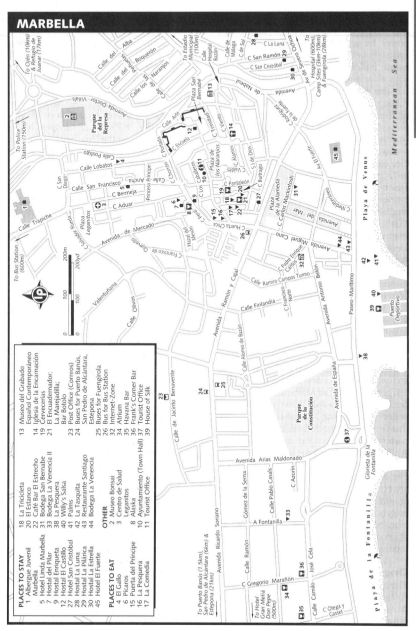

PLACES TO STAY
1 Albergue Juvenil Marbella
5 Hotel Linda Marbella
7 Hostal del Pilar
9 Hostal Enriqueta
12 Hostal El Castillo
27 Hotel San Cristóbal
28 Hostal La Luna
29 Hostal La Pilárica
30 Hostal La Estrella
45 Hotel El Fuerte

PLACES TO EAT
4 El Gallo
6 Pícaros
15 Puerta del Príncipe
16 La Pesquera
17 La Comedia
18 La Tricicleta
20 El Estanco
22 Café Bar El Estrecho
31 Bodega San Bernabé
33 Bodega La Venencia II
38 La Pesquera
40 Willy's Salsa
41 Palms
42 La Tasquita
43 Restaurante Santiago
44 Bodega La Venencia

13 Museo del Grabado Español Contemporáneo
14 Iglesia de la Encarnación
19 Cervecerías
21 El Encuadernador; La Marejadilla; Bar Botolo
23 Post Office (Correos)
24 Buses for Puerto Banús, San Pedro de Alcántara, Estepona
25 Buses for Fuengirola
26 Bus for Bus Station
32 Internet-Zone
34 Atrium
35 Havana Bar
36 Frank's Corner Bar
37 Tourist Office
39 House of Silk

OTHER
2 Museo Bonsai
3 Centro de Salud Leganitos
8 Alaska
10 Ayuntamiento (Town Hall)
11 Tourist Office

lamp post', has expressed the view that Spain was 'better off under Franco'. Having won power he set about restoring Marbella's image by laying marble pavements, planting palms, building underground car parks and, with notoriously heavy-handed police methods that would shock most holidaymakers, ridding the streets of petty criminals, prostitutes and drug addicts. Gil also encouraged property development and courted the wealthy and famous, including the Costa's recent wave of nouveau-riche. He was re-elected mayor in 1995 and 1999, but has had to face a growing mountain of lawsuits in which he has been accused of a welter of misdeeds ranging from town-planning irregularities to illegally diverting €27 million of Marbella council money to the Atlético Madrid football team (of which he was president). Gil spent a brief spell in jail in the Atlético case in 1999. His critics also argue that a lot of serious organised crime, related to drug trafficking and money laundering, goes on unchecked in the town.

In spite of the Costa's Byzantine politics, true justice may be closing in on Gil y Gil. In mid-2001 Gil was given a six-month jail sentence on a number of counts. In April 2002 he was finally jailed and his assets were seized by the courts. He posted bail and was released a few days later. He then resigned as mayor of Marbella, a hollow defiance since he would have been dumped within days anyway. Latest reports suggest that Gil may still be defiant, but that his supporters have melted away and he is isolated. At the time of writing his fate is not known.

In Marbella, however, to the innocent eye, all's right with the world. The beaches are clean, and although the celebrity circus around the nearby Puerto Banús waterfront is generally B-list verging on XYZ, the tourists have returned, there's a sheen of glamour still, the sun shines, and Marbella retains its appeal even for the most jaded.

Orientation

The N-340 through town goes by the names Avenida Ramón y Cajal and, farther west, Avenida Ricardo Soriano. The old town is centred on Plaza de los Naranjos, north of

Avenida Ramón y Cajal. The bus station is on the northern side of the Marbella bypass, about 1.2km north of Plaza de los Naranjos.

Information

The helpful **tourist offices** (☎ 95 282 35 50; *Plaza de los Naranjos 1 • ☎ 95 277 14 42; Glorieta de la Fontanilla; open 9am-8pm or 9pm daily*) are closed on holidays. There's another office (☎ 95 282 28 18; *open 10am-midnight daily*), in the 'Marbella' arch over the N-340 at the eastern entrance to the town; it's closed 1 January.

The main **post office** is on Calle de Jacinto Benavente. There is a good Internet centre at **Internet-Zone** (*Calle Padre Enrique Cantos 4; open 10am-midnight daily*) off Avenida Miguel Cano.

Emergency medical attention is available at the **Centro de Salud Leganitos** (☎ 95 277 21 84; *Plaza Leganitos; open 8am-5pm Mon-Fri, 9am-5pm Sat*). **Hospital Europa** (☎ 95 277 42 00; *Avenida de Severo Ochoa*) is 1km east of the centre. The **Policía Nacional** (☎ 091; *Avenida Doctor Viñals*) station is north of the town.

Things to See & Do

Marbella's beachfront is reached beyond the busy central throughway of Avenida Ramón y Cajal, through the Plaza de la Alameda and then down a broad walkway, the Avenida del Mar. The avenida is peppered with crazed sculptures by Salvador Dalí, that are somehow perfectly in tune with Marbella's likeable theatricality. The central **Playa de Venus**, immediately below Avenida del Mar and east of the Puerto Deportivo, is a fairly standard Costa beach, apart from the *in situ* model elephant peering from a clump of palm trees. For a longer, broader and usually less crowded stretch of sand walk to the 800m-long **Playa de la Fontanilla**, west of Glorieta de la Fontanilla or, even better, the 2km **Playa de Casablanca** beyond Playa de la Fontanilla.

Marbella's picturesque **Casco Antiguo** (old town) is largely closed to traffic, and has Muslim origins. At the heart of its pleasant web of narrow alleyways is pretty **Plaza de los Naranjos**, crammed with café

Lounge on Playa Burriana, one of Nerja's most enticing beaches

Málaga's stunning cathedral

The Costa del Sol is a haven for sun lovers

Café chic: breakfast the Spanish way

Flashy Puerto Banús, near Marbella, is the Costa del Sol's finest marina

Tile pictures on a wall, Córdoba

Córdoba's 14th-century Torre de la Calahorra

Reflect on the Río Guadalquivir from Córdoba's Puente Romano

tables. The 16th-century town hall is on its northern side and a 17th-century fountain on the southern side. Nearby, on Plaza de la Iglesia, is the **Iglesia de la Encarnación**, begun in the 16th century and later redone in baroque style.

A little farther east, the **Museo del Grabado Español Contemporáneo** *(Museum of Contemporary Spanish Prints; admission €2; open 10am-2pm & 5.30pm-8.30pm Mon-Fri, 10am-2pm Sun)*, in a 16th-century hospital on Calle Hospital Bazán, exhibits work by Picasso, Miró and Dalí, among others. Just to the north, along streets such as Calle Arte and Calle Portada, are remains of Marbella's old **Muslim walls**.

Northeast of the old town, in the watery Parque de la Represa, is the charming **Museo Bonsai** *(☎ 95 286 29 26; adult/child €3/1.50; open 10am-1.30pm & 4.30pm-8pm daily)*, devoted to Japanese miniature-tree art.

There are good walks in the **Sierra Blanca** starting from the Refugio de Juanar, a hotel 17km from Marbella. Just south of the hotel are the ruins of the original Refugio de Juanar, once a hunting lodge.

Special Events
Marbella's big week-long *feria* happens around 11 June. The Castillo de Cante flamenco song festival on the first or second Saturday of August (starting about 11pm) in Ojén village, 10km north of Marbella, always features some big names.

Places to Stay – Budget
Camping Marbella 191 *(☎ 95 277 83 91; N-340 Km 184.5; sites high season €20)*, on the beach 3km east, has a limited opening season. Three bigger and less expensive year-round sites are in the next 10km of the N-340 heading east; all are within walking distance of the beach.

Albergue Juvenil Marbella *(☎ 95 277 14 91, fax 95 286 32 27; Calle Trapiche 2; under 26/other mid-June–mid-Sept & holiday periods €12.90/17.25, Apr-June & Sept-Oct €10.90/15.20, rest of year €8.50/11.50)* is a hostel that holds about 140 in rooms for one to four people (half have bathrooms). It is modern and has a pool.

There are plenty of *hostales* in the old town.

Hostal El Castillo *(☎ 95 277 17 39, fax 95 282 11 98; Plaza San Bernabé 2; singles/doubles with bathroom €24/39)*, near the Islamic walls, has plain, old-fashioned but comfy rooms. The hotel's aerial photo of 1950s Marbella says a lot about Costa development.

Hostal Enriqueta *(☎ 95 282 75 52, fax 95 282 76 14; Calle De Los Caballeros 18; doubles/triples with bathroom & fan €36/52)* has pleasant rooms.

Hostal del Pilar *(☎ 95 282 99 36; w http://hostal@marbella-scene.com; Calle Mesoncillo 4; singles, doubles or triples per person €10)* is a popular and hugely friendly British-run place off Calle Peral. Prices depend on the season, and there's a bar with a pool table, a roof terrace for sunbathing and a log fire for the cooler months. Big English breakfasts start at €4.

Just southeast of the old town, small *hostales* cluster on narrow Calle San Cristóbal and nearby streets. Three of the better ones are **Hostal La Luna** *(☎ 95 282 57 78; Calle La Luna 7; doubles with bathroom €30-36)*, **Hostal La Estrella** *(☎ 95 277 94 72; Calle San Cristóbal 36; doubles with bathroom €42)* and **Hostal La Pilárica** *(☎ 95 277 42 52; Calle San Cristóbal 31; doubles with bathroom €36-42)*.

Places to Stay – Mid-Range & Top End
Above the *hostal* bracket you'll normally pay €70 or more for a double in summer.

Hotel San Cristóbal *(☎ 95 277 12 50, fax 95 286 20 44; e info@hotelsancristobal.com; Avenida Ramón y Cajal 3; singles/doubles €60/80.80)* is one of the less pricey of the upmarket hotels; you'll probably be better off with a room at the back or side, away from the noisy avenue.

Hotel Linda Marbella *(☎/fax 95 285 71 71; e lindamarbellasl@terra.es; Calle Ancha 21; singles/doubles €37.45/52.40)* is a traditional house that has been charmingly restored in a modern style, with much use of fresh pastel colours. Management is friendly and multilingual.

Hotel El Fuerte *(☎ 95 286 15 00, fax 95 282 44 11; Avenida El Fuerte s/n; doubles €132)*, a 263-room place, is close to Playa de Venus.

Hotel Gran Meliá Don Pepe *(☎ 95 277 03 00, fax 95 277 99 54; Calle José Meliá s/n; doubles €354.50)* is a five-star hotel just over a kilometre west of the town centre. Prices drop by more then a third in the low season.

Places to Eat

Dining in Marbella doesn't necessarily mean chichi interiors and bikini-size portions. There are some fabulous authentic tapas bars and a few trendy restaurants that do delicious, good-value cuisine.

Old Town Up in the picturesque streets of old Marbella, **El Gallo** *(☎ 95 282 79 98; Calle Lobatos 44; fish dishes €3; open 1pm-4.30pm & 7pm-11pm Wed-Mon)* is a real local adventure. Come here for delicious fish dishes.

Café Bar El Estrecho *(Calle San Lázaro 12; tapas €1.10)*, **El Estanco** *(☎ 95 292 40 11; Calle Buitrago 24; tapas €1.50)* and **Bar Bartolo** *(☎ 95 282 69 50; Calle San Lázaro)* are three good spots for varied tapas and strong viscous coffee. If they are busy, just elbow your way in.

Pícaros *(☎ 95 282 86 50; Calle Aduar 1; mains €7.20-11.85 plus IVA, 3-course Sunday lunch €21; open from 7.30pm)* has a dreamy open-air terrace for those romantic moments. Drool over the menu, which includes Mediterranean prawns with garlic butter and rice (€9).

La Comedia *(☎ 95 277 64 78; Calle San Lázaro; mains €11.10-20.25)* is a hip, sparsely decorated place run by a Swedish duo. It offers interesting international fare like tempting turbot with artichoke which costs €17.50.

La Tricicleta *(☎ 95 285 76 86; Calle San Lázaro; meat & fish mains €14.50-20; open 7.30pm-midnight Mon-Sat)*, located in the same alley as La Comedia, has a rustic downstairs dining area and a showy roof terrace. Dine on duck breast with a five-pepper sauce flambéd with Jerez brandy and you'll see why this eatery is a cracking choice.

Puerta del Príncipe *(☎ 95 277 49 64; Plaza de la Victoria; mains €5.40-21; open 10.30am-1.30pm daily)*, with its hulking stuffed bull in the lobby, rustles up good old-fashioned steaks. Satisfy the matador inside and go for a meaty platter here.

La Pesquera *(☎ 95 277 53 02; Plaza de la Victoria; mains €5.40-21; open 10.30am-1.30pm daily)* is the fish-fancier's version of the steakhouse next door. Sit under the awning outside and sizzle alongside the bamboo-skewered sardines (€5.40). There is another branch on Glorieta de la Fontanilla.

Plaza de los Naranjos, a giant patio dining area, is usually mobbed with tourists.

Elsewhere Soak up the authentic bodega vibe at **Bodega San Bernabé** *(Calle Carlos Mackintosh; tapas €1.60)*, which chooses to concentrate on two great Spanish staples: ham and cheese.

Playa de Venus has a throng of eateries on the sand. If you can cope with the skinny bronzed bodies then head for **Palms** *(salads from €5.70)*, which specialises in interesting salads, or **La Tasquita** *(mains €7-10)*, which serves fried and grilled seafood.

Willy's Salsa *(Puerto Deportivo; sandwiches €2)*, one of the shack-like bars in the marina, does tasty sandwiches in chilled surrounds. Refresh yourself with a glass of freshly squeezed orange juice (€2).

The seafront Paseo Marítimo is lined with restaurants all the way from Hotel El Fuerte to Glorieta de la Fontanilla.

Restaurante Santiago *(☎ 95 277 00 78; Paseo Marítimo 5; 2-course meal around €24)* cooks up gourmet seafood dishes in elegant surrounds. Sit by the window and survey the palms on Playa de Venus.

Bodega La Venencia *(Avenida Miguel Cano 15; montaditos from €1.05)*, just behind Playa de Venus, and **Bodega La Venencia II** *(Avenida Fontanilla 4)* serve lip-smacking ham tapas and *montaditos* (small sandwiches, often toasted).

Entertainment

House of Silk *(☎ 95 285 85 32; Puerto Deportivo; ⓦ www.houseofsilk.com; DJs 9pm-*

3am Thurs-Sat) has a Tibetan vibe and plays funky house and dance music. Sit back on the cushions with a fresh-fruit smoothie during the day or get something stronger at night.

El Encuadernador *(☎ 95 286 58 92; Calle San Lázaro 3)*, meaning 'The Bookbinder', is tucked away on a quaint alley and fosters a loyal following with its authentic beer-den feel.

La Marejadilla *(Calle San Lázaro)* rubs shoulders with El Encuadernador and is just right for a follow-up round of drinks to keep spirits soaring. The literal translation of *marejadilla* is 'slight swell', which says it all.

Calle Pantaleón, has a string of *cervecerías* (beer bars) buzzing late into weekend nights with a young crowd. Posey drinkers head for Calle Camilo José Cela and Calle Gregorio Marañón. Here you'll find **Frank's Corner Bar**, a US-themed joint with pool tables; **Havana Bar**, a laid-back joint with swish leather sofas; and slightly snooty **Atrium** *(☎ 95 282 85 89)*.

Alaska *(Calle Peral 6)*, one of the most popular hang-outs in Marbella, still manages to attract a hip bunch.

The free bimonthly publication *Marbella Día y Noche* (Ⓦ www.guiamarbella.com) contains useful information on concerts and exhibitions.

Shopping

If you've come here for sequinned swimwear, you're in luck. The winding streets of the old town are full of glittering boutiques full of brash clothing, enticing craft shops and fancy antique showrooms.

A lively street market takes place on Monday mornings around the Estadio Municipal football ground, east of the old town.

Getting There & Away

Bus Buses to Fuengirola, Puerto Banús (€0.90), San Pedro de Alcántara and Estepona leave about every 30 minutes from Avenida Ricardo Soriano. Services from the **bus station** *(☎ 95 276 44 00)* in the north of town include frequent buses to Benalmádena Costa, Torremolinos and Málaga (direct €4.20, 45 minutes; indirect €4, 1½ hours),

and a few a day to Ronda (€4, 1½ hours), Seville (€12.80, 3½ hours), Granada (direct €11.95, 2½ hours; indirect €11.80, 3½ hours), Córdoba (€14.10, five hours), La Línea (€4.50, 1½ hours), Algeciras (direct €5.10, one hour; indirect €5, 1½ hours) and Cádiz (direct €13.35, 2½ hours; indirect €13.30, 4½ hours).

Getting Around

From the bus station, bus No 7 (€0.85) runs to the **Fuengirola/Estepona bus stop** *(Avenida Ricardo Soriano)* near the town centre. Returning from the centre to the bus station, take No 2 from Avenida Ramón y Cajal (corner of Calle Huerta Chica). To walk from the bus station to the centre, cross the bridge over the bypass and carry straight on down Calle de Trapiche, which leads down to the Albergue Juvenil Marbella, then continue direct down Calle Bermeja.

PUERTO BANÚS

The coastal strip between Marbella and Puerto Banús, 5km west, is known as La Milla de Oro (the Golden Mile) because of its number of super-luxury properties – including the Marbella Club Hotel and King Fahd of Saudi Arabia's Mar Mar estate. Puerto Banús is the flashiest marina on the Costa del Sol, often a port of call for huge floating gin palaces that moor in Monte Carlo at other times of year. A few travellers get work on the boats – if they're not already working as time-share touts elsewhere. Puerto Banús is also a nightlife centre, though prices are high.

The marina's main entrance has security gates to prevent access by unauthorised cars. By the control tower at the western end of the harbour – where the swankiest boats tie up – is the **Aquarium de Puerto Banús** *(☎ 95 281 87 67; adult/child €4.80/3.60; open 11am-6pm daily)*, similar to Sea Life at Benalmádena Costa (see the earlier Torremolinos & Benalmádena section for details). While open most of the year, it may shut Monday to Friday in winter. As an optional extra, you can take a dive in the aquarium's tanks with rays, lobsters and small sharks.

Places to Eat & Drink

The marina is skirted by glam shops and not-so-glam restaurants, though some have a dash of class. Bars are crammed with dolled-up women trying to score gold-bejewelled yachtsmen. Most settle for golfers instead.

The Red Pepper (☎ 95 281 21 48; Calle de Ribera; dishes from €11.40; open daily) dishes up tasty Greek dishes, such as moussaka (€13), to the Puerto Banús gentility.

Restaurante Antonio (☎ 95 281 35 36; Calle de Ribera; mains €10-15) does a brisk trade in sizable seafood platters. Even though this place is huge, it gets packed, so book ahead.

Don Leone (☎ 95 281 17 16; Calle de Ribera 44-45; pasta mains €6-12) is the best of the marina's Italian-inspired eateries, with great home-made pasta.

The western end of the marina has a few fancy bars: **Salduba Pub** (☎ 95 281 10 92; Calle de Ribera) and **Sinatra Bar** (Calle de Ribera) are two of the most popular.

Old Joy's Pub (☎ 95 281 42 83; Calle de Ribera) gets the jewellery jangling, with its nightly live piano performances.

La Comedia (Calle de Ribera) plays the latest mix of disco pop to get you grooving.

Dreamer's (☎ 95 281 20 80; Carretera, Cádiz & Río Km 175; ⓦ www.dreamers-disco .com) brings house-music lovers a taste of clubbing paradise. With a mix of tribal house, vocal house, light shows, bongo beats and an ever-changing menu of DJs you'll be hard pushed to find somewhere better to let your hair down.

Getting There & Away

Several boats a day usually go to Puerto Banús from Marbella's Puerto Deportivo (look for signs there advertising the trip) for around €5.40 one-way or €7 return. For bus information, see the Marbella Getting There & Away section.

ESTEPONA

postcode 29680 • pop 37,500

Estepona has controlled its development relatively carefully and remains a fairly agreeable seaside town. Its fine main beach, Playa de la Rada, is backed by a broad promenade. Beyond this, a protective line of palm trees, shrubs and colourful flower beds, dampens the impact of traffic on the busy seafront road of Avenida de España. The oldish town centre around leafy, traffic-free Plaza Las Flores is also pleasant. A sizable fishing fleet and a large marina share the port beyond the lighthouse at the western end of town.

The **tourist office** (☎ 95 280 09 13; ⓦ www.infoestepona.com; Avenida San Lorenzo 1; open 9am-6pm Mon-Fri, 9am-2pm Sat) is in the town centre. The **bus station** (☎ 95 280 02 49; Avenida de España) is 400m west, on the seafront.

Selwo Costa del Sol (☎ 95 279 21 50; adult/child €16.50/11; open 10am-6pm Oct-May daily, 10am-8pm daily June-Sept, closed Mon Nov-Dec), a 1-sq-km safari park with 200 exotic animal species from around the globe, opened in 1999 at Las Lomas del Monte, 6km east of Estepona. Some you see on foot, others from 4WD vehicles. One feature is the walk-through Cañón de las Aves, a 300m-long natural canyon filled with birds. To get there from Estepona, a taxi is best. A direct daily bus runs from Málaga via Torremolinos, Fuengirola and Marbella (phone Selwo for information).

Centrally located accommodation in Estepona is limited.

Hostal Pilar (☎ 95 280 00 18; Plaza Las Flores 22; singles/doubles €25/45) is an old-fashioned, friendly place, nicely located on the old square.

Pensión Malagueña (☎ 95 280 00 11; Calle Castillo 1; singles/doubles €30/42), off Plaza Las Flores, has reasonable rooms.

Pensión San Antonio (☎ 95 280 14 76; Calle Adolfo Suárez 9; singles/doubles €10.30/22), a block east of the square, is an amiable place that offers basic rooms.

Hotel Buenavista (☎ 95 280 01 37, fax 95 280 55 93; Paseo Marítimo 180; singles/ doubles with bathroom €27/42) is on the seafront.

Hotel Aguamarina (☎ 95 280 61 55, fax 95 280 45 98; Avenida San Lorenzo 32; singles/doubles €53/73.80) is a sizable hotel just along from the bus station. Breakfast is included in the price.

Plaza Las Flores is a student hang-out that's home to a few tapas bars and restaurants. Nightlife focuses on the marina, which has a flush of popular bars including **Christopher Columbus** (☎ 95 280 56 25; *Puerto Deportivo*).

Getting There & Away

Bus Eleven buses run to Fuengirola, Torremolinos and Málaga (€5.40, two hours) daily, eight on Sunday. Buses run every half-hour between 6.40am and 10.30pm to Marbella (€1.60, 70 minutes). About 10 buses run to Algeciras (€2.95, 1 hour) and two to Cádiz (€11.10, 3½ hours), daily.

CASARES
postcode 29690 • pop 3200
• elevation 435m
Casares, 18km from Estepona (10km inland), is well worth an outing. Clinging to steep hillsides below the well-preserved remains of a Muslim castle, it affords wonderful views, and The Sierra Crestellina, to its northwest, offers good walking opportunities.

Pensión Plaza (☎ 95 289 40 88; *Plaza de España 6; doubles €20*) on the main square, has adequate rooms with bathroom.

Buses leave Estepona for Casares at 11am, 1.30pm and 7pm daily except Sunday (€1.56, 45 minutes). The last one back leaves Casares at 4pm.

Inland

Málaga province's interior is a far cry from the tourist-clogged coasts. Here you'll find spectacular gorges and remote mountainous areas with good walking; intriguing towns and villages, with winding streets and ancient castles; and traces of even earlier humanity in the form of impressive cave paintings and megalithic tombs.

EL CHORRO, ARDALES & AROUND
Fifty kilometres northwest of Málaga, the Río Guadalhorce carves its way through the awesome Garganta del Chorro (El Chorro Gorge). Also called the Desfiladero de los Gaitanes, the gorge is about 4km long, as much as 400m deep, and sometimes just 10m wide. Its often sheer walls and other rock faces nearby are the biggest magnet for rock climbers in Andalucía with hundreds of bolted climbs snaking their way up the limestone cliffs. Along the gorge run the main railway into Málaga (with the aid of 12 tunnels and six bridges) and a path called the Camino (or Caminito) del Rey, which for long stretches becomes a concrete catwalk clinging to the gorge walls up to 100m above the river. The Camino del Rey is in a dangerously decayed state and unless long-discussed repairs are actually made, you should not attempt to walk along it, although skilled guides organise special trips that require abseiling ability and some rock-climbing and scrambling experience. You *can* view much of the gorge and path by walking along the railway.

This craggy northwestern area of the province is full of other places of historic and natural interest. The pleasant town of Ardales is the main centre.

El Chorro
postcode 29552 • pop 100
• elevation 200m
El Chorro village is a tiny settlement in the midst of a spectacular and surreal landscape of soaring limestone crags that encircle an ugly dam on the Guadalhorce, just south of the gorge.

The Finca La Campana, run by experienced climbers and outdoor specialists (see Places to Stay & Eat), offers climbing courses and climbing, caving, walking, kayaking and mountain bike trips. (They do a trip along the Camino del Rey that requires abseiling at the beginning and end of the route). They also rent out mountain bikes for €10 a day. **Aventur El Chorro** (☎ 649 24 94 44), near the station, rents out mountain bikes for about €1.80 per hour. Camping El Chorro (see Places to Stay & Eat) rents out bikes for about the same.

Camino del Rey The 'King's Path' is so named because Alfonso XIII reputedly walked along it in 1921 when he opened the reservoirs above the gorge, which supply much of Málaga province's water. It has been officially closed since 1992 and, by 2000, gaping holes in its concrete floor had made it impassable for all but skilled rock climbers. There is always talk about 're-opening' the Camino del Rey, but that may be a long time away, if ever.

Places to Stay & Eat Amid eucalyptus trees 350m towards the gorge from the village is **Camping El Chorro** (*☎/fax 95 249 52 95; camping per adult/child €3.20/2, tent €1.75-3)*, which has room for 150 people. The **Albergue** *(adult/child under 12 €9.60/ 8, breakfast included)* is farther along the wooded slopes, approached by going left at the entrance gate. It has clean and smart rooms.

Pensión Estación (*☎ 95 249 50 04; singles/doubles €21/24)*, at El Chorro station, has four clean little rooms, and **Restaurante Estación**, also called **Bar Isabel**, a renowned climbers' gathering spot, serves *platos combinados* from €3.50-4.50.

Apartamentos La Garganta (*☎ 95 249 51 19, fax 95 249 52 98; e informacion@la garganta.com; apartments €72)*, a converted flour mill just south of the station, has small apartments for up to five people, plus a pool and a good restaurant with good meaty dishes for €5.25 to €12.25 and fish for €4.25 to €7.25.

Refugio de Escalada La Garganta (*☎ 95 249 51 01; e informacion@lagarganta.com; bunks €6)*, just below the station, is popular with climbers. It has its own climbing wall, and a kitchen. Bring a sleeping bag for your bunk.

Finca La Campana (*☎/fax 95 211 20 19, ☎ 626 963 942; w www.el-chorro.com; bunks €10, doubles €24, 2–8-person apartments €34-80)*, 2km from the station (signposted), is in a delightful location. It has a pool, climbing wall and guest kitchen; prepared breakfasts are available too. SGE maps and cycling route maps are on sale here.

Bobastro

Back in the 9th century, the rugged El Chorro area was the redoubt of a kind of Andalucian Robin Hood, Omar ibn Hafsun, who resisted the armies of Córdoba for nearly 40 years from the hill fortress of Bobastro. Ibn Hafsun came from a family of Muwallads (converts from Christianity to Islam) but turned to banditry after killing a neighbour. Quickly gaining popular support – partly, it's said, because he defended the peasants against taxes and forced labour – he at one stage controlled territory all the way from Cartagena to the Strait of Gibraltar.

To reach Bobastro from El Chorro village, follow the road up the valley from the western side of the dam, and after 3km take the signposted Bobastro turn-off. Nearly 3km up, an 'Iglesia Mozárabe' sign indicates the 500m footpath to the remains of a Mozarabic church cut out of the rock. Legend, supported by some historical sources, says that Ibn Hafsun converted to Christianity (thus becoming a Mozarab) before his death in 917, and was buried in this church. Mozarabs certainly played an important part in his uprising. When Bobastro was finally conquered by Córdoba in 927, Ibn Hafsun's remains were taken away for posthumous crucifixion outside Córdoba's Mezquita.

Faint traces of Ibn Hafsun's rectangular fortress remain on the highest point of the hill, a farther 2.5km up the road. The views are magnificent and you can take refreshments at **Bar La Mesa** *(open June-Sept)*.

Valle de Abdalajís

This village 9km east of El Chorro is Andalucía's paragliding capital: tuition is offered by the **Club-Escuela de Parapente** (*☎ 952 48 91 80; Calle Sevilla 4, Valle de Abdalajís)*.

Ardales
postcode 29550 • pop 3200
• elevation 450m

If you continue westwards past the Bobastro turn-off on the MA-444 from El Chorro, after 2.5km you reach a T-junction. A left turn here will take you south to Ardales (6km); a right turn leads to the Parque Ardales camping ground (600m), the Restaurante El Mirador (2km) and other restaurants near the picturesque Embalse del

Conde del Guadalhorce. This very large reservoir dominates the landscape and is noted for its carp fishing.

Things to See & Do The **Museo de la Historia y las Tradiciones** (☎ 95 245 80 46; adult/child €1/0.50 open 10.30am-2pm & 5pm-7pm Tues-Sun Oct-Mar; 10.30am-2pm & 5pm-8pm Tues-Sun Apr-Sept) at the entry to Ardales from the A-357, provides tourist information and has displays on local archaeology and customs.

The **Museo Municipal Cueva de Ardales** (Plaza Ayuntamiento; admission €0.70; open 10.30am-2pm & 4pm-6pm Tues-Sun Nov-May, 10.30am-2pm & 5pm-7pm Tues-Sun Jun-Oct) is located on the plaza adjoining Ardales' central Plaza de San Isidro. Devoted to the Cueva de Ardales, 3.5km southeast of the town, it has copies of its prehistoric rock paintings and carvings. For two-hour guided visits costing €4.80 to the **Cueva de Ardales** itself (possible between May and October) contact **Ardales town hall** (☎ 95 245 80 87) a week or two in advance. The caves contain 60 Palaeolithic paintings and carvings of animals, done between about 18,000 and 14,000BC, and traces of later occupation and burials from about 8000 BC to after 3000 BC.

Up near the top of the village, the **Iglesia de la Nuestra Señora de los Remedios** was originally a mosque and has a good Mudejar artesonado ceiling (wooden ceiling with interlaced beams). If it's closed ask at Plaza de la Iglesia 1, opposite, for the key. Above the church is **La Peña**, a crag with the remains of a 10th-century fort probably built by Omar ibn Hafsun.

A track leaving the road opposite the steps up to Restaurante El Mirador leads 600m to the start of a walking track on the right, which leads down to the northern end of **El Chorro** gorge in 1.5km.

Places to Stay Situated seven kilometres north of Ardales on the banks of the Embalse del Conde del Guadalhorce, **Parque Ardales** (☎ 95 211 24 01; camping 2 people, tent & car €9, apartments high season €64) has a large, appealing, shady

camp site, and apartments accommodating up to four people.

Pensión Bobastro (☎ 95 245 91 50; Plaza de San Isidro 13; singles/doubles €12/24), in the centre of Ardales, has spotless, comfy rooms with shared bathrooms. It's more like living with a local extended family, albeit a charming one.

Pensión El Cruce (☎ 95 245 90 12; singles/doubles €15/30), near the A-357, 500m from the centre, is a more standard roadhouse-style place, but with pleasant rooms and a busy bar with a menú for €6.

Hotel Mesón (☎ 95 211 24 11, fax 95 211 28 05; Pantano del Chorro 16; singles/doubles €51/70) is a comfortable, lodge-like hotel that also has a good restaurant.

Places to Eat For the best food in Ardales town, head to **Bar El Casino** (Plaza de San Isidro; raciones €4-6). Try the delicious huevos con bechamel (hard-boiled eggs in bechamel sauce) or pimientos rellenos de ternera (veal-stuffed peppers): both are rolled in breadcrumbs then deep fried.

Bar Millan (Calle Fray Juan 1; tapas €0.90) is a satisfyingly raucous place on the corner of the central square. A picture of Bob Marley oversees the full-on piped music.

Several restaurants along the road beyond Parque Ardales are very popular at the weekend and holidays.

Restaurante El Mirador (☎ 95 245 82 03; Parque de Ardales, Zona Cuarta; mains €5-10), overlooking the reservoir, serves economical salads and omelettes as well as meat dishes.

Mesón El Oasis (☎ 95 211 24 00; Zona de los Embalses; mains €4.30-9), a kilometre farther on from Restaurante El Mirador, across a dam, offers varied grilled meats, but the star item on its menu is paletillas de cordero en miel (shoulder of lamb in honey) costing €16.50.

Getting There & Away
Los Amarillos buses run from Málaga to Ronda (€3.60) and vice-versa, via Ardales, four times daily but there's no bus service to El Chorro.

Three trains a day run to El Chorro from Málaga (€3.30, 45 minutes), except Sunday and holidays. You can also reach El Chorro from Ronda (€4.80, 70 minutes) or Seville by one direct train daily in each case (except Sunday and holidays from Ronda). Only from Ronda (except Friday, Sunday and holidays) do schedules allow a round trip in one day. Timetables change from time to time, however.

To reach El Chorro, drivers from Málaga can branch off the A-357 onto the A-343 Antequera road near Pizarra. About 4km north of Pizarra, turn left for Álora and El Chorro. The road passes narrowly between houses, and you eventually hit a pot-holed road that takes you to El Chorro. Another approach from Málaga is to continue on the A-357 to the Ardales junction. Turn right here along the MA-444 with the reservoir on your left, then in about 5km turn off right, signed to El Chorro. Also from Ardales, a partly unpaved road leads 20km southwest along the remote Turón valley to El Burgo (see Around Ronda later in this chapter).

RONDA
postcode 29400 • pop 34,500
• elevation 723m

Old and new Ronda stand either side of the spectacular 100m-deep El Tajo gorge amid the beautiful Serranía de Ronda. The town is just an hour inland from the Costa del Sol and is a world away from the coastal hustle, although that same hustle is transferred each morning as countless day-trip coaches disgorge their Costa-based passengers. The best time to enjoy this wonderful town with some ease is in the honeyed light of evening. The popularity of Ronda has not detracted from its remarkable appeal although the arrival of a McDonald's right next to Ronda's Parador is a tasty irony.

Capital of a small Berber *taifa* after the collapse of the Córdoba caliphate, Ronda came under Sevillan rule in the mid-11th century but regained a large measure of independence after Seville's fall in 1248. Despite a near-impregnable location, it fell to Fernando El Católico in 1485 because its governor and army left to defend Málaga,

thinking that city was about to come under Christian attack.

Orientation & Information

The old Muslim part of town, known as La Ciudad, stands on the southern side of the El Tajo gorge, with the newer town, El Mercadillo, to the north. Three bridges cross the gorge, the main one being the Puente Nuevo linking Plaza de España with Calle de Armiñán. Both parts of town come to an abrupt end on their western sides with cliffs plunging away to the valley of the Río Guadalevín far below. Places of interest are mainly concentrated in La Ciudad while most places to stay and eat, along with the bus and train stations, are in El Mercadillo.

The **municipal tourist office** (☎ 95 218 71 19, fax 95 218 71 47; Paseo de Blas Infante; open 9.30am-6.30pm Mon-Fri, 10am-2pm & 3pm-6.30pm Sat, Sun & public holidays) has helpful and knowledgeable staff; the place can become busy by late morning. Also, there is a **Junta de Andalucía tourist office** (☎ 649 96 53 38; Plaza de España 1; open 9am-7pm Mon-Fri, 10am-2pm Sat). Banks and ATMs are mainly on Calle Virgen de la Paz (opposite the bullring) and Plaza Carmen Abela. The main **post office** is on Calle Virgen de la Paz 18-20. The **internet centre (Informatica Virtual System)** (Calle de Sevilla 7; open 10am-2pm & 5pm-8.30pm) charges €0.50 per half-hour. The **Comansur shop** (☎ 95 287 86 67; Calle Lauria 30) sells 1:50,000 SGE maps of the region. The **Policía Local** (☎ 95 287 13 69) station is in the **town hall** (Plaza Duquesa de Parcent).

Plaza de España & Puente Nuevo

Chapter 10 of Ernest Hemingway's *For Whom the Bell Tolls* tells how early in the civil war the 'fascists' of a small town were rounded up in the town hall. They were then clubbed and flailed as they were made to walk the gauntlet between two lines of townspeople 'in the plaza on the top of the cliff above the river'. At the end of the line the victims, dead or still alive, were thrown over the cliff. The episode was based on

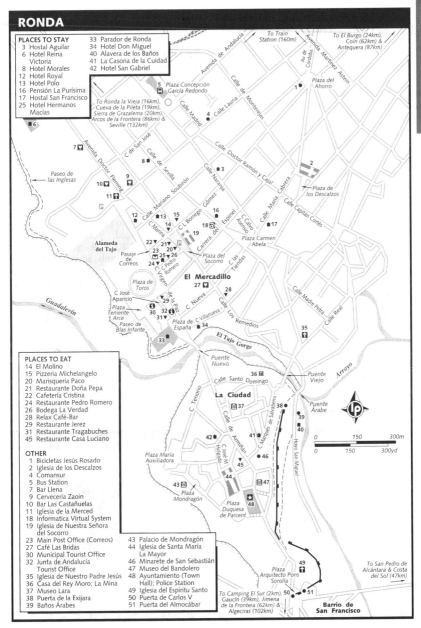

RONDA

PLACES TO STAY
3 Hostal Aguilar
6 Hotel Reina Victoria
8 Hotel Morales
12 Hotel Royal
13 Hotel Polo
16 Pensión La Purísima
17 Hostal San Francisco
25 Hotel Hermanos Macías
33 Parador de Ronda
34 Hotel Don Miguel
40 Alavera de los Baños
41 La Casona de la Cuidad
42 Hotel San Gabriel

To Ronda la Vieja (16km),
Cueva de la Pileta (19km),
Sierra de Grazalema (20km),
Arcos de la Frontera (86km) &
Seville (132km)

Plaza Concepción
García Redondo

Plaza del Ahorro

To Train Station (160m)

To El Burgo (24km),
Coín (62km) &
Antequera (87km)

Avenida de Andalucía

Avenida Martínez Astein

Av de Córdoba

Calle de Monterejas

Avenida de Andalucía

Calle Madrid

Calle Lauria

Plaza de los Descalzos

Calle Doctor Ramón y Cajal

Calle María Cabrera

Calle Capitán Cortés

Paseo de las Inglesas

Avenida Doctor Fleming

C de San José

Calle de Sevilla

Calle Naranja

Calle Mariano Soubrón

C L Borrego Gómez

Calle Espinel

Calvo Asenso

Plaza Carmen Abela

Alameda del Tajo

C Marina

Carrera del

Plaza del Socorro

C las Tiendas

Pasaje de Correos

C Pedro Romero

C Virgen de la Paz

El Mercadillo

Plaza de Toros

C José Aparicio

Plaza Teniente Arce

C Nueva

Calle Los Remedios

Calle Madre Petra

Calle Real

Paseo de Blas Infante

C Villanueva

Plaza de España

El Tajo Gorge

Guadalevín

Puente Nuevo

Puente Viejo

Puente Árabe

Calle Santo Domingo

La Ciudad

Arroyo

C Tenorio

Calle de Armiñán

C Marqués de Salvatierra

Hoyo San Miguel

Plaza María Auxiliadora

C José M Holgado

Plaza Mondragón

Plaza Duquesa de Parcent

Plaza Arquitecto Pons Sorolla

To San Pedro de Alcántara & Costa del Sol (47km)

To Camping El Sur (2km),
Gaucín (39km), Jimena
de la Frontera (62km) &
Algeciras (102km)

Barrio de San Francisco

0   150   300m
0   150   300yd

PLACES TO EAT
14 El Molino
15 Pizzeria Michelangelo
20 Marisquería Paco
21 Restaurante Doña Pepa
22 Cafetería Cristina
24 Restaurante Pedro Romero
26 Bodega La Verdad
28 Relax Café-Bar
29 Restaurante Jerez
31 Restaurante Tragabuches
45 Restaurante Casa Luciano

OTHER
1 Bicicletas Jesús Rosado
2 Iglesia de los Descalzos
4 Comansur
5 Bus Station
7 Bar Llena
9 Cervecería Zaoin
10 Bar Las Castañuelas
11 Iglesia de la Merced
18 Informatica Virtual System
19 Iglesia de Nuestra Señora del Socorro
23 Main Post Office (Correos)
27 Café Las Bridas
30 Municipal Tourist Office
32 Junta de Andalucía Tourist Office
35 Iglesia de Nuestro Padre Jesús
36 Casa del Rey Moro; La Mina
37 Museo Lara
38 Puerta de la Exijara
39 Baños Árabes
43 Palacio de Mondragón
44 Iglesia de Santa María La Mayor
46 Minarete de San Sebastián
47 Museo del Bandolero
48 Ayuntamiento (Town Hall); Police Station
49 Iglesia del Espíritu Santo
50 Puerta de Carlos V
51 Puerta del Almocábar

real events in Ronda, though the real perpetrators were, according to Hugh Thomas' authoritative *The Spanish Civil War*, a gang from Málaga. Ronda's Parador, on Plaza de España, was, before it became a hotel, the town hall.

The majestic Puente Nuevo (New Bridge) spanning El Tajo from Plaza de España is two centuries old. An unsubstantiated Ronda tradition relates that its architect, Martín de Aldehuela, fell to his death in 1793 while trying to engrave the bridge's date on its side – a legend no doubt encouraged by the incomplete hieroglyphics accompanying the word *año* (year) beside the shield on the side of the bridge.

Plaza de Toros & Around
Ronda's elegant bullring *(Calle Virgen de la Paz; admission €4; open 10am-6pm daily)* is a Mecca for aficionados. Opened in 1785, it's one of the oldest bullrings in Spain, has one of the biggest arenas, and has been the site of some of the most important events in bullfighting history (see the boxed text 'Ronda's Fighting Romeros'). It contains a **Museo Taurino** that is currently being expanded, and that is crammed with memorabilia such as costumes worn by Pedro Romero and 1990's star Jesulín de Ubrique, and photos of famous fans including Ernest Hemingway and Orson Welles.

Spectacular clifftop views open out from **Paseo de Blas Infante**, behind the Plaza de Toros, and the leafy **Alameda del Tajo** park nearby.

La Ciudad
Though most of its Muslim buildings have been heavily modified over the centuries, La Ciudad retains the character of a typical old Muslim town.

Casa del Rey Moro & La Mina From the Puente Nuevo, head along La Ciudad's main street, Calle de Armiñán, then take the first street on your left to visit the Casa del Rey Moro *(House of the Moorish King; Calle Santo Domingo 17)*. The house itself, which was built in the 18th century, supposedly over the remains of a Muslim palace, is closed to the public. But you can visit its terraced, gorge-side **gardens** *(adult/child €3.80/1.90; open 10am-7pm daily)* and also climb down **La Mina**, a Muslim-era stairway of over 300 steps cut into the rock all the way to the river at the bottom of the gorge. These steps enabled Ronda to maintain water supplies when it was under attack, and provided a hidden entry/exit into the old city – but were also one of the points where Christian troops forced entry when they finally took Ronda in 1485. The steps are not well-lit and are quite steep and wet in places. Care should be taken, even by the fit and able; the very young and the less able could have difficulty.

Ronda's Fighting Romeros

Ronda can bullishly claim to be the home of bullfighting – and it does. During the 18th and 19th centuries three generations of Ronda's Romero family enshrined forever most of the basics of modern bullfighting on foot (previously it was conducted on horseback as a kind of sporting cavalry training for the nobility). Francisco Romero, born in 1698, evolved the ballet-like use of the cape to attract the bull, and of the *muleta* for the kill. His son Juan introduced the matador's supporting team, the *cuadrilla*; and grandson Pedro (1754–1839) perfected an intellectual, elegant and classical style, still known as the Escuela Rondeña (Ronda School), in which matadors work as one with the bull. Pedro is said to have killed 5500 bulls in his career, without being gored once.

Museo Lara This art and antiques museum *(Calle de Armiñán 29; admission €2.50; open 10am-8pm daily)*, in a handsome old mansion, exhibits over 2000 diverse items that range from blunderbusses to opera glasses, archaeological remains to a pipe collection.

Palacio de Mondragón The Mondragón Palace *(Plaza Mondragón; admission €2; open 10am-6pm Mon-Fri, 10am-3pm Sat, Sun & holidays)* is thought to have been built for Abomelic, ruler of Ronda, in 1314. It was altered soon after the Christian conquest, and Fernando and Isabel lodged here at some point. Of the ground floor's three courtyards, the only one to preserve Islamic character is the Patio Mudejar, from which a horseshoe arch leads into a clifftop garden with splendid views. The dome above the main staircase is exquisite. Some rooms house a museum on prehistoric life in the Ronda area. There are more fine views from the nearby **Plaza María Auxiliadora**.

Iglesia de Santa María La Mayor A minute's walk southeast from the Palacio de Mondragón is this fine church *(Plaza Duquesa de Parcent; admission €2; open 10am-6pm daily Nov-May, 10am-8pm daily June-Oct)*, which stands on the site of Muslim Ronda's main mosque. Its tower displays Islamic origins and the galleries beside it, built for viewing festivities in the square, also date from Muslim times. Just inside the church entrance is an arch covered with Arabic inscriptions, which was part of the mosque's mihrab (prayer niche indicating the direction of Mecca). The church was begun in Gothic style but, as building went on over the centuries, tastes changed to the Renaissance style and finally to the baroque of the northern end.

Barrio de San Francisco In this southern quarter of La Ciudad you'll find the imposing late-15th-century **Iglesia del Espíritu Santo** *(Calle Espíritu Santo; admission €1; open 10am-7pm Mon-Sat)*, and a stretch of the old city walls pierced by two gates, the 16th-century **Puerta de Carlos V** and the 13th-century **Puerta del Almocábar**.

Museo del Bandolero This interesting museum *(Calle de Armiñán 65; admission €2.50; open 10am-7pm daily Nov-May, 10am-8pm daily June-Sept)* is dedicated to the banditry for which central Andalucía, including the Ronda area, was once renowned. Old prints seem to reflect that when the youthful bandoleros were not being shot, hanged or garrotted by the authorities they were stabbing each other in the back, literally as much as figuratively, with extremely wicked-looking knives.

Just off the same street, to the north, the little **Minarete de San Sebastián** was built in Granada style, as part of a mosque, in the 14th century.

Walls, Baths & More Bridges Beside the Museo del Bandolero, steps lead down to an impressive stretch of Ronda's old walls along the eastern side of La Ciudad. Following them, you pass through the **Puerta de la Exijara**, which was the entry to Islamic Ronda's Jewish quarter, outside the walls. A path continues down to the beautiful, almost intact, 13th- and 14th-century **Baños Árabes** *(Arab Baths; admission free; open 9.30am-1.30pm & 4pm-6pm Tues, 9.30am-3.30pm Wed-Sat)*.

From the northern side of the nearby Puente Viejo, you can make your way back up to Plaza de España via a small park along the gorge's edge.

Special Events

Ronda's famous old bullring stages relatively few fights, but in early September it holds some of the most celebrated and unusual in Spain. The Corridas Goyescas is one in which top matadors fight in early 19th-century-style costumes – just as in Goya's depictions of Ronda bullfights. The *goyescas* are the culmination of a fiesta starting in late August, and the Feria de Pedro Romero includes an important flamenco event, the Festival de Cante Grande.

Places to Stay – Budget

Camping El Sur *(☎ 95 287 59 39; A-369; camping 2 adults, tent & car €11.50)* is a good camping ground in a pleasant setting, 2km southwest of Ronda on the Algeciras road.

Budget rooms in Ronda generally don't offer great value.

Pensión La Purísima *(☎ 95 287 10 50; Calle de Sevilla 10; singles/doubles €15/27)* is clean, friendly and better than most with 10 rooms. The owner speaks French.

Hostal Aguilar *(☎ 95 287 19 94; Calle Naranja 28; singles/doubles €18/35)* is handy for the bus station and offers small but adequate rooms.

Hostal San Francisco *(☎ 95 287 32 99; Calle María Cabrera 18; singles/doubles with bathroom €15/27)* is another good option. It has just 16 reasonable rooms and offers a warm welcome.

A bit more money can buy you considerably better accommodation.

Hotel Royal *(☎ 95 287 11 41, fax 95 287 81 32; Calle Virgen de la Paz 42; singles/doubles €34.50/43)* in a good location has 29 plain but decent rooms with bathroom and TV.

Hotel Hermanos Macías *(☎ 95 287 42 38; Calle Pedro Romero 3; singles/doubles €23/39)* is another place with reasonable rooms; rates include breakfast.

Hotel Morales *(☎/fax 95 287 15 38, fax 95 218 70 02; Calle de Sevilla 51; singles/doubles with bathroom €22.50/41.70)* has 18 pleasant rooms. Its walls are decked with maps of the area, it has a room for bicycles, and the staff are full of information on the town and nearby natural parks.

Places to Stay – Mid-Range

Hotel San Gabriel *(☎ 95 219 03 92, fax 95 219 01 17; e sangabriel@ronda.net; Calle José M Holgado 19; singles/doubles €67.40/ 80.25)* is a tranquil and stylish hotel that occupies a converted 18th-century mansion at the heart of La Ciudad.

La Casona de la Ciudad *(☎ 95 287 95 95, fax 95 216 10 95; e reservas@lacasona delaciudad.com; Calle Marqués de Salvatierra 5; doubles €91)* is another old-town hotel in a handsome mansion. It is full of fine antique furnishings and paintings and has big, beautifully decorated rooms.

Alavera de los Baños *(☎/fax 95 287 91 43; w www.andalucia.com/alavera; Hoyo San Miguel s/n; singles €42, doubles €58-72)*,

owned by a friendly Spanish/German couple, is a small and individual hotel, in a converted tannery next door to the Baños Árabes. The rooms are attractive and rates include breakfast. The hotel restaurant offers delicious gazpacho and vegetarian options and, like the decor, it has some interesting Moroccan touches.

Hotel Polo *(☎ 95 287 24 47, fax 95 287 24 49; Calle Mariano Soubirón 8; singles/ doubles €41.70/65.60)*, another cheerful family-run hotel, offers 33 spacious rooms. It also has a busy restaurant.

Hotel Don Miguel *(☎ 95 287 77 22, fax 95 287 83 77; Calle Villanueva 8; doubles €67.50)* is the least expensive option overlooking the gorge.

Places to Stay – Top End

Hotel Reina Victoria *(☎/fax 95 287 12 40; Avenida Doctor Fleming 25; singles €80-113, doubles €135-174)*, a 90-room place, was built by a British company in the 1900s when Ronda was a popular outing from Gibraltar by the recently constructed railway from Algeciras. The old-fashioned comfort recalls far-flung parts of the British empire. The hotel has fine clifftop gardens.

Parador de Ronda *(☎ 95 287 75 00, fax 95 287 81 88; e ronda@parador.es; Plaza de España s/n; singles/doubles €97/121)* stands at the very edge of the gorge and has bright and airy rooms.

Places to Eat

Typical Ronda food is hearty mountain fare, with an emphasis on stews (called *cocido*, *estofado* or *cazuela*), trout *(trucha)*, game such as rabbit *(conejo)*, partridge *(perdiz)*, quail *(codorniz)*, and oxtail *(rabo de toro)*.

Marisquería Paco *(Plaza del Socorro)*, a block northeast of the bullring, does good seafood and *jamón* (cured ham) tapas.

El Molino *(Plaza del Socorro; platos combinados from €4.25)* is popular for its pizzas and pasta costing €3.65 to €5, and varied breakfasts from a good *tostada* and *café con leche* (coffee with hot milk) at €3.75 to *desayuno americano* (American breakfast) a gut-busting dish at €7.20 and marginally healthier than the Scottish version at €5.25.

Cafetería Cristina *(Pasaje del Correos; menú €6.25)* in an arcade running between Plaza del Socorro and Calle Virgen de la Paz, does *platos combinados* from €3.50 at the bar to €5.70 at tables, and has a tasty line in pastries.

Restaurante Doña Pepa *(Plaza del Socorro 10; menú €7.25-10)*, solid and old-fashioned in food and decor, has lots of à la carte choices including vegetarian options.

Restaurante Hermanos Macías *(Calle Pedro Romero 3; meat & fish mains €5.50-10)*, on a pedestrian street between Plaza del Socorro and Calle Virgen de la Paz, is a friendly mid-range eatery with decent if unspectacular food. The tapas bar **Bodega La Verdad**, next door, is popular with locals.

Pizzería Michaelangelo *(☎ 95 287 36 83; Calle Lorenzo Borrego Gómez 5)* is a busy place that offers tasty pizzas and pastas for €2.70 to €4.25.

Relax Café-Bar *(☎ 95 287 72 07; Calle Los Remedios 27; pastas & bakes €5.50; open 1pm-4pm & 8pm-midnight Mon-Fri)* is an oasis of good vegetarian food in meat-hungry Ronda. It is run by two friendly Englishwomen, who do a terrific range of tasty dishes, including salads from €3 to €4.50, soups for €3.90 and sandwiches with imaginative fillings from €3.60.

Restaurants in the bullring/Plaza de España area tend to be touristy but several are good.

Restaurante Pedro Romero *(☎ 95 287 11 10; Calle Virgen de la Paz 18; mains €9-15, set lunch €12)*, opposite the bullring, is a celebrated eatery dedicated to bullfighting, with blood-red tablecloths and decor of bulls' heads and fight photos. The food is classic *rondeño*, with à la carte mains and a set lunch (not including drinks).

Restaurante Jerez *(Plaza Teniente Arce 2; mains €9-12)*, on the corner of Calle José Aparicio, serves soups and salads costing €3.60 to €6.50, oxtail at €11.50 and partridge for €14.50.

Restaurante Tragabuches *(☎ 95 219 02 91; Calle José Aparicio 1; 2-course meal €19.50-32)* has a good reputation. For main course you might go for venison and sweet potatoes or pork trotters with squid and sunflower seeds.

Restaurante Casa Luciano *(Calle de Armiñán 42; 3-course menú €7.80)*, a pleasant little place in La Ciudad, serves salads and omelettes starting at €4.25.

Entertainment

A modest nightlife zone centres around the foot of Avenida Doctor Fleming, with **Bar Llena**, **Bar Las Castañuelas** and the youthful **Cervecería Zaoin** (with a pool table), among the more interesting spots. **Café Las Bridas** *(Calle Los Remedios 18)* sometimes puts on live flamenco or rock. Relax Café-Bar (see Places to Eat) has a good evening atmosphere.

Getting There & Away

Bus The bus station is at Plaza Concepción García Redondo 2. **Comes** *(☎ 95 287 19 92)* has buses to Arcos de la Frontera, Jerez de la Frontera and Cádiz five times daily; Gaucín, Jimena de la Frontera and Algeciras (€7.25, 1½ hours) at 4pm Monday to Friday; and Zahara de la Sierra. **Los Amarillos** *(☎ 95 218 70 61)* goes to/from Seville (€8.40, 2½ hours) via Algodonales three to five times daily; Grazalema (€1.95, 35 minutes), Benaocaz and Ubrique twice daily; and Málaga (€7, two hours) via Ardales four times daily. **Portillo** *(☎ 95 287 22 62)* runs to/from Málaga (€7.85, 1½ hours) via San Pedro de Alcántara and Marbella three or four times daily. Further services run to other hill towns and villages.

Train Ronda station *(☎ 95 287 16 73; Avenida de Andalucía)* is on the scenic line between Bobadilla and Algeciras. Five or more trains run daily to/from Algeciras (€5.65 to €10, 1½ to two hours) via Gaucín and Jimena de la Frontera; three daily to/from Granada (€10.10, 2½ hours) via Antequera; one runs daily except Sunday to/from Málaga (€7.45, two hours); two run daily to/from Córdoba (€13.50 to €14.50, 2½ hours) and Madrid (by day €52, 4½ hours; overnight €29.50, nine hours). For Seville and other trains to/from Granada, Málaga, Córdoba and Madrid, change at Bobadilla or Antequera.

Getting Around

It's less than 1km from the train station to most accommodation. Every 30 minutes town mini-buses run to Plaza de España from Avenida Martínez Astein, across the road from the station, but the walking distance is not great.

Parking in Ronda is, inevitably, difficult. There are a number of underground car parks and some hotels have parking deals for guests. Parking charges are about €1 per hour, €12 for 12 to 24 hours. Taxis are found in Plaza Carmen Abela.

Bicycle For bicycle rental, **Bicicletas Jesús Rosado** (*π/fax 95 287 02 21, π 637 45 77 56; e jrosado@ronda.net; 87 Plaza del Ahorro 1; open 10am-2pm & 5pm-8.30pm Mon-Fri, 10am-2pm Sat*) rents out well-equipped mountain bikes for €2.40 an hour, €9 a day or €18 for three days.

AROUND RONDA

Fine hill country, with plenty of walking and cycling possibilities, and dotted with picturesque mountain towns and villages, stretches in every direction from Ronda. These green, misty hills (including the Sierra de Grazalema and Los Alcornocales natural parks to the west and southwest – see the Cádiz Province chapter for details) are the western end of the Cordillera Bética.

Ronda la Vieja

This ruined hilltop Roman town (*Acinipo; π 630 42 99 49; admission free; open 10am-5pm or 6pm Tues-Sun*) about 22km northwest of Ronda, has a partly reconstructed theatre. A site plan you'll be given will help you decipher other buildings. It's wise to check opening hours. You'll need your own vehicle: the turn-off north of the A-376 is about 6km from Ronda.

Serranía de Ronda

The mountains and valleys south and southeast of Ronda that go by this name are not Andalucía's highest or deepest, but they're certainly among the greenest and prettiest. Any of the roads through them make a picturesque route between Ronda and southern

Cádiz province, Gibraltar or the Costa del Sol, and many of the white villages here have accommodation. **Cortés de la Frontera**, overlooking the Guadiaro valley, and **Gaucín**, looking across the Genal valley to the Sierra Crestellina, are among the most beautiful spots to stop.

Cueva de la Pileta & Benaoján Palaeolithic paintings of horses, goats, fish and even a seal, dating from 20,000 to 25,000 years ago, are preserved in the Cueva de la Pileta, an impressive cave 20km southwest of Ronda. Beautiful stalactites and stalagmites add to the effect, and you'll be guided by kerosene lamp by one of the knowledgeable Bullón family from the farm in the valley below. A member of the family discovered the paintings in 1905 when searching for bat dung to use as fertiliser.

The **Cueva de la Pileta** (*π 95 216 73 43*) is 4km south of Benaoján village, about 250m off the Benaoján-Cortes de la Frontera road. The turn-off is signposted. Visits are by one-hour guided tour at 10am, 11am, noon, 1pm, 4pm and 5pm daily, plus 6pm from 16 April to 31 October. They cost €6 or €6.50 per person, depending how many turn up; children under the age of 10 pay €2.50, student-card holders €3. Guides speak at least some English and German. The maximum group size is 25, so if you come on a busy day you may have to wait for a place. At peak seasons it's worth ringing ahead to try to book a particular time.

Molino del Santo (*π 95 216 71 51; e molino@logiccontrol.es; Barriada Estación s/n; B&B singles €88-94, doubles €103-118; open mid-Feb–mid-Nov*) in Benaoján is an attractive 17-room British-run hotel and restaurant in a converted water mill. Rates depend on the room. At popular times, such as mid-April to 3 June and in September, half-board (with breakfast, afternoon tea and dinner) is obligatory, from €168 a double. It's advisable to book ahead.

Benaoján is the nearest that you can get to the Cueva de la Pileta by public transport. It is served by two Los Amarillos buses (from Monday to Friday) and up to four daily trains to/from Ronda. Walking trails link Benaoján with Ronda and villages in the Guadiaro valley.

Parque Natural Sierra de las Nieves

This 180-sq-km park southeast of Ronda, the highest portion of the Serranía de Ronda, is noted for its stands of the rare Spanish fir, and fauna including some 1000 ibex and various species of eagle. The snow *(nieve)* after which the mountains are named usually falls between January and March.

El Burgo, a remote but attractive village 10km north of Yunquera on the A-366, makes a good base for visiting the east and northeast of the park. Information is available from Yunquera's **tourist office** *(☎ 95 248 25 01; Calle del Pozo 17; open 8am-3pm Tues-Fri)*, or the **town hall** in El Burgo *(☎ 95 216 00 02)*.

Torrecilla If you're prepared to take a vehicle on unpaved tracks the best starting point for climbing Torrecilla (1919m), the highest peak in the western half of Andalucía, is the Área Recreativa Los Quejigales, 10km east by unpaved road from the A-376 Ronda–San Pedro de Alcántara road. The turn-off, 12km from Ronda, is marked by 'Parque Natural Sierra de las Nieves' signs. Walking from Los Quejigales you have a steepish 470m ascent by the Cañada de los Cuernos gully, with its Spanish fir wood, to the Puerto de los Pilones pass. Then there's a fairly level section followed by the steep 230m to the summit – you'll be rewarded by marvellous views in decent weather. The walk takes about five hours in total.

An alternative approach, slightly longer, is from the Puerto del Saucillo (1200m), 6km west of Yunquera by dirt road. En route you can take in another landmark peak, Peñón de los Enamorados (1777m).

These walks *can* be done any time of year by the properly equipped, but the heat of July and August demands extra stamina, and in winter be prepared for temperatures close to freezing. Avoid cloud, mist, heavy rain or snow and high winds. Carry water to get you as far as Cerro del Pilar, at the foot of the final ascent, where there's a freshwater spring. The IGN/Junta de Andalucía

Parque Natural Sierra de las Nieves map (1:50,000) shows the relevant paths.

Places to Stay & Eat Eight hundred metres off the A-376 on the road to Los Quejigales is **Camping Conejeras** *(☎ 619 18 00 12; camping 1 person, tent & car €7.25; open Oct-June, & Sat & Sun July-Sept)*.

Camping Pinsapo Azul *(☎ 95 248 27 54; Yunquera 29410; camping 1 person, tent & car €7.80; open Apr-Oct)* is at Yunquera. The site has its own bar and swimming pool.

Hostal Asencio *(☎ 95 248 27 16; Calle Mesones 1; singles €13.50, doubles with bathroom €36.50)*, with a restaurant that does tasty local dishes with emphasis on meat, but with some vegetarian choices. The hotel is tucked away at the heart of Yunquera near the central Plaza de la Constitución.

Posada del Canónigo *(☎ 95 216 01 85; Calle Mesones 24; singles/doubles with bathroom €37.30/52)*, in El Burgo, is a delightful small hotel in a restored mansion; it has a good restaurant with a *menú* for €10.80. The friendly management has information on walking routes and can organise horse riding.

Hostal Sierra de las Nieves *(☎ 95 216 01 17; Calle Real 26; singles/doubles with bathroom €22/31)* is a cheaper, but equally friendly option at the heart of El Burgo.

Bar Isla de las Palomas next door to Hostal Sierra de las Nieves and the busy **Bar Casino** opposite do good tapas for about €0.90.

Getting There & Away Buses between Málaga and Ronda (€7.50, 2½ hours, two to three daily) through Yunquera and El Burgo are run by the **Sierra de las Nieves** line *(☎ 95 287 54 35)*.

ANTEQUERA

postcode 29200 • pop 40,000
• elevation 575m

Antequera lies 50km north of Málaga. It is an engaging, down-to-earth town, behind whose sometimes hectic modern face is one of the richest historic legacies in Andalucía.

The area's Neolithic and Bronze Age inhabitants of circa 2500 BC to 1800 BC erected some of Europe's largest dolmens (burial chambers built with huge slabs of rock). Later Antequera was an important Roman town. In Muslim times it was a favoured community of the Granada emirs, before it became their first town to fall to Castile in 1410. The commercial momentum that has contributed to Antequera's importance led to the town's later 'golden age' during the 16th and 17th centuries, when splendid churches and mansions were built.

Orientation & Information

The substantial remains of a hilltop Muslim castle, the Alcazaba, dominates the town. Down to the northwest is Plaza de San Sebastián, from which the main street, Calle Infante Don Fernando, runs northwest. The **bus station** (*Calle Sagrado Corazón de Jesús*) and **train station** (*☎ 95 284 32 26; Avenida de la Estación*) are 1km and 1.5km north of the centre, respectively.

The **tourist office** (*☎/fax 95 270 25 05; Plaza de San Sebastián 7; open 10am-2pm & 5pm-8pm Mon-Sat 16 June–30 Sept; 9.30am-1.30pm & 4pm-7pm Mon-Sat 1 Oct–15 June; 10am-2pm Sun & holidays year-round*) has excellent information.

There are plenty of banks and ATMs along Calle Infante Don Fernando. The **post office** is on Calle Nájera just east of the tourist office. There's an **internet centre** (*antakira.net; Calle Barrero 20; open 10.30am-2pm & 4.30pm-1am Mon-Thur, until 2am Fri, 11am-3pm & 4.30pm-2am Sat, 4.30pm-1am Sun*) with prices at €1.80 per hour.

Librería and Papelería (*San Agustín; Infante Don Fernando 15*) is a bookshop that has some maps and local books. Tucked away down a side street off Infante Don Fernande is **Sónar** (*Calle Comedias 2*) a great little music shop that has a good selection of Spanish music.

Things to See

The main approach to the hilltop Alcazaba is from Plaza de San Sebastián, up the stepped Cuesta de San Judas and then through an impressive archway, the **Arco de los Gigantes**, built in 1585 and incorporating stones with Roman inscriptions. Not a huge amount remains of the **Alcazaba** itself, but it has been turned into a pine-scented, terraced garden and you can visit the **Torre del Homenaje** (*Keep; admission free; open 10.30am-2pm & 4.30pm-6.30pm Tues-Fri, 10.30am-2pm Sat, 11.30am-2pm Sun*). There are great views from this high ground, especially towards the northeast and the Peña de los Enamorados (the Rock of the Lovers), a stony hill that has a startling resemblance to a giant human head. It earned its name from the legendary suicidal leap from its summit of a Christian girl and a Muslim youth in despair over parental opposition to their liaison. Just below the Alcazaba is the large 16th-century **Colegiata de Santa María la Mayor** (*Plaza Santa María; admission free; open 10am-2pm & 4.30pm-6.30pm Tues-Fri, 10.30am-2pm Sat, 11.30am-2pm Sun*). This church-cum-college played an important part in Andalucía's 16th-century humanist movement, and boasts a beautiful Renaissance facade, lovely fluted stone columns inside, and a Mudejar *artesonado* ceiling. It's no longer in use (Antequera has 32 other churches to serve its needs), but plays host to some excellent musical events. Beside the church is the excavated site of some Roman baths.

In the town below, the pride of the **Museo Municipal** (*Plaza Coso Viejo*) is a superb 1.4m bronze statue of a boy, 'Efebo', elegant, athletic and not entirely innocent. It is possibly the finest piece of Roman sculpture found in Spain. It was discovered on a local farm in the 1950s. The museum also displays some finds from a Roman villa in Antequera where a superb group of mosaics was discovered in 1998. Museum visits are by guided tour (€2) about every 30 minutes from 10am to 1.30pm and 4pm to 6pm Tuesday to Friday, 10am to 1.30pm Saturday, 10am to 1.30pm Sunday.

The **Museo Conventual de las Descalzas** (*Plaza de las Descalzas*), in the 17th-century convent of the Carmelitas Descalzas (Barefoot Carmelites), approximately 150m east of the Museo Municipal, displays highlights of Antequera's rich religious art heritage. Outstanding works include a painting by Lucas Giordano of St Teresa of Ávila (the

16th-century founder of the Carmelitas Descalzas), a bust of the Dolorosa by Pedro de Mena and a *Virgen de Belén* sculpture by La Roldana. The museum is open for guided visits only, costing €2.10. They go every 30 minutes from 10am to 1.30pm and 4pm to 6pm Tuesday to Friday, 10am to 12.30pm Saturday and Sunday.

Only the most jaded would fail to be impressed by the **Iglesia del Carmen** *(Plaza del Carmen; admission €1.20; open 10am-2pm & 4pm-7pm Mon-Sat, 10am-2pm Sun)*, about 400m farther southeast. The 18th-century Churrigueresque retable is a real marvel – one of the high points of Andalucian sculpture. Carved in red pine (unpainted) by *antequerano* Antonio Primo, it's spangled with statues of angels by Diego Márquez y Vega, and saints, popes and bishops by José de Medina.

The **Dólmen de Menga** and the **Dólmen de Viera** *(c. 2500 BC; admission free; open 9am-3.30pm Tues, 9am-6pm Wed-Sat, 9.30am-2.30pm Sun)* are a kilometre from the town centre within a small, wooded park beside the road leading northeast to the N-331. Head down Calle Encarnación from the central Plaza de San Sebastián and continue to follow the signs. You may find the dolmens periodically out of bounds as preservation work is carried out. Prehistoric people of the Copper-Bronze Age, transported dozens of huge slabs from nearby hills – you can spot one of the sources, a quarry atop a small hill to the west – to construct these burial chambers for their leading families. The stone frames were covered with mounds of earth. The engineering implications for the time are astonishing. Menga, the larger, is 25m long, 4m high and composed of 32 slabs, the largest of which weighs 180 tonnes. At midsummer the sun rising behind the Peña de los Enamorados to the northeast shines directly into the chamber mouth. A third chamber, the **Dólmen del Romeral** *(c. 1800 BC; admission free; open 9am-3.30pm Tues, 9am-6pm Wed-Sat, 9.30am-2.30pm Sun)*, is farther out of town. It is of later construction and features much use of small stones for its walls. To get there, continue 2.5km past

Menga and Viera through an industrial estate, then turn left following 'Córdoba, Sevilla' signs. After 500m, turn left at a roundabout and follow 'Dólmen del Romeral' signs for 200m.

Special Events

Antequera goes to town in a big way for its Real Feria de Agosto in mid-August.

Places to Stay

Camas El Gallo *(☎ 95 284 21 04; Calle Nueva 2; singles/doubles €9/15)*, just off Plaza de San Sebastián, is friendly and has clean, small, no-frills rooms.

Pensión Madrona *(☎ 95 284 00 14; Calle Calzada 25; singles/doubles with bathroom €17.70/24.75)*, another friendly place 400m northeast of Plaza de San Sebastián, near the market, has comfy rooms (plus a couple of small singles).

Hotel Colón *(☎ 95 284 00 10; Calle Infante Don Fernando 31; singles/doubles €20.65/34.25)*, a rambling place, has varied rooms with bathroom and TV costing more in August, at Easter and Christmas.

Hotel San Sebastián *(☎/fax 95 284 42 39; Plaza de San Sebastián 5; singles/doubles with bathroom €35/50)* was until recently the Hostal Manzanito. It's since been nicely refurbished, and is decidedly central; the singles are a touch cramped.

Hotel Castilla *(☎/fax 95 284 30 90; Calle Infante Don Fernando 40; singles/doubles €25/39)* offers comfy rooms with TV.

Parador de Antequera *(☎ 95 284 02 61; e antequera@parador.es; Paseo García del Olmo s/n; singles/doubles €71/88.50)*, in a quiet area north of the bullring and near the bus station, is set amid pleasant gardens.

Places to Eat

Local specialities you'll encounter on almost every Antequera menu include *porra antequerana*, a cold dip similar to gazpacho before the water is added; *bienmesabe* (literally 'tastes good to me'), a sponge dessert; and *angelorum*, another dessert incorporating meringue, sponge and egg yolk. Antequera is also one of the world capitals of the breakfast *mollete* (soft bread roll).

Hotel Castilla (Calle Infante Don Fernando 40; platos combinados €4) has a busy and popular restaurant that is a good-value place to head for any meal. Good helpings of eggs and chips, or chicken or pork with chips and vegies all cost €3.75 to €4; bocadillos are €2.40.

Pensión Madrona (Calle Calzada 25; fish & meat mains €4.80-7.25) has another fairly economical restaurant that, as well as fish and meat dishes, does salads starting at €3.60.

Telepizza (☎ 95 270 20 48; Calle Infante Don Fernando 41; pizzas €4.85-8.35) has a seating area as well as its busy delivery service.

Restaurante La Espuela (Calle San Agustín 1; open Tues-Sun; menú €11.50) is the place to head for something a bit classier. It is off Calle Infante Don Fernando and offers traditional dishes such as wild boar, venison and oxtail for €10 to €15, as well as pizzas and pasta from €4 to €6.70. Its menú típico is a fine selection of Antequera specialities for €14.50.

Restaurante La Espuela Plaza (Calle Infante Don Fernando; open daily), original and long-established, is in the bullring at the northwestern end of Calle Infante Don Fernando. It offers similar fare and prices to La Espuela but without the pizza or pasta.

Entertainment

Antequera's livelier, more interesting bars include **Le Bistrot** (Calle San Agustín) off Calle Infante Don Fernando, which goes on until 4am at least, and **La Guagua** (Calle Diego Ponce). Two excellent hang-outs are **La Madriguer** (Calle Calzada 16) and the **Manolo Bar** (Calle Calzada) opposite the Pensión Madrona, and a veritable picture gallery of famous faces.

Getting There & Around

Automóviles Casado (☎ 95 284 19 57) runs up to 12 buses a day to/from Málaga (€3, 50 minutes). **Alsina Graells** (☎ 95 284 13 65) runs five a day to/from Estepa, Osuna, Seville (Prado de San Sebastián; €9.25, 2½ hours) and five a day to/from Granada (€5.85, 1½ hours), three to/from Córdoba

(€7, 1½ hours) and five to/from Almería (€15.15, 4½ hours).

Two to four trains a day run to/from Granada, Seville, Ronda, Algeciras and Almería. For Málaga or Córdoba, change at Bobadilla. For information contact **Antequera station** (☎ 95 284 32 26).

Antequera can be a traffic nightmare and a team of formidable traffic wardens keep a tight grip on things. Buy tickets from them at streetside parking spots, €0.60 an hour. There is underground parking in Calle Diego Ponce north of Plaza de San Sebastián, €1 an hour, €12 for 12 to 24 hours. Taxis wait halfway along Calle Infante Don Fernando, or you can call ☎ 95 284 10 08.

AROUND ANTEQUERA
El Torcal

Millions of years of wind and water action have sculpted this 1336m mountain south of Antequera into some of the weirdest, most wonderful rock formations you'll see anywhere. A 12-sq-km area of gnarled, serrated and pillared limestone, formed as seabed 150 million years ago, constitute the protected Paraje Natural Torcal de Antequera. There are some deep ravines, and cliffs on most sides. There is an **El Torcal visitor centre** (☎ 95 203 13 89; open 10am-2pm & 3pm-5pm Nov-May, 10am-2pm & 4pm-6pm June-Oct).

Casual visitors are only allowed to follow a single marked walking trail, the 1.4km 'Ruta Verde', which starts and ends near the visitor centre. Longer tours require a paid-for guide. Details are erratic, so you should check with the visitor centre in advance, or ask at Antequera's tourist office.

Getting There & Away You will need a vehicle. Buses from Antequera will get you there, or back, but not both in the same day. Drivers should head south down Calle Picadero near the western end of Calle Infante Don Fernando, then follow the C-3310 towards Villanueva de la Concepción. Twelve kilometres from town a turn uphill to the right leads 4km to the visitor centre. A taxi costs €18 with one hour at El Torcal. It's best to get the tourist office to arrange a taxi for you.

Laguna de Fuente de Piedra

When it's not dried up by drought, this lake just south of the A-92, 20km northwest of Antequera, is the biggest natural lake in Andalucía and one of Europe's two main breeding grounds for the spectacular greater flamingo (the other is the Camargue in France). After a wet winter as many as 16,000 pairs of flamingos will breed at the lake. The birds arrive in January or February, with the chicks hatching in April and May. The flamingos stay till about August, when the lake, which rarely is more than 1m deep, no longer contains enough water to support them. They share the lake with thousands of other birds of some 170 species.

The **Centro de Información Fuente de Piedra** (☎ 95 211 17 15; open 10am-2pm & 4pm-6pm Wed-Sun Nov-Mar, 10am-2pm & 6pm-8pm Wed-Sun rest of year) is at the lakeside. It gives advice on the best spots for bird watching. It also sells a range of good maps and hires binoculars (an essential) at €1.45 for 45 minutes.

There is a **tourist office** (☎ 95 273 54 53; Calle Castillo 1; open 10am-2.30pm Wed-Sun) in the main square of Fuente de Piedra itself. It has leaflets and information and sells local wine, olive oil and handicrafts. The village is a pleasant, unassuming place; there are a number of old-fashioned bars around the square where you can get tapas for €1 and a menú for €5.

Camping La Laguna (☎ 95 273 52 94; Camino de la Rábita; camping 1 adult, tent & car €10.45, 4-6 person cabins €66, 4-person bungalows €62) is on the edge of Fuente de Piedra village and has pretty lake views.

Hostal La Laguna (☎ 95 273 52 92; singles/doubles €24/30), just off the A-92 at Fuente de Piedra, has fairly drab rooms. Its restaurant does a menú for €6.

Getting There & Away Buses run between Antequera bus station and Fuente de Piedra village (€0.90) nine times a day Monday to Friday, four times on Saturday and three times on Sunday and holidays.

East of Málaga

The coast east of Málaga, sometimes described as the Costa del Sol Oriental, is less developed than the coast west of the city. Along the grey-sand beaches is a string of medium-sized resort towns: Rincón de la Victoria, Torre del Mar, Torrox Costa and Nerja. The first two are mainly popular with Spaniards while Torrox is favoured by Germans and Nerja by the British. Sea water quality along this coast still leaves much to be desired – only Torrox has proper treatment facilities for sewage before it enters the sea (usually by outlets about 1.5km from the shore).

All the towns have *hostales*, hotels and holiday apartments – Nerja has the most – and there are several camping grounds too.

Behind the coast the attractive La Axarquía region climbs to the rugged mountains straddling the border of Granada province. A 406-sq-km area of these mountains was declared the Parque Natural Sierras de Tejeda, Almijara y Alhama, Andalucía's 23rd natural park, in 1999.

RINCÓN DE LA VICTORIA
postcode 29730 • pop 19,247

Rincón's **Cueva del Tesoro** (*Treasure Cave;* admission €4.20; open 10am-2pm & 3pm-6pm Mon-Fri, 10am-6pm Sat, Sun & holidays) is worth a stop. This series of underground caverns has stalagmites, stalactites, underground pools and some Palaeolithic wall paintings, though these last are off-limits to visitors. Gold was supposedly hidden here by Muslim emirs.

TORRE DEL MAR
postcode 29740 • pop 6600

Despite the ugly line of apartments facing its seafront, Torre del Mar is a likable place with more local flavour than the towns farther east. Its pleasant beachfront promenade continues a couple of kilometres east to Playa La Caleta, which has a marina. Torre fills up with Spanish holiday-makers in July and August. There's a **tourist office** (☎ 95 254 11 04; Avenida Andalucía 119) a few blocks west of the central boulevard, Paseo de Larios.

At the seafront end of Paseo de Larios is a line of **bars** and **discos** known as El Copo, which kick on all night on Friday and Saturday and attract crowds from far afield.

NERJA
postcode 29780 • pop 15,000

Nerja, 56km east of Málaga with the Sierra de Almijara rising close behind it, is older and more charming than the preceding towns, though tourism development has pushed it far beyond its old confines since the 1960s. Nerja continues to expand and has become increasingly popular with package holiday-makers as well as independents. The seafront western end of town is now a mass of standard high-rise hotels and apartment blocks.

There are good coastal views from the Balcón de Europa lookout point in the centre. From the Balcón, a delightful walk-way, the Paseo de los Carabineros, winds its way for nearly a kilometre to Playa Burri-ana, Nerja's biggest and best beach. The Paseo can be reached through a gapway to the right of the tourist office and then down steps. It wanders between pinnacles of con-glomerate rock that look like huge tumbled blocks of pebble dash.

Orientation & Information

Buses stop on the main road at the north edge of the town centre. Just below the bus stop is Plaza Cantarero. From here it is just over 500m to the Balcón de Europa and the tourist office. From Plaza Cantarero head straight down Calle Pintada. Nerja's streets are very narrow. For drivers who end up at the heart of the town, there is an under-ground car park off Calle La Cruz.

The **tourist office** (☎ 95 252 15 31; *Puerta del Mar; open 10am-2pm & 4.30pm-7pm Mon-Fri, 10am-1pm Sat*) has plenty of use-ful information leaflets. Nerja's **post office** *(Calle Cristo 6)* is a short distance north of

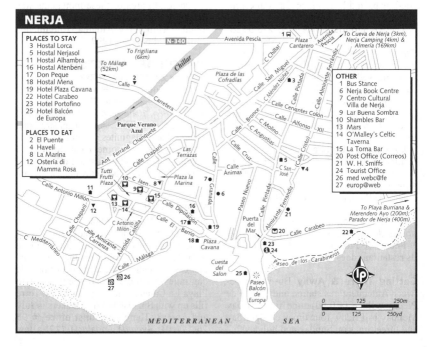

NERJA

PLACES TO STAY
3 Hostal Lorca
5 Hostal Nerjasol
11 Hostal Alhambra
16 Hostal Atenbeni
17 Don Peque
18 Hostal Mena
19 Hotel Plaza Cavana
22 Hotel Carabeo
23 Hotel Portofino
25 Hotel Balcón de Europa

PLACES TO EAT
2 El Puente
4 Havelí
8 La Marina
12 Osteria di Mamma Rosa

OTHER
1 Bus Stance
6 Nerja Book Centre
7 Centro Cultural Villa de Nerja
9 Lar Buena Sombra
10 Shambles Bar
13 Mars
14 O'Malley's Celtic Taverna
15 La Torna Bar
20 Post Office (Correos)
21 W. H. Smiffs
24 Tourist Office
26 med webc@fe
27 europ@web

To Cueva de Nerja (3km), Nerja Camping (4km) & Almería (169km)

To Frigiliana (6km)

To Málaga (52km)

Avenida Pescía

Plaza Cantarero

Plaza de las Cofradías

Parque Verano Azul

Las Terrazas

Tutti Frutti Plaza

Plaza la Marina

Plaza Cavana

Cuesta del Salon

Puerta del Mar

Paseo de los Carabineros

To Playa Burriana & Merendero Ayo (200m); Parador de Nerja (400m)

Paseo Balcón de Europa

MEDITERRANEAN SEA

0   125   250m
0   125   250yd

the tourist office. The **Europ@web** Internet centre *(Calle Málaga; open 10am-midnight daily)* charges €0.90 for 15 minutes, €3 for an hour. Close by is **med webc@fe**, with similar times and charges.

Nerja Book Centre *(Calle Granada 30)* has second-hand books in English and other languages and also stocks videos for rent. There is a good selection of Spanish-interest paperbacks and guidebooks at **W.H. Smiffs** *(Calle Almirante Fernándiz)*, in a small arcade along from the post office.

Nerja's annual *feria* (around 10 October) is one of the last of the year.

Places to Stay

Nerja Camping *(☎ 95 252 97 14; N-340; camping 2 people, tent & car €17)*, about 4km east of town, is pleasant. In August, try to arrive early in the day to ensure a spot.

Hostal Lorca *(☎ 95 252 34 26; e hostal lorca@teleline.es; Calle Méndez Núñez 20; singles/doubles €33/39)* is a charming place with comfy, spotless rooms. It's run by a friendly Dutch couple who have lots of local information, including details of walking routes.

Hostal Mena *(☎ 95 252 05 41; Calle El Barrio 15; singles/doubles with bathroom €19.50/30)*, a short distance west of the tourist office, is a good choice. The entrance hall houses an entertaining selection of paintings.

Hostal Atenbeni *(☎ 95 252 13 41; Calle Diputación 12; singles/doubles €20/25)* has reasonable rooms.

Don Peque *(☎/fax 95 252 13 18; Calle Diputación 13; doubles €27-35)* is opposite Hostal Atenbeni; it has pleasant rooms. There is no reduction for singles.

Hostal Alhambra *(☎ 95 252 21 74; Calle Antonio Millón 12; singles/doubles €29/39)* has pleasant rooms and is hidden away across Calle Chaparil and then a few metres up a broad alleyway.

Hostal Nerjasol *(☎ 95 252 22 21; Calle Pintada 54; singles/doubles €21/40)* is another good option.

Hotel Portofino *(☎ 95 252 01 50; Puerta del Mar 2; doubles high season €58)*, has some rooms with good beach views.

Hotel Carabeo *(☎ 95 252 54 44; e hcara beo@arrakis.es; Calle Carabeo 34; rooms or suites €128.50-154)* is a small, very stylish, family-run hotel with gardens and a pool overlooking the sea; room rates include breakfast.

Hotel Plaza Cavana *(☎/fax 95 252 40 00; Plaza Cavana 10; singles/doubles €77/107)* is a smart modern hotel at the heart of the town.

Hotel Balcón de Europa *(☎ 95 252 08 00, fax 95 252 44 90; e balconeuropa@spa.es; singles €95.40, doubles €119-203)* is right on the famous Balcón and has its own little beach.

Parador de Nerja *(☎ 95 252 00 50, fax 95 252 19 97; e nerja@parador.es; Calle Almuñécar 8; singles/doubles €99/125)* is nicely located above Playa Burriana.

Nerja has a number of apartments to let; inquire at the tourist office.

Places to Eat

There are dozens of places to eat in town.

Merendero Ayo *(Playa Burriana; mains €4-6)* is an open-air place above Nerja's best beach where you can enjoy a plate of paella cooked on the spot in great sizzling pans. It does reasonably priced salads too, and more expensive meat and fish dishes.

Havelí *(☎ 95 252 42 97; Calle Cristo 42; mains €8-10; open evenings)* is a good, medium-priced Indian restaurant with a roof terrace in summer. It has over 85 dishes to choose from.

Ostería di Mamma Rosa *(Edificio Corona, Calle Chaparil; mains €10-14; open Mon-Sat)* has some delicious starters and home-made desserts.

El Puente *(Calle Carretera 4; raciones €4)* is a great eating place despite being awkwardly placed on the west side of town where the Málaga road crosses a bridge over the Río Chillar; be careful when crossing the bridge on foot. The food makes up for it, with tapas at €1 and big helpings of everything.

La Marina *(Plaza la Marina; dishes €3-5)* is a terrific fish restaurant, popular with locals. It offers everything that swims, from squid to monkfish.

MÁLAGA PROVINCE

Entertainment

The **Centro Cultural Villa de Nerja** (☎ 95 252 38 63; **w** www.nerja.net; Calle Granada 45) runs an ambitious annual programme of classical, theatre, jazz and flamenco featuring international artistes. It also has a film programme of top current releases, in Spanish.

Nightlife is focused on the aptly named Tutti-Frutti Plaza, and the adjoining Calle Antonio Millón. There's a clutch of bars and discos with an eccentric internationalism, from **La Torna Bar** and its offer of 'A Taste of England in Spain' to **O'Malley's Celtic Taverna** and **La Buena Sombra**, with **Mars** making things extraterrestrial. Just up the road is the self-proclaimed 'Nerja's biggest', the **Shambles Bar**, which is how you may well end up at the end of the night. Things hot up after midnight.

Getting There & Away

Alsina Graells (☎ 95 252 15 04; N-340) has around 14 daily buses to/from Málaga (€2.90, one hour), eight to/from Almuñécar (€1.90, 25 minutes), five to/from Almería (€9.30, 2½ hours) and three to/from Granada (€7.10, 1½ hours).

AROUND NERJA

The area's really big tourist attraction is the **Cueva de Nerja** (☎ 95 252 95 20; admission adult/child €5/2.50; open 10am-2pm & 4pm-6.30pm daily), 3km east of Nerja, just off the N-340. An enormous cavern, hollowed out by water around five million years ago, it was inhabited by Stone Age hunters around 15,000BC. Their rock paintings are off-limits to visitors, but there are still lots of impressive rock formations to admire. Every July, Spanish and international ballet and music stars perform in the cave as part of the Festival Cueva de Nerja. You need to ask at Nerja tourist office for programme details. About 14 buses a day run from Málaga and Nerja.

Farther east, the coast becomes more rugged and scenic and with your own wheels you can head out to some good **beaches** reached by tracks down from the N-340, around 9km from Nerja. **Playa del Cañuelo**, immediately before the border

with Granada province, is one of the best, with a couple of summer-only restaurants.

Seven kilometres north of Nerja and linked to it by several buses daily (except Sunday) is the pretty village of **Frigiliana**. El Fuerte, the hill that climbs above the village, was the scene of the final bloody defeat of the Moriscos of La Axarquía in their 1569 rebellion (see the following La Axarquía section). Some of the Moriscos reputedly threw themselves from the hilltop rather than be killed or captured by the Spanish.

LA AXARQUÍA

The chief attractions of La Axarquía include hill and mountain scenery; pretty white villages; strong, sweet, local wine made from sun-dried grapes; and good walking in spring and autumn.

La Axarquía is riven by deep valleys lined with terraces and irrigation channels that go back to Muslim times. Nearly all the villages dotted around the olive, almond and vine-planted hillsides are of Muslim origin, with narrow, higgledy-piggledy streets. La Axarquía joined the 1569 Morisco rebellion (see Las Alpujarras in the Granada Province chapter) and afterwards its inhabitants were replaced with Christians from farther north.

You can pick up information on La Axarquía at the tourist offices in Málaga, Nerja or Torre del Mar. Prospective walkers should ask for the leaflet on walks in the Parque Natural Sierras de Tejeda, Almijara y Alhama. **Rural Andalus** (☎ 95 227 62 29) (see Accommodation in Facts for the Visitor chapter) and **Axartur** (☎ 95 254 20 58) have numerous **self-catering houses** and **apartments** in La Axarquía, typically costing around €50 per house per night.

The best maps for walkers are *Mapa Topográfico de Sierra Tejeda* and *Mapa Topográfico de Sierra Almijara* by Miguel Ángel Torres Delgado, both at 1:25,000. Useful guides include *25 Walks in and around Cómpeta & Canillas de Albaida* by Albert & Dini Kraaijenzank. You should be able to find the guide at Marco Polo in Cómpeta (see the Cómpeta section later in this chapter) and the maps at Marco Polo or

Papelería Ariza *(Avenida Constitución 57, Cómpeta).* Papelería Ariza may also have the Spanish walking guides *Sendas y Caminos por los Campos de la Axarquía* (Interguías Clave) and *Andar por La Axarquía* (El Búho Viajero).

Western Axarquía

The 'capital' of La Axarquía, **Vélez Málaga**, 4km north of Torre del Mar, is busy but unspectacular but its restored hilltop Muslim castle is worth a look. From Vélez the A-335 heads north past the Embalse de la Viñuela reservoir and up through the **Boquete de Zafarraya**, a dramatic cleft in the mountains, towards Granada. One bus a day each way between Torre del Mar and Granada makes its way over this road.

Some of the most dramatic Axarquía scenery is up around the highest villages, **Alfarnate** (925m) and **Alfarnatejo** (858m), with towering, rugged crags such as Tajo de Gomer and Tajo de Doña Ana rising to their south.

Places to Stay & Eat Hotel de La Viñuela (☎ 95 251 91 93; **e** hotel@hotelvinuela .com; singles/doubles €60/82) has a fine position on the eastern bank of the Embalse de la Viñuela and very comfortable rooms and a restaurant. Prices are raised in August.

Restaurante Vinuela *(Carretera Vé-Málaga a Alhama; mains €3.60-15)* is on the A-356 heading west from Embalse de la Viñuela. It does mainly meat dishes. Right next door is the smarter **Restaurante El Pantano** with fish and meat mains for €5.40 to €12. Both get very busy at weekends.

Venta de Alfarnate *(☎ 95 275 93 88; Antigua Carretera de Málaga-Granada; open 11am-7pm Tues-Thur & Sun, 11am-midnight Fri & Sat; mains €7.20-15)*, on the Loja road just outside Alfarnate, is probably Andalucía's oldest inn, dating from 1690. It displays mementos of past visitors including some of the bandits who used to roam these hills and, on occasions, took it over. Foodwise it's renowned for *huevos a la bestia*, which is a kind of hill-country mixed grill of fried eggs and assorted pork products (€9).

Comares

Comares sits like a snowdrift atop its lofty hill. You see it for mile after mile before a final twist in an endlessly winding road lands you below the hanging garden of its cliff. From a little car park, you can climb steep winding steps to the village. Look for ceramic footprints underfoot and simply follow them through a web of narrow, twisting lanes past the Iglesia de la Encarnación and eventually to the ruins of Comares' castle and a remarkable summit cemetery. The village has a history of rebellion against Muslim and Christian rulers, having been a stronghold of Omar ibn Hafsun (see the El Chorro, Ardales & Around section earlier in this chapter), but today there is a tangible sense of contented isolation. The views across the Axarquía are stunning.

For accommodation there's the **Hotel Atalaya** *(☎ 95 250 92 08; Calle Encinillas 4; singles/doubles with bathroom €24/42)* at the entrance to the village. It has a restaurant that does meat dishes from €4.25 to €9.60. A better bet farther in towards the village is **Mirador de la Axarquía** *(☎ 95 250 92 09; Calle Encinillas s/n; singles/doubles €18/30)*. It has good-value studio-style rooms and a friendly bar-restaurant that does tasty grills for €4.20 to €7.25, and salads from €2.40.

There are a couple of friendly bars at the heart of the village and the ceramic footprints will lead you eventually to the **Centro de Medicina Natural** in Calle Agua, where there's a little café offering delicious vegetarian snacks; the plum crumble is superb, and there are over 40 speciality drinks to choose from.

On weekdays only a bus leaves Málaga for Comares at 6pm and returns at 7am the next morning (€1.85).

Cómpeta

postcode 29754 • pop 2684
• elevation 625m

The highest mountains in the area stretch east from the Boquete de Zafarraya. The village of Cómpeta is one of the best bases for a stay in La Axarquía. It has some of the area's best local wine, and the popular

Noche del Vino (Night of the Wine) on 15 August features a programme of flamenco and Sevillana music and dance in the central Plaza Almijara, and limitless free wine. **Marco Polo** (Calle José Antonio 3), just off Plaza Almijara, sells books in English and several other languages, and maps. There is a large car park at the foot of the central part of the village.

Places to Stay On a hilltop 1km southeast of Cómpeta, **Hostal Alberdini** (☎ 95 251 62 41, 650 269 764; self-catering per person per night €36-45) is a delightful complex of self-catering apartments (turn right at the Venta de Palma bar on the Torrox road; the entrance is several hundred metres ahead and is unmissable). Some of the individual units are superb Gaudi-esque works of art in themselves.

Rooms are available in several homes: **Las Tres Abejas** (☎ 95 255 33 75; e bart333@teleline.es; Calle Panaderos 43; B&B singles/doubles with bathroom €30/40) is about 150m uphill from Plaza Almijara. The lovely, renovated **Casa Azahara** (☎/fax 95 251 61 53; Calle Carretería 9) has similar prices.

Hotel Balcón de Cómpeta (☎ 95 255 35 35; Calle San Antonio 75; doubles €67.50) has air-con rooms with balcony, and a restaurant, bar, tennis court and good pool.

Places to Eat There's cheap and cheerful fare at **Bar Marcos** at the foot of the village, opposite the bus stop.

Café Bar Perico (Plaza Almijara; fish & meat mains €5.10-12.30) does decent standard fare with omelettes and revueltos (scrambled-egg dishes) for €2 to €3.50 and bocadillos for €1.50 to €2.10.

El Pilón (Calle Laberinto; fish and meat mains €9), near Café Bar Perico, does very good Spanish and international food including prawn and avocado salad (€4.50) and solomillo a la pimienta verde (pork sirloin in green pepper sauce, €7.80).

Museo del Vino (Avenida Constitución) serves ham, cheese and sausage raciones and wine from the barrel. It's also something of an Aladdin's Cave of regional crafts and produce for sale.

Restaurante Asador Museo del Vino (Avenida Constitución; mains €5.40-15) next door to Museo del Vino, specialises in excellent grilled meats, such as pork and lamb chops.

Cortijo Paco (☎ 95 255 36 47; Avenida Canillas 6; mains €9-12) is another excellent restaurant, with views to the distant sea from its terrace. It's reached by continuing past the Hotel Balcón de Cómpeta then heading uphill and back right.

Getting There & Away Three buses a day (two on Saturday, Sunday and holidays) run from Málaga to Cómpeta and Canillas de Albaida, via Torre del Mar.

Around Cómpeta

A few kilometres down the valley, **Árchez** has a beautifully decorated Almohad-style minaret next to its church. A scenic road winding west from Árchez through Salares, Sedella and Canillas de Aceituno eventually links up with the A-335 north of Vélez Málaga. Another road leads southwest from Árchez to **Arenas** where a steep but driveable track climbs to the ruined Muslim **Castillo de Bentomiz**, crowning a hilltop with fine panoramas. Keep your eyes open for chameleons, which are more abundant around Arenas than anywhere else in Spain. In early October Arenas stages the Feria de la Mula, dedicated to that rapidly disappearing beast of burden, the mule.

Walking See the introductory paragraphs on La Axarquía for information on maps and walking guidebooks.

Perhaps the most exhilarating walk in the area is up the dramatically peaked **El Lucero** (1779m). From its summit on a clear day, there are stupendous views as far as Granada in one direction and Morocco in the other. This is a full, demanding day's walking with an ascent of 1150m from Cómpeta: start by climbing left along the track above Cómpeta football pitch. About 1½ hours from Cómpeta you pass below and west of a fire observation hut on the hill La Mina. Turn right through a gap in the rock 400m past the turning to the hut. This path leads in one hour to Puerto Blanquillo (1200m), from which a path climbs 200m to the Puerto de Cómpeta.

One kilometre down from the latter pass, past a quarry, the summit path (1½ hours) diverges to the right across a stream bed, marked by a sign board and map. El Lucero is topped by the ruins of a Guardia Civil post built to watch for anti-Franco rebels after the civil war. It's possible to drive as far up as Puerto Blanquillo on a rough mountain track from Canillas de Albaida, a village 2km northwest of Cómpeta, in 40 minutes or so.

Córdoba Province

Córdoba city stands in the fertile valley of the Río Guadalquivir, which runs through the middle of the province. The city has a fascinating and romantic history: it was capital of Al-Andalus (the Muslim-ruled parts of medieval Spain) when it was at its peak. Its former mosque, the Mezquita, is one of the most magnificent Islamic buildings in the world. The rest of Córdoba province contains many appealing rural areas where the combination of remote, ancient villages and rolling hills produces a rare beauty.

CÓRDOBA
postcode 14080 • pop 310,000
• elevation 110m

Córdoba lies on a curve of the Guadalquivir with countryside spreading out in every direction. It is by far the biggest settlement in what is essentially a rural province, and seems both provincial yet sophisticated at the same time. The labyrinthine medieval quarter, adjoining the Mezquita, is what fascinates most visitors, but the modern part of the city has its own special charm. To get an idea of what being *cordobés* is about, it is worth trying to experience the two Córdobas.

The city is quiet and withdrawn during the winter months, but it bursts into life from mid-April to mid-June. At this time of year the skies are blue and the heat is tolerable, the city's many trees and lovely patios drip with foliage and blooms, and Córdoba stages most of its major fiestas. September and October are also pleasant months climatically.

History

The Roman colony of Corduba, founded in 152 BC, became the capital of Baetica province, covering most of today's Andalucía. This Roman cultural centre was the birthplace of the writers Seneca and Lucan.

Córdoba fell to the Islamic invaders in AD 711 and soon became the Muslim capital on the Iberian Peninsula. It was here in 756 that

Highlights

- Lose yourself amid the glory of the Mezquita, one of the greatest of all Islamic buildings
- Wander the labyrinthine Jewish and Muslim quarters of Córdoba and enjoy the flowers of the city's patios and the Alcázar gardens
- Visit Medina Azahara, one of Andalucía's most impressive archaeological sites
- Head for Priego de Córdoba and its baroque extravaganzas
- Take the high road into the beautiful mountains of the Sierras Subbéticas or the wooded hills of Parque Natural Sierra de Hornachuelos

Abd ar-Rahman I set himself up as the independent emir of Al-Andalus, founding the Omayyad dynasty. Córdoba's – and Al-Andalus' – heyday came under Abd ar-Rahman III (912–61), who in 929 named himself caliph (the title of the Islamic successors of Mohammed), sealing Al-Andalus' longstanding de facto independence from the Abbasid caliphs in Baghdad. Córdoba was by now the biggest city in Western Europe, with a population somewhere between 100,000 and 500,000. Its economy flourished on the agriculture from its irrigated hinterland and

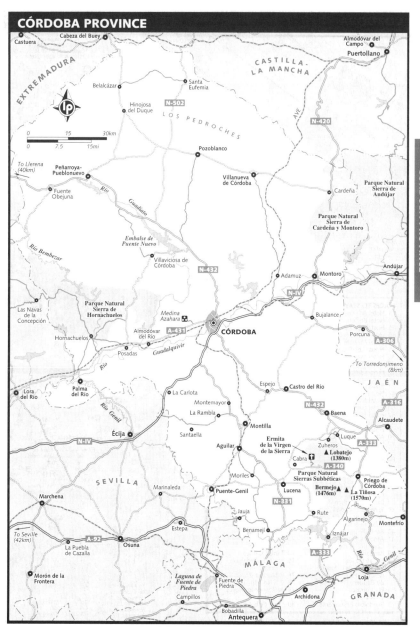

CÓRDOBA PROVINCE

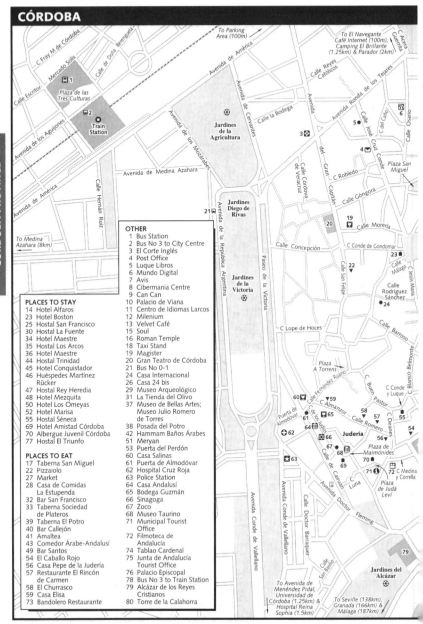

CÓRDOBA

To Parking Area (100m)
To El Navegante Café Internet (100m), Camping El Brillante (1.25km) & Parador (2km)

Jardines de la Agricultura

Jardines Diego de Rivas

Jardines de la Victoria

Plaza San Miguel

Plaza A Torrens

Plaza de Maimónides

Plaza de Judá Leví

Jardines del Alcázar

To Medina Azahara (8km)

To Avenida de Menéndez Pidal, Universidad de Córdoba (1.25km) & Hospital Reina Sophia (1.5km)

To Seville (138km), Granada (166km) & Málaga (187km)

PLACES TO STAY
14 Hotel Alfaros
23 Hotel Boston
25 Hostal San Francisco
30 Hostal La Fuente
34 Hotel Maestre
35 Hostal Los Arcos
36 Hotel Maestre
44 Hostal Trinidad
45 Hotel Conquistador
46 Huéspedes Martínez Rücker
47 Hostal Rey Heredia
48 Hotel Mezquita
50 Hotel Los Omeyas
52 Hotel Marisa
55 Hostal Séneca
69 Hotel Amistad Córdoba
70 Albergue Juvenil Córdoba
77 Hostal El Triunfo

PLACES TO EAT
17 Taberna San Miguel
22 Pizzaiolo
27 Market
28 Casa de Comidas La Estupenda
32 Bar San Francisco
33 Taberna Sociedad de Plateros
39 Taberna El Potro
40 Bar Callejón
41 Amaltea
43 Comedor Árabe-Andalusí
49 Bar Santos
54 El Caballo Rojo
56 Casa Pepe de la Judería
57 Restaurante El Rincón de Carmen
58 El Churrasco
59 Casa Elisa
73 Bandolero Restaurante

OTHER
1 Bus Station
2 Bus No 3 to City Centre
3 El Corte Inglés
4 Post Office
5 Luque Libros
6 Mundo Digital
7 Avis
8 Cibermania Centre
9 Can Can
10 Palacio de Viana
11 Centro de Idiomas Larcos
12 Milenium
13 Velvet Café
15 Soul
16 Roman Temple
18 Taxi Stand
19 Magister
20 Gran Teatro de Córdoba
21 Bus No 0-1
24 Casa Internacional
26 Casa 24 bis
29 Museo Arqueológico
31 La Tienda del Olivo
37 Museo de Bellas Artes; Museo Julio Romero de Torres
38 Posada del Potro
42 Hammam Baños Árabes
51 Meryan
53 Puerta del Perdón
60 Casa Salinas
61 Puerta de Almodóvar
62 Hospital Cruz Roja
63 Police Station
64 Casa Andalusí
65 Bodega Guzmán
66 Sinagoga
67 Zoco
68 Museo Taurino
71 Municipal Tourist Office
72 Filmoteca de Andalucía
74 Tablao Cardenal
75 Junta de Andalucía Tourist Office
76 Palacio Episcopal
78 Bus No 3 to Train Station
79 Alcázar de los Reyes Cristianos
80 Torre de la Calahorra

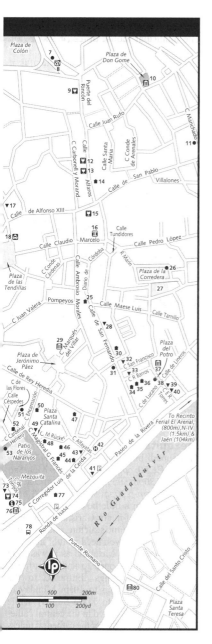

the products of its skilled artisans – leather and metalwork, textiles, glazed tiles and more. It had dazzling mosques, patios, gardens and fountains, plus aqueducts and public baths. Abd ar-Rahman III's court was frequented by Jewish, Arab and Christian scholars, and Córdoba's university, library, observatories and other institutions made it a centre of learning whose influence was still being felt in Christian Europe many centuries later. Abulcasis (936–1013), author of a 30-volume medical encyclopedia and considered the father of surgery, was the area's most remarkable scholar during this age.

One of Mohammed's arm bones, kept in the Mezquita, became a psychological weapon against the Christians and was partly responsible for the development of the opposing cult of Santiago (St James). Córdoba became a place of pilgrimage for Muslims who could not get to Mecca or Jerusalem.

Towards the end of the 10th century, Al-Mansur (Almanzor), a ruthless general whose northward raids terrified Christian Spain, took the reins of power from the caliphs. When he destroyed the cathedral at Santiago de Compostela, home of the Santiago cult, he had its bells carried to Córdoba by Christian slaves and hung upside down as gigantic oil lamps in the Mezquita. After the death of Al-Mansur's son Abd al-Malik in 1008, the caliphate descended into anarchy. Rival claimants to the title, Berber troops and Christian armies from Castille and Catalunya all fought over the spoils. The Berbers terrorised and looted the city and, in 1031, Omayyad rule ended.

Al-Andalus collapsed into dozens of *taifas* (petty kingdoms). Córdoba became part of the Sevilla *taifa* in 1069 (and has been overshadowed by that city ever since). But Córdoba's intellectual traditions lived on. The 11th-century philosopher-poets Ibn Hazm (who wrote in Arabic) and Judah Ha-Levi (Hebrew) both spent important parts of their lives here. Twelfth-century Córdoba produced the two most celebrated of all Al-Andalus' scholars – the Muslim Averroës (1126–98; see Literature in the Facts about Andalucía chapter) and the Jewish Maimonides (1135–1204). Both were men of multifarious talents, best remembered for their philosophical efforts to harmonise religious faith with Aristotelian reason. But while Averroës held high office under the Almohads in Córdoba and Sevilla, Maimonides fled Almohad intolerance and spent most of his career in Egypt.

When Córdoba was taken by Castille's Fernando III in 1236, much of its population fled. Fernando returned the bells to Santiago de Compostela and Córdoba became a provincial city of shrinking importance. Its decline was only reversed by the arrival of industry in the late 19th century – though Christian Córdoba produced one of the greatest Spanish poets, Luis de Góngora (1561–1627).

Orientation

The medieval city is immediately north of the Guadalquivir, a warren of narrow streets surrounding the Mezquita just a block from the river. Within the medieval city, the area northwest of the Mezquita was the *judería* (Jewish quarter), the Muslim quarter was north and east of the Mezquita, and the Mozarabic (Christian) quarter was farther to the northeast.

The main square of modern Córdoba is Plaza de las Tendillas, 500m north of the Mezquita, with the main shopping streets to its north and west. The train and bus stations are 1km northwest of Plaza de las Tendillas.

Maps The helpful and well-stocked **Luque Libros** (☎/fax 957 47 30 34; ℮ luquelibros @apepmeco.es; Calle José Cruz Conde 19) sells city and Michelin maps at about half the price of the tourist shops near the Mezquita. It also sells CNIG and SGE maps and Editorial Alpina maps.

Information

Tourist Offices The multilingual **Junta de Andalucía tourist office** (☎ 957 47 12 35; Calle de Torrijos 10; open 9.30am-8pm Mon-Fri, 10am-8pm Sat, 10am-2pm Sun & holidays) is in a 16th-century chapel facing the western side of the Mezquita. It closes at 7pm from Monday to Saturday in March, October and sometimes August and Septem-

ber, and at 6pm from November to February. The **municipal tourist office** (☎ 957 20 05 22; Plaza de Judá Leví; open 8.30am-2.30pm Mon-Fri), a block farther west, is helpful; it sometimes opens longer in summer.

There is a **tourist information kiosk** (open 10am-2pm & 4.15pm-8pm Mon-Fri) at the train station.

Money Most banks and ATMs are in the newer part of the centre, around Plaza de las Tendillas and Avenida del Gran Capitán. The bus and train stations have ATMs.

Post & Communications The main **post office** (open 8.30am-8.30pm Mon-Fri, 9.30am-2pm Sat) is at Calle José Cruz Conde 15. **Cibermania Center** (Plaza de Colón 34; open 10am-1pm & 5pm-10pm daily) and **Mundo Digital** (Calle Osario 9; open 10am-2.30pm & 4.30pm-10pm daily) both charge €1.80 per hour for online services.

Medical Services & Emergency The main general hospital, **Hospital Reina Sofia** (☎ 957 21 70 00; Avenida de Menéndez Pidal s/n), is located 1.5km southwest of the Mezquita. The **Hospital Cruz Roja** (Red Cross Hospital; ☎ 957 29 34 11; Avenida Doctor Fleming s/n) is more central. For an ambulance you can call ☎ 957 21 79 03 or ☎ 957 29 55 70.

The **Policía Nacional** station (☎ 957 47 75 00) is at Avenida Doctor Fleming 2.

Mezquita

This superb building (☎ 957 47 05 12; admission €6.50; open 10am-6.30pm Mon-Sat, 3.30pm-7.30pm Sun Apr-Sept; 10am-5.30pm Mon-Sat, 2pm-5.30pm Sun Oct-May & holidays) can seem a little bewildering to begin with. Because of major Christian alterations to the original Islamic structure, and the darkness they impose, you need a bit of imagination to picture the Mezquita as it was – an architectural unity open to and in harmony with its surroundings. Entrance to the Mezquita is free 9am to 10am Monday to Saturday and 9am to 11am Sunday while Mass is being celebrated in the central cathedral, but you cannot enter the cathedral unless you are attending the Mass in its entirety. The rest of the Mezquita is unlit during this time.

The Mezquita has some truly beautiful architectural features, among them the famous rows of two-tier arches assembled in mesmerising stripes of red brick and white stone, and the more elaborate arches, domes and decoration in and around the splendid prayer niche (mihrab).

From outside, the building looks like a fortress with thick stone walls punctuated by decorated portals; it's low-slung except for the protruding roofs of the cathedral within and the lower domes along the southern wall.

History Abd ar-Rahman I founded the Mezquita in 785 on the site of a church which had been partitioned between Muslims and Christians, reputedly purchasing the Christian half from the Christian community. Abd ar-Rahman II (821–52) and Al-Hakim II in the 960s extended the Mezquita southwards to cater for Córdoba's expanding population. Al-Hakim II also added the existing mihrab and, for extra light, built a number of domes with skylights over the area in front of it. Under Al-Mansur, eastward extensions were made and the mihrab lost its central position in the south wall.

What you see today is the building's final Islamic form with one major alteration – a 16th-century cathedral right in the middle (hence the often-used description 'Mezquita-Catedral'). Extensions made to the Mezquita under Abd ar-Rahman II and Al-Mansur were partly dismantled to make way for the cathedral.

For more information on the Mezquita's architectural qualities and importance, see the Muslim Architecture special section earlier in this book.

Orientation The main entrance is the Puerta del Perdón, a 14th-century Mudejar gateway on Calle Cardenal Herrero, with the ticket office immediately inside.

Beside the Puerta del Perdón is a 16th- and 17th-century tower built around the remains of the original minaret. Inside the gateway is the pretty **Patio de los Naranjos**

Opening Hours

Opening hours for Córdoba's sights change frequently, so check with the tourist offices for updated times. Most places except the Mezquita close on Monday. Closing times are generally an hour or two earlier in winter than summer.

(Courtyard of Orange Trees), from which a door leads inside the building itself.

A leaflet given free to visitors contains a map clearly outlining the stages of the building's construction. The first 12 east-to-west aisles inside the building, a forest of pillars and arches, comprise Abd ar-Rahman I's original 8th-century mosque, completed by his son Hisham I and extending a little over halfway across the existing building from west to east. The mihrab is visible straight ahead from the entrance door, in the far (southern) wall. In the centre of the building is the Christian cathedral, aligned east to west and surrounded by more Islamic aisles, pillars and arches. Just past the right-hand (western) end of the cathedral, heavier, more elaborate arches mark the approach to the mihrab.

Abd ar-Rahman I's Mezquita This original section incorporated columns and capitals – of various coloured marbles, granite and alabaster – from the site's previous Visigothic church, from Roman buildings in Córdoba and elsewhere, and even from ancient Carthage. The columns were of differing heights so the taller ones had to be sunk into the floor. They support two tiers of arches, giving an effect reminiscent of Roman aqueducts and/or date palms. The use of bicoloured materials for the arches was inspired. Most of the columns for other parts of the building were made by Cordoban artisans.

Mihrab & Maksura The bay immediately in front of the mihrab and the bay to each side form the *maksura*, the area where the caliphs and their retinues would have prayed (today enclosed by railings). The *maksura* and mihrab are the artistic pinnacle of the building. Each of the *maksura*'s three bays has a skylit dome with star-patterned stone vaulting. Because these domes were made of stone, rather than the wood used for the rest of the Mezquita's roofs, they rested on stronger, more elaborate arches. The mosaic decoration on the dome over the central bay is particularly beautiful. In the central bay is the arched entrance to the mihrab itself. This arch and its rectangular frame *(alfiz)* were superbly decorated with mosaic flower motifs and inscriptions from the Quran, all in gold, purple, green, blue and red, and rich stucco work. The mihrab itself, which you cannot enter, is octagonal with a shell-shaped dome. The mihrab served both to amplify the voice of the prayer leader and to indicate the direction of Mecca.

Cathedral The Mezquita was used as a cathedral after Fernando III took Córdoba. Early Christian modifications, such as the Mudejar tiling added in the 1370s to the Mozarabic and Almohad Capilla Real (nine bays north and one east of the mihrab), were carried out with restraint. But in the 16th century the centre of the Mezquita was ripped out to allow construction of the Capilla Mayor (the altar area) and choir *(coro)* designed by Hernán Ruiz the Elder. The Capilla Mayor has a rich 17th-century jasper and marble retable; the choir's fine mahogany stalls were carved in the 18th century by Pedro Duque Cornejo.

If you think of the whole building as a cathedral, the forests of Islamic arches and pillars provide a superb setting for the central structures. If you see it as a mosque, the Christian additions wreck its whole conception. King Carlos I overrode the wishes of Córdoba's city council in permitting the church authorities to build the Capilla Mayor and choir. Legend has it that when he saw the results he was horrified, exclaiming: 'You have destroyed something that was unique in the world'.

Other Sections The Mezquita contains many further chapels: one next to the

mihrab and others lining the eastern and western walls. Wandering around the rest of the Mezquita, it's possible to lose yourself in the aisles with views of only the incredible columns and arches, uninterrupted by the Christian alterations. The final Islamic building had 1300 columns, of which 850 remain. In Muslim times the Mezquita would have been better lit, with open doors along its sides.

Palacio Episcopal

The Bishops' Palace *(Calle de Torrijos)* is next door to the tourist office. It stages interesting exhibitions, often of regional pottery, in its handsome patio, to which admission is free. The Palace also houses the **Museo Diocesano** *(☎ 957 49 60 85; admission €1.20; open 9.30am-1.30pm & 4pm-6pm Mon-Fri, 9.30am-1.30pm Sat)* with a collection of religious art including some outstanding medieval woodcarving.

Judería

The old Jewish quarter extends west and northwest from the Mezquita, almost to the beginning of Avenida del Gran Capitán. It's a maze of narrow streets and small squares, of whitewashed buildings with flowers dripping from window boxes and wrought-iron doorways giving glimpses of plant-filled patios (see the boxed text 'Córdoba's Hidden Heart' for details). The tourist shops and restaurants around the Mezquita thin out quickly within one or two blocks.

The **Museo Taurino** *(Bullfighting Museum; Plaza de Maimónides; admission €2.95, free Fri; open 10am-2pm & 6pm-8pm Tues-Sat Apr-Oct; 10am-2pm & 4.30pm-6.30pm Tues-Sat Nov-May; 9.30am-3pm Sun & holidays year-round)*, in a 16th-century mansion, celebrates, with grim theatricality, Córdoba's legendary matadors, with rooms dedicated to El Cordobés and Manolete. Exhibits include the rather forlorn, pegged-out hide of Islero, the bull that killed the revered Manolete at Linares in 1947.

Just up from the Museo Taurino is the **Zoco** *(Calle de los Judíos)*, a group of craft workshops/showrooms around an old patio (see Shopping later in this chapter). The 14th-century **Sinagoga** *(Calle de los Judíos 20; admission €0.30, EU citizens free; open 10am-1.30pm & 3.30pm-5.30pm Tues-Sat, 10am-1.30pm Sun & holidays)* is one of very few medieval Spanish synagogues that survives reasonably intact. It's a beautiful little building, retaining its upstairs women's gallery and stucco work that includes Hebrew inscriptions and intricate Mudejar star and plant patterns. The **Casa Andalusí** *(Calle de los Judíos 12; admission €2.50; open 10.30am-8pm May-Sept; 10.30am-7pm Oct-Apr)* is a 12th-century house prettily decked out with a tinkling fountain in the patio and a variety of exhibits, mainly relating to Córdoba's medieval Muslim culture, but also including a Roman mosaic in the cellar.

Just to the left at the top of Calle de los Judíos is the **Puerta de Almodóvar**, an Islamic gate in a restored stretch of the old city walls.

Alcázar de los Reyes Cristianos

The Castle of the Christian Monarchs *(admission €1.90, free Fri; open 10am-2pm & 4.30pm-6.30pm Tues-Sat Oct-Apr, 10am-2pm & 6pm-8pm Tues-Sat May-Sept, 9.30am-2.30pm Sun & holidays year-round)*, southwest of the Mezquita, began as a palace and fort for Alfonso X in the 13th century. From 1490 to 1821 the Inquisition operated from here. Its large gardens, full of fish ponds, fountains, orange trees, flowers and topiary, are among the most beautiful in Andalucía. The building itself, much altered, houses an old royal bathhouse and a museum, with some interesting Roman mosaics.

Río Guadalquivir & Torre de la Calahorra

The Guadalquivir in Córdoba is not particularly impressive, except when it's swollen by winter rains. Just south of the Mezquita, it's crossed by the much-restored **Puente Romano** (Roman Bridge). Traffic is heavy across the bridge and the pedestrian walkways are narrow. At the southern end of the Puente Romano is the **Torre de la Calahorra** *(admission €4.80; open 10am-2pm & 5.30pm-8.30pm daily May-Sept, 10am-6pm daily Oct-Apr)*, a 14th-century tower with a curious museum highlighting the intellectual achievements of Islamic Córdoba and focusing on its reputation for religious tolerance.

Museo Arqueológico

Córdoba's archaeological museum *(Plaza de Jerónimo Páez 7; admission €1.50, EU citizen free; open 3pm-8pm Tues, 9am-8pm Wed-Sat, 9am-3pm Sun & holidays)* is in a Renaissance mansion with a large patio. A reclining stone lion takes pride of place in the Iberian section. The Roman period is well represented with large mosaics, elegant ceramics and tinted glass bowls. The upstairs is devoted to medieval Córdoba, including bronze animal figures from Medina Azahara.

CÓRDOBA PROVINCE

Córdoba's Hidden Heart

Concealed behind heavy wooden doors or partly hidden by wrought-iron gates are many examples of a beautiful Cordoban tradition.

For centuries, the patios of Córdoba have provided shade during the searing heat of summer, a haven of peace and quiet, and a place to talk and entertain.

In the first half of May you'll notice 'patio' signs in the streets and alleyways, which means that you're invited to enter and view what is for the rest of the year closed to the outside world. At this time of year the patios are at their prettiest as new blooms proliferate. Many patios are entered in the annual competition, the Concurso de Patios Cordobeses; a map of patios open for viewing is available from the tourist office. Some of the best are on and around Calle San Basilio, about 400m southwest of the Mezquita. During the competition, the patios are generally open from 5pm to midnight Monday to Friday and noon to midnight Saturday and Sunday. Admission is usually free but sometimes there's a container for donations.

Plaza del Potro

This attractive square 400m northeast of the Mezquita is mentioned in *Don Quixote*, whose author, Miguel Cervantes, lived for a spell in a nearby street. The square's heyday was in the 16th and 17th centuries when it was a hang-out for traders and adventurers. In the centre is a lovely 16th-century stone fountain topped by a rearing colt *(potro)*. On the western side of the square is **Posada del Potro**, formerly an inn but now an art gallery. Opposite, the former Hospital de la Caridad houses the **Museo de Bellas Artes** *(admission €1.50, EU citizen free; open 3pm-8pm Tues, 9am-8pm Wed-Sat, 9am-3pm Sun & holidays)*, with a collection by mainly Cordoban artists, and the **Museo Julio Romero de Torres** *(admission €2.95 Tues-Thur, free Fri; open 10am-2pm & 6pm-8pm Tues-Sat May-Sept, 10am-2pm & 4.30pm-6.30pm Tues-Sat Oct-Apr, 9.30am-2.30pm Sun & holidays year-round)*, devoted to local painter Julio Romero de Torres (1880–1930), hugely revered in Córdoba. His trademark portraits depict, with relish, sultry nudes and heavy-handed sexual symbolism. His voluptuous *Ofrenda al Arte del Toreo* (Offering to the Art of Bullfighting) says it all, and *Canto Hondo* with its stabbed victim and esoteric symbolism will give you reason to pause.

Plaza de la Corredera

This exhilarating 17th-century square, more northern Spanish in style than Andalucían, lies 200m north of Plaza del Potro. Córdoba's Roman amphitheatre stood here; later, Inquisition burnings and bullfights happened in the square and today rock concerts and other events are staged. Though extensively restored, there is still a small daily fruit market and on Saturdays a lively, colourful and very local flea market.

Palacio de Viana

This Renaissance palace *(Plaza de Don Gome 2; admission €6; open 9am-2pm Mon-Sat June-Sept, 10am-1pm & 4pm-6pm Mon-Fri, 10am-1pm Sat Oct-May)*, 500m north of Plaza de la Corredera, has 12 patios and a formal garden, which are lovely to visit in spring though unspectacular in midwinter.

The palace was occupied by the Marqueses de Viana until a couple of decades ago. The charge covers a one-hour guided tour of the rooms (packed with art and antiques) and access to the patios and garden (which take about half an hour to stroll round).

Plaza de las Tendillas & Around

Córdoba's busy main square features a clock with flamenco chimes, exuberant fountains and an equestrian statue – much loved by pigeons – of local lad Gonzalo Fernández de Córdoba, who rose to become the Catholic Monarchs' military right-hand man and earn the name El Gran Capitán. The streets running off from here are the main shopping zones. Calle Conde de Gondemar leads west into the broad and lengthy Avenida del Gran Capitán, undistinguished architecturally, but the scene of Córdoba's evening *paseo* and lively enough. A ruined Roman temple has been partly restored, with 11 columns standing, nearby on Calle Claudio Marcelo, to the east of Plaza de las Tendillas.

Language Courses

For information on monthly courses (except August) at Córdoba University, contact the Universidad de Córdoba **Servicio de Lenguas Modernas y Traducción Técnica** *(☎ 957 21 81 33, fax 957 21 89 96; ⓦ www .uco.es/webuco/ceucosa/lenguas; Edificio E U Enfermería, Avenida de Menéndez Pidal, 5 planta, 14071 Córdoba)*. Course fee is €361 and monthly accommodation can be arranged in shared apartments (€180), university residences, and lodgings with local families (€480).

A good private language school is **Centro de Idiomas Larcos** *(☎ 957 47 11 03; ⓦ www .larcos.net; Calle Manchado 9)*, offering a range of Spanish courses lasting from one or two weeks upwards, and varied accommodation options. A typical two-week course costs €257, and two weeks in a shared apartment costs about €156.

Special Events

Spring and early summer is the chief festival time in Córdoba. The major events are:

Semana Santa Every evening during Holy Week (from Palm Sunday to Good Friday) up to 12 *pasos* (religious images carried on platforms) and their processions file through the city, passing along the *carrera oficial* (official course) – Calle Claudio Marcelo, Plaza de las Tendillas, Calle José Cruz Conde – between about 8pm and midnight. The climax is the *madrugada* of Good Friday, when six *pasos* pass along the *carrera oficial* between 4am and 6am.

Cruces de Mayo During the first few days of May, squares and patios are decked with flower crosses, which become a focus for wine and tapas stalls, music and merrymaking.

Concurso & Festival de Patios Cordobeses During the first half of May, at the same time as the patio competition (see the boxed text 'Córdoba's Hidden Heart'), there's a busy cultural programme which, every three years (next in 2004), includes the Concurso Nacional de Arte Flamenco, an important flamenco competition.

Feria de Mayo During the last week of May and first days of June there is non-stop partying with concerts, a big fairground in the El Arenal area southeast of the city centre, and the main bullfight season in the Los Califas ring on Gran Via Parque.

Festival Internacional de Guitarra This is a two-week celebration of the guitar during late June and the first half of July, with live performances of classical, flamenco, rock, blues and more; top names play in the Jardines del Alcázar at night.

Places to Stay

Many Córdoba lodgings are built around the charming patios for which the city is famous. There are plenty of places near the Mezquita, with the cheaper ones chiefly in the streets to the east. Those mentioned here are just a selection. Booking ahead during the main festivals is essential. Córdoba draws increasing numbers of visitors throughout the year and from March to October booking ahead is also worth thinking about. Single rooms for a decent price are in short supply. Prices are generally reduced from November to mid-March; some places also cut their rates in the hot months of July and August.

Places to Stay – Budget

Camping About 1.25km north of Plaza de Colón is **Camping El Brillante** (☎ 957 40 38 36, fax 957 28 21 65; Avenida del Brillante 50; camping per adult/car/tent €3.60/3.60/3-3.60; open year-round).

Bus Nos 10 and 11 run to/from the train and bus stations and Plaza de Colón.

Hostels An excellent, modern place perfectly positioned in the Judería, **Albergue Juvenil Córdoba** (☎ 957 29 01 66, fax 957 29 05 00; Plaza de Judá Leví s/n; under 26/over 26 Mar-Oct & holiday periods €12.90/17.25, Nov-Feb €10.90/15.20) accommodates 167 people in double, triple, quadruple and quintuple rooms, all with air-con, heating and private bathroom. One wing is in a converted 16th-century convent.

Hostales The friendly, very old-fashioned **Huéspedes Martínez Rücker** (☎ 957 47 25 62; e reservation@hmrucker.com; Calle Martínez Rücker 14; singles/doubles €12/20) has a pretty patio and 12 small rooms. You get a 10% reduction for a three-day stay.

Hostal Rey Heredia (☎ 957 47 41 82; Calle de Rey Heredia 26; singles/doubles without bathroom €10/20, with bathroom €12/25) is simple, old-fashioned and friendly, with a plant-filled patio. There are nine decent rooms.

Hostal Trinidad (☎ 957 48 79 05; Calle Corregidor Luis de la Cerda 58; singles/doubles €13/26) is small and fairly basic.

Hostal Séneca (☎/fax 957 47 32 34; Calle Conde y Luque 7; singles/doubles without bathroom €20/34, with bathroom €31/40) is a 12-room place, a short distance north of the Mezquita. It is charming and friendly with a marvellous pebbled patio, filled with greenery. Rates include breakfast, and it's worth phoning ahead. Parking is available at €10 per night.

The following *hostales* are around Calle de San Fernando, away from the Mezquita and the main tourist crowds.

Hostal La Fuente (☎/fax 957 48 78 27; e hostallafuente@terra.es; Calle de San Fernando 51; singles/doubles €30/42) offers 40 decent rooms all with bathroom, TV, air-con and heating in an attractive 19th-century house. Rooms are compact, but there are courtyards for sitting in. A decent breakfast is served for €3 and a *menú* for €6.60.

Hostal Los Arcos (☎ 957 48 56 43, fax 957 48 60 11; Calle Romero Barros 14; singles/doubles €15/25, doubles with bathroom €31) is fairly modern, friendly and centred on a pretty courtyard.

Hostal Maestre (☎ 957 47 24 10, fax 957 47 53 95; Calle Romero Barros 4-6; singles/doubles with bathroom €21/33) is a pleasant place, with 20 clean spacious rooms.

Hostal San Francisco (☎/fax 957 47 27 16; Calle de San Fernando 24; singles or doubles with/without bathroom €43/37) is tiny. English and Dutch are spoken, and parking costs €6.

Places to Stay – Mid-Range

Hotel Los Omeyas (☎ 957 49 22 67, fax 957 49 16 59; Calle Encarnación 17; singles/doubles €38/62), half a block from the Mezquita, has fairly comfortable, good-sized rooms but without much character. It has a nice patio and café where breakfast is €3.50, and is popular with tour groups.

Hotel Marisa (☎ 957 47 31 42, fax 957 47 41 44; Calle Cardenal Herrero 6; singles/doubles €37.80/62), facing the northern side of the Mezquita, offers plain, comfy, sizable rooms.

Hostal El Triunfo (☎ 957 49 84 84, fax 957 48 68 50; e reservas@htriunfo.com; Calle Corregidor Luis de la Cerda 79; singles/doubles €40/61), facing the southern side of the Mezquita, has 70 rooms with air-con and TV, and there's a restaurant.

Hotel Mezquita (☎ 957 47 55 85, fax 957 47 62 19; e hotelmezquita@wanadoo.es; Plaza Santa Catalina 1; singles/doubles €36.40/70.60), across the street from the eastern side of the Mezquita, offers 21 good rooms. It's advisable to book ahead.

Hotel Boston (☎ 957 47 41 76, fax 957 47 85 23; Calle Málaga 2; singles/doubles €28.85/45.70) has bright pleasant rooms in a good location next to Plaza de las Tendillas.

Hotel Maestre (☎ 957 47 24 10, fax 957 47 53 95; Calle Romero Barros 4; singles/doubles €27/45), 400m east of the Mezquita, has plain but bright rooms with attached bathroom, and garage parking costing €6 a night.

Places to Stay – Top End

Hotel Conquistador (☎ 957 48 11 02, fax 957 47 46 77; Calle Magistral González Francés 15; doubles €155-173), an elegant 102-room place facing the eastern side of the Mezquita, has comfortable rooms.

Hotel Amistad Córdoba (☎ 957 42 03 35, fax 957 42 02 65; Plaza de Maimónides 3; singles/doubles €106/130) is an attractive place in the Judería. It occupies two modernised mansions.

Hotel Alfaros (☎ 957 49 19 20; e alfaros@maciahoteles.com; Calle Alfaros 18; doubles €120.50), north of the city centre, is a good 133-room place.

Parador (☎ 957 27 59 00, fax 957 28 04 09; e cordoba@parador.es; Avenida de la Arruzafa s/n; doubles €115) is 3km north of the city centre on the site of Abd ar-Rahman I's summer palace, where Europe's first palm trees were planted.

Places to Eat

Found on almost every Cordoban menu, *salmorejo* is a thick tomato-based gazpacho with bits of hard-boiled egg on top. *Rabo de toro* (oxtail stew) is another favourite. Some of the top restaurants feature recipes from Al-Andalus such as garlic soup with raisins, honeyed lamb, fried aubergine and meats stuffed with dates and pine nuts. The local wine from nearby Montilla and Moriles is similar to sherry and made by the same process but without being fortified. Like sherry, it comes *fino*, *amontillado* or *oloroso* (see Wine in the Facts for the Visitor chapter for details on the different types) and there's also the sweet Pedro Ximénez variety made from raisins.

Córdoba prides itself on its *tabernas*, busy bars where you can usually also sit down to eat.

There are loads of places to eat right by the Mezquita, some expensive, some mediocre and some awful. A few better-value places are a short walk west into the Judería. A longer walk east or north will produce even better options for the budget-conscious or inquisitive.

Around the Mezquita The busy **Bar Santos** (Calle Magistral González Francés 3;

tapas/raciones €0.90/3) might be tiny but it does a roaring trade in *bocadillos* (filled rolls; around €2.25), tapas and *raciones* (meal-sized servings of tapas). Wash down your snack with a glass of potent sangria.

El Caballo Rojo (☎ 95 747 53 75; *Calle Cardenal Herrero 28; mains €10.20-17.70)* specialises in Mozarabic food from caliphal times. You're guaranteed something out of the ordinary with the *menú* (fixed-priced meal; €17.70). Be prepared for a loud shock when the Mezquita bells ring.

Bandolero Restaurante (☎ 95 747 64 91; *Calle de Torrijos 6; media-raciones €2.40-7.20, mains €8.70-13.55)*, facing the western side of the Mezquita, has good *media-raciones* (half-*raciones*) and *platos combinados* (mixed platters). You can sit in the bar, the patio or the restaurant at the back.

Amaltea (☎ 95 749 19 68; *Ronda de Isasa 10; mains €6-10; open noon-4.30pm & 6.30pm-midnight)* specialises in natural, organic food. Tuck into a delicious green salad with avocado and walnuts, while cool jazz hums away in the background.

Judería Start off with a complimentary glass of Montilla wine on the patio at **Casa Pepe de la Judería** (☎ 95 720 07 44; *Calle Romero 1; mains €9.60-14.40; open 1pm-4pm & 8.30pm-11.30pm)*. This place can charm even the most demanding punter with its good service and fine food, including Cordoban-style ox tails (€10.80).

Restaurante El Rincón de Carmen (☎ 95 729 10 55; *Calle Romero 4)*, with its geranium-filled patio, is a good place for a moonlit supper. The food isn't spectacular, and the tuna steak with onion sauce (€12.50) is rather tough, but the ambience makes up for it.

El Churrasco (☎ 957 29 08 19; *Calle Romero 16; mains €12, menú €12)* is one of Córdoba's top restaurants. The food is rich, the portions generous and the service attentive. Meaty dishes include *churrasco* (barbecued fillet of pork) with exotic Arabian sauce (€9.60).

Casa Elisa (*Calle Almanzor 34; bocadillos €1-2)* is just a hole-in-the-wall place that does excellent take-away hot filled rolls.

Comedor Árabe-Andalusí (*Calle Alfayatas; bocadillos €3)* entrances diners with its dim lighting, Arabic music and mouth-watering falafel *bocadillos*. This place is a treat not to be missed.

East of the Mezquita The well-loved and roomy **Taberna Sociedad de Plateros** (☎ 95 747 00 42; *Calle San Francisco 6; tapas €1.50-2; open Tues-Sun)* serves a selection of tempting tapas. This place began life as a society for silversmiths, hence the name.

Bar San Francisco (*Calle de San Fernando 65; platos combinados €5.75)* does popular *platos combinados* and a good-value three-course *menú* for €8.

Casa de Comidas La Estupenda (☎ 95 747 04 94; *Calle de San Fernando 39; menú €6.60)* has a well-priced *menú* comprising two hearty dishes. The seafood platters (€7.70) are also popular with the fish-craving masses.

Bar Callejón (*Calle Enrique Romero de Torres; platos combinados €3-5.40, 3-course menú €7.20)*, on a pedestrian street with tables outside looking up to Plaza del Potro, does tasty omelettes (€4.30) and a range of fish dishes (€5.50 to €6.10).

Taberna El Potro (*Calle Enrique Romero de Torres; menú €6-17.50)*, next door to Bar Callejón, is a bit more expensive but does a choice of five set menus. Chat to the parrot perched outside while you eat.

City Centre Going strong since 1880, **Taberna San Miguel** (*Casa El Pisto;* ☎ 95 747 83 28; *Plaza San Miguel 1; tapas €1.50, media-raciones €3-6; open noon-4pm & 8pm-midnight Mon-Sat)* is one of Córdoba's most popular and atmospheric *tabernas*. You'll find a good range of dishes here, and inexpensive Moriles wine ready in jugs on the bar.

Pizzaiolo (☎ 95 748 64 33; *Calle San Felipe 5; pizza or pasta €3.95-6.70)* made *Guinness World Records* for having the world's longest menu (more than 360 dishes always available). It's bright and popular without reaching any great culinary heights.

CÓRDOBA PROVINCE

Entertainment

The magazines *¿Qué hacer en Córdoba?* and *Welcome & Olé!*, issued free by tourist offices, have some what's-on information, as does the daily newspaper *Córdoba*. Fliers are posted for live bands outside music bars and at the Albergue Juvenil Córdoba (see Places to Stay). Bands usually start around 10pm and there's rarely a cover charge. Most bars in the medieval city close around midnight.

Bodega Guzmán *(Calle de los Judíos 7)* is an atmospheric local favourite that oozes alcohol from every nook. Check out the bullfight/festival decor and don't leave without trying some wine from the barrel.

Casa Salinas *(Calle Fernández Ruano)*, just round the corner, is a cosy place with flamenco on some nights.

Tablao Cardenal *(☎ 957 48 33 20; Calle de Torrijos 10; admission €16.80)* vibrates with the sound of tapping heels when its flamenco shows (from 10.30pm nightly) get going. The performances are sometimes mediocre; nonetheless they're authentic.

Córdoba's liveliest bars are mostly scattered around the newer parts of town and come alive around 11pm or midnight at weekends. You'll be lucky to find any action early in the week.

Soul *(☎ 95 749 15 80; Calle de Alfonso XIII 3; open till 3am daily)* attracts a hip and arty crowd with its retro vibe and vanguard music. It also does coffee and toast (€1.50) for breakfast.

Velvet Café *(Calle Alfaros 29)* has a Bohemian '60s feel with whirling patterns and lazy music.

Milenium *(Calle Alfaros 33)* is a popular gay haunt that plays a good range of ambient House tunes.

Can Can *(Puerte del Rincón 7; open 8pm-3am)* might imply frilly knickers and leg waggling but this place is far too laid-back for that; relax and soak up the atmosphere.

Magister *(Avenida del Gran Capitán 2)* caters to the more mature drinker, playing soporific background music and brewing beer on the spot to assure patrons the alcohol won't run out. The beer comes in five tasty varieties: blond *rubia* and *tostada*, the dark *caramelizada* and *morenita*, and the *especial*, which varies from season to season.

Surfer Rosa *(☎ 95 775 22 72; Feria El Arenal 4; open 11pm-late)* is a riverbank warehouse in the Recinto Ferial El Arenal (the May fairgrounds). Live bands play frequently, the recorded music is infectious, and admission is often free.

Sala Level *(Calle Antonio Maura 58; tickets €9; open 8pm-late)*, west of the city centre in the Ciudad Jardín suburb, is another busy live-band venue. Prices vary depending on the talent.

Gran Teatro de Córdoba *(☎ 957 48 02 37; Avenida del Gran Capitán 3)* has a busy programme ranging from varied concerts and theatre to dance and film festivals.

Filmoteca de Andalucía *(☎ 957 47 20 18; Calle Medina y Corella 5; admission €0.90)*, situated at the end of a small courtyard, regularly shows subtitled (sometimes in Spanish, sometimes in English) foreign films.

Hammam Baños Árabes *(☎ 95 748 47 46; Calle Corregidor Luis de la Cerda; bath €12)*, the heavenly Arabic baths, are just right for a relaxing wallow. You can also get a bath and chiro-massage for €18. Don't forget your swimming costume; naked people are not admitted.

Shopping

Córdoba is known for its embossed leather products *(cuero repujado)*, silver jewellery (particularly filigree) and attractive pottery. Shops selling these and other crafts concentrate around the Mezquita. The **Zoco** *(Calle de los Judíos)* is a group of workshops/showrooms selling good but pricey crafts.

Meryan *(☎ 95 747 59 02; Calleja de las Flores)* is the best place for embossed leather, and you should be able to find a wallet or an attractive pair of slippers for €9 to €12.

Plaza de la Corredera has a few shops selling boots, music and bric-a-brac. **Casa 24 bis**, in the northern corner, is a treasure-trove of Spanish antiquities (and junk).

La Tienda del Olivo *(☎ 95 747 44 95; Calle de San Fernando 124B)* sells fancy soaps made from olive oil, plus oodles of Extra Virgin for those tapas nights back home.

Calle José Cruz Conde is the smartest central shopping street. There is also an excellent **El Corte Inglés** (Avenida del Gran Capitán) to fulfil those shopping whims.

Getting There & Away

Bus The bus station (☎ 957 40 40 40; Plaza de las Tres Culturas) is behind the train station. Minimum daily services by **Alsina Graells** (☎ 957 27 81 00) include 10 buses to/from Seville (€8, 1¾ hours), eight to/from Granada (€9.65, three hours) and five to/from Málaga (€9.45, 2½ hours). Alsina Graells also serves Écija, Carmona, Antequera, Cádiz, Nerja and Almería. **Bacoma** (☎ 957 27 98 60) runs to Baeza, Úbeda, Valencia and Barcelona. **Transportes Ureña** (☎ 957 40 45 58) serves Jaén five or more times daily (€5.85, 1½ hours). **Secorbus** (☎ 902 22 92 92) operates six buses to/from Madrid daily (€10.10, 4½ hours).

Autotransportes López y Lisetur (☎ 957 76 70 77) runs to Extremadura and northwestern Córdoba province. **Autotransportes Ureña** (☎ 957 27 81 00) serves central north Córdoba province, **Autotransportes San Sebastián** (☎ 957 23 67 71) and **Autocares Pérez Cubero** (☎ 957 68 40 23) go to western Córdoba province, and **Empresa Carrera** (☎ 957 40 44 14) heads south, with several daily buses to Priego de Córdoba and Cabra, and at least two a day to Zuheros, Rute and Iznájar.

Train Córdoba's modern train station (☎ 957 40 02 02; Avenida de América) is 1km northwest of Plaza de las Tendillas.

About 20 trains a day run to/from Seville, ranging from Andalucía Exprés regional trains (€7, 1¼ hours) to AVEs (€14.50 or €17.50 in the cheapest class, turista, 45 minutes). Options to/from Madrid range from several daily AVEs (€40 to €59.50 in turista, 1¾ hours) to a middle-of-the-night Estrella (€23.45 in a seat, 6¼ hours).

Several trains head to Málaga daily (€12 to €24, two to three hours), Cádiz and Barcelona. One or two trains a day go to Jaén, Huelva and Fuengirola. For Granada (€12, four hours) you need to change at Bobadilla.

Car Rental firms include **Avis** (☎ 957 47 68 62; Plaza de Colón 32), and **Europcar** (☎ 957 40 34 80), as well as **Hertz** (☎ 957 40 20 60), both at the train station.

Getting Around

Bus City buses cost €1. Bus No 3, from the street between the train and bus stations, runs to Plaza de las Tendillas and down Calle de San Fernando, 300m east of the Mezquita. For the return trip, pick it up on Ronda de Isasa, just south of the Mezquita, or Avenida Doctor Fleming.

Car & Motorcycle Córdoba's one-way system is nightmarish, and parking in the old city can be difficult. Metered streetside parking around the Mezquita and along the riverside is demarcated by blue lines. Charges are €0.30/0.65/1.25 for 30/60/75 minutes, from 8am to 9pm. Overnight parking outside these hours is free, but you need to be on the spot and feeding the meter by 8am. There is parking across the river, but it is not necessarily secure overnight. A tempting option (metered) is the walled space just below the Mezquita, abreast of the Puerta del Puente. This is fine by day, but overnight parking is not advised as it is not secure. There is secure parking just off Avenida Doctor Fleming costing €1.05/12.60 for one hour/24 hours. There is an underground car park on Avenida de América with similar prices.

The routes to many hotels and hostales are fairly well signposted, and the signs display a 'P' if the establishment has parking. Charges for hotel parking are about €6 to €10.

Taxi In the city centre, cabs congregate at the northeastern corner of Plaza de las Tendillas. The fare from the train or bus station to the Mezquita is around €4.50.

AROUND CÓRDOBA
Medina Azahara

In 936 Abd ar-Rahman III decided his new caliphate needed a new capital and duly had one built 8km west of Córdoba at the foot of the Sierra Morena. Records state that 10,000 labourers worked on its construction, setting

6000 stone blocks a day, and by 945 the caliph was able to install himself and his retinue. Stretching 1.5km from east to west and 700m from north to south, the new city was called Medina Azahara *(Madinat al-Zahra;* ☎ *957 32 91 30; admission €1.50, EU citizen free; open 10am-8.30pm Tues-Sat, 10am-2pm Sun May–mid-Sept; 10am-2pm Tues-Sat, 10am-2pm Sun mid-Sept–Apr).* The name was in celebration of Abd ar-Rahman's wife Azahara.

Medina Azahara's glory was short-lived. Al-Mansur transferred the seat of government to a new palace-complex of his own, east of the city, in 981. Then, between 1010 and 1013, Medina Azahara was wrecked by Berber soldiers who occupied it during the anarchic collapse of the caliphate. During succeeding centuries its ruins were plundered repeatedly for building materials.

Though less than one-tenth of the city has been excavated, and what's open to visitors is only about a quarter of that, Medina Azahara is still intriguing and its country location adds to the appeal.

The visitor route takes you down through the city's original northern gate to the **Dar al-Wuzara** (House of the Viziers), a partly restored building which would have been used by the caliphs' administrative advisers. It has several arches and is fronted by a square garden. Down to the east from here is a **portico**, a row of arches in red and white stripes similar to the Córdoba Mezquita, which fronted a military parade ground. From here your path leads downhill, with views over Medina Azahara's ruined caliphal **mosque**, to the most impressive building on the site, the much-restored **Salón de Abd ar-Rahman III**, facing a large garden. This was the caliphs' throne hall, a three-aisled affair with beautiful arches. Its floral, geometric and calligraphic stone carving (still being pieced back together) was of a lavishness unprecedented in the Islamic world. Richard Fletcher writes in *Moorish Spain* that in the centre of the hall stood a bowl containing mercury: when the caliph wished to impress visitors, he would have a slave rock the bowl so that reflected light flashed around the hall like lightning.

The route followed through the site is not circular and you have to retrace your steps from the Salón de Abd ar-Rahman III.

Getting There & Away The nearest you can get by bus is the Cruce de Medina Azahara, the turnoff from the A-431, from which it's a 3km walk, slightly uphill, to the site. This can be an uninspiring and dusty trudge in the heat of summer; more so when tour buses roar past in either direction crammed with visitors and school groups, although you might catch a lift from a passing car. City bus No 0-1 will drop you at the *cruce.* At the time of writing, this departed the northern end of Avenida de la República Argentina at 8am, 8.30am, 9.40am, 11.20am, 1pm, 2pm, 3.20pm and 6pm daily. A drinks kiosk is usually open in summer at the Medina Azahara car park.

A taxi costs €24 for the return trip, with one hour allowed to view the site. You can book an organised tour to Medina Azahara through many of the hotels or contact **Córdoba Vision** (☎ *957 23 17 34).* **Córdoba en Bici** (☎ *639 425 884)* organises various cycling tours including one to Medina Azahara.

If you're driving, take Avenida de Medina Azahara west from the city centre, leading out onto the A-431. The Medina Azahara turnoff is signposted 5km from the city centre. Parking at the site is €0.60.

NORTH OF CÓRDOBA

The Sierra Morena rises sharply just north of Córdoba city then rolls fairly gently over most of the north of the province.

Los Pedroches

You can have an interesting day or two exploring Los Pedroches, the province's northernmost district, between Belalcázar in the northwest and Cardeña in the northeast. Buses reach most of its villages from Córdoba, but to tour freely you need a vehicle.

Los Pedroches is a sparsely populated area of scattered granite-built settlements, occasional rocky outcrops and expanses of woodland pasture *(dehesa).* White storks nest precariously on church towers, castles and other vantage points around the district.

Two absorbing places to head for, if you enjoy off-the-beaten-track destinations, are the castles at Belalcázar and Santa Eufemia. Both villages have simple, inexpensive *hostales*. The **Castillo de los Sotomayor** looming over remote Belalcázar is one of the spookiest fortifications in Andalucía. Dominated by a huge top-heavy keep, with a later Renaissance palace tacked on to the side, it was built in the 15th century on the site of a Muslim fort. The castle is closed up and you can't go inside, but you can walk around the outside of it. The trip to Belalcázar is worth it just for the views of the castle from round about.

Santa Eufemia, 26km east of Belalcázar across empty countryside, is Andalucía's northernmost village. The **Castillo de Miramontes**, originally Muslim, on a crag above it to the north, is a tumbled ruin but the 360° views from it are stupendous. To reach the castle turn west off the N-502 main road at Hostal La Paloma in the village, and after 1km turn right at the 'Camino Servicio RTVE' sign, from which it's a 1.5km drive uphill to the castle.

The eastern end of Los Pedroches is occupied by the **Parque Natural Sierra de Cardeña y Montoro**, a hilly, wooded area that is one of the last Andalucian redoubts of the wolf and lynx.

WEST OF CÓRDOBA
Almodóvar del Río
postcode 14728 • pop 7,237
• elevation 123m

The castle-crowned **Almodóvar del Río** lies 22km down the Guadalquivir valley from Córdoba and is an attractive and busy agricultural town. There is a **tourist office** (*☎/fax 957 63 50 14; Calle Vicente Aleixandre 3; open 9am-2pm & 6pm-8pm Mon-Fri, 10am-1pm Sat, 10am-2pm Sun Apr-Oct; 9am-2pm & 5pm-7pm Mon-Fri, 10am-1pm Sat, 10am-2pm Sun Nov-Mar*) just round the corner from the pretty central square, Plaza de la Constitución.

Almodóvar's inescapable main feature is its monumental, and slightly sinister, eight-towered **castle** (*☎ 957 63 51 16; admission by donation; open 11am-7pm daily*) that

dominates the view from miles around. The castle was founded in 740 but owes most of its present appearance to post-Reconquista rebuilding. Pedro I (the Cruel) used it as a treasure store. The castle has been almost over-restored by its owner the Marqués de la Motilla. It was never taken by force and the sense of impregnability is still potent within the massive walls. The towers – with names such as 'the Bells', 'the School' and 'the Tribute' – have various stories attached to them and there are information placards in Spanish and English.

If you are driving, the best way to reach the castle (avoiding the crowded town centre) is to ignore signs ahead for *Centro Urbano* at the junction as you enter town. Instead, go right and follow the A-431 ring road, signed to Palma del Río and Posadas. There is ample parking below the castle, but you can also drive up the winding, stony approach track. You can easily walk down into the old town centre from the castle.

Hostal San Luis (*☎ 957 63 54 21; Carretera Palma del Río; singles/doubles €21/36*) is alongside the main A-431 by the turn-off for Almodóvar. It has decent rooms in a separate building attached to its busy restaurant. Don't be put off by the large number of trucks pulled up outside. Breakfast is €3 and you can get plentiful *platos combinados* for €5 to €6. In Almodóvar there are several good eating places.

Bar Tapón (*Calle Antonio Espín 18*) is just up from the tourist office and does good meat dishes such as *carne de monte* (local game, such as venison or wild boar) for €5. **La Taberna** (*☎ 957 71 36 84; Calle Antonio Machado 24*) is more upmarket and has fish and meat dishes for around €12.

Autocares Pérez Cubero (*☎ 957 68 40 23*) runs 10 buses to/from Córdoba on weekdays, five on Saturday and two on Sunday (€1.45, ½ hour).

Hornachuelos & the Parque Natural Sierra de Hornachuelos

The pleasant village of Hornachuelos is the ideal base for spending a couple of days enjoying the quiet charms of the **Parque Natural Sierra de Hornachuelos**, a 672-sq-km area of rolling hills in the Sierra Morena, northwest of Almodóvar del Río. The park is densely wooded with a mix of holm oak, cork oak and ash, and is pierced by a number of river valleys that are thick with willow trees. It is renowned for its eagles and other raptors, and harbours the second largest colony of black vultures in Andalucía. There are small numbers of wolves, lynxes and otters in the area, and large numbers of red deer and wild boar attract many hunters.

Hornachuelos is an appealing village that stands above a small reservoir on the banks of which is a charming little picnic area. The village is reached by a long winding approach road where traffic is controlled by lights. The main square is Plaza de la Constitución. The **tourist office** (☎/fax 957 64 07 86; Calle Antonio Machado 6; open 10am-2pm Mon-Thur, 10am-2pm & 4pm-6pm Fri-Sun) was located here at the time of writing, but there are plans to relocate it to the sports complex on Carretera de San Calixto, the main road to the west of the centre. From Plaza de la Constitución, a lane, La Palmera, with a charming palm tree pebble mosaic underfoot, leads up to the Iglesia de Santa Maride las Flores and a mirador on Paseo Blas Infante.

Heading northwest from Hornachuelos on the road to San Calixto takes you in about 1.5km to the **Centro de Visitantes Huerta del Rey** (☎ 957 64 11 40; open 10am-2pm & 4pm-7pm Mon-Fri, 10am-7pm Sat). The centre has interesting displays on the area and its creatures, and sells local produce, including honey. You can get information on the numerous walking trails that fan out from the centre and you can book for a **guided walk** (☎ 957 33 82 33, 617 23 77 00), hire bikes or arrange horse riding sessions here. There is a bar-restaurant just by the centre car park that does mains from €5 to €8.40.

Places to Stay & Eat At the heart of Hornachuelos village is **Casa Rural El Melojo** (☎ 957 64 06 29; Plaza de la Constitución 15; doubles €51), a traditionally furnished house, with substantial reductions for groups.

On the main road just west of the centre is **Hostal El Álamo** (☎ 957 64 04 76; Carretera Comarcal 141, also called Carretera de San Calixto; singles/doubles €32/51.45). There is a busy bar and restaurant but rooms are in separate units and are clean and pleasant. The restaurant does a *menú* for €6.90 and specialises in big creamy cakes. Further north along the main road, and at the northwest entrance to Hornachuelos, the cheaper **El Kiosco** (☎ 957 64 04 30; Explanada del Kiosco; singles/doubles €18/30) has dull but serviceable rooms. You can get breakfast for €2 and a *menú* for about €6 in its bar-restaurant.

Bar Casa Alejandro (Avenida Guadalquivir 4; raciones €3.60) is just south of the road that leads into the village. It's very popular with locals and the walls are heavy with hunting trophies; an alarmingly lifelike stuffed head of a horse protrudes from a bar-side pillar.

Autocares Pérez Cubero (☎ 957 68 40 23) runs four buses to/from Córdoba on weekdays, one on Saturday, and two on Sunday (€3.20, 50 minutes).

TOWARDS MÁLAGA

The N-331 to Antequera and Málaga crosses mainly unspectacular, rolling agricultural country known as La Campiña. **Montilla**, 45km from Córdoba, is the main production centre for Córdoba's sherrylike wines. You can visit **Bodegas Alvear** (☎ 957 65 01 00; Avenida María Auxiliadora 1), but you should call first to book. Montilla has several hotels and *hostales*.

LA SUBBÉTICA

The south of Córdoba province straddled the Muslim-Christian frontier from the 13th to 15th century and many towns and villages are crowned by castles. The beautiful, mountainous southeast is known as La Subbética after the Sistema Subbético range which crosses this corner of the province. The mountains, canyons and wooded valleys of the 316-sq-km Parque Natural Sierras Subbéticas offer some enjoyable walks. The CNIG 1:50,000 map *Parque Natural Sierras Subbéticas* is useful, but it's best to get a copy before arriving in the area (see Maps in the Facts for the Visitor chapter).

The southern boundary of the region is demarcated by the Embalse de Iznájar, a long, wriggling reservoir overlooked by the village of Iznájar from an imposing crag topped by a Muslim castle and a 16th-century church. The area has some good lakeside walking. The northern section of the park has a number of attractive settlements of which Zuheros and Priego de Córdoba are among the most appealing.

The park's **Centro de Visitantes Santa Rita** (☎ 957 33 40 34; A-340) is located, not very conveniently, 10km east of Cabra.

Zuheros & Around
postcode 14870 ● pop 930
● elevation 625m

Rising above a sea of olive trees south of the N-432, Zuheros is a beautiful base for exploring the northern section of the region. Tourist information is available from **Turismo Zuheros** (☎ 957 69 47 75; W www .zuheros.com; open 9am-2pm & 5pm-8pm Mon-Fri, 10am-2pm & 5pm-8pm Sat & Sun), a small office attached to a cheese-making factory; you can buy delicious varieties of local cheese – some cured with pepper or wood ash – for €6 to €10.50, complete hams for €53, wines, olive oil and honey. The Turismo has plenty of leaflets and information on walking and bike hire. It can put you in contact with a good walking guide (or to contact directly, phone ☎ 957 69 47 96). There is a **park information point** (☎ 957 33 52 55) open occasionally a few hundred metres up the road towards the Cueva de los Murciélagos. There is a good car park at the heart of the village below the castle.

Zuheros has a delightfully relaxed atmosphere. All round the western escarpment on which it perches there are miradors with exhilarating views of the dramatic limestone crags that tower over the village and create such a powerful backdrop for Zuheros' **castle**. The castle is of Muslim origin and retains a satisfying patina of age and decay in its rough stonework. Near the castle is a church that was once a mosque, and directly opposite the castle is the **archaeological museum** (castle & museum admission €1.80; open 10am-2pm & 5pm-8pm daily 16 Apr-14 Sept; 10am-2pm & 4pm-7pm daily 15 Sept-15 Apr). The museum custodian will give you a guided tour of the museum. To visit the castle you need to get the key from the museum. A 4km drive up the mountain – enjoyable in itself – behind the village is the **Cueva de los Murciélagos** (Cave of the Bats; ☎ 957 69 45 45), which was inhabited by Neanderthals more than 35,000 years ago. It's renowned for its rock paintings of goats and people from Neolithic times (6000–3000 BC). Guided visits for groups of up to 10 people take place at noon and 6pm Monday to Friday (individuals may be able to join these groups) and at 11am, 12.30pm, 2pm, 6pm and 7.30pm on Saturday, Sunday and holidays from 16 April to 14 September. The cost per person is €3.60, with guides catering for a maximum of up to 150 people a day.

Hotel Zuhayra (☎ 957 69 46 93; Calle Mirador 10; singles/doubles with bathroom €36.40/46) is an excellent base for exploring the area. It can supply a great deal of information on walking routes and on guided walks. The hotel's restaurant does good mains for €4 to €9. Just below the castle is the **Mesón Los Palancos** with raciones from €3.50.

Empresa Carrera (☎ 957 40 44 14) runs five buses to/from Córdoba on weekdays, four on Saturdays and two on Sundays (€5, one hour).

Zuheros Walk You need good maps, or an experienced guide, to explore the deeper reaches of the mountains around Zuheros, but there is a pleasant circular walk of just over 4km through the Cañon de Bailón, the rocky gorge behind the village, that gives a taste of it all. Just below Zuheros on its southwestern side, where the approach road CO241 from the A316 Doña Mencía junction bends sharply, there is a small car park at the Mirador de Bailón, right in front of the mouth of the gorge. From the entrance to the car park – with your back to the gorge – take the broad stony track heading up left. Follow the track as it winds uphill and then curves left along the slopes above the gorge. In about 500m the path descends and the valley of the Bailón opens out between rocky walls. The path crosses the stony riverbed to its opposite bank and, in about 1km, a wired-down stone causeway that recrosses the river appears ahead. A few metres before you reach this crossing, bear up left on what is at first a very faint path. It becomes much clearer as it zigzags past a big tree and a twisted rock pinnacle up on the right. Climb steadily, then, where the path levels off, and keep left through trees to reach a superb viewpoint. Continue on an obvious path that passes a couple of Parque Natural noticeboards and takes you to the road leading up to the Cueva de los Murciélagos. Turn left and follow the road back down to Zuheros.

Priego de Córdoba
postcode 14800 • pop 21,732
• elevation 650m

This sizable town is another possible base for exploring La Subbética, as well as being a delight in itself. Two of the province's highest peaks, 1570m La Tiñosa and 1476m Bermejo, rise to the southwest. Priego is blessed with a series of outstanding baroque churches, built in the 18th century. The town's old Muslim quarter, the Barrio de La Villa, is enchanting.

Priego's main square is the busy Plaza de la Constitución which merges with the smaller traffic junction of Plaza Andalucía. The helpful **tourist office** (☎ 957 70 06 25; Calle del Río 33; open 10am-1.30pm & 5pm-7.30pm Tues-Sun) is a short walk south of the central Plaza de la Constitución. The office's indefatigable chief, José Mateo Aguilera, is an enthusiastic fount of information.

Things to See There's much to see in Priego and all the town's churches and monuments have external information panels in English and French, as well as Spanish. Priego's churches are normally open 10am to 1pm daily, and some are open from about 6pm to 8pm; but be prepared for unpredictable closures.

The main area of monuments lies 200m northeast of Plaza de la Constitución and is reached by following Calle Solana and on through Plaza San Pedro. At a junction with Calle Doctor Pedrajas you can go left to visit the well-preserved 16th-century slaughterhouse, the **Carnicerías Reales** (admission free; open 10am-1pm & 5pm-7pm). It has an enclosed patio and a wonderful stone staircase; exhibitions of paintings are often held here. Turning right along Calle Doctor Pedrajas takes you to Plaza de Abad Palomino. On the square's northern side is Priego's **Castillo**, an Arabic fortress built on original Roman foundations in the 9th century and later rebuilt in the 16th century. Closed to the public for many years, the castle has had much archaeological investigation, which among other things turned up dozens of stone cannonballs. The good news is that it is likely to be open for visits from 2003.

Across the square from the castle is Priego's hidden glory, the **Parroquia de la Asunción** (Plaza de Abad Palomino; open 11am-1.30pm & 5.30pm-8pm Tues-Sun May-Sept; 10.30am-1.30pm & 4pm-7pm Tues-Sun Oct-Apr). The 16th-century exterior is unassuming and the main part of the interior is enjoyably ornate, but the 18th-century Sagrario chapel is one of the supreme works of Andalucían baroque, a lavish eruption of white stucco and sculpture surging upwards to a beautiful dome that is pierced by windows.

Behind La Asunción are the winding streets of the **Barrio de La Villa**, where cascades of potted geraniums transform the whitewashed walls, especially in Calle Real and in the Plaza de San Antonio. Other pretty alleyways lead down from the heart of the Barrio to the Paseo de Adarve where there are fine views across the rolling countryside and mountains. On the southern edge of the barrio and ending in a superb mirador is the lovely **Paseo de Colombia** (literally, 'Promenade of the Roses') with fountains, flower beds and an elegant pergola.

Priego's sumptuous baroque churches also include the **Iglesia de San Pedro** (Plaza San Pedro), the **Iglesia de San Francisco** (Calle Buen Suceso) and the particularly splendid **Iglesia de la Aurora** (Carrera de Álvarez).

Another splendid Priego treasure is the **Fuente del Rey** *(Calle del Río)*, an elegant fountain which would be more at home in the gardens of Versailles than in a small town in provincial Andalucía. The Fuente originated in the 17th century but dates in its present form from 1803. It is reached from Plaza Andalucía by following Calle del Río to where the fountain occupies the centre of a small leafy square. Glittering water flows from 139 spouts – the upper ones in the form of grotesque stone faces – into three terraced pools adorned with a centrepiece sculpture depicting Neptune and Amphitrite. Behind the Fuente del Rey is the late-16th-century **Fuente de la Virgen de la Salud**, less flamboyant, but further enhancing the square's delightful tranquillity.

Also worth a visit is the **Museo Histórico** *(Carrera de las Monjas 16; admission free; open 10am-2pm & 6pm-8pm Tues-Fri, 11am-2pm Sat & Sun)*, just west of Plaza de la Constitución. Its imaginative displays cover mainly the local archaeology of the prehistoric to the medieval periods. The museum organises archaeological tours in the area.

Places to Stay & Eat Just east of Plaza de la Constitución, **Hostal Rafi** *(☎ 957 54 70 27, fax 957 54 07 49; e htelrafi@arrakis.es; Calle Isabel La Católica 4; singles/doubles €20.60/33; breakfasts €3, menú €6, fish & meat dishes €5.40-9)* has pleasant rooms and a busy restaurant.

Río Piscina *(☎ 957 70 01 86; Carretera Monturque-Alcalá La Real Km 44; doubles €44)* is located on the eastern edge of town.

Villa Turística de Priego *(☎ 957 70 35 03; 2-person apartments €72)*, 7km north on the road to Zagrilla, is a modern, Muslim-style place with self-catering apartments.

Priego has some good restaurants to supplement its lively local bars and cafés.

Balcón del Adarve *(☎ 957 54 70 75; Paseo de Colombia 36; menú €9)* has lovely yellow, blue and green tiling and a terrace. Fish and meat dishes range from €7 to €12 and include such specialities as *solomillo de ciervo al vino tinto con Grosella* (venison in gooseberry and red wine sauce), and *salmón en supremas a la naranja* (salmon in orange sauce). It also does stir-fries for €5 to €7.

El Ajibe *(☎ 957 70 18 56; Calle Abad Palomino; raciones €4-9, menú €6.75)* is next to the Castillo. Part of the downstairs has a glass floor above Roman foundations and the outside terrace is shaded by vines; salads start at €4.55.

Bar Cafetería Río *(Calle Río; raciones €5.40-7.20)* is a busy central option with *revueltos* for €6.60 to €7.20, and fish and meat dishes from €6 to €11. The same people run **Pizzeria-Bagueteria Varini** *(Calle Torrejón 7)* just round the corner where there's a huge range of pizzas from €8 to €9.70, pastas from €3.60 to €5.10 and baguettes from €2.70 to €3.30.

Getting There & Around The centre of Priego can get very busy. There is parking just by the football and basketball pitches in Calle Cava north of Plaza de la Constitución. There is a small car park in Plaza Palenque along Carrera de las Monjas, the street that runs east from Plaza de la Constitución. At the time of writing, a multistorey car park was under construction here.

Priego's bus station is about 1km west of Plaza de la Constitución on Calle Nuestra Señora de los Remedios, off Calle San Marcos. Bus No 1 from the Plaza Andalucía will take you there. **Empresa Carrera** *(☎ 957 40 44 14)* runs up to 12 buses to/from Córdoba weekdays, (€5.70, 1¼ hours), five on Saturday and Sunday, two or more to Granada, and others to Cabra and elsewhere.

Granada Province

As well as the world-famous city of Granada, this enthralling province includes Andalucía's highest mountains (in the Sierra Nevada) and the beautiful Las Alpujarras valleys to their south.

Granada

postcode 18080 • pop 243,000
• elevation 685m

The Alhambra palace-fortress, dominating the Granada skyline from its hilltop perch, and the fascinating Albayzín, Granada's old Islamic quarter, are highlights of any visit to Andalucía. Granada also possesses many impressive and historic post-Reconquista (Reconquest) buildings, and the city's setting, with the often snow-clad Sierra Nevada as backdrop, is magnificent. Its greenness is a delight in often-parched Andalucía, and its climate pleasant, especially in spring and autumn. With a large and vibrant Spanish and international student population, Granada also boasts a buzzing cultural life, some excellent bars and a hopping nightlife.

HISTORY

Granada began life as an Iberian settlement, referred to as Elibyrge or Illiberis. Under the Romans the town was called Illiberia Florentia. Muslim forces took over from the Visigoths in AD 711, with the aid of the Jewish community around the foot of the Alhambra hill in what was called Garnata al-Jahud, from which the name Granada derives. (*Granada* also happens to be the Spanish for pomegranate, the fruit on the city's coat of arms.) The Muslims initially established a provincial capital, Elvira, 10km northwest of Granada on the site of modern Atarfe. In the 11th century the Zirid dynasty, rulers of the local kingdom *(taifa)*, moved back to the more easily defensible Albayzín.

When the Almohad state ruling Al-Andalus (the Muslim-controlled areas of the Iberian Peninsula) crumbled in the 13th

Highlights

- Indulge your senses at the Alhambra and Generalife, the legendary palace and gardens of Spain's last Muslim dynasty

- Ramble round the Albayzín, Granada's bohemian, warren-like old Islamic quarter, with sunset views of the Alhambra

- Admire Granada's Capilla Real, burial place of the Catholic Monarchs (Reyes Católicos)

- Get out on the town in the buzzing bars and clubs of after-dark Granada

- Explore the beautiful, mysterious Las Alpujarras valleys and climb the snow-capped Sierra Nevada

century, a minor potentate called Mohammed ibn Yusuf ibn Nasr managed to establish an independent emirate, known as the Nasrid emirate, centred on Granada. After the fall of Córdoba (1236) and Seville (1248) to Christian Castile (Castilla), Muslims sought refuge in Granada. The Nasrid emirate became the final remnant of Al-Andalus, stretching from the Strait of Gibraltar to east of Almería. Mohammed began to develop the Alhambra as his royal court, palace and fortress, and the Nasrids were to rule from this increasingly lavish complex for 250 years. Throughout their rule they played off Castile and Aragón

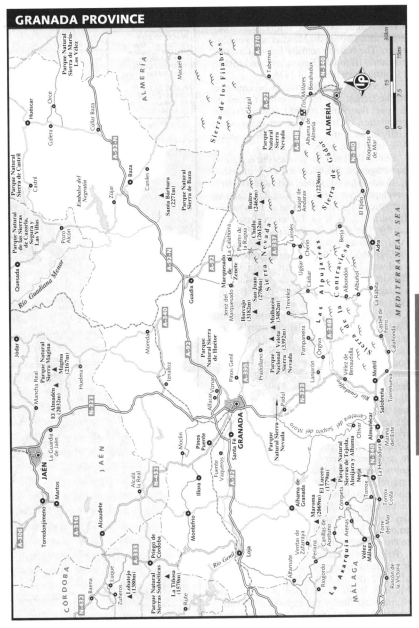

(the Iberian Peninsula's main Christian states) against each other, at times also seeking assistance from the Merenid rulers of Morocco. The Nasrids actually helped Castile's Fernando III to take Seville and paid tribute to Castile from then until 1476.

Under the Nasrids Granada became one of the richest and most populous cities in Europe, flourishing on the talents of its big population of traders and artisans, especially under emirs Yusuf I and Mohammed V in the 14th century.

But by the late 15th century the economy had stagnated, the rulers led a life of hedonism inside the Alhambra, and violent rivalry developed over the succession. One faction supported emir Abu al-Hasan and his harem favourite, Zoraya (a Christian from the north). The other faction backed Boabdil, Abu al-Hasan's son by his wife Aixa. In 1482 Boabdil rebelled, setting off a confused civil war. The Christian armies that invaded the Granada emirate that year took full advantage. The scene had been set for war by Abu al-Hasan's refusal to pay tribute to Castile from 1476, and the unification of Castile and Aragón through the marriage of the Catholic Monarchs, Isabel and Fernando.

The Christians captured Boabdil in 1483 and extracted from him a promise to surrender much of the emirate if they would help him regain Granada. Following Abu al-Hasan's death in 1485, Boabdil won control of the city. The Christians pushed across the rest of the emirate, devastating the countryside. Then in 1491 they laid siege to Granada. After eight months Boabdil agreed to surrender the city in return for the Alpujarras valleys, 30,000 gold coins and political and religious freedom for his subjects. He allowed Castilian troops into the Alhambra on the night of 1 January 1492, and the next day Isabel and Fernando entered the city ceremonially in Muslim dress. They set up court in the Alhambra for several years.

Religious persecution soon soured the scene. Jews were expelled from Spain soon after the fall of Granada; persecution of Muslims led to revolts across the former emirate and finally the expulsion of Muslims in the early 17th century. Granada thus

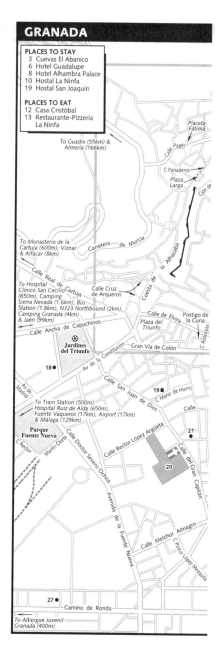

GRANADA

PLACES TO STAY
3 Cuevas El Abanico
6 Hotel Guadalupe
8 Hotel Alhambra Palace
10 Hostal La Ninfa
19 Hostal San Joaquín

PLACES TO EAT
12 Casa Cristóbal
13 Restaurante-Pizzería La Ninfa

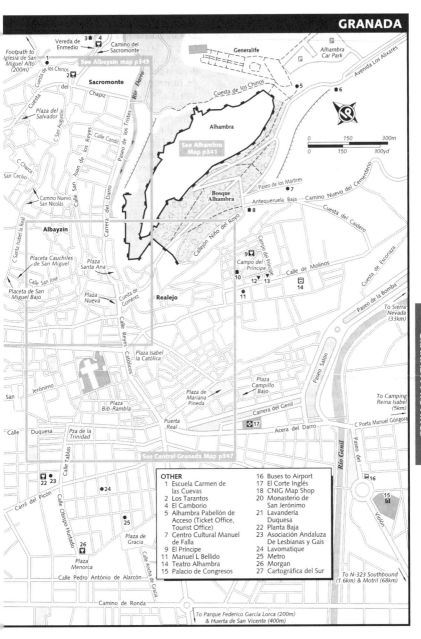

GRANADA

OTHER
1 Escuela Carmen de las Cuevas
2 Los Tarantos
3 El Camborio
4 El Camborio
5 Alhambra Pabellón de Acceso (Ticket Office, Tourist Office)
7 Centro Cultural Manuel de Falla
9 El Príncipe
11 Manuel L Bellido
14 Teatro Alhambra
15 Palacio de Congresos
16 Buses to Airport
17 El Corte Inglés
18 CNIG Map Shop
20 Monasterio de San Jerónimo
21 Lavandería Duquesa
22 Planta Baja
23 Asociación Andaluza De Lesbianas y Gais
24 Lavomatique
25 Metro
26 Morgan
27 Cartográfica del Sur

GRANADA PROVINCE

lost much of its talented populace and fell into a decline that was only arrested by the interest drummed up by the Romantic movement in the 1830s. This set the stage for the restoration of Granada's Islamic heritage and the arrival of tourism.

Early-20th-century Granada frowned on liberalism, leading to the horrors unleashed after the Nationalists took the city at the start of the civil war in 1936. An estimated 4000 *granadinos* with left-wing or liberal associations were killed, among them Federico García Lorca, Granada's – and Andalucía's – most famous writer. Granada still has a reputation for conservatism.

ORIENTATION

The two major central streets, Gran Vía de Colón and Calle Reyes Católicos, meet at Plaza Isabel La Católica. From here, Calle Reyes Católicos runs southwest to Puerta Real, an important intersection, and northeast to Plaza Nueva. The street Cuesta de Gomérez leads northeast up from Plaza Nueva towards the Alhambra on its hilltop. The old Muslim district, the Albayzín, rambles over another hill rising north of Plaza Nueva, separated from the Alhambra hill by the valley of the Río Darro. Below the south side of the Alhambra is the old Jewish district, Realejo.

Less ancient parts of the city stretch to the west, south and east. From Puerta Real, Acera del Darro, an important artery, heads southeast to the Río Genil.

Places to stay are scattered all round the central areas. Plaza Nueva is one important focus (it's also, incidentally, a focus for 'New Age travellers', who may ask you for money).

Most major sights are within walking distance of the city centre though there are buses if you get fed up with walking uphill. The bus station (northwest) and train station (west) are out of the centre but linked to it by plenty of buses.

INFORMATION
Tourist Offices

Granada's **Oficina Provincial de Turismo** (☎ 958 24 71 28; e *infotur@dipgra.es; Plaza de Mariana Pineda 10; open 9.30am-7pm*

Mon-Fri, 10am-2pm Sat) is a short walk east of Puerta Real. The very helpful staff have plenty of free maps and material on Granada and its province. The Junta de Andalucía runs a slightly more central **Oficina de Turismo** (☎ *958 22 10 22; Corral del Carbón, Calle Mariana Pineda; open 9am-7pm Mon-Sat, 10am-2pm Sun & holidays)* with information on all of Andalucía. Bus and train information is posted in an adjacent room. The Junta operates another **tourist office** (☎ *958 22 95 75; Avenida del Generalife s/n; open 8am-7.30pm Mon-Sat, 9am-1pm Sun Mar-Oct; 8.30am-4pm Mon-Fri, 9am-1pm Sat & Sun Nov-Feb)* in the Alhambra ticket-office building. There's also a useful municipal **tourist information kiosk** *(Plaza Nueva; open 10am-8pm Mon-Sat)* in the city centre.

Money

Banks and ATMs abound on Gran Vía de Colón, Plaza Isabel La Católica and Calle Reyes Católicos. On Calle Reyes Católicos you will also find a few exchange offices and **American Express** (☎ *958 22 45 12; Calle Reyes Católicos 31).*

Post & Communications

The **main post office** *(Puerta Real s/n; open 8.30am-8.30pm Mon-Fri, 9.30am-2pm Sat)* often has long queues. If stamps are all you want, you can pop round the corner to the nearby *estanco* (tobacconist) **Expendeduría No 37** *(Acera del Casino 15).*

N@veg@web *(Calle Reyes Católicos 55; open 10am-11pm daily)*, a prominent and large Internet centre just off Plaza Isabel La Católica, charges €0.90 per half-hour or part thereof (but, at the time of writing, €1.05 an hour to students). It also offers fax and photocopying. You pay about €0.50 per 30 minutes at **Madar Internet** *(Calle Calderería Nueva 10; open 10am-midnight Mon-Fri, noon-midnight Sat & Sun)*, **Internet Elvira** *(Calle de Elvira 64; open noon-1am daily)* and **Net** *(Plaza de los Girones 3).*

Digital Resources

Granada city hall's website (w www .granada.org) has good, clickable maps and a broad range of information on what to do, where to stay and so on, with plenty of links. For English, click 'Turismo', then 'Local Tourist Guide'.

Travel Agencies

Usit Unlimited (☎ 902 25 25 75; Calle Navas 29) specialises in student and youth travel.

Bookshops

Metro (☎ 958 26 15 65; Calle Gracia 31) stocks an excellent range of English-language novels, guidebooks and books on Spain, plus plenty of books in French and some in German, Italian and Russian. Some books in English are available at **Librería Urbano** (Calle Tablas 6). Granada's best map shop, also good for Spanish guide-books, is **Cartográfica del Sur** (☎ 958 20 49 01; Calle Valle Inclán 2), just off Camino de Ronda.

Laundry

You can wash a machine-load for €4.20 and dry it for €0.60 at **Lavomatique** (Calle Paz 19; open 10am-2pm & 5pm-8pm Mon-Fri, 10am-2pm Sat). **Lavandería Duquesa** (Calle Duquesa 24), open similar hours, does the washing and drying for you at a cost of €8.50.

Medical Services & Emergency

Two central hospitals with good emergency facilities are **Hospital Ruiz de Alda** (☎ 958 02 00 09; Avenida de la Constitución 100) and the **Hospital Clínico San Cecilio** (☎ 958 02 30 00; Avenida del Doctor Oloriz 16).

The most central police station is the **Policía Nacional** (☎ 958 80 80 00; Plaza de los Campos).

ALHAMBRA

Stretched along the top of the hill known as La Sabika, the Alhambra (☎ 902 44 12 21; ⚏ www.alhambra-patronato.es; admission €7, EU senior €5, disabled & child under 8 free; open 8.30am-8pm daily Mar-Oct; 8.30am-6pm daily Nov-Feb; closed 25 Dec & 1 Jan) is the stuff of fairy tales. From outside, its red fortress towers and walls appear plain if imposing, rising from woods of cypress and elm, with the Sierra Nevada forming a magnificent backdrop. Inside the Alhambra, you're in for a treat, especially in the marvellously decorated emirs' palace, the Palacio Nazaríes (Nasrid Palace), and the Generalife, the Alhambra's gardens. Water is an art form here and even around the outside of the Alhambra the sound of running water and the greenery take you to a world far away from the bustle of the city and the general dryness of much of Spain.

Granada's Bono Turístico

Granada's tourist voucher, the Bono Turístico Granada, gives admission to several of the city's major sights plus 10 rides on city buses for €15 – a saving of nearly €14 on what you'd pay for each monument and ride individually. It's a worthwhile investment if you plan to stay a few days.

The Bono covers admission to the Alhambra, cathedral, Capilla Real, La Cartuja and San Jerónimo monasteries, and the Parque de las Ciencias. You can buy it at the Alhambra or Capilla Real ticket offices; at the **Caja General de Ahorros de Granada bank** (Plaza Isabel La Católica 6; 10am-2pm & 5.30pm-8pm Mon-Sat) for the slightly higher charge of €16.80; by credit card over the telephone from the **Bono information line** (☎ 902 10 00 95; English spoken); or on the Internet at ⚏ caja.caja-granada.es/bono.

When you buy your Bono you are given a half-hour time slot for entering the Alhambra's Palacio Nazaríes, as with all Alhambra tickets.

If you stay two nights or more in one of the scheme's participating hotels, paying the hotel's regular room rate, you are entitled to one free Bono per double room. You must request it when you book the room. Information on participating hotels (mostly three- and four-star) is available from the Bono information line and on the Internet at ⚏ www.granada.org.

This tranquillity can be completely shattered by the hordes of visitors who traipse through (an average of 6000 a day), so it's a good idea to visit early in the morning or late in the afternoon or – a magical experience – make a night visit to the Palacio Nazaríes (see Admission, later, for more details).

The Alhambra has two outstanding sets of buildings, the Palacio Nazaríes and the Alcazaba (Citadel). Also within the complex are the Palacio de Carlos V, the Iglesia de Santa María de la Alhambra, two hotels (see Places to Stay), several book and souvenir shops and lots of lovely gardens, among which those of the Generalife are supreme.

There's a small snack bar by the ticket office but nowhere to eat inside the Alhambra except in the Parador de Granada hotel.

History

The Alhambra takes its name from the Arabic *al-qala'at al-hamra* (red castle). The first palace on the site was built by Samuel Ha-Nagid, the Jewish grand vizier of one of Granada's 11th-century Zirid sultans (whose own fortress was in the Albayzín). It was the Nasrid emirs of the 13th and 14th centuries who turned the Alhambra into a fortress-palace complex adjoined by a small town (medina). (Of the medina, only ruins remain.) The founder of the Nasrid dynasty, Mohammed ibn Yusuf ibn Nasr, set up home on the hilltop, rebuilding, strengthening and enlarging the Alcazaba. His successors Yusuf I (r. 1333–54) and Mohammed V (r. 1354–59 and 1362–91) built the Alhambra's crowning glory, the Palacio Nazaríes.

After the Christian conquest the Catholic Monarchs appointed a Muslim to restore the decoration of the Palacio Nazaríes. In time the Alhambra's mosque was replaced with a church and the Convento de San Francisco (now the Parador de Granada) was built. Carlos I, grandson of the Catholic Monarchs, had a wing of the Palacio Nazaríes destroyed to make space for the huge Renaissance palace, the Palacio de Carlos V (using Carlos' title as Holy Roman Emperor).

In the 18th century the Alhambra was abandoned to thieves and beggars. During the Napoleonic occupation it was used as a barracks and narrowly escaped being blown up. In 1870 it was declared a national monument as a result of the huge interest taken in it by Romantic writers such as Washington Irving, who wrote *Tales of the Alhambra* (a wonderful book to read while you're in Granada) in his study in the Palacio Nazaríes during his stay in the 1820s. Since then the Alhambra has been salvaged and heavily restored.

Admission

Some areas of the Alhambra can be visited at any time without a ticket. These include the open area around the Palacio de Carlos V and the courtyard inside it, the Plaza de los Aljibes in front of the Alcazaba, and Calle Real de la Alhambra. But the highlights of the complex – the Palacio Nazaríes and the adjacent Jardines del Partal, the Alcazaba and the Generalife – can only be entered during official opening hours and with a ticket. A maximum of between 6300 and 8260 tickets is available for each day, depending on the season and day of the week. At least 2000 of these tickets are sold at the ticket office each day, but in the busiest seasons (Easter week, July, August and September) these sell out early and you need to start queueing by 7am, an hour before the ticket office opens, to be reasonably sure of getting one. Demand is high from April to October. In winter, you may well get a ticket almost immediately at any time of day or week.

It's highly advisable to book in advance, even though this costs a commission of €0.90 per ticket. You can book up to a year ahead, and there are three ways to do it:

- In person at any branch of the BBVA bank, which has some 4000 branches around Spain and others in London, Paris, Milan and New York. Buying your ticket from BBVA saves queueing to pick it up at the Alhambra ticket office. BBVA has a convenient Granada branch on Plaza Isabel La Católica; it's open from 8.30am to 2.15pm Monday to Friday, 8.30am to 1pm Saturday from October to March.
- On the Internet at W www.alhambratickets .com. This website provides information, in English, Spanish and French, about tickets for the Alhambra.

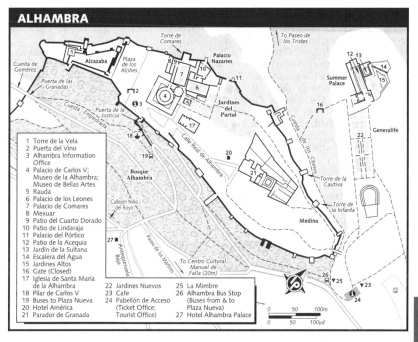

ALHAMBRA

1 Torre de la Vela
2 Puerta del Vino
3 Alhambra Information Office
4 Palacio de Carlos V; Museo de la Alhambra; Museo de Bellas Artes
5 Rauda
6 Palacio de los Leones
7 Palacio de Comares
8 Mexuar
9 Patio del Cuarto Dorado
10 Patio de Lindaraja
11 Palacio del Pórtico
12 Patio de la Acequia
13 Jardín de la Sultana
14 Escalera del Agua
15 Jardines Altos
16 Gate (Closed)
17 Iglesia de Santa María de la Alhambra
18 Pilar de Carlos V
19 Buses to Plaza Nueva
20 Hotel América
21 Parador de Granada
22 Jardines Nuevos
23 Cafe
24 Pabellón de Acceso (Ticket Office; Tourist Office)
25 La Mimbre
26 Alhambra Bus Stop (Buses from & to Plaza Nueva)
27 Hotel Alhambra Palace

• By telephone at Banca Telefónica BBVA on ☎ 902 22 44 60 from within Spain or ☎ 00-34-91 346 59 36 from outside Spain. It's open from 8am to 5.55pm daily and English speakers are available on these numbers, but you may have to wait some time for one on the Spanish domestic number.

For Internet or phone bookings you need a Visa card, MasterCard or Eurocard. You receive a reference number which you must show, along with your passport, national identity card or the credit card with which you paid for the ticket, at the Alhambra ticket office when you pick up the ticket on the day of your visit. Note that you cannot buy same-day tickets by Internet or by phone or from BBVA, nor can you buy advance tickets at the Alhambra ticket office.

Every ticket is stamped with a half-hour time slot during which you must enter the Palacio Nazaríes. Once inside the Palacio Nazaríes, you can stay as long as you like. Each ticket is also either a *billete de mañana* (morning ticket), valid for entry up until 2 pm, or a *billete de tarde*, for entry after 2pm. These are the periods during which you can enter the Generalife or Alcazaba. Again, once inside these sections, you can stay as long as you like. In summer, your time slot for entering the Palacio Nazaríes may be several hours after you buy a ticket at the ticket office, and with an afternoon ticket you won't be able to enter the Alcazaba or Generalife until 2pm.

The Palacio Nazaríes is open for **night visits** *(10pm-11.30pm Tues-Sat Mar-Oct; 8pm-9.30pm Fri & Sat Nov-Feb)*. For each night 560 tickets are available, at the same prices as daytime tickets, with the ticket office open from 30 minutes before the palace's opening time until 30 minutes after it. You can book ahead for night visits in exactly the same way as for day visits.

Ticketing arrangements change from time to time as the authorities strive to cope with the numbers of visitors.

Getting There & Away

Walking There are two main ways to walk up to the Alhambra; both take 20 to 30 minutes from Plaza Nueva. One is the path **Cuesta de los Chinos**, also called Cuesta del Rey Chico, which leads up from Paseo de los Tristes, emerging about 50m from the ticket office. The other is **Cuesta de Gomérez**, which leads up through the **Puerta de las Granadas** (Gate of the Pomegranates), built by Carlos I, and the **Bosque Alhambra** (the woods below the south side of the Alhambra). Immediately after the Puerta de las Granadas, veer left up the Cuesta Empedrada path to a beautiful Renaissance fountain, the **Pilar de Carlos V**.

If you already have your Alhambra ticket, you can turn sharp left after the fountain and enter the Alhambra without going to the ticket office, through the austere **Puerta de la Justicia** (Gate of Justice), constructed by Yusuf I in 1348 as the Alhambra's main entrance. There's an **Alhambra information office** a short distance inside this gate.

For the ticket office, continue outside the Alhambra walls from the Pilar de Carlos V for about 600m. The office is in the Pabellón de Acceso (Access Pavilion), where you'll also find a tourist information office and bookshop. From the Pabellón de Acceso you can enter the Generalife, and move on from there to other parts of the complex. If you like, come back to the soothing gardens of the Generalife later.

Bus Bus Nos 30 and 32 from Plaza Nueva both run every 10 minutes from 7.15am to 11pm up Cuesta de Gomérez to the Alhambra, stopping near the ticket office (eastern end of the complex). The buses return to Plaza Nueva via a stop near the Puerta de la Justicia. No 32 continues from Plaza Nueva on a second loop through the Albayzín.

Car & Motorcycle 'Alhambra' signs on the approach roads to Granada will conduct you circuitously to the Alhambra car parks (€1.25/12.50 per hour/day), which are just off Avenida de los Alixares, a short distance uphill from the ticket office. From the city centre you would have to drive out by Paseo de la Bomba and follow 'Sierra Nevada' then 'Alhambra' signs to the same car parks.

Ignore people who try to wave you into other parking places as you approach, perhaps telling you that the official car parks are full. They'll demand €10 or more for 'looking after' your car in what might really even be a tow-away zone.

Alcazaba

What remains of the Alcazaba is chiefly its ramparts and several towers, the most important and tallest being the **Torre de la Vela** (Watch Tower), with a narrow staircase leading to the top terrace which has splendid views of the city and surrounds. The cross and banners of the Reconquista were raised here in January 1492. The tower's bell rings on festive occasions only, but in the past it tolled to control the irrigation system of the Vega, the plain on which Granada stands. One of the Alhambra's many dungeons is set in the ground just inside the Alcazaba's eastern walls.

Palacio Nazaríes

This is the Alhambra's true gem, the most impressive Muslim building in Europe. With its perfectly proportioned rooms and courtyards, intricately moulded stucco walls, beautiful tiling, fine carved wooden ceilings and elaborate *muqarnas* (honeycomb or stalactite) vaulting, all worked in mesmerising, symbolic, geometrical patterns, the Nasrid Palace stands in marked contrast to the austere Alcazaba. Arabic inscriptions, especially the endlessly repeated '*wa la galiba illa Allah*' ('there is no conqueror but Allah'), proliferate in the stuccowork, which, like the wood, was originally mostly painted in bright colours.

Mexuar This room, through which you normally enter the palace, dates from the 14th century. It was used as a ministerial council chamber and as an antechamber for those awaiting audiences with the emir. The public would generally not have been allowed beyond here. The chamber has been much altered; it was converted into a chapel in the 16th century, and now contains both Muslim and Christian motifs. At its far end is the small, lavishly decorated Oratorio (Prayer Room), which overlooks the Río Darro.

Patio del Cuarto Dorado From the Mexuar you pass into this courtyard, with a small fountain and the Cuarto Dorado (Golden Room) on the left. This patio was where the emirs would give audiences to their subjects. The Cuarto Dorado takes its name from its beautiful wooden ceiling, which was gilded and redecorated in the time of the Catholic Monarchs, as is shown by their emblems, the yoke and the sheaf of arrows. On the other side of the patio is the entrance to the Palacio de Comares through a beautiful facade of glazed tiles, stucco and carved wood.

Palacio de Comares Built for Emir Yusuf I, this section of the Palacio Nazaríes served as a private residence for the ruler. It's built around the **Patio de los Arrayanes** (Patio of the Myrtles), named after the hedges flanking its rectangular pool and fountains. The rooms along the sides may have been quarters for the emir's wives. Finely carved arches atop marble pillars form porticos at both ends of the patio. Through the northern portico, inside the Torre de Comares (Comares Tower), is the **Sala de la Barca** (Hall of the Boat), with a beautiful inverted boat–shaped wooden ceiling. This room leads into the square **Salón de Comares** (Comares Hall), also called the Salón de los Embajadores (Hall of the Ambassadors), where the emirs would have conducted their negotiations with Christian emissaries. The stuccowork on the walls contains repeated inscriptions in praise of Allah, and the marvellous domed marquetry ceiling contains more than 8000 cedar pieces in a pattern of stars representing Islam's seven heavens, through which the soul ascends before reaching the eighth (in the centre) where Allah resides.

The southern end of the patio is overshadowed by the walls of the Palacio de Carlos V.

Palacio de los Leones From the Patio de los Arrayanes you move into the Palace of the Lions, another private palace-within-a-palace, built in the second half of the 14th century under Mohammed V, when the Granada emirate reached its political and artistic peak. Many other buildings in the Palacio Nazaries were redecorated in Mohammed's reign. It's not known what, if any, difference in function the Palacio de Comares and Palacio de los Leones had, but by some accounts the Palacio de los Leones was the royal harem.

The rooms of the palace surround the famous **Patio de los Leones** (Lion Courtyard), with its marble fountain that channelled water through the mouths of 12 carved marble lions. Carved especially for this palace, the fountain was originally brightly painted, chiefly in gold. In 2002 the fountain was turned off and its lions were being taken away in ones and twos for tests and restoration work. Acid rain is one reason why the 14th-century lions and the basin they surround have deteriorated faster in the last couple of decades than in the previous six centuries.

The Palacio de los Leones symbolises the Muslim paradise, which is divided into four parts separated by rivers (here represented by water channels meeting at the central fountain). The patio's gallery, including the beautifully ornamented pavilions protruding at its eastern and western ends, is supported by 124 slender marble columns.

Of the four halls bordering the patio, the **Sala de los Abencerrajes** on the southern side is the legendary site of the murders of the noble Abencerraj family, who favoured Boabdil in the palace power struggle and whose leader, the story goes, dared to dally with Zoraya, Abu al-Hasan's harem favourite. The room's lovely high-domed ceiling features *muqarnas* vaulting in an eight-point star formation.

At the very eastern end of the patio is the **Sala de los Reyes** (Hall of the Kings), whose inner alcoves have leather-lined ceilings painted by 14th-century Christian artists, probably from the Italian city of Genoa. The room's name comes from the painting on the ceiling of the central alcove, thought to depict 10 Nasrid emirs. On the northern side of the patio is the **Sala de Dos Hermanas** (Hall of Two Sisters), as beautiful and richly decorated as the Sala de los Abencerrajes, and probably named after the two slabs of white marble sitting on either side of its fountain. This may have been the room of the emir's favourite para-mour. It features a fantastic *muqarnas* dome with a central star and 5000 tiny cells, reminiscent of the constellations. At its far end is the **Sala de los Ajimeces** with a beautifully decorated little lookout area, the **Mirador de Lindaraja**. Through the low-slung windows of the mirador, the room's occupants could look out over the Albayzín and countryside while reclining on ottomans and cushions. In Islamic times, nearby buildings did not obstruct the view.

Other Sections From the Sala de Dos Hermanas a passageway leads through the **Estancias del Emperador** (Emperor's Chambers), built for Carlos I in the 1520s; some of them were later used by Washington Irving. From here you descend to the Patio de la Reja (Patio of the Grille) which leads to the pretty **Patio de Lindaraja**, originally created as a lower garden for the Palacio de los Leones. In the southwestern corner of the patio is the entrance (only sometimes open) to the **Baño de Comares**, the Palacio de Comares' bathhouse, with its three steam rooms lit by star-shaped skylights.

From the Patio de Lindaraja you emerge into the **Jardines del Partal**, an area of terraced gardens created in the early 20th century around various old structures, ruined and standing. The small **Palacio del Pórtico** (Palace of the Portico), from the time of Mohammed III (1302–09), is the oldest surviving palace in the Alhambra. You can leave the Jardines del Partal by a gate facing the Palacio de Carlos V (next to the site of the **Rauda**, the emirs' cemetery), or continue along a path to the Generalife, which runs parallel to the Alhambra's ramparts, passing several towers.

KELLI HAMBLET

The huge Palacio de Carlos V has a two-tiered circular courtyard with 32 columns

Palacio de Carlos V

This huge Renaissance palace is the dominant Christian building in the Alhambra. Were it in a different setting its merits would be more readily appreciated. Begun in 1527 by Pedro Machuca, an architect from Toledo who studied under Michelangelo, it was financed from taxes on the Granada area's Morisco (converted Muslim) population. Funds dried up after the Moriscos rebelled in 1568, and the palace remained roofless until the early 20th century when work restarted. The main (western) facade features three porticos divided by pairs of fluted columns, with bas-relief battle carvings at their feet. The building is square but contains a surprising two-tiered circular courtyard with 32 columns. This circle inside a square is the only Spanish example of a Renaissance ground plan symbolising the unity of earth and heaven.

Inside are two museums. The ground-floor **Museo de la Alhambra** (*☎ 958 22 75 25; admission free; open 9am-2.30pm Tues-Sat*) has a wonderful collection of Muslim artefacts from the Alhambra, Granada province and Córdoba, with explanatory texts in English and Spanish. Highlights include the elegant Alhambra Vase, decorated with gazelles, and the door from the Sala de Dos Hermanas.

Upstairs, the **Museo de Bellas Artes** (*☎ 958 22 48 43; admission €1.50, EU citizen free; open 2.30pm-8pm Tues, 9am-8pm*

Wed-Sat, 9am-2.30pm Sun Apr-Sept; 2.30pm-6pm Tues, 9am-6pm Wed-Sat, 9am-2.30pm Sun Oct-Mar) has an impressive collection of Granada-related paintings and sculptures. Notable are the carved wooden relief of the Virgin and child (c. 1547) by Diego de Siloé, several 17th-century works by Alonso Cano, including the modern-looking *Ecce Homo*, and the portraits and landscapes by Granada's two early-20th-century José Marías – López Mezquita and Rodríguez Acosta.

Other Christian Buildings

The **Iglesia de Santa María de la Alhambra** was built between 1581 and 1617 on the site of the Muslim palace mosque. The **Convento de San Francisco**, now the Parador de Granada hotel, was erected over a small Islamic palace. Isabel and Fernando were laid to rest in a sepulchre here while their tombs in the Capilla Real were being built.

Generalife

The name means 'Architect's Garden'. This beautiful, soothing composition of pathways, patios, pools, fountains, trimmed hedges, tall, long-established trees and, in season, flowers of every imaginable hue, on a hillside facing the Alhambra, is the perfect place to end an Alhambra visit. The Muslim rulers' summer palace is in the corner furthest from the entrance. On the way to it you pass through the Generalife's 20th-century **Jardines Nuevos** (New Gardens). Within the palace, the **Patio de la Acequia** (Court of the Water Channel) has a long pool framed by flower beds and 19th-century fountains whose shapes sensuously echo the arched porticos at each end. Off this patio is the **Jardín de la Sultana** (Sultana's Garden), almost as lovely and with the trunk of a 700-year-old cypress tree, where Abu al-Hasan supposedly caught his lover, Zoraya, with the head of the Abencerraj clan, leading to the murders in the Sala de los Abencerrajes of the Palacio Nazaríes. Above here are the modern **Jardines Altos** (Upper Gardens), with the **Escalera del Agua** (Water Staircase), a set of steps with water running down beside them.

CAPILLA REAL

The Royal Chapel *(☎ 958 22 92 39; Calle Oficios; admission €2.50; open 10.30am-1pm & 4pm-7pm Mon-Sat, 11am-1pm & 4pm-7pm Sun Apr-Oct; 10.30am-1pm & 3.30pm-6.30pm Mon-Sat, 11am-1pm & 3.30pm-6.30pm Sun Nov-Mar; closed Good Friday)*, adjoining the cathedral, is Granada's outstanding Christian building. Commissioned by the Catholic Monarchs as their own mausoleum, it was built in elaborate Isabelline Gothic style, but not finished until 1521, so they had to be temporarily interred in the Alhambra's Convento de San Francisco.

The monarchs lie with three relatives in simple lead coffins in the crypt beneath their marble monuments in the chancel. The chancel is divided from the chapel's nave by a gilded screen made in 1520 by Maestro Bartolomé de Jaén – a masterpiece of wrought-iron artisanry. The coffins, from left to right, belong to Felipe El Hermoso (Philip the Handsome; the husband of the monarchs' daughter Juana la Loca), Fernando, Isabel, Juana la Loca (Joanna the Mad) and Miguel, the eldest grandchild of Isabel and Fernando.

The marble effigies reclining above the crypt were a tribute by Carlos I to his parents and grandparents. The slightly lower of the two monuments, representing Isabel and Fernando and with a Latin inscription lauding them as 'subjugators of Islam and extinguishers of obstinate heresy', was carved by a Tuscan, Domenico Fancelli. The other monument, to Felipe and Juana, is higher, apparently because Felipe was the son of Holy Roman Emperor Maximilian. This is the work (1520) of Bartolomé Ordóñez from Burgos.

The chancel's densely decorated plateresque retable (1522), with a profusion of gold paint, is by Felipe de Vigarni. Note its kneeling figures of Isabel (lower right, with the name 'Elisabeth') and Fernando (lower left), attributed to Diego de Siloé, and the brightly painted bas-reliefs below depicting the defeat of the Muslims and subsequent conversions to Christianity. Cardinal Cisneros is there too.

The sacristy contains an impressive small museum with Fernando's sword and Isabel's sceptre, silver crown and personal art collection, which is mainly Flemish but also including Botticelli's *Prayer in the Garden of Olives*. Also here are two fine statues of the Catholic Monarchs at prayer by Vigarni.

CATHEDRAL

Adjoining the Capilla Real but entered separately, from Gran Vía de Colón, is Granada's cavernous Gothic/Renaissance cathedral (☎ 958 22 29 59; admission €2.50; open 10.45am-1.30pm & 4pm-8pm Mon-Sat, 4pm-8pm Sun Apr-Oct; 10.45am-1.30pm & 4pm-7pm Mon-Sat, 4pm-7pm Sun Nov-Mar). Construction of the cathedral began in 1521 and lasted until the 18th century. It was directed from 1528 to 1563 by Renaissance pioneer Diego de Siloé, and the main facade on Plaza de las Pasiegas, with four heavy square buttresses forming three great arched bays, was designed in the 17th century by Alonso Cano. De Siloé carved the statues on the lavish Puerta del Perdón on the northwestern facade, and much of the interior is also his work, including the gilded, painted and domed Capilla Mayor. The Catholic Monarchs at prayer (one above each side of the main altar) were carved by Pedro de Mena in the 17th century. Above the monarchs are busts

of Adam and Eve by Cano. In the cathedral museum, be sure to see Cano's fine *San Pablo* sculpture and the golden Gothic monstrance given to Granada by Isabel La Católica.

LA MADRAZA

Opposite the Capilla Real is part of the old Muslim university, La Madraza (Calle Oficios). Now with a painted baroque facade, the much-altered building retains an octagonal domed prayer room with stucco lacework and pretty tiles. The building is part of the modern university but you can take a look inside whenever it's open.

CENTRO JOSÉ GUERRERO

Just along the street from La Madraza, this art museum (☎ 958 24 73 75; Calle Oficios 8; admission free; open 11am-2pm & 5pm-9pm Tues-Sat, 11am-2pm Sun) is dedicated to the most celebrated artist to come out of Granada, abstract expressionist José Guerrero (1914–91), who was born in the city but found fame in New York in the 1950s. The centre, which opened in 2000, exhibits good temporary shows as well as a permanent collection of Guerrero's dramatic and colourful canvases, and it's very much worth a visit.

How to Handle Unwanted Gifts

Many visitors to Andalucía feel uncomfortable and/or intimidated when *gitanas* (Roma women) step across their paths and thrust a sprig of rosemary or some other herb into their hands. In Granada, this happens a lot around the Capilla Real and cathedral and on the pedestrian approaches to the Alhambra. The best thing to do if you don't want to hand over any money is to resolutely ignore any advance. The minute you allow the sprig to be pressed into your hand, you will be expected to pay something. Before you know it, your palm may have been read and payment demanded. I got caught, allowing a youngish woman to tell my fortune. She spoke rapidly in a soothing tone for about 20 seconds before putting out her hand for money. I handed over €1. The woman's tone changed to displeasure. She hissed that coins are bad luck and that she wanted paper money. I insisted that coins are part of the economy (how could they be bad luck?) and refused to hand over a note. The woman took off angrily, but held on to the €1.

Several readers have commented on similar incidents in Seville and Granada and their embarrassment about them. Many people are caught off guard because they don't know who is accosting them.

Shoe shiners hang out in the same places and may demand outrageous fees for feeble efforts; they can be particularly mean with the polish!

Susan Forsyth

CENTRAL GRANADA

PLACES TO STAY
3 Hostal Navarro Ramos
4 Hostal Landázuri
5 Hotel Molinos
8 Hostal Gomérez
9 Hostal Viena
12 Hostal Britz
13 Hostal Austria
14 Hostal Venecia
28 Hotel Anacapri
43 Hostal-Residencia Lisboa
45 Hotel Navas
51 Hotel Los Tilos
55 Pensión Romero
56 Huéspedes Capuchinas
58 Hostal Zurita
59 Hostal Lima
60 Hostal Sevilla
61 Hostal Meridiano
62 Hotel Reina Cristina

PLACES TO EAT
17 Al Andalus
18 Grand Café Central
19 Antigua Castañeda
20 Bodegas Castañeda
22 La Nueva Bodega
25 Vía Colón
27 Jamones Castellano
40 Mercado Central San Agustín; Parking San Agustín
50 Café Bib-Rambla
52 Pizzeria Gallio
53 Cunini
54 El Cepillo
57 Bar Reca

OTHER
1 Puerta de las Granadas
2 Iglesia de Santa Ana
6 Net
7 Centro de Lenguas Modernas
10 Tourist Information Kiosk
11 Buses to Albayzín & Sacromonte
15 Buses to Alhambra
16 ATA Rent A Car
21 La Taberna del Irlandés
23 Bar Avellano
24 Granada 10
26 Buses to Bus & Train Stations; Camping Sierra Nevada; Albergue Juvenil Granada & Airport
29 N@veg@web
30 Iberia Office
31 BBVA
32 Catholic Monarchs & Columbus Monument
33 Caja General de Ahorros de Granada
34 Policía Nacional
35 Corral del Carbón; Oficina de Turismo (Junta de Andalucía); Artespaña

36 American Express
37 Centro José Guerrero
38 La Madraza
39 Capilla Real
41 Herb & Spice Stalls
42 La Sabanilla
44 Usit Unlimited
46 Oficina Provincial de Turismo
47 Expendeduría No 37
48 Teatro Isabel La Católica
49 Main Post Office (Correos)
63 Librería Urbano

GRANADA PROVINCE

ALCAICERÍA, PLAZA BIB-RAMBLA & PLAZA DE LA TRINIDAD

The Alcaicería was the Muslim silk exchange but what can be seen here now is a 19th-century restoration filled with tourist shops – but charming in the early morning light and quiet. Its buildings, divided by narrow alleys, are just south of the Capilla Real. Just southwest of the Alcaicería is the large, pleasant Plaza Bib-Rambla with restaurants, flower stalls, and a central fountain with statues of giants. This square has been the scene of jousting, bullfights and Inquisition burnings. Pedestrianised Calle Pescadería and Calle de los Mesones lead northwest to leafy Plaza de la Trinidad, another lively square.

CORRAL DEL CARBÓN

This building (Calle Mariana Pineda) began life as a 14th-century inn for merchants. It has since had a chequered history, being used as an inn for coal dealers (hence its modern name, meaning 'Coal Yard') and later a theatre. It houses a tourist office and a government-run crafts shop, Artespaña. You can't miss the lovely Islamic facade with its elaborate horseshoe arch.

ALBAYZÍN

A wander around the hilly streets and the fascinating alleys of Granada's old Muslim quarter, the Albayzín (also spelt Albaizín, Albaycín or Albaicín), is a must. The Albayzín, covering the hill facing the Alhambra across the Darro valley, was where Granada began, as an Iberian settlement in about the 7th century BC. It was also where the Zirid Berber dynasty set up their fortress when they moved the seat of local power back from Elvira (10km northwest) to Granada in the 11th century. The Albayzín's name derives from 1227, when Muslims from Baeza (Jaén province) moved here after their city was conquered by the Christians. It became a densely populated residential area with 27 mosques, and it survived as the Muslim quarter for several decades after the Christian conquest in 1492. Muslim ramparts, houses, gates, fountains and cisterns remain, and many of the churches and villas (cármenes) of the Albayzín incorporate Islamic remains. The Albayzín is a favourite area for foreign students in Granada to live, and it's a marvellous area to ramble around, but to be on the safe side, stay on the more major streets after dark.

Bus Nos 31 and 32 both run circular routes from Plaza Nueva around the Albayzín (Paseo de los Tristes, Cuesta del Chapiz, Plaza del Salvador, Plaza de San Nicolás, Placeta de San Miguel Bajo, Arco de Elvira) and back to Plaza Nueva about every 10 to 12 minutes. No 32 follows this with another loop up to the Alhambra and back. No 32 runs from 7.30am to 11pm; No 31 goes from 6.27am to 11pm or later.

Walking Tour

This tour of the Darro valley and the Albayzín, starting from Plaza Nueva, should take four or five hours including visits to some of the sights and a stop for something to eat and drink.

Plaza Nueva extends northeast into Plaza Santa Ana, where the **Iglesia de Santa Ana** incorporates a mosque's minaret in its bell tower (as do several churches in the Albayzín). Along narrow Carrera del Darro, have a look at the 11th-century Muslim bathhouse, the **Baños Árabes El Bañuelo** (☎ 958 02 78 00; Carrera del Darro 31; admission free; open 10am-2pm Tues-Sat), one of Granada's oldest buildings. Further along is the **Museo Arqueológico** (Archaeological Museum; ☎ 958 22 56 40; Carrera del Darro 43; admission €1.50, EU citizen free; open 3pm-8pm Tues, 9am-8pm Thur-Sat, 9am-2pm Sun), housed in a Renaissance mansion, the Casa de Castril. On display are finds from Granada province from Palaeolithic to Muslim times, with all-Spanish explanatory material. It's curious to find ancient Egyptian amulets (brought by the Phoenicians) so far from home.

Just past the museum, Carrera del Darro becomes Paseo de los Tristes (also called Paseo del Padre Manjón). Several cafés and restaurants here have outdoor tables and, with the Alhambra's fortifications looming above, it makes a good spot to pause. From

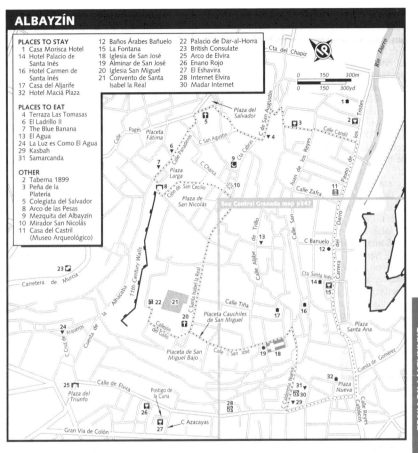

ALBAYZÍN

PLACES TO STAY
1 Casa Morisca Hotel
14 Hotel Palacio de
    Santa Inés
16 Hotel Carmen de
    Santa Inés
17 Casa del Aljarife
32 Hotel Maciá Plaza

PLACES TO EAT
4 Terraza Las Tomasas
6 El Ladrillo II
7 The Blue Banana
13 El Agua
24 La Luz es Como El Agua
29 Kasbah
31 Samarcanda

OTHER
2 Taberna 1899
3 Peña de la
    Platería
5 Colegiata del Salvador
8 Arco de las Pesas
9 Mezquita del Albayzín
10 Mirador San Nicolás
11 Casa del Castril
    (Museo Arqueológico)

12 Baños Árabes Bañuelo
15 La Fontana
18 Iglesia de San José
19 Alminar de San José
20 Iglesia San Miguel
21 Convento de Santa
    Isabel la Real

22 Palacio de Dar-al-Horra
23 British Consulate
25 Arco de Elvira
26 Enano Rojo
27 El Eshavira
28 Internet Elvira
30 Madar Internet

See Central Granada map p347

GRANADA PROVINCE

here several narrow lanes head up into the Albayzín – try Calle Candil, which leads up into Placeta de Toqueros where the **Peña de la Platería** flamenco club is located (see Entertainment, later, for more information).

If you turn right at the top of Placeta de Toqueros, left at the fork soon afterwards, then left again, you emerge on Carril de San Agustín. Go left and after about 100m the street turns 90° to the right. Continue 200m (initially uphill) to Plaza del Salvador, dominated by the **Colegiata del Salvador** (☎ 958 27 86 44; admission €0.75; open 10.30am-1pm & 4.30pm-6.30pm Mon-Sat), a 16th-

century church on the site of the Albayzín's main mosque. The mosque's patio, with three sides of horseshoe arches, survives at the church's western end. From here Calle Panaderos leads west to **Plaza Larga**, with lively bars offering cheap *menús* (fixed-price meals).

Leave Plaza Larga through the **Arco de las Pesas**, an impressive Islamic gateway in the Albayzín's 11th-century defensive wall, and take the first street to the left, Callejón de San Cecilio. This leads to the **Mirador San Nicolás**, a lookout point with fantastic views of the Alhambra and Sierra Nevada.

You might like to come back here later for sunset (you can't miss the trail then!), but at any time of day keep a tight hold on your belongings. Skilful, well organised wallet-lifters and snatchers of bags and cameras operate here. One of their tactics is to distract people with 'impromptu' flamenco dance routines; another is for pillion riders on passing motorbikes to stand up and grab bags lying on the mirador's side walls.

The Albayzín's first new mosque in many centuries, the **Mezquita del Albayzín**, is being built just east of Mirador San Nicolás, off Cuesta de las Cabras, to serve modern Granada's growing Muslim population.

Take the steps down beside the west end of the lookout, turn right and follow the street down to Camino Nuevo de San Nicolás. Turn right, passing the **Convento de Santa Isabel la Real** (☎ 958 27 78 36; Calle Santa Isabel la Real 15), founded in 1501 on the site of the 12th-century Zirid palace, and with a Gothic chapel that is open erratically. A few more steps down the street is **Placeta de San Miguel Bajo**, whose cafés and restaurants with outdoor tables are great places to relax over something to eat or drink. The plaza's **Iglesia de San Miguel** is another church on the site of a former mosque. Leave Placeta de San Miguel Bajo by Callejón del Gallo, turn right at the end of this short lane and you'll come to the door of the 15th-century **Palacio de Dar-al-Horra** (Callejón de las Monjas s/n; admission free; open 10am-2pm Mon, Wed & Sat), the abode of the mother of Granada's last Muslim ruler, Boabdil. With its patio, pool, arched doorways, coffered ceilings, and friezes with decorative inscriptions, it is said to be like a mini-Alhambra. Unfortunately we have never found it open even during its limited published hours, but it's always worth a try. You can try telephoning ☎ 958 22 14 37 or ☎ 651 86 22 49 for current opening-hours information.

Return to Placeta de San Miguel Bajo and head down Placeta Cauchiles de San Miguel, which becomes Calle San José, where the lovely little **Alminar de San José** (San José Minaret) survives from the 11th-century mosque that stood here before the neighbouring Iglesia de San José was built in the 16th century. Calle San José meets the top of **Calle Calderería Nueva**, lined by *teterías* (Arabic-style tearooms) and craft shops and full of bohemian atmosphere – stop for an infusion or head on down to Calle de Elvira and back to Plaza Nueva.

SACROMONTE

The Sacromonte district occupies the north side of the Darro valley northeast of the Albayzín, below a city perimeter wall dating from Nasrid times. Many of the dwellings here are cave homes, burrowed out of the hillside since the 18th century and mostly occupied by *gitanos* (Roma people). Some of the abandoned caves higher up the hill are now occupied by homeless people. Some caves on or near Sacromonte's main street, Camino del Sacromonte, are venues for expensive tourist-oriented flamenco shows or house lively dance clubs (see Entertainment, later, for more details). By day, it's interesting to stroll around the area, and you can work your way up to the Iglesia de San Miguel Alto, at the top of the hill, for fine views. Bus No 31 (see the Albayzín section, earlier) detours along Camino del Sacromonte eight times daily; times are posted at its stops.

MONASTERIO DE SAN JERÓNIMO

This 16th-century monastery (☎ 958 27 93 37; Calle Rector López Argueta 9; admission €2.50; open 10am-1.30pm & 4pm-7.30pm daily Apr-Oct; 10am-1.30pm & 3pm-6.30pm daily Nov-Mar), 500m west of the cathedral, features some beautiful stone carving and a spectacularly decorated church. Specially to be admired in the cloister are two lovely plateresque doorways carved by the monastery's chief architect, the talented Diego de Siloé.

The church, in a combination of Isabelline Gothic and Renaissance styles, features an incredible profusion of brightly painted sculpture on the enormous retable and the towering vaults at the eastern end. This was the first church in the world to be dedicated to the Immaculate Conception, and the retable, with La Inmaculada (Mary the Immaculate) occupying the central position, was the inspiration for generations of Andalucian retables. Before it, at the foot of the steps, is the tombstone of El Gran Capitán (the Great Captain), Gonzalo Fernández de Córdoba, the military right-hand man of the Catholic Monarchs. Statues of El Gran Capitán and his wife, the Duquesa de Sesa, at prayer stand either side of the retable. It was the duchess's commissioning of Diego de Siloé to provide her husband's resting place that resulted in the splendour of the monastery's decoration.

MONASTERIO DE LA CARTUJA

Another architectural gem stands 2km northwest of the centre, reached by bus No 8 from Gran Vía de Colón. La Cartuja Monastery (☎ 958 16 19 32; Paseo de la Cartuja; admission €2.50; open 10am-1pm & 4pm-8pm Mon-Sat, 10am-noon & 4pm-8pm Sun Apr-Oct; 10am-1pm & 3.30pm-6pm Mon-Sat, 10am-noon & 3.30pm-6pm Sun Nov-Mar), with an imposing, sand-coloured stone exterior, was built between the 16th and 18th centuries. It's the lavish baroque monastery church that people come to see, especially the Sagrario (Sanctuary) behind the main altar, a confection of red, black, white and grey-blue marble, columns with golden capitals, profuse sculpture and a beautiful frescoed cupola; and, to the left of the main altar, the Sacristía (Sacristy), the ultimate expression of Spanish late baroque, in effusive 'wedding-cake' stucco and brown-and-white Lanjarón marble (resembling a melange of chocolate mousse and cream). The Sacristía's cabinets, veneered and inlaid with mahogany, ebony, ivory, shell and silver by Fray José Manuel Vázquez in the 18th century, represent a high point of Granada marquetry art.

HUERTA DE SAN VICENTE

This house (☎ 958 25 84 66; Calle Virgen Blanca s/n; admission €1.80, free Wed; admission only by guided tour in Spanish every 30 minutes, 10am-12.30 pm & 4pm-6.30pm Tues-Sun), where Federico García Lorca spent summers and wrote some of his best-known works, is a 15-minute walk from the centre and was once surrounded by orchards. Today the Parque Federico García Lorca separates it from whizzing traffic in an attempt to recreate the tranquil environment that inspired him.

The house contains some original furnishings, including Lorca's writing desk and piano, some of his drawings and other memorabilia, and exhibitions connected with his life and work. To get there, head 700m down Calle de las Recogidas from Puerta Real, turn right along Calle del Arabial then first left into Calle Virgen Blanca.

LANGUAGE & FLAMENCO COURSES

With its many attractions and youthful population, Granada is a good place to study Spanish. It also has several schools of Spanish dance. The Oficina Provincial de Turismo can provide lists of schools, many with their own websites, and some are listed on W www.granada.org (see Digital Resources, earlier in this chapter).

Granada University's **Centro de Lenguas Modernas** (Modern Languages Centre; ☎ 958 21 56 60; W www.ugr.es/~clm; Placeta del Hospicio Viejo s/n) offers a variety of Spanish language and culture programmes from intensive beginner's courses to classes for teachers of Spanish. Its teachers are highly qualified, and Spanish language students use the same centre, in the historic Realejo district, providing plenty of opportunities for cultural interchange. Some classes contain lots of American college students apparently in Spain to drink, but others attract a more alert clientele. Intensive language courses, at all levels, range from 10 days (40 hours of classes) for €310 to 2½ months (160 hours) for €862.

Escuela Carmen de las Cuevas (☎ 958 22 10 62; W www.carmencuevas.com; Cuesta de los Chinos 15, Sacromonte) is one private school that gets good reports. It teaches Spanish language and culture, and flamenco dance and guitar, all at several levels from beginner upwards. A two-week intensive language course (30 hours' tuition) costs €255.

ORGANISED TOURS

Granavisión *(☎ 958 53 58 72)* offers guided tours of the Alhambra and Generalife (€30), Historic Granada tours (€35) and excursions further afield. Phone direct or book through a travel agent.

SPECIAL EVENTS

The big two are **Semana Santa** (Holy Week) and the **Feria de Corpus Christi** (Corpus Christi Fair) nine weeks later. Benches are set up in Plaza del Carmen to view the Semana Santa processions. Fairgrounds, drinking, bullfights and *sevillanas* (traditional Andalucian dances with high, twirling arm movements) are features of Corpus Christi.

Día de la Cruz (Day of the Cross) is held on 3 May, when squares, patios and balconies are adorned with floral crosses (Cruces de Mayo) which become the focus for music, drinking, horse riding, polka-dot dresses and sevillana dancing.

Festival Internacional de Música y Danza is a festival of mainly classical music and dance, with many events (some free) held in the Generalife, Palacio de Carlos V and other historical sites,. It runs for 2½ weeks from late June to early July. Tickets go on sale in May at the festival box office *(☎ 958 22 18 44)* in the Corral del Carbón, Calle Mariana Pineda s/n. Internet applications can be made at W www.granadafestival.org.

PLACES TO STAY

There should be no problem finding a room except during Semana Santa, but from March to October it's worth booking ahead.

PLACES TO STAY – BUDGET

At busy times rooms tend to fill up before noon, especially on Cuesta de Gomérez. Most places keep more or less the same prices year-round except for a few days over Easter.

Camping

There's one camping ground in the city, which holds 600 people, and half a dozen smaller ones within a few kilometres, most of them accessible by bus.

Camping Sierra Nevada *(☎ 958 15 00 62; Avenida de Madrid 107; camping per adult/tent/car €4.25/4.25/5.40)* is just a short walk from the bus station, 2.5km northwest of the centre. It has big clean bathrooms, a pool and laundrette. Bus No 3 runs between here and Gran Vía de Colón in the centre.

Camping Reina Isabel *(☎ 958 59 00 41; Carretera Granada-La Zubia Km 4; camping per adult/tent/car €3.60/3.60/5.70)*, about 5km south of the centre, is clean and has a pool and good bathrooms. Take the La Zubia exit from the Ronda Sur ring road, or the La Zubia bus, about 20 every minutes from Paseo del Salón in the city.

Hostels

Albergue Juvenil Granada *(☎ 958 27 26 38; Calle Ramón y Cajal 2; under 26/other €12.90/17.25 Mar-Sept & holiday periods, €10.90/15.20 Oct-Feb)* is 1.7km west of the centre. It's a large, modern, building with 89 comfy double and triple rooms, all with bathroom. Get there by bus No 10 from the bus station or bus No 11 from the centre (Gran Vía de Colón) or from Avenida de la Constitución, 150m from the train station. The hostel is 100m down a side street off Camino de Ronda.

Hostales & Pensiones

Near Plaza Nueva Half a dozen *hostales* (budget hotels) are strung along Cuesta de Gomérez, between Plaza Nueva and the Alhambra.

Hostal Britz *(☎/fax 958 22 36 52; Cuesta de Gomérez 1; singles/doubles €17/27, with bathroom €26/37)* is friendly, with 22 clean, adequate rooms and a lift.

Hostal Venecia *(☎ 958 22 39 87; Cuesta de Gomérez 2; singles/doubles/triples/quads €13/24/36/48)* is an exceptionally welcoming place whose owners even bring you a soothing herbal infusion to drink each morning. Relaxing background music plays, incense wafts, it's warm in winter and the nine rooms are all individually and prettily decorated.

Hostal Viena *(☎/fax 958 22 18 59; Calle Hospital de Santa Ana 2; singles/doubles/*

Grand designs: Granada's imposing cathedral

Patio de la Acequia and gardens, Granada

Vibrant shopfront, Calle de los Mesones, Granada

Choose from a tempting selection of tapas dishes and dine Andalucian style

Said to be the highest village in Spain, Trevélez is a starting point for ascents of the Sierra Nevada peaks

Ski slopes, Sierra Nevada, Granada province

Oak woods near Trevélez, Granada province

Characteristic whitewashed houses dot Granada province's verdant landscape

triples/quads €23/33/45/51, doubles/triples/ quads with bathroom €40/54/57), just off Cuesta de Gomérez, has 16 simple, old-fashioned, clean rooms. Staff are obliging, English and German are spoken, and parking is available for €6. Loud music from the bar below won't help your slumbers, though.

Hostal Austria (☎ 958 22 70 75; e aus tria@arrakis.es; Cuesta de Gomérez 4; singles/ doubles/triples €23/33/45, doubles/triples with bathroom €40/54) is run by the same people as Hostal Viena and is similar but a little more modern in style.

Hostal Gomérez (☎/fax 958 22 44 37; Cuesta de Gomérez 10; singles/doubles/ triples €13/20/25) has nine very plain and bare rooms with shared bathrooms, but good prices.

Hostal Navarro Ramos (☎ 958 25 05 55; Cuesta de Gomérez 21; singles/doubles €11.50/18, doubles with bathroom €27) offers 16 good, clean, simple rooms at excellent prices.

Hostal Landázuri (☎/fax 958 22 14 06; Cuesta de Gomérez 24; singles/doubles €20/24, singles/doubles/triples with bathroom €28/36/48) boasts a terrace with Alhambra views, a pretty patio-garden and a café serving inexpensive breakfasts. Many of the 15 rooms are recently renovated and the triples are large, bright and comfortable. It's well heated in winter, and parking is available for €6.

Hostal-Residencia Lisboa (☎ 958 22 14 13, fax 958 22 14 87; Plaza del Carmen 27; singles/doubles €17/26, with bathroom & TV €29/38), a few blocks south of Plaza Nueva, is a friendly place with 28 clean rooms. Some beds are a bit wobbly. The paintwork is in dull greys and browns, but the bathrooms sport blue and white tiles. Most rooms overlook the plaza or Calle Navas.

The streets between Calle de Elvira and Gran Vía de Colón, west of Plaza Nueva, have several more *hostales* and are worth a look if you're having difficulty finding a room.

Plaza de la Trinidad & Around Some of the many *hostales* in this area fill up with university students in term time. The following should have rooms year-round.

Pensión Romero (☎ 958 26 60 79; Calle Sillería 1; singles/doubles €12/20), homely and family-run, has eight neat, clean rooms, some with ceiling fan and nearly all with external windows.

Huéspedes Capuchinas (☎ 958 26 53 94; Calle Capuchinas 2; singles/doubles €18/27) is a welcoming, clean abode with five simple rooms sharing bathrooms.

Hostal Zurita (☎ 958 27 50 20; Plaza de la Trinidad 7; singles/doubles/triples €17/ 29/41, doubles/triples with bathroom €36/ 50) has 14 quiet, pretty rooms with heating and air-con, nearly all with little balconies. Everything is very clean. Parking costs €7.20 a day.

Hostal Lima (☎ 958 29 50 29; Calle Laurel de las Tablas 17; singles/doubles/triples with bathroom €24/36/48), on a quiet side street, has bright, predominantly yellow, decor, brass bedsteads, firm mattresses, heating and air-con.

Hostal Sevilla (☎ 958 27 85 13; Calle Fábrica Vieja 18; singles/doubles €14/20, with bathroom €17/29.50) is a friendly, clean, straightforward, 14-room *hostal* run by a young family.

Hostal Meridiano (☎/fax 958 25 05 44; e hostalmeridiano@telefonica.net; Calle Angulo 9; singles €15, doubles €24-27, doubles with bathroom €33) is a modernised former student residence that is run by a helpful couple tuned to travellers' needs. Six of the 18 attractive rooms have bathrooms; there's a bathroom for each pair of other rooms. A sitting room with free Internet access was being prepared when we visited.

Hostal San Joaquín (☎ 958 28 28 79; e informacion@hostalsanjoaquin.com; Calle Mano de Hierro 14; rooms with bathroom per person €15-18) rambles in old-fashioned style around a couple of leafy patios. The spacious, clean rooms, for up to four people, are cool in summer but can be cold in winter. Accoutrements vary: some have air-con and heating, others sport a fridge.

PLACES TO STAY – MID-RANGE

Private bathroom, TV, air-con and heating are standard in this range.

GRANADA PROVINCE

Hotel Maciá Plaza (☎ 958 22 75 36; w www.maciahoteles.com; Plaza Nueva 4; singles/doubles €50/72) has plain rooms but a great location. Try for a double overlooking the plaza. The singles are small. Rates fall to €35/50 at slow times in winter, and there are weekend discounts in July and August.

Hotel Anacapri (☎ 958 22 74 77, fax 958 22 89 09; Calle Joaquín Costa 7; singles/doubles/triples €64/90/109 Apr–June & Sept–Oct, €58/77/96 other months), just a minute's walk from Plaza Nueva, has 49 quite pretty rooms in varied colours, with cork floors. Buffet breakfast is €6 and the reception staff are notably friendly.

Hotel Los Tilos (☎ 958 26 67 12, fax 958 26 68 01; Plaza Bib-Rambla 4; singles/doubles €36/52) provides comfy rooms (the 26 doubles are a good size, the four singles small). Eleven doubles overlook the plaza and there's a small but panoramic roof terrace. Buffet breakfast is €5.

Hotel Reina Cristina (☎ 958 25 32 11; w hotelreinacristina.com; Calle Tablas 4; singles/doubles €59/89), just off Plaza de la Trinidad, is in a renovated 19th-century mansion that once belonged to the Rosales family, friends of Lorca. The writer spent his last days here before being arrested by the Nationalists. Rooms are very comfortable and the hotel has a good restaurant. Parking costs €9.65.

Casa del Aljarife (☎/fax 958 22 24 25; w www.granadainfo.com/most; Placeta de la Cruz Verde 2; singles/doubles/triples €67/90/116) is a beautifully restored 17th-century house in the atmospheric Albayzín, with just four spacious, characterful rooms, helpful hosts, and a pretty patio where you can take breakfast in warmer weather.

Hotel América (☎ 958 22 74 71, fax 958 22 74 70; Calle Real de la Alhambra 53; singles/doubles €74/96.50; open Mar–Nov) is within the Alhambra grounds, but it has only 17 rooms; reservations are essential.

Hotel Guadalupe (☎ 958 22 34 23; e guadalupeh@infonegocio.com; Avenida Los Alixares s/n; singles/doubles/triples €61/95/103) is almost on the Alhambra's doorstep. Some of the 42 comfy rooms have Alhambra views.

Hotel Navas (☎ 958 22 59 59; e h-navas@jet.es; Calle Navas 22; singles/doubles/triples €64/86/107) is a perfectly adequate but unexciting city-centre hotel. With 44 rooms, it's on a manageable scale, and all rooms have external windows.

Hotel Molinos (☎ 958 22 73 67; e hotel molinos@usa.net; Calle Molinos 12; singles/doubles €45/64), in the interesting Realejo district, is neat, clean and tiny – it has just nine rooms and it once made the *Guinness Book of Records* as the world's narrowest hotel.

Hostal La Ninfa (☎ 958 22 79 85; Campo del Príncipe s/n; double/twin rooms €51/64), also in Realejo, is covered in brightly painted ceramic stars, both outside and in. The hotel has a pretty lobby-cum-breakfast-room and 10 clean, cosy rooms. The friendly owners speak English and German.

Cuevas El Abanico (☎/fax 958 22 61 99, 608 84 84 97; w www.el-abanico.com; Vereda de Enmedio 89, Sacromonte; singles/doubles/triples €55/55/70, 2-bedroom cave for 4 €85) offers something different – cave lodgings in the Sacromonte *gitano* neighbourhood. The five cave apartments are comfortably decorated and kitted out with heating, kitchen, bathroom, hot water and outdoor terraces, and the owner is friendly and helpful. There's normally a two-night minimum stay (longer at peak periods).

PLACES TO STAY – TOP END

Some of Granada's most charming lodgings are small hotels in renovated mansions in the lower Albayzín. The following three all have English-speaking staff and offer breakfast for around €6.

Casa Morisca Hotel (☎ 958 22 11 00; e casamorisca@terra.es; Cuesta de la Victoria 9; singles/doubles interior €92/116, exterior €113/141) occupies a mansion that dates back to the late 15th century, centred on a patio with a pool and wooden galleries. It has 14 rooms, which aren't huge but are full of atmosphere.

Hotel Carmen de Santa Inés (☎ 958 22 63 80; e sinescar@teleline.es; Placeta de Porras 7; singles/doubles €77/103, doubles with sitting room €128-225) is an old Muslim house that was extended in the 16th and 17th centuries. Its nine rooms are furnished with antiques and the lovely patio opens onto a garden of myrtles, fruit trees and fountains.

Hotel Palacio de Santa Inés (☎ 958 22 23 62; e sinespal@teleline.es; Cuesta de Santa Inés 9; singles/doubles €77/103, doubles with sitting room €128-225) has 35 rooms in an early-16th-century building, with reception installed in the Renaissance patio.

Parador de Granada (☎ 958 22 14 40; w www.parador.es; Calle Real de la Alhambra s/n; singles/doubles €173/217) is the Alhambra's San Francisco monastery converted into a hotel. Originally built in the time of the Catholic Monarchs, whose initial burial place was here, it's the most expensive parador in Spain. You can't beat its location within the Alhambra and its historical connections. Book ahead.

Hotel Alhambra Palace (☎ 958 22 14 68; w www.h-alhambrapalace.es; Peña Partida 2; singles/doubles/triples €123/160/217, suites €231), a large and luxurious neo-Islamic edifice dating from 1910, close to the Bosque Alhambra, has wonderful views over the city.

PLACES TO EAT

Granadino cuisine blends seafood and tropical fruits from the nearby coast, meats and sausages from the interior (particularly from Las Alpujarras) and plump fresh vegetables from the market gardens of La Vega, the fertile plain that surrounds Granada. A hint of the Muslim past is evident in pastries such as syrup cakes, aniseed doughnuts and almond meringues, and in sorbets *(granizados)* – Muslim rulers liked their ices to be made with snow from the mountains.

Granadinos enjoy hearty soups and stews flavoured with herbs such as fennel. *Rabo de toro* (oxtail stew) and *habas con jamón* (broad beans with ham) are typical dishes. Granada's most famous dish, *tortilla Sacromonte*, is an omelette combining cured ham, prawns or oysters, greens and offal (traditionally, calf brains and bull testicles!).

Bar flies will be pleased to find that tapas are often free at night, though at many places (especially around Plaza Nueva) you may need to be drinking up at the bar from 8pm to qualify for these titbits. Food and drink prices are higher in choice locations such as in and around the Alhambra, Plaza Bib-Rambla, Plaza Nueva and some of the tea rooms on Calle Calderería Nueva.

Hunt through the Albayzín for a restaurant with a terrace – the reward is a spectacular view of the Alhambra, which is theatrically floodlit at night.

Near Plaza Nueva

Grand Café Central (☎ 95 822 97 06; Calle de Elvira; menú from €6.60) faces bustling Plaza Nueva and satisfies Alhambra-bound sightseers with good breakfasts (around €5). In the afternoon it does vegetable paella (€5.90) and a selection of tapas (€6.90).

Al Andalus (☎ 95 822 67 30; Calle de Elvira; mains around €6) shaves off hunks of meat from the kebab grill to eat in or take away. Hearty Arabic fast food includes warm felafel in pitta bread (€1.80).

La Nueva Bodega (Calle Cetti Meriém 3; menú from €6.75) mainly functions as a meeting place for the family who own it. However, the chefs cook great paella even if the rest of the food swims in oil.

Bodegas Castañeda (Calle Almireceros; tapas €1.20-1.80), an institution among locals and tourists alike, does classy food in a typical bodega (traditional wine bar) setting. Fill up on Spanish tortilla and *alioli*.

Antigua Castañeda (Calle de Elvira; mains around €10.20) has barrels of potent 'Costa' (Coastal) wine from the Sierra de la Contraviesa and offers a range of delicious, eye-catching food. Try the *montaditos* (€1.95), slices of bread with a variety of toppings.

Vía Colón (☎ 958 22 98 42; Gran Vía de Colón 13; tapas around €2.50), decorated with winged cherubs and angels, is a smart, popular café-bar serving up fancy crepes (€3 with thick chocolate sauce and cream), coffee and snacks.

Jamones Castellano (Cnr Calle Almireceros & Calle Joaquín Costa) sells basic groceries that are ideal for picnics. Get a few slices of *jamón serrano* (cured ham) and some cheese to fill your own *bocadillo* (bread roll).

GRANADA PROVINCE

For fresh fruit and vegies, the large covered **Mercado Central San Agustín** *(Calle San Agustín)* is a block west of the cathedral.

Inhale the lingering aroma of the herb and spice stalls along the Calle Cárcel Baja side of the cathedral. The bulging sacks contain everything from camomile to saffron.

Alhambra

La Mimbre *(☎ 958 22 22 76; Cnr Paseo del Generalife & Cuesta de los Chinos; mains around €10-15)*, under the sheer walls of the Alhambra, has pleasant outdoor tables in a leafy garden. Unwind here after the Alhambra experience.

Parador de Granada *(☎ 958 22 14 40; Calle Real de Alhambra s/n; open 11am-11pm daily; bocadillos from €4.95)* has a swanky restaurant and a terrace bar attached. Stare out at the marvellous views as you quaff your coffee (€1.60).

Albayzín

The labyrinthine Albayzín holds a wealth of eateries, all tucked away in the narrow streets – some behind gates with inconspicuous bells and missable signs. Atmospheric Calle Calderería Nueva is a muddle of *teterías* and Arabic-influenced takeaways.

Kasbah *(Calle Calderería Nueva 4; teas €1.80)* is a dark tea den, lit only by candles at night, where the aroma of herbal infusions and incense makes your nose twitch. Sit on one of the cushion-covered benches and absorb the atmosphere.

Samarcanda *(☎ 958 21 00 04; Calle Calderería Vieja 3; mains around €5.40)* offers excellent Lebanese cuisine in small but filling portions. Hummus and falafel are among the tantalising dishes on offer (€3 each).

Near the top of the Albayzín, Plaza Larga and nearby Calle Panaderos have lively cafés and bars with cheap *menús* (around €6). **The Blue Banana** *(☎ 958 20 37 60; Calle Panaderos 3)* is a great place for a cool juice after the sweaty hike up to the top of the Albayzín.

El Ladrillo II *(☎ 958 29 26 51; Calle Panaderos 35; seafood platters €7.20, menú €4.50)* cooks up popular seafood platters

(barcos) and some extravagant dishes, such as marinated small shark (€6.60).

El Agua *(☎ 958 22 33 58; Plaza Aljibe de Trillo 7; fondues €13 per person, minimum 2 people; open 1.30pm-3.30pm & 8pm-11.30pm Wed-Mon, 8pm-11.30pm Tues)* is the place for wild fondue feasts. Melt along with the cheese as you dunk your chunks of juicy ham and take in the fabulous Alhambra views. After all that (and the chocolate fondue dessert) you're guaranteed to leave satisfied.

Terraza las Tomasas *(☎ 958 22 41 08; Carril de San Agustín 4; mains around €10-15; open 2pm-3.30pm & 9pm-11pm Tues-Sun)* is hard to find in the Albayzín jungle, but ring the little bell when you get there and prepare to be astonished. This classy restaurant is blessed with the best views of the Alhambra, impeccable service and commendable food. Dishes, such as squid in black Andalucian sauce (€10.80), are tasty though your mind will probably be focused elsewhere.

La Luz es Como el Agua *(☎ 958 20 13 68; Calle Cruz de Arqueros 3; menú around €10; open from 8pm Wed-Sat, 2pm-5.30pm Sun)*, close to Plaza del Triunfo, is a relaxed, slightly offbeat place run by a multilingual Belgian. Before making a special trip, phone to check that it's open.

Plaza Bib-Rambla & Around

Café Bib-Rambla *(☎ 958 71 0076; Plaza Bib-Rambla 3)* has a clutch of outdoor tables, just right for breakfast alfresco. Wash down toast and marmalade (€2.40) with a strong coffee (€1.20).

Pizzeria Gallio *(☎ 958 52 10 15; Plaza Bib-Rambla 14; pizzas around €5.35-8.75)* is Plaza Bib-Rambla's slice of Italy, with tasty pizzas to prove it. Try pizza florentina, with spinach and béchamel sauce (€5.35).

Cunini *(☎ 958 25 07 77; Plaza de Pescadería 14; menú €14.40)* might have a tank of terrified lobsters outside but the punters seem quite happy. Fritura Cunini comprises a selection of delicious seafood and costs €24 for two people.

El Cepillo *(Plaza de Pescadería; menú €6.50; open Mon-Sat)*, a few doors from Cunini, is less swanky but just as popular. Its seafood *menú* attracts a crowd at lunch time.

Bar Reca *(☎ 958 29 60 35; Plaza de la Trinidad; raciones €5.40-6.60)* occupies a compact corner spot on Plaza de la Trinidad and swarms with punters tucking into ham *bocadillos* (€2.10). The messy tissue-strewn floor indicates a good time.

Campo del Príncipe

Casa Cristóbal *(☎ 958 22 30 53; Campo del Príncipe 19; menú from €9)* throbs with sangria-giddy diners enjoying dishes such as tender rabbit with garlic.

Restaurante-Pizzería La Ninfa *(Campo del Príncipe 14; pizzas around €6; open noon-3.30pm & 7pm-10pm daily)* cooks up tempting pizzas in a wood-fired oven. Look out for the strings of garlic and red peppers clustered above the entrance.

ENTERTAINMENT

The excellent monthly *Guía de Granada* (€0.75), available from kiosks, lists entertainment venues and places to eat, including tapas bars.

Bars, Music & Dancing

Granada buzzes with heel-clicking flamenco dancers, bottle-clinking hippies and grooving students out on the pull. Chilled bars line the Río Darro at the base of the Albayzín and Campo del Príncipe attracts a sophisticated bunch. The city's large, youthful university population includes plenty of aspiring musicians who keep the gig circuit alive. Look out for posters and leaflets advertising live music and non-touristy flamenco. The bi-weekly flyer *YOUthING* lists many live-music venues, some of which are also dance clubs where DJs spin the latest tracks.

Around Plaza Nueva Get your evening off to a swinging start by indulging in cerveza and free tapas at the bars just west of Plaza Nueva. **Bodegas Castañeda** and **Antigua Castañeda** (see Places to Eat, earlier, for details) are the most inviting, with swaying crowds and slopping drinks. Other entertaining bars can be found on Placeta Sillería and Calle Joaquín Costa.

Bar Avellano *(Cnr Calle de Elvira & Calle Cárcel Baja)* whips up a post-midnight storm with its interesting play list. How about rhythmic blues with African beats and a smattering of pop classics?

La Taberna del Irlandés *(Calle Almireceros)* is a hybrid Spanish/Irish bar that melds local tipples with international

---

Granada's Flamenco Hot Spots

It's difficult to see flamenco that's not geared to tourists but some shows are more authentic than others and attract Spaniards as well as foreigners. The quality of flamenco shows depends on who is performing. If some of Granada's top professionals are dancing, you're in for a good evening. If not, you may be disappointed.

El Eshavira *(☎ 958 29 08 29; Postigo de la Cuna 2; W www.eshavira.com)* is a smoky den that has live flamenco some nights. Check online for the latest programme.

Los Tarantos *(☎ 958 22 45 25 day, 958 22 24 92 night; Camino del Sacromonte 9; tickets €18)* is a frenzy of flamenco delights all tightly packed in a cave. Midnight shows on Friday and Saturday draw fewer foreigners; most tour and hotel groups opt for the 10pm performance. For these shows, you can prebook tickets through hotels and travel agents. Wear your dancing shoes if you want to sit in the first few rows: you'll be pulled up on stage before you know it! A string of other flamenco haunts can be found at the Sacromonte caves, though some are a rip-off. Remember to watch your back if you go up there alone at night.

Peña de la Platería *(☎ 958 21 06 50; Placeta de Toqueros)*, with its large outdoor patio, is buried deep in the Albayzín warren. Catch a 10pm performance on Thursday or Saturday.

Flamenco dancers and singers also perform in some of Granada's more highbrow venues – see under Other Entertainment later in this chapter for details.

flavours. Whether you choose Tetley's Bitter or wine from the Spanish coast you're likely to leave legless.

Granada 10 (Calle Cárcel Baja; admission €6; open around midnight), housed inside a plush cinema, brims with trendy wannabes strutting their stuff. If that's not enough, you can watch a movie beforehand.

La Sabanilla (Calle San Sebastían 14), Granada's oldest bar, might be slightly rough around the edges but it still draws an energetic crowd. Watch out for wobbly bar flies.

Elsewhere Duck down the dark alley off Calle Azacayas and turn the corner to reach **El Eshavira** (☎ 95 829 08 29; Postigo de la Cuna 2; w www.eshavira.com; open from 10pm daily), which reflects the granadino penchant for dark, smoky haunts that ooze cool jazz and sultry flamenco.

Enano Rojo (Calle Elvira 91; open from 10pm daily), with its toadstool emblem, plays riotous jazz and funk to a hip crowd. The later you get there the better. **Planta Baja** (Calle Horno de Abad 11; w www .planta-baja.com; open from midnight daily), near Plaza de la Trinidad, offers deprived beat-lovers a well-needed fix. Catch DJ Toner scratching on Friday or Sergio's Saturday funkclub and enjoy everything from exotic pop to garage and lounge.

Morgan (Calle Obispo Hurtado 15; open 4pm-4am Tues-Sun) is the place to sample house, deep house, funky house and soulful house. It's a house-hunter's dream.

La Fontana (Carrera del Darro 19), next to the first bridge over the River Darro, is shaded by the bulk of the Alhambra. Inside you can huddle round the pool table, drink beer (or coffee) and listen to rock ballads. Well, when the heat gets too much...

Taberna 1899 (Paseo de los Tristes) may be on 'Sad People Promenade' but this drinking den, with its buffed wood and bodega vibe, has a range of spirit-lifting Spanish wines and liqueurs.

El Príncipe (Campo del Príncipe; admission around €10) entertains Granada's well-dressed bunch of party girls and suave bachelors. Inhale the aftershave and show off your moves.

El Camborio (Camino del Sacromonte; admission around €5; open from 11pm Sat & Sun year-round) mixes modern sounds with prehistoric surroundings – yes, you can finally rave in a cave. There are two dance floors (one at cave level) playing a variety of dance and pop tracks.

Other Entertainment

The notice board in the foyer of **La Madraza** (Calle Oficios), opposite the Capilla Real, has large posters listing forthcoming cultural events.

Centro Cultural Manuel de Falla (☎ 958 22 00 22; Paseo de los Mártires s/n), near the Alhambra, is a venue for weekly orchestral concerts.

The **Teatro Alhambra** (☎ 958 22 04 47; Calle de Molinos 56) and the more central **Teatro Isabel La Católica** (☎ 958 22 15 14; Acera del Casino) have ongoing programmes of theatre and concerts (sometimes flamenco).

SHOPPING

A distinctive local craft is marquetry (taracea), used on boxes, tables, chess sets and more – the best have shell, silver or mother-of-pearl inlays. Marquetry experts can be seen at work in the shop opposite the Iglesia de Santa María in the Alhambra. Other granadino crafts include embossed leather, guitars, wrought iron, brass and copper ware, basket weaving, textiles and, of course, pottery. Places to look out for Granada handicrafts include the Alcaicería, the Albayzín and Cuesta de Gomérez. Also try the government-run **Artespaña** in the Corral del Carbón.

Strum your way home with a handmade guitar from **Manuel L Bellido** (Calle Molinos) – peer in the workshop window for a glimpse of the guitar makers at work.

The Plaza Nueva area is awash with jewellery vendors, selling from rugs laid out on the pavement, and ethnic clothes shops. Go on, satisfy the hippy inside.

For general shopping, try pedestrianised Calle de los Mesones and the ever useful department store **El Corte Inglés** (Acera del Darro).

GETTING THERE & AWAY
Air
Iberia (☎ *958 22 75 92; Plaza Isabel La Católica 2*) flies daily to/from Madrid and Barcelona.

Bus
Granada's **bus station**, on Carretera de Jaén, is nearly 3km northwest of the centre. All services operate from here except a few to nearby destinations such as Fuente Vaqueros (see Around Granada, later in this chapter). **Alsina Graells** (☎ *958 18 54 80*) runs buses to Córdoba (€9.65, three hours direct, nine times daily), Seville (€14.90, three hours direct, nine daily), Málaga (€7.55, 1½ hours direct, 17 daily), Las Alpujarras (see that section later in this chapter for details), Jaén, Baeza, Úbeda, Cazorla, Salobreña, Almuñécar, Nerja and Almería. The Alsina desk also handles buses to Madrid.

Buses to Guadix (€3.80, 1½ hours), Baza and Mojácar are run by **Autedia-Maestra** (☎ *958 15 36 36*), which also provides tickets and information for Transportes Agobe's service to Portugal.

Other buses run to Alicante, Valencia, Barcelona and many international destinations (see the introductory Getting There & Away chapter, earlier in this book, for more details on international buses).

Train
The **station** (☎ *958 20 40 00; Avenida de Andaluces*) is 1.5km west of the centre, off Avenida de la Constitución. Four trains run daily to/from Seville (€15.10 to €16.65, three hours) and to/from Almería (€10.10 to €11.10, 2¼ to 2½ hours) via Guadix, and seven to/from Antequera (€5.65 to €6.25, 1½ hours). Three go to Ronda (€10.10, 2½ hours) and Algeciras (€15.10, four to 4½ hours). For Málaga (€10.25) or Córdoba (€13.10) take an Algeciras train and change at Bobadilla. Four trains go to Linares/Baeza daily. Just one or two daily trains go to Madrid, Valencia and Barcelona.

Car
Car rental is expensive. **ATA** (☎ *958 22 40 04; Plaza Cuchilleros 1*) has small cars such as Renault Clios for €61/84/220 for one/two/seven days.

GETTING AROUND
To/From the Airport
The **airport** (☎ *958 24 52 23*) is 17km west of the city on the A-92. At least five buses daily (€2.85), operated by **Autocares J González** (☎ *958 13 13 09*), run between the airport and a stop near the Palacio de Congresos, stopping in the centre on Gran Vía de Colón, where a schedule is posted at the outbound stop, opposite the cathedral. A taxi costs €18.

GRANADA PROVINCE

Be Warned! – Driving in Granada

Vehicle access to the Plaza Nueva area, and therefore to the narrow streets leading up from Plaza Nueva to the Alhambra and Albayzín, is restricted by red lights and little black posts known as *pilonas* that block certain streets during certain times of day (typically 11am to 1pm and after 8pm). Residents and other authorised drivers slot cards into a box, causing the posts to slide down into the ground to let one car (only) pass. You'll see the warning sign '*Obstáculos en calzada a 20 metros*' and will have to detour. The only exception is if you are going to stay at one of the Plaza Nueva area hotels – in which case, press the button by your hotel's name beside the *pilonas* to engage in a disembodied long-distance conversation with your hotel's reception, which will be able to lower the *pilonas* for you.

It's a good idea to ask advice beforehand from your hotel (if you have booked one) about parking. Many hotels, especially in the middle range and above, have their own parking facilities for which they might charge you anything from €6 per day. There are centrally placed public car parks just off Gran Vía de Colón (Parking San Agustín, Calle San Agustín; €0.95/16 per hour/day) and on Acera del Darro (Parking Plaza Puerta Real; €1/10 per hour/day), as well as the Alhambra car parks (see Getting There & Away in the Alhambra section, earlier).

Bus

City buses cost €0.85. Tourist offices give out a leaflet showing routes. The Bono Turístico voucher (see the boxed text earlier in this chapter) includes 10 bus rides. On the buses you can buy a six-ride pass *(bono)* for €4 or a 20-ride pass for €10.

Bus No 3 runs between the bus station and Gran Vía de Colón in the centre. To reach the centre from the train station, walk straight ahead to Avenida de la Constitución and pick up bus No 4, 6, 7, 9 or 11 going to the right (east). From the centre (Gran Vía de Colón) to the train station, take No 3, 4, 6, 9 or 11.

Taxi

Taxis line up on Plaza Nueva. Most fares within the city cost between €3 and €4.50.

AROUND GRANADA

Granada is surrounded by a fertile plain known as La Vega, planted with poplar groves and crops ranging from potatoes and maize to melons and tobacco. The Vega has always been vital to the city and was an inspiration to the writer Federico García Lorca, who was born and died here. The **Parque Federico García Lorca**, a memorial park between the villages of Víznar and Alfacar (about 2.5km from each), marks the site where Lorca and hundreds of others are believed to have been shot and buried by the Nationalists at the start of the civil war.

Fuente Vaqueros

The house where Lorca was born in 1898, in Fuente Vaqueros village, 17km west of Granada, is now the **Museo Casa Natal Federico García Lorca** (☎ 958 51 64 53; W www .museogarcialorca.org; Calle Poeta Federico García Lorca 4; admission €1.80; guided visits hourly 10am-1pm & 5pm-7pm Tues-Sun Apr-Jun; 10am-2pm Tues-Sun July-Aug; 10am-1pm & 6pm-8pm Tues-Sun Sept; 10am-1pm & 4pm-6pm Tues-Sun Oct-Mar). The place makes his spirit come alive, with numerous charming photos, posters and costumes for plays that he wrote and directed, and paintings illustrating his poems. A short video captures him in action with the touring Teatro Barraca.

Buses to Fuente Vaqueros (€1.10, 20 minutes) by **Ureña** (☎ 958 45 41 54) leave from Avenida de Andaluces in front of Granada train station. A timetable is posted outside the Fricama office near the stop. Departures from Granada at the time of research were at 9am daily then hourly (every two hours on Saturday, Sunday and holidays) from 11am to 9pm.

East of Granada

The A-92 northeast from Granada crosses the forested, hilly Parque Natural Sierra de Huétor before entering an increasingly arid landscape. Outside Guadix the A-92 veers southeast towards Almería, crossing the Marquesado de Zenete district below the north flank of the Sierra Nevada, while the A-92-N heads northeast across the Altiplano, Granada's 'High Plain', which breaks out into mountains here and there and affords superb long-distance views on the way to northern Almería province.

GUADIX
postcode 18500 • pop 19,500
• elevation 915m

Guadix (gwah-**deeks**), 55km from Granada, is famous for its cave dwellings – not prehistoric remnants but the homes of about 3000 present-day townsfolk. Cave living is in fact fairly widespread in eastern Granada and Guadix has the biggest concentration of underground homes. There's a **tourist office** (☎ 958 66 26 65; Carretera de Granada s/n; open 8am-3pm Mon-Fri) on the Granada road leaving the town centre.

Things to See

At the centre of Guadix is a fine sandstone **cathedral** (admission €1; open 11am-1pm & 4pm-6pm Mon-Sat), built in the 16th to 18th centuries on the site of the town's former main mosque. Gothic pointed arches and ceiling tracery predominate in one part of the interior, while the rest of the inside and much of the exterior, constructed later to plans by Diego de Siloé, exhibit the round arches and flourishes of Renaissance and baroque. Nearby, **Plaza de las Palomas** is beautiful when floodlit at night.

A short distance south is the entrance to the 10th- and 11th-century Muslim castle, the **Alcazaba** *(Calle Barradas 3; admission by donation; open 10am-2pm Mon-Sat)*, which gives views over the main cave quarter, the Barriada de las Cuevas, some 700m south.

The typical 21st-century cave has a white-washed wall across the entrance, a chimney and TV aerial protruding from the top, and all mod cons inside. Some have many rooms. The caves maintain a comfortable temperature around 18°C year-round. The **Cueva Museo Municipal** *(Plaza de Padre Poveda; admission €1.30; open 10am-2pm & 4pm-6pm Mon-Sat, 10am-2pm Sun)* in the Barriada de las Cuevas recreates typical cave life.

Places to Stay & Eat

Hotel Comercio *(☎ 958 66 05 00; Calle Mira de Amezcua 3; singles €33, doubles €45-51)* is a long-standing central hotel that had a complete makeover a few years ago and offers very comfy rooms and a good restaurant with a wide variety of medium-priced Spanish fare.

Hotel Mulhacén *(☎ 958 66 07 50; Avenida Buenos Aires 41; singles/doubles €31/40)* is a straightforward place on the Murcia road 600m from the centre.

Cuevas Pedro Antonio de Alarcón *(☎ 958 66 49 86; ⓦ www.andalucia.com/cavehotel; Barriada San Torcuato; singles/doubles/quads €33.50/46.50/70)* offers the genuine Guadix experience: accommodation in caves. This is in fact a comfy, modern cave-apartment-hotel with a pool and restaurant. It's 2.5km past Hotel Mulhacén along the same road towards the A-92 (look for 'Alojamiento en Cuevas' signs). During Semana Santa and August, prices go up a bit and there's a four-night minimum.

Getting There & Away

Guadix is about one hour from Granada and 1½ hours from Almería by any of 10 buses or four trains daily in each direction. At least two daily buses head to Baza, Murcia, Madrid, Jaén and Mojácar. The bus station is at the end of Calle Concepción Arenal,

off Avenida Medina Olmos about 700m southeast of the centre. The train station is off the Murcia road about 2km northeast of the town centre.

MARQUESADO DE ZENETE

This bleak, flat area between Guadix and the Sierra Nevada was a prosperous agricultural district in Muslim times. After the Reconquista it was awarded to Cardinal de Mendoza, chief adviser to the Catholic Monarchs during the war against Granada. His illegitimate son Rodrigo de Mendoza became its first *marqués* (marquis).

The main town, **Jerez del Marquesado**, served by daily buses from Granada and Guadix, is a starting point for ventures into the high Sierra Nevada.

Thirteen kilometres east of Jerez, the forbidding **Castillo de La Calahorra** *(admission by donation; open 10am-1pm & 4pm-6pm Wed; other times by appointment with caretaker Antonio Trivaldo ☎ 958 67 70 98)* looms above the village of La Calahorra. The castle was built between 1509 and 1512 by Rodrigo de Mendoza, whose tempestuous life included a spell in Italy unsuccessfully wooing Lucrezia Borgia. The building's domed corner towers and blank walls enclose an amazingly elegant Italian Renaissance courtyard with a staircase of Carrara marble. There are at least two **hostales** and one **hotel** in La Calahorra village, from which the A-337 heads south over the **Puerto de la Ragua** pass to Las Alpujarras.

BAZA

postcode 18800 • pop 21,000
• elevation 850m

The market town of Baza, 44km northeast of Guadix, dates back to Iberian times. Its attractive Plaza Mayor is dominated by the 16th-century **Iglesia Concatedral de la Encarnación**. Baza's **tourist office** is in the **Museo Municipal** *(Plaza Mayor; museum & tourist office open 10am-2pm & 5pm-7pm daily except holidays)*, whose archaeological collection includes a copy of the *Dama de Baza*, a person-size Iberian goddess statue unearthed locally in 1971 and one of the outstanding pieces of Iberian art (the original is housed in Madrid's Museo Arqueológico Nacional).

Hostal Avenida (☎ 958 70 03 77; Avenida José de la Mora 26; singles/doubles €12/24, with bathroom €18/36) is about 500m south of Plaza Mayor.

Hotel Anabel (☎ 958 86 09 98; Calle María de Luna s/n; singles/doubles with bathroom €21/36) is a friendly place near Hostal Avenida.

La Solana (Calle Serrano) is one of the best of a handful of beer and tapas bars close to Plaza Mayor.

The **bus station** (Calle Reyes Católicos) is 200m north of Plaza Mayor. There are about 15 buses a day to/from Guadix and Granada in one direction and Vélez Rubio and Murcia in the other.

Sierra Nevada

The Sierra Nevada mountain range, with mainland Spain's highest peak, Mulhacén (3482m), forms an almost year-round snowy, southeastern backdrop to Granada. The range extends about 75km from west to east, crossing from Granada into Almería province.

All the highest peaks (3000m or more) are towards the range's western (Granada) end, and it's on the northern flank of this end of the range that the Sierra Nevada ski resort, Europe's most southerly, stands. In the warmer seasons the mountains and the valleys beneath them (especially Las Alpujarras, to the south) offer some wonderful walking. Lonely Planet's *Walking in Spain*

Orce Man

The dusty Altiplano village of Orce, on a country road between Baza and María (Almería province), styles itself the 'Cradle of European Humankind'. This modest claim rests on a fossilised bone fragment probably between one and two million years old, found in 1976 at nearby Venta Micena. The bone is widely accepted to be part of the skull of an infant *Homo erectus* that had probably been taken to lunch by a giant hyena. *Homo erectus* was an ancestor of *Homo sapiens*, and the bit of bone would therefore be the oldest known human remnant in Europe. Many palaeontologists have taken this 'Hombre de Orce' (Orce Man) as evidence that humans reached Europe much earlier than was previously believed, and direct from Africa, instead of via Asia as had been thought. Others, however, say the fragment more likely came from a horse or deer and could be less than a million years old.

What's not disputed is that for most of the last four million years, much of the Hoya de Baza, the now arid basin in which the Baza-Orce area lies, was a lake. Wildlife drinking at the edge of the lake was vulnerable to attack by larger animals, and the fossilised bones of dozens of species, including mammoth, rhinoceros, sabre-tooth tiger, hippopotamus, giant hyena, wolf, bear, elephant and buffalo, relics of such encounters between one and two million years ago, have been found at Venta Micena and nearby sites. It's quite a thrill to know that the landscape you're crossing was once roamed by such creatures.

A good selection of the finds – including enormous mammoths' teeth and a replica of the 'Hombre de Orce' fragment (the original is under lock and key in Orce town hall) – are on show in Orce's interesting **Museo de Prehistoria y Paleontología** (☎ 958 74 61 83; admission €1.50; open 11am-2pm daily year-round; 6pm-8pm daily June-Sept; 4pm-6pm daily Oct-May), in a Muslim-era castle just off the village's central square.

If you need accommodation in Orce, try **Cueva del Tío Ciñao** (ⓦ www.vivegranada.com/orce; Barrio San Marcos 52; 2/4/6 people €48/84/120), a recently renovated, century-old, three-bedroom cave holiday apartment.

Fans of the distant past could also seek out the Bronze Age sites of El Castellón Alto and El Cerro de Real, at Galera on the A-330, 8km west of Orce.

details eight days of good walking in the Sierra Nevada and Las Alpujarras.

The best overall map of the area is Editorial Alpina's *Sierra Nevada, La Alpujarra* (1:40,000), available in English as *Map & Tourist Guide Sierra Nevada*. It comes with a booklet describing 32 walking, mountain bike and cross-country skiing routes.

The best period for walking in the high mountains is early July to early September: only then is the high ground reliably snow-free and the weather relatively settled. Unfortunately this doesn't coincide with the most comfortable months down in the valleys (see the following Las Alpujarras section). Late June/early July and the first half of September are the best compromise periods. The Sierra Nevada is a serious mountain range and the temperature on the summits averages 14°C less than in the highest Alpujarras villages: you should come well equipped, and prepared for cloud, rain or strong, icy winds at *any* time.

Nearly all the upper reaches of the Sierra Nevada are included in the 862 sq km Parque Nacional Sierra Nevada, the biggest of Spain's dozen national parks. This rare high-altitude environment is home to about 2100 of Spain's 7000 plant species including 66 endemics, among them unique types of crocus, narcissus, thistle, clover, poppy and gentian. Andalucía's largest ibex population (about 5000) is here too – in summer, walkers may come across ibex anywhere above about 2800m.

Surrounding the national park, at lower altitudes, is the 848 sq km Parque Natural Sierra Nevada, which has a lesser degree of protection.

ESTACIÓN DE ESQUÍ SIERRA NEVADA

The A-395 leads from Granada to the Estación de Esquí Sierra Nevada (Sierra Nevada Ski Station), with high peaks rising behind it. About 10km before the ski station is the **Centro de Visitantes El Dornajo** (☎/fax 958 34 06 25; open 10am-2pm & 4pm-6pm daily), which has plenty of information on Sierra Nevada possibilities and facilities, and maps for sale.

Skiing

The **ski station** (☎ 902 70 80 90; ⓦ *www .sierranevadaski.com*), at Pradollano, 33km from Granada, is an ugly modern construction and very crowded at weekends in the season, but the skiing and facilities are good enough for it to have hosted the World Alpine Skiing championships in 1996.

The season normally lasts from December to April or early May. Prices of accommodation and ski passes (*forfaits*; €18 to €29.50 for one day) are lowest in the 'promotional' periods at the beginning and end of the season, and highest around Christmas/New Year and other holiday periods, and on Saturdays and Sundays from January to March.

The station has 51 marked downhill runs totalling 65km – four graded black (very difficult), 23 red (difficult), 20 blue (easy) and four green (very easy). The highest start almost at the top of 3392m Veleta, the second highest peak in the Sierra Nevada. Cable cars (€9 return for nonskiers) run up from Pradollano (2100m) to Borreguiles (2645m); other lifts go higher. There are cross-country routes too, and a dedicated snowboard area *(parque de surf)* above Borreguiles. During the ski season the resort has a thriving nightlife.

Rental of skis, boots and poles costs €15.50 for one day; a snowboard and boots cost €18. The resort has a dozen ski and snowboard schools: at the Escuela Oficial de Esquí (Official Ski School), a six-hour weekend course is €49.30. There's an **information office** (☎ 958 24 91 19) next to the ticket office at the resort.

Places to Stay & Eat

Room reservations are highly advisable in the ski season. Outside the ski season only a few hotels stay open.

Albergue Juvenil Sierra Nevada (☎ 902 51 00 00; under 26/other €12.90/17.25 Dec-Apr & holiday periods; €8.50/11.50 rest of year), the youth hostel near the top of the ski station, is the cheapest place to stay, with 214 places in rooms holding two or four people. Prices include breakfast. It's quite a hike up to the hostel after an evening in the resort's bars, though!

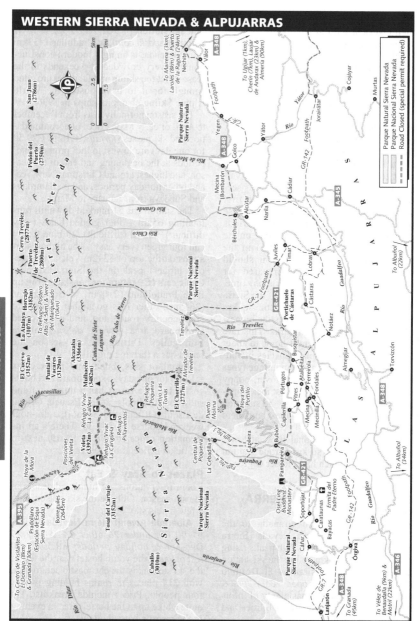

WESTERN SIERRA NEVADA & ALPUJARRAS

The resort has around 18 hotels, *hostales* and apartment-hotels. Less expensive ones, with doubles costing around €75 to €90, include **Hotel Telecabina** (☎ 958 48 20 00), **Hostal El Ciervo** (☎ 958 48 04 09) and **Hotel-Apartamentos Trevenque** (☎ 958 48 08 62). The best deals are ski packages which you should try to book at least two weeks ahead on the station's phone number or website. A two-night half-board package with two days' ski passes costs from about €120 to €270 per person.

Getting There & Away

In the ski season **Autocares Bonal** (☎ 958 46 50 22) runs three daily buses (four at weekends) to the ski resort from Granada bus station (€3/5.50 one way/return, one hour). Outside the ski season there's just one bus daily (9am from Granada, 5pm from the ski station). A taxi from Granada costs about €40.

MULHACÉN & VELETA

The Sierra Nevada's two highest peaks – Mulhacén (3482m) and Veleta (3392m), even in summer usually marked out by patches of snow – rise to the southeast of the ski station. They also crown the head of the Poqueira valley in Las Alpujarras on the south flank of the range. Mulhacén, the highest peak in mainland Spain, is named after Moulay Abu al-Hasan, father of the ill-fated Boabdil. Its summit supports a small shrine and a roofless chapel, a few metres from the edge of a near-perpendicular 500m drop to the Hoya de Mulhacén basin. The views, on a good day, are incredible, taking in such distant ranges as the Sierra de Cazorla and the Rif Mountains of Morocco.

A road climbs right over the Sierra Nevada from the ski station to Capileira, the highest village in the Poqueira valley, but it's closed to motor vehicles (except with a special permit) between Hoya de la Mora (2475m), some 3km up from Pradollano, and Hoya del Portillo (2150m), 12.5km above Capileira. From about late June to the end of October the Sierra Nevada national park operates **information offices** (*open approximately 8.30am-2.30pm & 3.30pm-7.30pm daily*) at Hoya de la Mora and Hoya del Portillo. During approximately the same periods national-park shuttle bus services, called the Servicio de Interpretación Ambiental Altas Cumbres (High Peaks Environmental Interpretation Service), run about 6km up the road from Hoya de la Mora (to the Posiciones del Veleta, at 3020m), and some 16km up from Capileira (to Puerto Molina, 3km above Hoya del Portillo, at 2400m). Tickets (€4/6 one way/return on either route) are sold at the Hoya de la Mora information post and at the Altas Cumbres office beside the main road in Capileira.

One or two early and late runs from Capileira continue beyond Puerto de Molina as far as the Mirador de Trevélez at about 2670m. Details of these services are subject to change but some form of bus service carrying visitors to the road's higher altitudes can be expected to continue. For further information, call ☎ 630 95 97 39 for the northern route or ☎ 686 41 45 76 for the south side.

Many exciting walks start from the near the bus routes, and the national park offices have leaflets summarising them. From the Posiciones del Veleta it's about 4km to the top of Veleta, an ascent of some 370m with about 1½ hours' walking; or 14km to the top of Mulhacén, with four to five hours' walking; or about 24km (about nine hours) all the way over to Puerto Molina. From Puerto Molina it's around 4½ hours to the top of Mulhacén (11km, 1100m ascent), or you could reach the Cañada de Siete Lagunas, a lake-dotted basin below the eastern side of Mulhacén, in about three hours.

If you want to make more than a day trip of it, there are four high-mountain refuges where you can spend the night.

Refugio Poqueira (☎ 958 34 33 49; *per person €7.80; breakfast/dinner €3.50/10; open year-round*), a modern place with 87 bunks, is towards the top of the Poqueira valley at 2500m. Phone ahead if possible. Blankets are provided and there are hot showers. You can get to the refuge by walking the 7km from Puerto Molina (about two hours), or following the Río Mulhacén for 2.3km down from the road beneath the west side of Mulhacén, then following a path veering 750m southeast to the refuge.

Sleeping in the three *refugios vivac* – simple stone or brick shelters with boards for around 12 people to sleep on – is free, and they're always open, but reservations are not possible. **Refugio Vivac La Caldera** is below the west flank of Mulhacén, a 1½-hour walk up from Refugio Poqueira; **Refugio Pillavientos** is about a 20-minute walk southwest along the road from Refugio La Caldera; and **Refugio Vivac La Cariguëla** is about a 2¼-hour walk further west along the road, at the 3200m Collado del Veleta pass below the summit of Veleta.

Overnight camping in the mountains is allowed only above 1600m, at least 50m from high-mountain lakes and at least 500m from staffed refuges and vehicle tracks. You must give prior notification by email, fax or letter to the **Director-Conservador del Parque Nacional Sierra Nevada** (fax 958 02 63 10; ℮ *pn.snevada@cma.junta-andalucia.es; Carretera Antigua de Sierra Nevada Km 7, 18191 Pinos Genil, Granada)*, stating the name and identity card or passport number of the person responsible, the location and the number of people and tents. It's advisable to check the latest regulations at park information offices.

You can of course reach the refuges and high altitudes without using the summer bus service. A straightforward route is to take path No 3, with yellow marker posts, from Capileira (shown on the Editorial Alpina map/booklet): this path starts from a small picnic area on the Sierra Nevada road 250m above Capileira's Finca Los Llanos hotel, and makes it way up the east side of the Poqueira valley to Cortijo Las Tomas, from which it is about 45 minutes further up to the Refugio Poqueira – about five hours' walking from Capileira in all. A good route from Trevélez is to head northwestward up to the Cañada de Siete Lagunas, from which you can ascend Mulhacén via the rocky Cuesta del Resuello ridge – it will take around seven hours' of walking from Trevélez.

Las Alpujarras

The wrinkled landscape along the southern flank of the Sierra Nevada, a 70km-long jumble of valleys known as Las Alpujarras or La Alpujarra, forms one of the oddest and most picturesque crannies of all Andalucía. Arid hillsides split by deep ravines alternate with oasis-like white villages set amid gardens, orchards and woodlands watered by rapid streams. It's a particularly delightful area to explore on foot and is the starting point for some of the best routes up into the Sierra Nevada (see the preceding section).

Despite a recent burst of tourism, Las Alpujarras remains a world apart, with a rare sense of timelessness and mystery. The Berber-style villages and the terraced and irrigated hillsides are ubiquitous reminders of its flourishing Muslim past.

History
In Muslim times Berber migrants to the Alpujarras introduced the cultivation of silk-worms (the mulberry-leaf-eating caterpillars of the silk moth). Thread spun from the silk-worms' unravelled cocoons was the raw material of the thriving silk workshops of 10th- and 11th-century Almería and, later, Nasrid Granada. Together with irrigation-based agriculture, the production of silk thread supported a population of probably over 150,000 in at least 400 villages and hamlets in Las Alpujarras by the late 15th century.

On his surrender to the Catholic Monarchs in 1492, Boabdil, the last Granada emir, was awarded the Alpujarras as a personal fiefdom. He settled at Laujar de Andarax in the eastern Alpujarras (Almería province), but left for Africa the next year. Christian promises of tolerance gave way to forced mass conversions and land expropriations; in 1500, Muslims rebelled across the former Granada emirate, with the Alpujarras in the thick of things. When the revolt failed, Muslims were given the choice of exile or conversion. Most converted – to become known as Moriscos – but the change was barely skin deep. A new repressive decree by Felipe II in 1567 forbade the use of Arabic names and dress and even the Arabic language, leading to a new revolt in 1568, led by an Alpujarras Morisco named Aben Humeya and aided by North African Muslims.

Two years of vicious guerrilla war in the Alpujarras ended only after Don Juan of Austria, Felipe's half-brother, was brought in to quash the insurrection and Aben Humeya was assassinated by his cousin Aben Aboo.

Almost the whole Alpujarras population was deported to Castile and western Andalucía, and some 270 villages and hamlets were re-peopled with settlers from northern Spain. The other villages were abandoned. Over the following centuries, the silk industry fell by the wayside and swaths of the Alpujarras' woodlands were lost to mining and cereal growing.

Books

In the 1920s literary Englishman Gerald Brenan settled in the Alpujarras village of Yegen with 'a good many books and a little money', to escape the weight of British traditions. His *South From Granada* is a fascinating picture of a very isolated and superstitious corner of Spain, leavened by visits from Virginia Woolf and other literati. Another Englishman, Chris Stewart, settled in Las Alpujarras in the 1990s, as a sheep farmer near Órgiva; his *Driving over Lemons* tells entertainingly of modern life as a foreigner in Las Alpujarras.

Walking

The best times for walking in Las Alpujarras are April to mid-June and mid-September to early November, when the temperatures are just right and the vegetation at its most colourful.

There's a wealth of good walks linking valley villages or heading up into the Sierra Nevada, and two long-distance footpaths traverse Las Alpujarras. One is the GR-7, which crosses Europe from Tarifa (Cádiz province) to Greece: you could follow it through the Granada Alpujarras from Lanjarón to Laroles in one week. The 144km GR-142 runs from Lanjarón to Fiñana on the northern flank of the Sierra Nevada in Almería province.

See the Sierra Nevada section, earlier, for information on maps.

Accommodation

It's worth booking ahead for rooms in Las Alpujarras during Semana Santa and from July to September. Many villages have apartments and houses for short-term rental; ask in information offices, look for signs or ask around.

Food & Drinks

Most Alpujarras food is straightforward, hearty country fare, with lots of good meat and local trout. Trevélez is famous for its *jamón serrano*, but many other villages produce good hams too. A *plato alpujarreño* consists of fried potatoes, fried eggs, sausage, ham and maybe a black pudding, and usually costs around €4 to €5.

'Alpujarras' or 'Costa' wine comes from the Sierra de la Contraviesa, on the south flank of Las Alpujarras, and tends to be strong and fairly raw.

Getting There & Away

Bus Buses to the Alpujarras are run by **Alsina Graells** (*Granada* ☎ 958 18 54 80 • *Órgiva* ☎ 958 78 50 02). From Granada, buses leave at 10.30am, noon and 5.15pm daily for Lanjarón, Órgiva (€3.50, 1½ hours), Pampaneira (€4.30, two hours), Bubión (€4.50, 2¼ hours), Capileira (€4.70, 2½ hours) and Pitres (€5, 2¾ hours). The last two continue to Trevélez (€5.25, 3¼ hours) and Bérchules (€6.25, 3¾ hours). Return buses start from Bérchules at 5am and 5pm and from Pitres at 3.30pm. Alsina also runs a twice-daily Granada–Ugíjar service (€7.60, four hours) via Lanjarón, Órgiva, Cádiar, Yegen and Válor, a Málaga–Lanjarón service via Órgiva (daily except Sunday), a daily Almería–Bérchules service via Adra and a daily Almería–Ugíjar bus via Berja.

Car & Motorcycle The main road into the Alpujarras from the west is the A-348 (C-333 on some signs). The GR-421 road turns north off the A-348 just west of Órgiva to wind along the northern slopes of the Alpujarras, rejoining it a few kilometres north of Cádiar.

From the Motril direction, turn east off the N-323 just north of Vélez de Benaudalla.

LANJARÓN
postcode 18420 • pop 3750
• elevation 660m

Las Alpujarras' westernmost town, a spa, has a good setting on the southern slopes of the Sierra Nevada, but what most people see is a straggly place along the A-348 (Avenida Andalucía). Numerous *hostales* and hotels, with doubles costing between €20 and €50, are strung along Avenida Andalucía, but only a few stay open during winter. The cheaper ones tend to be towards the eastern end of town.

ÓRGIVA
postcode 18400 • pop 5000
• elevation 725m

The main town of the western Alpujarras, Órgiva is a scruffy but bustling place. On Thursday mornings locals and the Alpujarras' sizable international community (which has a big hippy/New Age element) gather to buy and sell everything from vegetables to bead necklaces at a colourful market in the upper part of town, the Barrio Alto.

From the Alsina Graells bus station and office at Avenida González Robles 67, walk up the street and around to the right to reach Órgiva's central traffic lights. You will find several banks and ATMs on and near Plaza García Moreno and its continuation, Calle Doctor Fleming, which head uphill here.

The 16th-century twin-towered **Iglesia de Nuestra Señora de la Expectación** stands beside Plaza García Moreno.

Places to Stay & Eat
Camping Órgiva (☎ 958 78 43 07; A-348 Km 18.9; camping per adult/tent/car €3.80/3.70/3.10, cabins & bungalows from €32.10), 2km south of the centre on the A-348 towards the Río Guadalfeo, has a nice pool area but there is only a small area for camping.

Pensión Alma Alpujarreña (☎ 958 78 40 85; Avenida González Robles 49; singles/doubles €15/30), just below the central traffic lights, remains refreshingly unmod-

ernised, with Franco-era bedspreads and clean bathrooms. Some rooms have private bathroom.

Hostal Mirasol (☎ 958 78 51 59; Avenida González Robles 3; singles/doubles €13/25.50), near the bridge over the Río Chico on the west side of town, has plain, though adequate, rooms with bathroom.

Hotel Mirasol (☎ 958 78 51 08; Avenida González Robles 5; singles/doubles €22.50/38.50) offers newer, more comfortable, all-white rooms with TV.

Hotel Taray (☎ 958 78 45 25; A-348 Km 18.5; singles/doubles from €46/60), a few hundred yards up the road from Camping Órgiva, provides pleasant pastel rooms in Alpujarras-style buildings. There's a lovely big pool at the bottom of the grassy garden.

Mesón Casa Santiago (Plaza García Moreno; mains €5.40-7.20) is good for grilled meats at indoor or outdoor tables.

La Zahona (Plaza García Moreno) sells good cakes and pastries, which go well with a drink at the pavement tables of **Café Galindo Plaza**, next door.

PAMPANEIRA, BUBIÓN & CAPILEIRA
postcodes (respectively) 18411, 18412, 18413 • pops 330, 370, 520
• elevations 1050m, 1300m, 1440m

These villages, clinging to the side of the deep Barranco de Poqueira ravine 14km to 20km northeast of Órgiva, are among the prettiest, most dramatically sited, and most touristed, in Las Alpujarras. Their white-washed stone houses seem to clamber over each other in an effort not to slide down into the gorge, while streets decked with flowery balconies wriggle between.

Capileira, the highest of the three, is the best base for walks if you don't have your own vehicle.

Information
The **Punto de Información Parque Nacional de Sierra Nevada** (☎ 958 76 31 27; Plaza de la Libertad; open 10am-2pm & 5pm-7pm Tues-Sat Semana Santa–mid-Oct; 10am-2pm & 4pm-6pm Tues-Sat rest of year; 10am-3pm Sun & Mon year-round), on

Pampaneira's square, has a wealth of information about the Alpujarras and Sierra Nevada, including maps for sale, and can inform you about walks and mountain refuges. Some information on the national park is available at the office of the **Servicio de Interpretación de Altos Cumbres** *(open 7.45am-2pm & 3.15pm-8pm daily, approx late June–end Oct; variable rest of year)*, by the main road in Capileira.

There are ATMs just outside the car park entrance in Pampaneira, and in Capileira at **La General** *(Calle Doctor Castilla)*. Internet use costs €1/1.50/2 per 15/30/60 minutes at Ciber Monfí Café Morisco in Bubión (see Places to Stay & Eat, later).

Things to See

All three villages – like many others in Las Alpujarras – have solid 16th-century **Mudejar churches** (open at mass times, posted on the doors). They also have small **weaving workshops** which you can poke your head into: an interesting little one in Bubión is French-owned **Taller del Telar** *(Calle Santísima Trinidad)*, with ancient looms from Granada. Also in Bubión, don't miss the **Casa Alpujarreña** *(Calle Real; admission €1.80; open 11am-2pm daily, 5pm-7pm Fri, Sat & holidays)*, beside the church. This is an excellent little folk museum in a village house that was left untouched from the 1950s until its recent adaptation as a museum – a marvellous glimpse of bygone Alpujarras life!

Given the somewhat Himalayan character of the Poqueira landscape, it's not entirely surprising that a small Tibetan Buddhist monastery, **Osel Ling** *(Place of Clear Light;* ☎ *958 34 31 34)*, stands about 1550m high on the far side of the valley from Pampaneira. The monastery welcomes visitors at certain times: call for hours. You can walk to it from any of the villages or drive up from the turn-off marked 'PN Sierra Nevada' opposite the Ermita del Padre Eterno, a wayside chapel on the GR-421, 5km below Pampaneira.

Walking

Eight trails ranging from 4km to 23km (two to eight hours) are marked by little colour-coded posts in the beautiful Barranco de Poqueira. Although their starting points can be hard to find, they are marked and described on the recommended Editorial Alpina map. Most routes start from Capileira.

Route No 4 (8km, 3½ hours) takes you from Capileira up to the hamlet of La Cebadilla, then down the western side of the valley and back up to Capileira. To find its start, walk down to the end of Calle Cubo at the northern end of Capileira, turn right at Apartamentos Vista Veleta and follow the street out into the countryside. Fork up to the right 125m after the last village building on your right. Route No 2 starts at the end of Calle Cerezo in Capileira.

Nevadensis *(*☎ *958 76 31 27;* W *www .nevadensis.com)*, based at the information centre in Pampaneira (see Information, earlier), offers hikes and treks with knowledgeable guides, including a combined 4WD and foot ascent of Mulhacén for €27 per person.

Other Activities

Depending on the season, Nevadensis (see the preceding section for details) can organise horse riding (around €30 for two hours), mountain biking (€27/45 per half-day/day), climbing, ski touring and snowshoeing. Horse-riding with **Rafael Belmonte** *(*☎*/fax 958 76 31 35;* W *www.ridingandalucia.com)* and **Dallas Love** *(*☎ *958 76 30 38, fax 958 76 30 34)* gets good reports. Both are Bubión-based, speak English and offer trail rides lasting anywhere up to nine days or so.

Places to Stay & Eat

All rooms mentioned have private bathroom.

Pampaneira Two good-value *hostales* face each other at the entrance to the village.

Hostal Pampaneira *(*☎ *958 76 30 02; Avenida Alpujarra 1; singles/doubles €20/30)* has a friendly local owner, clean, good-sized rooms and one of the cheapest restaurants in the village (trout €5.40, *menú* €7.25).

Hostal Ruta del Mulhacén *(*☎ *958 76 30 10;* e *rutamul@arrakis.es; Avenida Alpujarra 6; singles/doubles €27/32)* has uninterrupted valley views from some rooms.

Restaurante Casa Diego (*Plaza de la Libertad 15; mains €4.50-7.50*), with a pleasant upstairs terrace, is a good choice out of the three restaurants just along the street. Trout with ham, and local ham and eggs, are good bets among the cheaper dishes.

Bubión Below the main road, **Hostal Las Terrazas** (☎ 958 76 30 34; ⓦ *www.terrazas alpujarra.com; Plaza del Sol 7; singles/ doubles €20/25.20, double/quad apartments €37/54*) has pleasant though smallish rooms, and apartments nearby.

Ciber Monfí Café Morisco (☎ 958 76 30 53; *Calle Alcalde Pérez Ramón 2; light dishes €2.50-4; closed Tues*), a converted old village house in the maze of narrow streets below Hostal Las Terrazas, is a tea-and-coffee-house-cum-bar serving great Arabic food to cool background music. With a pretty garden terrace, board games, Internet, log fire in winter and live music on weekend nights, it's the Poqueira valley's coolest hangout. Try the *plato Monfí* (€10), combining a brochette of your choice with rice, couscous and salads.

Capileira Just off the main road, **Hostal Poqueira** (☎/fax 958 76 30 48; *Calle Doctor Castilla 6; singles/doubles €18/24*) is a friendly place with good-value rooms – and winter heating.

Hostal Atalaya (☎ 958 76 30 25; *Calle Perchel 3; singles/doubles €15/28, exterior doubles €30*), 100m down the main road from Hostal Poqueira and recently modernised, offers pleasant rooms with breakfast included.

Finca Los Llanos (☎ 958 76 30 71; *Carretera de Sierra Nevada; singles/doubles €38.50/64.50, apartments for 2 €77*), at the top of the village, offers classier, comfortable accommodation. The apartments have terrace, kitchen, sitting room and parking. Breakfast is included.

Cortijo Catifalarga (☎ 958 34 33 57; *singles €40, doubles €55.50-79.50, apartments from €72*) is the choicest base. The signposted 500m driveway to this charmingly renovated old farmstead begins 750m up the Sierra Nevada road from the top of

the village. Chestnut beams, stone floors and Moroccan rugs set the tone, and some rooms have their own terraces. You can dine indoors or out, and hear live music some nights – and the views are fabulous.

Most places to stay have restaurants but there are alternatives.

Bar El Tilo (*Plaza Calvario*) serves good-value *raciones* (meal-sized servings of tapas, for €3 to €5) such as melon and ham, lamb chops or *patatas a lo pobre*, a potato dish with peppers and garlic.

Casa Íbero (☎ 958 76 32 56; *Calle Parra 1; salads €4.50-5.10; mains €6-10; open 1.30pm-3.30pm Fri-Sun, 7.30pm-10.30pm daily*) below the church, makes original international food ranging from varied couscous dishes to Saharan turkey with dates and apples. The adjoining **Íbero Fusión** bar provides juices, music, tarts and salads.

Shopping

All three villages have plentiful craft shops selling, among other things, colourful, inexpensive, homespun Alpujarras cotton rugs. In Capileira **J Brown** (*Calle Doctor Castilla*) sells slinky handmade leather and suede clothing at good prices, including waistcoats from €60.

Alpujarras Houses

Travellers who have been to Morocco may notice a resemblance between villages in the Alpujarras and those in the Atlas Mountains. The typical Alpujarras building style was introduced by Berber settlers during Muslim times.

Most houses have two storeys, with the lower one still often used for storage and animals. The characteristic flat roofs (*terraos*), with their protruding chimney pots, consist of a layer of *launa* (a type of clay) packed onto flat stones which are laid over beams of chestnut, ash or pine. Nowadays there's often a layer of plastic between the stones and the *launa* for extra waterproofing. Whitewash is a fairly modern introduction too: the villages all used to be stone-coloured.

PITRES & LA TAHA

postcode 18414 • population (Pitres) 400
• elevation 1250m

Pitres is almost as pretty as the Poqueira gorge villages but less touristed. It has a bank and ATM on the main square. The five hamlets in the valley just below Pitres – Mecina, Mecinilla, Fondales, Ferreirola and Atalbéitar – are grouped with it in a municipality called La Taha, a name that recalls the Muslim emirate of Granada, when the Alpujarras was divided into 12 administrative units called *tahas*. Ancient paths between these hamlets wend through some of the Alpujarras' lushest woods and orchards, to the ubiquitous tinkle of running water, and the air seems thick with accumulated centuries. A few minutes' walk below Fondales is an old Muslim bridge over the Río Trevélez gorge, with a ruined Muslim mill beside it (ask for the *puente árabe*).

Places to Stay & Eat

Camping El Balcón de Pitres (☎ 958 76 61 11; camping per adult/tent/car €3.90/3.90/ 2.90, cabins & cottages from €30 for 2; open year-round), just above by the GR-421 on the western side of Pitres, is shady and fairly spacious. It also has a pool and a decent, inexpensive restaurant.

Refugio Los Albergues (☎ 958 34 31 76; bunks €7; open 16 Feb-14 Dec), is a small walkers' hostel in a beautiful setting 200m (signposted) down a path from the GR-421 main road on the eastern side of Pitres. It has 12 bunks, one double room (€21), an equipped kitchen, hot showers and interesting outdoor toilets. The friendly German owner is full of information on the area's many good walks.

Hotel Albergue de Mecina (☎ 958 76 62 54; www.hotelalberguedemecina.com; Calle La Fuente s/n; singles/doubles with bathroom €47/59) is a tasteful 21-room hotel in Mecina, modern and comfortable but with touches of traditional Alpujarras style.

L'Atelier (☎ 958 85 75 01; www.ivu.org/ atelier; Calle Alberca s/n; singles €30, doubles with bathroom €36-42), also in Mecina, is the last thing you might expect to stumble upon in this remote neck of the woods: a welcoming French-run vegetarian guesthouse, serving gourmet meatless meals and with an art gallery next door. It has five rooms and breakfast is included.

Sierra y Mar (☎ 958 76 61 71; www .sierraymar.com; Calle Albaicín; singles/ doubles with bathroom €25/45), in Ferreirola, is a really charming guesthouse in a wonderfully tranquil little village. Its nine highly individual rooms are set around multiple patios and gardens. Room rates include breakfast. The welcoming, multilingual Danish and Italian owners have been here since the 1980s and you couldn't ask for more helpful or knowledgeable hosts, especially when it comes to planning walks in the district.

El Jardín (☎ 689 63 35 29; Calle Escuelas Viejas; open 6pm-10pm Tues-Thur, 1pm-10pm Fri-Sun Semana Santa–late autumn; mains €6.30-7.20) is a British-run vegetarian restaurant with a lovely shady garden, 200m east of Pitres' plaza. The evolving menu ranges from staples like lasagne and stuffed pancakes to exotica such as brie Curaçao, a hard-to-resist combination of brie, tropical fruits and vegetables, red-pepper sauce and coconut.

TREVÉLEZ

postcode 18417 • pop 775
• elevation 1476m

Trevélez, set in a gash in the mountainside almost as impressive as the Poqueira gorge, is famous for three reasons: it's a frequent starting point for ascents of the high Sierra Nevada peaks; it produces some of Spain's best *jamón serrano*, with hams trucked in from far and wide for curing in the dry mountain air; and it's often said to be the highest village in Spain. Other Spanish villages, notably Valdelinares, Aragón, which reaches above 1700m, have better claims to the 'highest' title, but the Trevélez municipality is certainly the highest on the mainland as it includes Mulhacén.

Along the main road you're confronted by a welter of ham and souvenir shops, but an exploration of the upper parts reveals a lively, typically Alpujarran village. La General bank just above the main road has an ATM.

Walking

Aside from routes up Mulhacén and to other Alpujarras villages, Trevélez is also one end of an old pack-animal route over the 2800m Puerto de Trevélez pass to Jerez del Marquesado, (see the Marquesado de Zenete section, earlier in this chapter), 22km northeast. This could be walked in a long day or you could sleep at the staffed **Refugio Postero Alto** (☎ 958 34 51 54) before Jerez.

Places to Stay & Eat

Camping Trevélez (☎ 958 85 87 35; camping per adult/tent/car €3/2.40/2.70; open year-round) is 1km south of Trevélez along the GR-421 towards Busquístar. It's set on a terraced hillside with lots of trees and has ecologically minded owners and a good-value restaurant.

Restaurante González (☎ 958 85 85 31; Plaza Francisco Abellán s/n; singles/doubles/triples €15/25/35; mains €5-9) is by the main road at the foot of the village, with basic rooms in a separate building down a nearby side street. The good-value restaurant serves trout, ham, plato alpujarreño and other local fare.

Hostal Pepe Álvarez (☎ 958 85 85 03; Plaza Francisco Abellán s/n; singles/doubles with bathroom €21/39), just along from Restaurante González, has more comfortable rooms, some with terraces overlooking the busy plaza.

Hostal Fernando (☎ 958 85 85 65; Pista del Barrio Medio s/n; singles/doubles with bathroom €15/25), by the road going up towards the top of the village, is friendly and clean, with just five rooms, most enjoying good views.

Hotel La Fragua (☎ 958 85 86 26; Calle San Antonio 4; singles/doubles with bathroom €19/30) has comfortable rooms but if a walking group decides to clatter forth at 6am, you stand little chance of sleeping through it. The hotel is signposted from Plaza Barrio Medio, above Hostal Fernando.

Mesón La Fragua (mains €5-10), just along the street from Hotel La Fragua, offers relatively exotic fare such as partridge in walnut sauce and fig ice cream, and some good vegetarian dishes as well as

excellent solomillo (pork steaks). Also good is **Mesón Joaquín** (GR-421 western side of village; 3-course menú with wine €7.70), but mind your head on the hanging hams.

Jamón de Trevélez crops up on every menu. If you're tempted to buy some to take away, the shops up in the village tend to be cheaper than those on the main road.

EAST OF TREVÉLEZ

Seven kilometres south of Trevélez the GR-421 crosses the low Portichuelo de Cástaras pass and turns east into a harsher, barer landscape, yet still with oases of greenery around the villages. The central and eastern Alpujarras have their own magic, but see far fewer tourists than the western villages.

From **Juviles**, 12km from Trevélez, you can walk in half an hour to the top of Fuerte, a rocky hill rising east of the village which was its fortress in Muslim times.

Café Bar Pensión Tino (☎ 958 76 91 74; Calle Altillo Bajo 38; singles/doubles €15/27), just off the main road at the southwestern end of Juviles, has seven straightforward but pleasant rooms with bathroom.

Five kilometres further east is **Bérchules**, in a green valley which stretches a long way back into the hills and offers attractive walks.

La Posada (☎ 958 85 25 41; e laposada berchules@wanadoo.es; Plaza del Ayuntamiento 7; B&B per person €15; closed July-Aug) is Bérchules' sturdy 18th-century village inn, adapted by villager Miguel and his wife to provide simple but comfortable lodgings geared to walkers. English is spoken and vegetarian food is available.

Hotel Los Bérchules (☎ 958 85 25 30; Carretera de Bérchules 20; singles/doubles with bathroom €24/36), by the main road at the bottom of Bérchules, has comfier rooms, a good restaurant, English-speaking hosts and a cosy sitting room with a bookcase full of books on Spain.

Cádiar, down by the Río Guadalfeo 8km south of Bérchules, is one of the bigger Alpujarras villages (2000 people). Nearby is perhaps the most charming place to stay in the Alpujarras.

Alquería de Morayma (☎/fax 958 34 32 21; w www.alqueriamorayma.com; double rooms & apartments €50-63, 4-person apartments €78-87), 2km from Cádiar just off the A-348 towards Órgiva, is an old farmstead lovingly renovated and expanded by its *granadino* owners to provide a dozen comfortable and unique rooms and apartments. There's good, moderately priced food, a library of Alpujarras information, great views across the valley towards the mountains, and fascinating art and artefacts everywhere.

Yegen, where Gerald Brenan made his home in the 1920s, is about 12km east of Bérchules along the GR-421. Parts of the valley below Yegen have a particularly moonlike quality. Brenan's house, just off the village square, is marked by a plaque. Several walking routes have been marked out locally including a 2km 'Sendero de Gerald Brenan'.

Café-Bar Nuevo La Fuente *(☎ 958 85 10 67; Calle Real 38; singles/doubles €12/24)*, on Yegen's village square, is a friendly place with eight very clean rooms and leaflets on the walks.

Hostal El Tinao *(☎ 958 85 12 12; rooms €25-30)*, on the main road, has just two rooms (with bathroom) but its new British owners plan to add two more and a public Internet service.

El Rincón de Yegen *(☎ 958 85 12 70; singles/doubles €22/36, 4-person apartments €60)*, above the road at the eastern edge of the village, has Yegen's most comfortable accommodation, as well as a good, medium-priced restaurant.

Válor, 5km northeast of Yegen, was the birthplace of Aben Humeya, leader of the 1568 rebellion, and is the setting for the most celebrated of several Moros y Cristianos (Moors & Christians) festivities in Las Alpujarras, recreating the 1568–70 rebellion. On 14 and 15 September, colourfully costumed 'armies' battle it out noisily on and off from midday to evening.

Hostal Las Perdices *(☎/fax 958 85 18 21; Calle Torrecilla s/n; singles or doubles with bathroom €26)*, in the centre of Válor, has clean, straightforward rooms.

Ugíjar (population 2600), 7km southeast of Válor, is the main market town hereabouts, but for another attractive place to

stay, venture a few kilometres off the Válor-Ugíjar road to the unspoiled village of **Mairena**, on the GR-7 long-distance path and with superb views from its elevated position.

Las Chimeneas *(☎ 958 76 03 52; W www .moebius.es/contourlines; Calle Amargura 6; rooms for up to 3 with breakfast or apartments with kitchen €50-60; dinner €15)* is a Mairena village house renovated in charming, uncluttered style. The helpful young British owners are full of information on the many things to do in the area, offering guided walks, mountain biking, horse riding, painting excursions and camping in the mountains. They serve good dinners using organic local produce. If you're lucky they may be able to pick you up from Granada.

East of Mairena or Ugíjar you encounter the A-337 which heads north over the Sierra Nevada by the 2000m Puerto de la Ragua pass (occasionally snowbound in winter) to La Calahorra (see the Marquesado de Zenete section, earlier). Continuing eastward you soon enter Almería province (see Las Alpujarras in the Almería province chapter, later in this book).

The Coast

Granada's 80km coastline is rugged and cliff-lined, with spectacular views from the coastal N-340 highway as it winds up and down between scattered seaside towns and villages. This coast is called the Costa Tropical because of the hot-climate crops such as sugar cane, custard apples, avocados and mangos that are grown where the coastal plain broadens out a bit. The N-323 from Granada arrives near the coast just west of Motril after threading through an impressive gorge carved by the Río Guadalfeo. East of uninspiring Motril, the mountains often come right down to the sea, but the settlements are mostly drab and the beaches pebbly. If you're driving from the east, a road to Las Alpujarras heads north across the Sierra de la Contraviesa from La Rábita.

West of Motril the terrain is a bit less abrupt and there are a few quite attractive beach towns.

SALOBREÑA
postcode 18680 • pop 10,500
Salobreña's huddle of white houses rises on a crag between the N-340 and the sea, 2km west of the N-323 junction. At the top is an impressive Muslim castle and below is a long and wide dark-sand beach. It's a low-key place for most of the year but jumps in July and August.

Orientation & Information
From the N-340, Avenida Federico García Lorca skirts the eastern and lower part of the town as it heads a kilometre or so south to the seafront. Just 200m along is the helpful **tourist office** (☎ 958 61 03 14; Plaza de Goya; open 9.30am-1.30pm Mon-Sat & 4.30pm-7pm Mon-Fri Nov-May; 9.30am-1.30pm & 4.30pm-7pm daily June-Oct). The Alsina Graells bus stop is diagonally across the street from the tourist office.

Market days are Tuesday and Friday.

Things to See & Do
A 20-minute walk uphill from the tourist office, the **Castillo Árabe** (Arab Castle; admission €2.55 including Museo Arqueológico; Castillo & Museo open 11am-1.30pm & 4pm-7pm Tues-Sun) dates from the 12th century, though the site was fortified as early as the 10th century. The castle was used as a summer residence by the Granada emirs. Legend has it that Emir Mohammed IX had his three daughters, Zaida, Zoraida and Zorahaida, held captive here too; Washington Irving gives a version of this story in Tales of the Alhambra. The inner Alcazaba, a setting for many cultural events, retains much of its Nasrid structure. You can walk along parts of the surrounding parapets. The **Museo Arqueológico** (Plaza del Ayuntamiento), is nearby, in the former town hall, below the church.

Immediately below the castle is the 16th-century Mudejar **Iglesia de Nuestra Señora del Rosario** with a striking arched doorway. The old Muslim town (the original Albayzín and the later Broval and Bóveda districts) spills out below the castle, ending on one side in steep cliffs. There's a **mirador** in the Albayzín and another one on Paseo de las Flores below the castle.

The tourist office offers two-hour guided walking tours (€6) of the old town and its sights on Thursday and Friday (minimum four people).

Special Events
Semana Santa processions through the steep old town streets attract a lot of visitors. The Día de la Cruz (Day of the Cross) on 3 May is a lively, colourful affair with horse riders, polka-dot dresses and sevillana dancing, as in Granada. Salobreña's feria takes place in the last week of June. Around 20 August, the one-day Lucero de Alba features rock and flamenco acts in the castle and elsewhere.

Places to Stay
Pensión Mari Carmen (☎ 958 61 09 06; Calle Nueva 30; singles/doubles with bathroom & TV €10/21) is about a 10-minute uphill walk from Plaza de Goya. It's newly refurbished. There's a communal terrace with great views across the cane fields and out to sea.

Pensión Castell-Mar (☎ 958 61 02 27; Calle Nueva 15; per person €10), a bit lower down the same street, has several rooms with terrace or balcony, some with private bathroom.

Hotel Salambina (☎ 958 61 00 37; doubles €38.50), just west of town on the N-340, has better rooms than Mari Carmen or Castell-Mar, but without the old-world charm.

Hotel Salobreña (☎ 958 61 02 61; N-340; singles/doubles €49/70.50), a couple of kilometres west of and flashier than Hotel Salambina, has 130 comfortable doubles. A big oval-shaped pool and an old watchtower feature in the substantial grounds.

Places to Eat
Restaurante Pesetas (☎ 958 61 01 82; Calle Bóveda s/n; mains €8), a little place on the street below the Iglesia de Nuestra Señora del Rosario, serves good tapas, raciones and meals. There's a terrace.

Restaurante Yusuf (☎ 958 82 82 37; Plaza del Ayuntamiento) is a smart, more upmarket place.

La Bodega (Plaza de Goya; menú €7.25), down by the tourist office, is a popular place and has outdoor tables.

There are loads of restaurants, beach-side eateries *(chiringuitos)* and bars, and a spot of nightlife, on and near the beachfront. **Restaurant El Peñón** *(☎ 958 61 05 38; Paseo Marítimo s/n)* just by the big rock which divides Salobreña's main beach, does good medium-priced seafood. **Bar Sunen**, on the beach opposite Restaurant El Peñón, is a good place to sip a sunset drink.

Getting There & Away
Alsina Graells *(☎ 958 61 25 21)* has plenty of buses along the coast in both directions (€6 to Málaga; €7 to Almería), and at least six daily to Granada (€4.60). There are also daily buses to Lanjarón, Seville, Córdoba, Jaén and Madrid.

ALMUÑÉCAR
postcode 18690 • pop 18,000
Fifteen kilometres west of Salobreña, Almuñécar may appear uninviting but there's an attractive old section around its 16th-century castle. Popular with Spanish tourists and with a growing community of northern Europeans, it's bright and not too expensive, although the beaches are pebbly. Adventure activities from paragliding to diving and hiking are heavily promoted in the area.

History
The Phoenicians set up a colony called Ex or Sex here in the 8th century BC to obtain oil and wine from interior Andalucía for trade. The Roman Sexi Firmum Iulium was founded in 49 BC. It was here that Abd ar-Rahman I arrived from Damascus in AD 755, going on to found the Muslim emirate of Córdoba. Later, the town served as a coastal fortress for the Granada emirate. And it was from Almuñécar that Granada's last emir, Boabdil, with 1130 supporters, finally abandoned Spain for North Africa in 1493.

Orientation & Information
The **bus station** *(☎ 958 63 01 40; Avenida Juan Carlos I No 1)* is just south of the N-340. Plaza de la Constitución, the main square of the old part of town, is a few minutes walk southwest, with little Plaza de la Rosa a few minutes further southeast. The **tourist office**

(☎ 958 63 11 25; Avenida de Europa; open 10am-2pm & 6pm-9pm daily June-Sept; 10am-2pm & 4pm-7pm daily Oct-May) is at the other end of town in the neo-Mudejar Palacete de La Najarra, just back from the eastern end of Playa de San Cristóbal.

Almuñécar's beachfront is divided by a rocky outcrop, the Peñón del Santo, with Playa de San Cristóbal, the best of the beaches, to the west, and Playa Puerta del Mar to the east. Further east is the separate Playa de Velilla with lots of apartment blocks, but quite a good beach.

Things to See
Just behind Playa de San Cristóbal is a tropical bird aviary, the **Parque Ornitológico Loro-Sexi** *(adult/child €2/1.40; open 11am-2pm & 4pm-7pm daily)*. The top of the hill just inland is occupied by the **Castillo de San Miguel** *(admission €2 including Museo Arqueológico; Castillo & Museo open 10am-12.30pm & 7pm-10pm Tues-Sun July–mid-Sept; 10.30am-1.30pm & 4pm-7pm Tues-Sat, 10.30am-2pm Sun mid-Sept–June)*, built by the conquering Christians over Muslim and Roman fortifications. The climb up through narrow streets to the entrance (on the northern side) is well worthwhile: the castle commands excellent views and contains a museum which has displays that add up to a quick history of Almuñécar. The **Museo Arqueológico** *(Calle Málaga)* is in 1st-century Roman galleries called the Cueva de Siete Palacios. The museum has local Phoenician, Roman and Islamic finds plus a rare 3500-year-old Egyptian amphora, probably brought by the Carthaginians. One hundred metres along Avenida de Europa from the tourist office, in the Parque Botánico El Majuelo, is the **Factoría de Salazones de Pescado**, the remains of a Carthaginian and Roman fish-salting workshop.

Further afield, off Avenida del Mediterráneo about a 1.8km walk west of the old town, is the **Necrópolis Puente de Noy**, a Phoenician and Roman cemetery, where over 200 tombs have been excavated. Out near the N-340 are several lengths of **Roman aqueduct**.

GRANADA PROVINCE

Activities
You can windsurf, dive, ride a horse, walk, run or cycle in and around Almuñécar. The tourist office's leaflet *Turismo Deportivo* details relevant companies.

Places to Stay
Camping Carambolo (☎ 958 63 03 22; *Carretera N-340, Km 315; camping 2 people with tent & car €24*) is east of the centre on the main highway.

Budget *hostales* are in the streets between the bus station and Plaza de la Rosa.

Hostal Plaza Damasco (☎ 958 63 01 65; *Calle Cerrajeros 16; singles/doubles with bathroom & TV €22/42*) is a good 18-room place in a distinctive neo-Muslim building.

Hotel Goya (☎ 958 63 05 50; *Avenida de Europa 31; singles/doubles with bathroom €25/44*), opposite the tourist office, has bright and spacious rooms.

Hotel Casablanca (☎ 958 63 55 75; *Plaza San Cristóbal 4; singles/doubles with bathroom €36/54*) is almost on Playa de San Cristóbal, opposite the monument to Abd ar-Rahman I. It has 35 spacious, quite attractive rooms, and a good restaurant.

Hotel Altamar (☎ 958 63 03 46; *Calle Alta del Mar 21; doubles €48*), with good rooms, is above a cybercafé, 15m north of Plaza de la Rosa.

Hotel California (☎ 958 88 10 38; w *www.hotelcaliforniaspain.com; Carretera N-340 Km 313; singles/doubles €33/48; closed Jan*) is run by a friendly young English/Belgian couple. Its bar, lounge and restaurant, overlooking the town and sea, are decorated with colourful Andalucian/Moroccan furnishings. The 10 rooms come with bathroom, TV and private balcony. The Belgian owner is an experienced paraglider; accommodation/flying packages are available.

Places to Eat
Plaza de la Constitución has a few popular restaurants with tables outside.

Bodega Francisco (*Calle Real 15; menú €6*), between Plaza de la Constitución and Plaza de la Rosa, is a typical bar with a long tapas list.

Just east of Plaza de la Rosa is Plaza Kelibia, which has several bars with tables on the square: **La Trastienda** (*Plaza Kelibia*) serves a generous tapa with your drink. Their wonderful salmon and cheese canapes (€3.20) come with a delicious salad.

Directly south of Plaza de la Rosa, Acera del Mar has a line of eateries facing Playa Puerta del Mar.

La Galería (☎ 958 63 41 18; *Paseo Puerta del Mar 3; menú €15*) is run by a talented, young Belgian chef. A tangy appetiser appears unsolicited. The menu includes various fish dishes (€11 to €17.50) and even snails (€7.25 a half-dozen).

Or you could head for the restaurants opposite Playa de San Cristóbal: **Restaurant Hotel Casablanca** (*see Places to Stay; menú €5.71*), with tables on the square at the eastern end of Paseo de los Flores, does good meat dishes.

Hotel California (*See Places to Stay; mains €7*) offers tasty dishes and vegetarian options. Expect something different here.

Entertainment
Plaza Kelibia and Acera del Mar buzz at night.

Auditorio Martín Recuerda (*Calle Puerta de Granada*), in the Casa de la Cultura, hosts musical events, theatre, poetry readings and a cine club.

Venta Luciano (☎ 958 63 13 79; *Carretera Suspiro del Moro*), 3km north of Almuñécar, has a barbecue followed by a flamenco show (€24) at 8pm on Friday. Reservations are essential.

Getting There & Away
Several buses a day run along the coast to Nerja, Málaga and Almería, and inland to Granada. There's also one bus each to Lanjarón, Orgiva, Jaén and Úbeda, and two to Seville. There is a direct service to/from Madrid (€12.47; five hours).

If you're driving to or from Granada, consider going by the Carretera del Suspiro del Moro, a spectacular road across the mountains to the Puerto del Suspiro del Moro on the N-323 Granada–Motril road, via Otívar.

MARINA DEL ESTE

West of Almuñecar, the N-340 winds between the mountains and the coast for 7km to La Herradura. Shortly before La Herradura is the turn-off to Marina del Este on the Punta de la Mona promontory. The 4km access road winds uphill then descends steeply to the coast and the beautiful marina, which has lost the exclusive feel it originally had. It was backed by a hillside covered in tall eucalypts. Now, the whole hillside is urbanised and the elegant gums have gone.

One dive outfit remains. **Buceo La Herradura** (☎ 958 82 70 83; W www.buceola herradura.com) charges around €40 for a dive including the boat and equipment, or €360 for a four-day PADI course.

El Barco (mains €12-16; open noon-4pm daily) does excellent seafood. **Barlovento** (fish mains €8-16.50) is at least as good.

LA HERRADURA

postcode 18697 • pop 1900

The little resort town of La Herradura attracts paragliders from far and wide for the thermals that rise around the hills backing its pretty, horseshoe-shaped bay, and is popular locally for water sports (it has a windsurfing school and several dive outfits) and seafront restaurants. Its sheltered beach is packed during July and August. In January the town hosts the Andrés Segovia international classical guitar competition.

Orientation & Information

The Alsina Graells bus stop is at the top of Calle Acera del Pilar, right by the N-340. Calle Acera del Pilar heads south to the seafront Paseo Andrés Segovia, also called Paseo Marítimo, which runs right along the bay. There's a **tourist information kiosk** (open 10am-2pm & 4pm-6pm Mon-Fri, 11am-2pm Sat) at this junction. The town, with a few shops and services, spills down the gentle slope between the N-340 and the beach, and along Paseo Andrés Segovia. On this street, head to **Windsurf La Herradura** (☎ 958 64 01 43) for windsurfer/canoe/dinghy rentals (€9/9/18 an hour). Dive out-

fits include **Granada Sub** (☎ 958 64 02 81) and **Mar Azul** (☎ 958 64 06 18).

Places to Stay

Two camping grounds, **Camping La Herradura** (☎ 958 64 00 56; Paseo Andrés Segovia; camping 2 adults, tent & car €13.25) and **Nuevo Camping La Herradura** (☎ 958 64 06 34; Paseo Andrés Segovia; camping 2 adults, tent & car €17), are opposite the beach.

Hostal Peña Parda (☎ 958 64 00 66; Paseo Andrés Segovia 65; doubles with bathroom €48), with basic rooms at the western end of the beach, and **Hostal La Caleta** (☎ 958 82 70 07; Paseo Andrés Segovia; doubles with bathroom €60-72), towards the eastern end, both have good restaurants.

Hotel Sol Los Fenicios (☎ 958 82 79 00; Paseo Andrés Segovia; doubles €119), a few doors east of Hostal La Caleta, has better rooms, with terrace or balcony, set around an interior patio.

Places to Eat

Most restaurants on Paseo Andrés Segovia serve good food at reasonable prices, though they mark up drinks. The following are all along the eastern half of the beachfront.

Casa Antonio & Evelyn (closed Thur) has a mixed menu; try one of their excellent soups, or jabalí (wild boar).

Café Luciano (open from 1pm) is a relaxed and eccentric place (newspaper decorates the ceiling) to linger over a coffee.

Mesón El Tinao (☎ 958 82 74 88; Edificio Bahía II; mains €11-20; closed Mon) prepares excellent Alpujarras food and a few unusual dishes like duck with raspberries.

El Chambao de Joaquín (☎ 958 64 00 44; weekend paella & drink €5.70), with a beachside garden, is at the far eastern end of the beach. Paella is dished out from a giant pan at 2.30pm every Saturday and Sunday. You need to book for Sunday.

Getting There & Away

Plenty of Alsina Graells buses head east and west along the coast and a few go to Granada.

GRANADA PROVINCE

Jaén Province

There are two special reasons to venture on from Granada or Córdoba to the comparatively isolated province of Jaén (ha-**en**). One is the Parque Natural de Cazorla, perhaps the most beautiful of all Andalucía's mountain regions. The other is a wonderful Renaissance architectural heritage that owes its richness and style to a master of classical architecture, Andrés de Vandelvira. The best examples are to be found in Úbeda and Baeza, as well as the capital city, Jaén. These main features apart, the province has numerous villages and tucked-away places that do not see many visitors, yet which have great charm and interest.

The Jaén landscape alternates between impressive mountain ranges and a rolling agricultural *campiña* (countryside under cultivation) covered with olive trees. The Río Guadalquivir rises among the Cazorla mountains, then flows west across the province. The Desfiladero de Despeñaperros pass – a gap in the Sierra Morena on Jaén's northern border – has, from time immemorial, been the most important northern gateway to Andalucía.

JAÉN
postcode 23080 • pop 113,000
• elevation 575m

The provincial capital, set among rugged mountains and olive groves, is a likable, busy and fairly lively place with plenty to keep you interested for a day or two.

Castile's Fernando III ('El Santo', the Saint) took Jaén from the emirate of Granada after a siege in 1246. Fernando agreed to respect the emirate's frontiers in return for tribute of half the emir's annual income. But in the 15th century the Catholic Monarchs made Jaén a base for their successful final war against the Granada emirate. Centuries of decline set in after the Reconquista (Reconquest), with many *jiennenses* emigrating to Spanish colonies – hence the existence of other Jaéns in Peru, the Philippines and elsewhere. Only since the 1960s has Jaén seen

Highlights

- Lose yourself amid the exquisite Renaissance architecture of Úbeda and Baeza
- Explore the ruggedly beautiful Parque Natural de Cazorla, a haven for wildlife, with excellent walking among craggy mountains and green river valleys
- Sample city life in down-to-earth Jaén and merge with the rural bustle of the town of Cazorla
- Visit impressive Muslim and Reconquista castles at Jaén, Baños de la Encina, Cazorla and Segura de la Sierra

much growth. The opening of a university in 1993 helped enliven the city.

Orientation

Old Jaén, with narrow, winding streets, huddles around the foot of Cerro de Santa Catalina, the wooded, castle-crowned hill above the western side of the city. Jaén's monumental cathedral is near the southern end of the old city. From here, Calle de Bernabé Soriano leads northeast and downhill to Plaza de la Constitución, the focal point of the newer part of the city, complete with metal palm trees that light up at night.

From Plaza de la Constitución, Calle Roldán y Marín, soon becoming Paseo de la

JAÉN PROVINCE

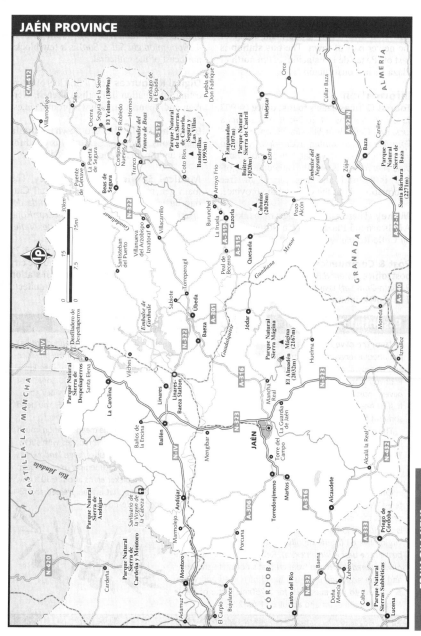

Estación, heads northwest to the **train station** 1km away. This is the main artery of the newer part of town. The **bus station** is east off Paseo de la Estación, 250m north of Plaza de la Constitución.

Information

Tourist Offices Jaén's **tourist office** (☎ 953 19 04 55, fax 953 24 26 24; e ot@jaenanda lucia.org; Calle de la Maestra 13; open 10am-7pm Mon-Fri in winter, 10am-8pm Mon-Fri in summer, 10am-1pm Sat, Sun & public holidays year round) is near the cathedral. The office is helpful and has plenty of free information about the city and the province.

Money There's no shortage of banks or ATMs around Plaza de la Constitución and on Calle Roldán y Marín.

Post & Communications The city's **main post office** (open 8.30am-8.30pm Mon-Fri, 9.30am-2pm Sat) is at Plaza de los Jardinillos. The **Cu@k internet centre** (Melchor Cobo Medina; €1.50 for 1 hour; open 10.30am-3pm & 5pm-1am Mon-Fri, 11am-3pm & 4.30pm-midnight Sat & Sun) is a few blocks northeast of the cathedral.

Digital Resources You'll find lots of interesting information in English, French, German and Spanish on w www.promojaen.es.

Bookshops In the old town, **Librería Metrópolis** (Calle del Cerón 17) is good for maps and Spanish-language guidebooks.

Medical Services & Emergency The main general hospital is the **Hospital Ciudad de Jaén** (☎ 953 29 90 00; Avenida del Ejército Español). The **Red Cross** (Cruz Roja; ☎ 953 25 15 40; Plaza Sta. Maridel Valle) provides emergency advice.

The **Policía Municipal station** (☎ 953 21 91 05; Carrera de Jesús) is just behind the city hall. There is also a **Policía Nacional station** (☎ 953 26 18 50), on Calle del Arquitecto Berges.

Essential Oil

In Jaén, the olive (aceituna) rules. You can smell the astringent odour of olive oil (aceite de oliva) just about everywhere you go. Over 40 million olive trees (olivos) stud the rolling hills of the province and occupy almost every scrap of fertile land. A third of Jaén province – more than 4500 sq km – is devoted to olive groves (olivares). In an average year these trees produce 900,000 tonnes of olives, most of which are turned into some 200,000 tonnes of olive oil. Thus, Jaén provides about half of Andalucía's olive oil, one-third of Spain's and 10% of that used in the entire world. You need some of the best Verde Mágina virgen extra oil just to digest those statistics.

The olives are harvested from late November to January. Though there's some mechanisation, much is still done traditionally by spreading nets beneath the trees, then beating the branches with sticks. The majority of Jaén's (and Andalucía's) olive groves are owned by a handful of large landowners and the dominance of this one crop in the province's economy means that unemployment in Jaén rises from 10% during the harvest to around 45% in summer. An olive picker earns about €30 a day.

Once harvested, olives are taken to oil mills to be mashed into a pulp that is then pressed and filtered. Modern machinery and stainless-steel vats have replaced mule-driven presses that once squeezed the oil through esparto-grass mats. Oil that is considered good enough for immediate consumption is sold as virgin olive oil (aceite de oliva virgen), the finest grade (the best of the best is virgen extra). Refined olive oil (aceite de oliva refinado) is made from oil that's not quite so good, and plain aceite de oliva is a blend of refined and virgin oil. Expect to pay about €5 for a 750mL bottle of Verde Mágina virgen extra and about €11 for 2.5L.

NICK KELLY

Cathedral

Jaén's huge cathedral *(open 8.30am-1pm & 4pm-7pm Mon-Sat in winter; 8.30am-1pm & 5pm-8pm Mon-Sat rest of year; 8.30am-1.30pm & 5pm-7pm Sun & holidays year-round)* was built mostly in the 16th and 17th centuries, and mainly to the designs of Andrés de Vandelvira, on the site of Muslim Jaén's main mosque. Its highlight is the superb twin-towered **southwestern facade** *(Plaza de Santa María)*, which is more baroque than Renaissance and features an array of 17th-century statuary, much of it by Sevilla's Pedro Roldán.

The interior of the cathedral is cavernous and gloomy, but the clusters of soaring Corinthian columns lend it great power and the choir stalls display beautiful carving. Directly behind the main altar, the **Capilla Mayor** *(Capilla del Santo Rostro)* houses the Reliquia del Santo Rostro de Cristo, a cloth with an image of Christ's face, with which St Veronica is believed to have wiped Christ's face on the road to Calvary. The Reliquia is said to have been carried to Jaén from Constantinople in the 14th century. It is contained behind glass and is kept in a strongbox. A painting of the cloth replaced the original during the Napoleonic Wars. Both painting and cloth were stolen during the Spanish Civil War and (ironically, considering previous Napoleonic fears) later turned up hidden in a garage outside Paris. On Fridays at 11.30am and 5pm long queues of the faithful assemble to kiss the cloth. You can visit the **Museo Catedral** *(Cathedral Museum; admission €3; open 10am-1pm & 5pm-7pm Mon-Sat, 10am-1.30pm & 6pm-7pm Sun)* in the mausoleum beneath the chapter house for an excess of religious art and artefacts, including some fine baroque-period paintings and Renaissance sculpture.

Palacio de Villardompardo

This handsome Renaissance palace *(☎ 953 23 62 92; Plaza de Santa Luisa de Marillac)*, 500m northwest of the cathedral, houses two museums and what's claimed to be the largest Islamic bathhouse open to visitors in Spain. All three sections are closed on holidays. Admission is free to all nationalities with a passport or national identity card. There are pamphlets, in French and English, giving some information on the baths and the museums.

The complex is Jaén's most rewarding attraction and is one of the most intriguing collections of artefacts and archaeological remains to be found under one roof in Andalucía. There are even traces of Roman stonework, cleverly displayed beneath a glass floor. The initial gallery of the complex has a fascinating display of black-and-white photographs of people at work in rural Jaén of the early 20th century and earlier.

The **Baños Árabes** *(Arab Baths; open 9am-8pm Tues-Fri, 9.30am-2.30pm Sat & Sun)*, in the bowels of the building, are beautified by horseshoe arches and star-shaped skylights. Their most impressive section is the temperate room *(sala templada)*. Built in the 11th century, then turned into a tannery by the Christians, the baths disappeared in the 16th century when the Conde de Villardompardo built a palace over the site. They were rediscovered in 1913.

The **Museo Internacional de Arte Naïf** *(International Museum of Naïf Art; open 9am-8pm Tues-Fri, 9.30am-2.30pm Sat & Sun)*, opened in 1988, is the only museum in Spain devoted to this very colourful, perspective-free school of painting. It is a remarkably cheering experience to wander through the numerous salons past scores of such brilliantly coloured, lucid and witty paintings. The work and collection of the museum's founder, Manuel Moral, a native of Jaén province, forms the basis of the display. Village life and the countryside are constant themes: the paintings from Haiti are the most vivid.

The **Museo de Artes y Costumbres Populares** *(Museum of Popular Art & Customs; open 9am-8pm Tues-Fri, 9.30am-2.30pm Sat & Sun)* is devoted to pre-industrial Jaén province. The displays are spread over a basement and three floors and you may become pleasantly lost for a while. Rural crafts, old wagons and carts, and fine 19th-century clothes are the most eye-catching items.

Iglesia de la Magdalena

Jaén's oldest church is on Calle Santo Domingo, a short walk west of the Palacio de Villardompardo. Originally a mosque, it has a Gothic main facade and interior. Its tower is the mosque's minaret, reworked in the 16th century. Keeping a low profile, you can enter the church daily during mass, usually from 6pm to 8pm. The outstanding internal feature is the retable. Behind the church is a lovely Islamic courtyard with Roman tombstones and a pool used for ritual ablutions in Muslim times.

Iglesia de San Ildefonso

The 'home church' *(Plaza de San Ildefonso; open 8.30am-noon & 6pm-9pm daily)* of Jaén's patron saint, the Virgen de la Capilla, stands 200m northeast of the cathedral, after which it is the second-largest church in the city. San Ildefonso was founded in the 13th century, but has been remodelled several times. An inscription on the bottom (northeastern) end of its exterior marks the spot where the Virgin is believed to have appeared on 10 June 1430. Her much-venerated image stands in a special chapel.

Museo Provincial

Jaén's Provincial Museum *(Paseo de la Estación 27; admission €1, EU citizen free; open 3pm-8pm Tues, 9am-8pm Wed-Sat, 9am-3pm Sun)* has an excellent archaeological collection covering the cultures of Jaén province from pre–3000 BC hunter-gatherers to Muslim times. The highlight is a room of fine 5th-century-BC Iberian sculpture from Porcuna, showing a clear Greek influence in the fluidity of their forms. The museum is closed on public holidays.

Castillo de Santa Catalina

Undoubtedly in Jaén's most spectacular location, this former Muslim fortress *(admission free; open 10am-2pm & 3.30pm-6pm Thur-Tues)* is perched atop the cliff-girt Cerro de Santa Catalina, the high hill that towers above the city. If you don't have a vehicle for the circuitous 4km drive up from the city centre, you can take a taxi (€6) or walk (about 40 minutes from the city centre) by heading

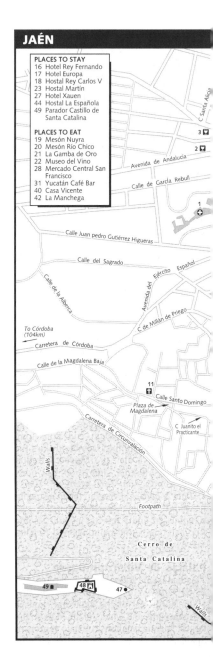

JAÉN

PLACES TO STAY
16 Hotel Rey Fernando
17 Hotel Europa
18 Hostal Rey Carlos V
23 Hostal Martín
27 Hotel Xauen
44 Hostal La Española
49 Parador Castillo de Santa Catalina

PLACES TO EAT
19 Mesón Nuyra
20 Mesón Río Chico
21 La Gamba de Oro
22 Museo del Vino
28 Mercado Central San Francisco
31 Yucatán Café Bar
40 Casa Vicente
42 La Manchega

JAÉN

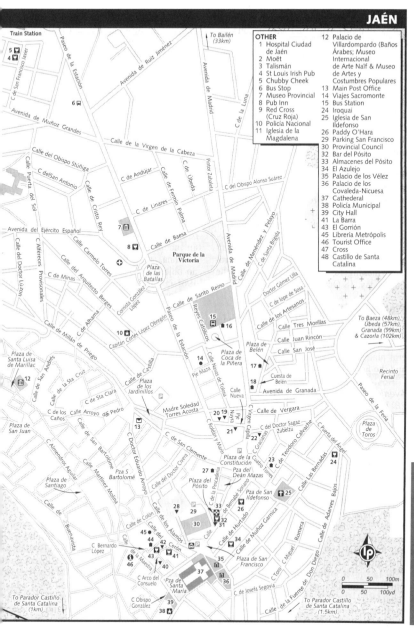

OTHER
1 Hospital Ciudad de Jaén
2 Moët
3 Talismán
4 St Louis Irish Pub
5 Chubby Cheek
6 Bus Stop
7 Museo Provincial
8 Pub Inn
9 Red Cross (Cruz Roja)
10 Policía Nacional
11 Iglesia de la Magdalena
12 Palacio de Villardompardo (Baños Árabes; Museo Internacional de Arte Naïf & Museo de Artes y Costumbres Populares
13 Main Post Office
14 Viajes Sacromonte
15 Bus Station
24 Iroquai
25 Iglesia de San Ildefonso
26 Paddy O'Hara
29 Parking San Francisco
30 Provincial Council
32 Bar del Pósito
33 Almacenes del Pósito
34 El Azulejo
35 Palacio de los Vélez
36 Palacio de los Covaleda-Nicuesa
37 Cathedral
38 Policía Municipal
39 City Hall
41 La Barra
43 El Gorrión
45 Librería Metrópolis
46 Tourist Office
47 Cross
48 Castillo de Santa Catalina

JAÉN PROVINCE

uphill from the Cathedral to join Calle de Buenavista. Go up right and at a junction with Carretera de Circunvalación, cross over; a short distance along to the right, take the path that heads off steeply uphill to the left.

Inside the castle you can check out the keep, a chapel and some underground water tanks.

Past the castle at the end of the ridge stands a large cross from where there are magnificent views over the city and the olive groves beyond.

Special Events

Semana Santa (Holy Week) is celebrated in a big way, with processions through the old city by members of 13 brotherhoods *(cofradías)*. The week climaxes in the early hours of Good Friday. Jaén's biggest party is the Feria y Fiestas de San Lucas, with concerts, funfairs, bullfights and general merrymaking for about 10 days up to the saint's day, 18 October.

Places to Stay

From May to October mosquitoes can be a nuisance in Jaén hotels, especially the cheaper ones; arm yourself. Prices in several places rise a bit during Semana Santa and the Feria y Fiestas de San Lucas.

Hostal Rey Carlos V *(☎ 953 22 20 91; Avenida de Madrid 4; singles/doubles €18/ 28)* has basic rooms and there can be noise from the busy street outside. However, it's handy for the bus station and is still quite close to the centre.

Hostal Martín *(☎ 953 24 36 78; Calle Cuatro Torres 5; singles/doubles €16/25)*, in a narrow street just east of Plaza de la Constitución, has basic but adequate rooms.

Hostal La Española *(☎ 953 23 02 54; Calle Bernardo López 9; singles/doubles €18/26, doubles with shower & toilet €30- 32)* is near the cathedral at the heart of the old town and has a grimly gothic interior that includes a creaking spiral staircase. Add to this a loftily indifferent welcome, plus drab furnishings, and you've got real 'character', if that's what you're after.

Hotel Europa *(☎ 953 22 27 00;* [e] *pem ana@ofijaen.com; Plaza de Belén 1; singles/*

doubles €34/57.50) has bright, modern rooms with air-con, TV and bathroom. It also has a garage.

Hotel Xauen *(☎ 953 24 07 89;* [e] *cliente@ hotelxauen.com; Plaza del Deán Mazas 3; singles/doubles €40.65/52.45)*, just off Plaza de la Constitución, is also good and more central than Hotel Europa. Rooms here have air-con, TV and bathroom. It has a restaurant where breakfast is €3 and evening meal €8.

Hotel Rey Fernando *(☎ 953 25 18 40, fax 953 26 51 22; Plaza de Coca de la Piñera 5; singles/doubles €48/61)*, next to the bus station, has comfortable rooms and an interestingly lavish decor.

Parador Castillo de Santa Catalina *(☎ 953 23 00 00, fax 953 23 09 30;* [e] *jaen@ parador.es; singles/doubles €93.50/115)* has an incomparable site atop Cerro de Santa Catalina, and is the place to stay if money is no object and you have a vehicle. Built in 1965 in imitation of the castle next door, the parador has spacious, comfortable rooms, a pool and Islamic-style decorative touches.

Places to Eat

Several of the atmospheric old bars on Calles Cerón, Arco del Consuelo and Bernardo López, near the cathedral, serve tapas and *raciones* (meal-sized servings of tapas). One such place is **La Manchega** *(☎ 953 23 21 92; Bernardo López 12; platos combinados €4)*, which also does breakfast coffee and toasted rolls for €1 to €1.50.

Casa Vicente *(Calle Francisco Martín Mora; menú €30)*, near La Manchega in a restored mansion with patio, is one of the best restaurants in town. Its specialities are pork and venison.

Yucatán Café Bar *(Calle de Bernabé Soriano; platos combinados up to €5.45)* isn't a bad place for breakfast at €2.50. It serves sandwiches and hamburgers for around €2.

Short Calle Nueva, off Calle Roldán y Marín, has several good places to eat and drink, including **Mesón Río Chico** *(☎ 953 24 08 02; Calle Nueva 2; menú €8)*, a top choice, is very popular. The downstairs *taberna* serves delicious tapas and *raciones* of meat, *revueltos* (scrambled-egg dishes)

The rolling fields of Jaén province are speckled with over 40 million olive trees

Autumn colours, Jaén province

Minding the flock in rural Andalucía

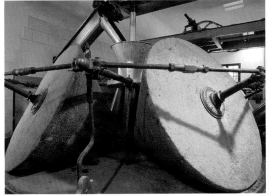

Olive oil is pressing business in Jaén province

Although Cabo de Gata (Almería province) is the driest place in Europe, it supports abundant flora

Two old amigos watch the day go by

Mini Hollywood, Almería province

Rustic windmill, Cabo de Gata, Almería province

and fish from €7 to €12 and various salads from €6 to €7.50. There is a more expensive restaurant upstairs.

La Gamba de Oro *(Calle Nueva 5; raciones €3-6)* is just along the street and is a terrific seafood place for this far inland. There are baskets underfoot for discarded shells, and a selection of fried fish costs €4 to €8.

Mesón Nuyra *(☎ 953 27 31 31; fish & meat mains €10.80-13.25)*, downstairs in Pasaje Nuyra, a passageway off Calle Nueva, is a bit more formal. Salads cost between €7.80 and €9.

Museo del Vino *(☎ 953 24 26 88; Calle del Doctor Sagaz Zubelzu 4; mains from €9)* is another good taberna-cum-restaurant establishment and, as its name suggests, has good wines.

You can buy almost any type of fresh food at the large, modern **Mercado Central San Francisco** *(Calle de los Álamos)*.

Entertainment

Jaén stages numerous, and excellent, cultural events featuring local and national performers at various venues. The tourist office has monthly programmes of concerts, dance, film and theatre performances.

For general socialising, several atmospheric old bars are clustered just northwest of the cathedral on Calle Cerón and narrow Calles Arco del Consuelo and Bernardo López. Among them are **La Barra** *(Calle Cerón 7)*, **El Gorrión** *(Calle de Arco del Consuelo 7)* and **La Manchega**, with entrances on both Calle de Arco del Consuelo and Calle Bernardo López. These last two have both been in action since the 1880s. Several of the establishments on Calle Nueva (see Places to Eat) are also excellent if you are on a tapas tour.

Bar del Pósito *(Plaza del Pósito 10)* is an entertaining place on the pleasant little square off Calle de Bernabé Soriano. It's a regular hangout for Jaén's cultural movers and you may even be buttonholed by the odd poet reciting quite serious stuff in several languages. **El Azulejo** bar *(Calle de Hurtado 8)* is another place with good atmosphere.

For a bit more action, **Iroquai** *(☎ 953 24 36 74; Calle de Adarves Bajos 53)* usually has live rock, blues, flamenco or fusion on Thursdays (look out for its posters) and plays good recorded music other nights. It also has an entrance on Calle Las Bernardas.

Paddy O'Hara *(Calle de Bernabé Soriano 30)* has the trappings of all trans-national Irish bars and the Irish beers to go with it, but any Irish music is likely to be piped pop-folk. It does good tapas to make up for it.

The main nightlife zone is farther away, towards the train station and university, whose students add some zip to the bar life. **Pub Inn** *(Paseo de la Estación 23)*, **Moët** *(Avenida de Andalucía 10)*, **Talismán** *(Avenida de Muñoz Grandes 5)*, **St Louis Irish Pub** *(Calle de San Francisco Javier 5)* and the very popular **Chubby Cheek** *(☎ 953 27 38 19; Calle de San Francisco Javier 7)*, which is more appealing to an older set and has live jazz most weeks, are all places where you'll find a lively scene towards the end of the week.

Shopping

The main shopping areas focus on Calle Roldán y Marín, Paseo de la Estación and Calle de San Clemente (off Plaza de la Constitución). Jaén's trademark olive oil can be bought at **Almacenes del Pósito** *(Plaza del Pósito)*, where a 750ml bottle of Verde Mágina *virgen extra* costs about €5 and 2.5 litres €11. A big flea market *(mercadillo)* is held on Thursday mornings at the **Recinto Ferial** *(Avenida de Granada)*, northeast of Plaza de la Constitución.

Getting There & Away

Bus From the **bus station** *(☎ 953 25 01 06; Plaza de Coca de la Piñera)*, Alsina Graells runs 11 or more daily buses to Granada (€5.90, 1½ hours), seven or more to Baeza (€2.90, 45 minutes) and Úbeda (€3.60, 1¼ hours), and buses to Cazorla (€6.15, two hours) at noon and 4.30pm. The Ureña line travels up to eight times daily to Córdoba and three times to Seville. Other buses head for Guadix, Málaga, Almería, Madrid, Valencia, Barcelona and many smaller places in Jaén province.

Train Jaén **train station** *(☎ 953 27 02 02)* is at the end of a branch line and there are only four departures most days. One train leaves at 8am for Córdoba (€7.45, 1½ hours), Seville (€14.10, three hours) and Cádiz (€21.15, 4¾ hours). Three go to Madrid.

Car & Motorcycle Jaén is 92km north of Granada by the fast N-323. This road continues to Bailén where it meets the Córdoba–Madrid N-IV. To get to or from Córdoba, take the A-306 via Porcuna.

Viajes Sacromonte (☎ 953 22 22 12; *Paseo de la Estación 12*), in the Pasaje Maza arcade, is a car-rental agent as well as a general travel agent. **Avis** (☎ 953 28 09 37; *Avenida de Madrid*) and **Atesa** (☎ 953 28 16 40; *Calle Ortega Nieto 9*) have local offices.

Getting Around

There's a **bus stop** (*Paseo de la Estación*) south of the train station: bus No 1 will take you to Plaza de la Constitución, the central point for all city buses, for €1.

Driving in Jaén can be stressful for strangers to the city. If you end up in the centre, there is underground parking at Plaza de la Constitución and at Parking San Francisco, off Calle de Bernabé Soriano near the cathedral. Costs are €0.80 per hour or €10 for 24 hours.

Taxis gather on Plaza de la Constitución, Plaza de San Francisco, near the cathedral, and at the bus and train stations. Call **Radio Taxis** (☎ 953 22 22 22).

THE NORTHWEST

The N-IV Córdoba–Madrid highway slices across the northwest of Jaén province. If you're travelling this way there are a few places, not far off the highway, that are worth a visit.

Parque Natural Sierra de Andújar

This 740-sq-km natural park north of Andújar is claimed to have the biggest expanses of natural vegetation in the Sierra Morena. Evergreen oaks grow in sunny areas, gall oaks in shady ones, and the park is home to plenty of bull-breeding ranches and a few wolves, lynx and boars, plus deer, mouflon and various birds of prey. Information is available from the **Centro de Visitantes**

(☎ 953 54 90 30), at Km 12 on the road from Andújar to the Santuario de la Virgen de la Cabeza, and from Andújar's **tourist office** (☎ 953 50 49 59; *Plaza de Santa María*).

The **Santuario de la Virgen de la Cabeza**, within the park and a 31km drive north of Andújar, is a 13th-century shrine, now largely rebuilt after an eight-month siege by Republicans in the civil war. It's the scene of one of Spain's biggest religious events, the Romería de la Virgen de la Cabeza, on the last Sunday of April. Half a million people converge to witness a small statue of the Virgin Mary – known as **La Morenita** (The Little Brown One) – being carried around the Cerro del Cabezo for about four hours from about 11am. It's a festive, emotive occasion: children and items of clothing are passed over the crowd to priests who touch them to the Virgin's mantle.

The small **Hotel la Mirada** (☎ 953 54 91 11; *doubles* €40) and **Pensión Virgen de la Cabeza** (☎ 953 12 21 65; €32), both near the sanctuary, could be bases for exploring the park at normal times of year. There's also a range of accommodation in Andújar.

At least four buses a day run from Jaén to Andújar and there are buses from Andújar to the sanctuary on Saturday and Sunday.

Baños de la Encina

One of Andalucía's finest Muslim castles dominates the quiet ridge-top town of Baños de la Encina, a few kilometres north of unexciting Bailén.

Built in 967 on the orders of the Cordoban caliph Al-Hakim II, the oval castle has 14 wall towers and a large keep entered through a double horseshoe arch. It fell to the Christians in 1212 just after the battle of Las Navas de Tolosa. Tourist information – and the key to the castle – are available at the 16th-century **town hall** (☎ 953 61 30 04; *Plaza de la Constitución; open 9am-1pm Mon-Fri*) on the village's main square. The interior of the castle has an unprotected parapet encircling the walls that is definitely not for the uncertain. Several mansions and churches – including the Ermita del Cristo del Llano, with spectacular rococo decoration almost reminiscent of the Alhambra – make a ramble through Baños' old streets worthwhile. The **Restaurante Mirasierra** *(Calle Bailen 6)* does good fish and meat dishes for €6 to €8.

PARQUE NATURAL SIERRA MÁGINA & HUELMA

This little-visited natural park, prominently visible from the Jaén–Granada and Jaén–Baeza roads and crossed by the A-301 south of Úbeda, is full of rugged mountains and topped by Mágina (2167m), the highest peak in Jaén province. There are a number of marked walking trails in the park. In autumn the area is famous for its wild mushrooms, of which 300 kinds grow here. The **Centro de Visitantes** *(☎ 953 78 76 56; open 6pm-8pm Thur & Fri, 10am-2pm & 6pm-8pm Sat & Sun)* is in the castle at Jódar, northeast of the park.

The small town of Huelma, in the southern foothills, is one base for a visit. It has an old quarter of typically Muslim narrow winding streets, and its ruined castle remained in Muslim hands till 1438, much later than places not far north such as Jaén and Baeza.

Andrés de Vandelvira and Diego de Siloé both had a hand in the design of the nearby **Iglesia de la Inmaculada**.

Hostal Marce *(☎ 953 39 10 06; Calle Santa Ana 17; doubles with bathroom around €18)* is an accommodation option.

BAEZA

postcode 23440 • pop 16,000
• elevation 790m

Standing on the northern side of the Guadalquivir valley, 48km northeast of Jaén, this relaxed country town is packed with stunning Gothic and Renaissance buildings.

The seat of a bishopric under the Visigoths, Baeza (ba-**eh**-thah) developed into a trade centre, renowned for its bazaars, during the Muslim period. In 1227 it became the first sizable Andalucian town to fall to the Christians when it was conquered by Fernando III. Its heyday was during the 16th century, when the Baeza nobility, having finally ended centuries of feuding, ploughed much of the profit from booming textile and grain industries into grand buildings. On occasional summer evenings you could be mistaken for thinking Baeza is the most heavily policed town in Spain, as dozens of uniformed Guardia Civil officers stroll through the streets and relax at café tables. Most are students from the nearby Academia de Guardias de la Guardia Civil.

Orientation & Information

The heart of town is Plaza de España, with the long, wide Paseo de la Constitución stretching to its southwest.

The **bus station** is about 700m east of Plaza de España on a street officially called Avenida Alcalde Puche Pardo.

The **tourist office** *(☎ 953 74 04 44; open 9am-2.30pm Mon-Fri, 10am-1pm alternate Sat)* is in a beautiful 16th-century building on Plaza del Pópulo (Plaza de los Leones), just southwest of Paseo de la Constitución. The **main post office** is at Calle Julio Burell 19. You can check email at **Speed Informatica** *(Portales Tundidores 2; open 9am-2pm & 5pm-7pm; €1.80 per hour)* on the north side of Paseo de la Constitución. Another Internet place is **Microware** further up the street, but it tends to draw crowds of game players.

You'll find banks and ATMs on Paseo de la Constitución and to the east on Calle San Pablo.

You could walk around the following sequence of sights in a leisurely day. The opening hours of some of the buildings are unpredictable.

Plaza de España & Paseo de la Constitución

On Plaza de España stands the **Torre de los Aliatares**, one of the few remaining bits of Muslim Bayyasa, whose walled fortress it helped to fortify. Somehow this tower survived Isabel la Católica's 1476 order to demolish Baeza's fortifications in order to end the feuds between the town's Benavide and Carvajal noble families.

Once Baeza's marketplace and bullring, Paseo de la Constitución is lined with attractive arcades. Its central area is a fine open space that is free of traffic. On summer evenings youngsters play exuberant football here.

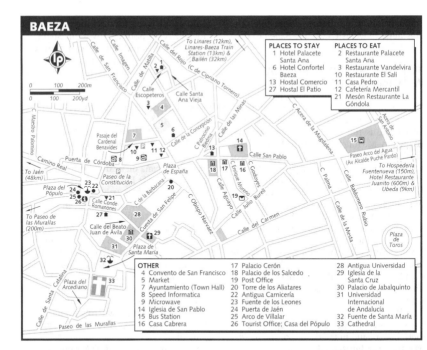

BAEZA

PLACES TO STAY	PLACES TO EAT
1 Hotel Palacete Santa Ana	2 Restaurante Palacete Santa Ana
6 Hotel Confortel Baeza	3 Restaurante Vandelvira
13 Hostal Comercio	10 Restaurante El Sali
27 Hostal El Patio	11 Casa Pedro
	12 Cafetería Mercantil
	21 Mesón Restaurante La Góndola

OTHER		
4 Convento de San Francisco	17 Palacio Cerón	28 Antigua Universidad
5 Market	18 Palacio de los Salcedo	29 Iglesia de la Santa Cruz
7 Ayuntamiento (Town Hall)	19 Post Office	30 Palacio de Jabalquinto
8 Speed Informatica	20 Torre de los Aliatares	31 Universidad Internacional de Andalucía
9 Microwave	22 Antigua Carnicería	32 Fuente de Santa María
14 Iglesia de San Pablo	23 Fuente de los Leones	33 Cathedral
15 Bus Station	24 Puerta de Jaén	
16 Casa Cabrera	25 Arco de Villalar	
	26 Tourist Office; Casa del Pópulo	

Plaza del Pópulo

This beautiful square, a few steps west of
Paseo de la Constitución, is also named
Plaza de los Leones after the **Fuente de los
Leones** (Fountain of the Lions) in its centre.
The fountain, constructed with carvings
from the Iberian and Roman village of Cás-
tulo, 15km west of Baeza, is topped by a
statue that is traditionally believed to represent Imilce, an Iberian princess from Cás-
tulo who was the wife of Carthaginian
leader Hannibal. Imilce, if it is she, wears a
suitably enigmatic smile.

On the southern side of the square is the
lovely plateresque **Casa del Pópulo**, built in
about 1540. Formerly a courthouse, it's now
Baeza's tourist office. Adjoining it is the
1526 **Arco de Villalar** (Villalar Arch), next
to which is the originally Muslim **Puerta de
Jaén** (Jaén Gate).

On the eastern side of the square stands
the **Antigua Carnicería** (Old Slaughterhouse), a fine 1548 building with a Renais-

sance gallery and the large two-headed
Habsburg eagle shield of Carlos I.

If you have time to spare you could go
through the Puerta de Jaén and along the
street to the **Paseo de las Murallas**, a path-
cum-road which loops round the old city
walls to a point near the cathedral. From here,
Baeza's sometimes deceptive position on a
steep escarpment can be appreciated through
splendid views over the surrounding country.

Antigua Universidad

Baeza's Old University *(Calle del Beato Juan
de Ávila; admission free; open 10am-1pm &
4pm-6pm Thur-Tues)* is a short walk southeast of Plaza del Pópulo. Founded in 1538,
the university was a fount of progressive
ideas that ran counter to the conservative
tendencies of Baeza's dominant families. It
was closed in 1824 and since 1875 the building has housed an *instituto de bachillerato*
(high school). The main patio has two floors
of elegant Renaissance arches and a plaque

outside one classroom telling us that the poet Antonio Machado taught French here from 1912 to 1919.

Palacio de Jabalquinto
Around the corner is the finest of Baeza's noble mansions *(Plaza Santa Cruz; admission free; open 10am-2pm & 4pm-6pm Thur-Tues)*. Probably built in the early 16th century for one of the Benavides clan, it has a spectacular facade in the flamboyant Isabelline Gothic style, topped by a Renaissance gallery. The patio has been in decay for years and has been under restoration for some time, but you can soon capture the sense of its grandeur. It, too, is Renaissance-style, with marble columns, two tiers of elegant arches and a fountain. A majestic baroque stairway ascends from one side.

Iglesia de la Santa Cruz
Across the square from the Palacio de Jabalquinto, the mid-13th-century Church of the Holy Cross *(open 11am-1pm & 4pm-6pm Mon-Sat, noon-2pm Sun & holidays)* was one of the first churches built in Andalucía after the Reconquista. It was one of the last in Spain, and one of the very few in Andalucía, to be built in the Romanesque style, which was already starting to give way to the Gothic of most early post-Reconquista Andalucian churches. Santa Cruz's round-arched portals and semicircular apse set it quite apart from Gothic. There are enchanting traces of the mosque that the church replaced. Opening times are not very reliable, but late morning is probably the best chance of finding it open. Inside are some 15th-century paintings.

Plaza de Santa María
This handsome square southwest of, and uphill from, the Palacio de Jabalquinto is dominated by the cathedral, but also worth a pause are the **Fuente de Santa María** in the middle and the **Universidad Internacional de Andalucía** on the northern side. The attractive fountain, built in 1569 by *baezano* Ginés Martínez, is in the form of a miniature Roman triumphal arch. The university, which mainly conducts short courses for postgraduates, is housed in the sober 17th-century Seminario (Seminary) de San Felipe Neri.

Cathedral
Baeza's cathedral *(admission free, donations welcome; open 10.30am-1pm & 4pm-6pm Thur-Tues, 10.30am-1pm & 4pm-6pm in winter)* is an aesthetic hotch-potch, albeit with some fascinating features. The predominant style is 16th-century Renaissance, well displayed in the **main facade** on Plaza de Santa María, and in the basic design of the three-nave interior (by Andrés de Vandelvira and Jerónimo del Prado). The oldest feature is the 13th-century Gothic/Mudejar **Puerta de la Luna** (Moon Doorway) at the western end, above which is a nice 14th-century Gothic rose window. The **Puerta del Perdón** (Pardon Doorway) on the southern side is 15th-century Gothic.

A lavish baroque **retable** backs the main altar and a 13th-century Romanesque/Gothic **Crucifixion sculpture** – rare in Andalucía – stands high on the retable of the adjacent Capilla del Sagrario. At the cathedral's western end, the **grille** on the **Antiguo Coro** (Old Choir) is one of the masterpieces of Jaén's 16th-century wrought-iron supremo, Maestro Bartolomé. The centre of the grille, from the bottom up, depicts with pleasing simplicity St Andrew, the coronation of the Virgin (holding the infant Jesus) and the Crucifixion. To the right of the grille you can pop a coin into a slot by an unremarkable painting: the painting slides noisily aside, a recording of holy music begins and the 18th-century **Custodia del Corpus**, a large silver monstrance used in Baeza's Corpus Christi processions, is revealed in all its glory.

The **cloister** has four Mudejar chapels with Arabic inscriptions.

Town Hall
The town hall *(Ayuntamiento; Paseo del Cardenal Benavides 9)*, a block north of Paseo de la Constitución, has a marvellous plateresque facade. The four finely carved balcony portals on the upper storey are separated by the coats of arms of Felipe II (in the middle), the magistrate Juan de Borja, who had the place built, and that of the

town. The building was originally a courthouse and prison (entered by the right- and left-hand doors respectively).

Convento de San Francisco

The San Francisco convent (Calle de San Francisco), a short walk from the town hall, was apparently one of Andrés de Vandelvira's masterpieces, conceived as the funerary chapel of the Benavides family. But it stood in ruins for a long time after being devastated by an earthquake and being sacked by French troops in the early 19th century. It's now partly restored and, at the eastern end, a striking arrangement of curved girders traces the outline of its dome over a space adorned with Renaissance carvings. The cloister, occupied by the Restaurante Vandelvira (see Places to Eat for details), is worth a look, too.

Calle San Pablo

This street leading east from Plaza de España is strung with handsome 16th-century mansions including the **Palacio de los Salcedo** (Calle San Pablo 18); the **Palacio Cerón** (Nuevo Casino; Calle San Pablo 24), with a nice two-tier patio; and the **Casa Cabrera** (Calle San Pablo 30), with a good plateresque front. Across the street from the Casa Cabrera is the 15th-century Gothic **Iglesia de San Pablo**.

Organised Tours

Guided tours (☎ 953 74 43 70) of Baeza take place each day at 11am and 5pm (€6, children under 12 free). The tours take about two hours and start from outside the tourist office. Commentary is in Spanish.

Special Events

Baeza stages picturesque Semana Santa and Corpus Christi processions and an annual feria (fair) from 10 to 15 August. Most renowned is the Romería de La Yedra. On the morning of 7 September the image of the Virgen del Rosell is carried from the Iglesia de San Pablo through Baeza's streets, accompanied by a singing and dancing crowd. In the afternoon, a colourful procession of riders and decorated carts follows the image

to La Yedra village, 4km to the north, to continue celebrations there.

Places to Stay

Some prices go up a few euros from about June to September.

Hostal El Patio (☎ 953 74 02 00, fax 953 74 82 60; Calle Conde Romanones 13; singles/doubles €12/18, with shower €15/21, doubles with bathroom €24) occupies a fine old 17th-century mansion with a covered patio that has one of the most extensive lounge suites you've ever seen. The place has an oddly pleasing air of decline and fall about it, but some rooms are drab and poorly lit.

Hostal Comercio (☎ 953 74 80 67, 953 74 01 00; Calle San Pablo 21; doubles €21, with shower & toilet €24, with bathroom €27) is slightly gloomy and creaky, but the welcome is gracious and the place has decent, old-fashioned rooms, some with their own little entrance hall. There's heating in winter, and plenty of hot water. The poet Antonio Machado stayed in room 215 in 1912.

Hotel Confortel Baeza (☎ 953 74 81 30, fax 953 74 25 19; e com.confortel@once.es; Calle de la Concepción 3; singles/doubles €62.60/80.25) occupies the old Hospital de la Purísima Concepción – very modernised but still with a large, arcaded central patio that, unfortunately, acts as an echo chamber late at night. The cosy, air-con rooms are nothing special for the price, but included in the rate is a fill-up breakfast buffet that will keep you going for the day.

Hospedería Fuentenueva (☎ 953 74 31 00, fax 953 74 32 00; e fuentenueva@ mx4.redestb.es; Paseo Arco del Agua s/n; singles/doubles €43/67.40), about 300m beyond the bus station, used to be a women's prison but is now a beautifully restored and decorated small hotel, all subdued orange and salmon-pink colours and stencilling; wholly relaxing. The 12 rooms are comfortable, bright, have air-con, and are mostly large, with marble bathrooms. Rates include breakfast.

Hotel Juanito (☎ 953 74 00 40, fax 953 74 23 24; Paseo Arco del Agua s/n; singles/ doubles €32/44), 450m farther along the street, next to a petrol station and opposite Baeza's football ground, offers rooms with bathroom, air-con, heating and TV. Its restaurant is the most celebrated in the province (see Places to Eat for details).

Hotel Palacete Santa Ana (*☎/fax 953 74 16 57;* e *info@palacetesantaana.com; Calle Santa Ana Vieja 9; singles/doubles €38.70/ 65*) is Baeza's most stylish hotel, contained within a 16th-century mansion and with beautifully furnished rooms. Lounges, dining salons and hallways are veritable galleries of fine art. The nearby restaurant of the same name is under the same management.

Places to Eat

Cafetería Mercantil (*Portales Tundidores 18, Paseo de la Constitución; raciones €6.60-7.20*) is busy from morning to night with amiable *baezano* men (few women, it seems) and serves a long list of generous *raciones*, plus *media-raciones* (half-*raciones*), tapas and *bocadillos* (long, filled white-bread rolls) for €2.40. This is your chance to sample *criadillas* (bull or lamb testicles) or *sesos* (brains), but there are plenty of more straightforward things too.

Mesón (*☎ 953 74 29 84; Portales Carbonería 13, Paseo de la Constitución; fish & meat mains €8-13.25*) has a terrific local atmosphere helped along by the glowing woodburning grill behind the bar, cheerful service and good food. Try *patatas baezanas*, a vegetarian delight that mixes a huge helping of sautéed potatoes and mushrooms for €8.

Casa Pedro (*Paseo del Cardenal Benavides 3; menú €8*), a place where you can eat inexpensively, offers fried eggs and ham for €3.90, and omelettes for €2.40 to €4.80.

Restaurante El Sali (*☎ 953 74 13 65; Pasaje del Cardenal Benavides 15, menú €7.80*) does a three-course *menú* with lots of choice. À la carte main dishes range from chicken or pork loin at €4.80 to partridge at €13.80.

Restaurante Vandelvira (*Calle de San Francisco 14; mains €9.50-15*), in part of the remodelled Convento de San Francisco (see earlier for details), is one of the classier places in town. If you want to spoil yourself you

might go for the partridge pâté salad at €9, followed by *solomillo al carbón* (char-grilled steak €15).

Hospedería Fuentenueva (*3 courses €18*) is the stylish restaurant of the hotel of the same name (see Places to Stay for details). It offers Jaén cuisine leavened by exotica such as couscous. It does themed weeks of specialities from other nations. The bar-café has some tasty snacks such as *suelas* (sizable toasted sandwiches) for around €3.60.

Restaurante Juanito (*☎ 953 74 00 40; Paseo Arco del Agua s/n; 3 courses €30*), in the Hotel Juanito (see Places to Stay, earlier), is where Juan Antonio Salcedo and his wife Luisa have been dishing up traditional Jaén fare for four decades. People come from far and wide to eat here. Specialities include *alcachofas Luisa* (Luisa's artichokes) and partridge salad as starters, and *cabrito al horno* (roast kid) to follow. The Juanito is closed Sunday and Monday evenings.

Restaurante Palacete Santa Ana (*☎ 953 74 16 57; Calle Escopeteros 12; fish & meat mains €11-15*) is a large restaurant and bar complex that occupies several floors and is run by the same management as Hotel Palacete Santa Ana. There are excellent flamenco nights staged here.

Getting There & Around

From the **bus station** (*☎ 953 74 04 68; Paseo Arco del Agua*), Alsina Graells runs up to 11 buses daily to Jaén (€2.90, 45 minutes), up to 15 to Úbeda (€0.70, 30 minutes) and at least five daily to Granada. There are two buses to Cazorla daily at 1pm and 5.30pm (€5.80, 2¼ hours). Other buses go to Madrid, Córdoba, Seville and Málaga.

The nearest train station is **Linares-Baeza** (*☎ 953 65 02 02*), 13km northwest, where a few trains a day leave for Granada, Córdoba, Seville, Málaga, Cádiz, Almería, Madrid and Barcelona. Buses connect with most trains from Monday to Saturday.

Parking in Baeza is fairly restricted, but there are parking spots around the Paseo de la Constitución and in Paseo del Cardenal Benavides. Taxis wait for fares in Paseo de la Constitución.

ÚBEDA

postcode 23400 ● pop 32,000
● elevation 760m

Just 9km east through the olive groves from Baeza, with which it has a neighbourly rivalry, Úbeda (oo-be-dah) has an even larger heritage of marvellous buildings from bygone centuries. Plaza Vázquez de Molina is the finest ensemble of Renaissance buildings in Andalucía.

History

Úbeda was taken from the Muslims by Fernando III in 1234. In the 14th century a group of local knights earned the title Lions of Úbeda for their heroics during the conquest of Algeciras, which is why lions are a common motif on Úbeda buildings.

Just as in Baeza, the town's leading post-Reconquista families, among them the Molinas, the de la Cuevas and the Cobos, spent

---

Andrés de Vandelvira

Born in 1509 at Alcaraz, 150km northeast of Úbeda, Andrés de Vandelvira almost single-handedly brought the Renaissance to then-wealthy towns of the Jaén region. Influenced by the pioneering Spanish Renaissance architect Diego de Siloé, Vandelvira designed a number of marvellous buildings in Úbeda, Baeza, Jaén and elsewhere, which add up to one of the outstanding groupings of Renaissance architecture in Spain. His work spanned all three main phases of Spanish Renaissance architecture and three of Úbeda's finest buildings illustrate this with a flourish. In buildings of the ornamental early Renaissance phase known as plateresque, such as the Capilla de El Salvador, a predilection for sculpted coats of arms lingered from the Isabelline Gothic era. A much purer line and more classical proportions emerge in the later Palacio de Vázquez de Molina. In his last building, the Hospital de Santiago (completed in 1575, the year he died), Vandelvira displays almost as much sobriety as did Juan de Herrera in El Escorial, the paradigm of the austere Spanish late Renaissance.

---

much time and energy quarrelling with each other and entangling themselves with the factions competing for the Castilian throne. In 1506 most of Úbeda's fortifications were razed, on Isabel La Católica's orders, to put an end to these quarrels. But the Cobos and the Molinas had by now patched things up enough to intermarry, and one of their line, Francisco de los Cobos y Molina, rose to be first secretary to King Carlos I; his nephew Juan Vázquez de Molina succeeded him in the job and kept it under Felipe II. High office exposed these men to international culture just as the Renaissance was reaching Spain from Italy. Consequently, much of the wealth that they (and a flourishing local agriculture) brought to 16th-century Úbeda was spent on the profusion of lavish Renaissance mansions and churches that remain its greatest glory today.

Orientation & Information

Most of Úbeda's splendid buildings – the main reason for visiting the town – are among the warren of narrow, winding streets and expansive squares that constitute the old town, in the southeast. The cheaper accommodation and the bus station are about 1km away, in the drab new town to the west and north. Plaza de Andalucía marks the boundary between the two parts of town.

The **tourist office** (☎ 953 75 08 97; Calle Baja del Marqués 4; open 8am-3pm Mon-Sat) is in the 18th-century Palacio Marqués de Contadero, in the old town.

There is a **post office** (open 8.30am-2.30pm Mon-Fri, 9.30am-1pm Sat) at Calle Trinidad 4. You'll find the biggest concentration of banks and ATMs on Plaza de Andalucía and nearby Calle Rastro.

There's a **health centre** (Centro de Salud; ☎ 953 75 11 03; Calle Explanada), with an emergency section, in the new part of town; and a **general hospital** (☎ 953 79 71 00; Carretera de Linares Km 1) on the northwestern edge of town. The **Policía Nacional** (☎ 091; Plaza Vázquez de Molina) occupy the Antiguo Pósito. The **Policía Municipal** (☎ 953 75 00 23; Plaza de Andalucía) are in the busy centre.

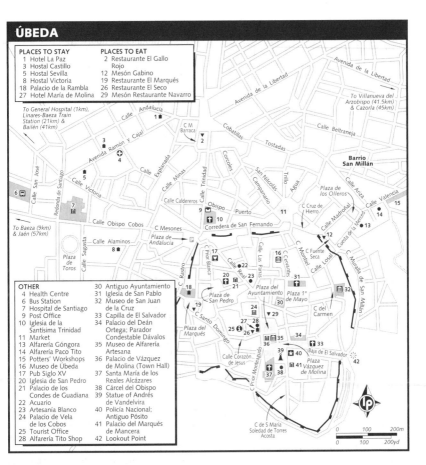

ÚBEDA

PLACES TO STAY
1 Hotel La Paz
3 Hostal Castillo
5 Hostal Sevilla
8 Hostal Victoria
18 Palacio de la Rambla
27 Hotel María de Molina

PLACES TO EAT
2 Restaurante El Gallo Rojo
12 Mesón Gabino
19 Restaurante El Marqués
26 Restaurante El Seco
29 Mesón Restaurante Navarro

OTHER
4 Health Centre
6 Bus Station
7 Hospital de Santiago
9 Post Office
10 Iglesia de la Santísima Trinidad
11 Market
13 Alfarería Góngora
14 Alfarería Paco Tito
15 Potters' Workshops
16 Museo de Úbeda
17 Pub Siglo XV
20 Iglesia de San Pedro
21 Palacio de los Condes de Guadiana
22 Acuario
23 Artesanía Blanco
24 Palacio de Vela de los Cobos
25 Tourist Office
28 Alfarería Tito Shop
30 Antiguo Ayuntamiento
31 Iglesia de San Pablo
32 Museo de San Juan de la Cruz
33 Capilla de El Salvador
34 Palacio del Deán Ortega; Parador Condestable Dávalos
35 Museo de Alfarería Artesana
36 Palacio de Vázquez de Molina (Town Hall)
37 Santa María de los Reales Alcázares
38 Cárcel del Obispo
39 Statue of Andrés de Vandelvira
40 Policía Nacional; Antiguo Pósito
41 Palacio del Marqués de Mancera
42 Lookout Point

Plaza Vázquez de Molina

Enclosed by beautiful 15th- and 16th-century buildings in richly textured stone, this 180m-long square is Úbeda's crown jewel. Floodlighting after dark makes it even more picturesque. A lookout point (mirador), 150m east of the square along Baja de El Salvador, gives fine views across the olive fields, with the Cazorla mountains in the distance to the east.

Capilla de El Salvador Facing along Plaza Vázquez de Molina from its western end, this church (admission €2; open 10.30am-2pm & 4.30pm-7pm daily, last hour free admission) was Andrés de Vandelvira's first work in Úbeda. Commissioned by Francisco de los Cobos y Molina as a funerary chapel for his family, it today belongs to the Sevilla-based Duques de Medinaceli, descendants of the Cobos and one of Andalucía's major landowning families. Vandelvira built the chapel in the 1540s to designs by Diego de Siloé, but he added plenty of his own touches, including the portals and the sacristy.

The **main facade** (Plaza Vázquez de Molina) is a pre-eminent example of the plateresque style, modelled on Siloé's Puerta del Perdón at Granada cathedral. The portal is topped by a carving of the transfiguration of Christ, flanked by statues of St Peter and St Paul. On the underside of the arch immediately above the door, the French sculptor Esteban Jamete placed representations of Greek gods – a Renaissance touch that would have been inconceivable a few decades earlier. A Gothic penchant for heraldry lingers, however, in the sculptures flanking the portal. To the left, soldiers bear the five-lion coat of arms of Francisco de los Cobos y Molina; to the right, two women hold the shield of his wife María Manrique.

The church's side portals, though they are smaller, also bear intricate carving, including, on the northern Portada del Evangelio, Santiago Matamoros incarnated as Carlos I, beneath a medallion of Christ.

The entrance is on the southern side. The sacristy, designed by Vandelvira and with much classical sculpture by Jamete, has a portrait of Francisco de los Cobos y Molina. The richly decorated chancel is modelled on Siloé's Capilla Mayor in the Granada cathedral, with a frescoed dome. The main retable, by Alonso de Berruguete, was damaged in the civil war and only one statue, the *Transfiguración del Monte Tabor* (Transfiguration on Mount Tabor), is original. A fine 1557 grille (some say it's by Jaén's Maestro Bartolomé) divides the chancel from the nave, beneath which is the Cobos family crypt, containing the tomb of Francisco de los Cobos y Molina.

Palacio del Deán Ortega Next to the Capilla de El Salvador stands what was the house of its chaplains, a palace by any other name and one of Vandelvira's finest works. Partly remodelled in the 17th century, the mansion became Úbeda's luxurious parador in 1930 and its typically Vandelvira two-tier courtyard is about the most elevated spot in town for a drink (a beer is €1.80).

Palacio de Vázquez de Molina This beautiful mansion *(Plaza Vázquez de Molina; open 9am-2.30pm & 5pm-9pm daily)*, now Úbeda's town hall, dominates the western end of Plaza Vázquez de Molina. Vandelvira built it in about 1562 for Juan Vázquez de Molina, whose coat of arms surmounts the doorway.

The uncluttered facade, deeply Italian-influenced, has superbly harmonious proportions. Horizontally, it's divided into three tiers by slender cornices. Vertically, Esteban Jamete's caryatids, separating the oval windows of the top level, continue the lines of the pilasters flanking the rectangular windows of the middle tier.

You can enter the building by its northern entrance on Plaza del Ayuntamiento to admire the fine patio, with two storeys of rounded arches on slender pillars.

In one side of the building, the **Museo de Alfarería Artesana** *(admission €1.80; open 10.30am-2pm & 4.30pm-7pm Tues-Sat, 10.30am-2pm Sun)* is devoted to Úbeda pottery, a craft whose green glaze dates back to Muslim times.

Santa María de los Reales Alcázares This large church facing the Palacio de Vázquez de Molina is one of Úbeda's finest, but has been closed for restoration for several years. Built over Muslim Úbeda's main mosque, it has a Renaissance facade but is mainly 15th-century Gothic. Inside are grilles by Maestro Bartolomé and a lovely Gothic cloister occupying what was the mosque's ritual ablutions courtyard.

Other Buildings Next door to Santa María stands the **Cárcel del Obispo** (Bishop's Prison), where nuns who stepped out of line used to be incarcerated. It is now a courthouse. Under the trees in front is a **statue of Andrés de Vandelvira**, the man who made Úbeda worth visiting. By the statue, fronting the main square, the 16th-century **Antiguo Pósito**, originally a communal store for surplus grain, is now the local headquarters of the Policía Nacional. Calle de Santa María Soledad de Torres Acosta leads south from here into the area that was the Muslim fortress.

Plaza del Ayuntamiento & Around

This broad square on the northern side of the Palacio de Vázquez de Molina is overlooked from its northwestern corner by the **Palacio de Vela de los Cobos**, with handsome middle-floor windows and top-floor gallery – built by Vandelvira for another of the Cobos clan, Francisco Vela de los Cobos.

Three blocks northwest up Calle Real (once Úbeda's main commercial street) stands the 17th-century **Palacio de los Condes de Guadiana**, another of the town's best mansions, with a tower and some good carving round the windows and balconies.

Plaza 1° de Mayo & Around

A couple of blocks northeast of Plaza del Ayuntamiento, this area used to be the market square, bullring and site of Inquisition burnings. Local worthies watched the gruesome events from the gallery of the elegant 16th-century **Antiguo Ayuntamiento** (Old Town Hall) in the southwestern corner. Along the top (northern) side of the square is the **Iglesia de San Pablo**, with a fine late-Gothic portal (1511). Its 13th-century western front is in Romanesque-cum-Gothic style, and the tower at the eastern end (1537) is plateresque. You can enter the church between 7pm and 9pm daily: look for the 1530s Capilla de Camarero Vago, by Vandelvira, and some elegant grilles.

Just north, a 14th-century Mudejar house with an attractive patio houses the **Museo de Úbeda** (Calle Cervantes 4; admission €1.50, EU citizen free; open 3pm-8pm Tues, 9am-8pm Wed-Sat, 9am-3pm Sun), with archaeological exhibits from Neolithic to Muslim times.

Museo de San Juan de la Cruz

This museum (Calle del Carmen; admission free; open 11am-1pm & 5pm-7pm Tues-Sun), in the 17th-century Oratorio de San Juan de la Cruz, a block east of Plaza 1° de Mayo, is devoted to the 16th-century mystic, poet and religious reformer St John of the Cross (San Juan de la Cruz).

St John of the Cross, born in Castilla y León in 1542, founded the breakaway monastic order of Carmelitos Descalzos (Barefoot Carmelites – they wore sandals instead of shoes) in an effort to return to the austerity and contemplative life from which

he felt mainstream Carmelites had lapsed. He wrote of the 'dark night of the soul', leading to the bright dawn of experience of God, and taught that mysticism was the simple understanding and accepting of the way things are.

Mainstream Carmelites opposed this thinking, and he was imprisoned several times. St John came to Úbeda from Baeza in September 1591, suffering from gangrene in his leg. He died here three months later.

On the museum's ground floor is the chapel where he was originally buried; an effigy lies on the spot. Upstairs is the room in which he died – with some of his bones in a glass case. Other rooms hold prints recording the key events of his life, early editions of his writings, and art connected with his life and teachings. In a reconstructed monk's cell, a lifelike figure of St John sits at a writing table he used – facing a cabinet containing not only letters written by him, but a couple of fingers from his right hand.

Visits, guided by Spanish-speaking monks, last about half an hour.

Hospital de Santiago

Vandelvira's last building, begun in 1562 and completed in 1575, is the farthest from the heart of old Úbeda, but is one of his masterpieces. The Hospital de Santiago (Calle Obispo Cobos; open 8.30am-2pm & 4pm-10pm Mon-Fri, 11am-2.30pm & 6pm-9.30pm Sat & Sun) is a very sober, grand-scale, late-Renaissance building that has been dubbed the Escorial of Andalucía, after Felipe II's contemporary palace-monastery near Madrid.

The lack of decoration focuses attention on the building's fine proportions, from the long facade crowned by end towers to the classic Vandelvira two-level patio with marble columns.

You can wander into the hospital (it's not a hospital now – it houses a library, the municipal dance school and an exhibition hall) between opening times.

Special Events

Semana Santa processions are colourful, and Úbeda celebrates early summer with the Festival Internacional de Música y Danza

Ciudad de Úbeda, bringing varied music and dance performers to the town through the month of May. The biggest festivities are the Fiestas de San Miguel from 27 September to 4 October, with firework shows, parades, concerts, a bullfight season and more.

Places to Stay

Hostal Victoria (☎ 953 75 29 52; Calle Alaminos 5; singles/doubles €17/32), 200m west of Plaza de Andalucía, has reasonable rooms with bathroom, TV, air-con and heating. Parking can be arranged.

Hostal Castillo (☎ 953 75 04 30; Avenida Ramón y Cajal 16; singles/doubles €17/32, with washbasin/bathroom €15/23), farther from the centre and under the same ownership, has similar rooms to Hostal Victoria, with bathroom, air-con and heating (no TV). Parking can be arranged.

Hostal Sevilla (☎ 953 75 06 12; Avenida Ramón y Cajal 9; singles/doubles €18/33), a pleasant family-run hostal, has clean, fairly modern rooms with bathroom and heating.

Hotel La Paz (☎ 953 75 08 48; Calle Andalucía 1; singles/doubles €31.50/52) is located in a rather anonymous part of town, but is comfortable and well-appointed, although the singles are a bit small.

Parador Condestable Dávalos (☎ 953 75 03 45, fax 953 75 12 59; e ubeda@parador .es; Plaza Vázquez de Molina; singles/doubles €108/121.30, special doubles €131-187) is a 30-room place in the old Palacio del Deán Ortega. It is now comfortably modernised and appropraitely luxurious. The 'special doubles' rise in price according to the level of luxury.

Palacio de la Rambla (☎ 953 75 01 96; Plaza del Marqués 1; singles/doubles €77/ 99.50, suite €115.55) is located in a splendid 16th-century palace. Rates for the large doubles include breakfast. Home of the Marquesa de la Rambla, the eight-room hotel centres on a lovely Vandelvira patio and has a pleasant garden. Strict security means guests need to use an intercom for entry.

Hotel María de Molina (☎ 953 79 53 56; e hotelmm@hotel-maria-de-molina.com; Plaza del Ayuntamiento; singles/doubles

€47/73.85, about 10% more on Fri & Sat) is another sumptuous hotel in a beautiful old mansion right at the heart of the old town.

Places to Eat

Hostal Castillo (see Places to Stay, earlier), in the new town, serves a reasonable three-course menú with salad and a drink for €7, and breakfast for €1.80.

Restaurante El Gallo Rojo (☎ 953 75 20 38; Calle Manuel Barraca 3; fish & meat mains €6-10, 3-course menú €9.65), just off the northern end of Avenida Ramón y Cajal, is one of the best places in the new part of town, with a cheerful atmosphere. Giant bocadillos with various fillings are €2 to €3.

Restaurante El Marqués (Plaza del Marqués; platos combinados €5-7) in the old town, 150m downhill from Plaza de Andalucía, does reasonable-value platos combinados that are 20% more if you eat them at a table.

Mesón Restaurante Navarro (Plaza del Ayuntamiento 2; bar raciones €4-9, restaurant mains €8-12.25) has a bar at the front that can get very smoky and noisy, but has excellent and varied raciones, media-raciones and bocadillos (€1.50 to €4.50) and a restaurant serving typical local fare in the back. Note that the sign just says 'Mesón Restaurante'.

Mesón Gabino (Calle Fuente Seca; fish & meat mains €6-10) is a cellar restaurant with old stone pillars and decent food, including salads, vegetable and egg dishes at €5.40 to €6.70.

Restaurante El Seco (Calle Corazón de Jesús 8; 3-course menú €12) is another mid-priced option in the old town and is beside a pretty square filled with orange trees. Tortillas and revueltos are €4 to €7.80.

Parador Condestable Dávalos (see Places to Stay; lunch or dinner around €25) has a restaurant that serves the finest food. The price for lunch or dinner is fair for some of the excellent local dishes, such as carrué-cano (green peppers stuffed with partridge) or cabrito guisado con piñones (stewed kid with pine nuts) for €14 to €16, and some scrumptious desserts.

Entertainment

Pub Siglo XV *(Calle Prior Blanca)* is an atmospheric bar with old stone pillars and sometimes live flamenco or other music.

Shopping

The typical green glaze on Úbeda's varied and attractive pottery, and the tradition of embroidering coloured patterns into esparto-grass mats *(ubedíes)*, both date from Muslim times.

Several workshops sell pottery in the San Millán *barrio* (district), the potters' quarter northeast of the old town, and the potters are often willing to explain some of the ancient techniques they use. **Alfarería Paco Tito** *(Calle Valencia 22)* is one of the best known, but several others on the same street, and nearby **Alfarería Góngora** *(Cuesta de la Merced 32)*, are worth a look. **Alfarería Tito** *(Plaza del Ayuntamiento 12)* also has a large shop in the old town. Prices for smaller pottery pieces that you could comfortably carry home start at about €6.

For esparto mats and baskets, costing from about €5, visit **Artesanía Blanco** *(Calle Real 47)* in the old town. The nearby **Acuario** *(Calle Real 61)* has some good antiques, and bits and pieces of fine tiling.

The main shopping streets are Calle Mesones and Calle Obispo Cobos, between Plaza de Andalucía and the Hospital de Santiago.

Getting There & Around

Bus The bus station (☎ 953 75 21 57; *Calle San José 6)* is in the new part of town. Alsina Graells runs to Baeza up to 15 times daily (€0.70, 30 minutes), to Jaén up to 13 times daily (€3.60, 1¼ hours), to Cazorla three or four times and to Granada up to seven times. Bacoma goes to Córdoba and Seville four times daily. Other buses head to Málaga, Madrid, Valencia, Barcelona and small places around Jaén province.

Train The nearest station is **Linares-Baeza** (☎ 953 65 02 02), 21km northwest, which you can reach by Linares-bound buses. See the Baeza section for information on trains.

Car & Motorcycle

Parking is difficult in the narrow streets of the old town and not much easier in the streets that radiate from Plaza de Andalucía. However, at the time of writing Plaza de Andalucía was a major construction site as refurbishment and the building of an underground car park forged ahead. Completion was promised for 2003.

PARQUE NATURAL SIERRA DE DESPEÑAPERROS

The road north out of Andalucía to Madrid, the N-IV, passes through indifferent countryside to the north of Jaén until the hills of the Sierra Morena appear on the horizon. Ahead lies the **Desfiladero de Despeñaperros**, the 'Pass of the Overthrow of the Dogs'; or more precisely the 'throwing over' or 'hurling down'. It was here that the Christian victors of a key battle of the Reconquista at nearby Las Navas de Tolosa, in 1212, are said to have tossed from the cliffs many of the Muslim occupants of the area. Enshrined in the one name is brutal insult and vicious reprisal.

The full drama of the pass is not appreciated until the last minute, when the road from the south descends suddenly and swoops down between rocky towers and wooded slopes to slice through tunnels and defiles. Its southbound carriageway wriggles its way along the wooded slopes to the west, both roads more than a kilometre apart in places. The carriageway through the deep pass runs alongside the railway for most of the way.

Road and rail have robbed the Desfiladero de Despeñaperros of much of its historic romance, but the splendid hill country to either side is one of Spain's most beautiful and remote areas, a wilderness clothed with dense woods of pine, holm oak and cork trees from which protrude dramatic cliffs and pinnacles of fluted rock. The area is home to deer and wild boar, and the occasional wolf and lynx have been reported. There are no local buses, so you need your own transport to get the best from the area. The main visitor centre is the **Centro de Visitantes Puerta de Andalucía** (☎ 953 66 43 07; *Carretera Santa Elena a Miranda del Rey; open 10am-2pm & 4pm-8pm Apr-Sept; 10am-2pm & 3pm-7pm*

JAÉN PROVINCE

Oct-Mar) on the outskirts of **Santa Elena**, the small town just south of the pass. The centre is a large building and has excellent displays on the wildlife and geology of the park. It has information and maps on walking routes in the area.

Santa Elena is an ideal base for exploring the park. It is a friendly place, bypassed by the motorway and all the better for it. It has shops, bars and cafés.

Camping Despeñaperros *(☎ 953 66 41 92; e campingdesp@navegalia.com; camping per 2 adults, tent & car €12)* has a great location among pine trees. The friendly and helpful owner can advise on walking and arrange guiding, or you can contact a park guide direct on ☎ 610 28 25 31.

Hotel El Mesón de Despeñaperros *(☎ 953 66 41 00, fax 953 66 41 02; e meson@ serverland.com; Avenida de Andalucía 91; singles/doubles €22.50/36)* is at the north end of Santa Elena and has comfy rooms and a busy restaurant with *platos combinados* starting at €3.80 and a *menú* for €9.50.

Hotel Restaurante Alfonso VIII *(☎ 953 66 42 31, fax 953 66 41 02; e complejo@ wanadoo.es; Carretera N-IV, Km 259; singles/doubles €37/45.60)* is a huge modern building just off the motorway to the south of Santa Elena. It has good rooms and its very popular restaurant does meat and fish dishes at €8.40 to €11 and salads at €5.80 to €7.80.

Bar Restaurante Santa Elena *(Carretera N-IV, Km 258; menú €9)* is just along from the Alfonso VIII.

There are no trains to Santa Elena and there is no direct bus from Jaén; several buses from Jaén run on weekdays to La Carolina, about 12km south of Santa Elena, from where **La Sepulvedana** *(☎ 953 66 03 35)* runs about four or five buses to Santa Elena, weekdays only. It's best to check the current schedules.

CAZORLA
postcode 23470 • pop 9700
• elevation 836m

Cazorla, 45km southeast of Úbeda, is the main gateway to the Parque Natural de Cazorla, which begins dramatically amid the cliffs of **Peña de los Halcones** (Falcon Crag) that tower above the town. It's a busy, bustling place with terrific appeal, a halfway house between the passive landscape of the plains and the great rugged swathe of mountain and valley that unfolds enticingly to the north and east. There's an imposing castle, a sequence of three plazas – each one delightfully different from the other and linked by narrow streets – and a range of worthwhile places to stay, eat and drink. Cazorla becomes crowded during Spanish holiday times and on weekends from spring to autumn.

Orientation & Information
The A-319 from the west winds up into Cazorla as Calle Hilario Marco, which in turn ends at Plaza de la Constitución, the often frantically busy main square of the newer part of town. The second important square is Plaza de la Corredera, 150m south of Plaza de la Constitución. It is reached along Calle Doctor Muñoz, Cazorla's narrow, but shop-lined, main street. Plaza de Santa María, 300m farther southeast, and reached along even more-narrow, winding streets, is the heart of the oldest part of town, and stands directly below the castle and crags.

The **Oficina de Turismo Municipal** *(☎ 953 71 01 02; Paseo del Santo Cristo 17)*, 200m north of Plaza de la Constitución, has information on the Parque Natural de Cazorla as well as Cazorla town, but it only opens from about April to October. There is also a **tourist information kiosk** *(Calle Hilario Marco; open 10am-2pm & 5pm-9pm in summer, 10am-2pm & 4pm-8pm in winter)* located on the right-hand side of the road, just past the sharp right-hand bend as you come into town along the A-319 from the west.

The privately run **Quercus** *(☎ 953 72 01 15, fax 953 71 00 68; Calle Juan Domingo 2; open 10am-2pm & 5pm-8pm, until 9pm in summer)*, just off Plaza de la Constitución, provides some tourist information and sells maps, Spanish-language guidebooks and souvenirs. It also offers excursions into the park (see Organised Tours under Parque Natural de Cazorla later in this chapter).

The **post office** *(Calle Mariano Extremera 2)* is behind the town hall, just off Plaza de la Corredera. You'll find several banks with ATMs on and between Plaza de la Constitución and Plaza de la Corredera.

There's a health centre, **Centro de Salud Dr José Cano Salcedo** (☎ 953 72 10 61), at Calle Ximénez de Rada 1. The **Policía Local** (☎ 953 72 01 81) are in the town hall just off Plaza de la Corredera.

There is a convenient car park in Plaza del Mercado, below Plaza de la Constitución.

Plaza de la Corredera

The 17th-century **Iglesia de San José** at the northern end of the square contains six copies of El Greco paintings by Rafael del Real. In the square's top corner, with its landmark clock tower, stands the **town hall**, a former monastery. A theatre occupies the monastery's old church. The **Iglesia del Carmen**, 200m up Calle del Carmen from here, is Cazorla's best-looking church. It's mainly a 17th- and 18th- century construction, but with an earlier, plateresque tower. Plaza de la Corredera is full of life at most times.

Plaza de Santa María

Calle Gómez Calderón heads south from Plaza de la Corredera along canyon-like streets to the **Balcón de Zabaleta**, a little mirador, like a sudden window in the blank walls, with stunning views over the town and up to the Castillo de la Yedra. Along from here is the seductive Plaza de Santa María (or Plaza Vieja) where you can soon lose a pleasant hour or two in the early evening amid café tables and ancient plane trees. The large, ruined **Iglesia de Santa María** at the square's far end was built by Andrés de Vandelvira in the 16th century, over a river that runs under the square. The church was wrecked by Napoleonic troops in reprisal for Cazorla's tenacious resistance and is now used for occasional open-air concerts. Also on the square is a 400-year-old fountain, the **Fuente de las Cadenas**.

Castillo de la Yedra

The shortest way to the castle from Plaza de Santa María used to be up the steep and narrow Calle del Castillo, but this is now closed off at its top. Access is now by a much longer hike starting along the street to the right of the ruined Iglesia de Santa María. From here a concrete road winds steeply upwards – a solitary seat halfway draws fierce competition on busy days, like musical chairs without the music – to the impressive Castle of the Ivy (*Castillo de las Cuatro Esquinas, Castle of the Four Corners; admission €1.50, EU citizen free; open 3pm-8pm Tues, 9am-8pm Wed-Sat, 9am-3pm Sun & holidays*). The castle is of Roman origin, though it was largely built by the Muslims, then restored in the 15th century after the Reconquista. Much money has been spent on a modern restoration, and the castle houses the **Museo del Alto Guadalquivir** (Museum of the Upper Guadalquivir), a mishmash of art, artefacts and relics of local life. Included are a reconstructed traditional kitchen, models of old oil mills and a chapel featuring a life-sized Romanesque/Byzantine Crucifixion sculpture. The guided tours are more like the outings of a captive audience than a pleasant browse: a relentlessly silent custodian shepherds groups around the exhibits and rooms.

Special Events

On 14 May, in a pilgrimage called La Caracolá, the image of San Isicio (a Christian apostle supposedly stoned to death at Cazorla in Roman times), is carried from the Ermita de San Isicio to the Iglesia de San José, and the streets are lit with oil lamps. Cazorla's main annual fiesta, from 17 to 21 September, features bullfights and music. On the first day a 17th-century painting of the Cristo del Consuelo (Christ of Consolation), which was rescued from the Napoleonic destruction of the Iglesia de Santa María, is carried in procession.

Places to Stay

Camping Cortijo San Isicio (☎ 953 72 12 80; *camping per adult/tent/car €3/3.30/2.40; open Mar-Oct*), is a charming little place amid pine trees, off the Quesada road 4km southwest of central Cazorla. It has room for just 54 people. The access road is narrow and twisting.

Albergue Juvenil Cazorla (☎ 953 72 03 29; *Plaza Mauricio Martínez 6; under 26/other*

€12.90/17.25 holiday periods; €10.90/15.20 June-Sept; €8.50/11.50 rest of year), 200m uphill from Plaza de la Corredera, is a spick-and-span youth hostel in a former 16th-century convent. It has a pool and places for 120 people in rooms holding between two and six, most with shared bathrooms. The top-floor doubles, with wood-beamed ceilings, are as attractive as any budget room in town.

Pensión Taxí (☎ 953 72 05 25; Travesía de San Antón 7; singles/doubles €18/33), just off Plaza de la Constitución, is another friendly place. Breakfast is €2 and evening meal €8.

La Cueva de Juan Pedro (☎ 953 72 12 25; Calle La Hoz 2; singles/doubles €15/30), on a corner of Plaza de Santa María, is an atmospheric old building with only a handful of rooms.

Hotel Guadalquivir (☎/fax 953 72 02 68; e info@hguadalquivir.com; Calle Nueva 6; singles/doubles €31/41.30), just off Calle Doctor Muñoz, is a cheerful place that has prettily decorated rooms with bathroom, TV, air-con and heating. The singles are a touch small. It has a café with breakfast at €3.30.

Hotel Andalucía (☎ 953 72 12 68; Calle Martínez Falero 42; singles/doubles €24/33) is a friendly, family-run place with good, sizable rooms with bathroom and TV. The hotel does delicious breakfasts for €3. Parking is available.

Hotel Ciudad de Cazorla (☎ 953 72 17 00, fax 953 71 04 20; Plaza de la Corredera 9; singles/doubles €59/70.75) has 35 modern rooms with air-con, heating, bathroom and TV. Breakfast is included and there is a restaurant, pool and garage.

Hotel Peña de los Halcones (☎ 953 72 02 11, fax 953 72 13 35; Travesía del Camino de La Iruela 2; singles/doubles €51.70/63.30), 400m uphill from Plaza de la Corredera, has good-sized, pine-furnished rooms with air-con, bathroom and TV. Some rooms have great views. The hotel has a restaurant, café and pool.

A few other hotels are a 1km hike down Calle Hilario Marco from Plaza de la Constitución. The small **Hotel Parque** (☎/fax 953 72 18 06; Calle Hilario Marco 62; singles/ doubles €25.85/43.30), and the 23-room **Hotel Don Diego** (☎ 953 72 05 31; Calle Hilario Marco 163; singles/doubles €22/34), almost opposite, have rooms with bathroom.

Villa Turística de Cazorla (☎ 953 71 01 00; Ladera de San Isicio; singles/doubles €48/75) has rooms with kitchen and fireplace. It has a good restaurant and a pool too.

Places to Eat

In late summer or autumn, after rain, locals disappear into the woods to gather large, deliciously edible mushrooms that they call *níscalos*. If these appear in restaurants, get your share.

Mesón Don Chema (☎ 953 72 00 68; Calle Escaleras del Mercado 2; mains €7-9), down a lane off Calle Doctor Muñoz, is a cheerful place that serves good, typical local fare, such as the sizzling *huevos cazorleña*, a mixed stew of sliced boiled eggs and chorizo with vegetables.

La Forchetta (Calle de las Escuelas 2; pizza €3.60-5.40), just down from Plaza de la Constitución, serves tasty pizza, plus pasta at similar prices.

Restaurante La Sarga (☎ 953 72 15 07; Plaza del Mercado s/n; 4-course menú €18) is one of the more upmarket eateries in town. Mains are €9 to €11.50 and specialities include *caldereta de gamo* (venison stew).

La Cueva de Juan Pedro (Plaza de Santa María; raciones €9), an ancient, wood-beamed place hung with countless clumps of garlic and drying peppers, serves up very traditional Cazorla fare such as *conejo* (rabbit), *trucha* (trout), *rin-rán* (a mix of salted cod, potato and dried red peppers), *jabalí* (boar), *venado* (venison) and even mouflon. All are available as *raciones*, prepared in a variety of ways.

Several of the bars on Cazorla's three main squares serve good tapas and *raciones*, including **Bar Las Vegas** (Plaza de la Corredera 17; raciones €6), where besides *lomo de jabalí* (loin of wild boar) there's an item called *gloria bendita* (blessed glory), which is a tasty prawn-and-capsicum *revuelto*. The Las Vegas has the town's best breakfast *tostadas* (toasted rolls), too.

La Montería *(Plaza de la Corredera 18)* has tapas of *choto con ajo* (veal with garlic) and venison. Other tapas stops include bright **Café-Bar Rojas** *(Plaza de la Constitución 2)* and down-to-earth **Taberna Quinito** *(Plaza de Santa María 6)*.

A daily **market** is held in the Plaza del Mercado just down from the Plaza de la Constitución.

Entertainment
As well as its tapas bars, Cazorla has a number of music bars that get lively on weekend nights, among them the popular **Clan Bar** *(Paseo del Santo Cristo)*, which has a remarkable collection of Irish and Scottish bottled beers among a wide range. Other spots are **La Rana Verde** *(Calle San Juan 12)*, above the youth hostel, and **Pub Liberty** *(Calle Hilario Marco 4)*.

Getting There & Away
Bus Alsina Graells runs two daily buses to/from Úbeda, Baeza, and Jaén (€6.15, two hours) and Granada (€11.65, 3½ hours). The main stop in Cazorla is Plaza de la Constitución; Quercus has timetable information. Buses to Cazorla leave Granada at 10.30am and 3pm, Jaén 1½ hours later, Baeza 2½ hours later and Úbeda three hours later. Departures from Cazorla are at 5.30pm daily, 7am Monday to Saturday and at 8am Sunday and holidays. A couple more daily buses run just between Úbeda and Cazorla.

AROUND CAZORLA
The village of **La Iruela**, 100m higher than Cazorla on the hill to the east, is less than 1km from Plaza de la Corredera – head up Calle del Carmen and its continuation, Camino de la Iruela. The picturesque ruins of La Iruela's Knights Templar castle stand atop a sheer crag at the far (eastern) end of the village.

Hotel La Finca Mercedes *(☎ 953 72 10 87; singles/doubles €22.50/35.30)*, a friendly place beside the main A-319 just beyond a turning up to La Iruela, has good views from rear windows. Breakfast is €2.70 and main meals are about €8.

Hotel Finca *(☎ 953 72 05 01; singles/ doubles €30/39)* is the smaller hotel next door, run separately by members of the same family as La Finca Mercedes.

For details of walks in the Cazorla– La Iruela district, see the following section.

PARQUE NATURAL DE CAZORLA
The 2143-sq-km Parque Natural de las Sierras de Cazorla, Segura y Las Villas (to give it its full title) is the biggest protected area in Spain. It's a corrugated, craggy region of several complex mountain ranges – not extraordinarily high, but memorably beautiful – divided by high plains called *navas* and deep river valleys and lakes, and in many places thickly forested. The chief ranges run roughly north to south.

The park's attractions include enjoyable walking, picturesque villages with historical interest, and better prospects of seeing wildlife in the wild than almost anywhere else in Andalucía. Red and fallow deer, wild boar, mouflon and ibex are all here in good numbers (partly because they are protected in order to be hunted). You may even see deer or boar from a car on some of the roads. Some 140 bird species nest in the park, including several types of eagle, vulture and falcon, and efforts are being made to reintroduce the majestic lammergeier (bearded vulture).

Exploring the park is a lot easier if you have a vehicle, but some bus services exist (see Getting There & Around at the end of this section) and there are plenty of places to stay inside the park. Those without vehicles have the option of guided excursions to reach the more remote areas.

The Río Guadalquivir, Andalucía's longest river, rises between the Sierra de Cazorla and Sierra del Pozo in the south of the park and flows northwards into the Embalse del Tranco de Beas reservoir, from which it emerges westbound for the Atlantic Ocean.

The best times to visit the park are April to June, and September and October: the vegetation is at its most colourful and you avoid most of the winter rain and the heat of July and August. In winter a lot of the park is often covered in snow. When walking, go properly equipped, with enough water and appropriate clothes. Temperatures up in the hills are several degrees lower than down in the valleys, and the wind can be cutting at any time.

The park is hugely popular with Spanish tourists and attracts an estimated 600,000 visitors a year – some 50,000 of them during Semana Santa. The other peak periods are July and August, and weekends from April to October.

Maps & Guides

Lonely Planet's *Walking in Spain* details three of the best Cazorla walks.

The best maps are Editorial Alpina's 1:40,000 *Sierra de Cazorla*, covering the southern one-third of the park (€5.40) and *Sierra de Segura*, covering the northern two-thirds (€7.40). Selected walking and mountain-bike routes are specially marked, and described in accompanying booklets. The Sierra de Cazorla map is available in English. You may be able to get these and other maps and guides at the Torre del Vinagre information centre (see The Centre of the Park later in this section) and at some shops in Cazorla town, but do not rely on it. See Maps in the Facts for the Visitor chapter for information on buying maps before you arrive.

Information

The main park information centre is at Torre del Vinagre. There are seasonal tourist offices at Cortijos Nuevos, Hornos, Santiago de la Espada, Segura de la Sierra, Orcera and Siles. Tourism offices in Cazorla also provide information on the park.

Organised Tours

A number of outfits offer guided trips to some of the park's less accessible areas, plus other activities. Hotels and camp sites in the park can often arrange for you to be picked up.

The highest-profile operator is **Quercus** (☎ 953 72 01 15; e *quercus@excursiones quercus.com; Calle Juan Domingo 2, Cazorla*), which has English- and French-speaking guides. Quercus offers 4WD trips from its

Cazorla base and from Torre del Vinagre to *zonas restringidas* (areas where vehicles are not normally allowed, with chained-off tracks) for €19 per person a half-day or €33 a full day, as well as guided hikes and *'caza fotográfica'* (photographic hunting) outings. Quercus can also be contacted through the Torre del Vinagre information centre.

Excursiones Bujarkay (☎ 953 71 30 11; *Calle Borosa 81, Coto Ríos*) offers walking, 4WD, biking and horse-riding trips with local guides *(guías nativos)*. It also has a roadside kiosk in Arroyo Frío.

Accommodation & Food

The park has plenty of accommodation but few places in the budget range, except for camp sites, of which there are at least 10. During peak visitor periods it's worth booking ahead.

Camping is not allowed outside the organised camp sites. These don't always stick to their published opening dates and from October to April it's always worth ringing ahead or checking with one of the tourist offices.

Virtually all hotels, *hostales* and camp sites in the park have restaurants, mostly serving local fare. There's also a variety of other restaurants and kiosks around the park.

See the later Places to Stay sections for details on what's available.

The South of the Park

The park begins just a few hundred metres up the hill east of Cazorla town, and the footpaths and dirt roads working their way between the pine forests, meadowlands, crags, streams and valleys of the Sierra de Cazorla offer heaps of scope for day walks or drives, with fine panoramas.

The main A-319, northeast from Cazorla, doesn't enter the park until Burunchel, after 7km. From Burunchel it winds 5km up to the 1200m Puerto de las Palomas pass, with the breezy Mirador Paso del Aire lookout a little farther on. Five twisting kilometres downhill from here is Empalme del Valle, a junction where the A-319 turns north towards Arroyo Frío to pick up the north-flowing Guadalquivir.

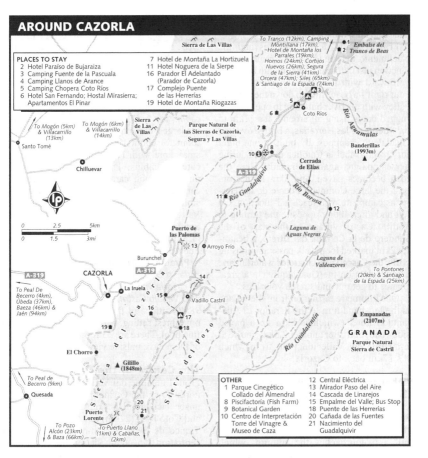

AROUND CAZORLA

PLACES TO STAY
2 Hotel Paraíso de Bujaraiza
3 Camping Fuente de la Pascuala
4 Camping Llanos de Arance
5 Camping Chopera Coto Ríos
6 Hotel San Fernando; Hostal Mirasierra;
   Apartamentos El Pinar
7 Hotel de Montaña La Hortizuela
11 Hotel Noguera de la Sierpe
16 Parador El Adelantado
   (Parador de Cazorla)
17 Complejo Puente
   de las Herrerías
19 Hotel de Montaña Riogazas

OTHER
1 Parque Cinegético
   Collado del Almendral
8 Piscifactoría (Fish Farm)
9 Botanical Garden
10 Centro de Interpretación
   Torre del Vinagre &
   Museo de Caza
12 Central Eléctrica
13 Mirador Paso del Aire
14 Cascada de Linarejos
15 Empalme del Valle; Bus Stop
18 Puente de las Herrerías
20 Cañada de las Fuentes
21 Nacimiento del
   Guadalquivir

Sierra de Cazorla by Car This 60km itinerary is a good introduction to the parts of the park nearest Cazorla town. Much of it is on unpaved roads, but it's all quite passable for ordinary cars, if a little bumpy in places.

Head first up to La Iruela (see Around Cazorla, earlier) and turn right along Carretera Virgen de la Cabeza soon after entering La Iruela. You reach the **Merenderos de Cazorla** lookout, with fine views over Cazorla, after about 700m. After another 4km you pass the Hotel de Montaña Riogazas; 7km farther is **El Chorro**, a gorge that's good for watching Egyptian and griffon vultures.

Just beyond El Chorro, ignore another dirt road forking down to the right. The track you are on winds round over the **Puerto Lorente** pass and down to a junction after 12km. Fork right here and after a couple of hundred metres a 'Nacimiento del Guadalquivir' sign points down some steps towards the river on your left. A plaque on the far bank marks the official **source of the Guadalquivir**. In dry periods you can apparently identify the stream emerging from underground. The road heads a short distance past the Nacimiento to the **Cañada de las Fuentes** picnic area. (If you have extra time and energy you could

JAÉN PROVINCE

continue 8km from here to Cabañas – see the later Cabañas Walk section.)

From Cañada de las Fuentes and the Nacimiento del Guadalquivir, return to the junction just before the Nacimiento and head northward with the infant Guadalquivir on your right – a beautiful trip down the wooded valley with the river bubbling to one side and rugged crags rising all around. It's 11km to the **Puente de las Herrerías**, a bridge over the Guadalquivir supposedly built in one night for Queen Isabel la Católica to cross during her campaigns against Granada. Here the road becomes paved, and 3km farther on, past the large Complejo Puente de las Herrerías camp site, you reach a T-junction. Go left and after 400m, opposite the turning to Vadillo Castril village, is the start of the **Sendero de la Cerrada del Utrero**, a beautiful 2km marked loop walk passing imposing cliffs, the **Cascada de Linarejos** waterfall and a small dam on the Guadalquivir – a great chance to get out and stretch your legs.

One kilometre farther on from the village is the left-hand turn to the Parador El Adelantado hotel (which is 5km up a paved side-road) and after another 2.5km you're at Empalme del Valle junction, from which it's 17km back to Cazorla.

Cabañas Walk This 2028m peak, one of the highest in the park, is a two-hour round-trip walk from the road at Puerto Llano, 8km south of Cañada de las Fuentes. The route loops round the southern end of the hill and approaches the summit, which offers superb views, from the southeast.

Sierra del Pozo & Barranco del Guadalentín Walks Further good walks in the south of the park are to be had in the Sierra del Pozo, which rises above the eastern side of the upper Guadalquivir valley, and in the Barranco del Guadalentín, a deep river valley farther east. The latter is particularly rich in wildlife, but you need either your own vehicle, or a guide with one, to reach these areas.

Places to Stay Accommodation options in the southern part of the park are limited.

Hotel de Montaña Riogazas (☎ 953 12 40 35; singles/doubles €30/40; open Apr-Oct), at Km 4.5 on the road from La Iruela to El Chorro, is an old hunting lodge converted into an attractive little hotel.

Complejo Puente de las Herrerías (☎/fax 953 72 70 90; camping per adult/tent/car €4/3.60/3.60, doubles with bathroom €45, cabins for 2/12 people €42.80/143.40) is the largest camping ground in the park, with room for about 1000 people. It also has a small hotel with 11 double rooms, and self-catering cabins. There's a restaurant and pool, and you can arrange horse riding, canoeing, canyoning and climbing. It's possible to walk here from the Empalme del Valle bus stop by following the signed Sendero de El Empalme del Valle path (1.5km) then the signed Sendero de la Fuente del Oso path (1.4km).

Parador El Adelantado (Parador de Cazorla; ☎ 953 72 70 75, fax 953 72 70 77; e cazorla@parador.es; at end of JF-7094, near Vadillo Castril; singles/doubles €79.50/98.40) offers all the parador comforts in a pine forest setting, with a grassy garden and fine pool. There are 33 rooms, but only nine of them have outside views.

The Centre of the Park

From Empalme del Valle the A-319 heads north down the Guadalquivir valley to the unspectacular villages of Arroyo Frío (6km) and Coto Ríos (22km) and the Embalse del Tranco de Beas reservoir. The main concentration of accommodation and visitor facilities in the park is dotted along this road and the most popular day hike, up the Río Borosa, is accessible from it. The bus from Cazorla goes as far as Coto Ríos.

Torre del Vinagre Sixteen kilometres northeast of Empalme del Valle, the roadside **Centro de Interpretación Torre del Vinagre** (☎ 953 71 30 40; open 10am-2pm & 5pm-8.30pm daily in summer; 11am-2pm & 4pm-7pm daily in spring & autumn; 11am-2pm & 4pm-6pm Tues-Sun in winter) was built as a hunting lodge for Spain's high and mighty, including Franco, in the 1950s. Today it offers displays and information on the park, with opening hours that vary by the year and season. In an adjoining building is the **Museo de Caza** (Hunting Museum; admission free; open 11am-2pm & 5pm-8pm daily in summer; 11am-2pm & 4pm-7pm daily in spring & autumn; 11am-2pm & 4pm-6pm Tues-Sun in winter), with a welter of stag antlers, boar tusks and stuffed wildlife, plus ibex and deer heads staring dolefully from the walls. As if to counter all this lifelessness, just up the road is a **botanical garden** (admission free; open 11am-noon daily, 4pm-6pm Wed-Sun) exhibiting the park's flora.

Río Borosa Walk Though it can get very busy at weekends and holiday times, this 24km, seven-hour walk (return, not counting stops) is popular for good reason. It follows the Río Borosa upstream, through scenery that progresses from the pretty to the majestic, via a gorge and two tunnels (a torch is useful) to two beautiful mountain lakes – an ascent of 500m in the course of 12km from Torre del Vinagre. Using the bus to Torre del Vinagre (see Getting There & Around later in this section), you can do it as a day trip from Cazorla. You should carry plenty of water with you.

A road signed 'Central Eléctrica', east off the A-319 opposite the information centre, crosses the Guadalquivir after about 500m and within 1km from the river, reaches a **fish farm** (piscifactoría), with parking areas close by. The marked start of the walk is on your right, shortly past the fish farm.

The first section is an unpaved road, criss-crossing the tumbling, trout-rich river on bridges. After about 4km diverge to the right along a path signed 'Cerrada de Elías'. This takes you through a beautiful 1.5km section where the valley narrows to a gorge (the **Cerrada de Elías**) and the path takes to a wooden walkway to save you from swimming. You re-emerge on the dirt road and continue for 3km to the **Central Eléctrica**, a small hydroelectric station.

The path passes between the power station and river, and crosses a footbridge, where a 'Nacimiento de Aguas Negras, Laguna de Valdeazores' sign directs you ahead. About

1.5km from the station, the path turns left and zigzags up into a **tunnel** cut inside the cliff for water flowing to the power station. A narrow path, separated from the watercourse by a fence, runs through the tunnel, which takes about five minutes to walk through. Then there's a short section in the open air before you enter a **second tunnel**, which takes about one minute to get through. You emerge just below the dam of **Laguna de Aguas Negras**, a picturesque little reservoir surrounded by hills and trees. Cross the dam to the other side of the lake then walk about 1km south to reach a similar-sized natural lake, the **Laguna de Valdeazores**.

Parque Cinegético Collado del Almendral & Tranco Seven kilometres north of Coto Ríos, on a spur of land between the A-319 and the Embalse del Tranco de Beas, the parque cinegético (game park) is a large enclosed area where ibex, mouflon and deer are kept. A 1km footpath leads from the parking area to three lookout points where you might see animals – your chances are highest at dawn and dusk.

Fifteen kilometres farther north, the A-319 crosses the dam that holds back the reservoir. The small village of Tranco stands on the northern side of the dam.

Places to Stay In Arroyo Frío two modern, medium-sized hotels are **Hotel Cazorla Valle** (☎ 953 72 71 00, fax 953 72 06 09; doubles €40.30) and **Hotel Montaña** (☎ 953 72 70 11, fax 953 72 70 01; doubles €46).

Complejo Turístico Los Enebros (☎ 953 72 71 10, fax 953 72 71 34; singles/doubles with bathroom, TV & heating €49/78, apartments for 4-12 people €99.50-163.70), at the northern end of the village, has a hotel, apartments and a small camp site. There are also two pools and a playground.

Hotel Noguera de la Sierpe (☎ 953 71 30 21, fax 953 71 31 09; e lfhotels@lfhotels .com; singles/doubles €63/97), 5km north of Arroyo Frío along the A-319, is a favourite of the hunting community. It's decked with trophies, including a surprisingly alert-looking stuffed lion in the lobby; clearly not a local catch. The rooms are comfortable but not exactly cosy. You can arrange riding sessions from 30 minutes to six hours (€6 to €72).

Hotel de Montaña La Hortizuela (☎/fax 953 71 31 50; singles/doubles €35.31/47) is a 27-room, cosy hotel in a tranquil setting 1km off the main road. The turn-off is 2km north of Torre del Vinagre. The rooms are medium-sized with bathroom, and the hotel has a restaurant, with a €9 menú.

A farther 1km north on the A-319 are the comfortable, modern **Hotel San Fernando** (☎ 953 71 30 69; singles/doubles €45/53), and the older **Hostal Mirasierra** (☎/fax 953 71 30 44; singles/doubles €28.90/34; both have pools. Adjoining the Mirasierra is **Apartamentos El Pinar** (☎ 953 71 30 68; 4-8 person apartments €57-102).

Within the next 4km on (or just off) the A-319 are three medium-sized camping grounds beside the Guadalquivir: the first is **Camping Chopera Coto Ríos** (☎ 953 71 30 05; camping per 2 adults, tent & car €11.77), with a rather cramped but shady site by the side road into Coto Ríos; then **Camping Llanos de Arance** (☎ 953 71 31 39; camping per 2 adults, tent & car €14.35), just across the Guadalquivir; and finally **Camping Fuente de la Pascuala** (☎ 953 71 30 28; camping per 2 adults, tent & car around €13.90), beside the A-319.

Hotel Paraíso de Bujaraiza (☎ 953 12 41 14; singles/doubles with bathroom €40/60) is in a fine position by the reservoir.

North of Tranco along the road towards Hornos are the **Hotel de Montaña Los Parrales** (☎ 953 12 61 70; singles/doubles with bathroom €21/33), overlooking the reservoir, with a pool and rates including breakfast, and **Camping Montillana** (☎ 953 12 61 94; camping per adult/tent/car €3.20/3.40/4.55).

The North of the Park

North of the Embalse del Tranco de Beas the main valley widens out and the hills are less rugged.

Hornos & Around Twelve kilometres north of the dam at Tranco, the A-319 runs into a T-junction from which the A-317 winds 4km up to Hornos, a village atop a high rock outcrop with panoramic views. Hornos' castle, which dates from Islamic times, looks more impressive from a distance than it really is.

The A-317 winds 45km southeast across the Sierra de Segura from Hornos to the small town of Santiago de la Espada near the park's eastern boundary. About 10km northeast of Hornos on the A-317 is the Puerto de Horno de Peguera pass and junction. One kilometre up the road to the north (towards Siles), a dirt road turns left at some ruined houses to the top of **El Yelmo** (1809m), one of the most distinctive mountains in the northern part of the park. It's 5km to the top – an ascent of 360m. At a fork after 1.75km, go right (the left fork goes down to El Robledo and Cortijos Nuevos). Both the climb and the summit of El Yelmo afford superb long-distance views. You should see griffon vultures wheeling around the skies – and, at the weekend and holidays, paragliders and hang-gliders. The road is OK for cars, if narrow, but is also a good walk.

Segura de la Sierra Easily the most spectacular and interesting village in the park, Segura de la Sierra sits on a high hill crowned by a castle dominating the countryside. By road it's 20km north of Hornos: turn east off the A-317 4km after Cortijos Nuevos.

Segura, a small place of just a few narrow streets, is possibly of Phoenician origin. The Romans mined silver in the area, and in Muslim times Segura was briefly the capital of a taifa (small kingdom). When taken in 1214 by the Knights of Santiago, it was one of the very first Christian conquests in Andalucía.

The incredibly sinuous road that wriggles its way upwards to Segura is deceptive. You begin to feel you'll never get there. As you approach the upper, older part of the village, there's a **tourist office** (☎ 953 48 02 80), open during Semana Santa and summer only, beside the Puerta Nueva, an arch which was one of four gates in Segura's Muslim walls. In other seasons tourist information is available from the **town hall** (☎ 953 48 02 80; open 8am-3pm Mon-Fri), just through the arch. The two main attractions, the castle and the Baño Moro, are normally left open all day every day, but you should check before heading for the castle especially.

Along and across the street from the town hall is the **Iglesia de Nuestra Señora del Collado**, the parish church, built about 1400 but much reconstructed since. In front of the church is the Fuente Carlos V, a handsome Renaissance fountain. The deconsecrated **Iglesia de los Jesuitas**, adjoining it below, has a good Renaissance facade. Continue down from here, then left along Calle Caballeros Santiaguistas, to the **Baño Moro** (Muslim Bath), built about 1150, probably for the local ruler Ibn ben Hamusk. It has three rooms (for cold, temperate and hot baths), a barrel vault with skylights, and horseshoe arches. Nearby is the **Puerta Catena**, the best preserved of Segura's four Muslim gates.

If you're walking up to the **castle**, at the top of the village, take the first narrow street up to the right after the parish church, Calle de las Ordenanzas del Común. After a few minutes you'll emerge beside Segura's tiny bullring, with the castle track heading up to the right. Do not underestimate the bullring, Famous fighters, such as Enrique Ponce, have fought here during Segura's October festival. You can drive most of the way up to the castle by heading past the parish church and round the perimeter of the village.

The main feature of the castle is its three-storey keep from which there are great views across to El Yelmo and far to the west. There's also a chapel with supposedly marvellous acoustics, but it is rarely opened outside special events at the castle. The castle's origins are Muslim or earlier. Take care on the castle's unlit stairways, even in daylight.

Places to Stay & Eat At the entrance to the village of Hornos, **Bar El Cruce** (☎ 953 49 50 03; Puerta Nueva 27; single/doubles with bathroom €12/24) is a cheerful place with decent rooms and a good menú for €8.40.

El Mirador (☎ 953 49 50 19; Puerta Nueva 11, Hornos; singles/doubles €15/24), around the corner from Bar El Cruce and into the village, also has eight rooms with bathroom, but is definitely a second choice.

Camping El Robledo (☎ 953 12 61 56; camping per adult/tent/car €3/3.30/2.40)

is at El Robledo, about 4km east of Cortijos Nuevos on a road leading up to El Yelmo.

Los Huertos de Segura (☎ 953 48 04 02, fax 953 48 04 17; e antonpeer@arrakis.es; Calle Castillo 11, Segura de la Sierra; 2-person studio €45, 2/4 person apartment €54/60) has excellent self-catering studio rooms and apartments with terrific views. The friendly owners are a good source of information about organised tours and walking in the area.

La Mesa Segureña (☎ 953 48 21 01; Calle Postigo 13; menú €10) is a good restaurant in Segura de la Sierra close to Los Huertos de Segura. Breakfast is €3.

Getting There & Around

Bus Buses are run daily (except Sunday) by **Carcesa** (☎ 953 72 11 42) from Cazorla's Plaza de la Constitución to Empalme del Valle, Arroyo Frío (€1.50, 45 minutes), Torre del Vinagre (€2.40, one hour) and Coto Ríos (€2.40, 70 minutes) (The timetable changes from time to time so check with the company or with Quercus in Cazorla – see Orientation & Information under Cazorla earlier in this chapter for details). At our last check, the buses left Cazorla at 5.45am and 3pm Monday to Friday from mid-September to late June, 6.30am and 2.40pm from late June to mid-September, and Saturday year-round. Buses back to Cazorla left Coto Ríos at 7.10am (at 8am late June to mid-September and on Saturday all year) and 4.30pm.

No buses link the northern part of the park with the centre or south, and there are no buses to Segura de la Sierra. However, coming from Jaén, Baeza or Úbeda, you could get an Alsina Graells bus to La Puerta de Segura (leaving Jaén daily at 9.30am and returning from La Puerta at 3pm). From La Puerta the best bet is a **taxi** (☎ 953 48 08 30, 619 06 04 09) onwards to Segura de la Sierra (€10).

Car & Motorcycle Approaches to the park include the A-319 from Cazorla, roads into the north from Villanueva del Arzobispo and Puente de Génave on the N-322, and the A-317 to Santiago de la Espada from Puebla de Don Fadrique in northern Granada province. There are at least seven petrol stations in the park.

Almería Province

Andalucía's easternmost province is its hottest and driest, with over 3000 hours of annual sunshine beating down relentlessly upon large expanses of mountainous semi-desert. Northwest of the coastal capital, Almería city, the eastern outliers of the wooded Alpujarras give way to a succession of mountain ranges rising to over 2000m, their slopes pierced by the ravines of often dry river beds. East of Almería city these arid mountains meet the coast on the hilly Cabo de Gata peninsula, where magnificent beaches are strung between dramatic cliffs and headlands. Attractive coastal resorts such as San José and Mojácar, and inland villages such as Níjar enhance the appeal of this otherwise desolate environment. In recent decades Almería has harnessed its bountiful sunlight to regenerate a once-moribund economy through tourism and the intensive cultivation, on its coastal plains, of vegetables, fruit and flowers under thousands of polythene greenhouses, a plastic sea that adds another bizarre element to an already remarkable landscape.

ALMERÍA

postcode 04080 • pop 171,000

The cliff-ringed Alcazaba is a linked series of fortified compounds that dominates Almería and its sea approaches. It is the most dramatic reminder of the city's long-lost glory. Islamic Almariya was initially a port for the Córdoba caliphate, and, as the capital of an 11th-century *taifa* (small kingdom), it grew wealthy from international trade and the weaving of silk from Alpujarras thread. The city was taken by the Catholic Monarchs in 1490 and its Muslim populace was expelled a year later. Neglect and a devastating earthquake in 1522 led to Almería's decline. Recovery began only in the 19th century, mainly from the profits of mineral extraction. Today Almería is a likable and lively port city, where the Alcazaba and a tangle of 19th-century streets and plazas around the late-medieval cathedral provide a heart of rich

Highlights

- Spend time exploring the beaches, coast and villages of the unique and dramatic Cabo de Gata peninsula
- Soak up the past at the Alcazaba of Almería, one of Andalucía's most impressive Muslim castles
- Search out the colourful pottery at Níjar and Sorbas
- Relax at Mojácar's traditional village and its modern beach resort
- Make the trip to Los Vélez, a little-visited area that has fascinating historical relics and beautiful mountain scenery
- Enjoy the contrasting landscapes of the wooded Almerian Alpujarras and of the arid mountains of the Tabernas area

character to a city whose outer reaches have been brutally modernised. The Mediterranean Games of 2005 are being staged in Almería, another promising step towards regeneration.

Orientation & Information

Old and new Almería lie to either side of the Rambla de Belén, a *paseo* (walk) which runs down the centre of Avenida de Federico García Lorca. A broad airy boulevard, Rambla de Belén is punctuated by water channels, fountains, palm trees and dramatic sculptures, and descends gently towards the sea above the course of a once-dry river bed. East of Rambla de Belén lies Almería's architecturally bland commercial district. West of the Rambla lie the city centre, the cathedral, the Alcazaba and the oldest and most interesting streets and plazas. The old city's main artery, Paseo de Almería, leads diagonally north from Rambla de Belén to a busy intersection called Puerta de Purchena. The bus and train stations share the same reception concourse on Carretera de Ronda, a few hundred metres east of the seaward end of Rambla de Belén.

The tourist information office of the **Patronato Provincial de Turismo** (☎ 950 62 11 17; Plaza Bendicho; open 10am-2pm & 5pm-8pm Mon-Fri) is helpful, as is the Junta de Andalucía **tourist office** (☎ 950 27 43 55; Parque de Nicolás Salmerón s/n; open 9am-7pm Mon-Fri, 10am-2pm Sat & Sun). Both have many free leaflets and brochures. The **Oficina Turística Municipal** (Municipal Tourist Office; ☎ 950 28 07 48; Rambla de Belén, Avenida de Federico García Lorca s/n; open 10am-2pm & 6pm-8pm Mon-Fri, 10am-noon Sat) is below ground level and is not well signed. It has useful information and

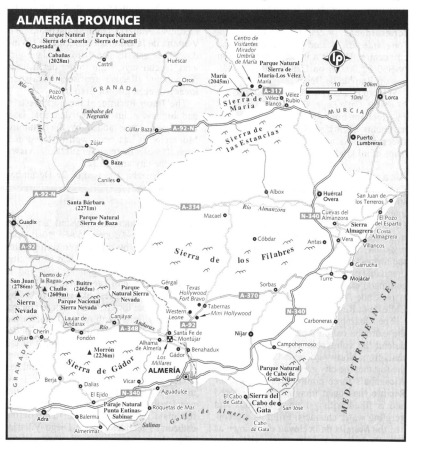

ALMERÍA PROVINCE

is also worth visiting for its regular displays of excellent artwork and regional pottery.

There are numerous **banks** on Paseo de Almería and a **post office** (Plaza de Juan Cassinello 1) just off it. The **dc-9 internet centre** (☎ 950 25 71 96; Calle Martínez Almagro 8; open 9am-10pm Mon-Sat, 11am-10pm Sun; €1.80 per hour) is worth visiting just for its layout, which includes the entire fuselage of a Shorts 360, the kind of small carrier aircraft that was used by the British Post Office in the early 1980s. You can tap out your emails from aircraft seats inside the plane. **Travel agencies** cluster along Paseo de Almería and Avenida de la Estación.

The main public hospital is **Hospital Torcárdenas** (☎ 950 21 21 00; Pasaje Torcárdenas), located 4km northeast of the city centre. There's a **Policía Local station** (☎ 950 21 00 19) on Calle Santos Zárate, just off Rambla de Belén.

El Libro Picasso (☎ 950 23 56 00, fax 950 27 05 02; Calle Reyes Católicos 17 & 18) is an excellent bookshop with separate departments facing each other across the street. It stocks a vast range of books and maps of all kinds.

Alcazaba

Earthquakes and the ravages of time have spared little of the original splendour of the interior of the Alcazaba (admission €1.50, EU citizen free; open 9am-8.30pm daily mid-June–Sept; 9.30am-6.30pm daily Oct–mid-June). Yet the solid walls and towers of the fortress still rise triumphantly from impregnable cliffs to dominate the city and to command exhilarating views. The entrance is on Calle Almanzor, up the hill west of Calle de la Reina.

The Alcazaba was founded in AD 955 by the Córdoba caliph Abd ar-Rahman III to defend the vulnerable coast from Fatimid raids from North Africa, and it was around the fort that the city grew. The lowest of the Alcazaba's three compounds, the **Primer Recinto**, has been imaginatively restored and is filled with gardens, fountains and gurgling water channels. From its top corner, the **Muralla de la Hoya** (also known as Muralla de Jairán) – a fortified wall built in

the early 11th century by Jairán, Almería's first *taifa* ruler – descends the valley on the northern side of the Alcazaba and climbs the slopes of Cerro de San Cristóbal opposite, a parched and barren hill crowned with a ruined church and a giant statue of Christ.

The **Segundo Recinto** was the heart of the Alcazaba. Built against the wall at its eastern end are the **Aljibes Califales** (Caliphal Water Cisterns) and a chapel, the **Ermita de San Juan**, converted from a mosque by the Catholic Monarchs. On the northern side of the enclosure are the remains of the Muslim rulers' palace, the **Palacio de Almotacín** – named after Almotacín (r. 1051–91), the ruler under whom medieval Almería reached its peak. The **Ventana de la Odalisca** (Concubine's Window) here gets its name from a slave girl who, legend says, leapt to her death from the window after her imprisoned Christian lover had been thrown from it.

The **Tercer Recinto**, at the northwestern and highest point of the Alcazaba, is a fortress that was added by the Catholic Monarchs. It has been well restored and from its walls there are breathtaking views across the city and the sea.

The Alcazaba is closed on 25 December and 1 January.

Cathedral

Almería's monumental cathedral (admission €2; open 10am-4.30pm Mon-Fri, 10am-1pm Sat) is fronted by ranks of towering palm trees at the heart of the old part of the city. The cathedral was begun in 1524 and is mainly a mixture of late-Gothic and Renaissance styles. Its fortress-like walls, linked by six formidable towers, were built to counter pirate raids from North Africa. Look for the exuberant **Sol de Portocarrero** (Calle del Cubo), a splendid 16th-century relief of the sun, carved on the eastern end of the building.

The spacious interior of the cathedral has a Gothic ribbed ceiling; jasper and local marble are used in some of its baroque and neoclassical trimmings. The chapel behind the main altar contains the tomb of the cathedral's founder, Bishop Diego Villalán, whose broken-nosed image is a work of the

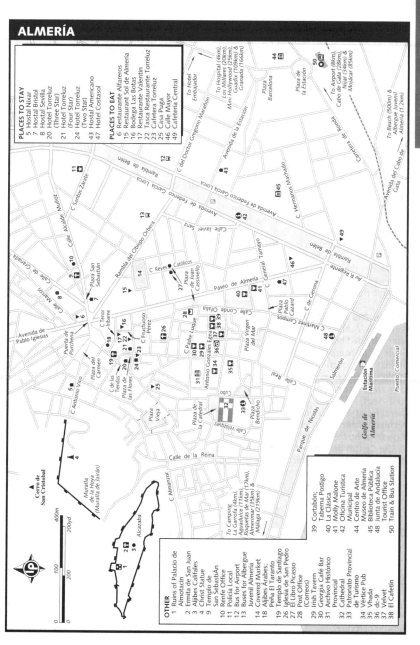

ALMERÍA

PLACES TO STAY
5 Hostal Nixar
7 Hostal Bristol
8 Hostal Sevilla
20 Hotel Torreluz
 (Three Star)
21 Hotel Torreluz
 (Four Star)
24 Hotel Torreluz
 (Two Star)
43 Hostal Americano
47 Hotel Costasol

PLACES TO EAT
6 Restaurante Alfareros
15 Restaurant Sol de Almería
16 Bodega Las Botas
17 Restaurante Valentín
22 Tasca Restaurante Torreluz
23 Cafetería Torreluz
25 Casa Puga
46 Calle Mayor
49 Cafetería Central

OTHER
1 Ruins of Palacio de
 Almotacín
2 Ermita de San Juan
3 Aljibes Califales
4 Christ Statue
9 Templo de
 San Sebastián
10 Renfe Office
11 Policía Local
12 Bus for Airport
13 Buses for Albergue
 Juvenil Almería
14 Covered Market
18 Aljibes Árabes;
 Peña El Taranto
19 Templo de Santiago
26 Iglesia de San Pedro
27 El Libro Picasso
28 Post Office
 (Correos)
29 Irish Tavern
30 Georgia Café Bar
31 Archivo Histórico
 Provincial
32 Cathedral
33 Patronato Provincial
 de Turismo
34 Centro Arte
35 Vhada
36 dc-9
37 Velvet
38 El Cafetín
39 Cortabón;
 Taberna Postigo
40 La Clásica
41 Molly Malone
42 Oficina Turística
 Municipal
44 Centro de Arte
45 Museo de Almería
 Biblioteca Pública
48 Junta de Andalucía
50 Tourist Office
 Train & Bus Station

16th-century architect and sculptor, Juan de Orea, as are the choir, with its walnut stalls, and the Sacristía Mayor, with its carved stone roof, windows and arches. A door in the south wall opens onto a small Renaissance courtyard crammed with shrubs and flowers.

Plaza Vieja

Around 200m up from the cathedral is this arcaded square, also known as Plaza de la Constitución, a charming and serene 17th-century enclosure, its walls hung with vivid bougainvillea and geraniums. It has plenty of seats to dream away an hour or two in the sun. Almería's endearingly theatrical-looking Ayuntamiento (City Hall) is on its northwest side. The centre of the plaza is filled with tall palm trees that encircle the bone-white Monumento a los Colorgos (Monument to the Redcoats), which commemorates the execution in 1824 of 24 liberals who took part in a rebellion against the despotic rule of Fernando VII.

Museums & Exhibitions

Almería's Archaeological Museum is currently divided between two temporary sites. Finds from nearby Los Millares and other prehistoric material are in the **Biblioteca Pública** (Calle Hermanos Machado; admission free; open 9am-2pm Mon-Sat mid-June–Sept, Tues-Sat Oct–mid-June). The Iberian and Roman collections are in the **Archivo Histórico Provincial** (Calle Infanta 12; admission free; open 9am-2pm Mon-Fri).

The **Centro de Arte – Museo de Almería** (Plaza Barcelona; admission free; open 11am-2pm & 6pm-8pm Mon-Fri, 6pm-9pm Sat, 11am-2pm Sun) stages temporary exhibitions and houses the city's permanent art collection.

Beach

A long, grey-sand beach fronts the palm-lined Paseo Marítimo, east of the city centre.

Special Events

Almería's big bash is the summer *feria* (fair) in late August – 10 days and nights of music, bullfights, fairground rides, exhibitions and full-on partying.

Places to Stay – Budget

Camping La Garrofa (☎ 950 23 57 70; camping per person/tent/car €3.10/3.10/3.10; open year-round) is on the coast 4km west of town on the Aguadulce road. It has room for 200 people.

Albergue Juvenil Almería (☎ 950 26 97 88, fax 950 27 17 44; Calle Isla de Fuerteventura s/n; under 26/other €12.90/17.25 mid-June–Aug & holiday periods, €10.90/15.20 rest of year), clean and well kept, can accommodate 170 people, nearly all in double rooms. It's 1.5km east of the city centre, beside the Estadio de la Juventud stadium and three blocks north of Avenida del Cabo de Gata. Take bus No 1 'Universidad' from the eastern end of Rambla del Obispo Orbera and ask the driver for the *albergue*, or stadium.

Hostal Americano (☎ 950 28 10 15; Avenida de la Estación 6; singles/doubles with washbasin €21/36, with bathroom €26/42), near the mid-point of Rambla de Belén, has decent-sized but slightly drab rooms. It is close to the bus and train stations and to the bus stand for the airport.

Hostal Sevilla (☎ 950 23 00 09; Calle de Granada 23; singles/doubles €27/40.30) is a cheerful place that offers clean, air-con rooms with TV and private bathroom.

Hostal Bristol (☎ 950 23 15 95; Plaza San Sebastián 8; singles/doubles €30/43) has a comfortable, old-fashioned charm.

Hostal Nixar (☎/fax 950 23 72 55; Calle Antonio Vico 24; singles/doubles €23.80/40.30, doubles with bathroom €43) is a well-kept place, but it has a rather gloomy decor that is matched occasionally by the welcome. You have to ring for entrance, even in the middle of the day.

Places to Stay – Mid-Range & Top End

In this range you can count on a private bathroom, satellite TV, air-con in summer and heating in winter.

Hotel Torreluz (☎ 950 23 43 99, fax 950 28 14 28; e torreluz@torreluz.com; Plaza de las Flores; singles/doubles in 2-star €38.80/57.30, in 3-star €55.50/74) comprises separate but adjacent hotels of two and three stars under the same management. Secure garaging is available for both.

Hotel Embajador (☎ 950 25 55 11, fax 950 25 93 64; Calzado de Castro 4; singles/doubles €54.70/80.40) is very handy for the bus and train stations. It has pleasant rooms, but the overall decor is slightly dated.

Hotel AM Torreluz (☎ 950 23 49 99, fax 950 23 47 09; e recep.torreluz-IV@laural.es; Plaza de las Flores; singles/doubles €67.40/114.50) is a four-star place with all the trimmings and is under a different management to its namesake neighbours. Prices are reduced by up to 40% at weekends. It has its own underground garage.

Hotel Costasol (☎/fax 950 23 40 11; e recepcion@hotelcostasol.com; Paseo de Almería 58; singles/doubles €63.25/73.90), in a convenient central location, has comfortable rooms. Parking is available.

Places to Eat

Cafetería Torreluz (Calle de las Flores; breakfast €3) is a smart local breakfast favourite, where varied tostadas (toasted rolls or slices of toast) and mini bocadillos (small sandwiches) cost from €1 to €1.50 and you can get a desayuno continental (continental breakfast) of orange juice, coffee and tostada.

Tasca Restaurante Torreluz (Calle Concepción Arenal; raciones €4.30-19) has a pleasant wood-panelled bar offering good tapas and raciones (meal-sized servings of tapas), including tasty fish dishes such as boquerones fritos (deep fried anchovies). Platos combinados (mixed platters) include patatas con huevos estrellados (fried eggs and chips; €5.69) or solomillo de cerdo al ajo (pork sirloin in garlic; €10).

Restaurante Valentín (Calle Tenor Iribarne 19; fish & meat mains €10-15) is a secluded little restaurant with stylish service. It specialises in good fish dishes, but langosta (lobster) will set you back €52.

Bodega Las Botas (Calle Fructuoso Pérez 3; media-raciones €4.20-5.40, raciones €7-9.80) is a popular sherry bar with old sherry casks serving as table tops. A ración of the finest jamón ibérico (cured ham) costs €16.80.

Restaurante Alfareros (Calle Marcos 6; fish & meat mains €7; open daily), a no-nonsense place near Puerta de Purchena, serves a good three-course lunch and dinner menú (fixed-price meal), including wine and a decent choice of fish and meat main courses.

Cafetería Central (Avenida de Federico García Lorca; platos combinados or mains €5.70-11), a big, bright place beside Rambla de Belén, also does salads and pastas for €4.40 to €5.40.

Casa Puga (Calle Jovellanos 7; tapas about €1) has few rivals as Almería's best tapas bar. Shelves of ancient wine bottles and traditional azulejo (glazed blue tile) wall covering set the tone.

Entertainment

A dozen or so music bars are clustered in the streets between the post office and the cathedral. Some of them open from late afternoon.

Georgia Café Bar (☎ 950 25 25 70; Calle Padre Luque 17) has terrific ambience. It has been running for more than 20 years and stages occasional live jazz, although even the piped music is great.

La Clásica (☎ 950 26 70 25; Calle Poeta Villaespesa 4), a little away from the main group, stays open to the small hours, with dancing to salsa and pop on the patio.

Despite its famous Irish name, **Molly Malone** (Paseo de Almería 56), just round the corner from La Clásica, has a far more English-orientated decor, with old London theatre posters fading in the fog of cigarette smoke.

Velvet (☎ 950 26 33 51; Calle Trajano 14) is a dance club that stays open to the early hours. It has mainly piped music, but weekend DJs do a fair job of keeping Almería abreast of the latest trends.

Peña El Taranto (☎ 950 23 50 57; Calle Tenor Iribarne), in the renovated Aljibes Árabes (Arab Water Cisterns), is Almería's top flamenco club. Live performances, open to the public, often happen at weekends.

Other popular **bars** on Calle Antonio González Eea include El Cafetín, the Irish Tavern and Taberna El Postigo.

Getting There & Away

Air Almería's **airport** (☎ 950 21 37 00) receives charter flights from several European countries. Scheduled services go to/from Dusseldorf with **LTU International Airways** (☎ 950 21 37 80), and to Barcelona, Madrid and Melilla with **Iberia** (at the airport ☎ 950 21 37 90). You can pick up inexpensive outbound international fares from agencies such as **Viajes Cemo** (in Roquetas de Mar ☎ 950 33 35 02 • at the airport ☎ 950 21 38 47) or **Tarleton Direct** (in Roquetas ☎ 950 33 37 34 • in Mojácar ☎ 950 47 22 48 • at the airport ☎ 950 21 37 70).

Bus Daily departures from the **bus station** (☎ 950 26 20 98) include nine or more buses to Guadix (€6.60, 1¼ hours); five or more to Granada (€10, 2¼ hours); eight to Málaga (€12.40, 3¼ hours); three to Seville (€24.30, five hours); and 10 or more to Murcia (€13, 2½ hours). There are four buses daily to Madrid and at least one bus daily each to Jaén, Úbeda, Córdoba, Valencia, Barcelona and – except Sunday – Ugíjar (via Berja) and Bérchules (via Adra).

For buses to places within Almería province, see under Getting There & Away in individual destinations.

Train You can buy tickets at the town centre **Renfe (Spanish National Railways) office** (☎ 950 23 18 22; Calle Alcalde Muñoz 7; open 9.30am-1.30pm Mon-Fri & 9.30am-1pm Sat), as well as at the **train station** (☎ 902 24 02 02). Direct trains run to/from Granada (€11.10, 2¼ to three hours, four times daily), Seville (€26.65, 5½ hours, three times daily) and Madrid (€35 to €46.50, 6¾ to 10 hours, twice daily). All trains go through Guadix (€5.80 to €13, 1¼ to 1¾ hours).

Boat From the Estación Marítima, **Trasmediterránea** (☎ 950 23 61 55, 902 45 46 45) sails to/from Melilla six days a week and three times daily from mid-June to late August or early September. The trip takes up to eight hours. The cheapest passenger accommodation, a *butaca* (seat), costs €26.30 one way; the fare for a car starts at €112 for a small vehicle. You can buy tickets at the Estación Marítima. The Moroccan lines **Ferrimaroc** (☎ 950 27 48 00, fax 950 27 63 66), **Comarit** (☎ 950 23 61 55) and **Limadet** (☎ 950 27 07 71) sail to/from Nador, the Moroccan town neighbouring Melilla, with similar frequency and prices.

Getting Around

To/From the Airport The airport is 9km east of the city, off the N-344; the No 14 'Aeropuerto' bus (€0.70) runs between the city (the end of Calle del Doctor Gregorio Marañón) and airport every 30 to 45 minutes daily from 7am to 10.30pm, but less frequently on Saturday and Sunday. It runs from the airport to the city every 30 to 45 minutes from 7am to 10.08pm Monday to Friday, and from 7am to 11.03pm Saturday and Sunday.

Car & Motorcycle There are several car rental agencies in the city. Avis, Europcar, Hertz and local company **Atesa** (☎ 950 29 31 31) have desks at the airport.

Almería has the same difficult streetside parking as most Andalucían cities. There are, however, large underground car parks beneath the Rambla de Belén and on the eastern side of the Rambla at its seaward end. Fees are €0.85 per hour, €10.20 for 24 hours.

Taxis There are taxi stands on Puerta de Purchena and Paseo de Almería and at the joint bus and train station (☎ 950 22 61 61, 950 25 11 11; night taxis ☎ 950 42 5757).

AROUND ALMERÍA
West of Almería

There are two neat but run-of-the-mill beach resorts to the west: **Aguadulce**, 11km from Almería, and **Roquetas de Mar**, 17km from Almería around the coast. Both do a sizable northern-European package-holiday trade. Almerimar, further west, is popular with Spanish vacationers. The wetlands of the **Paraje Natural Punta Entinas-Sabinar**, between Roquetas and Almerimar, are a good place to see greater flamingos and other water birds – around 150 species have been recorded there. A vast area west of Almería and a lesser one to its east are covered in plastic-sheeting greenhouses (see the boxed text 'The Plastic Sea').

Los Millares

You need to be an enthusiast for archaeological sites to consider a visit to Los Millares (☎ 608 95 70 65; admission free; open 9.30am-4pm Tues-Sat), on the N-324, 20km northwest of Almería between the villages of Gádor and Santa Fé de Mondújar. Your own transport is necessary as there is no viable public transport for a trip there and back. The site is not particularly scenic and there is a 1.5km trek from the main road. It can be searingly hot in summer, so take water and protect yourself against sunburn. All this aside, Los Millares is a compelling place and is of world significance archaeologically.

The site covers 19 hectares and stands on a 1km-long spur between the Río Andarax and Rambla de Huéchar. It was occupied from possibly 2700 to 1800 BC during a period when the Río Andarax was navigable from the sea. Its metalworking people may have numbered up to 2000 during optimum periods of occupation. They hunted, bred domestic animals and grew crops; their skills included pottery and jewellery-making, and certain finds indicate trading links with other parts of the Mediterranean.

The site is enclosed within four lines of defensive walls (reflecting successive enlargements of the settlement). Inside lie the ruins of the stone houses typical of the period. Outside the living area are the ruins (and some reconstructions) of typical passage graves of the Neolithic and pre–Bronze Age period: domed chambers entered by a low passageway.

Do not be discouraged by a notice on the roadside wall of the gate house stating that you should contact the Delegación de Cultura de Almería for permission to enter the site. It is essential, however, that you check that someone will be on duty at the Los Millares gate house to give access. Phone ☎ 608 95 70 65 before setting out. To get there, take the A-92 north from Almería to Benahadux, then head northwest on the A-348. Signs indicate the Los Millares turning, shortly before Alhama de Almería.

Wild West Towns

North of Benahadux, Almería's increasingly savage semidesert landscape resembles the deeply riven 'badlands' of the American West. In the 1960s and '70s, makers of Western movies spotted the resemblance and shot dozens of films here, including *A Fistful of Dollars*, *The Magnificent Seven* and *The Good, the Bad and the Ugly*. Locals played Indians, outlaws and cavalry, while Clint Eastwood, Raquel Welch, Charles Bronson

---

The Plastic Sea

With the aid of fertiliser, and using water pumped up from as deep as 100m, Almería's farmers have used polythene greenhouses to turn barren coastland into some of Europe's most intensive horticultural zones. It is an industry that since the 1970s has brought untold wealth to parts of Almería province. Most of the vegetables, fruit and flowers that are produced are trucked out early in the year to northern Europe, where the demand from supermarkets and the shopping public is for unblemished and uniformly shaped produce.

The capital of this bizarre *'plasticultura'* is the sprawling town of El Ejido, west of Almería. El Ejido reputedly has Spain's highest ratio of bank branches to population, but is also the scene of considerable tension between Spaniards and the Moroccan labourers on whom the greenhouse industry now relies.

The environmental price of such intensive forcing of produce is also high. The water deep below the plains is not being allowed to replenish itself and mountain villages such as Níjar have long been concerned about the pressure on their once-abundant water supplies.

and other lesser stars took centre stage. Movie makers come here less often now, but the surviving shells of three Wild West sets remain as tourist attractions of a sort, although much of the original character has been 'themed' out of them.

Mini Hollywood *(☎ 950 36 52 36; adult/child €16/9, ticket includes Reserva Zoológica; open 10am-9pm daily Apr-Oct, 10am-7pm Tues-Sun Nov-Mar)*, the best known and most expensive of these sets, is 25km from Almería on the Tabernas road and has all the features you'd expect of a Wild West movie town. Youngsters love every minute of it, but adults may have to grit their teeth at what has become a very costly outing. At noon and 5pm (and 8pm from mid-June to mid-September) a mock bank hold-up, shoot out and hanging is staged – or hammed up outrageously – to off-key music. Brace yourself for the equally hammy cancan show in the saloon. A djoining the Wild West town is the **Reserva Zoológica** with lions, elephants and numerous other species of African and Iberian fauna.

Three kilometres further towards Tabernas, then a few minutes along a track to the north, **Texas Hollywood Fort Bravo** *(☎ 950 16 54 58)* boasts a Western town, a stockaded fort, a Mexican village and Indian tepees. There's also **Western Leone** *(☎ 950 16 54 05)* on the A-92 about 1km north of the A-370 turning. Both places played a part in some of the same films as Mini Hollywood and have a more authentic if slightly worn-out air, not least on their approach tracks so it's best to drive slowly. Prices are cheaper than those at Mini Hollywood.

There are several weekday buses, fewer at weekends, between Almería and Tabernas (€1.70, one hour), but check first that the driver will not only drop you near the attractions, but also stop for you on the way back. The best option for a visit to any of the theme parks is with your own transport.

Just northeast of Tabernas the A-349 strikes northeast across the Sierra de los Filabres. The road initially passes the **Centro Solar**, a huge solar energy development aimed at harnessing all that Almerían

sunlight. The route through the arid mountains makes for an entertaining drive and lands you amid the wrecked quarrying landscape around the industrial town of Macael and on the A-334 that leads west to Baza and east to Huércal-Overa.

Níjar & Sorbas

Some of Andalucía's most attractive and original glazed pottery and colourful striped cotton rugs known as *jarapas* are made in Níjar, a small town nestling below the rugged peaks of the Sierra Alhamilla 4km north of the N-340, 31km northeast of Almería.

Shops and workshops selling these products line the main street, Calle García Lorca, and are dotted along the adjoining Barrio Alfarero (Potters' Quarter) along Calle Las Eras, off Calle García Lorca. From the top end of the main street, the narrow Calle Carretera leads into the heart of old Níjar and to Plaza la Glorieta and the church of Santa María de la Anunciación, which has a handsome coffered wooden ceiling. Beyond Plaza la Glorieta, up Calle Colón, is the delightful Plaza del Mercado with a huge central plane tree and a superb blue-tiled fountain with big fish-head faucets. Beyond here again, in Calle Lavadero, is a ceramics shop, La Tienda de los Milagros, which specialises in some very fine and colourful pottery.

Accommodation is limited but **Hostal Asensio** *(☎ 950 36 10 56; Calle Parque 2; singles/doubles €21/42)* has bright, pleasant rooms. The less cheerful **Hostal Montes** *(☎ 950 36 01 57; Avenida García Lorca 26; singles/doubles €24/30)* is just down the road. In Plaza la Glorieta **Café Bar Glorieta** *(plato combinados €4.80)* does *bocadillos* for €2.40. Across the plaza, **Bar Restaurante El Pipa** has much the same food at similar prices. **Café Bar La Curva** *(Calle Parque; platos combinados €6)* is diagonally opposite Hostal Asensio.

Níjar is served by two buses a day (one only on Saturday), but times make a day trip from Almería impossible. There are parking bays all the way up Avenida García Lorca, but check for parking restriction signs.

Another pottery town, Sorbas, lies about 34km by road from Níjar and can be reached from here by a pleasant drive through the compact mountains of the Sierra de Alhamilla. Sorbas stands along the edge of a dramatic limestone gorge. There is a very helpful **tourist information office** (☎ 950 36 44 76; Calle Terraplén 9; open 10am-2pm daily) on the road up to the centre. It is best to park here than in the town centre, which is very cramped.

Old Sorbas has a quietly persuasive charm, which is enhanced by a number of handsome 17th-century mansions, their neglected facades still retaining their original colours and features. Sorbas pottery is less colourful than that of Níjar and is more functional. There are several workshops and salesrooms located at the lower end of town beyond the pleasant central Plaza de la Constitución.

The only accommodation option is **Hostal Sorbas** (☎ 950 36 41 60; singles/doubles €15/22) on the main road, a drab but cheap place, right at the entrance to the village. The **Café Bar Teide** (☎ 950 36 44 56; Calle San Andrés), just off the main square, does platos combinados for €5.50.

There are four buses on weekdays and two on Saturday from Almería to Sorbas and back (€3, 1¾ hours).

LAS ALPUJARRAS

West of the small spa town of Alhama de Almería, the A-348 winds up the Andarax valley into the Almería Alpujarras (for more information see the Las Alpujarras section in the Granada Province chapter earlier in this book).

The landscape is at first relentlessly barren, with arid, serrated ridges stretching to infinity, but gradually it becomes more vegetated as you approach Fondón, where the small **Camping Puente Colgante** (☎ 950 51 42 90; camping per person/tent/car €3/3/3; open year-round) is located.

For information on walking routes and refuges in the mountain range, visit the **Centro de Visitantes Laujar de Andarax** (☎ 950 51 35 48), on the A-348, just west of Laujar de Andarax.

Laujar de Andarax
postcode 04470 • pop 1800
• elevation 920m

This pleasant 'capital' of the Almería Alpujarras is where Boabdil, the last emir of Granada, settled briefly after losing Granada. It was also the headquarters of Aben Humeya, the first leader of the 1568–70 Morisco uprising, until he was assassinated by his cousin Aben Aboo. Today it produces Almería's best wine.

The handsome **Casa Consistorial** (Town Hall) on the central Plaza Mayor de la Alpujarra was built in 1792. It has a facade of three tiers of arches crowned by a distinctive belfry-cum-weathervane. To the left of the town hall is a splendid 18th-century fountain. The large 17th-century brick **Iglesia de la Encarnación** is a stately building that has a minaret-like square tower and a lavish golden retable. A signposted road leads 1km north to **El Nacimiento**, a series of waterfalls in a deep valley, with a couple of restaurants nearby.

The falls are the starting point for some walking trails which the Centro de Visitantes can tell you about.

Places to Stay & Eat Just off Plaza Mayor de la Alpujarra, **Hostal Fernández** (☎ 950 51 31 28; Calle General Mola 2; singles/doubles €15/32) is a friendly place overlooking the main square. It has a good restaurant, with mains from about €5.

Hotel Almirez (☎ 950 51 35 14; e almihost@larural.es; singles/doubles €23.55/35.30), 1km west of town on the A-348, is a nicely situated modern hotel. It has a bar and a large restaurant that offers a reasonable menú for €8.40.

Fonda Nuevo Andarax and **Café Bar Carmela**, both near the junction of Calle José Antonio and Calle Aben Humeya, are popular local bars.

Getting There & Away A bus to Laujar (€3.80, 1¼ hours) leaves Almería bus station at 9am daily except Saturday, starting back from Laujar at 3.45pm. Between Laujar and the Granada Alpujarras, take a bus to Berja, then another to Ugíjar or beyond.

CABO DE GATA

East of Almería city the stark, volcanic hills of the Sierra del Cabo de Gata tumble down to a sparkling turquoise sea around the Cabo de Gata peninsula. At the tip of the peninsula a lonely lighthouse, the Faro de Cabo de Gata, overlooks the jagged reefs of the **Arrecife de las Sirenas** (Reef of the Mermaids). Some of Spain's most beautiful and least crowded beaches are strung between the awesome cliffs and capes of this dramatic coastline. With just 100mm of rain in an average year, Cabo de Gata is the driest place in Europe. Yet the area supports a remarkable variety of flora and fauna adapted to life in such an arid, salty environment. The area's scattered whitewashed settlements and flat-roofed houses add to its haunting North African character and the fairly low-key level of tourist development has not spoiled its refreshing sense of remoteness.

You can walk along the coast for 61km all the way from Retamar (east of Almería city) round the southern tip of Cabo de Gata and then northeast to Agua Amarga, but in summer there's very little shade (the route is described in Lonely Planet's *Walking in Spain*).

There is a broad coastal plain on the western side of Cabo de Gata that flanks the wide bay, **Golfo de Almería**, on which Almería city stands; superb sandy beaches line most of its length as far as La Almadraba de Monteleva, but the area is often subject to fierce, localised winds that can make sitting on the beach uncomfortable. The southern tip of the peninsula and its eastern side are more rugged, and the eastern side has plenty of good beaches, which are less windy. There's also good snorkelling in several places.

It's worth calling ahead for accommodation anywhere on Cabo de Gata during Easter, July and August. Camping is only allowed in official camping grounds.

The Editorial Alpina 1:50,000 map *Cabo de Gata-Níjar Parque Natural* is the best for the area.

Information

About 2.5km before Ruescas on the road from Almería, is **Centro de Interpretación Las Amoladeras** (☎ 950 16 04 35; open 10am-2pm & 5pm-9pm daily mid-July–mid-Sept; 10am-3pm Tues-Sun mid-Sept–mid-July), the main information centre for the Parque Natural de Cabo de Gata-Níjar, which covers Cabo de Gata's 60km coast, plus a thick strip of hinterland. The centre has displays on the area's fauna, flora and human activities, as well as tourist information and maps. It also sells a range of souvenirs and local craft work.

El Cabo de Gata

Officially called San Miguel de Cabo de Gata, this is the main village on the western side of the promontory. Fronted by an attractive stretch of sandy beach, it's composed largely of one- and two-storey holiday homes, but has an old nucleus with a small fishing fleet at the southern end. A bank on Calle Iglesia has an ATM.

South of the village are the **Salinas de Cabo de Gata** (salt-extraction lagoons). In spring, many greater flamingos and other water birds call in here while migrating from Africa or Huelva's Doñana area to breeding grounds further north (such as France's Camargue, in the case of the flamingos). A few flamingos and many other species stay on here to breed, then others arrive in summer but by late August there can be as many as 1000 flamingos here. Autumn brings the biggest numbers of migratory birds as they pause on their return south. A good place to watch the birds is the hide in a wood-fenced area just off the road 3km south of the village. You should see a good variety of birds any time of year, except winter, when the salinas are drained after the autumn salt harvest.

Another flamingo-viewing spot, where you'll probably get closer to the birds, is the small lagoon where the stream **Rambla de Morales** reaches the beach, 2km northwest of El Cabo de Gata village.

Places to Stay & Eat Near the beach, **Camping Cabo de Gata** (☎/fax 950 16 04 43; camping per person/tent/car €3.50/3.50/3.50, electrical hook-up €2.70; open year-round) is 2km down a signposted side road southwest of Ruescas. It has a pool, a restaurant and 250 sites.

Hostal Las Dunas (☎ 950 37 00 72; Calle Barrio Nuevo 58; singles/doubles €38.50/55), at the northern end of Cabo de Gata village, has well-kept, modern rooms with bathroom. Its surroundings are dull, but the excellent beach is just a short stroll down the road.

Blanca Brisa (☎/fax 950 37 00 01; Las Joricas 49; singles/doubles €38.50/64.30) is a modern hotel, with comfortable rooms, at the entrance to the village. It has a decent restaurant with breakfast for €3 and platos combinados for about €5.

El Naranjero (☎ 950 37 01 11; Calle Iglesia 1; meat dishes €9.50-15, fish dishes €12-25) is a popular, mainly fish and seafood restaurant at the entrance to the village.

Pizzeria Pedro (Calle Islas de Tabarca 2), located just around the corner from Blanca Brisa, serves fine pizzas and pasta at middling prices, but it's open only from June to August.

Faro de Cabo de Gata & Around

The salt collected from the salinas is piled up in great heaps at La Almadraba de Monteleva, a desolate-looking village with an equally desolate-looking church, the Iglesia de las Salinas, whose extremely tall tower dominates the area for miles around.

South of La Almadraba the coast becomes abruptly more rugged and the road winds airily round the cliffs to reach the lighthouse on the southern tip of the peninsula. A turning by Bar José y María (open Easter to October), just before the lighthouse, leads up to the **Torre Vigía Vela Blanca**, an 18th-century watchtower atop 200m cliffs. The tower is not open to the public, but there are spectacular views from the cliffs.

Here the surfaced road ends, but a walking and cycling track continues down to Playa de Mónsul (about 2km away), Playa de los Genoveses (4.5km) and San José (8.5km).

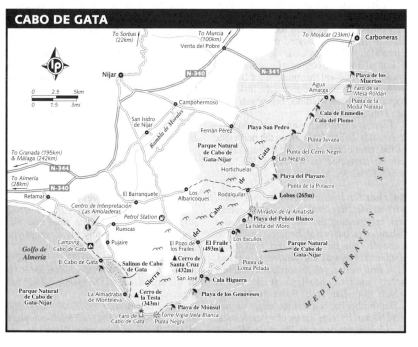

San José

postcode 04118

The attractive resort of San José lies on a small sandy bay on the eastern side of Cabo de Gata, a few kilometres northeast of the lighthouse. It is becoming increasingly popular in summer and on weekends out of season, but it retains its pleasant, relaxing atmosphere. Apart from an intrusive hotel right on the main beachfront, San José is low-rise with an open layout.

The road from the north becomes San José's main street, Avenida de San José, with the beach a couple of blocks down to the left. On Avenida de San José, in the main block of shops and cafés, just before the central Plaza Génova, you'll find a **natural park information office and visitor centre** (☎ 950 38 02 99; open 10am-2pm & 5pm-9.30pm Mon-Sat, 10am-2pm Sun). It sells maps and a range of books, souvenirs and craft work.

Also on Avenida de San José, in the village centre, are a **Caja Rural bank**, an **ATM** and a **Spar supermarket**. At the time of writing the post office was closed and a temporary post office van, open for an hour only each morning, was located on Calle de la Plaza alongside Plaza Génova.

For a good selection of second-hand books and for local information try **David's** on Avenida de San José above the little Moroccan gift shop **Aladino**, but watch your head on the stairs.

There is a reasonable amount of parking in Avenida de San José and on the north side of the main beach and at the harbour. Taxis can be contacted on ☎ 950 38 97 37 or ☎ 608 05 62 55.

Beaches San José has a sandy central beach, with an attractive little harbour at its eastern end, representing the village's origins as a fishing cove, but two of the finest beaches on Cabo de Gata lie along a dirt road to the southwest. **Playa de los Genoveses**, a broad, 1km strip of fine yellow sand, with shallow waters, and rocky headlands at each end, is 4.5km from San José. **Playa de Mónsul**, 2.5km further on, is a shorter length of grey sand backed by huge lumps of volcanic rock. Two kilometres west of Playa de Mónsul,

the road is blocked to motor vehicles – but not to walkers or bicycles – as it climbs to the Torre Vigía Vela Blanca (see Faro de Cabo de Gata & Around earlier).

Activities The information office can tell you about bicycle rental, horse riding, boat trips, 4WD tours and diving.

Places to Stay With room for 185 people, **Camping Tau** (☎/fax 950 38 01 66; @ e@parquenatural.com; camping per person/tent/car €3.50/3.50/3.50; open Apr-Sept) has a shady site 250m back from the beach. Follow the 'Tau' sign pointing left along Camino de Cala Higuera as you approach central San José from the north, and go about 800m.

Albergue Juvenil de San José (☎ 950 38 03 53, fax 950 38 02 13; Calle Montemar s/n; bunks €8; open 1 Apr-1 Oct) is a friendly, non-Inturjoven youth hostel run by the local municipality. It also opens for Christmas, New Year and long weekends. To find it, head towards Camping Tau but turn right after crossing a dry river bed, then take the first left up the hill.

Hostal Bahía (☎ 950 38 03 07, fax 950 38 03 06; singles/doubles €36/48), and its sister establishment **Hostal Bahía Plaza** (☎ 950 38 03 07; Avenida de San José; singles/doubles €36/48), across the street, are in the centre of San José and have 34 attractive, clean rooms with bathroom and TV, in bright, modern buildings.

Hostal Costa Rica (☎ 950 38 01 03, fax 950 38 00 59; Avenida de San José; singles/doubles €38/54) is a spick-and-span place just along from Hostal Bahía.

Hostal Puerto Genovés (☎/fax 950 38 03 20; Calle Arrastre; singles/doubles €39/57), just southeast of the main road into San José, is a bright, friendly place where you get breakfast included in the price.

Hostal Ágades (☎ 950 38 03 90; Calle Sidi Bel Abbes 1; singles/doubles €39/50) is on the inland side of the main road and has pleasant rooms.

Hostal Eldorado (☎ 950 38 01 18, fax 950 38 02 46; doubles €54), a French-run place above the road towards Playa de los

Genoveses, has pretty, well-equipped rooms, all with good views, and a French/Spanish/Mexican restaurant.

Plenty of apartments are available for rent (ask the tourist office or look for signs); two people can pay as little as €18 a day for a few days' stay off season, though it's more like €60 during July and August.

Places to Eat Under the same ownership as the Bahía *hostales*, **Restaurante El Emigrante** (☎ 950 38 03 07; *Avenida de San José; fish & meat mains €6-12*) has tasty food. Tortillas or a mixed salad cost €3 to €4.80. Breakfast of orange juice, toast and coffee costs €3.

Cafetería Restaurante El Ancla (☎ 950 38 00 69; *Calle La Olla; mains €9-14*), just back from the eastern end of the beach, is a popular seafood restaurant, with some shellfish costing less than normal mains.

Just beyond El Ancla, on the north side of the beach and near the harbour, is a line of eateries with outdoor tables including two **Italian places** (*pizza or pasta €5.40-6*) and **El Tempranillo** (*platos combinados €4.81, meat & fish mains €7.20-10.80, salads €4-7.50*).

San José to Las Negras

The rugged coast northeast of San José has only two small settlements, the odd fort and a few beaches before the slightly bigger village of Las Negras, 17km away as the crow flies. The road spends most of its time diverting inland.

The hamlet of **Los Escullos** has a short, mainly sandy beach and a restored old fort, the Castillo de San Felipe. You can walk here from San José along a track from Cala Higuera.

Camping Los Escullos (☎ 950 38 98 11; *camping per 2 adults, tent, car & electrical hook-up €18.70 high season; open year-round*), a large, moderately shaded place 900m back from the beach, has a pool, grocery store, ATM and bikes for hire. It also has a restaurant with a *menú* for €6.25.

Near the beach are two reasonable, small hotels: **Hotel Los Escullos** (☎ 950 38 97 33; *rooms €51-60*), and **Casa Emilio** (☎ 950 38 97 32; *singles/doubles €39/48*). Both have

restaurants offering tortillas and salads for €3.10 to €5 and meat and fish mains for €8 to €15.

La Isleta del Moro, 1km further northeast, is a tiny fishing village on the western arm of a wide bay with the Playa del Peñón Blanco stretching to its east.

Hostal Isleta del Moro (☎ 950 38 97 13; *fax 950 38 97 64; singles/doubles with bathroom €21/43*) has a restaurant with fresh seafood.

Casa Café de la Loma (☎ 950 52 52 11; *singles/doubles €30/42, all rooms an additional €6 in Aug*), on a small hill above the village, is a friendly, relaxed place with terrific views. The six rooms can be booked by groups. In summer a restaurant opens and offers vegetarian dishes as well as a general *menú*. There are occasional flamenco nights.

From here, the road climbs to a good viewpoint, the **Mirador de la Amatista** before heading inland past the former goldmining village of Rodalquilar. About 1km past Rodalquilar is the turning for **Playa del Playazo**, 2km away along a level track. This attractive sand beach stretches between two headlands, one topped by the Batería de San Ramón fortification (now a private home). From here you can walk alongside the coast to Camping La Caleta and Las Negras.

The tiny but engaging village of **Las Negras** stands above a pebbly beach that runs north towards Punta del Cerro Negro, an imposing headland of volcanic rock.

Camping La Caleta (☎ 950 52 52 37; *camping per adult/child/tent/car €3.60/ 3.45/4.20/3.75; open year-round*) is 1km south in a separate cove and is reached down a paved road. It lies in a valley and can be fiercely hot in summer, but there is a good swimming pool. There is a bar-restaurant and a supermarket.

Hostal Arrecife (☎ 950 38 81 40; *Calle Bahía 6; singles/doubles with bathroom €26/38*), on the main street, has decent rooms, some of which have sea views from their balconies.

Other accommodation is mostly holiday apartments and houses to let, but you may find a few signs offering rooms by the night.

Restaurante La Palma (☎ 950 38 80 42), overlooking the beach, is a relaxed place that plays good background music and serves excellent fish dishes at medium prices.

Pizza y Pasta (☎ 950 38 80 97; open Mar-Nov; mains €5-6), just down from the main street, is a bright, friendly place that offers tasty pizza, pasta and lasagne, and salads at €3 to €5.

Las Negras to Agua Amarga

There's no road along this cliff-lined and most secluded stretch of the Cabo de Gata coast, but walkers can take an up-and-down path of 11km. **Playa San Pedro**, one hour's walk from Las Negras, is the site of a ruined hamlet whose buildings (including a castle) once housed an international colony of two or three dozen hippies and the occasional wandering naturist, now long gone. There is talk of plans to establish a road to San Pedro from inland, though potential development should be low-key. It's 1½ hours' walk on from San Pedro to **Cala del Plomo**, a beach with another tiny settlement, then 1½ hours more to Agua Amarga. You could stop at the nice little **Cala de Enmedio** beach half an hour after Cala del Plomo.

Drivers from Las Negras to Agua Amarga must head inland through Hortichuelas. From the bus shelter on the eastern side of the road in Fernán Pérez, you can head northeast cross-country for 10km on a mostly unpaved but reasonable road (keep to the main track all the way) to meet the paved road running down to Agua Amarga from the N-341.

Agua Amarga

The most northerly settlement on the eastern side of Cabo de Gata, Agua Amarga is a pleasant, more-tourist-than-fishing village, but still with an unspoiled feel to it, standing alongside a good sandy beach. It has a supermarket and post office.

Three kilometres east up the Carboneras road is a turning to a clifftop lighthouse, the Faro de la Mesa Roldán (1.25km), with an old watchtower for a neighbour. The views up here are marvellous. From the car park by the turning you can walk down to the

naturist Playa de los Muertos. The road continues north through Carboneras, a minor resort, but with a huge cement factory looming balefully over its southern approaches, to Mojácar.

Places to Stay & Eat At the eastern end of the beach, **Hostal Restaurante La Palmera** (☎ 950 13 82 08; Calle Aguada s/n; rooms €48-84) has 10 pleasant rooms with bathroom, with prices depending on the views. The restaurant has a nice beach terrace and offers meat and fish mains at €6.60 to €15 and salads at €4 to €8.

Hotel Family (☎ 950 13 80 14, fax 950 13 80 70; Calle La Lomilla; singles/doubles €50/55, with sea views €80/85), just up from the western end of the beach amid trees, is run by a friendly French family and has nine lovely rooms with bathroom. Prices include a big breakfast. An excellent four-course menú (€16), including drinks, is served in the **restaurant** nightly at 7pm, also at weekends at 1pm.

Hotel Las Calas (☎ 950 13 82 35; singles/doubles €79/98) is behind Chiringuito Las Tarahis at the southwestern end of the beach; it also has houses and apartments for rent.

Hotel El Tio Kiko (☎ 950 13 80 80, fax 950 13 80 67; Calle Embarque; singles/doubles €96/138) is a top-of-the-range place with spectacular, if expensive, views.

Chiringuito Las Tarahis ((☎ 950 13 82 35; fish & meat mains from €7) is run by the Hotel Las Calas and is at the southwestern end of the resort overlooking the beach. It serves tortillas from €3.60.

La Plaza (Calle Ferrocarril Minero; plato combinados €5.40), in the village square, is a cheerful down-to-earth place. Try the fish soup for authentic local taste.

Getting There & Away

Bus schedules can be obtained from Almería city tourist offices or from Almería bus station. Some useful bus services are listed in the table.

The only petrol station on Cabo de Gata is halfway along the Ruescas–San José road. San José has a couple of car-rental agencies.

Bus Information

from	to	company	price (€)	departures	duration (hrs)
Almería	Agua Amarga	Bergasan	3.70	7.45pm Mon & Fri	1¼
Agua Amarga	Almería	Bergasan	3.70	6.15am Mon & Fri	1¼
Almería	El Cabo de Gata	Becerra	1.80	4 buses daily	½
Almería	La Isleta del Moro	Bernardo	2.50	6.30pm Mon, 2.15pm Sat*	1
La Isleta del Moro	Almería	Bernardo	2.50	6.30am Mon & Sat	1
Almería	Las Negras & Rodalquilar	Alsa	3.40	6pm Mon-Fri, 1pm Sat	1¼
Las Negras	Almería	Alsa	3.40	7.30am Mon-Sat	1¼
Almería	San José	Bernardo	2.40	10am, 1.15pm, 6.30pm Mon-Fri; 10am, 2.15pm, 6.30pm Sat; 10am, 6.30pm Sun	1¼
San José	Almería	Bernardo	2.40	7am, 11am, 3pm, 7.30pm Mon-Fri; 8am, 11am, 3.15pm, 7.30pm Sat; 11am, 7.30pm Sun	1

Bus Companies:

Autocares Bergasan	(☎ 629 51 28 28)
Autocares Becerra	(☎ 950 22 44 03)
Autocares Bernardo	(☎ 950 25 04 22)
Alsa	(☎ 950 28 16 60)

* on other days, drivers of San José buses might be persuaded to detour

MOJÁCAR
postcode 04638 • pop 4400

Mojácar lies on the coast to the northeast of Cabo de Gata and 85km from Almería. There are two Mojácars: old Mojácar Pueblo, a jumble of white cube-shaped houses on top of a steep-sided hill 2km inland, and Mojácar Playa, a modern coastal resort 7km long but only a few blocks wide. Mojácar Pueblo is dominated by tourism, but retains its picturesque charms and can still captivate with its bougainvillea-draped balconies and its maze-like streets. Mojácar Playa is a relentless strip of hotels, apartments, shops, bars and restaurants, but the predominantly low-rise buildings give it a cheerful airy appeal. There is a good long beach, marred in places by the rattle of heavy traffic on the main road, the Paseo del Mediterráneo, separating the beach from the main strip. There is a lively summer scene all along Paseo del Mediterráneo, but life slows down here from October to Easter.

From the 13th to 15th century, Mojácar Pueblo stood on the Granada emirate's eastern frontier and suffered several Christian attacks, including a notorious massacre in 1435, before finally succumbing to the Catholic Monarchs in 1488. Tucked away in an isolated corner of one of Spain's most backward regions, it was decaying and almost abandoned by the mid-20th century before its mayor lured artists and others with give-away property offers.

Orientation & Information

Mojácar Playa and Mojácar Pueblo are joined by a road which heads uphill from a junction by the Parque Comercial shopping centre towards the northern end of Mojácar Playa.

The **tourist office** (☎ 950 47 51 62, fax 950 61 51 63; e info@mojacar.com; Calle Glorieta; open 9.30am-2pm & 5pm-7.30pm Mon-Fri, 10.30am-1.30pm Sat) is in Mojácar Pueblo, just north of the main square, Plaza Nueva, and is very helpful. A summer information booth (☎ 950 47 87 26; Paseo del Mediterráneo), opposite the Parque Comercial in Mojácar Playa, opens similar hours to the Pueblo office from Easter to October. In the same building as the Pueblo tourist office is a **post office** and the **Policía Local station** (☎ 950 47 20 00). Banesto, next door, and Unicaja, across the square, have **ATMs**, as does Banco de Andalucía in the Parque Comercial. There's another post office in the Parque Comercial.

Things to See & Do
Seeing Pueblo is mainly a matter of wandering the quaint streets with their flower-decked balconies, and browsing through the craft shops, galleries and boutiques. **El Castillo**, at the very top of the village, is private property (and not a castle), but there are great views from the public terraces around it. The fortress-style **Iglesia de Santa María** (Calle Iglesia), just south of Plaza Nueva, dates from 1560 and may previously have been a mosque. On Calle La Fuente, in the lower part of the Pueblo is the remodelled, though still expressive Fuente Mora (Moorish Fountain), a fine example of the Spanish Muslim tradition of enhancing function with artistry. An inscription records the noble plea for Mojácar Muslims to be allowed to remain in their home, made by Alavez, the last Islamic governor of Mojácar, to the Catholic Monarchs who usurped him in 1488.

Apart from Mojácar Playa's long, sandy main **beach**, a number of more secluded beaches are strung out to the south of the town. Some of those beyond the Torre de Macenas, an 18th-century fortification, are naturist beaches.

Special Events
The Moros y Cristianos festival, on the weekend nearest 10 June, re-enacts the Christian conquest of Mojácar, along with dances, processions and other festivities.

Places to Stay
Mojácar Pueblo Two kilometres west of Mojácar Pueblo on the Turre road, **Camping El Quinto** (☎ 950 47 87 04; e camping_elquinto@hotmail.com; camping per 2 adults, tent & car €16.85; open year-round) is small but in a pleasant location.

Pensión Casa Justa (☎ 950 47 83 72; Calle Morote 7; singles/doubles €18/36, doubles with bathroom €45) is reasonable value.

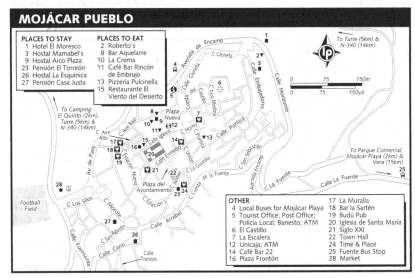

MOJÁCAR PUEBLO

PLACES TO STAY	PLACES TO EAT
1 Hotel El Moresco	2 Roberto's
3 Hostal Mamabel's	8 Bar Aquelarre
9 Hostal Arco Plaza	10 La Crema
23 Pensión El Torreón	11 Café Bar Rincón de Embrujo
26 Hostal La Esquinica	13 Pizzeria Pulcinella
27 Pensión Casa Justa	15 Restaurante Viento del Desierto

OTHER	
4 Local Buses for Mojácar Playa	17 La Muralla
5 Tourist Office; Post Office; Policía Local; Banesto; ATM	18 Bar la Sartén
	19 Budú Pub
6 El Castillo	20 Iglesia de Santa María
7 La Escalera	21 Siglo XXI
12 Unicaja; ATM	22 Town Hall
14 Café Bar 22	24 Time & Place
16 Plaza Frontón	25 Fuente Bus Stop
	28 Market

To Turre (5km) & N-340 (14km)

To Camping El Quinto (2km), Turre (5km) & N-340 (14km)

To Parque Comercial, Mojácar Playa (2km) & Vera (15km)

Football Field

Hostal La Esquinica (☎ 950 47 50 09; Calle Cano 1; singles/doubles €30/42) is near Pensión Casa Justa.

Hostal Arco Plaza (☎ 950 47 27 77; Calle Aire Bajo 1; singles/doubles €42/54), just off Plaza Nueva, has 16 pretty rooms painted a variety of pastel shades and with bathroom, TV, air-con and heating.

Hostal Mamabel's (☎/fax 950 47 24 48; e hotel@mamabels.com; Calle Embajadores 5; doubles/suites €64.70/87) is a charming place to stay, with a fine restaurant and excellent, spacious rooms. All are individually and tastefully decorated and have sea views, bathroom, heating and TV. Some have their own terraces.

Pensión El Torreón (☎ 950 47 52 59; Calle Jazmín 4; doubles €42) has great views from its bougainvillea-draped balcony, and just five rooms, with shared bathroom. This is the alleged birth house of Walt Disney (see the boxed text 'Walt Disney's Cartoon Connection' later in this chapter).

Hotel El Moresco (☎ 950 47 80 25, fax 950 47 82 62; Avenida de Encamp; singles/doubles €83/108.54) is a 147-room modern hotel favoured by tour groups.

Mojácar Playa Almost everything here is on Paseo del Mediterráneo, the main road running along the back of the beach.

Camping El Cantal (☎ 950 47 82 04; camping per 2 adults, tent & car €12.60; open year-round), 1km south of the Parque Comercial (near El Cantal bus stop), has room for 800 people.

Hostal Bahía (☎ 950 47 80 10; doubles with bathroom €48.35) is just to its south.

Hotel El Puntazo (☎ 950 47 82 65; Paseo del Mediterráneo 257; 3-star doubles €72-88, 1-star doubles €45-52), 2km south of the Parque Comercial, comprises separate but adjacent hotels of one and three stars under the same management. There is a restaurant serving both.

Parador (☎ 950 47 82 50, fax 950 47 81 83; e mojacar@parador.es; singles/doubles €78.60/98.40), a few hundred metres south of the Parque Comercial, is a modern building with lavish gardens and its own swimming pool.

Places to Eat

Mojácar Pueblo By the church, **Restaurante El Viento del Desierto** (Plaza Frontón; mains €5-6) is good value; fish soup is €2.70 and main courses such as beef bourguignon, pork fillet with mushrooms, or rabbit in mustard are available.

Café Bar Rincón de Embrujo (Calle Iglesia 4; platos combinados or seafood raciones from €4) is down the street from Restaurante El Viento del Desierto.

Bar Aquelarre, up in the shopping precinct above Plaza Nueva, serves up reasonable meat and seafood dishes for €5 to €6. **La Crema**, in the same precinct, is one of the few places offering an early breakfast out of season, for €2.70.

Pizzeria Pulcinella (Calle Puntica 5) has pizzas from €5.49, pastas from €6.50 and salads from €6.

El Horno (☎ 950 47 24 48; Calle Embajadores 5; 3-course menú €12.90, mains €10.50-16) is the stylish restaurant of Hostal Mamabel's (see Places to Stay). It offers probably the best food in Mojácar.

Roberto's (Avenida de Encamp; meat & fish mains from €7.80) has occasional flamenco which enlivens this popular eatery where you can get a roast dinner on Sunday for €10.

Mojácar Playa There are dozens of places to eat along Paseo del Mediterráneo, especially south of the Parque Comercial.

Restaurante Chino La Gran Muralla (set meals €7.50-15.60), 2km south of the Parque Comercial near the Pueblo Indalo bus stop, serves a tasty selection of fish and meat dishes.

Antonella (open evening Mon-Sun, lunch Sun), on the seaward side of the main road just above the beach near the Cueva del Lobo bus stop, pulls in customers with its medium-priced pizzas and pasta.

The Codfather is a determinedly British-flavoured fish and chip shop towards the southern end of Mojácar Playa. It offers cod, chips and mushy peas for €6, steak and kidney pie and chips for €5 and kids' portions of fish and chips for €4. Next door is **Jijonenca Heladería**, an ice-cream parlour to really make the youngsters' day.

Entertainment

Classical music and jazz concerts are staged at **El Castillo** in Mojácar Pueblo. For information call ☎ 950 47 20 33. Lively bars in Mojácar Pueblo include **La Escalera** *(Calle Puntica)*, **Budú Pub** *(Calle Estación Nueva)*, **La Muralla** *(Calle Estación Nueva)* and **Nora's Bar** *(Calle Enmedio)*. For good conversation and late-night drinking, the stylish **Time & Place** *(Plaza de las Flores)* keeps going to the early hours, as does **Café Bar 22** *(Calle Enmedio)*, while **Bar la Sartén** *(Calle Estación Nueva)*, the 'Frying Pan' but better known as 'Gordon's Bar', keeps going even longer, with a terrific stir of conversation and character. On weekends and holidays from Easter to October you can burn energyafter midnight by heading for one of Mojácar's open-air discos such as **Master**, halfway between Mojácar Pueblo and Mojácar Playa or **Pascha** on the beach just north of Camping El Cantal. The lively, long-established **Tito's** bar, overlooking the beach, is near Las Ventánicas bus stop towards the southern end of Mojácar Playa and features live music, including jazz. Tito's also has Internet access.

Getting There & Away

Bus Long-distance buses stop at the Parque Comercial and at the Fuente bus stop at the foot of Mojácar Pueblo. The tourist office has timetables.

Two or more buses run daily to/from Murcia (€8, two to three hours), Almería (€5, 1¾ hours), Granada (€13.50, 4¼ hours) and Madrid (€27, eight hours). There's a bus to Málaga daily except Sunday and holidays. For Almería, Granada and Murcia you buy tickets on the bus; for Málaga and Madrid you must book at a travel agency such as **Viajes Cemo** *(☎ 950 47 28 35; Paseo del Mediterráneo)*, 2km south of the Parque Comercial (Pueblo Indalo bus stop). Buses to Alicante, Valencia and Barcelona go from Vera, 16km north, which is served by several daily buses from Mojácar (€1, 45 minutes).

Car & Motorcycle Mojácar is 14km east of the N-340. A winding, scenic coastal road approaches Mojácar from Agua Amarga and Carboneras to the south.

Getting Around

A local bus service (€0.60) runs a circuit from the southern to northern ends of Mojácar Playa (Hotel Indalo to La Rumina stop), then back to the Parque Comercial, up to the Pueblo (stopping at the junction of Avenida de Encamp with Calle Glorieta, near the tourist office), then back down to the Parque Comercial and Hotel Indalo. It runs every half-hour from 9am to 11.30pm, April to September, and every hour from 9.30am to 7.30pm, October to March, reaching the Pueblo in 15 minutes.

In Mojácar Playa parking is fairly informal especially along the seaward side of the main road. In Mojácar Pueblo you should head for the main car park by following the one-way system along Avenida de Paris to reach the car park at Plaza Rey Alabez. Mojácar's Wednesday market takes over the car park. It is not advisable to leave your car in the official car park overnight Tuesday, when parking is transferred to the nearby football stadium for the duration of the next day's market. Taxis hang about in Plaza Nueva, or can be called on ☎ 950 47 81 84. There are several car rental offices strung out along Mojácar Playa.

VERA & AROUND
postcode 04620 • pop 6400
• elevation 102m

Almería's once neglected stretch of coast from Mojácar to the provincial border with Murcia is fast attracting holiday-makers, both clothed and unclothed, especially around the big sandy beaches to either side of the Río Almanzora. Here, one of the largest naturist resorts in Europe is still developing within a vast complex of apartments, villas and hotels. Further north again is the sombre, yet intriguing, Costa Almagrera, backed by the dark, brooding hills of the Sierra Almagrera, where locals, and visitors, thin out appreciably. The main centres of the area are the inland towns of Vera and its neighbour, Cuevas del Almanzora, where there are ancient cave dwellings.

Mojácar to Vera

Five kilometres north of Mojácar is the fishing port of **Garrucha**, hardly scenic, but bustling and colourful, especially round the harbour where there is a clutch of good fish restaurants. There are beaches at the southern entrance to the town. **Hostal Cortés** (☎ 950 13 28 13; Paseo Marítimo 200; singles/ doubles €40/60) is at the southern end of the seafront. It has clean, well-kept rooms and a restaurant that does platos combinados from €5.40.

Just beyond Garrucha the main road heads inland for 8km to Vera where the modern **Vera Hotel** (☎ 950 39 30 08; e verahotel@ interbook.net; singles/doubles €57/76) on the southern approach to the town is in a bleak roadside location but has comfortable rooms and a good restaurant with a decent menú for €7.80. There is little to interest the visitor in Vera itself other than the town's main church, the handsome **Iglesia de la Encarnación**. In front of the church is a charming, pedestrianised square, a haven amid Vera's otherwise traffic-logged streets. The town has a complicated one-way traffic system and, if you plan to stop off during the busy morning period, it's best to park on the outskirts and walk in.

Cuevas de Almanzora Lying 6km north of Vera, Cuevas is today a busy agricultural town but has a history of human settlement from earliest times. There is a **tourist information kiosk** (☎ 950 45 81 35; Avenida de Atrales 28; open 10am-2pm & 5pm-7pm daily) that has limited parking alongside. The bus station and taxi rank are just along from the information kiosk, where Avenida de Atrales branches left and leads into the centre of town. Cuevas' old town centre is a maze of narrow streets, but you can usually find parking in the side streets to the east of Avenida Atrales as it approaches the centre.

The handsome **Castillo Marqués de Los Velez** at the heart of the town has medieval features and today houses a **Museo Arqueológico** and the **Museo Antonio Manuel Campoy** (☎ 950 45 80 63; admission free; open 10am-1.30pm & 5pm-8pm Tues-Sat, 10am-1.30pm Sun). The Manuel Campoy museum exhibits a large and fascinating selection of art works, from the outstanding private collection of Antonio Manuel

Campoy, a native of Cuevas who was one of Spain's greatest art critics.

The town's other big attraction is the **Cuevas del Calguerín** (☎ 950 45 66 51, 639 10 19 48; admission €5; guided visits 11am, 2pm, 4pm & 9pm daily), several layers of cliff-face cave dwellings on the northern outskirts of the town. If you are driving, follow signs from the town for 'Cuevas Históricas' and take the road alongside the dried-up bed of the Río Almanzora from where you can see the caves on your left. There are no buses and the walk to the site from town is a dusty 2km. The price for the cave tour is fairly stiff for what you get, but it is fascinating all the same. The regular tour guide was born in the caves. Commentary is in Spanish only. One of the caves is being prettily decked out for what is likely to be pricey holiday accommodation and should be available by 2003; inquire at the Cuevas del Calguerín.

There is not much accommodation in Cuevas itself, but **Hotel La Parra** (☎ 950 45 71 05; Avenida de Atrales 28; singles/doubles €38/52), beside the tourist information kiosk, has reasonable rooms. Its lively restaurant does mainly meat mains for about €8.

Vera Playa & the Sierra Almagrera

Back on the coast, Vera Playa comprises the good beaches to either side of the mouth of the Río Almanzora and is exuberantly naturist. There is big money to be made in putting a roof over the unclothed it seems. Huge frothy-looking developments are still springing up, and complexes like **Vera Playa Club** (☎ 950 46 74 75; Carretera de Garrucha a Villaricos; doubles from €180) and a clutch of equally expensive apartments shut off the beaches from the main road, although there are access points for all.

The big **Camping Almanzora** (☎/fax 950 46 74 25; Carretera de Garrucha a Villaricos; camping per adult/child/tent/car €3.90/ 3.30/3.90/3.80) has a zona naturista for naturists and a zona textiles for the clothed, although the beach is healthily all-embracing.

Just to the north is the pleasant village of Villaricos, which is a sudden return to traditional buildings after the vast architectural confections of Vera Playa. It has a pebbly beach and two hotels with good rooms and excellent restaurants, **Hostal Restaurante Playa Azul** (☎ 950 46 70 75; Calle Barea 62; singles/doubles €24/42) and **Hostal Restaurante Don Tadeo** (☎/fax 950 46 71 05; Calle Baria 37; singles/doubles €24/36).

You'll need your own transport to explore further north from here where the road winds on for 8km between the coast and the gaunt, wrenched-looking slopes of the Sierra Almagrera. Amid these dark, shaley hills, silver, lead, bauxite and iron ore were mined from the 1830s to the 1950s. You still find traces of mine buildings along the coast, but there are small beaches of dark sand and there is a rare sense of isolation until the road reaches the charming village of El Pozo del Esparto with its smart little harbour. Here the **Hostal Restaurante Esperanza** (☎ 950 46 72 11; Calle La Esperanza; singles/doubles €30/40) has a good restaurant overlooking the harbour. It offers fish and meat mains for €6 to €21. Just next to the hotel is **Diving Vivariva** (☎ 950 46 75 72), a diving shop and café that runs diving trips and courses in the crystal clear waters of the Almagrera coast. Beyond El Pozo the coast road wanders on for a few kilometres towards Almería's final beach resort of San Juan de los Terreros and the border with Murcia.

Getting There & Away

About 10 buses a day go each way between Almería and Vera (€6, 2¾ hours) and between Mojácar, Garrucha (€0.75, 30 minutes) and Vera (€1, 50 minutes). Several buses a day go each way between Vera and Cuevas de Almanzora (€0.40, 15 minutes) but there are no regular bus connections to Villaricos and north along the Almagrera coast. In July and August there are infrequent connections to Villaricos from Vera. Schedules change each year so best to contact **Vera bus station** (☎ 950 39 04 10).

VÉLEZ BLANCO & AROUND
postcode 04830 • pop 2300
• elevation 1070m

The intriguing district called Los Vélez is north of the A-92-N Granada–Murcia road

in the north of the province. Its main settlements are three small towns – Vélez Rubio, Vélez Blanco and María. To their west lies the remote Sierra de María mountain range whose highest peak is María (2045m). Vélez Blanco, with a dramatic castle overlooking a scramble of red-tiled houses, is easily the most attractive and interesting of the towns. Much of the mountains and countryside is under protection in the Parque Natural Sierra de María-Los Vélez.

Information

At Vélez Blanco's **Centro de Visitantes Almacén del Trigo** (☎ 950 41 56 51; Avenida del Marqués de los Vélez; open 10am-2pm Wed-Thur, 10am-2pm & 4pm-6pm Fri, Sun & public holidays), information on walking routes, refuges and other attractions is available. The centre is on the northern edge of town. If arriving by car from the south, reaching it is easier by following the main road that bypasses Vélez Blanco, then entering the town by its northern access road. Another natural park visitor centre, the **Centro de Visitantes Mirador Umbría de María** (☎ 950 52 70 05) is 2km west of María off the A-317 and has similar opening times.

In Vélez Blanco there is a **post office** in Calle Clavel and an **ATM** at the start of Calle Vicente Sánchez, at the eastern end of the main street, Calle La Corredera. It's behind a solid metal grille, so don't get your hand stuck.

Things to See

Vélez Blanco is crowned by the very imposing **Castillo de los Fajardo** (adult/child €1/0.30; open 11am-1pm & 4pm-7pm Mon, Tues, Thur & Fri, 11am-4pm Sat, Sun & holidays). The castle seems to spring naturally from its rocky pinnacle and confronts, across the tiled roofs of the village, the great Sphinx-like mountain butte of La Muela. The castle is built over an earlier Muslim fort and dates from the 16th century. The interior is now rather bare (impoverished owners sold off the decorations around 1900), but if you're really determined you can see the lovely marble main patio next time you're in New York, where it has been reconstructed in that city's Metropolitan Museum of Art.

A stroll round Vélez Blanco is rewarding, not least for its delightful maze of streets and its many attractive houses. From the far end of the tree-lined main street, Calle La Corredera, you can head up Calle Vicente Sánchez to reach the castle. On the way, Calle Palacio, first left, is a good example of Vélez Blanco's stylish domestic architecture, all overhanging tiles and handsome wrought-iron balconies.

Just south of Vélez Blanco on the road from Vélez Rubio, signs point to the **Cueva de Los Letreros** (A-317; admission free), an ancient rock shelter with the most outstanding of several groups of 7000-year-old rock paintings in the district. The paintings, which would have had a sacred or magical purpose, show abstract symbols and animals and people engaged in hunting. They include the now ubiquitous Indalo figure (see the boxed text 'Walt Disney's Cartoon Connection' later in this chapter). Though they're not very big and not all distinct, they are fascinating. For a close-up look, contact the Centro de Visitantes Almacén del Trigo and arrange a time for them to open the iron fence around the shelter for you. From the A-317 you can drive 500m along the signposted dirt track, then it's a 10-minute walk up to the shelter.

Vélez Rubio centres on the handsome Plaza de la Constitución, which is dominated by the lavishly baroque Iglesia de la Encarnación. There's an archaeological, geological and ethnographic museum, the **Museo Miguel Guirao** (Carrera del Carmen 27).

The upland town of **María** is a plain little place but has a fine position against the awesome backdrop of the Sierra de María and is a good base from which to explore the mountains. The town is surrounded by almond groves that are a glorious froth of pink and white blossom in spring.

About 6km west of María, the A-317 heads north onto a high plateau towards the lonely village of **Cañada de Cañepla**, from where it continues, by a superbly scenic road, into the Parque Natural de Cazorla (see the Jaén Province chapter).

Places to Stay & Eat

Hostal La Sociedad (☎ 950 41 50 27; Calle Corredera 5; doubles with bathroom €24), in the centre of Vélez Blanco, has good rooms. If it seems closed in winter, check with the owners at the Bar Sociedad just across the road, where they serve good tapas for €1.50, a decent menú for €9 and breakfast for €1.50.

Hotel Velad Al-Abyadh (☎ 950 41 51 09, fax 950 41 50 98; Calle Balsa Parra 28;

Walt Disney's Cartoon Connection

The world's greatest purveyor of cartoons, Walt Disney, has an intriguing connection with eastern Almería, where there is an enduring belief that he was born in Mojácar, allegedly the result of a secret liaison between a village girl and a wealthy landowner. Legend says that the child was taken by his mother to America and was there adopted by the Disney family of Chicago, although the Disneys have always fiercely rejected such claims.

Disney's fame as a cartoonist makes for a tenuous but fascinating link with Almería's famous Indalo symbol, the strange little 'stick' figure, cartoon-like in its simplicity, that is a prominent feature of the prehistoric paintings at the Cueva de Los Letreros, the 'Cave of the Signs', near Vélez Blanco. One theory suggests that the word Indalo derives from the prefix inda, meaning the 'all powerful', a term that was used by the Iberians of southern Spain when referring to great leaders, or to forces of nature. Numerous males in eastern Almería are called Indalecío and the appeal of the little Indalo figure seems to have survived triumphantly, from ancient cave painting to 21st-century souvenir motif. The Indalo has even been adopted as the official marketing symbol of Almería tourism and it is a popular symbol on craftwork and souvenirs, especially in Mojácar, where it is often painted above doorways as a good luck sign. Disney would probably have transformed it into a mouse.

singles/doubles at the back €45/62, at the front €51.40/68.50), at the entrance to Vélez Blanco from Vélez Rubio, resembles a hunting lodge inside and has comfortable rooms. Brace yourself for the admirable water pressure in the showers. The hotel has a restaurant that does tasty tapas and meat dishes.

Restaurante Los Vélez *(Calle Balsa Parra 15; mains €8-10)*, along the street from Hotel Velad Al-Abyadh, does satisfying meals.

Mesón el Molino *(☎ 950 41 50 70; Calle Curtidores; fish & meat mains €12-15)*, tucked away up a narrow lane near the centre of Vélez Blanco, is a superb restaurant but is definitely the place for meat-eaters, with big displays of raw beef and hung hams. The heads of bulls and stags watch balefully from the walls. The patio has a gurgling stream channelled through it. Choice ranges from partridge and duck, to steak and hake.

Hotel Jardín *(☎ 950 41 01 06; N-342; doubles with bathroom €30)*, is on the old main road at the eastern end of Vélez Rubio.

Hostal Zurich *(☎ 950 41 03 35; N-342; doubles €42.80)* is near the western end of Vélez Rubio at busy junction of the A-317 to Vélez Blanco and has a restaurant.

Mesón El Candil *(Puerta de San Nicolás)*, a few hundred metres along Avenida de Andalucía, to the east of Hostal Zurich, serves good-value *platos combinados* for about €4.

Hostal Torrente *(☎ 950 41 73 99; Camino Real 10; singles/doubles €16/34)*, in María, is on the main road. It is family run and extremely well-kept, if a touch austere. The singles are rather small. The hotel's bar-restaurant does decent, mainly meat *raciones* for €4.80 to €7.

Hotel Sierramaría *(☎ 950 41 71 26; e sierramaria@cajamar.es; singles/doubles €34/54)*, also in María, is a stylish, modern hotel with superb mountain views. It is reached along a turning left, just before Hostal Torrente.

Getting There & Away

Alsina Graells *(☎ 968 29 16 12)* runs three or four buses daily each way through Vélez Rubio en route between Granada (€9.30, 3½ hours), Guadix (€7, 2½ hours) and Murcia (€6.60, 2¼ hours). Other Alsina services run to/from Sevilla and Córdoba.

Enatcar leaves from Almería at 3.30pm on Monday to Friday, 2pm on Saturday and 7.30pm on Sunday to Vélez Rubio (€10, 2¼ hours), Vélez Blanco (€10.25, 2½ hours) and María (€10.70, 2½ hours).

Autobuses Giménez García *(☎ 968 44 19 61)* has a bus from María (7.30am Monday to Friday, 9.30am Saturday) to Vélez Blanco, Vélez Rubio and Lorca. Returning, these stop at Vélez Rubio at 3.40pm Monday to Friday and 12.55pm Saturday.

The bus stop in Vélez Rubio is on Avenida de Andalucía at the junction by the Hostal Zurich.

Language

Spanish, or Castilian (castellano), as it is often and more precisely called, is spoken throughout Andalucía. English isn't as widely spoken as many travellers expect, though you are more likely to find people who speak some English in the main cities and tourist areas. Generally, however, you'll be better received if you try to communicate in the local language.

Andalucian Pronunciation

Pronunciation of Spanish isn't difficult, given that many Spanish sounds are similar to their English counterparts, and there's a clear and consistent relationship between pronunciation and spelling. However, few Andalucians pronounce Castilian as it is used in other parts of Spain or as it is taught to foreigners. Local accents vary too but if you stick to the following rules you should have very few problems making yourself understood.

Vowels

Unlike English, each of the vowels has a uniform pronunciation that doesn't vary. For example, **a** has one pronunciation rather than the numerous ones we find in English, such as in 'cake', 'care', 'cat', 'cart' and 'call'. Many words have a written accent. This acute accent (as in *días*) indicates a stressed syllable; it doesn't change the sound of the vowel. Vowels are pronounced clearly even if they are in unstressed positions or at the end of a word.

a	similar to the 'a' in 'art' but shorter
e	as in 'met'
i	between the 'i' in 'marine' and the 'i' in 'flip'
o	similar to the 'o' in 'hot'
u	as in 'put'

Consonants

Some consonants are the same as their English counterparts. The pronunciation of other consonants varies according to which vowel follows. The Spanish alphabet also contains the letter ñ, which is not found in the English alphabet. Until recently, the clusters **ch** and **ll** were also officially separate consonants, and you're likely to encounter many situations – eg, in lists and dictionaries – in which they are still treated that way.

b	soft, as the 'v' in 'van'; also (less commonly) as in 'book' when word-initial or when preceded by a nasal such as 'm' or 'n'
c	as 'k' before 'a', 'o' and 'u'; as 's' when followed by 'e' or 'i' (not 'th' as in standard Castilian)
ch	as in 'choose'
d	when word-initial it's as in 'do'; elsewhere as the 'th' in 'then', and sometimes not pronounced at all – thus *partido* (divided) becomes 'partio'
g	as in 'go' when initial or before 'a', 'o' or 'u'; elsewhere much softer. Before 'e' or 'i' it's a harsh, breathy sound, similar to the 'ch' in Scottish *loch*
h	always silent
j	a harsh, guttural sound similar to the 'ch' in Scottish *loch*
ll	similar to the 'y' in 'yellow' but often closer to a 'j' in Andalucía
ñ	a nasal sound like the 'ni' in 'onion' or the 'ny' in 'canyon'
q	always followed by a silent 'u' and either 'e' (as in *que*) or 'i' (as in *aquí*); the combined sound of 'qu' is like the 'k' in 'kick'
r	a rolled 'r' sound; longer and stronger when initial or doubled
s	often not pronounced at all, especially when not initial; thus *pescados* (fish) can be pronounced 'pecao' in Andalucía
v	same sound as Spanish **b** (see above)
x	as the 'x' in 'taxi' when between two vowels; as the 's' in 'say' before a consonant

z pronounced as 's' (not 'th' as in standard Castilian); often silent when at the end of a word

Semiconsonant

Andalucian Spanish also has the semiconsonant **y**. It's pronounced as **i** when at the end of a word or when it stands alone as a conjunction. As a consonant, its sound is somewhere between the 'y' in 'yonder' and the 'g' in 'beige', depending on the region.

Greetings & Civilities

Hello.	*¡Hola!*
Goodbye.	*¡Adiós!*
Yes.	*Sí.*
No.	*No.*
Please.	*Por favor.*
Thank you.	*Gracias.*
That's fine/ You're welcome.	*De nada.*
Excuse me.	*Perdón/Perdóneme.*
I'm Sorry/Forgive me.	*Lo siento/Discúlpeme.*

Useful Phrases

Do you speak English?	*¿Habla inglés?*
Does anyone here speak English?	*¿Hay alguien que hable inglés?*
I understand.	*Entiendo.*
I don't understand.	*No entiendo.*
Just a minute.	*Un momento.*
Could you write it down, please?	*¿Puede escribirlo, por favor?*
How much is it?	*¿Cuánto cuesta/vale?*

Getting Around

What time does the ... leave/arrive?	*¿A qué hora sale/ llega el ...?*
boat	*barco*
city bus	*autobús/bus*
intercity bus	*autocar*
train	*tren*
next	*próximo*
first	*primer*
last	*último*
I'd like a ... ticket.	*Quisiera un billete ...*
one-way	*sencillo*
return	*de ida y vuelta*

1st-class	*de primera clase*
2nd-class	*de segunda clase*

Directions

Where is the bus stop?	*¿Dónde está la parada de autobús?*
I want to go to ...	*Quiero ir a ...*
Can you show me (on the map)?	*¿Me puede indicar (en el mapa)?*
Go straight ahead.	*Siga/Vaya todo derecho.*
Turn left.	*Gire a la izquierda.*
Turn right.	*Gire a la derecha.*
near	*cerca*
far	*lejos*

Around Town

I'm looking for ...	*Estoy buscando ...*
a bank	*un banco*
the city centre	*el centro de la ciudad*
my hotel	*mi hotel*
the market	*el mercado*
the museum	*el museo*
the police	*la policía*
the post office	*los correos*
public toilets	*los servicios/ aseos públicos*
a telephone	*un teléfono*
the tourist office	*la oficina de turismo*
the beach	*la playa*
the bridge	*el puente*
the castle	*el castillo*
the cathedral	*la catedral*
the church	*la iglesia*
the hospital	*el hospital*
the lake	*el lago*
the main square	*la plaza mayor*
the old city	*la ciudad antigua*
the palace	*el palacio*
the ruins	*las ruinas*
the sea	*el mar*
the square	*la plaza*
the tower	*la torre*

Accommodation

Where is a cheap hotel?	*¿Dónde hay un hotel barato?*
What's the address?	*¿Cuál es la dirección?*
Could you write it down, please?	*¿Puede escribirla, por favor?*

Do you have any rooms available?	*¿Tiene habitaciones libres?*
I'd like to reserve a room for two people.	*Quisiera reservar una habitación para dos personas.*
I'll be arriving about 7pm.	*Yo llegaré sobre las siete de la tarde.*
What's your fax number?	*¿Cuál es su número de fax?*
What's your email address?	*¿Cuál es su dirección de correo electrónico?*
Please turn on your fax machine.	*Por favor encienda su fax.*

I'd like ...	*Quisiera ...*
a bed	*una cama*
a single room	*una habitación individual*
a double room	*una habitación doble*
a room with a bathroom	*una habitación con baño*
to share a dorm	*compartir un dormitorio*

How much is it ...?	*¿Cuánto cuesta ...?*
per night	*por noche*
per person	*por persona*

Can I see it?	*¿Puedo verla?*
Where is the bathroom?	*¿Dónde está el baño?*

I need ...	*Necesito ...*
soap	*jabón*
toilet paper	*papel higiénico*
a towel	*una toalla*
more blankets	*más mantas*

Time & Dates

What time is it?	*¿Qué hora es?*
today	*hoy*
tomorrow	*mañana*
in the morning	*de la mañana*
in the afternoon	*de la tarde*
in the evening	*de la noche*

Monday	*lunes*
Tuesday	*martes*
Wednesday	*miércoles*

Signs

Entrada	**Entrance**
Salida	**Exit**
Información	**Information**
Abierto	**Open**
Cerrado	**Closed**
Prohibido	**Prohibited**
Comisaria	**Police Station**
Servicios/Aseos	**Toilets**
Hombres/Caballeros	**Men**
Mujeres/Damas	**Women**

Thursday	*jueves*
Friday	*viernes*
Saturday	*sábado*
Sunday	*domingo*

January	*enero*
February	*febrero*
March	*marzo*
April	*abril*
May	*mayo*
June	*junio*
July	*julio*
August	*agosto*
September	*setiembre/septiembre*
October	*octubre*
November	*noviembre*
December	*diciembre*

Health

I'm ...	*Soy ...*
diabetic	*diabético/a*
epileptic	*epiléptico/a*
asthmatic	*asmático/a*

I'm allergic to ...	*Soy alérgico/a a ...*
antibiotics	*los antibióticos*
penicillin	*la penicilina*

antiseptic	*antiséptico*
aspirin	*aspirina*
condoms	*preservativos/ condones*
contraceptive	*anticonceptivo*
diarrhoea	*diarrea*
medicine	*medicamento*
nausea	*náusea*

Emergencies

Help!	¡Socorro/Auxilio!
Call a doctor!	¡Llame a un doctor!
Call the police!	¡Llame a la policía!
I'm ill.	Estoy infermo/a.
I'm lost.	Estoy perdido/a.
Go away!	¡Vete!

sunblock cream	crema protectora contra el sol
tampons	tampones

Numbers

0	cero
1	uno, una
2	dos
3	tres
4	cuatro
5	cinco
6	seis
7	siete
8	ocho
9	nueve
10	diez
11	once
12	doce
13	trece
14	catorce
15	quince
16	dieciséis
17	diecisiete
18	dieciocho
19	diecinueve
20	veinte
21	veintiuno
22	veintidós
23	veintitrés
30	treinta
31	treinta y uno
40	cuarenta
50	cincuenta
60	sesenta
70	setenta
80	ochenta
90	noventa
100	cien/ciento
1000	mil

one million	un millón

FOOD

breakfast	desayuno
lunch	almuerzo/comida
dinner	cena
menu	carta
waiter/waitress	camarero/a

I'd like the set lunch.	Quisiera el menú del día.
Is service included in the bill?	¿El servicio está incluido en la cuenta?
I'm a vegetarian.	Soy vegetariano/a.

Food Glossary

Andalucía has such a variety of foods and food names that you could travel for years and still find unfamiliar items on almost every menu. The following guide should at least help you sort out what's what.

Basics

botella – bottle
cocina – kitchen
comida – lunch, meal, food
copa – glass, especially a wine glass
cuchara – spoon
cuchillo – knife
cuenta – bill (check)
media-ración – half a ración
menú del día – fixed-price set meal
mesa – table
plato – plate
ración – meal-sized serving of a tapa dish
taza – cup
tenedor – fork
vaso – glass

aceite (de oliva) – (olive) oil
azúcar – sugar
caliente – hot
confitura – jam
frío/a – cold
hierba buena/menta – mint
mayonesa – mayonnaise
mermelada – jam
miel – honey
picante – hot (spicy)
pimienta – pepper
sal – salt
salsa – sauce
soja – soy

vegetal – vegetable (adjective)
vinagre – vinegar

arroz – rice
bollo – bread roll
empanada – pie
espagueti – spaghetti
fideo – vermicelli noodle
harina – flour
macarrones – macaroni
mollete – soft bread roll
pan – bread
panecillo – bread roll
tostada – toasted roll
trigo – wheat

Cooking Methods & Common Dishes

a la brasa – grilled
a la parrilla – grilled
a la plancha – grilled on a hotplate
adobo – a marinade of vinegar, salt, lemon and spices, usually for fish before frying
ahumado/a – smoked
albóndiga – meatball or fishball
aliño – in a vinegar and oil dressing
alioli – garlic mayonnaise
asado/a – roasted
caldereta – stew
caldo – broth, stock
casero/a – home-made
cazuela – casserole
cocido – cooked; also hotpot/stew
croqueta – croquette
crudo – raw
escabeche – a marinade of oil, vinegar and water for pickling perishables, usually fish or seafood
estofado – stew
flamenquín – rolled and crumbed veal or ham, deep fried
frito/a – fried
guiso – stew
horneado/a – baked
horno – oven
migas – simple dish basically composed of fried flour and water
olla – pot
paella – rice, seafood and meat dish
pavía – battered fish or seafood
pil pil – garlic sauce usually spiked with chilli
potaje – stew
rebozado/a – battered and fried

relleno/a – stuffed
salado/a – salted/salty
seco/a – dry/dried
tierno/a – tender/fresh
zarzuela – fish stew

Soups, Starters & Snacks – *Sopas, Entremeses & Meriendas*

bocadillo – bread roll with filling
ensalada – salad
gazpacho – cold, blended soup of tomatoes, peppers, cucumber, onions, garlic, lemon and breadcrumbs
montadito – small bread roll with filling, or a small sandwich, or an open sandwich – often toasted
pincho – a tapa-sized portion of food, or a *pinchito* (see Meat & Poultry)
pitufo – small filled baguette or roll
sopa de ajo – garlic soup
tabla – selection of cold meats and cheeses on a board
tapa – snack on a saucer

Fruits – *Frutas*

aceituna – olive
aguacate – avocado
cereza – cherry
frambuesa – raspberry
fresa – strawberry
granada – pomegranate
higo – fig
lima – lime
limón – lemon
mandarina – tangerine
manzana – apple
manzanilla – camomile (also a type of olive or a type of sherry)
melocotón – peach
melon – melon
naranja – orange
pasa – raisin
piña – pineapple
plátano – banana
sandía – watermelon
uva – grape

Vegetables – *Vegetales/Verduras/ Hortalizas*

ajo – garlic
alcachofa – artichoke
apio – celery
berenjena – aubergine, eggplant

calabacín – courgette, zucchini
calabaza – pumpkin
cebolla – onion
champiñones – mushrooms
col – cabbage
coliflor – cauliflower
espárragos – asparagus
espinacas – spinach
guindilla – chilli pepper
guisante – pea
hongo – wild mushroom
judías blancas – butter beans
judías verdes – green beans
lechuga – lettuce
maíz – sweet corn
patata – potato
patatas a lo pobre – 'poor man's potatoes', a potato dish with peppers and garlic
patatas bravas – spicy fried potatoes
patatas fritas – chips, French fries
pimiento – pepper, capsicum
pipirrana – salad of diced tomatoes and red peppers
puerro – leek
seta – wild mushroom
tomate – tomato
verdura – green vegetable
zanahoria – carrot

Pulses & Nuts – *Legumbres & Nueces*
almendra – almond
alubia – dried bean
anacardo – cashew nut
cacahuete – peanut
garbanzo – chickpea
haba – broad bean
lentejas – lentils
nuez (pl: *nueces*) – nut, walnut
piñón – pine nut
pipa – sunflower seed

Fish – *Pescados*
aguja – swordfish
anchoas/boquerones – anchovies
atún – tuna
bacalao – salted cod; it's soaked before cooking, prepared many different ways and can be succulent
caballa – mackerel
cazón – dogfish
chanquetes – whitebait (illegal, but not uncommon)
dorada – sea bass

lenguado – sole
merluza – hake
mero – halibut, grouper, sea bass
mojama – cured tuna
pescadilla – whiting
pescaíto frito – small fried fish
pez espada – swordfish
platija – flounder
rape – monkfish
rosada – ocean catfish, wolf-fish
salmón – salmon
salmonete – red mullet
sardina – sardine
trucha – trout

Seafood – *Mariscos*
almejas – clams
bogavante – lobster
búsano – sea snail, whelk
calamares – squid
camarón – shrimp
cangrejo – crab
chipirón – small squid
choco – cuttlefish
cigala – crayfish
frito variado – a mixture of deep-fried seafood
fritura – same as *frito variado*
gamba – prawn
langosta – lobster
langostino – large prawn
mejillones – mussels
ostra – oyster
peregrina – scallop
pulpo – octopus
puntillita/o – small squid, fried whole
quisquilla – shrimp
sepia – cuttlefish
venera – scallop

Meat & Poultry – *Carne & Aves*
beicon – bacon (usually thin-sliced and pre-packaged; see *tocino*)
bistek – thin beef steak
butifarra – thick sausage (to be cooked)
cabra – goat
cabrito – kid, baby goat
callos – tripe
caracol – snail
cerdo – pig, pork
chacinas – cured pork meats
charcutería – cured pork meats
chorizo – red sausage

choto – veal
chuleta – chop, cutlet
codorniz – quail
conejo – rabbit
cordero – lamb
embutidos – the many varieties of sausage
filete – fillet
hamburguesa – hamburger
hígado – liver
jamón (serrano) – (mountain-cured) ham
lengua – tongue
lomo – loin (of pork unless specified otherwise – usually the cheapest meat dish on the menu)
morcilla – black pudding
pato – duck
pavo – turkey
pechuga – breast, of poultry
picadillo – minced meat
pierna – leg
pinchito – Moroccan-style kebab
pollo – chicken
rabo (de toro) – (ox) tail
riñón – kidney
salchicha – fresh pork sausage
salchichón – cured sausage
sesos – brains
solomillo – sirloin (usually of pork)
ternera – beef, veal
tocino – bacon (usually thick; see *beicon*)
vaca, carne de – beef

Dairy Products & Eggs – *Productos Lácteos & Huevos*
leche – milk
mantequilla – butter
nata – cream
queso – cheese
revuelto de ... – eggs scrambled with ...
tortilla – omelette
tortilla española – potato omelette
yogur – yoghurt

Desserts & Sweet Things – *Postres & Dulces*
bizcocho – sponge cake
churro – long, deep-fried doughnut
flan – creme caramel
galleta – biscuit, cookie
helado – ice cream

natillas – custards
pastel – pastry, cake
tarta – cake
torta – round flat bun, cake
turrón – almond nougat or rich chocolatey sweets that appear at Christmas
yema – yolk, or candied yolk

DRINKS
Nonalcoholic

water	*agua*
fizzy mineral water	*agua mineral con gas*
plain mineral water	*agua mineral sin gas*
tap water	*agua del grifo*
tiger nut drink	*horchata*
fruit juice	*zumo*
soft drinks	*refrescos*
coffee ...	*café ...*
... with liqueur	*... carajillo*
... with a little milk	*... cortado*
... with milk	*... con leche*
iced coffee	*café helado*
black coffee	*café solo*
long black	*doble*
decaffeinated	*café descafeinado*
tea	*té*
hot chocolate	*chocolate*

Alcoholic

anisette	*anís*
beer	*cerveza*
brandy	*coñac*
champagne	*champán/cava*
cider	*sidra*
cocktail	*combinado*
rum	*ron*
sangría (red wine punch)	*sangría*
sherry	*jerez*
whisky	*güisqui*
a glass of ... wine	*un vino ...*
red	*tinto*
white	*blanco*
rosé	*rosado*
sweet	*dulce*
sparkling	*espumoso*

Glossary

alameda – avenue or boulevard
albergue juvenil – youth hostel; not to be confused with *hostal*
alcázar – Muslim-era fortress
andaluz – Andalucian
apartado de correos – post office box
apnea – snorkelling
autopista – motorway (toll charged)
autovía – toll-free motorway
AVE – Alta Velocidad Española; the high-speed train between Madrid and Sevilla
ayuntamiento – city or town hall

bailaor/a – flamenco dancer
baile – flamenco dance
bakalao – Spanish techno music (not to be confused with *bacalao*, salted cod)
balneario – bathing place, usually an inland spa
barrio – district or quarter (of a town or city)
biblioteca – library
bici todo terreno (BTT) – mountain bike
bodega – cellar, winery or traditional wine bar likely to serve wine from the barrel
bota – sherry cask or animal-skin wine vessel
buceo – scuba diving
bulería – upbeat type of flamenco song

cajero automático – automatic teller machine (ATM)
calle – street
callejón – lane
cama – bed
cambio – change/currency exchange
campo – countryside, field
caña – small beer in a glass; also a cane
cantaor/a – flamenco singer
cante jondo – 'deep song', the essence of flamenco
capilla – chapel
capilla mayor – chapel containing the high altar of a church
carnaval – carnival; a pre-Lent period of fancy-dress parades and merrymaking
carretera – road, highway
carta – menu

casa de huéspedes – guesthouse
casa rural – a village house or farmstead with rooms to let
casco – literally 'helmet'; used to refer to the old part of a city (*casco antiguo*)
castellano – Castilian; the language also called Spanish
caza – hunting
cercanías – local trains serving suburbs and nearby towns
cervecería – beer bar
chiringuito – small, often makeshift bar or eatery, usually in the open air
Churrigueresque – ornate style of baroque architecture named after the brothers Alberto and José Churriguera
claustro – cloister
cofradía – same as *hermandad*
colegiata – collegiate church, a combined church and college
comedor – dining room
consejo de gobierno – cabinet of the *Junta de Andalucía*
consigna – left-luggage office or lockers
converso – Jew who converted to Christianity in medieval Spain
copla – flamenco song
cordillera – mountain chain
coro – choir (part of a church, usually in the middle)
corrida de toros – bullfight
cortes – parliament
cortijo – country property
costa – coast
costumbristas – 19th-century Andalucian painters and writers who dealt with local customs and manners
coto – area where hunting rights are reserved for a specific group of people
cuenta – bill (check)
cuesta – sloping land, road or street
custodia – monstrance (receptacle for the consecrated Host)

dehesa – woodland pastures with evergreen oaks
ducha – shower

duende – the spirit or magic possessed by great flamenco performers

embalse – reservoir
embarcadero – pier, landing stage
encierro – running of bulls Pamplona-style (also happens in many other places around Spain)
ermita – hermitage or chapel
escalada – climbing
estación de autobuses – bus station
estación de esquí – ski station or resort
estación de ferrocarril – train station

farmacia – pharmacy
faro – lighthouse
feria – fair; can refer to trade fairs as well as to city, town or village fairs
ferrocarril – railway
fiesta – festival, public holiday or party
fin de semana – weekend
flamenco – means flamingo and Flemish as well as flamenco music and dance
fonda – basic eatery and inn combined
fuente – fountain, spring

gitano – the Spanish word for Roma people, formerly called Gypsies

hermandad – brotherhood, in particular one that takes part in religious processions
hospedaje – guesthouse
hostal – simple guesthouse or small place offering hotel-like accommodation; not a youth hostel

infanta – princess
infante – prince
IVA – *impuesto sobre el valor añadido*; value-added tax (VAT)
jardín – garden
judería – Jewish *barrio* in medieval Spain
Junta de Andalucía – executive government of Andalucía

laberinto – maze
latifundio – huge estate
lavabo – washbasin
lavandería – laundry
librería – bookshop
lidia – the art of bullfighting

lista de correos – poste restante
litera – bunk or (on a train) couchette
llegada – arrival
lucio – pond or pool in the Doñana *marismas*

madrugada – the 'early hours', from around 3 am to dawn – a pretty lively time in some Spanish cities!
marcha – action, life, 'the scene'
marismas – wetlands, marshes
marisquería – seafood eatery
medina – Arabic word for town or inner city
menú del día – fixed-price meal available at lunch time, sometimes in the evening
mercadillo – flea market
mezquita – mosque
mihrab – prayer niche in a mosque indicating the direction of Mecca
mirador – lookout point
morería – former Islamic quarter in a town
morisco – Muslim converted to Christianity in medieval Spain
moro – 'Moor' or Muslim (usually in a medieval context)
movida – similar to *marcha*; a *zona de movida* is an area of a town where young people gather to drink and have a good time
mozárabe – Mozarab; Christian living under Muslim rule in medieval Spain
Mudejar – Muslim living under Christian rule in medieval Spain; also refers to their decorative style of architecture
muelle – wharf, pier
muladí – Muwallad; Christian who converted to Islam, in medieval Spain

palo – literally a stick; also refers to the categories of flamenco song
panadería – bakery
papelería – stationery shop
parador – one of the Paradores de Turismo, a chain of luxurious hotels, often in historic buildings
paseo – avenue; park-like strip
paso – literally 'step'; also the platform an image is carried on in a religious procession
peña – a club, usually supporters of a football club or flamenco enthusiasts; sometimes a dining club
pescadería – fish shop

pícaros – dice tricksters and card sharps, rogues

pinsapar – forest of Spanish firs

piscina – swimming pool

plateresque – early phase of Renaissance architecture noted for its decorative facades

plato combinado – 'combined plate'; seafood/omelette/meat with trimmings

plaza de toros – bullring

presa – dam

provincia – province; Spain is divided into 50 of them

pueblo – village, town

puerta – gate, door

puerto – port, mountain pass

quinto real – the royal fifth: the 20% of the bullion from the New World to which the Spanish Crown was entitled

ración – meal-sized serving of tapas

rambla – stream

rastro – flea market, car-boot (trunk) sale

Reconquista – the Christian reconquest of the Iberian Peninsula from the Muslims (8th to 15th centuries)

reembolso – reimbursement

refugio – shelter or refuge, especially a mountain refuge with basic accommodation for hikers

reja – grille, especially a wrought-iron one over a window or dividing a chapel from the rest of a church

Renfe – Red Nacional de los Ferrocarriles Españoles, Spain's national rail network

reserva – reserve

retablo – retable (altarpiece)

ría – estuary

río – river

romería – festive pilgrimage or procession

ronda – ring road

s/m – on menus, abbreviation for *según mercado*, 'according to market price'

s/n – sin numero (without number), sometimes seen in addresses

sacristía – sacristy, the part of a church in which vestments, sacred objects and other valuables are kept

saeta – outburst of adoration by an onlooker at Santa Semana processions

salinas – salt lagoons

Semana Santa – Holy Week, the week leading up to Easter Sunday

sendero – path or track

sevillana – a woman from Sevilla; also a popular Andalucian dance

sevillano – a man from Sevilla; also means Sevillan (adjective)

sida – AIDS

sierra – mountain range

Siglo de Oro – Spain's cultural 'Golden Century', beginning in the 16th century and ending in the 17th century

supermercado – supermarket

taifa – small Muslim kingdom in medieval Spain

tapas – bar snacks, traditionally served on a saucer or lid *(tapa)*

taquilla – ticket window

tarjeta de crédito – credit card

tarjeta de residencia – residence card

tarjeta de telefónica – telephone card

terraza – terrace; often means an area with outdoor tables at a bar, café or restaurant

tetería – teahouse, often in Middle Eastern style with low seats around low tables

tienda – shop, tent

tocaor/a – flamenco guitarist

torno – revolving counter in a convent where nuns sell cakes, sweets and other products without being seen

trascoro – screen behind the *coro*

trono – throne; also the platform on which an image is carried in a religious procession

turismo – means both tourism and saloon car; *el turismo* can also mean the tourist office

v.o.s. (versión original subtitulada) – foreign-language film subtitled in Spanish

valle – valley

zoco – large market in Muslim cities

zona de acampada – free country camp site with no facilities or supervision

zonas restringidas – restricted areas

Thanks

Many thanks to the travellers who used the last edition and wote to us with helpful hints, useful advice and interesting anecdotes.

Isabelle Béjin, Eve Addis, Sabine Agena, Rosey Aindow, Abe Akresh, Jan Alexander, Neil Allies, Sine Andersen, Ted Angell, Robert Angert, Joy Armstrong, Chris Baldwin, Peter Baldwin, Martin Bamford, Michael Barry, Mike Bell, Tony Bellette, Alessandro Benvenuti, Edward Benz, Magda Biesemans, Tamas Biro, John Birthistle, Jeroen Blansjaar, Julien Bodart, Danny Boer, Jennifer Boger, Andre Bookelmann, A Th Bookleman, Figa Borova, Joseph Bosco, Pauline Bourhill, Julie Bowden, Glenn Boyes, Nathaniel S. Brigham, Evan Brinton, Dr Olivier Brunel, Peter Bubbear, Ian Buchanan, Jane Buenaventura, Philippa Burbeck, Larry Burrows, Belinda Byrne, James Calladine, Janet Calladine, Camino Galan Camon, Mauro Carlieri, George Casley, Jarret Cassaniti, J C Cazorla, Bryan Chambers, Cherie Chaperon, Michael Chapman, Rita Chawdhuri, Alfred Choy, Mollie Churchill, Mary Clarke, Barbara Coddington, Clark Colahan, Mary Collow, Anna Cooper, Robin Cooper, Maria Benedita Costa, Nicholas Covelli, Elisabeth Cox, John Cox, Stuart Cruickshank, Drew Cummings, Elizabeth Cunliffe, P Cuypers, Kathy Davidow, Boris de Wolf, Christophe Delaunay, Liz De-Loughrey, Dr Mike Dodd, Thomas Donegan, Kate Downer, Elizabeth Downing, Stephen Edwards, Jack Egerton, Martin Egerup, Henrik Elonheimo, Erik En Inez Van Ginneken, Marleen Enschede, Jacobien Erbrink, Jacobien Erdrink, Silvina Errecalde, Iain Fielden, Jennifer File, Karel Fluijt, Marek Fodor, Jay Fonkert, Arsenio Formoso, Saul Gallagher, Graeme Galloway, Elizabeth Garber, Julio Garcia Lopez, Alejandro Garduno, Mr & Mrs Gaudet, Kathleen Gillett, Nicole Goodfellow, Alexander Goutbeek, Meahan Grande, Gordon Grant, Tom Gray, Kate Greenwood, Catherina Grunwald, Paul Gurn, Bud Haas, Samantha Hack, Benjamin Hagard, Janet Hall, Jill hardy, Chris Harkensee, I W Harris, W Harrison, Georg Hasse, Adrian Hervey, Kaj Heydorn, Michael Hicks, Sarah Hird, Suzanne Hudson, Kimberly Huie, Barbara Huppauf, Sara Huston, Ted & Pixie James, Peter Jaskiewicz, Craig Jenkins, Robin Jett, Judith Johnson, Kirk Johnson, Linds Johnson, Anita Jones, Cynthia Karena, Erin Kelli, Manon Kerssemeeckers, Yu Fay Khan, Zia Asad Khan, Phil Kirkley, Alison Kirsch, Amanda Kliefoth, Brent Knevett, Suzanne Kocher, George Koenig, Heike Koenig, Sharon Kristoff, Petra Kubalcik, Lucien Lahaye, Fernando Landro, Vince Lauzon, Annette Lawrence, Gail Lefever, Ken Lefever, Rebecca LeSeelleur, Hui Ling, Zhiyu Liu, Jonathan Lord, Matt Loughney, Christine Mackay, Sara Macmillan, Linda Magno, Edith Maker, Fay Mander-Jones, Brian Mannix, Marisa Manzin, Giles Marshall, Jordi Sanchez Marti, Dubravka Martinovic, Jeremy May, Kirsty McFarlane, Mary McGinn, Annette McGuinness, Andrew McMenamin, Mrs Mcpryer, Janet Mead, Karen Mealer, Loyal Mealer, Brett Mitchell, Glen Mitchell, Naomi Mitchell, Charlene Mogdan, Jordi Vidal Morgades, Johnny Morgan, Nicole Morris, Bea Morrow, Raymond Mosher, Greg Mossop, Stuart Mould, Schloy Mualem, K Mulzer, Casey Murphy, Roberta Murray, Seth Nagel, Phil Nery, Brad & Rhea Ng, Julie Nichols, Maria Mejer Nielsen, Michael O Donoghue, Christopher O'Brien, Don O'Hara, Ros Osbourne, Alyson O'Shannessy, Ian Ostbye, Mark Parkes, Nikolaos Patelis, Jorge Peixoto, Ilan Peri, Janet Perkins, Neil Perkins, David Pickering, Martin Pilon, Tiago Pinto, Mark Pitt, L Podlesak, Scott Pope, LaMont Powell, Millie Powell, Elise Power, Duncan Purvis, Mobeena Rahmatullah, John S Ramsay, Paul Ratcliffe, Priyadarshini Rath, Cadence Reed, Jon Reimer, Spela Repic, Riccardo Ricci, Dave Richards, Tony Richmond, Petro Rinaldi, Janis Ringuette, Graham Rinzai, Barbara Roberts, Daniella Robinson, Cynthia Rocha, Kelly Rose, Orea Roussis, Gustavo Rubio, Antje Runschke, Julie Sadigursky, Helen Sage, Eric Sarlet, Joy Sarte, Benny Schiller, Guy Seinet, Heather Selin, Selina Serio, Tasha Seuren, Chris Seymore, Eyal Shaham, Gwen & Norm Shannon, Sue Shelley, Mike Shillitoe, Adele Sidhom, Ann Silverstein, Emma Smith, Margot Smith, Paul Smith, Richard Smith, Danielle Snyder, Rael Solomon, Christiana Souza, Eve Spence, Simon Spence, Suzanne Stahlie, Alberto Di Stefano, Giorgio Stenner, Rebecca Stephenson, Bill Stoughton, Bill & Ann Stoughton, Rafael Iglesias Stoutz, Michael Stringer, Philip Stynen, Eil Synnott, Terence Tam, Alan Tan, Christine Tanhueco, Margaret Thresh, Michel Thuis, Chris Thurman, Nenad Tkalec, Michael Tobin, Markus Tomschitz, Clayton Trapp, Kristian Tryggvason, Heidi Tsao, Liz Turner, Andreas Uthmann, Javier Valbuena, Joost van Iersel, Holly Venable, J D R Vernon, Jacques Vialla, Mari Christina Di Vito, Jason Muir Walker, N C Walker, Rob Walker, Barbara Walter, Gwyn Welles, James Whaley, Kristin White, B M Whitehead, Roy Wiesner, Hannah Wilberforce, Ed Wilde, Mark Wildon, Claire Wilhelm, Catherine Williamson, Fiona Wilson, Kori Wolfard, Glen Woods, Lucy Woodward, Nicholas Woyevodsky, Roger Wu, Mark Zappala, Sue Zyrich

LONELY PLANET

You already know that Lonely Planet produces more than this one guidebook, but you might not be aware of the other products we have on this region. Here is a selection of titles that you may want to check out as well:

Madrid map
ISBN 1 74059 322 7
US$5.99 • UK£3.99

Barcelona Condensed
ISBN 1 74059 335 9
US$11.99 • UK£5.99

Spanish phrasebook
ISBN 0 86442 719 0
US$7.99• UK£3.99

Spain
ISBN 1 74059 337 5
US$24.99 • UK£14.99

Madrid
ISBN 1 74059 174 7
US$14.99 • UK£8.99

World Food Spain
ISBN 1 86450 025 5
US$12.95 • UK£7.99

Catalunya & the Costa Brava
ISBN 1 74059 381 2
US$18.99 • UK£12.99

Valencia & the Costa Blanca
ISBN 1 74059 032 5
US$17.99 • UK£11.99

Canary Islands
ISBN 1 86450 310 6
US$15.99 • UK£9.99

Mediterranean Europe
ISBN 1 74059 302 2
US$27.99 • UK£16.99

Europe on a shoestring
ISBN 1 74059 314 6
US$24.99 • UK£14.99

Walking in Spain
ISBN 1 74059 245 X
US$19.99 • UK£14.99

Available wherever books are sold

Index

Text

Bold indicates maps.

443

Bold indicates maps.

Boxed Text

MAP LEGEND

CITY ROUTES

Freeway .... Freeway
Highway .... Primary Road
Road .... Secondary Road
Street .... Street
Lane .... Lane
.... On/Off Ramp

==== ...... Unsealed Road
.... One Way Street
.... Pedestrian Street
.... Stepped Street
⇒=== .... Tunnel
.... Footbridge

REGIONAL ROUTES

.... Tollway, Freeway
.... Primary Road
.... Secondary Road

.... Minor Road
– – – – .... Unsealed 4WD track
==== ...... Unsealed Road

BOUNDARIES

.... International
.... Autonomous Community
.... Province
.... Fortified Wall

HYDROGRAPHY

.... River, Creek
.... Lake
.... Spring; Rapids
.... Waterfalls

TRANSPORT ROUTES & STATIONS

—O— .... Local Railway
.... Underground Rlwy
.... Disused Railway
—Ⓜ— .... Subway, Station
.... Lightrail Tram

.... Cable Car, Chairlift
– – – – .... Ferry
– – – – .... Walking Trail
.... Walking Tour
.... Path

AREA FEATURES

.... Building
⊕ ...... Park, Gardens
.... Market
.... Sports Ground
.... Beach
+ + + ... Cemetery
.... Plaza
.... Swamp

POPULATION SYMBOLS

○ **CAPITAL** .... National Capital
◉ **CAPITAL** .... Provincial Capital
● **City** .... City
● **Town** .... Town
● Village .... Village
.... Urban Area

MAP SYMBOLS

● .... Place to Stay
▼ .... Place to Eat
● .... Point of Interest

✈ .... Airport
☮ .... Bank
🚌 .... Bus Terminal
🚠 .... Cable Car, Funicular
🏰 .... Castle
✝ .... Cathedral, Church
🎬 .... Cinema

☎ .... Embassy, Consulate
⚓ .... Fountain
⌂ .... Gate
✚ .... Hospital
@ .... Internet Cafe
☼ .... Lookout
▲ .... Monument

🏛 .... Museum
)(.......... Pass
✚ .... Police Station
✉ .... Post Office
🍺 .... Pub or Bar
.... Ruins
🏛 .... Stately Home

☒ .... Shopping Centre
✡ .... Synagogue
🚕 .... Taxi
☎ .... Telephone
🎭 .... Theatre
■ .... Tomb
ℹ .... Tourist Information

LONELY PLANET OFFICES

Australia
Locked Bag 1, Footscray, Victoria 3011
☎ 03 8379 8000 fax 03 8379 8111
email: talk2us@lonelyplanet.com.au

USA
150 Linden St, Oakland, CA 94607
☎ 510 893 8555 TOLL FREE: 800 275 8555
fax 510 893 8572
email: info@lonelyplanet.com

UK
10a Spring Place, London NW5 3BH
☎ 020 7428 4800 fax 020 7428 4828
email: go@lonelyplanet.co.uk

France
1 rue du Dahomey, 75011 Paris
☎ 01 55 25 33 00 fax 01 55 25 33 01
email: bip@lonelyplanet.fr
www.lonelyplanet.fr

World Wide Web: www.lonelyplanet.com or AOL keyword: lp
Lonely Planet Images: www.lonelyplanetimages.com